COMMITMENT AND COMPLIANCE

COMMITMENT AND COMPLIANCE

*The Role of Non-Binding Norms
in the International Legal System*

Edited by
DINAH SHELTON

OXFORD
UNIVERSITY PRESS

*This book has been printed digitally and produced in a standard specification
in order to ensure its continuing availability*

OXFORD
UNIVERSITY PRESS

Great Clarendon Street, Oxford OX2 6DP

Oxford University Press is a department of the University of Oxford.
It furthers the University's objective of excellence in research, scholarship,
and education by publishing worldwide in

Oxford New York

Auckland   Cape Town Dar es Salaam Hong Kong Karachi
Kuala Lumpur Madrid Melbourne Mexico City Nairobi
New Delhi Shanghai Taipei Toronto
With offices in
Argentina Austria Brazil Chile Czech Republic France Greece
Guatemala Hungary Italy Japan South Korea Poland Portugal
Singapore Switzerland Thailand Turkey Ukraine Vietnam

ISBN 0-19-829808-0

Foreword

Commitment and Compliance: The Role of Non-Binding Norms in the International Legal System is the culmination of a three-year study project organized by the American Society of International Law with the support of the National Science Foundation and the Ford Foundation. We are grateful for their support for this ground-breaking study that adds an important piece to the growing literature on compliance in the international legal system.

The project was initiated by Professor Edith Brown Weiss of the Georgetown University Law Center during her term as President of the American Society of International Law from 1994 to 1996. It builds on her work with Professor Harold K. Jacobson of the University of Michigan on compliance with international environmental accords which culminated in their edited volume, *Engaging Countries: Strengthening Compliance with International Environmental Accords* (MIT Press, 1998). Professor Weiss guided the early development of what came to be called the 'soft law project' by convening a workshop in May 1996 to identify issues raised by state compliance with non-binding norms and to develop a research agenda for elucidating and analyzing the problem area.

Drawing from this and other discussions, the project managers made several decisions about the direction of the ASIL soft law project including that the project would (1) be collaborative, multidisciplinary, and international; (2) provide a broad legal context within which to position issues of compliance with 'soft law'; and (3) undertake some comparative analyses of the use of soft law and compliance in several topic areas within international law. These decisions reflect the ASIL's strong research tradition of being cross-cutting, multidisciplinary, and international.

Throughout the study, the participants in this project held several meetings to discuss their contributions and the issues under consideration. These meetings were impeccably organized by Sandra Liebel of the ASIL, who also was instrumental in collecting and distributing manuscripts and keeping in touch with all the authors. She and others at Tiller House have been enormously helpful throughout the project. Thanks also to Brian Murray (J.D. 2000, Notre Dame Law School) for his assistance on the manuscript.

Although collaboration is a hallmark of ASIL's research program, the effectiveness and success of any particular project depends greatly on the leadership and guidance provided by the project director, in this instance Professor Dinah Shelton of Notre Dame Law School. And in Professor Shelton, the project found a fine and dedicated director. Contributors to the project probed issues, challenged received wisdom, and pushed the boundary of our knowledge. Working with each contributor and throughout the study,

Professor Shelton remained unflagging in her commitment to produce a volume of thoughtful and inter-related studies on what at times seemed a subject that could not be grasped. The value of this book as a collection of studies reflects her intellectual breadth and editorial skill. The ASIL is grateful to her and to all those who have contributed to this volume for working to deepen our understanding of the complexities of the contemporary international legal system.

CHARLOTTE KU
Executive Director
American Society of International Law
Washington, D.C.
August 1999

Contents

List of Contributors	xi
Abbreviations	xvii
Table of Treaties and Other International Documents	xix

Introduction: Law, Non-Law and the Problem of 'Soft Law'   1
Dinah Shelton

PART I. THE INTERNATIONAL SYSTEM

1. Normative Development in the International Legal System   21
   Christine Chinkin

2. Compliance Theories   43

   Choosing to Comply: Theorizing from International Relations and Comparative Politics   43
   Peter M. Haas

   Beyond Compliance: Helping Nations Cooperate   65
   Richard B. Bilder

3. Challenges to the International Legal System   75

   Interdependence, Globalization, and Sovereignty: The Role of Non-binding International Legal Accords   75
   Wolfgang H. Reinicke and Jan Martin Witte

   The Role of Soft Law in a Global Order   100
   Mary Ellen O'Connell

4. Commentary: Compliance with International Soft Law   115
   Jonathan L. Charney

PART II. PERSPECTIVES ON COMPLIANCE WITH NON-BINDING NORMS

5. The Environment and Natural Resources   121

   The General Assembly Ban on Driftnet Fishing   121
   Donald R. Rothwell

Pesticides and Chemicals: The Requirement of Prior Informed   146
Consent
Mohamed Ali Mekouar

The Legal Status and Effect of Antarctic Recommended   163
Measures
Christopher C. Joyner

Selected Agreements Concluded Pursuant to the Convention on   196
the Conservation of Migratory Species of Wild Animals
Clare Shine

Commentary and Conclusions   223
Alexandre Kiss

6. Trade and Finance   243

International Efforts against Money Laundering   244
Beth Simmons

'Soft Law' in a 'Hybrid' Organization: The International   263
Organization for Standardization
Naomi Roht-Arriaza

Policy Guidance and Compliance: The World Bank Operational   281
Standards
Laurence Boisson de Chazournes

Environmental Norms in the Asia-Pacific Economic Cooperation   303
Forum
Lyuba Zarsky

Commentary: Compliance with Non-Binding Norms of Trade and
Finance   330
David A. Wirth

7. Human Rights   345

A Hard Look at Compliance with 'Soft' Law: The Case of the OSCE   346
Erika B. Schlager

International Labor Organization: Recommendations and Similar   372
Instruments
Francis Maupain

Inter-American Human Rights Law, Soft and Hard   393
Douglass Cassel

Human Rights Codes for Transnational Corporations: The
Sullivan and McBride Principles   418

Christopher McCrudden

Commentary and Conclusions   449

Dinah Shelton

8. Multilateral Arms Control   465

Dinah Shelton

The System of Non-proliferation Export Controls   467

David S. Gualtieri

Protection of Nuclear Materials   486

Barry Kellman

International Regulation of Land Mines   505

Richard L. Williamson, Jr.

Commentary   521

Abram Chayes and Dinah Shelton

9. Conclusions: Understanding Compliance with Soft Law   535

Edith Brown Weiss

Editor's Concluding Note: The Role of Non-binding Norms
in the International Legal System   554

Dinah Shelton

Index   557

List of Contributors

Richard B. Bilder is Foley & Lardner Emeritus Professor of Law at the University of Wisconsin-Madison. He previously was an attorney in the Office of Legal Adviser at the U.S. Department of State. Professor Bilder has served as a Vice-President of the American Society of International Law, on the Board of Editors of the *American Journal of International Law*, on the Executive Council of the Law of the Sea Institute, as Chair of the International Law Association's Committee on Diplomatic Protection of Persons and Property, on U.S. delegations to international conferences and as an arbitrator in international and domestic disputes.

Laurence Boisson de Chazournes is a professor of international law at the University of Geneva. Between 1995 and 1999 she served as Senior Counsel in the Environment and International Law Unit of the Legal Department at the World Bank.

Douglass Cassel is Director of the Center for International Human Rights of Northwestern University School of Law in Chicago. From 1992 to 1993 he was Legal Adviser to the United Nations Commission on the Truth for El Salvador. He has written extensively on human rights in the Americas, appeared before the Inter-American Commission and the Inter-American Court of Human Rights, and been a consultant to non-governmental organizations, to the United States Mission to the Organization of American States, and to the OAS Secretariat.

Jonathan L. Charney is the Alexander Heard Distinguished Service Professor at the Vanderbilt University School of Law in Nashville, Tennessee. He is Co-editor in Chief of the *American Journal of International Law*, and has served as a member of the Board of Editors of the *Journal* since 1986. He is a member of the Council on Foreign Relations, the American Law Institute, and the Board of Editors of the journal *Ocean Development and International Law*. He has served as a Vice-President of the American Society of International Law and directs the Society's International Maritime Boundary project. He was a member of the United States delegation to the Third United Nations Conference on the Law of the Sea and served as Chief of the Marine Resources Section in the Land and Natural Resources Division of the United States Department of Justice.

Abram Chayes was Felix Frankfurter Professor of Law Emeritus at Harvard Law School. He was a life member of the American Law Institute and has served on the Executive Council of the American Society of International Law. He was a practicing attorney and served as the Legal Adviser of the U.S. Department of State. He participated in numerous international arbitrations and published extensively in the field of international law, especially in the area of arms control, disarmament, and dispute settlement.

Christine Chinkin is professor of international law at the London School of Economics and Political Science. She was previously Dean and Head of Department at the University of Southampton. She is a member of the Board of Editors of the *American Journal of International Law* and has written in areas of human rights, especially the human rights of women, international and domestic dispute resolution, and other aspects of international law.

David S. Gualtieri serves as a trial attorney with the Environment and Natural Resources Division of the United States Department of Justice. Previously he was an associate with Mayer, Brown & Platt and prior to that served as an Energy and Environmental Programs Attorney at Argonne National Laboratory. He also worked as a staff attorney in support of the Chairman of the United Nations Commission of Experts to Investigate Violations of International Humanitarian Law in the Former Yugoslavia. He has written in the areas of weapons control, international criminal law, and environmental regulation. Mr Gualtieri's contribution was written solely in his individual capacity and does not necessarily reflect the views of the United States Department of Justice, Argonne National Laboratory, or any other agency of the United States Government.

Peter M. Haas is a professor of political science at the University of Massachusetts at Amherst. He has published widely on international environmental subjects and on international relations theory. His recent work has focused on the interplay between international institutions and scientific involvement in the creation and enforcement of international regimes addressing transboundary and global environmental risks. He has consulted for the Commission on Global Governance, the United Nations Environment Programme, United States Department of State, United States Environmental Protection Agency, United States National Academy of Sciences, the American Association for the Advancement of Science, and the World Resources Institute.

Christopher C. Joyner is professor of international law in the Government Department at Georgetown University. He has also taught at George Washington University, Dartmouth College, and the University of Virginia, and served as a Senior Research Fellow at the Marine Policy Center, Woods Hole Oceanographic Institution, and at the Institute of Antarctic and Southern Ocean Studies at the University of Tasmania. He has published extensively on Antarctic law and politics.

Barry Kellman teaches at DePaul University College of Law and is co-director of the International Criminal Justice and Weapons Control Center. He chairs the ABA Committee on Law and National Security, is Chair of the Arms Control Section of the American Society of International Law, and also served as Chair of the Committee of Legal Experts on the Chemical Weapons Convention. He has been a consultant to the Defense Nuclear Agency on issues relating to the legal implementation of the Chemical Weapons Convention and the Strategic Arms Reduction Treaty, and to the Department of Energy on issues relating to verification procedures under the Nuclear Non-Proliferation Treaty. Since 1995, he has participated in the Group of Experts on Regional Security and Arms Control in the Middle East, serving as Chair of the Working Group on Elements of a Weapons of Mass Destruction Free Zone. Professor Kellman has numerous authored articles and book chapters on the laws of armed conflict, Middle East arms control, nuclear non-proliferation, and weapons smuggling.

Alexandre Charles Kiss is Director of Research Emeritus at the French National Center for Scientific Research and is President of the European Council on Environmental Law. He has specialized in international environmental law since the end of the 1960s, authored several books and more than 250 articles in this field. He is a consultant for numerous international institutions and for the French and Hungarian Governments. He is active in numerous environmental associations and serves as a vice-president of the International Institute of Human Rights.

Francis Maupain is former Legal Adviser to the International Labour Organization. He has a LL.M from Harvard Law School and a doctorate in law from the Sorbonne University in Paris. He is widely published in the field of international labor law.

Christopher McCrudden is Reader in Law at Oxford University, a Fellow at Lincoln College, Oxford, and a visiting professor at the University of Michigan Law School. He served as a member of the Standing Advisory Commission on Human Rights between 1984 and 1988 and has been an adviser to the Fair Employment Commission. He testified to the U.S. Congress, House of Representatives, International Relations Committee in March 1995 on economic justice in Northern Ireland.

Mohamed Ali Mekouar is Senior Legal Officer for natural resources and environmental law with the Legal Office of the United Nations Food and Agriculture Organization. He previously was professor at the Faculty of Law of Casablanca where he taught and researched in the field of environmental law. He has been a consultant providing technical assistance on environmental law and natural resources to governments throughout the world. He has lectured widely in Africa, South America, and Europe and published books and articles on natural resources and environmental law.

Mary Ellen O'Connell is an associate professor at The Ohio State University College of Law. She previously was a visiting professor at the University of Cincinnati College of Law, the University of Munich, and the Bologna Center of the Johns Hopkins University School of Advanced International Studies. She has also been a member of the faculties of Indiana University-Bloomington and the George C. Marshall European Center for Security Studies. She has authored books and more than two dozen articles on international law, especially on the use of force, enforcement of international law, and international environmental law.

Wolfgang H. Reinicke is a Senior Partner and Senior Economist in the Corporate Strategy Group of the World Bank, Director of the U.N. Project on Global Public Policy, and a Nonresident Senior Fellow in the Foreign Policy Studies program at the Brookings Institution in Washington D.C. Dr. Reinicke is a fellow of the World Economic Forum, a member of the Academic Council of the American Institute for Contemporary German Studies, and an advisor to several U.S. and European foundations. Dr. Reinicke previously was a Senior Scholar at the Brookings Institution (1991–98), a strategic management consultant for Roland Berger in Munich, in the operations department at Dresdner Bank in London, and a consultant to the National Academy of Sciences and the U.S. Agency for International Development.

Naomi Roht-Arriaza is a professor of law at the University of California, Hastings College of Law, San Francisco. Professor Arriaza teaches in the areas of domestic and international environmental law, international human rights, and torts. She is an associate editor of the *Yearbook of International Environmental Law* and has written widely on ISO 14000, among other issues. During 1995, she was a Senior Fulbright Scholar in Spain.

Donald R. Rothwell is an associate professor at the Faculty of Law, University of Sydney. His major research interests include constitutional and international law, with a specific focus on federalism, international environmental law, law of the sea, and law of the polar regions. He is widely published in these fields and since 1996 he has been the Editor-in-Chief of the *Asia Pacific Journal of Environmental Law*.

Erika B. Schlager joined the staff of the U.S. Commission on Security and Cooperation in Europe in September 1987 and serves as Counsel for International Law. Her responsibilities include developing Commission policy recommendations to the Department of State; participating in U.S. delegations to OSCE negotiations and specialized OSCE meetings on human rights, democracy-building and the peaceful settlements of disputes; authoring and editing reports and briefing papers on human rights, European institutional development, conflict and crisis management and the International Criminal Tribunal for the Former Yugoslavia; analyzing policy and legal issues relating to the OSCE and the Council of Europe; and lecturing to academic and public policy constituencies, including the U.S. Foreign Service Institute.

Dinah Shelton is professor of international law at the University of Notre Dame Law School. She is director of the doctoral program at the University's Center for Civil and Human Rights and a Fellow of the Kroc Institute for International Peace Studies. She has lectured throughout the United States, Europe, Africa and Asia and is widely published in the field of international law, particularly concerning human rights, international environmental law, and international institutions. She has served on the Executive Council of the American Society of International Law, the International Institute of Human Rights, and various other international law and human rights associations. She is a contributor to the *Yearbook of International Environmental Law* and a member of the Environmental Law Commission of IUCN. She is a consultant to numerous international organizations and has participated in cases before several international tribunals.

Clare Shine is a British barrister now practicing as a consultant in environmental law and policy in Paris. She has worked for several international organizations, including the CMS, Ramsar and CITES Secretariats, IUCN, European Union, Council of Europe, UNITAR and the U.N. Regional Activity Centre for Specially Protected Areas, and for the French Coastal Areas Conservancy. She is a contributing author to the *Yearbook of International Environmental Law* and a member of the IUCN Commission of Environmental Law.

Beth Simmons is an associate professor of political science at the University of California, Berkeley. She has written and published extensively in the area of international political economy and her recent research focuses on compliance with international law. Her first book, *Who Adjusts? Domestic Sources of Foreign Economic Policy During the Interwar Years*, won the American Political Science Association's 1995 Woodrow Wilson Prize for the best book published in the previous year on government, politics, or international relations. She has recently held fellowship positions at the International Monetary Fund and the United States Institute of Peace.

Richard L. Williamson, Jr. is Associate Dean and Professor of Law at the University of Miami. He was in the United States Foreign Service and later Division Chief of the U.S. Arms Control and Disarmament Agency. He served as an attorney in private practice between 1984 and 1988. He has taught and written extensively on arms control and international environmental law.

Edith Brown Weiss is the Frances Cabell Brown Professor of International Law at Georgetown University Law School. She is past president of the American Society of International Law, a member of the Board of Editors of the American Journal of International Law, and a member of the Council on Foreign Relations and the U.S. National Academy of Sciences. Between 1990 and 1992 she was Associate General Counsel for International Activities in the U.S. Environmental Protection Agency. She was previously an attorney advisor for the U.S. Arms Control and Disarmament Agency. She has lectured and published widely on international environmental law.

David A. Wirth is a professor of law at Boston College, Newton, Massachusetts. He also has taught at Washington and Lee and the University of Virginia law schools. He previously served as senior attorney with the Natural Resources Defense Council and the Office of Legal Advisor, U.S.

Department of State. He has published extensively in the field of international environmental law and international trade law. His work for this volume was supported by a research grant from Boston College Law School and he draws in part on his previously published writings.

Jan Martin Witte is a graduate student at the Johns Hopkins University, School of Advanced International Studies, Washington, D.C. and a Research Associate with the U.N. Vision Project on Global Public Policy Networks. He received a diploma in Political Science from the University of Potsdam. During his studies in Germany he was a scholar of the Friedrich-Ebert Foundation (FES). He specializes in international relations theory and international political economy.

Lyuba Zarsky is Co-director of the Nautilus Institute for Security and Sustainable Development in Berkeley, California and manages the Institute's Globalization and Governance Program. She has written widely on innovative approaches to the environmental and social governance of international markets, especially in Asia, and twice served on the U.S. delegation to meetings of APEC Environment Ministers. Her current research focuses on developing international investment rules which promote sustainable development and new approaches to enhance corporate social accountability.

Abbreviations

APEC	Asia-Pacific Economic Cooperation Forum
ASIL	American Society of International Law
ATCM	Antarctic Treaty Consultative Meeting
ATCP	Antarctic Treaty Consultative Party
CBD	Convention on Biological Diversity
CCAMLR	Commission for the Conservation of Antarctic Marine Living Resources
CCSBT	Commission for the Conservation of Southern Bluefin Tuna
CITES	Convention on International Trade in Endangered Species
CMS	Convention on the Conservation of Migratory Species of Wild Animals
COP	conference of the parties
DFI	direct foreign investment
DNA	designated national authority
ECJ	European Court of Justice
ECOSOC	Economic and Social Council
EMS	environmental management standards
FAO	Food and Agriculture Organization
FATF	Financial Action Task Force
GATT	Global Agreement on Tariffs and Trade
GEF	Global Environmental Facility
GFCM	General Fisheries Commission for the Mediterranean
GNP	gross national product
IAEA	International Atomic Energy Agency
I-ATTC	Inter-American Tropical Tuna Commission
ICCAT	International Commission for the Conservation of Atlantic Tunas
ICCPR	International Covenant on Civil and Political Rights
ICESCR	International Covenant on Economic, Social and Cultural Rights
ICJ	International Court of Justice
ICRC	International Committee of the Red Cross
IGO	intergovernmental organization
ILO	International Labor Organization
IMF	International Monetary Fund
INC	intergovernmental negotiating committee
IPTP	Indo-Pacific Tuna Programme
IRPTC	International Register of Potentially Toxic Chemicals
ISO	International Organization for Standardization
LDC	Lesser developed countries

MTCR	missile technology control regime
MNC	multinational corporations
MOP	meeting of the parties
NAFO	North Atlantic Fisheries Organization
NASCO	North Atlantic Salmon Conservation Organization
NBILA	non-binding international legal agreement
NEAFC	Northeast Atlantic Fisheries Commission
NGO	non-governmental organization
NIC	newly industrializing countries
NPAFC	North Pacific Anadromous Fish Commission
NPT	Nuclear non-proliferation treaty
OAS	Organization of American States
OAU	Organization of African Unity
OECD	Organization of Economic Cooperation and Development
OECS	Organization of Eastern Caribbean States
OLDEPESCA	Organization for Latin American Fishing Development
OSCE	Organization for Security and Cooperation in Europe
PIC	prior informed consent
R&D	research and development
REIO	regional economic integration organization
SFDI	Societé français de droit internationale
SPAR	South Pacific Albacore Research Working Group
SPC	South Pacific Commission
SPF	South Pacific Forum
UDHR	Universal Declaration of Human Rights
UN	United Nations
UNCED	United Nations Conference on Environment and Development
UNDP	United Nations Development Program
UNEP	United Nations Environment Program
UNGA	United Nations General Assembly
US or USA	United States of America
WECAFC	Western Central Atlantic Fishery Commission
WHO	World Health Organization
WMD	weapons of mass destruction
WTO	World Trade Organization

Table of Treaties and Other International Documents

1919

ILO, Maternity Protection Convention, 1919 (No. 3) 379–80

1945

United Nations Charter, 26 June 1945, 59 Stat. 1031 ....26, 102, 450, 455
Statute of the International Court of Justice.........................6, 21, 32, 174

1946

Constitution of the International Labor Organization, 9 Oct. 1946 62
    Stat. 3485, T.I.A.S. 1868, 15 U.N.T.S. 35 375–6
International Convention for the Regulation of Whaling, 2 Dec. 1946),
    161 U.N.T.S. 72, U.K.T.S. 5 (1949), Cmd. 7604; 62 Stat. 1716,
    T.I.A.S. No. 1849, 4 Bevans 248..200

1948

Charter of the Organization of American States, 30 Apr. 1948,
    2 U.S.T. 2394, T.I.A.S. No. 2361, 119 U.N.T.S. 3, amended
    27 Feb. 1970, 21 U.S.T. 607, T.I.A.S. No. 6847, amended
    25 Sept. 1997 ....396–7, 451
American Declaration of the Rights and Duties of Man, 2 May
    1948, O.A.S. Res. XXX, O.A.S. Off. Rec. OEA/Ser.L/V/I.4
    Rev. 346, 393–418, 450–1, 458
Universal Declaration of Human Rights, 10 Dec. 1948, U.N.G.A. Res.
    217A (III), UN Doc. A/810 at 71 (1948).....95, 449, 450, 451, 453, 455–6

1949

Convention Relative to the Protection of Civilian Persons in Time
    of War, 12 Aug. 1949, 6 U.S.T. 3516, T.I.A.S. No. 3365,
    75 U.N.T.S. 287.. 411

1952

ILO, Maternity Protection Convention (Revised), 1952 (No. 103)..379–80

1955

Standard Minimum Rules for the Treatment of Prisoners, adopted by
    the First United Nations Congress on the Prevention of Crime and
    the Treatment of Offenders, 1955, approved by the Economic and
    Social Council Res. 663C (XXIV), 31 July 1957..........450, 452, 453, 458

1956

Statute of the International Atomic Energy Agency, 26 Oct. 1956,
8 U.S.T. 1093, T.I.A.S. 3873, 276 U.N.T.S. 3 225–6

1959

Antarctic Treaty, 1 Dec. 1959, 12 U.S.T. 794, T.I.A.S. No. 4780, 402
U.N.T.S. 71...112, 163–96, 229, 231, 239

1964

Agreed Measures on the Conservation of Antarctic Fauna and Flora,
13 June 1964, 17 U.S.T. 992, T.I.A.S. No. 6058 ....173, 178, 180–81

1965

Convention on the Elimination of All Forms of Racial Discrimination, 21
Dec. 1965, 660 U.N.T.S. 195, (1966) 5 I.L.M. 352..............345, 450, 453

1966

ILA, Helsinki Rules on the Use of the Waters of International Rivers, 20
Aug. 1966, (1967) 52 I.L.A. 484...226
International Covenant on Civil and Political Rights, 16 Dec. 1966, 999
U.N.T.S. 171, (1967) 6 I.L.M. 368 ....345, 355, 407, 411, 449, 450
International Covenant on Economic, Social and Cultural Rights,
16 Dec. 1966, 993 U.N.T.S. 3, (1967) 6 I.L.M. 360..............345, 449, 450

1967

1968

Treaty on the Non-Proliferation of Nuclear Weapons, 1 July
1968, 21 U.S.T. 483, T.I.A.S. No. 6839, 729 U.N.T.S.
161 ....467, 468, 471–4, 492–3, 522, 536

1969

Vienna Convention on the Law of Treaties, 23 May 1969, 1155 U.N.T.S.
331 8
American Convention on Human Rights, 22 Nov. 1969,
OEA/Ser.L/V/II.23, Doc. 21, rev. 6 (1969), O.A.S.T.S. No. 36 ..393–419

1972

Convention on the Prohibition of the Development, Production and
Stockpiling of Bacteriological (Biological) and Toxin Weapons and on
Their Destruction, 10 Apr. 1972, 26 U.S.T. 583, T.I.A.S. 8062, 1015
U.N.T.S. 163...467, 523

Stockholm Declaration on the Human Environment, 16 June 1972,
U.N. Doc. A/Conf. 48/14/Rev. 1 (U.N. Pub. E.73, II.A.14) (1973) ...230
Convention Concerning the Protection of the World Cultural and
Natural Heritage, 23 Nov. 1972, 27 U.S.T. 37, T.I.A.S. 8225,
(1972) 11 I.L.M. 1358 298

1973
Convention on International Trade in Endangered Species, 3 Mar. 1973,
993 U.N.T.S. 243, (1983) 12 I.L.M. 1085 12
International Convention for the Prevention of Pollution by Ships
(MARPOL) 2 Nov. 1973, U.N. Legislative Series ST/LEG/SER.B/18,
at 461; (1973) 12 I.L.M. 1319 227

1975
Final Act of the Helsinki Conference on Security and Cooperation in
Europe, 1 Aug. 1975, (1975) 14 I.L.M. 1292 ....26, 346

1978
UNEP Principles of Conduct in the Field of the Environment for the
Guidance of States in the Conservation and Harmonious Utilization of
Natural Resources Shared by Two or More States, 19 May 1978,
(1978) 17 I.L.M. 1097 228–9

1979
ILO, Minimum Age Convention, 1973 (No. 138) 376
Convention on the Conservation of Migratory Species of Wild
Animals, 23 June 1979, (1980), 19 I.L.M. 15.....................196–223, 227
Convention on the Conservation of European Wildlife and Natural
Habitats, 19 Sept. 1979, E.T.S. 104 200
Convention on the Elimination of All Forms of Discrimination against
Women 18 Dec. 1979, U.N.G.A. Res. 34/180 (XXXIV), 34 U.N.
GAOR, Supp. (No. 46) 194, U.N. Doc. A/34/830 (1979), (1980) 19
I.L.M. 33...345, 453

1980
Convention on the Physical Protection of Nuclear Material, 3 Mar.
1980, (1980)18 I.L.M. 1419..493
Protocol on Prohibitions or Restrictions on the Use of Mines, Booby
Traps and Other Devices (Protocol II) to the United Nations
Convention on Prohibitions or Restrictions of Use of Certain
Conventional Weapons Which May be Deemed to be Excessively
Injurious or to Have Indiscriminate Effects, 10 Oct. 1980, 19 I.L.M.
1524..510, 514–15

1981

ILO, Occupational Safety and Health Convention, 22 June 1981
(No. 155) 381
Declaration on the Elimination of All Forms of Intolerance and
Discrimination Based on Religion or Belief, 25 Nov. 1981,
G.A. Res. 36/55, 36 U.N. GAOR Supp. (No. 51) at 171,
UN Doc. A/36/51 (1981)... 450, 452, 453

1982

ILO, Termination of Employment Convention, 1982 (No. 158)... 376, 378
Convention on the Law of the Sea, 10 Dec. 1982), U.N. Doc.
A/CONF.62/122, (1982) 21 I.L.M. 1261 ....230, 537

1984

Convention against Torture and Other Cruel, Inhuman and Degrading
Treatment or Punishment, 10 Dec. 1984, U.N.G.A. 39/46 Annex,
39 U.N. GAOR, Supp. (No. 51) 197, U.N. Doc. A/39/51 at 197,
(1984) 23 I.L.M. 1027 ....345, 453

1985

ILO, Occupational Health Services Convention, 26 June 1985
(No. 161) 381
FAO Code of Conduct on the Distribution and Use of Pesticides,
28 Nov. 1985, UN Doc. M/R8130, E/8.86/1/5000
(1986)..146–63, 229, 335
Standard Minimum Rules for the Administration of Juvenile Justice
(Beijing Rules), 29 Nov. 1985, G.A. Res. 40/33 450

1986

Convention on Early Notification of a Nuclear Accident, 23 Sept. 1986,
(1986) 25 I.L.M. 1370 493
Convention on Assistance in the Case of a Nuclear Accident or
Radiological Emergency, 26 Sept. 1986, (1986) 25 I.L.M. 1377 493–4

1987

Montreal Protocol to the Vienna Convention for the Protection of the
Ozone Layer, 16 Sept. 1987, (1987) 26 I.L.M. 1541 ....12, 27, 224, 239
London Guidelines for the Exchange of Information on Chemicals in
International Trade, 17 June 1987, UN Doc. UNEP/GC 14/17,
Annex IV...146–63, 229
Cairo Guidelines and Principles for the Environmentally Sound
Management of Hazardous Wastes, 17 June 1987, UNEP Governing
Council Decision 14/30..229

1988
  Vienna Convention Against Illicit Traffic in Narcotic Drugs
    and Psychotropic Substances, 20 Dec. 1988, (1989)
    28 I.L.M. 483 ....249, 255, 257, 333

1989
  Convention on the Control of Transboundary Movements of
    Hazardous Wastes and Their Disposal, 23 Mar. 1989, (1989)
    28 I.L.M. 657 ....229, 336
  Tarawa Declaration of the South Pacific Forum (11 July 1989)............124
  Convention on the Rights of the Child, 20 Nov. 1989, U.N.G.A.
    Res. 44/25 Annex (XLIV), 44 U.N. GAOR Supp. No. 49 at 167,
    U.N. Doc. A/44/49 (1989), (1989) 28 I.L.M. 1448 ....345, 450, 453
  Convention for the Prohibition of Fishing with Long Drift Nets in the
    South Pacific 24 Nov. 1989, (1990), 29 I.L.M. 1449 ....122, 125, 239, 537
  Castries Declaration of the OECS, 24 Nov.,1989 125
  UNGA Resolution 44/225 on driftnet fishing, 22 Dec. 1989 ......126–7, 128

1990
  OECD FATF Forty Recommendations, February 1990 ....245, 255–6
  ILO, Convention concerning Safety in the Use of Chemicals at
    Work, 6 June 1990...161
  Agreement on the Conservation of Seals in the Wadden Sea, 16 Oct.
    1990, EmuT 990:77 198–9
  UNGA Resolution 45/197 on driftnet fishing, 21 Dec. 1990 ......127, 128–9

1991
  Agreement on the Conservation of Bats in Europe, 10 Sept.
    1991, EmuT 991:90 ....199, 206–7, 210–11, 215
  Agreement on the Conservation of Small Cetaceans of the Baltic and
    North Seas 13 Sept. 1991, EmuT 992:21..199
  Protocol on Environmental Protection to the Antarctic Treaty
    of 1 Dec. 1959, 4 Oct. 1991, EMuT 991:74, (1991) 30 I.L.M.
    1455..112, 176 , 180–1, 229
  UNGA Resolution 46/215 on driftnet fishing, 20 Dec. 1991 ..... 127, 129–30

1992
  Framework Convention on Climate Change, 9 May 1992,
    EmuT 992:35; (1992) 31 I.L.M. 849..230
  Convention on Biological Diversity, 5 June 1992, EmuT 992:42,
    (1992) 31 I.L.M. 818...230, 298–9
  Agenda 21, UNCED, 13 June 1992, A/Conf.151/4
    (1992)...11, 161, 231, 299

Rio Declaration on Environment and Development, 14 June
1992, A/CONF.151/26 (Vol.I), 8; (1992) 31 I.L.M.
874...10, 229–30, 231–5, 299
European Charter for Regional or Minority Languages, 5 Nov.
1992, E.T.S. No. 148...370–1
Declaration on the Rights of Persons Belonging to National
or Ethnic, Religious and Linguistic Minorities, 18 Dec. 1992,
GA Res. 47/135 450
General Comment No. 19 (1992), Committee on the Elimination of
Discrimination against Women...31

1993
Convention on the Prohibition of the Development, Production,
Stockpiling and Use of Chemical Weapons and on Their
Destruction, 13 Jan. 1993, (1993) 32 I.L.M. 800.....................467, 475–7
Memorandum of Understanding concerning Conservation Measures
for the Siberian Crane, 16 June 1993 ....199, 201, 207–8
Agreement to Promote Compliance with International Conservation
and Management Measures by Fishing Vessels on the High Seas,
29 Nov. 1993, EMuT 993:89..131

1994
Declaration on the Elimination of All Forms of Violence against Women,
G.A. Res. 48/104, U.N. Doc. A/Res/48/104, (1994) 33 I.L.M. 1049 31
Memorandum of Understanding concerning Conservation Measures
for the Slender-billed Curlew, 10 Sept. 1994.............199, 208–9, 211–14
Convention on Nuclear Safety, 20 Sept. 1994, (1994)
33 I.L.M. 1514..494

1995
Framework Convention for the Protection of National Minorities,
1 Feb. 1995, E.T.S. No. 15..370–1
Agreement for the Implementation of the Provisions of the United
Nations Convention on the Law of the Sea of 10 Dec. 1982
relating to the Conservation and Management of Straddling
Fish Stocks and Highly Migratory Fish Stocks, 4 Aug. 1995,
A/CONF.164/38 131
Agreement on the Conservation of Africa-Eurasian Migratory
Waterbirds, 15 Aug. 1995, EmuT 995:45 ....199, 209–10, 214, 217–18
Global Program of Action for the Protection of the Marine
Environment from Land-based Activities, 3 Nov. 1995.....................299

1996

Agreement on the Conservation of Cetaceans of the Black Sea,
Mediterranean Sea,and Contiguous Atlantic Area, 24 Nov.
1996, EmuT 979:55C 199

1997

Convention on the Law of the Non-Navigational Uses of International
Watercourses, 21 May 1997, EMuT 997:39 300
Joint Convention on the Safety of Spent Fuel Management and
on the Safety of Radioactive Waste Management, 5 Sept. 1997,
(1997) 36 I.L.M. 1431 494

1998

Statute of the International Criminal Court, 17 July 1998,
A/CONF.183/9...35
Convention on the Prior Informed Consent Procedure for Certain
Hazardous Chemicals and Pesticides in International Trade,
11 Sept. 1998 (1999) 38 I.L.M. 1 ....112, 146, 161–3, 229, 523
Revised Memorandum of Understanding concerning Conservation
Measures for the Siberian Crane, 13 Dec. 1998 ....199, 211–12

1999

Memorandum of Understanding concerning Conservation Measures
for Marine Turtles of the Atlantic Coast of Africa, 29 May 1999 200

European Union Laws

EC Regulation 2455/92 of 23 July 1992 concerning Community exports
and imports of certain dangerous chemicals, OJ 1992, L 251/13 157–8
EC Regulation 1836/93 of 29 June 1993 Establishing an Eco-
Management and Audit Scheme, O.J. L 168/1 of 10 July 1993 272
EEC Regulation 3094/86 on driftnet fishing..141
EC Directive on the Prevention of the Use of the Financial System for
the Purposes of Money Laundering (June, 1991)................................259

National Laws

U.K. Antarctic Treaty Act of 1964..170
U.S. High Seas Driftnet Fisheries Enforcement Act, Public Law
192–582 of 1992..139
U.S. High Seas Driftnet Fishing Moratorium Protection Act Public
Law 104–43 of 1995...139
U.S. Land Mine Moratorium Act, Public Law No. 102-484 (1992),
106 Stat 2561-6..511

Jurisprudence

Aegean Sea Continental Shelf Case (Greece v. Turkey) 1978
  I.C.J. Rep. 3. 38–9
Case of the S.S. 'Lotus,' 1927 P.C.I.J., ser. A, No. 10 ....5, 23
Case Concerning Maritime Delimitation and Territorial Questions
  between Qatar and Bahrain, 1994 I.C.J. Rep. 6. 38–9
Humane Society of the United States v. Brown, 920 F.Supp. 178
  (Court of International Trade 1996)..135
Legality of the Threat or Use of Nuclear Weapons, 1996 I.C.J. Rep.
  (Adv. Op. 8 July), (1996) 35 I.L.M. 809 ....32, 465–6
Military and Paramilitary Activities against Nicaragua
  (Nicaragua v. U.S.) 1986 I.C.J. Rep. 3 462
NFTC v. Baker, *et al.*, 26 F. Supp.2d 287 (D. Mass., 1998) 439
Prosecutor v. Dŭsko Tadić, IT-94-IT, 7 May 1997,
  (1997) 36 I.L.M. 908... 36

Introduction

Law, Non-Law and the Problem of 'Soft Law'

DINAH SHELTON

The studies in this volume concern three interrelated issues: (1) the nature of international law, (2) the role of legally non-binding norms or 'soft law' in the international system, and (3) compliance with international norms. The interaction of the three issues raises questions about law-making and the boundaries of international law in the modern world. The subject of compliance with non-binding norms draws the issues together, being concerned with why states and other international actors choose to conclude non-binding rather than binding normative instruments and whether or to what extent that choice affects their consequent behavior.

Non-binding norms have complex and potentially large impact in the development of international law. Customary law, for example, one of the two main sources of international legal obligation, requires compliance (state practice) not only as a result of the obligation, but as a constitutive, essential part of the process by which the law is formed. In recent years, non-binding instruments sometimes have provided the necessary statement of legal obligation (*opinio juris*) to evidence the emergent custom and have assisted to establish the content of the norm. The process of drafting and voting for non-binding normative instruments also may be considered a form of state practice.

Considerable recent scholarship on compliance has questioned what motivates governments and other actors to give effect to international law, but few of the studies have concerned compliance with non-binding norms.[1] As discussed below by Peter Haas, many scholars question whether conforming acts result from habit or motivated, self-interested decision. Others ask whether sanctions or other forms of coercion are necessary to achieve compliance or

---

[1] Several scholars have considered the theoretical legal effect of non-binding norms without examining whether in fact such norms are followed. See e.g. Dupuy, R.J., 'Droit déclaratoire et droit programmatoire: de la coûtume sauvage à la "soft law"', in SFDI, *L'Elaboration du droit international publique* (1973) 132; Seidel-Hohenveldern, I., 'International Economic "Soft Law"', 1979–II *RCADI* 173; Bothe, M., 'Legal and Non-Legal Norms—A Meaningful Distinction in International Relations?' (1980) XI *Neth. YB Int'l L.* 65; Weil, P., 'Towards Relative Normativity in International Law?' (1983) 77 *Am. J. Int'l L.* 413; Francioni, F., 'International "Soft Law": A Contemporary Assessment', in Lowe, V., and Fitzmaurice, M. (eds.), *Fifty Years of the International Court of Justice, Essays in Honor of Sir Robert Jennings* (1996) 167.

whether managing problems through incentives is more effective.[2] Managerial approaches suppose that states comply with rules in regulatory regimes out of enlightened self-interest and respond to non-coercive tools such as reporting and monitoring. The existence of international bureaucracies created and driven by treaty regimes they supervise makes compliance possible and likely, helping resolve ambiguity or indeterminacy of norms, assisting regulatory targets to overcome deficits in capacity to comply through technical assistance, and otherwise inducing conforming behavior. International institutions thus are a focal point for maximizing compliance and reducing the likelihood of defection.[3]

The present introduction sets forth a framework for the present study, beginning with a discussion of the traditional characteristics of international law. It then looks at recent changes in the international system and the difficulties they pose for resolving problems through traditional international law-making, leading to a discussion of the role of law and the rule of law generally, including the importance of compliance. It suggests several hypotheses about the reasons states have recourse to non-binding norms and what may be expected from a study of compliance with them. First, the background and scope of the ASIL project is presented.

A. BACKGROUND AND SCOPE OF THE STUDY

The project to study compliance with international non-binding norms or 'soft law' began with a workshop held on May 8–10, 1996. The workshop brought together participants from several disciplines to identify and explore issues raised by compliance with 'soft law' and to design the elements of a research agenda. In part, the meeting sought to test the hypothesis that countries sometimes comply with non-binding legal instruments as well as they do with binding ones. The term 'soft *law*' itself seems to contain a normative element leading to expectations of compliance.[4]

The workshop paid particular attention to environmental soft law, due to the recent work of Edith Brown Weiss and Harold Jacobson on compliance with international environmental treaties.[5] Participants also looked at ques-

---

[2] Compare e.g. Downs, G., *et al.*, 'Is the Good News About Compliance Good News About Cooperation' (1996) 50 *Int. Org.* 379, with Chayes, A., and Chayes, A.H., *The New Sovereignty: Compliance with International Regulatory Agreements* (1995) and Young, O., *International Governance: Protecting the Environment in a Stateless Society* (1994).

[3] See Abbott, K.W., 'Modern International Relations Theory: A Prospectus for International Lawyers' (1989) 14 *Yale J. Int'l L.* 335.

[4] Elements in a possible definition of soft law are addressed in Chapter 1 by Christine Chinkin. Throughout the project, the participants debated the appropriateness of using the term 'soft law', given its ambiguity and questionable correctness as a legal term. The various usages in this volume reflect the unresolved discussions.

[5] Jacobson, H.K., and Brown Weiss, E, 'Compliance with International Environmental Accords' (1995) 1 *Global Governance* 119.

tions of compliance in other subject areas of international law.[6] They identified numerous issues as needing study: do states comply with soft law; what
factors compel states to comply; do these factors differ depending on whether
law is hard or soft; do states respond to soft law in ways that look like
responses to hard law? A hypothesis emerged from the workshop that 'soft
law' is used more frequently in some fields of international law than others.
Some suggested that soft law norms are more frequently utilized in the subject areas of environment and human rights than in trade and arms control.

The project took up the questions raised by the workshop. The initial aim
was to study compliance with soft law in general, with a focus on environmental law because soft law has played a particularly important role in that
new field. After further reflection, however, a decision was made to compare
four subject areas: human rights, environment, arms control, and trade and
finance. Each of the fields has particularities that result in different uses for
non-binding norms and a different ratio of non-binding norms to 'hard' law.
Human rights law has developed over the past fifty years into a broad code of
behavior for states and state agents, not only in their relations with other
states, but primarily as non-reciprocal, unilateral commitments towards all
those within the jurisdiction of the state. Environmental law, in contrast, aims
more at regulating non-state behavior: most environmental harm is caused by
private entities and not by state agents. Arms control is a classic inter-state
issue related to securing international peace and security, requiring regulation
of both state and private entities. Trade and finance is perhaps the most varied of the four areas, one where there are examples of a high degree of regulation and others where there is virtually no law. *Quid pro quo* is more easily
perceived in the trade and arms control subject areas than in environment and
human rights. Consequently, bilateral enforcement is easier in the former and
perhaps compliance is easier to measure and to ensure. With incorporation of
human rights and environmental concerns into the trade and finance area,
and linkage of human rights and security in the OSCE, greater complexity
appears.

The limited time and resources available also led to a methodology that
confines the project to drawing out relevant factors from specific cases rather
than from a broad empirical study. Within each subject area, cases were chosen for analysis on the basis of hypotheses about factors that might influence
compliance. Those factors are:

(1) The institutional setting. Soft law has been adopted by global general
organizations, global specialized organizations, regional organizations, and
private groups. The project participants discussed at length whether or not to
include norms adopted by non-state actors. Ultimately it was decided to

---

[6] Papers from the workshop have been published by the American Society of International
Law as No. 29 in its *Studies in Transnational Legal Policy: International Compliance with
Nonbinding Accords* (Weiss, E.B., ed., 1997).

include them because they are usually intended to impact on state behavior or to circumvent state policies. In addition, with increasing globalization, transnational entities that make their own rules prepare and enter into normative instruments that look much the same as state-adopted norms. Our hypothesis was that the participation of the relevant stakeholders in the creation of the norm would lead to greater compliance.

(2) Regional diversity. We sought to examine norms from different regions where there are different levels of economic development and thus varying capacity to comply. In addition cultural differences in attitudes towards informal agreements might affect compliance.

(3) Type of obligation. Some of the cases call for state abstention from action (e.g. not violating human rights) while others demand positive measures (e.g. pesticide labeling). We assumed that costly positive measures would produce less compliance because lack of capacity to comply would become a greater factor.

(4) Generality and specificity. Some of the norms are very general while others (e.g. the driftnet fishing ban) are detailed and specific. We assumed that compliance would be better for specific norms that clearly convey what behavior is expected than with ambiguous or vague norms.

The grouping of the cases by topic is based on the original assumption that subject matter is a factor in use of and compliance with non-binding norms. The study could be re-sorted according to the type of actor adopting the norm or nature of the target group. These may be significant factors, but may themselves depend on the nature of the subject matter.

Throughout the project, participants debated whether binding instruments (law) and non-binding ones (soft law or non-law) are strictly alternative, or whether they are two ends on a continuum from legally binding to complete freedom of action. Recent inclusion of soft law commitments in hard law instruments suggests that both form and content are relevant to the sense of legal obligation. Some soft law instruments may have a specific normative content that is 'harder' than the soft commitments in treaties. Other non-binding instruments may never be intended to have normative effect, but are promotional, serving as a catalyst to further action. This appears to be the case with some of the concluding acts of international conferences. It may be suggested that the interplay of form and substance lead to four possible alternatives:

Table 0.1: Normative Intent

Content:	Form:	Legal instrument	Non-binding instrument
	Normative	Law	Commitment
	Promotional	Hortatory language	Freedom of action

Throughout the study, we attempted to distinguish compliance, enforcement, implementation, monitoring, supervision, and effectiveness. **Implementation** of international norms refers to incorporating them in domestic law through legislation, judicial decision, executive decree, or other process. **Compliance** includes implementation, but is broader, concerned with factual matching of state behavior and international norms: 'compliance refers to whether countries in fact adhere to the provisions of the accord and to the implementing measures that they have instituted'.[7] **Effectiveness** is the question whether the goals of the norm are achieved, and may be independent of compliance. **Norms** includes all rules of conduct, while **standards** refer to the measures of compliance or technical objectives. **Instruments** are the variety of texts in which they are contained. It should be noted that there can be compliance without implementation (not stockpiling chemical and biological weapons) and implementation without compliance (legally, but not in fact, banning trade in endangered species). **Monitoring** and **supervision** refer to the procedures and institutions which are used to assess compliance.

Part I of the study introduces the topic of compliance with soft law by first attempting to define the terms, then presenting an overview of the recent changes that have occurred in international society and the international legal system, focusing on the role of non-binding norms. Part II of the book presents the four subject areas, with the select cases in each one. The limited number of cases means that the conclusions must be tentative. Further studies and evaluations will be needed. Future research could undertake comparative national studies of state compliance, including the issue of the extent to which the autonomy of state agencies and mechanisms serves to diffuse shared understandings. Such studies can help elucidate the nature and meaning of international law in the next century. For the present, consideration of the international legal system as a whole, in its past and present forms, can provide necessary background.

B. THE INTERNATIONAL LEGAL SYSTEM

Scholars and judicial decisions have characterized the international legal system as a system of equal and sovereign nation states whose actions are limited only by rules freely accepted as legally binding.[8] Brierly defines international law as 'the body of rules and principles of action which are binding upon civilized

---

[7] Jacobson, H.K., and Brown Weiss, E., *supra* note 5; Brown Weiss, E., and Jacobson, H.K., *Engaging Countries: Strengthening Compliance with Environmental Accords* (1998).

[8] See the Case of the S.S. 'Lotus,' 1927 P.C.I.J., ser. A, No. 10, at 18 ('International law governs relations between independent states. The rules of law binding upon States therefore emanate from their own free will as expressed in conventions or by usages generally accepted as expressing principles of law and established in order to regulate the relations between these coexisting independent communities or with a view to the achievement of common aims').

states in their relations with one another'.[9] Traditionally, this state-centered system excluded any role for non-state actors and was based upon a belief in the factual as well as legal independence of states. Obligations were largely bilateral and reciprocal in nature, enforced by self-help. Thus, breach of an obligation by one state could lead to a withdrawal of equivalent benefits by the offended state. The subject-matter of international legal regulation was limited, largely concerned with diplomatic relations, the seas and other international waterways, trade, and extradition.

At the close of World War I, states agreed upon the means to identify binding international obligations for the purpose of resolving their disputes. As formulated in the Statute of the Permanent Court of International Justice, the Court should decide an international dispute primarily through application of international conventions and international custom.[10] This formulation remains in the Statute of the present Court. Although the Statute is directed at the Court, it is the only general text in which states have articulated the authoritative procedures by which they agree to be legally bound to an international norm. Treaties and custom thus must be recognized by scholars and other non-state actors as the means states have chosen to create international legal obligations for themselves. A question posed in this study is whether state behavior in adopting and complying with non-binding instruments evidences acceptance of new modes of law-making not reflected in the Statute of the Court. *Ab initio*, however, we take the view that international law is created through treaty and custom, and thus 'soft law' is not legally binding *per se*.

It has become commonplace to note that the international system has undergone tremendous recent changes. From a community of predominately western states, the global arena now contains more than four times the number of states that existed at the beginning of the last century. In addition, other communities have emerged to play important international roles: inter-governmental organizations, non-governmental organizations, professional associations, transnational corporations, and mixed entities comprised of members of different communities. They both contribute to the making of international norms and increasingly are bound by them.

The subject matter of international concern similarly has expanded, paralleling developments within states where governments have taken on an increasing number of tasks. Subjects once deemed private passed into the public sector and from there into issues of transnational concern. International law now governs human rights, environmental protection, weapons systems, and the use of force. It directly regulates individual conduct through

---

[9] Brierly, J., *The Law of Nations* 1 (Waldock, H., 6th edn., 1963).

[10] General principles of law are a third, more rarely used, source of international law, with judicial decisions and teachings of highly qualified publicists providing evidence of the existence of a norm. For the present Court, see Art. 38, Statute of the International Court of Justice.

the development of international criminal law and criminal tribunals. Most of these topics, as well as the expanding management of the commons areas, are regulated through complex multilateral regimes with supervisory organs established to monitor implementation and compliance. Some of the commitments are non-reciprocal in nature, e.g. human rights, where the duties are owed towards those within the territory and jurisdiction of the state and less towards other states parties to the instrument. In such a system, the traditional method of self-help to induce compliance through withdrawal of benefits is untenable.

Technological change also has made possible communications and travel that place new problems rapidly on the global agenda, including issues of transnational crime and the spread of disease. More information exists and that information is more readily available, creating an awareness of the multiplicity of problems that require international solutions. The relative simplicity of traditional international law necessarily has given way to complex forms, processes, instruments, and norms. Successful or unsuccessful attempts to resolve problems that arise in one subject area cannot always be projected into other subject areas. The needs and approaches of international environmental law, for example the notion of 'common but differentiated responsibilities', may not be appropriate to the human rights field or that of arms control. On the other hand, there has been considerable cross-over, from national law to international law and back (vertical cross-over) as well as from one subject area of international law to another (horizontal cross-over). An example of the latter is state reporting as a supervisory mechanism, which began in the human rights field and has become widespread in instruments concerning environmental protection.

C. THE ROLE OF LAW AND NON-LEGAL APPROACHES TO RESOLVING PROBLEMS

The proposed solutions to problems are not always in the form of law. All human societies strive to maintain order, prevent and resolve conflicts, and assure justice in the distribution and use of resources. The specific problems that arise in achieving each of these aims differ from one society to another and within every society over time. The threats to order and justice that emerge over time can give rise to a number of responses, of which legal regulation has become perhaps the most prevalent this century. Laws reflect the current needs and recognize the present values of society. As such, legal regulation is almost inevitably responsive; it can rarely anticipate or imagine future problems. Regulation of outer space activities, for example, only became a matter of interest and concern when such activities became possible. Guarantees of a right to privacy were articulated only when the threats to privacy from technology and government intrusion necessitated a response. While it may be possible to anticipate some emerging problems from current human activities, the ability to design responsive laws still requires defining the problem and identifying potential solutions to it.

Law is not the only means of seeking to prevent or resolve social problems. Issues of justice can and are also addressed through market mechanisms and private charity, while conflict resolution can be promoted through education and information, as well as negotiations outside legal institutions. Maintenance of order and societal values can occur through moral sanctions, exclusion, and granting or withholding of benefits, as well as by use of legal penalties and inducements. In the international arena, law is not the only form of social control or normative claim. Other basic requirements of behavior emerge from morality, courtesy, and social custom. They form part of the expectations of social discourse. Compliance with such norms may be expected and violations sanctioned. Like legal norms, they grow out of the understanding and values of society.

Law, however, is often deemed a necessary, if usually insufficient, basis for ordering behavior. The language of law, especially written language, most precisely communicates expectations and produces reliance, despite inevitable ambiguities and gaps. It exercises a pull toward compliance by its very nature. Its enhanced value and the more serious consequences of non-conformity lead to the generally accepted notion that fundamental fairness requires some identification of what is meant by 'law', some degree of transparency and understanding of the authoritative means of creating binding norms. A law perceived as legitimate and fair is more likely to be observed.

Identifying law can be problematic in a decentralized, some might say anarchic, system like the international society of states. It is not always clear where law ends and non-law begins, or, to use the current terminology, where 'soft' law should be placed. The issue can be important for compliance. Effective application of the principle *pacta sunt servanda*—that legal agreements should be carried out in good faith—proceeds from some basic agreement on what constitute '*pacta*' or legal agreements. The question then becomes whether or not it is necessary for a norm to be contained in a legally binding instrument in order for it to be accepted as binding (*pacta*). Traditional international law clearly distinguished between binding and non-binding instruments, but the distinction may be blurring, as discussed below.

D. COMPLIANCE WITH LAW

The half century since the end of the Second World War has witnessed the proliferation of international norms, not only in traditional areas of international regulation, but in new fields once thought within the exclusive domestic jurisdiction of states. As the systematization and codification of norms becomes relatively complete in some subject areas, it is natural that attention then turns to the implementation and effectiveness of the norms adopted. Compliance with international law is thus a subject of increasing interest, enhanced as concern with the rule of law emerges from within states to become an inter-state issue.

The rule of law requires compliance in order for law to be effective and makes compliance a matter of general international concern. Although any given state may be unaffected by non-compliance with a particular norm, all states are concerned to uphold the rule of law to ensure they are not affected by non-compliance in the future. It may not be necessary for all those subject to the law to comply all of the time, but upholding the rule of law as a general principle requires that measures be taken to encourage compliance, deter non-compliance, and remedy injury caused by violations of legal norms. Consistent non-compliance with a law not only impugns the particular norm, but undermines the rule of law generally. Understanding the factors that compel and condition compliance is thus important to international lawyers and motivates this study, which generally seeks to determine whether states comply with soft law and, if so, why.

States enter into a variety of international commitments, some of which they have chosen to label law. States negotiated the Vienna Convention on the Law of Treaties to govern the most formal of these undertakings. The variety of international commitments, together with concern for compliance, generally raises the question whether the form of a normative instrument, or the formality with which it is approved, as opposed to its language and its content, is crucial to securing compliance. Does formalism, or adoption of a norm according to approved 'law-making' methods, make a difference in compliance with the norm being asserted, with state decisions to comply or not comply? Does it matter to non-state actors, who may be more or less willing to pressure states to comply with a given norm?

The question being asked may recall debates in the post-war period over form and function in architecture. Functionalism has inherent limits imposed by the laws of physics and human knowledge, but it has nonetheless had an important impact on the visual landscape, as many architects subordinate form to function. Form in law may also follow function. It is generally assumed that denominating something 'law' makes a difference in expectations of compliance and consequences of non-compliance. While some modern critics deny that law is significant to international commitment and the behavior of states, recent activity in the international political arena does not support this conclusion.[11] It was clear at the Rio Conference on Environment and Development, for example, that the non-governmental representatives

---

[11] See Johnston, D.M., *Consent and Commitment in the World Community* (1997).

had a strong preference for a binding Earth Charter over the ultimately-adopted Rio Declaration, and that states were unwilling to accept a legally binding text because of the consequences flowing from legal obligations. Both groups clearly felt that the form of the commitment made a difference.

While legal obligation brings with it greater expectation of conforming behavior and consequences for non-compliance, states also are demonstrating concern about compliance with other forms of international commitment. The Heads of State and Government of the Member States of the Council of Europe, meeting for their first summit conference in Vienna in 1993, reaffirmed that accession to the Council of Europe presupposes compliance with basic principles of democracy, the rule of law and respect for human rights, including freedom of expression and the media, and protection of national minorities. The Summit Statement of October 9, 1992 emphasized: '[w]e are resolved to ensure full compliance with the commitments accepted by all member states within the Council of Europe' and referred to three specific instruments, two of which are legally non-binding.[12]

E. HARD LAW AND SOFT LAW

The line between law and not-law may appear blurred. Treaty mechanisms are including more 'soft' obligations, such as undertakings to endeavor to strive to cooperate. Non-binding instruments in turn are incorporating supervisory mechanisms traditionally found in hard law texts. Both types of instrument may have compliance procedures that range from soft to hard. The result seems to be a dynamic interplay between soft and hard obligations similar to that which exists between international and national law. In fact, it is rare to find soft law standing in isolation; instead, it is used most frequently either as a precursor to hard law or as a supplement to a hard law instrument. Soft law instruments often serve to allow treaty parties to authoritatively resolve ambiguities in the text or fill in gaps. This is part of an increasingly complex international system with variations in forms of instruments, means, and standards of measurement that interact intensely and frequently, with the common purpose of regulating behavior within a rule of law framework. The development of complex regimes is particularly evident in international management of commons areas, such as the high seas and Antarctica, and in ongoing intergovernmental cooperative arrangements. For the latter, the memorandum of understanding has become a common form of undertaking, perhaps 'motivated by the need to circumvent the political constraints, eco-

---

[12] See Council of Europe, *Monitoring of Compliance with Commitments Entered Into by Council of Europe Member States: An Overview*, 27 March 1997, Monitor/Inf (97) 1 at 9.

nomic costs, and legal rigidities that often are associated with formal and legally binding treaties'.[13]

In many cases, hard law instruments can be distinguished from soft law by internal provisions and final clauses, although the characteristics of each are increasingly difficult to identify. Recently, supervisory organs have been created to oversee compliance with non-binding norms. The Commission on Sustainable Development, for example, supervises implementation of Agenda 21. In other instances, states have been asked to submit reports on implementation of and compliance with declarations and programs of action, in a manner that mimics if it does not duplicate the mechanisms utilized in treaties. Some scholars have distinguished hard law and soft law by stating that breach of law gives rise to legal consequences while breach of a political norm gives rise to political consequences. Such a distinction is not always easy to make. Testing normativity based on consequences can be confusing, since breaches of law may give rise to consequences that may be politically motivated. A government that recalls its ambassador can either be expressing political disapproval of another state's policy on an issue, or sanctioning non-compliance with a legal norm. Terminating foreign assistance also may be characterized either way. Even binding UN Security Council resolutions based on a threat to the peace do not necessarily depend upon a violation of international law.

While the systematization and interpretation of rules and principles are crucial, it is first necessary to identify the process by which those rules and principles are authoritatively created. If states expect compliance and in fact comply with rules and principles contained in soft law instruments as well as they do with norms contained in treaties and custom, then perhaps the concept of international law, or the list of sources of international law, requires expansion. Alternatively, it may have to be conceded that legal obligation is not as significant a factor in state behavior as some would think. A further possibility is that law remains important and states choose a soft law form for specific reasons related to the requirements of the problem being addressed and unrelated to the expectation of compliance. Each of these possibilities is explored in the studies that follow.

It seems clear that compliance with soft law cannot be separated from the issue of why states have recourse to soft law forms for their international commitments. There are several possible reasons that could explain the choice of soft law over hard law.[14]

---

[13] Johnston, *supra* note 11 at p. xxiv.

[14] See Lipson, C., 'Why are Some Agreements Informal?' (1991) 45 *Int. Org.* 495. Lipson suggests four reasons for choosing informal agreements: to avoid formal and visible pledges; to avoid ratification; to be able to renegotiate or modify as circumstances change; and to achieve a result. He sees speed, simplicity, flexibility and privacy as part of informal agreements.

(1) Bureaucratization of international institutions has led to law that is 'deformalized' through programs of action and other policy instruments. The reason for the growth of international institutions, bureaucracies and institutions is that they serve a purpose, in the same way that administrative agencies have become an essential part of national societies. Technical details, need for flexibility, and rapid response necessitate permanent institutions with the competence and mandate to initiate norm-creation, monitor and assist performance, and secure compliance. Where institutions can assess performance, hard law may not be necessary because state behavior is likely to change in response to the assessments. Moreover, international institutions generally lack the power to adopt binding instruments and can only have recourse to soft law.

(2) The choice of non-binding norms and instruments may reflect respect for hard law, which states and other actors view cautiously. They may use the soft law form when there are concerns about the possibility of non-compliance, either because of domestic political opposition, lack of ability or capacity to comply, uncertainty about whether compliance can be measured, or disagreement with aspects of the proposed norm. When states do not feel they can comply with a norm, they are largely unwilling to put that norm in a binding instrument. Thus soft law may be the homage states pay to hard law and the result may be the adoption of more progressive norms than would be drafted if a hard law form were chosen.[15]

(3) Soft law instruments may be intended to induce states to participate or to pressure non-consenting states to conform. Some environmental treaties, e.g. CITES and the Montreal Protocol, have sought to influence the behavior of non-parties, but, in general, treaty rules preclude binding non-consenting states. Pressure on dissenting states through adoption of soft law instruments may be seen in particular as motivation for the UN General Assembly driftnet fishing resolutions.

(4) Soft law also may be emerging due to a growing strength and maturity of the international system. In on-going cooperative societies, from families to nations, it is recognized that not all relations need to be governed by law but some may be left to etiquette, social discourse, or informal commitments. Compliance is expected with all agreed norms, but 'law' is reserved for the serious or fundamental rules where its formality and binding-ness are important.

---

[15] David Victor suggests that non-binding norms may be better in regulating complex environmental problems because their actual influence in changing behavior may be better than that of treaties. Generally compliance is high with treaties because states negotiate treaties with which they can comply. The process of earning consent to binding commitments leads to commitments that are excessively modest or ambiguous and thus less effective than they could be. This is particularly the case where there is a high degree of uncertainty in goals, means or capacity or where exogenous factors may impact. States seem more willing to adopt clear and ambitious commitments when they are in non-binding form. Being clear, they are more effective.

(5) Legally binding norms may be inappropriate when the issue or the effective response is not yet clearly identified, due to scientific uncertainty or other causes, but there is an urgent requirement to take some action. Similarly, it may be necessary where diverse legal systems preclude legally binding norms. Thus, soft law may be increasingly utilized because it responds to the needs of the new international system. In national legal systems, law-creating methods have always varied, from constitution-writing, to legislation, executive decrees, administrative regulation, and private contract, as well as common law. International law-making itself has changed over time. Where it was once almost entirely customary in origin, treaty-making, first bilateral, then multilateral, has come to be seen as the predominant form of law-making in the modern world.

(6) Soft law allows for more active participation of non-state actors. Where states once created and applied international norms through processes that lacked transparency, participation, and accountability, non-state actors have become a significant source of power alongside, if not outside, state control. Public participation is not only a goal but a reality in the development and implementation of international norms. Soft law permits non-state actors a role that is possible only rarely in traditional law-making processes.

(7) Soft law generally can be adopted more rapidly because it is non-binding. It can also be quickly amended or replaced if it fails to meet current challenges. Its flexibility extends to implementation and compliance where the dynamic interaction of the various actors can play a crucial role. Soft law may thus substitute for hard law when no agreement on hard law can be achieved or when recourse to the hard law form would be ineffective (less progressive norms or less likelihood they would be acceptable in the national political arena). It may be that an increased number of negotiating states makes it more likely that there will be few hard law agreements in the global setting. If this is the case, we would expect to see more soft law on the global than the regional level, and that appears to be the case.

F. COMPLIANCE WITH SOFT LAW

In this study of compliance with soft law, several factors were identified in advance as possibly affecting state performance. While most of them apply to all subject areas in the study, the relative importance of each varies from one subject to another. The hypotheses center on the form or process of adoption, the content of the instrument, the institutional setting, and the follow-up procedures envisaged. All the hypotheses stem from a general theory that states adopt and accept international norms when it is in their self-interest and they comply for the same reason. When they do not comply, the interests of others lead to various responsive actions. The notion of self-interest can include survival, domestic politics, moral values, altruism, and economic progress. Further, compliance may result not from the possibility of sanctions but from recognition of the need to ensure sustainability of the common good. Public goods theory may be more appropriate, in fact, to the subjects of environment and human rights than game theory, which may apply to arms control and trade.[16] The factors that were hypothesized to affect compliance include:

(1) The context of the norm-creation, especially the relationship between soft law and hard law. Soft law can be used to fill in gaps in hard law instruments or supplement a hard law instrument with new norms. Conversely, a soft law instrument may be adopted as a precursor to a treaty. Our hypothesis is that soft law adopted pursuant to a widely-accepted hard law agreement will reflect greater commitment and therefore produce better compliance than a new norm in soft law form chosen because there was no agreement on a hard law text. On the other hand, in subject areas of rapid change, where states agree that action needs to be taken without delay, compliance may be high even in the absence of a binding norm. The contextual setting also includes the overall level of compliance. It is assumed that the greater the consensus in the international community for the norms and the more compliance, the greater the likelihood that any single state will comply.

It also may be expected that the process of norm-creation, which by itself can induce some compliance, would probably have less impact when the norms are non-binding than when they are binding. People are conditioned to obey the law and feelings of obligation often play a significant role in compliance choices.[17] Thus, the form of the rules may play a role in decision making.[18]

(2) Content of the norm. We assume that the harder the content of the obligation the better compliance is likely to be. Ambiguity and open-endedness of international standards can limit efforts to secure compliance, because states may be unsure of the required conduct or unwilling to move beyond minimal efforts to implement the perceived norm. Ambiguity may also reflect lack of agreement, in which case compliance will be uneven.[19] Content also varies in its impact on state sovereignty. The more intrusive the rule, the harder it may be to comply. Thus, compliance with international 'non-binding' norms may be greatest for 'rules of the road' on common

---

[16] See Brown Weiss and Jacobson, *supra* note 7.

[17] Young, O., *Compliance and Public Authority: A Theory with International Applications* (1979) 23. 'Rules constitute an essential feature of bureaucracies and . . . routinized compliance with rules is a deeply ingrained norm among bureaucrats.' *Ibid.* at 39.

[18] See Kratochwil, F.V., *Rules, Norms and Decisions* (1989), 15, 95–129.

[19] Normative ambiguity may be a deliberate strategy, however, to ensure maximum agreement, especially when coupled with processes of review that can lead to normative strengthening of the provisions over time. The stability of the process and the institutional matrix for making and applying decisions on environment and development are crucial. See Handl, G, 'Controlling Implementation of and Compliance with International Environmental Commitments: The Rocky Road from Rio' (1994) 5 *Col.J.Int'l Envtl. & Pol'y* 305.

spaces, where the ability of all to use the road depends on each respecting the rules and only international rules will work.

The perceived economic costs of compliance or non-compliance also must be considered. 'Positive' obligations to take action may have costs that are absent when states are merely obliged to refrain from certain actions. Capacity thus may be crucial to achieving compliance with positive obligations. The majority of nations, for example, face issues of capacity to combat and remediate harm from local pollution, preventing full compliance with international norms.[20] Where capacity is the issue, compliance may be improved by increasing opportunities to engage in desirable behavior.

Competition in the international economy introduces incentives to non-compliance with some obligations, particularly in the area of trade. States may choose to lure investment, for example, by reducing legal controls over environmental protection, treatment of workers, or financial accountability. Incentives to defect can be very high in some areas, e.g. money laundering, but linkage of subject areas may overcome some of the disincentives. The OSCE process, coupling human rights and security concerns, demonstrated how separate subject areas may be linked in ways that promote greater compliance with the different sets of norms than would likely be achieved if each subject area was regulated on its own. Incentives also may be built into the normative instrument.[21]

(3) The institutional setting. Institutions and mechanisms capable of giving authoritative interpretations may foster compliance because they can 'harden' the norm through judicial or quasi-judicial rulings. It has been asserted that '[the] normal way of inducement of compliance with legal obligations is . . . to submit allegations of non-compliance to a court'.[22] While this model may be challenged as overly litigious, supervisory mechanisms are crucial, especially in subject areas where the norm is accompanied by strong incentives not to comply. Monitoring and publicly revealing non-compliance may be the most effective, if not the only, method of inducing compliance in the face of strong disincentives. It may even be possible that some stronger monitoring mechanisms exist in soft law precisely because it is non-binding and states are therefore willing to accept the scrutiny they would reject in a binding text.

Compliance review mechanisms are an intermediate phase in treaty implementation, between domestic application and sanctions for non-compliance. They have a significant impact on the level of compliance because the expec-

---

[20] Parker, R.W., *Choosing Norms to Promote Compliance and Effectiveness: The Case for International Environmental Benchmark Standards* (unpublished paper on file).

[21] See Mitchell, R.B., 'Regime Design Matters: Intentional Oil Pollution and Treaty Compliance' (1994) 48 *Int. Org.* 425.

[22] Fleischhauer, C.A., 'Inducing Compliance', in I United Nations Legal Order 231, 236 (Schachter, O. & Joyner, C., eds. 1995).

tation of being identified as not complying with a norm, *i.e.* verification by reliable sources, helps deter violations. The nature of the norm also is highly related to the need for and ability to undertake compliance review. In this regard, the compliance with the norm must be verifiable (the difficulty of measuring freedom of speech compared to mercury content of discharges into water makes it easier to conceal non-compliance with the former) and the information must be receivable by the relevant institutions. At the same time, the less precise the obligation, the more important the review to clearing up ambiguity and filling in gaps in the normative instrument.[23]

Other factors increase the importance of compliance mechanisms for specific subject areas. In the field of environmental law, compliance review is important because of the risk of irreversibility and potential magnitude of environmental problems, the lack of reciprocity as a tool for enforcing environmental norms, the failure to operationalize state liability and responsibility, and the need for compliance to be precisely measured and quantified.[24]

(4) Targets of the norm. States may find it easier to comply with norms that govern official behavior than with obligations to regulate non-state behavior. States have various direct sanctions available to control the behavior of state agents, from disciplinary measures to dismissal. States may be less willing to comply, however, if the requirements are perceived as undermining governmental power, as in the fields of human rights and arms control.

The regulation of non-state behavior is likely to require legislation that prohibits, requires, or regulates the specific conduct. Passage of such legislation may be difficult when the non-state actors play a powerful role in the domestic political arena. On the other hand, compliance by non-state actors may be easier to achieve when they are part of the drafting process, which is difficult to achieve through traditional law-making processes. Stake-holders who participate in drafting the norms that govern their behavior are more likely to feel a commitment to the norms adopted. While the need for and existence of organized non-state participation is important, it appears from hard law studies that decentralization does not necessarily affect compliance.

Among the questions addressed in the study are the relationship between negotiations (the reasons for recourse to soft law) and compliance and the extent to which concern with compliance drives both the form and the content of the norm. The impact or incentives and disincentives, which make a difference to compliance, will depend on the subject areas and different

---

[23] See Charpentier, J., 'Le contrôle par les organisations internationales de l'exécution des obligations des états', in 182 *R.C.A.D.I.* [1983–IV] 172. See also Imperiali, C. (ed.), *L'Effectivité du droit international de l'environnement: Contrôle de la mise en œuvre des conventions internationales* (1998); Sands, P., *The Effectiveness of International Environmental Agreements: A Survey of Existing Legal Instruments* (1992); Wolfrum, R., *Means of Ensuring Compliance with and Enforcement of International Environmental Law* (1998) 272 RCADI .

[24] Lang, W., 'Compliance Control in International Environmental Law: Institutional Necessities' (1996) 56 *Heidelberg J. Int'l L.* (ZaöRV) 685.

results may be expected at different points in time. Soft law may be used precisely because compliance is expected to be difficult; it begins a dynamic process over time that may lead to hard law or the norm may remain soft at the international level but become hard law internally.

CONCLUSION

The growing complexity of the international legal system is reflected in the increasing variety of forms of commitment adopted to regulate state and non-state behavior with regard to an ever-growing number of transnational problems. It is unlikely that we will see the return of a law/freedom of action dichotomy. Instead, the various international actors will create and attempt to comply with a range of international commitments, some of which will be in legal form, others of which will be contained in non-binding instruments. The lack of a binding form may reduce the options for enforcement in the short term (*i.e.* no litigation), but this does not deny that there can exist sincere and deeply held expectations of compliance with the norms contained in the non-binding form.

Various incentives and disincentives to compliance may be identified but there is little that can be done to quantify these factors, as the decisions of states and non-state actors to comply or not comply involve complex and holistic determinations, not always based on rational preferences. While this study seeks to identify the elements that go into the decisions of states and non-state actors to comply with soft law norms, quantification was not attempted, given the impossibility of identifying the causal relevance of international commitments at any particular time for any given state: correspondence of behavior with legal rules is not the same as compliance.[25]

The study is not premised on deriving a 'recipe' for success that will ensure the effective resolution of international problems and conflicts. While there may be particular factors that appear to influence state behavior across the four subject areas, determinants of implementation, compliance, and effectiveness vary even in a single subject area. Ultimately, the study is concerned with international legal commitments, whether binding or non-binding, as tools to prevent and resolve conflict and promote international justice. It implies that once international regulation has been perceived as necessary and action has been taken, compliance is expected and necessary, but not always sufficient, for the norm to become effective. The implications of this for particular states, especially the most powerful, in particular cases needs further study. States are not unitary actors and there may be elements of compliance

---

[25] In this regard, we agreed with Chayes and Chayes that 'the general level of compliance with international agreements cannot be empirically verified.' Chayes, A., and Chayes, A.H., 'On Compliance,' (1993) 47 *Int. Org.* 175 at 176.

and non-compliance simultaneously within a given state. The role of civil society, transparency, and participatory governance are broader themes that emerge from the project. In the end, the international legal system appears to be a complex, dynamic web of interrelationships between hard and soft law, national and international regulation, and various institutions that seek to promote the rule of law. In this system, soft law is playing increasingly important and varied roles.

Part I The International System

The authors in Part I discuss the problem of law-making and compliance in the global system, beginning with an analysis of the current legal framework within which states and, to some extent, non-state actors make various types of commitments. That framework is then placed in the larger context of international politics and economics, especially the phenomenon of globalization.

Christine Chinkin first analyzes the structure of traditional international law and the conceptual bases for a distinction between legally binding and non-binding norms. She enters the debate over whether 'hard' and 'soft' law are distinct categories, or end points on a continuum. She reviews the variety of non-binding instruments and their uses, developing criteria for identifying 'soft law' among the multitude of international texts adopted by international actors. In Chapter 2, Peter Haas discusses what is meant by compliance and what factors affect state decisions to comply with international norms. He questions whether differences should be expected between compliance with legally binding and non-binding norms. Richard Bilder presents an alternative approach to the same issue.

Chapter 3 looks at current challenges to the global system and what they may mean for the future of international law. Wolfgang Reinicke and Jan Martin Witte first discuss the differences between interdependence and globalization in economic activities and the impact of economic globalization on state sovereignty and the international legal order. Mary Ellen O'Connell expands the discussion to look at globalization of other issue areas and the role of non-binding norms in the light of current trends. Part I concludes with a commentary by Jonathan Charney.

Chapter 1

Normative Development in the International Legal System

CHRISTINE CHINKIN

INTRODUCTION

Current debates about the forms and functions of international law-making are a continuation of long-standing tensions between those who assert the paramountcy of state consent and those who urge limitations on state action in favor of international regulation. The first two sources listed in Article 38(1) of the Statute of the International Court of Justice (ICJ), treaties and custom, ensure complete coincidence between those who make the law and those who are bound by it.[1] This exclusive state control was challenged by the inclusion in Article 38(1)(c) of 'general principles of law'. The formulation of this paragraph was a compromise between exponents of expanding the scope of international law-making and adherents of the positivist stance that international law derives solely from the will of states.[2] The compromise allows the ICJ to seek principles common to systems of national law that have not been enshrined in custom or treaty, without authorizing unfettered recourse to notions of objective justice.[3]

Similar controversy and compromise have occurred with respect to the ways in which states manifest their consent and the arenas within which they conduct international affairs. Collective diplomatic negotiation even before the twentieth century necessitated relaxation of the requirement of unanimity in favor of some form of consensus in order to secure at least the benefits of discussion.[4] Such consensus was recorded in a conference *voeux*, declaration,

---

[1] Cassese, A., *International Law in a Divided World* (1986) 169.

[2] The former sought to authorize reference to general principles drawn from the conscience of civilized nations, that is natural law and justice, while the latter rejected the concept of binding obligations that had not been 'developed into positive rules supported by an accord between all States'. Root, E., American member of the Advisory Committee of Jurists that drafted the Statute of the Permanent Court of Justice, cited in *ibid.*, at 171.

[3] The Court has been restrained in its use of this freedom, most recently in its 1996 advisory opinion on the Legality of the Threat or Use of Nuclear Weapons where the majority made no reference to general principles of law to fill the lacuna caused by the lack of any relevant treaty obligations and by conflicting state practice. *Legality of the Threat or Use of Nuclear Weapons*, 1996 ICJ Rep. (Adv. Op. July 8) reprinted in (1996) 35 I.L.M. 809.

[4] Tammes, A., 'Decisions of International Organs as a Source of International Law' (1958) 94 *Rec. des Cours* 261. Tammes says that it was at the Second International Peace Conference in

or recommendation that was understood as having less significance than a 'perfect legal act',[5] but represented a functional compromise. Beginning about the 1960s newly independent states made a more deliberate attempt to affirm a law-making, rather than merely recommendatory, nature of institutional resolutions, in particular those of the United Nations General Assembly (UNGA).[6] They sought to use their numerical majority within the General Assembly to amend substantive international law with new principles that better upheld their interests,[7] and in so doing to revolutionize the basis of international norm-creation.[8]

The inadequacies of treaties and custom as modes of international law-making have become increasingly exposed.[9] The broadening subject matter of international regulation, the claims by and against non-state actors, and the global challenges posed by, *inter alia*, environmental degradation, decreasing natural resources, sustainable development, human rights violations, and disarmament have created an international setting that requires diversified forms and levels of law-making. International organizations have provided the fora for addressing these issues and for the evolution of international bureaucracies charged with performance of the institutional mandate. States have accepted institutional restraints on their freedom of action in efforts to devise and implement practicable solutions to the dilemmas facing them. These restraints themselves become part of the fabric of international practice. In the 1990s international law has been further transformed by the political changes following the end of the Cold War, the emergent demands of nationalism and tribalism, globalization and fragmentation, and by the communications revolution.[10] Debates about the legal effect of institutional resolutions and directives have merged with broader assertions of the existence and importance of a range of what have become known as 'soft law' instruments.[11] Their importance is that they generate expectations about the future behavior and attitudes of international actors, providing a measure of stability within the evolving system while still maintaining some flexibility.

1907 that this practice became explicit but that it can be seen as far back as the Congress of Paris, 1856; *ibid.*, at 292.

   [5] *Ibid.*, at 285.   [6] United Nations Charter, Art. 10.
   [7] In particular they sought a New International Economic Order and the right to development; see Seidl-Hohenveldern, I., 'International Economic Soft Law' (1980) 163 *Rec. des Cours* 164; Rich, R., 'The Right to Development: A Right of Peoples?', in Crawford, J. (ed.), *The Rights of Peoples* (1988) 39.
   [8] Garibaldi, O., 'The Legal Status of General Assembly Resolutions: Some Conceptual Observations' (1979) 73 *Proc. Am. Soc. Int'l L.* 324.
   [9] See *e.g.* Palmer, G., 'New Ways to Make International Environmental Law' (1992) 86 *Am.J. Int'l L.* 259; Gunning, I., 'Modernizing Customary International Law: the Challenge of Human Rights' (1991) 31 *Va. J. Int'l L.* 211.
   [10] See Chs. 3 and 4. See also Koh, H., 'Why Do Nations Obey International Law?' (1997) 106 *Yale L.J.* 2599.
   [11] Lord McNair is credited with first using this expression; Tammes, A., 'Soft Law' in *Essays on International and Comparative Law in Honour of Judge Erades* (1983) 187.

A range of opinion exists on the theoretical and practical desirability of soft law. Some authors have long rejected formal distinctions between international law and policy;[12] others acknowledge that the contemporary international law-making process is complex and deeply layered, that there is a 'brave new world of international law' where 'transnational actors, sources of law, allocation of decision function and modes of regulation have all mutated into fascinating hybrid forms. International Law now comprises a complex blend of customary, positive, declarative and soft law.'[13] From this perspective, drawing a formal distinction between hard and soft obligations is less important than understanding the processes at work within the law-making environment and the products that flow from it. More broadly, Jonathan Charney has urged acceptance of 'universal' international law to supplement the traditional methods of international law-making.[14] He derives universal law from global multilateral fora, giving weight to the extent to which participating states are made aware that the proposed rule is a refinement, codification, crystallization, or progressive development of existing principles of law, and by the level of widespread support for the rule. Another approach identifies an intermediate concept of 'declarative' law in norms that have been announced by a majority of states but are not actually enforced by them, or rules that are both practiced and accepted as law, but only by a minority of states.[15]

In an impassioned backlash to the perceived blurring of the binary (positivist) division between law and non-law, other theorists reject outright the notion of law-making through non-binding instruments.[16] The idea of different categories of law is seen to weaken the objectives of stability and certainty, creating a 'gliding bindingness'[17] and even undermining the international rule of law. They uphold the exclusive criteria of formal legal validity listed in Article 38(1) of the Statute of the ICJ and applied in the *Lotus* case,[18] strongly reiterating that they are not 'some esoteric invention but rather they provide criteria by which the actual expectations and commitments of States can be tested'.[19] Klabbers argues for the redundancy of the concept of soft law,[20]

[12] Most notably the New Haven law and policy approach; in the context of law-making see MacDougal, M., and Reisman, M., 'The Prescribing Function in the World Constitutive Process: How International Law is Made' (1980) 6 *Yale Studies in World Public Order* 249.

[13] Koh, H., 'A World Transformed' (1995) 20 *Yale J. Int'l L.* p. ix.

[14] Charney, J., 'Universal International Law' (1993) 87 *Am. J. Int'l L.* 529.

[15] Chodosh, H., 'Neither Treaty nor Custom: The Emergence of Declarative International Law' (1991) 26 *Texas Int'l L.J.* 88.

[16] *e.g.* Weil, P., 'Towards Relative Normativity in International Law?' (1983) 77 *Am. J. Int'l L.* 413; Danilenko, G., *Law-making in the International Community* (1993).

[17] Ingelse, C., 'Soft Law' (1993) 20 *Polish YB Int'l L.* 75.

[18] *The Lotus Case (France v. Turkey)*, 1927 PCIJ ser. A No. 10 (Judgment of September 7).

[19] Brownlie, I., 'The Rights of Peoples in Modern International Law', in Crawford, J. (ed.), *The Rights of Peoples* (1988) 15.

[20] Klabbers, J., 'The Redundancy of Soft Law' (1996) 65 *Nordic J. Int'l L.* 167.

asserting that to denote an instrument as 'soft law' is to impute legal character to it, albeit of a different nature (or degree) than that of hard law. This necessarily raises difficult questions about further legal consequences, such as whether violation of a principle of soft law amounts to an internationally wrongful act and thus incurs responsibility that can be imputed to the state, or whether it has some other 'softer' consequence? Klabbers asserts that:

> The self-contained nature of the soft legal order . . . is not just a by-product of the soft law thesis, but is one of essential foundations. For, if it could be claimed that soft law leads, in its application, to either hard law (hard responsibility, hard sanctions) or to non-law (no responsibility and no sanctions), soft law loses its distinctiveness, and therewith its reason of existence.

Klabbers contends that neither state practice nor judicial decision making shows evidence of acceptance or application of soft law; instead, soft law is recast into the traditional positivist sources of international law. He maintains, however, that the category of law itself is nuanced. Legal norms are not monolithic[21] and it is intuitively accepted that some norms are accorded greater weight than others and some are precisely framed, while others are open-ended, indeterminate, and incapable of creating precise predictions of future behavior. Compliance and non-compliance with law cannot be divorced from these extra-legal factors. He therefore considers that:

> Our binary law is well capable of handling all kinds of subtleties and sensitivities; within the binary mode, law can be more or less specific, more or less exact, more or less determinate, more or less serious, more or less far-reaching; the only thing it cannot be is more or less binding.

His conclusion is coupled with a very broad view of what constitutes a treaty, which thus reduces the 'grey area of uncertainty' by assuming the existence of binding obligations.[22] Accordingly, the crucial issue in each case is to determine the exact scope and strength of obligation.

The concept of international soft law thus remains controversial. On an overtly political level, acceptance of normative standards articulated through soft forms of law-making entails recognition that the rigid control of states over that process is weakening. Yet public international law is not alone in seeking a variety of techniques and devices for changing, predicting, and monitoring behavior.[23] Social systems utilize both binding principles and substrata of non-binding principles that are not and need not be incorporated within formal law-making processes, but still create normative standards and

---

[21] Cf. Reisman, M., 'The Concept and Functions of Soft Law in International Politics', in Bello, E., and Ajibola, B.A. (eds.), *Essays in Honour of Judge Taslim Olawale Elias* (1992) 135 at 136.

[22] Klabbers, J., *The Concept of Treaty in International Law* (1996).

[23] See for discussion of similar developments in international commercial law Goode, R., 'Usage and its Reception in Transnational Commercial Law' (1997) 46 *Int'l & Comp.LQ.* 1.

expectations of appropriate behavior. Indeed the priority accorded to law and legal sanction by western societies is not universal; other cultures readily employ non-legal forms of social control.[24] Domestic legal systems avail themselves of diverse means of regulating conduct. Some are widely applicable, others appertain to societal sub-groups, often in forms of self-regulation, for example through codes of conduct of professional associations. Similar distinctions are inherent in European Community law-making.[25] That international law has progressed in a similar fashion may be a sign of a maturing system breaking free of the limitations of exclusive law-making through treaty and custom and recognizing a decline of the consensual system.

There is an inevitable paradox in examining compliance with international soft law instruments: in many instances standards have been concluded in legally non-binding form precisely and deliberately to avoid any obligation to comply.[26] What forces then promote compliance with non-binding instruments? Should our understanding of compliance be modified in the context of non-binding instruments? The case studies in this volume further our understanding of how non-traditional forms of international law-making lead to behavioral and attitudinal change. Nevertheless, the richness and texture of contemporary international law and the broad differences in its form, purpose, style, and participants make illusory attempts to construct any systematic framework for the analysis of soft law that is not interspersed with exceptions, or framed at such a high level of abstraction that its usefulness is diminished.

A. FORMS OF SOFT LAW

1. Diversity of Soft Law Forms

Soft law appears in an 'infinite variety' of forms.[27] Most such law is written, but unwritten principles such as comity and good faith may be included. Lack of *opinio juris* prevents comity becoming merged with custom, but failure to comply may lead to acts of retorsion against the non-complying entity— indeed acknowledgment that retorsion is applicable against actions not contrary to international law testifies to the weight accorded to non-legal norms.

The conclusion of an agreement in treaty form does not ensure that a hard obligation has been incurred.[28] Treaties with imprecise, subjective, or

---

[24] Brierly, J., and David, R., *Major Legal Systems in the World Today: An Introduction to the Comparative Study of Law* (3rd edn. 1985).

[25] Wellens, K., 'Soft Law in European Community Law' (1989) 14 *Eur. L. Rev.* 267.

[26] Indeed, acceptance of soft law forms arguably lessens the pressures upon states to conclude binding agreements. *Ibid.*, at 269.

[27] Baxter, R., 'International Law in her "Infinite Variety"' (1980) 29 *Int'l & Comp. L.Q.* 549.

[28] A treaty is defined in the Vienna Convention on the Law of Treaties (1969) 1155 U.N.T.S. 331, Art. 2(1)(a).

indeterminate language have been termed 'legal soft law' in that they fuse legal form with soft obligations. Some writers reject this classification arguing that the treaty form is conclusive of binding obligation.[29] A compromise position is that a treaty with soft provisions creates an obligation of good faith performance,[30] although this is barely borne out by state practice.

States may deliberately eschew the form or intention of legally-binding obligation and reach agreement in diverse ways, such as memoranda of understanding, joint communiqués, minutes, or 'gentlemen's agreements'. Baxter discusses explicitly 'political treaties', such as the Yalta agreement, as an early form of soft law where the participants all recognized that they were acting in the political, rather than strictly legal, sphere.[31] In this sense, anticipated reactions to non-compliance were also politically framed. Schachter similarly refers to the 'rules of the game or tacit understandings' that were operative during the Cold War.[32] The Helsinki Final Act was deliberately drafted as a legally non-binding document,[33] although reliance upon it through the Conference on Security and Cooperation in Europe,[34] and especially by non-state actors, far exceeded that accorded many binding instruments. In 1993, the Middle East peace process was reactivated by a political agreement between Israel and the PLO; although the Declaration of Principles on Interim Self-Government Arrangements in many ways mirrored a Peace Treaty, the lack of Palestinian statehood ensured the Declaration's non-treaty status.[35]

An overtly political dimension explains the non-legal form of the instruments mentioned. A variety of motives influences the choice of form in other contexts. Participants may choose a non-binding agreement to avoid national legal requirements for the incorporation of treaties, or international provisions relating to treaties, such as registration pursuant to the United Nations Charter, Article 102.[36] The choice also may be a reflection of ease of amendment and termination,[37] or a desire simply to buy time. In some situations,

---

[29] See Ingelse, *supra* note 17 for a summary of such views. For a practical application see the High Court of Australia opinions in *The Commonwealth* v. *Tasmania* (1983) 46 A.L.R. 625 concerning whether the UNESCO Convention for the Protection of the World Cultural and National Heritage imposes hard or soft obligations.

[30] Ingelse, *supra* note 17.   [31] Baxter, *supra* note 27.

[32] Schachter, O., 'Towards a Theory of Obligation', in Schwebel, S. (ed.), *The Effectiveness of International Decisions* (1971) 9 at 13.

[33] Bastid, S., 'The Special Significance of the Final Act', in Buergenthal, T. (ed.), *Human Rights, International Law and the Helsinki Accords* (1977) 11.

[34] Since 1994 the Organization for Security and Cooperation in Europe; see Dronov, V., 'From CSCE to OSCE: Historical Retrospective', in Evans, M. (ed.), *Aspects of Statehood and Institutionalism in Contemporary Europe* (1997) 105.

[35] Meighan, K., 'The Israel–PLO Declaration of Principles: Prelude to a Peace?' (1994) 34 *Va. J.Int'l L.* 435 at 448–59.

[36] A state may deliberately register an agreement to enhance its claim that it is a binding treaty; alternatively failure to register does not alter the binding nature of a treaty.

[37] This may become more significant since the ICJ has affirmed that treaty law does not allow

preliminary draft texts may acquire a separate life as a form of soft law, before the drafters have decided upon the final form.[38]

Alternatively, states may opt to conclude a binding agreement. Within the Council of Europe conventions are favored where immediate unification or harmonization of law is sought. States also may choose to continue a long tradition of treaty law, for example in humanitarian law,[39] or there may be a change of direction. In this volume, Francis Maupain describes the plea within the International Labor Organization for completion of non-binding instruments because of the poor ratification record of recent conventions.

Different forms of instrument may be combined. Environmental law-making[40] often combines a framework convention with an accompanying (or subsequent) detailed protocol(s). Typically, the framework convention establishes a structure for further co-operation between the parties through monitoring and implementation procedures, exchanging data, and facilitating scientific research, while protocols provide for greater specificity in complex regulation. They also permit ease of response to changed scientific knowledge and circumstances. A convention also may anticipate subsequent conference resolutions, administrative agreements, or even memoranda of understanding when further agreement can be reached. As Clare Shine elucidates in her case study, the legal character of the last is especially controversial.

Conventions can generate 'secondary' or 'delegated' soft law, that is the statements and practice that develop around a treaty to supplement or correct the text.[41] The Montreal Protocol to the Vienna Convention for the Protection of the Ozone Layer provides a framework for a non-compliance procedure the details of which were prepared by a working party and adopted by the Fourth Meeting of the Parties to the Protocol in 1992.[42] The internal practices and administrative decisions of the Implementation Committee form secondary soft law.[43]

for unilateral termination; *Case Concerning the Gabcikovo-Nagymaros Project (Hungary/Slovakia)*, 1997 ICJ Rep. (Judgment of September 25).

[38] It may be difficult to determine whether draft texts have become accepted as (hard) customary international law, or are taken account of as soft law. In the *Case Concerning the Gabcikovo-Nagymaros Project (Hungary/Slovakia)*, 1997 ICJ Rep. (Judgment of September 25) the ICJ drew upon the International Law Commission's Draft Articles on State Responsibility, 1996.

[39] International humanitarian law has been developed through treaty law since the Geneva Red Cross Conventions of 1864. However where an instrument moves outside the terms of the Geneva Conventions a non-binding instrument may be preferred, *e.g.*, Declaration on the Protection of Women and Children in Emergency and Armed Conflict, 1974.

[40] *e.g.* the Vienna Convention for the Protection of the Ozone Layer, 1985, the Convention on Climate Change, 1992, and the Convention on Biodiversity, 1992.

[41] The concept of a 'living treaty' as enunciated by D. Bethlehem, in a paper presented to the International Law Association, British Branch, 1996, entails the notion of secondary soft law.

[42] Report of the Fourth Meeting of the Parties to the Montreal Protocol on Substances that deplete the Ozone Layer, UNEP/OZL.Pro.4/15, November 25, 1992, (1992) 3 Y.B.I.E.L. 819.

[43] There are numerous examples of secondary soft law but this project is examining only primary soft law.

As is evident from the case studies, the use of soft law forms has been closely associated with the growth of international institutions. Resolutions, declarations, codes of conduct, and guidelines articulated by global international or regional organizations have been termed 'non-legal soft law'.[44] Such instruments vary enormously. Their subject matter is as broad as that of international regulation, and indeed they have been widely used to intrude upon areas once accepted as falling within domestic jurisdiction. Some appear coercive in that they include deadlines for implementation,[45] targets for performance, and mechanisms for monitoring. Some are worded at a high level of abstraction and generality, others have a greater degree of specificity; some are narrow and highly specialist, others are broad in scope and vision; some are programmatic, others more immediate. There is a danger of over-proliferation, or 'rival' texts with instruments on the same topics emanating from different institutions. Textual variation, or even inconsistency, weakens the authority of all and creates incoherence. There is therefore a need for institutional coordination and cooperation.

During the 1990s a multiplicity of non-binding instruments in the form of declarations, agendas, programs, and platforms for action emanated from global summit conferences.[46] The subject matter of these conferences—human rights, population, environment, development, human habitation, the empowerment of women—could suggest that issues of social justice are deemed by states as inherently soft, or perhaps too intrusive into domestic jurisdiction to be the subject of binding obligations. Despite high governmental participation in the conferences and preparatory meetings, the normative weight of the final conference documents is uncertain. Usually, they have been adopted only after heated negotiation, and have been subject to reservations and interpretative statements, a development somewhat inconsistent with their legally non-binding character.[47] The texts are both declaratory and programmatic, targeting governments, international organizations, and non-governmental organizations (NGOs) for future action. They cut across established legal categories in ways that may mold future international legal discourse.[48] NGO fora have been held parallel to each of these confer-

---

[44] Decisions of the Security Council create binding obligations under the United Nations Charter, Art. 25. Other Security Council resolutions, such as authorization of the use of force without requiring all states to participate in action, may be considered a form of soft law.

[45] *e.g.* GA Res. 46/215, December 20, 1991 provided a deadline for the cessation of all drift-net fishing by December 31, 1992.

[46] *e.g.* the World Summit for Children, New York 1990; the World Conference on the Environment and Development, Rio de Janeiro, 1992; the World Conference on Human Rights, Vienna, 1993; the International Conference on Population and Development, Cairo, 1994; the World Summit for Social Development, Copenhagen, 1995; the Fourth World Conference on Women, Beijing, 1995; and Habitat II, Istanbul, 1996.

[47] In the context of the Fourth World Conference on Women see Otto, D., 'Holding up Half the Sky: But for Whose Benefit?' (1996) 6 *Australian Feminist L.J.* (1996) 6.

[48] *e.g.* the Beijing Platform for Action emphasizes the linkages between armed conflict, other forms of violence, civil and political, and economic, social, and cultural rights, sustainable

ences, attended by representatives of international NGOs in unprecedented numbers and ensuring maximum publicity for the official proceedings.[49] This level of activity perhaps suggests both a new institutional forum for international law-making and the inclusion of new participants within it. NGO observer status and the publicity generated by NGOs enhanced the openness of the governmental proceedings and prompted claims of the democratization of international law-making by the inclusion of voices not generally heard in international arenas. Yet, NGOs have not become part of the formal conference negotiations and their inclusion remains dependent upon government acquiescence. In addition, international civil society is neither monolithic nor democratic, different non-state actors have different agendas and priorities, and there is the danger of over-representation by those with the greatest resources. Nevertheless their input in regional and global preparatory meetings, as well as during the final conferences, may be a significant factor in maintaining informed pressure upon governments to comply with the expectations articulated, thus ensuring greater weight for the agreed statements.

Perhaps the most controversial claimants to international soft law status are those that emanate neither directly nor indirectly from states but are nonetheless intended to modify transnational behavior. Private norm-making initiatives such as the MacBride and Sullivan Principles, discussed by Chris McCrudden, statements of principles from individuals in non-governmental capacity,[50] texts prepared by expert groups,[51] the establishment of 'peoples' tribunals',[52] and self-regulating codes of conduct for networks of professional peoples[53] and multinational corporations come within this category. NGOs also sometimes wish to disassociate themselves from a government line.[54] The use of the non-legal form is dictated by lack of formal law-making capacity and the impact of a non-binding text depends upon the political and economic interests of the relevant players.

---

economic development, equality between women and men, political power-sharing, and accountability.

[49] *e.g.* it is estimated that over 1,500 organizations participated at the World Conference on Human Rights and 30,000 (mainly) women representatives went to the Fourth World Conference on Women.

[50] *e.g.* the Bangalore Declaration, 1988, the Victoria Falls Declaration of Principles for the Promotion of the Human Rights of Women, 1994, agreed by judges of the Commonwealth, reprinted in Commonwealth Secretariat, *Promotion of the Human Rights of Women and the Girl Child through the Judiciary, Commonwealth Declarations and Strategies for Action* (1997).

[51] *e.g.* the Helsinki Rules on the use of international rivers prepared by the International Law Association.

[52] Cassese, *supra* note 1 at 414, describes the Russell tribunal.

[53] See Bianchi, A., 'Globalization of Human Rights: The Role of Non-State Actors', in Teubner, G. (ed.), *Global Law Without a State* (1997) 179.

[54] The NGO Bangkok Declaration on Human Rights, 1993, challenges the assertions of some Asian governments with respect to an Asian approach to human rights.

2. Categorization of Soft Law Forms

There are various ways of categorizing international soft law. Instruments may be included within this generic term for a number of reasons:

(i)   they have been articulated in non-binding form according to traditional modes of law-making;

(ii) they contain vague and imprecise terms;

(iii) they emanate from bodies lacking international law-making authority;

(iv) they are directed at non-state actors whose practice cannot constitute customary international law;

(v)   they lack any corresponding theory of responsibility;

(vi) they are based solely upon voluntary adherence, or rely upon non-juridical means of enforcement.

A possible model for classification is to locate soft law according to its relationship with hard law. Categories might include:

(i) Elaborative soft law, that is principles that provide guidance to the interpretation, elaboration, or application of hard law.[55] This may be envisaged by a treaty such as a framework convention, or simply refer back to treaty obligations with the inference that the hard and soft law are inter-dependent and that the latter derives authority from, and extends the meaning of, the former.[56]

(ii) Emergent hard law, that is principles that are first formulated in non-binding form with the possibility, or even aspiration,[57] of negotiating a subsequent treaty, or harden into binding custom through the development of state practice and *opinio juris*.[58] This process can be part of a deliberate strategy. The programmatic, educative, and evolutionary functions are widely accepted as one among the benefits of

---

[55] *e.g.* General Assembly resolutions that elaborate the United Nations Charter such as General Assembly Declaration on Principles of International Law Concerning Friendly Relations and Co-operation among States in Accordance with the Charter of the United Nations, GA Res. 2625, October 24, 1970.

[56] *e.g.* the Vienna and Beijing Conferences called for ratification of the Convention on the Elimination of All Forms of Discrimination Against Women and removal of crippling reservations.

[57] The articulation of such aspiration can itself have catalytic effect. Cf. '[o]ne should never underestimate the focalizing and authoritizing effect of the use of legal symbols in these communications'; Reisman, *supra* note 21.

[58] *e.g.* the Universal Declaration of Human Rights, GA Res. 217A (III), December 10, 1948 and the Stockholm Declaration on the Human Environment, adopted by the United Nations Conference on the Human Environment, UN Doc. A/CONF.48/14 and Corr. 1 (1972) 11 I.L.M. 1416 have both hardened through treaty and custom.

the soft form of recording consensus.[59] It is unclear whether 'piloting' a treaty through an earlier soft declaration (as has become regular practice in the field of human rights) is a significant factor in inducing compliance. Voluntary compliance lacks the necessary will to change status from soft to hard law, unless a new form of law-making is asserted.

(iii) Soft law as evidence of the existence of hard obligations.[60]

(iv) Parallel soft and hard law, that is similar provisions articulated in both hard and soft forms allowing the soft version to act as a fall-back provision.[61]

(v) Soft law as a source of legal obligation, through acquiescence and estoppel, perhaps against the original intentions of the parties.

This categorization is problematic in that it defines soft law in terms of its distinction from hard law, and not in its own terms. It excludes what may be termed 'autonomous' soft law, principles that stand alone. It also assumes that the transformation into hard obligation is desirable. This may not always be the case, for example where ongoing flexibility is required, or the consequences of state responsibility for non-compliance are not warranted.

3. The 'Hardening' of Soft Law

Soft law is a device that can be deliberately used by non-state actors to influence state behavior when there is little prospect of successfully concluding a treaty. The enthusiasm with which NGOs seek articulation of norms, albeit in non-binding form, suggests that they view the soft/hard law distinction as carrying little weight. The campaign with respect to state responsibility for failure to eliminate violence against women is a good example. NGOs and individual experts collaborated in producing the first draft texts of what became the General Assembly Declaration on the Elimination of all Forms of Violence against Women, 1993. This resolution, in conjunction with the Committee on the Elimination of Discrimination Against Women's General Comment No. 19 (1992) and consistent wording in the Vienna Programme of Action and the Beijing Platform for Action (all legally non-binding) are viewed by women's NGOs as having successfully placed the issue on the international agenda and requiring state response. Although a regional

[59] Dupuy, R.J., 'Declaratory Law and Programmatory Law: from Revolutionary Custom to "Soft Law"', in Horn, N. (ed.), *Studies in Transnational Economic Law: Legal Problems of Codes of Conduct for Multinational Enterprises* (1980) 247.

[60] *e.g.* the ICJ has given weight to General Assembly resolutions prohibiting the use of force and illegal intervention as evidence of both state practice and *opinio juris*; *Military and Paramilitary Activities in and against Nicaragua (Nicaragua v. United States)*, Merits, 1986 ICJ Rep. 14 at paras 183–6.

[61] *e.g.* the prohibition of the use of force is expressed in both United Nations Charter, Art. 2(4) and GA Res. 2625, October 24, 1970.

convention on violence against women was adopted within the framework of the Organization of American States in the same period, it remains hard to envisage global acceptance of a treaty on this subject.

Once a prospective norm has been formulated in soft form it can become a catalyst for the development of customary international law. To many commentators this is the *raison d'être* of soft law and its entry point into the traditional sources of law. However this leaves open its status before that transformation and, further, the 'sliding scale' of required consistent state practice might in fact lower the level of compliance deemed necessary,[62] even while the obligation is deemed to have hardened. Also the relationship between customary international law and soft law is ambiguous. Some jurists regard custom itself as soft because of its vagueness and imprecision, but its inclusion within Article 38(1)(b) of the Statute of the ICJ and constitutional incorporation into the domestic law of many states weighs against this labeling.

Since categories of hard and soft law are not polarized but lie within a continuum that itself is constantly evolving,[63] it may be impossible to know whether or not an instrument has the character of emerging hard law, or whether it has achieved this status at a precise point in time. Georges Abi-Saab has identified three significant criteria for determining whether this process has occurred:[64] the circumstances of the adoption of the instrument, including voting patterns and expressed reservations, the concreteness of the language, and the existence of follow up procedures. Using similar criteria, in its advisory opinion on the *Legality of Nuclear Weapons*, the ICJ considered that conflicting state practice had prevented the emergence of any customary rule despite many relevant General Assembly resolutions. It also rejected the argument that such resolutions constituted *opinio juris* since several had been adopted 'with substantial numbers of negative votes and abstentions'.[65] Although non-binding instruments do not become binding merely through repetition, 'a series of resolutions may show the gradual evolution of the opinio juris required for the establishment of a new rule' and may influence behavior, e.g. in promoting treaty negotiations.[66] This is not necessarily a one way process and claims of soft law becoming hard obligations can lose, as well as gain, credence over time.

Multiple strategies may be pursued in an endeavor to transform soft law into binding norms.[67] These may include critical use of secondary soft law, NGO and civil society targeting, and institutional practices. It may be within

---

[62] Kirgis, F., 'Custom on a Sliding Scale' (1987) 81 *Am. J. Int'l L.* 147.

[63] Riphagen, W., 'From Soft Law to Jus Cogens and Back' (1987) 17 *Vict. U. W L. Rev.* 81.

[64] Abi-Saab, G., 'Cours Général de Droit International Public' (1987) 207 *Rec. des Cours* 160–1.

[65] Legality of the Threat or Use of Nuclear Weapons (1996) 35 I.L.M. 809 at para. 71.

[66] *Ibid.*

[67] Cf. 'legal soft law may become more narrowly interpreted and become more enforceable'; Ingelse, *supra* note 17.

the mandate of one or more international institutions to carry forward the principles of a non-binding instrument.[68] For example the Commission on the Status of Women has sought to give effect to sections of the Beijing Platform for Action through the acceptance of recommendations of groups of experts established for this purpose.[69]

Internal institutional policies and practices may become binding through external pressures created by multiple actors. The creation of the World Bank Inspection Panel, for example, has transformed general guidelines and objectives effectively into law, because that is the way in which outsiders have viewed them.[70] Institutional compliance also may harden internal policies and practices, motivated by the importance accorded a particular instrument by the institutional management and enhanced by institutional structures such as quality insurance mechanisms, or desired for institutional convenience. Thus, a desire to avoid requests for inspection may encourage internal compliance with World Bank operational standards.

Soft treaty law may undergo a similar hardening process. The changed perception of the 1966 International Covenant on Economic, Social and Cultural Rights (ICESCR) is illustrative. It contained relatively weak language of obligation,[71] had no monitoring committee and no complaints mechanism comparable to that established under the First Optional Protocol to the ICCPR. Economic and social rights were widely regarded as lacking legal specificity, subjective and non-justiciable. However, external pressure led to the establishment in 1986 by ECOSOC of the Committee on Economic, Social and Cultural Rights to which states were required to report. This new institutional base has concentrated attention and the Committee has amplified the minimalist terms of the Convention through its thoughtful and detailed General Comments. Sufficient legal content has been given, *inter alia*, to the right to housing that it has been the basis of decision within Indian domestic courts. The Committee also has adopted stronger concluding comments and suggested steps to take against states that fail to comply with their reporting obligations.[72] An optional protocol providing for an individual complaints mechanism has been drafted and is under consideration. The combined impact of these measures has been to raise the level of obligation under the Covenant far beyond that originally envisaged. A number of

[68] For the implementation of Agenda 21 see A. Kiss, commentary, in this volume.
[69] Thematic Issues before the Commission on the Status of Women, Report of the Secretary-General, UN Doc. E/CN.6/1998/5, January 23, 1998.
[70] See Boisson de Chazournes, L., Policy Guidance and Compliance: the World Bank Operational Standards, below, p. 281.
[71] *e.g.* ICESCR, Art. 2(1) provides the obligation to 'take steps . . . with a view to achieving progressively the full realization of the rights in contrast with the immediate obligation' to respect and ensure the rights within the ICCPR, Art. 2(1).
[72] Steiner, H., and Alston, P., *International Human Rights in Context Law, Politics and Morals* (1993) 256–329 for the evolution of the ICESCR.

factors have contributed to the on-going transformation: greater political acceptance of economic and social rights,[73] NGO activity, academic analysis of economic and social rights,[74] institutional structures, the practice of similar bodies, notably the Human Rights Committee, and the drive, expertise, and vision of a few individuals. It is the potential for such refinement of obligation that in many instances motivates the adoption of soft law.

Finally, hard obligations may be deliberately softened to ensure some change in behavior without producing the harsh and possibly counter-productive consequences of breach. Negotiated agreements and amicable settlements between disputing parties within the framework of a dispute resolution clause, for example a conciliated agreement, may be inconsistent with the strict terms of the treaty. Such practice can undermine the expectations engendered by the treaty and change binding into non-binding obligations.

B. THE ACTORS

1. The Proponents of Soft Law

The origin of soft law is context specific and different actors are likely to promote binding or non-binding instruments in different circumstances according to their political, economic, and military interests. Inevitably the focus among the participants will be on what is politically possible or desirable, a matter subject to constant change and requiring that close attention be paid to unfolding international and domestic events.

Economically and militarily powerful states may favor hard obligations that they can impose and enforce. When the duties imposed are not deemed in their interest such states might still favor a legally binding treaty to which they can refuse to adhere, or they may become parties with appropriate reservations. Alternatively, international or domestic pressure might convince such states of the political desirability of participating in the drafting of a soft law instrument that allows them to present a co-operative attitude while requiring no formal steps of adherence. Weaker states might promote a soft law instrument on matters of concern to themselves, realistically accepting it as the best they can politically achieve and in the hope that it might gain greater force over time. Growing diversity in the geo-political and economic circumstances of those states that gained independence after 1945 means that common interests can no longer be assumed and that there is a more nuanced

---

[73] The affirmation in the Vienna Declaration and Programme of Action, June 25, 1993 (1993) 32 I.L.M. 1661, of the indivisibility and interdependence of civil and political and economic, social, and cultural rights is an example of non-legal soft law being used to enhance the transformation of legal soft law.

[74] Craven, M., *The International Covenant on Economic, Social and Cultural Rights* (1995).

approach to the desirability of law-making through soft instrumentalities. Disparate concerns may mean that a soft law instrument is the best that can be accomplished, acknowledging that changed behavior is required without making concrete concessions.[75] Contradictions between claims based on disadvantage and those of sovereign equality and independence continue to muddy conceptual thinking and law-making, especially in the contexts of economic development and environmental regulation.[76]

Where possible, non-state actors are likely to lobby states to conclude binding agreements that they can then use to pressure state compliance through domestic litigation, lobbying, and international procedures.[77] Seeking the support of influential states that will carry the process forward is therefore an important strategy. Where a binding agreement is not deemed politically possible or desirable, non-state actors have worked effectively for the conclusion of a non-binding instrument. NGOs also help change the political environment in driving for a binding agreement that has been previously thought unlikely to succeed. NGO activities with respect to the Rome Statute for a Permanent International Criminal Court, 1998 and the Landmines Convention are examples.

NGOs may also target other non-state actors to persuade them to change their behavior. This can cause the emergence of soft law through the interactions of diverse non-state actors. For example NGOs may use the power of actual or threatened consumer boycott to force change in corporate practice, giving rise to self-regulating codes or standards to stave off more coercive, external regulation.[78]

2. The Targets and Reliance upon Soft Law

The targets of soft law instruments are equally diverse. They include states, business and trade institutions,[79] NGOs,[80] IGOs,[81] officials of

[75] This may be especially so in the environmental area, *e.g.*, the Statement of Principles for a Global Consensus on the Management, Conservation, and Sustainable Development of All Types of Forest rather than a binding agreement on forests.

[76] See further Chinkin, C., 'The Challenge of Soft Law: Development and Change in International Law' (1989) 38 *Int'l & Comp. L.Q.* 850 at 854–5.

[77] See Maupain, p. 373 below, for the resistance of the workers' representatives in the ILO to the suggestion of greater use of soft law because they feared this would weaken ILO influence.

[78] Spiro, P., 'New Global Potentates: Nongovernmental Organizations and the "Unregulated" Marketplace' (1996) 18 *Cardozo L. Rev.* 957. Spiro illustrates this point by reference to the Greenpeace action over Brent Spar; see also Spiro, P., 'New Actors on the International Stage' (1998) 2 *Hofstra L. & Pol'y Symp.* 101 at 115.

[79] *e.g.* WHO Code on the International Marketing of Breastmilk Substitutes, 1981; the Forty Recommendations of the Financial Action Task Force on Money Laundering.

[80] *e.g.* there are a number of instruments concerning NGO relationships with UN agencies in the field.

[81] *e.g.* GA Res. 3232 (XXIX), November 12, 1974 that is directed at the ICJ recommending that it take account of progressive developments in international law and consider use of its power to decide *ex aequo et bono*, if the parties so decide.

IGOs,[82] government officials,[83] and individuals.[84] Soft law that is targeted at private actors cannot be transformed into customary international law as it has no intended impact upon state behavior. It may be used specifically to target private actors, including corporations, in ways that would not be possible through treaties, especially in legal systems that have no doctrine of self-executing treaties. Soft law thus straddles international (traditionally targeted at states) and national (traditionally targeted at individuals) regulation and fills gaps. In this way it can be seen as a 'bridge' between international legality and legitimacy.[85] The response of the target is all important in establishing that legitimacy and, where states are the target, in transforming the principles into binding international obligations.

Normative standards articulated through soft forms are relied upon by a variety of actors in both domestic and international fora. Advocates may argue for adherence by state agencies and thus become instrumental in developing state practice, while government and corporate lawyers advise on compliance with international expectations, and international bodies invoke them in their dealings with governmental or non-governmental agencies. Development banks, for example, can determine appropriate standards for bank-financed projects or technical assistance programs from international soft law instruments.[86] Normative provisions from international guidelines or codes of conduct can be incorporated into private contracts and financial loans and implemented into domestic law through formal prescription or the enunciation of standards by administrative and judicial decision-makers. International decision-makers too can rely upon soft law principles. The International Tribunal for War Crimes in the Former Yugoslavia, for example, has drawn upon a wide variety of non-binding, as well as binding, instruments in its molding of international criminal law. In *Prosecutor* v. *Dŭsko Tadić* the Trial Chamber used a range of non-binding materials—the Report of the Secretary-General, the Report of the *ad hoc* committee on the Permanent International Criminal Court, the ILC Draft Articles on Crimes against the Peace and Security of Mankind—to assist it in defining the elements of the offences charged and issues of jurisdiction.[87] This practice shows how those assessing conformity with international standards of behavior do not always differentiate between hard and soft obligations, but draw upon all

---

[82] *e.g.* the Secretary-General of the UN is often the target of Security Council and General Assembly resolutions directing him to take certain actions.

[83] The Memorandum of Understanding Concerning Conservation Measures for the Slender-billed Curlew, 1994 is addressed to environment ministries; C. Shine, n. 212.

[84] *e.g* International Chamber of Commerce, Uniform Customs and Practice for Documentary Credits (UCP); Uniform Rules for Demand Guarantees.

[85] Ingelse, C., *supra* note 17.

[86] *e.g.* the Draft Declaration on Indigenous Persons might be used in the context of resettlement programmes or the Forest Declaration in development projects: Boisson de Chazournes, L., at 298–9 below.

[87] *Prosecutor* v. *Dŭsko Tadić a/k/a/ Dule*, IT–94–IT, May 7, 1997 (1997) 36 I.L.M. 908.

available instruments across the continuum of legality to present as full a picture as possible of appropriate expectations.

Not all reliance upon soft law accords with the original intentions of those involved. Krut explains, for example, how the FAO and WHO jointly established the Codex Alimentarus Commission in 1963 to establish food and health standards to assist developing countries in improving health and environmental safety. Codex decision-making, however, has since become dominated by multinational corporations for their own purposes and research has shown the increasing degree of corporate involvement in setting standards to meet their own needs, not those of the intended beneficiaries. He argues that the GATT Uruguay Round elevated the Code from 'a relatively minor body that recommended standards to governments to a critically important body that works for standards to be globally "harmonized"'.[88]

C. DETERMINING THE LEVEL OF SOFTNESS OR HARDNESS OF OBLIGATION

A wide range of factors can assist in determining whether an instrument constitutes a binding agreement. The criteria are fluid, cumulative, and interlocking. None are determinative and all are context specific.[89] The following section examines the relevance of some such indicators: the form of the instrument, the intention of the parties as evidenced by the language employed and their subsequent behavior, and the subject matter and content of the instrument.

1. Form

It is axiomatic that neither the form nor the nomenclature of an instrument is determinative of its legal status. As has been pointed out by the ICJ,[90] the International Law Commission,[91] commentators,[92] and documentation of state practice[93] binding legal agreements take many forms. Form is determinative in the sense that a formally concluded treaty between states is *per se* legally binding under international law, while an institutional resolution or

---

[88] Krut, R., *Globalization and Civil Society: NGO Influence in International Decision-Making* (1997) 21.

[89] Van Hoof has formulated a mechanistic 'check-list' of manifestations that the parties intended to be bound; cited in Ingelse, *supra* note 17.

[90] *e.g. Temple of Preah Vihear (Cambodia* v. *Thailand)* 1961 ICJ Rep. 17 at 32; *Nuclear Tests Cases (Australia* v. *France)* 1974 ICJ Rep. 253 at para. 45.

[91] *e.g.* [1966] 2 Y.B.I.L.C. 172.

[92] *e.g.* Jennings, R., and Watts, A., *Oppenheim's International Law*, I (9th edn. 1992) 1200; Brownlie, I., *Principles of Public International Law* (5th edn. 1998) 610.

[93] See Aust, A., 'The Theory and Practice of Informal International Instruments' (1986) 35 *Int'l & Comp. L.Q.* 787 at 799.

agreement between non-state actors is not.[94] Form is not determinative in that binding obligations can be created in numerous other ways, for example through oral agreements, unilateral statements, minutes of a meeting, exchange of letters, and even through an intermediary.[95] In *Qatar* v. *Bahrain* the ICJ upheld the binding character of the signed minutes of a meeting and apparently reduced the grey area between soft and hard law by determining that the words of the bilateral agreement overrode any contrary intentions.

2. Intention of the Parties

A reluctance to abandon the consensual basis of international law is apparent in the weight that traditionally is accorded to whether states parties intended to create a legal relationship. Intention to be bound may be deduced from the language employed in the agreement, the circumstances of its conclusion, and, occasionally, the subsequent actions of the parties. The ICJ has affirmed that in determining the binding nature of an agreement it 'must have regard above all to its actual terms and to the particular circumstances in which it was drawn up'.[96] However in *Qatar* v. *Bahrain* the Court highlighted the words of the agreement, perhaps even contrary to the intentions of the parties. 'Whatever may have been the motives of each of the Parties, the Court can only confine itself to the actual terms of the Minutes as the expression of their common intention, and to the interpretation of them which it has already given.'[97]

The language of instruments tends to be more specific in denying legal obligation than in accepting it.[98] It is therefore comparatively easy to identify when all those involved deny creating any legally binding obligation, but less so when there is disagreement, deliberate ambiguity, or indeterminacy.[99] Texts in different languages may add further uncertainty[100] and the language of diplomacy and 'UN speak' often is deliberately imprecise.

Other ways of determining the parties' intentions include the negotiation history and the parties' subsequent behavior. Soft law instruments may be as

[94] The Vienna Convention on the Law of Treaties between States and International Organizations or between International Organizations 1986 affirms that international governmental organizations can enter into treaties.

[95] *Case Concerning Maritime Delimitation and Territorial Questions between Qatar and Bahrain* (Jurisdiction and Admissibility) 1994 ICJ Rep. 6.

[96] *Aegean Sea Continental Shelf Case (Greece* v. *Turkey)* 1978 ICJ Rep. 3 at para. 96 cited in *Case Concerning Maritime Delimitation and Territorial Questions between Qatar and Bahrain* 1994 ICJ Rep. 6 at paras. 22 and 23. See Chinkin, C., 'Mirage in the Sand? Distinguishing Binding and Nonbinding Relations between States' (1997) 10 *Leiden J.Int'l L.* 223.

[97] 1995 ICJ Rep. 6 at para. 41.

[98] Aust refers to the 'slightly tiresome, if harmless—even quaint—British obsession' of adhering strictly to unequivocal form and wording for binding agreements: Aust, A., *supra* note 93.

[99] Franck, T., *Fairness in International Law and Institutions* (1995) 30–4.

[100] See *Case Concerning Maritime Delimitation and Territorial Questions between Qatar and Bahrain* 1994 ICJ Rep. 6.

intensely negotiated as treaties and great weight subsequently may be given to the voting patterns and the number and character of dissenting voices.[101] *Travaux préparatoires* may provide subjective and contemporaneous evidence of the debates and circumstances of negotiations. In the *Aegean Sea Continental Shelf* case the background to the negotiations and prior diplomatic exchanges were seen as crucial in determining the parties' intentions, whereas in *Qatar v. Bahrain* the Court largely discounted the usefulness of the *travaux préparatoires* because of their 'fragmentary nature'. The Court paid little heed to the Bahrain pleadings in which the negotiations were analyzed and Bahraini intentions explained. Instead it concentrated upon the language of the recorded minutes of the meeting. The dilemma is that emphasis upon parties' intentions allows any party to reinterpret those intentions and to act accordingly, but emphasis upon the surrounding circumstances enables those intentions to be discounted, even while the decision maker purports to determine them through interpretation of the words used.

The intentions of drafters may be irrelevant where they lack international law-making capacity, or where those intentions are concealed by institutional procedures. The decision in *Qatar v. Bahrain* was in the context of bilateral negotiations where the parties were deciding their own future course of action, but many soft law instruments are much more widely directed. Formal means of adherence to a treaty serve to identify parties, but this does not apply to soft law instruments.

Some writers evoke consent itself as the basis for distinction, thus associating consent-based norms with hard law and non-consensual sources with soft law, with no predetermination as to which forms of law-making are consensual.[102] Just as the concept of state consent is a myth, so too is that of relying upon the intentions of the parties, or even the language of the agreement, to determine its status. Subjective will can be determined only through objective assessment, supplemented by notions of rationality and justice. The decision-maker must rely on a 'strategy of evasion'.[103] As Koskenniemi explains, '[t]he difficulty . . . is that statements or contexts do not demonstrate their objective nature automatically' and construction inevitably denies the subjectivity of at least one of the parties, in the guise of the decision-maker 'knowing better'.

3. Content and Subject-matter

The inclusion of certain provisions or institutional structures may indicate the hardness of the obligations incurred, *e.g.*, processes for amendment, modification, uniform interpretation, or termination may suggest the existence of binding obligations. Even within the framework of hard law, however,

[101] F. Maupain describes this process within the ILO; see p. 372 below.
[102] Kennedy, D., *International Legal Structures* (1987).
[103] Koskenniemi, M., *From Apology to Utopia* (1988) 300.

interpretative and other techniques may be espoused to avoid binding obligations. The 'margin of appreciation' doctrine mediates between subjective
implementation and objective obligations and its use by the European Court
of Human Rights illustrates the employment of soft law approaches within
authoritative decision-making processes. Reservations and interpretative
declarations are other ways of denying or undermining legal obligations
drafted in treaties and even soft law instruments. The latter suggests that
states are reluctant to rely upon the legalistic assertion that they have incurred
no binding obligation through acceptance of a non-binding instrument, perhaps in response to the high profile accorded to some such instruments
through the activities of non-state actors. Nonetheless, it clouds the distinction between hard and soft law. Blurring is also caused by the creation of
institutional structures through use of non-binding instruments, the clearest
example being the Organization on Security and Co-operation in Europe.

Processes for dispute resolution, monitoring, implementation, and sanctions also have been devised across a continuum from soft to hard procedures, thus reducing their importance in determining the nature of the
underlying obligation. Reliance on the existence or otherwise of these indices
of compliance misses the point that most international law does not rely upon
Austinian sanctions. Soft dispute resolution processes (negotiation, mediation, conciliation) should not be viewed as 'mistakes or pathologies' but
rather as reasoned decisions to avoid the confrontation of the adversarial
process and the consequences of a win/lose outcome.[104] Similarly 'soft' sanctioning systems[105] might be deemed preferable to demands for redress for
their potential to foster constructive dialogue and conforming behavior. On
the other hand, those offering financial incentives or special arrangements for
compliance might find it politically expedient at home to present such
arrangements as required by international obligation. The range of international instruments allows for such maneuverability without demanding
compartmentalization between them.

The perceived seriousness of the topic also might be indicative, although
here again there are contradictions. The paradox is that claims of *jus cogens*
are often introduced through soft law instrumentalities, or underlie these
statements, *e.g.*, the right to a secure existence, to self-determination, to
development.[106] International legal regulation does not move on a linear
scale from non-law at one end to norms of *jus cogens* at the other, but rather
there is a complex interlocking between the two.[107] The social justice agen-

---

[104] Reisman, *supra* note 21 at 138.

[105] Birnie, P., 'Legal Techniques of Settling Disputes: The Soft Settlement Approach', in
Butler, W. (ed.), *Perestroika and International Law* (1990). Examples of soft sanctioning procedures are requirements for reporting to human rights committees rather than individual complaint or adjudicatory mechanisms.

[106] Riphagen, *supra* note 63.   [107] *Ibid.*

das of the global summit conferences are illustrative: they concern matters of intense importance, even of global survival, but fall outside the parameters of traditional international law. They challenge the traditional paradigms of international law-making, state responsibility, international legal personality, dispute resolution, and sovereign equality. Soft law instruments to some extent answer the demands of international civil society that action be taken, while preserving to political elites the freedom to curtail their obligations.[108]

D. DOES INTERNATIONAL LAW NEED A CATEGORY OF SOFT LAW?

Despite scepticism about the juristic basis of the concept of international soft law, the reality is that states and other international actors have recourse to diverse methods of setting agendas, influencing behavior, and supplementing and shading international obligations. All of the growing number of participants in matters of international concern need to be able to make informed assessments of the likely actions and reactions of other actors, so as to make reasoned choices with respect to their behavior. Soft law helps fashion those choices by indicating the restraints upon behavior that may be self-imposed or demanded by others. The various instruments do not exist in a vacuum but form part of the many indicators of behavior. Practice shows that these can all be manipulated to serve different interests.

Soft law can be seen as a tool for negotiators and those who set, or wish to set, international agendas.[109] It can be used to break a deadlock in negotiations where disparities in wealth, power, and interests make binding agreement impossible. Different cultural and economic structures and interests can be accommodated through the subjective application of 'soft' language such as 'appropriate measures', 'best efforts', 'as far as possible', or 'with a view to achieving progressively'.[110] The programmatic use of soft law allows open-ended measures to be concluded, while affording time for their further elaboration within the agreed framework and timetable.[111] This can be especially significant where some states are resisting international legal regulation but there is a political awareness, perhaps engendered by civil society, that

---

[108] Disarmament is another example; in the *Legality of the Threat or Use of Nuclear Weapons* advisory opinion the ICJ discounted the effect of GA Resolutions on constituting a legal prohibition of nuclear weapons despite the potential impact of such weapons on the right to life and to a sustainable environment.

[109] Reisman, *supra* note 21.

[110] Gold, J., 'Strengthening the Soft International Law of Exchange Agreements' (1983) 77 *A.J.I.L.* (1983) 443.

[111] However the experience of UNCED plus five in Kyoto, 1997, suggests that while the timetable might be observed the commitment of some states to maintaining the process might be minimal.

'something must be done'. In this sense soft law can be presented 'as the only alternative to anarchy'.[112]

The complexity of international legal affairs has outpaced traditional methods of law-making, necessitating management through international organizations, specialized agencies, programmes, and private bodies that do not fit the paradigm of Article 38(1) of the Statute of the ICJ. Consequently the concept of soft law facilitates international co-operation by acting as a bridge between the formalities of law-making and the needs of international life by legitimating behavior and creating stability. Behavior in conformity with soft law principles is unlikely to be denounced, even by those who have remained outside their enunciation, while the appropriateness of rigid adherence to hard obligations may be undermined by emerging soft law. Even the expectation that soft law instruments will be ignored is an important factor in anticipating future behavior. Their negotiation requires response, even negative response, that clarifies the stance of others.

These developments also have a negative aspect. The contradictions both within the concept of soft law and, more specifically, between provisions articulated within different fora and by different protagonists lack coherence. Claimants can pick and choose between these instruments to support their position while decision-makers can either assert their validity or resort to formalism. Soft law may maintain the fiction of a universal international law, while in reality leading to its destruction through the formulation of relative standards. The end of the Cold War has reduced the polarized political use of arguments of relativity, but they remain potent in North/South dialogue. The conclusion of negotiations in soft form may conceal real substantive differences between states and deflect attention away from the slow pace at which principles of international responsibility and accountability are evolving. There may be a dislocation between the 'popular' civil society view that all such instruments constitute binding international obligations and that of governments that uphold the sanctity of treaties and custom. In this sense the distinction between hard and soft obligations creates a smoke screen behind which governments can shelter when demands for compliance are made. On the other hand such endeavors are not entirely cynical. As shown by the studies in this project, the motivations that cause the negotiation of these instruments may be supplemented by extraneous factors fostering compliance, and thus promoting international stability through regulatory forms.

---

[112] Gold, *supra* note 110.

Chapter 2
Compliance Theories

Choosing to Comply: Theorizing from International Relations and Comparative Politics

PETER M. HAAS

INTRODUCTION

This chapter discusses possible elements for understanding patterns of compliance with international non-binding norms (soft law), focusing on manipulable variables that may influence individual states' decisions to comply. States construct (or choose) their compliance, and such choices (or constructs) are now generally the consequence of international ideational and institutional forces, at times mediated by domestic politics and structures. It begins with conceptual discussions of compliance and soft law, followed by a review of perspectives from comparative politics and international relations about what induces states to comply with non-binding instruments. While a domestic and state-based account offers a baseline estimate of states' propensity to comply with a particular soft law instrument in isolation from any other influences, such an analysis is inadequate for most contemporary efforts because domestic influences do not operate in a vacuum; systemic and transnational factors now exercise a strong influence on the origin of many domestic factors and the political context in which they operate.

International lawyers have encountered difficulty in understanding compliance with 'hard law', making it perhaps useful to focus on factors that may influence compliance with international commitments in general. Indeed, Charles Lipson argues that the distinction between international and domestic law is much more significant than between forms of international law, because we do not know what proportion of hard and soft law obligations are converted into legally binding domestic obligations in which aggrieved parties have the right to sue.[1] Hard law and soft law share a set of features insofar as they emerge out of the same impulse of states needing to signal their commitments to other states in a setting of international anarchy. Thus this chapter looks at factors that influence choice under such circumstances.

---

[1] Lipson, C., 'Why Are Some International Agreements Informal?' (1991) 45 *Int. Org.* 495–538; Bull, H., *The Anarchical Society* (2nd edn., 1995).

Very little is known about the degree to which states comply with international commitments and empirical studies suggest that national compliance is uneven at best.[2] Even in the E.U., where compliance with environmental directives should be strongest because of overriding public concern combined with strong international institutions, implementation varies by country.[3] Moreover, George Downs and others argue that estimations of compliance with international injunctions are systematically overstated because instances where states comply in the absence of strong incentives for non-compliance are less important to signal state willingness to comply than is compliance in the face of material incentives for violations.[4] The lawyers' dictum that 'most treaties are complied with most of the time' is surely premature, and probably exaggerated. Studies of compliance find variation in compliance along a number of dimensions. Not all countries comply with the same legal instruments, the same country may vary in its compliance with different legal instruments across functional areas and even within the same issue area, and such patterns may change over time.

In the absence of well-established patterns of compliance, or well-defined expectations for patterns of compliance on the part of decision makers, this chapter relies on theoretically-informed foundations to identify factors that may influence compliance. Overall levels of compliance would be measured by whether most states vary their behavior consistently with international commitments. Operationalizing such concepts faces the problem that some treaties are ambiguous, often intentionally, about what targets or procedures are expected so that it is difficult to specify with any precision whether states are in compliance or not. National compliance could be measured in terms of state resources committed to the specified goal after ratification, *i.e.* whether a state changes its policy, laws, organizational routines, and practices in accordance with international commitments. While the best evidence for compliance with most types of international commitments is based on changes in investment

---

[2] On human rights see: Donnelly, J., *Universal Human Rights in Theory and Practice* (1989); McCormick, J.M., and Mitchell, N.J., 'Human Rights Violations, Umbrella Concepts, and Empirical Analysis' (1997) 49 *World Politics* 510–25; Brannum, K., *Compliance with Human Rights Norms*, Ph.D dissertation in political science, University of Massachusetts at Amherst (1998). On trade see: Jackson, J.H., *et al.*, *Implementing the Tokyo Round* (1984); Hudec, R.E., *Enforcing International Trade Law: The Evolution of the Modern GATT Legal System* (1993); Jackson, J., *The World Trading System* (1989). On arms control see: Nolan, J. (ed.), *Global Engagement: Cooperation and Security in the 21st Century* (1994); Spector, L.S., *Nuclear Ambitions* (1990). On environment see: Sand, P. (ed.), *The Effectiveness of International Environmental Agreements* (1992); Weiss, E.B., and Jacobson, H.K. (eds.), *Engaging Countries* (1998); Victor, D., *et al.* (eds.), *The Implementation and Effectiveness of International Environmental Commitments* (1998).

[3] Haigh, N., *et al.*, *Comparative Report: Water and Waste in Four Countries* (1986); Ward, N., *et al.*, 'Implementing European Water Quality Directives' in Baker, S., *et al.* (eds.), *The Politics of Sustainable Development* (1997) 202.

[4] Downs, G.W., *et al.*, 'Is the Good News About Compliance Good News About Cooperation?' (1996) 50 *Int. Org.* 379–406.

patterns and bureaucratic budgets, such evidence is often absent or extremely difficult to obtain in terms of time or money, so that research is based on the weaker evidence of enforcement. It is important to distinguish cases of deliberate compliance from serendipitous compliance, where states' actions fit international obligations but without deliberate choice. This distinction may be accomplished through process tracing, identifying whether credible causal mechanisms affect the choice by which compliance occurs.

The actual measurement of compliance may be difficult because domestic political systems vary in the actual location of enforcement and because states may submit false reports or refuse to submit data which they anticipate to be embarrassing. Highly federal systems locate authority for compliance at local levels, which are difficult to research and usually far from the direct influence of the central state.[5] Enforcement of air pollution policy in Austria, Germany, and Switzerland, for example, occurs at the level of the state, *Länder*, or canton, and in Denmark water pollution standards are enforced by municipal and local water courts, over which the national government has little direct influence.

Compliance is a matter of state choice. While some choices may be easy because compliance is manifestly in the national interest and there is little organized opposition, as may be the case regarding ISO standards, most decisions are potentially much more difficult. Compliance entails the state committing scarce resources, either in terms of staff time, political energy and attention, or money, a decision with distributional consequences. Even if a state believes that signing a treaty is in its best interest, the political calculations associated with the subsequent decision to comply with international agreements are distinct and different.[6] As long as states do not anticipate stringent political retribution for failing to comply with a commitment, they may well commit to obligations which they know they cannot meet, or which are crafted so ambiguously that their duties cannot be interpreted uniformly. In fact there are a host of self-interested reasons why states may adopt norms in soft law instruments, independently of any expectation of subsequent compliance. States may recognize that they are unable to comply, and commit out of a hope that others will help them comply—*e.g.* many Eastern European governments in the area of the environment—or signal their commitment in related areas of national importance, to strengthen a leader's political

---

[5] Michelman, H.J., and Soldatos, P. (eds.), *Federalism and International Relations* (1990); Hanf, K., 'Enforcing Environmental Laws', in Hill, M. (ed.), *New Agendas in the Study of the Policy Process* (1993); Hanf, K., and Toonen, T.A.J. (eds.), *Policy Implementation in Federal and Unitary Systems* (1985); Downing, P.B., and Hanf, K. (eds.), *International Comparisons in Implementing Pollution Laws* (1983); Harrison, K., 'Is Cooperation the Answer? Canadian Environment Enforcement in Comparative Context' (1995) 14 *J. Pol'y Analysis & Management*, pp. 221–44; Gross, A.C., and Scott, N.E., 'Comparative Environmental Legislation and Action' (1980) 2 *Int'l & Comp. L.Q.*, pp. 619–63.

[6] A U.S. diplomat, discussing WTO negotiations on National Public Radio, said that 'reaching agreement on the pact was relatively easy. The real negotiations began the day after, when China wouldn't enforce its intellectual property obligations.'

potential for domestic implementation, or because agreement is part of a broader diplomatic culture with which leaders wish to be associated.

A. DOMESTIC SOURCES OF COMPLIANCE

Compliance is, more to the point, a matter of choice by the state to discipline civil society, often at the request of activist sources in civil society. Yet while states may wish to comply, not all are capable. Technical and political factors intervene in the choice to comply. States may lack the technical capacity to fulfill obligations because they lack the competence to develop and enforce technical regulations consistent with international commitments. Many developing countries and formerly centrally planned economies have greater difficulties in complying with international obligations than have industrialized countries, due to less developed administrative systems and fewer monitoring and financial resources to devote to enforcement. Technical capacity may be less of a factor when a state is asked to forgo an activity rather than to halt an ongoing activity.

Cases remain where capable states willfully flaunt international rules, such as Norwegian and Japanese whaling practices, and Greek practices in licensing ships. Lack of political will to comply may come from the magnitude of expected resistance at home or because the state lacks the political wherewithal to induce behavioral change by its citizenry. One possible indicator of the political capacity of the state to comply is measured by the legitimacy of the state's claim to rule, operationalized through a calculation of the proportion of government revenue which is drawn from income taxes and other direct sources of taxation (and thus a measure of voluntary acceptance of the state) as against customs duties or other indirect sources of taxation that do not require voluntary acquiescence to the state. To fully flesh out this social dimension of state capacity it would be necessary to take account of the amount of resources that the state had to deploy in order to collect domestic taxes; it is always possible that a large majority of the tax revenues go into police and military to enforce the order on which voluntary payment of taxes is based. Compliance with international obligations in such a country would also be poor, because a large proportion of state political energy would be channeled into domestic surveillance and suppression rather than enforcement of international commitments. Compliance patterns would thus vary as a consequence of the political costs of inducing compliance and the state capacity to inflict those costs. Table 2.1 offers a conceptual taxonomy of the likelihood for compliance across these dimensions.

Assuming that states are capable of enforcement, the willingness to comply may still vary by the anticipated political costs of eliciting compliance. Students of comparative politics and of American politics have drawn from

Table 2.1: Likelihood of state compliance

	costly compliance	compliance not costly
state is capable and willing	possible	most likely
state is capable but unwilling	unlikely	unlikely
state is incapable and willing	state may try to comply and expect to fail in order to attract resources from international institutions to improve capacity	state may try to comply
state is incapable and unwilling	highly unlikely	unlikely

game theory, economic institutionalism, and social choice theory to focus on such matters of social choice.[7] The state generally is treated as a unitary actor dealing with a pluralistic society. Variation in state choices, from the domestic perspective, lies largely with the ability of diffuse domestic interests to forge dominant coalitions with which to pressure the government. The degree of political will necessary to comply varies according to the anticipated degree of domestic resistance, due in part to the identity, number and influence of those actors who will have to change their behavior.

A key potential source of variation in compliance is the nature of the issue being regulated and whose activities a state is seeking to influence, because the array of interests vary accordingly, as does the array of policy networks and the resistance ability of those bearing the costs of enforcement. It is not *a priori* clear which classes of issues will have a greater likelihood of compliance than others, but the dynamics of state choice should be quite different by issue, as the constellation of policy networks, actors, and potential influence varies by issue, even for the same state. For instance, the political costs of states enforcing compliance on the private sector and of individuals may be much higher than those of enforcing compliance on the activities by parastatals or the state itself. Most arms control and human rights actions are

[7] Shepsle, K., 'Studying Institutions: Some Lessons from Rational Choice Analysis' (1989) *J. Theor. Pol.* 131–47; Moe, T.M., 'The New Economics of Organization' (1984) 28 *Am. Pol. Sci. Rev.* 739–76; Koelble, T.A., 'The New Institutionalism in Political Science and Sociology' (1995) 27 *Comp. Pol.* 231–43; Noll, R. (ed.), *Regulatory Policy and the Social Sciences* (1985).

taken by the state itself, so compliance is in a sense a matter of self-regulation. Most environmental and trade activities are conducted by the private sector. States would be expected to downplay compliance obligations for issues in which anticipated political backlash from powerful domestic sectors and actors would be high.[8] Domestic factors would seemingly militate against strong compliance with environmental obligations, because of the heavy costs imposed on industry and its high degree of political representation, with a diffuse concentration of benefits on more poorly organized and represented tourists and individuals. Compliance with arms control regimes would largely be a matter of jockeying for influence between arms producers and citizens' groups. Compliance with human rights treaties would be a matter of human rights activists and NGOs seeking to exercise some degree of leverage on the state. Table 2.2 applies this framework to the various cases in this volume. Cases having multiple dimensions are presented according to the most salient dimension from the perspective of enforcement.

Table 2.2: Types of cases by source of activity and source of regulation

Source of Regulation	Source of Activity		
	state & state owned firms	firms (private)	individuals
IOs	money laundering? nuclear materials	money laundering? nuclear materials	money laundering
state	Antarctica nuclear materials OSCE treatment of minorities land mines missile technology	Antarctica ISO standards GA driftnet ban ILO labor standards nuclear materials land mines missile technology	Antarctica—private science, tourism GA driftnet ban
firms		ISO standards	
individuals/ NGOs		McBride/Sullivan Principles	

[8] Goldstein, J., *Ideas, Interests, and American Trade Policy* (1993); Milner, H.V., and Yoffie, D.B., 'Strategic Trade Policy and Corporate Trade Demands' (1989) 43 *Int. Org.* 239–72; Oye, K., and Maxwell, J.H., 'Self-Interest and Environmental Management', in Keohane, R.O., and Ostrom, E. (eds.), *Local Commons and Global Interdependence* (1995) 191–222.

Issues in which many actors are responsible for the targeted activities may elicit selective compliance according to the political costs of compliance for the state: *i.e.* states would extract compliance more easily from state actors than private actors, but it is less clear how different targets would respond to compliance demands from international organizations. Table 2.2 suggests that the cases will vary in terms of the extent of anticipated domestic resistance, and thus establishes an *ex ante* intertial baseline against which the international forces are directed.

More sweeping views of comparative politics look outside the institutional linkages within the state to patterns of state–society relations. They suggest that the willingness of a state to comply has to do with the nature of its relations to civil society[9] and to the administrative organization of the state itself.[10] From this perspective variation in compliance would vary by state, rather than by issue. States that command respect from domestic society would be more likely to allocate resources to enforcement than would states with feeble claims to legitimacy, where every enforcement action is politically costly. Few contemporary states have sufficient resources to squander signs of power when such actions engender political resentment. From this perspective legitimate states would be more likely to comply than would less legitimate states. Propositions from this perspective would also suggest that obligations worked out through antagonistic state–society relations would be more difficult to enforce than those worked out within the state. In instances where state administrative capacity varies by issue it is further possible that the same state would demonstrate different compliance patterns for different issue areas because the responsible agency is not the same, and the constellation of interests whose behavior must be disciplined varies by issue.

B. INTERNATIONAL SOURCES OF STATES' CHOICE TO COMPLY WITH SOFT LAW OBLIGATIONS

Compliance choices seldom are based solely on domestic considerations. States' choices are strategic, contingent on expectations of others' independent behavior. International relations scholars have looked at the systemic factors which influence states' expectations and choices. They argue that arrays of domestic influences are intimately intertwined with international realities. Domestic groups may anticipate international effects of compliance, and international factors amplify some domestic forces while suppressing others. Even the configuration of domestic interests can be the consequence

---

[9] Migdal, J.S., *Strong Societies and Weak States* (1988); Lijphart, A., *Electoral Systems and Party Systems* (1994); Schmitter, P., and O'Donnell, G., *Transitions from Authoritarian Rule* (1986).

[10] Noll, *supra* note 7; Risse-Kappen, T. (ed.), *Bringing Transnational Relations Back* (1995).

of international factors.[11] Compliance with liberal free-trade rules has been encouraged by industrial sectors that rely on free trade and foreign markets for their sales. Such accounts may help to explain recent compliance with pollution control treaties. Potential leaders with highly competitive pollution control technologies may anticipate market opportunities being created by the treaties. Such an account also would suggest differential compliance within the environmental sphere between pollution control regimes, where there are potential economic rewards, and conservation regimes, which offer more limited opportunities for the private sector.

International relations theorists differ in their identification of the international causes or reasons for why states choose to comply or not.[12] The most prominent contemporary efforts involve Realist and Neorealist efforts to stress the systemic distribution of material capabilities that provide the basis for interstate leverage, Neoliberal institutionalists focus on the formal organizational rules that guide strategic behavior, and social constructivists focus on the shared understandings that shape state behavior.

These approaches differ in their essential theories of the state. Realists and Institutionalists regard states as unitary rational actors, whose behavior and choices may be understood in terms of the array of incentives and choices available to the states. Social constructivists have a different notion of the state, treating it in more sociological and Weberian terms as a weak bureaucratic animal. They relax many of the rationalist assumptions that inform Neorealist and Neoliberal Institutionalist analysis. Social constructivists assume that states are not monolithic; instead their characteristics vary according to the extent to which the state is accountable to domestic society. At one extreme is the rare case of a totalitarian regime, impervious to influence. Much more common are various forms of pluralism. Moreover, states are functionally differentiated; made up of multiple competing bureaucratic elements each with its own functional jurisdiction or domain. For constructivists, states are not substantively or procedurally rational. Rather they make decisions subject to bounded rationality, the easiest choices are taken at any one point in time, and choices persist until new state action is galvanized

---

[11] Milner, H.V., *Resisting Protectionism* (1988); Destler, I.M., and Odell, J.S., *Anti-Protection: Changing Forces in United States Trade Politics* (1987).

[12] Caporaso, J.A., 'International Relations Theory and Multilateralism' (1992) 46 *Int. Org.* 599–632; Hansenclever, A., *et al.*, 'Interests, Power, Knowledge: The Study of International Regimes' (1996) 40 *Mershon Int'l Stud. Rev.* 177–228; Krause, K., and Williams, M.C., 'Broadening the Agenda of Security Studies' (1996) 40 *Mershon Int'l Stud. Rev.* 229–54. A similar display of theoretical disagreements about the future of European security appears in Mearsheimer, J.J., 'The False Promise of International Institutions' (1994–95) 19 *Int'l Security* 5–49; Mearsheimer, J.J., 'A Realist Reply' (1995) 20 *Int'l Security* 82–93; Keohane, R.O., and Martin, L.L., 'The Promise of Institutionalist Theory' (1995) 20 *Int'l Security* 39–51; Ruggie, J.G., 'The False Premise of Realism' (1995) 20 *Int'l Security* 62–70; Wendt, A., 'Constructing International Politics' (1995) 20 *Int'l Security* 71–81.

by political crises. Choices persist, and are seldom returned to until political crises catalyze a response.

None of these perspectives are deterministic; rather, they are contingent on the interplay between domestic and foreign politics, between comparative politics and international relations.[13] International pressures play off existing domestic conditions by creating, amplifying or inhibiting domestic pressures, while variations in the intensity of national preferences and state capabilities to influence others often are based, in part, on available domestic coalitions and available issue linkages. Possibly a country would choose not to comply, even if it had been complying earlier, if the international inducements were withdrawn, but exposure to such inducements over time may lead to new habits on the part of states, so that they would comply even with the removal of institutional incentives to comply.

Propositions from the various approaches can be evaluated in practice by several techniques. First, process tracing for a given country will focus over time on the decision to comply with a given treaty or set of treaties, seeking to determine if the institutional factor correlates with the decision to comply and if there is a plausible causal mechanism between the institution and the decision. Secondly, aggregate analysis of treaties with these characteristics correlated with compliance levels offers a statistical appraisal of the propositions. Thirdly, and more ambitiously, multivariate analyses taking account of changes in institutional factors over time and of state choices over time offer a more convincing appraisal of the propositions, capable of taking account of changes in state behavior and the presence or absence of each factor, as well as identifying where more factors correspond with higher levels of compliance. Finally, counterfactuals applied to individual state choices could also contribute to an appraisal of these propositions.

1. Realism, Power Based Factors, and Choices to Comply

Classical Realists argue that states seek to protect territorial integrity above all other goals. Compliance depends on threats of sanctions for non-compliance levied by a powerful state.[14] Consequently, compliance patterns should vary based upon the extent to which such integrity is potentially at risk and power is available to enforce compliance or deter non-compliance. It would be expected that compliance, in the absence of the exercise of power or leadership by a dominant country, would be strongest in the area of human

---

[13] Keohane, R.O., and Milner, H. (eds.), *Internationalization and Domestic Politics* (1996); Evans, P.B., *et al.* (eds.), *Double-Edged Diplomacy* (1993); Gourevitch, P.A., *Politics in Hard Times* (1986); Gourevitch, P.A., 'Domestic Sources of International Cooperation' (1996) 50 *Int. Org.* 349–73; Katzenstein, P.J. (ed.), *Between Power and Plenty* (1977); Risse-Kappen, *supra* note 10.

[14] Austin, J., *The Province of Jurisprudence. Determined Lecture I* (1954).

rights, slightly less strong in the environment, followed by trade and with arms control the issue with the lowest level of compliance. Within the area of trade, compliance levels would vary relative to the nature of the regulated products, where compliance would be lower for dual use technologies and technologies with potential military applications.

Measures of power and its concentration, in terms of the capabilities that would confer potential influence on a state, may well vary from issue to issue. A number of methodological and conceptual debates persist regarding the appropriate measures of influence for each issue, and the extent to which there exist modes of influence distinctive to each, as well as what universal sources of influence may be applicable to all areas of international relations.[15]

Neorealists focus on the extent to which policy autonomy is threatened, arguing that states are jealous of such autonomy and must be compelled to sacrifice it. Thus all compliance would be a matter of compulsion, but compliance could still be high in substantive domains that entail less perceived sacrifice of autonomy. While most Neorealists presume that states are loathe to cooperate, out of anticipation of free-riding, and all states comply only if compelled to do so, Realists suggest that compliance will only occur if a dominant country—a hegemon—exercises some degree of pressure on a country to comply, either through rewards for compliance or threatened sanctions for breach. Compliance levels, possibly taking into account the differences among issues, would vary according to the presence of hegemony and its use. In general compliance would be spotty, because enforcement would require constant vigilance and the exercise of power by a dominant party over weaker participants in the regime. If we assume that hegemons are rational in the use of their capabilities, we would expect threats to be used when states appeared likely to comply while rewards would be used only when non-compliance appeared likely, thus not having to expend them unnecessarily on parties who would probably comply even without external inducements.[16]

More pragmatically, it is possible that the role of power in compliance may be directly related to the manner of concluding the agreement. If it was adopted by truly voluntary agreement then the impediments to compliance might be less. If it was contentious, and resolved to some extent through the exercise of power, then compliance would be difficult and power would have to be deployed to extract compliance.

2. Functional Institutionalism and Institutional Inducements to Comply

State choices also can be influenced by international institutions, defined as 'persistent and connected sets of rules (formal and informal) that prescribe

---

[15] Baldwin, D.A., *Economic Statecraft* (1985); Nye, J.S., *Bound to Lead* (1990).
[16] Oye, K., *Economic Discrimination and Political Exchange* (1993) ch. 3.

behavioral roles, constrain activity and shape expectations'.[17] Neoliberal institutionalists and similarly inclined international lawyers seek to design institutions to perform functions that may induce states to comply.[18] There is a strong *ceteris paribus* basis to the research from which these propositions are drawn. most Neoliberal Institutionalist analysts presume that states already desire to cooperate (or comply) and merely require reinforcement to indulge their initial inclinations. Institutions serve a therapeutic role in encouraging compliance and deterring noncompliance by eliminating barriers to self-interested compliance. However, they may not exercise a direct influence on state preferences that were formed previously.

Research on international institutions and their potential influence on national choice has identified three principal functions performed by international institutions: enhancing the contractual environment within which state choices are made (including voting rules, suffrage provisions, number of parties, frequency of meetings, etc.), building state concern and building national capacity.[19] The contractual environment relates principally to the initial decision to sign or not to sign an agreement rather than subsequent decisions regarding compliance, and thus is not discussed in any greater detail below. It is difficult to weigh the influence of each institutional property or factor on state choice; presumably more is better. Institutional settings in which many factors are present may well command higher compliance levels than settings in which fewer factors are present or the institutions lack many of the more influential properties.

Clearly, some degree of institutional design improves the likelihood that each factor could contribute to state decisions to comply. For instance, public activities are best verified or enforced by private parties, and private actions by public authorities.[20] Monitoring and verification is easier with small numbers. Third party cross-checking of monitoring and verification data may contribute to confidence in the accuracy of such data, and thus increase their potential political impact on compliance decisions. Effective monitoring and policy surveillance, often through the involvement of non-state parties, may also compensate for sometimes willful gaps in national reporting, such as Russia's failure to report on dumping of decommissioned nuclear submarines' core reactors in coastal waters and whaling catches.

In the real world these variables are not so easily manipulated for policy purposes. Many international institutions were not designed to perform such

[17] Keohane, R.O., *International Institutions and State Power* (1989) 3.
[18] Chayes, A., and Chayes, A.H., 'On Compliance' (1993) 47 *Int. Org.* 175–206; Chayes, A., and Chayes, A.H., *The New Sovereignty* (1995); Bilder, R.B., *Managing the Risks of International Agreement* (1981). See Schelling, T., *The Strategy of Conflict* (1960) for many of the initial insights.
[19] Haas, P.M., Keohane, R.O., and Levy, M.A. (eds.), *Institutions for the Earth* (1993).
[20] Russell, C.S., 'Monitoring and Enforcement of Pollution Control Laws in Europe and the United States', in Tietenberg, T. (ed.), *Innovation in Environmental Policy* (1992) 219.

functions[21] and few scholars have tried to think systematically about which issues command sufficient concern by major states that they are likely to be endowed with strong institutions and thus capable of inducing compliance.[22] Researchers, including those on this project, are thus left with inductive techniques to identify issues in which institutionally powerful international organizations are capable of inducing compliance.[23]

Monitoring

Information may affect political will by publicizing state actions to potentially critical domestic and foreign audiences. It may also affect capacity by giving governments more and better information with which to act. Monitoring efforts worldwide remain largely the domain of governments, with most human rights and environmental treaties requiring states parties to submit periodic reports to secretariats about their activities. The quality of the environmental reports, which may include information on monitoring environmental quality or compliance efforts, is often poor, and many secretariats lack the resources or authority to check data submitted by governments.[24]

Many environmental treaties contain monitoring provisions for environmental quality. Explicit concern with monitoring is a reasonably recent phenomenon; the median year for treaties requiring environmental monitoring is 1982. Table 2.3 summarizes the monitoring provisions of environmental treaties.[25]

Monitoring data are most likely to be accurate and command political attention when they are collected and disseminated and verified by impartial third parties. When states or principal actors are responsible for monitoring the effects of their own actions they face too many incentives for misrepresentation. Many NGOs are now capable of monitoring environmental quality and national compliance, and are becoming involved as a source of shadow verification of government obligations. Their activities help

[21] Haas, P.M., and Haas, E.B., 'Learning to Learn' (1995) 1 *Global Governance* No 3.

[22] The few exceptions include Gallarotti, G., 'The Limits of International Organization' (1991) 45 *Int. Org.* 183–220; Murphy, C.N., *International Organization and Industrial Change* (1994); Ruggie, J.G., *Winning the Peace* (1997).

[23] Levy, M.A., *et al.*, 'The Study of International Regimes' (1995) *Eur. J. Int'l Relations* 267–330; Zacher, M.W., with Sutton, B.A., *Governing Global Networks* (1996).

[24] Sand, *supra* note 2 at 13–14; United States General Accounting Office, *International Environment International Agreements are not Well Monitored* (1992) GAO/RCED–92–43. A 1991 U.S. General Accounting Office survey found that only about 60% of the parties to the 1972 London Dumping Convention complied with reporting obligations; only 30% of the members of the MARPOL convention on operational oil pollution submitted reports; and many reports under the Montreal Ozone Protocol and the Helsinki sulfur dioxide protocol are incomplete and impossible to verify.

[25] Calculated from Kiss, A.C., *Selected Multilateral Treaties in the Field of the Environment* (1983); Rummel-Bulska, I., and Osafo, S., *Selected Multilateral Treaties in the Field of the Environment* (1991).

Table 2.3: Monitoring provisions in multilateral environmental treaties

what is monitored (n of treaties)	who does it	voluntary or mandatory	frequency
environmental quality (48)	governments (69%) governments must provide to IOs (4%) IOs (8%) unspecified (19%)	81% mandatory 19% voluntary	annually 17% biannually 19% triennially 2% unspecified 62%

compensate for the dearth of effective data on environmental quality, as well as providing an independent quality check on data collected through other sources.[26]

Much of the environment can be monitored remotely from satellites and does not require the active collection and submission of data by governments. Remote sensing and satellite monitoring can enhance verification of trends in natural resource use, marine pollution from organic sources and from oil, as well as levels of greenhouse gases, although ground truthing is still necessary to confirm remote sensing data. Satellite and airplane based monitoring is less effective at monitoring inorganic marine contamination and urban air quality, for instance, which requires localized sampling and monitoring.

Verification

Direct verification of state compliance may directly affect state choices to comply.[27] By providing prompt information about other states' actions, early warning of violations is available, reducing the fear of free riding and confirming countries' reputations. Verification also may indirectly deter non-compliance by increasing the likelihood of detection. To seriously influence compliance, verification data must be accurate, timely, and reliable. Verification may not be equally feasible in all cases; it is easier when the actions to be verified are large, and verifying arms control measures thus is easier with large weapons than with small ones. Remote sensing works well for the environment and for arms control, less well for trade and human

[26] Greenpeace International seeks to keep track of national compliance with many treaties and the Natural Resources Defense Council collects data on national compliance with the 1992 climate change treaty (UNFCCC). The IUCN and Greenpeace also try to track national compliance with many of the species conservation treaties. Natural Resources Defense Council and CAPE 2000, *Four in '94 Assessing National Actions to Implement Agenda 21: A Country-by-Country Progress Report* (1994).

[27] Fischer, W., *The Verification of a Greenhouse Gas Convention, Verification Report 1991* (1991); Chayes and Chayes (1995), *supra* note 18; United Nations Department for Disarmament Affairs, *Verification and the United Nations* (1991); Ausubel, J., and Victor, D., 'Verification of International Environmental Agreements' (1992) 17 *Ann. Rev. Energy & Env't*, pp. 1–44.

Table 2.4: Verification provisions in multilateral environmental treaties

what is monitored (n of treaties)	who does it	voluntary or mandatory	frequency
national compliance (58)	governments 72% governments provide to IO 7% IO 3% unspecified 18%	95% mandatory 5% voluntary	annually 29% biannually 18% triennially 2% unspecified 51%

rights. Table 2.4 summarizes the verification provisions of international environmental treaties, dealing with appraisals of state compliance.[28]

NGOs increasingly are active in verifying state compliance with environmental accords. Greenpeace now regularly monitors trade in hazardous wastes and in endangered species, and publicizes shipments that violate international treaties. The publicity generated by NGOs is often sufficient to inform recipient governments of violations of which they may have been unaware, as well as pressuring them to enforce their international commitments and to refuse entry of such products. Many NGOs have become virtual watchdogs over private activities, replacing or supplementing the activities of national enforcement agencies. Because governments are often unwilling to cede the semblance of authority to NGOs, private monitoring of governments' actions and of the environment may best be accomplished through independent scientific panels, which have access to a variety of sources of information. Surprise visits by independent inspectors are used in some regimes as a means of verification, and have long been a part of the nuclear non-proliferation regime and the Antarctic Treaty System. The concept is accepted by eastern European and OECD countries, but not by LDCs.

Horizontal Linkages

Linkages among institutions involved in an issue area may contribute to compliance. Dense networks of institutional factors, including such factors as numbers of international institutions involved in negotiations, and frequency of interactions could contribute to stronger levels of compliance. Such factors would improve the likelihood of compliance by encouraging states to build up their reputation to anticipate reciprocity in other areas of potential importance.[29] Dense networks also amplify the number of institutional factors

---

[28] International concern about verification of compliance is relatively recent: the median year for treaties requiring verification of national compliance is 1981.

[29] The U.K. proved willing to accept compromises in the EU Large Scale Power Plant Directive out of a perceived need to escape the reputation of being the 'dirty man of Europe'; a reputation which had impeded U.K. diplomatic efforts in other functional domains. Levy, M.A., 'The Power of Tote-Board Diplomacy', in Haas *et al.* (1993).

affecting state compliance: the existence of many institutions may strengthen the possible rewards for compliance and states may have better chances to shape the choices of other states through clever decisions about which institution to support to encourage others to comply.[30]

Similarly, actions taken in one area may positively or negatively affect the potential for compliance in another area. Human rights obligations that improve the domestic political influence of NGOs, for example, may contribute to compliance with treaties in other areas because the political influence of non-human rights NGOs is also enhanced and they gain in their potential to exercise domestic influence on their governments.

Nesting

State choices to comply may be affected by the issue-related context in which such choices are taken. Vinod Aggarwal refers to the array of hierarchical influences on states' compliance with international obligations as 'nesting'.[31] Nesting can take two forms: it may be conceptual, reflecting the causal connections that state decision makers believe tie together various issues. If leaders hold a tightly coupled view of international politics, then such high level beliefs will exercise a strong influence over state choice in lower-level conceptual areas. As an example, many LDCs endorsed similar positions and presumably share similar compliance patterns in the variety of issue areas that were addressed during debates over the new international economic order, including population, environment, and trade because they shared a tightly coupled view of international political and economic relations. They were all nested below this broader conceptual organization of issues. If the higher order conception is only loosely coupled, then the higher level cognitive map would be less likely to effect choice.

Nesting may also be legal in nature, meaning that choices to comply in one issue area may be legally prescribed by another domain that has legal precedence, or is politically more influential, much as the Supreme Court in the USA exercises ultimate determination over lower level judgments. In the area of trade, the new WTO may be able to exercise such influence. The ECJ is acquiring the authoritative power of an independent court able to overrule national legal decisions.[32]

---

[30] For instance, the densely overlapping networks within which G7 finance ministers operate—the BIS, OECD working groups, IMF working groups, and G7 summits—provide multiple sources of influence over state choice. In the environmental area, the overlapping memberships in the Baltic and North Sea environmental regimes by Denmark, Sweden, and Germany led each country to comply with both regimes (rather than considering each separately) as well as pushing other parties in each to comply. Haas, P.A., 'Protecting the Baltic and the North Sea', in Haas, P.M., *et al.* (eds.), *Institutions for the Earth* (1993).

[31] Aggarwal, V., *Liberal Protectionism* (1985) 186.

[32] Burley, A.M., and Mattli, W., 'Europe Before the Court' (1993) 47 *Int. Org.* 41–76; Sweet, A.C., and Caporaso, J.A., *From Free Trade to Supranational Polity: The European Court and*

Capacity building

The provision of various capacity-building resources accruing as a consequence of compliance, or the anticipation of such resources, may induce compliance. Thus, the opportunity of acquiring technology, training, financing,
and more general resource transfers may encourage compliance. The fear that
such resources will be withheld from non-complying states, such as occurs
through conditionality, may also encourage states to comply. Capacity building alone is unlikely to sway compliance decisions by any but the smallest and
weakest countries, whose decisions may not have a discernible impact on the
internationally shared problem being collectively addressed by international
soft law.

National Concern

Concern about the issue by elites and the mass public may positively affect a
state decision to comply. In the short term institutions publicize events and
engage in public education to catalyze opinion about issues for which mass
concern already exists. In the longer term institutions may build such concern
ab initio through public education and information campaigns, spreading literacy, the creation and strengthening of NGOs, and promoting the findings
and individual status of epistemic community members.

Institutional profile

The institutional profile may also influence national compliance choices. High
level institutions, if domestic conditions are satisfied, provide an opportunity
for politically opportunistic entrepreneurial civil servants to encourage compliance if they anticipate domestic rewards for public commitments. For
instance, Robert Putnam notes how the high profile public exchange of commitments at G7 Summits may strengthen the hand of each leader in subsequent policy battles at home, while also increasing the stakes of failing to
implement international commitments, and thus enhancing their commitment
in the domestic political battle.[33] Similarly, in the North Sea and Baltic Sea the
move from low-level bureaucratic coordination to periodic ministerial conferences greatly enhanced the potential for making public commitments.[34]

C. NATIONAL SENSITIVITY TO INSTITUTIONAL INCENTIVES

Such institutional factors are unlikely to be equally influential over all states'
choices. The potential influence of international institutions is contingent, in

---

Integration, University of Washington Political Relations and Institutions Group Working
Paper 2.45 (1996).

[33] Putnam, R.D., and Bayne, N., *Hanging Together* (1987).   [34] Haas, *supra* note 30.

this regard, on whether their information functions mesh with concerns of potentially powerful domestic groups. Institutional analysis is insufficient on its own to account for patterns of national compliance. Even holding institutional factors constant, one encounters wide variation in national enforcement with the same regulations. States vary in terms of their vulnerability to institutional inducements.[35] Not all states are vulnerable to external influence, although with increasing globalization this number is probably declining. State vulnerability can be measured in terms of relatively high levels of national trade/GNP, Direct Foreign Investment (DFI) as a percentage of Gross Fixed Capital Formation (GFCF), and foreign indebtedness. High levels of any of these increases the degree of foreign interest and the vulnerability of target states to influence from outside. Some states are relatively impervious to such direct and indirect leverage. Without pluralistic societies and without the need to seek credit or finance from international institutions, governments of many Newly Industrializing Countries (NICs) are relatively insensitive to the array of international and domestic political influences on governments to protect the environment.

Assuming some degree of vulnerability to external inducements, the degree to which specific institutional incentives are likely to exercise a direct impact on different states' choice is elaborated in Table 2.5. It indicates states that are sensitive to specific institutional inducements for compliance with international environmental soft law. It distinguishes states by state capacity, state/society relations and the extent of domestic environmental concern. State capacity is a measure of a state's technical capacity to formulate and monitor environmental policies. This is a multi-dimensional measure, based on bureaucratic measures of budgets of functional agencies, staffing, resources, administrative influence of functional agencies, and ability to monitor and enforce decisions in civil society. State capacity is measured by the numbers of scientists and engineers per million population and proportion of GNP devoted to research and development (R&D). High capacity is 0.4 percent of GNP for R&D or more than 300 scientists and engineers per million population.[36] State–society relations is a measure of the extent to which the state is responsive and accountable to domestic society, and thus is a measure of the extent to which the state is liable to respond to demands for compliance from domestic sources. The obvious measure is whether the government is coded as democratic or nondemocratic.[37] Public environmental concern is an indicator of the extent to which external pressures will resonate with domestic political forces, and thus the ability of international institutions to amplify

---

[35] Risse Kappen, *supra* note 10; Evangelista, M., 'Domestic Structure and International Change' in Doyle, M., and Ikenberry, G. (eds.), *New Thinking in International Relations Theory* (1997).

[36] The data are from the UNESCO Statistical Yearbook, various years.

[37] The data are from Russett, B., *Grasping the Democratic Peace* (1994).

Table 2.5: Variation in national sensitivity to institutional incentives for compliance with environmental soft law

	state is capable of making and enforcing policy	state is incapable of making and enforcing policy
state is responsive domestically	effective institutional functions include: verification, monitoring, national concern, institutional profile	effective institutional functions include: verification, monitoring capacity building, national concern, institutional profile
	capacity building is less influential here, because state capacity is already high.	Botswana **Colombia** **Costa Rica** Greece **Jamaica** **Mauritius** **Venezuela**
	Argentina **Australia** **Austria** **Belgium** **Canada*** **Denmark*** **Finland*** **France** **Germany*** **Ireland*** **Israel** **Italy** **Japan*** **Netherlands*** **New Zealand** **Norway*** **Portugal*** **Spain** **Sweden** **Switzerland*** **UK*** **USA***	
state is not responsive domestically	effective institutional functions include: verification, monitoring	effective institutional functions include: verification, monitoring capacity building
	Brazil* **Bulgaria** **Chile*** **China** **Czechoslovakia** **El Savador** **Ghana** **Guatemala** **Hungary*** **India*** **Kenya** Kuwait **S. Korea*** **Mexico*** **Nepal** **Pakistan** **Poland** **Russia*** Rwanda Saudi Arabia **Senegal** **Singapore** **S. Africa** **Togo** **Trinidad & Tobago** Turkey* Vietnam Yugoslavia **Zambia**	**Algeria** Afghanistan Albania Angola **Bangladesh** Burundi Central African Republic Chad Congo **Côte d'Ivoire** Cuba **Dominican Republic** **Ecuador** **Egypt** Gabon **Guinea** Guyana Haiti Honduras **Indonesia** Iran Iraq Jordan Laos Lebanon Lesotho Libya Malawi **Malaysia** **Mali** **Nicaragua** Niger **Nigeria** Panama **Paraguay** **Peru** **Philippines** Sri Lanka **Sudan** **Tanzania** **Thailand** Uganda **Uruguay** Yemen

domestic pressures for compliance. Environmental concern is measured by a 1992 Gallup survey of public environmental opinions in twenty-four countries[38] and the existence of environmental NGOs, indicated by whether more than two environmental NGOs attended UNCED from that country, or any country.[39] Bold type indicates countries with more than two environmental NGOs attending UNCED. Asterisks indicate countries in which over 40 per cent of the population expressed a 'great deal' or 'fair amount' of concern about the environment.[40]

Short term efforts fall within each cell. Longer term efforts, which are more indirect in focus, would strive to move states between cells, improving state capacity and opening up public access. It is for this reason that democratization is widely hailed as a world order strategy with multiple benefits beyond the area of human rights and liberties.

In sum, institutional factors as elaborated by functional institutionalists are likely to vary in their impact on state compliance choices by issue and by country. While verification and monitoring appear to be the most widely applicable institutional factors affecting state compliance, they will operate through different channels in different countries. In democratic or representative societies (pluralistic, parliamentary, presidential, corporatist, or consociational) the information will be converted to leverage through domestic and international channels, while in nondemocratic or nonrepresentative societies the information will be converted to pressure on compliance through international channels, either between states, from international institutions, or from MNCs and international banks. NGOs and other transnational actors may exercise an indirect effect through their ability to influence or use influential states, international institutions, or firms. Institutional factors are probably richest in the areas of trade and economic harmonization, followed by the environment and human rights.

D. SOCIAL CONSTRUCTIVISM AND KNOWLEDGE-BASED COMPLIANCE

International relations has recently returned to focus on the role of ideas and understanding in shaping choices by goal-seeking states. As international politics becomes increasingly complex and uncertain, it becomes farfetched to assume that states are capable of clearly anticipating how national welfare will be affected by policy choice at home and in conjunction with others. Social constructivism is a recent research program,[41] which looks at the

[38] The data are from Dunlap, R.E., *et al.*, *Health of the Planet* (1993).
[39] The data come from *Who is Who at the Earth Summit 1992* (1992).
[40] Dunlap *et al.*, *supra* note 38.
[41] Adler, E., 'Seizing the Middle Ground' (1997) 3 *Eur. J. Int'l Relations* 319–64; Wendt, *supra* note 12; Haas, P.M., 'Introduction: Epistemic Communities and International Policy Coordination' (1992) 46 *Int. Org.* 1–36; Haas and Haas, *supra* note 21. See also Franck, T., *The*

process by which collective representations of the world are constructed and diffused. Constructivists assume that states are incapable of searching for new information each time a decision is demanded, and that they rely on prior cognitive frames to understand how national interests are likely to be affected by any particular decision. Thus, decisions to comply are not based on rational calculations of interest, but compliance is rather a matter of applying socially generated convictions and understandings about how national interests are likely to be achieved in any particular policy domain.

Collective understandings are thus the source of state choices. Conviction can have two bases: an ethical or moral sense of obligation or a causal belief in how the world works and how a country's interests will be effected by compliance. *Pacta sunt servanda* (pacts made in good faith are binding) is too general a norm to fit the empirical record of spotty national compliance. States may share moral norms, which precede the choice to comply.[42] Morality may play a stronger role in the case in human rights, and be less likely to apply to other issues, because the very justification of the treaty is grounded on normative claims. International institutions that are regarded as legitimate can reinforce the operation of such norms on compliance through monitoring and verification.

The most important sources of influence for social constructivists are the shared causal understandings, or consensual knowledge, that help guide decision makers facing complex and unfamiliar domains. Such domains are increasingly common in international politics, particularly in the areas of economic and environmental policy. Obligations in these issue areas are grounded as much on causal and instrumental warrants as on normative ones. Appreciation of new causal factors in the policy environment which affect state interests may teach states to comply as they learn to recognize undesirable international conditions that detrimentally affect their national interest, while mastering new practices by which to alleviate or ameliorate such conditions.

From a constructivist's perspective compliance is more likely if there exist relevant widely shared causal beliefs about the operation of the issue to be controlled, and the degree to which the actual rules promote valued ends. The likelihood of compliance with economic regimes is increased if states believe that the regimes accurately reflect the way in which economies behave. Similarly, the potential for compliance may be improved if state officials share beliefs about the operation of ecosystems and the desirability of their preservation.

The principal mechanism by which such ideas are developed and dissemi-

Power of Legitimacy Among Nations (1990); Brunnee, J., and Toope, S.J., 'Environmental Security and Freshwater Resources: Ecosystem Regime Building' (1997) 91 *Am. J. Int'l L.* 26–59.

[42] Finnemore, M., *National Interests in International Society* (1996); Katzenstein, P.J. (ed.), *The Culture of National Security* (1996); Raymond, G.A., 'Problems and Prospects in the Study of International Norms' *Mershon Int'l Stud. Rev.* 41 (1997, Supp. 2), 205–46; Lumsdaine, D., *Moral Vision in International Politics* (1993).

nated is by epistemic communities: transnational networks of policy professionals who share common values and causal understandings. Members of epistemic communities will seek to introduce national measures consistent with their beliefs, and utilize the enforcement mechanisms of the bureaucratic units in which they operate.[43] Patterns of compliance are thus based on the extent to which epistemic community members are able to acquire influential positions in national administrations and in international institutions from which to encourage compliance.[44] Epistemic communities are most likely to gain prompt entry in democratic countries which have a high degree of technical competency in the substantive area in question.

International negotiations for particular legal or political commitments may then directly affect the prospects for compliance by including new groups in the process of negotiation, and by alerting states to new ideas, and recruiting and institutionalizing groups associated with those ideas. Negotiations may contribute to transforming the beliefs and interests of the parties engaged in the negotiations, and thus influence their subsequent choices regarding compliance.[45]

States may engage in three related types of learning about compliance. States may learn to comply with particular instruments, following the adoption of new consensual knowledge about how state interests are to be achieved. States also may learn to comply with related instruments in the same area of activity. For instance, they may recognize that national interests are protected by arms control or environmental protection, and thus find it easier to comply with other arms control or environmental commitments. States can learn as well about the connection between issues and thus change compliance patterns over time due to the acceptance of new 'policy maps' which identify goals that must be achieved in order to promote national goals.

As perceived causal connections are drawn between issue areas, compliance decisions will come to reflect the broader notion of how national interest is affected by concurrent activity in causally related areas. Of course, principal states may learn to reject linkages as well, although most new policy consensus focuses on previously unrecognized connections. Consequently, decisions to comply in one area may depend on the nature of the perceived linkages with other functional domains. Such linkages can be

[43] Haas, P.M., *Saving the Mediterranean* (1990); Haas, *supra* note 30.

[44] For instance, the U.K. moved from non-compliance to compliance with EU water quality standards following the penetration of an epistemic community able to convince the U.K. that compliance was in the country's interest. Richardson, J., 'EU Water Policy' (1994) 3 *Envtl. Pol.* 139–68; Bressers, H., *et al.*, 'Networks as Models of Analysis' (1994) 3 *Envtl Pol.* 1–24. Mediterranean governments came to embrace marine pollution controls following the influence of a regional ecological epistemic community, operating concurrently through national governments and through the United Nations Environment Program. Haas (1990), *supra* note 43.

[45] Haas, P.M., 'Do Regimes Matter?' (1989) 43 *Int. Org.*, pp. 377–404; Sjostedt, G., 'Environmental Aid Negotiations as a Process of Collective Learning', in Lofstedt, R.E., and Sjostedt, G. (eds.), *Environmental Aid Programmes to Eastern Europe* (1996).

created or contrived; that is compliance in one area can be made contingent on compliance or non-compliance in another area, thereby linking the decisions to comply. Such links were made in the Organization for Security and Cooperation in Europe. The use of trade sanctions as an enforcement device in environmental treaties has been challenged on these grounds.

Consensus seems to be crystallizing internationally around the linkages between environment and development activities,[46] as policy elites in national governments and international institutions as well as NGO activists increasingly recognize that efforts to promote economic growth are contingent on assuring some degree of environmental protection. Some analysts have stressed the obverse of this connection, that environmental protection may require some minimal economic growth as well. Appreciation of these linkages would lead states to comply in the newly highlighted policy domains, out of an appreciation of the complementary causal influences between them. Conversely, such new consensus might precipitate a backwards movement questioning compliance if stipulated activities in economic areas were deemed to undermine environmental quality.

E. CONCLUSION

Questions of compliance—to what extent states comply, which states are likely to comply, what patterns of compliance exist within and across areas of regulation—have not been extensively investigated and remain poorly understood. This chapter argues that compliance is a matter of state choice, and that that choice is often subject to institutional and constructivist forces. While there may be more compliance than skeptics believe, there is also probably less than many international lawyers and international relations scholars would like. Future compliance with international soft law is likely to continue to be driven by institutional and constructivist forces so long as globalization and democratization continue. States are likely to retain their legal sovereignty even in the face of global pressures so long as they remain the sole authoritative source for compliance decisions. Further research is called for to combine institutional and constructivist analysis to better understand how institutional design can enhance learning; on prior state beliefs that influence decisions about institutional design; on comparative national studies of state competence, on the degree of autonomy of agencies in different governments; and on the various mechanisms, such as persuasion, recruitment patterns, policy emulation, and third party inducements, by which shared understandings diffuse more broadly.

---

[46] Baker, S., *et al.* (eds.), *The Politics of Sustainable Development* (1997); Haas, P.M., 'Is "Sustainable Development" Politically Sustainable?' (1996) III *Brown J. World Aff.* 239–48; Nelson, J., and Eglinton, S.J., *Global Goals, Contentious Means* (1995).

Beyond Compliance:
Helping Nations Cooperate

RICHARD B. BILDER

This volume significantly contributes to our understanding of the international normative order. It calls attention to the diversity of normative techniques that states and other international actors use to determine their relations and establish cooperative arrangements, the complex interaction among the various norms, the way states and other international actors actually behave, and the long-overlooked, pervasive, and important role that non-legally binding norms play in the international normative process.

At the same time, I believe that it is necessary to question several of the basic ideas that appear to underlie this study. In particular, I would suggest that approaching issues of the international normative order from the perspective of 'compliance' risks obscuring or distorting an understanding of how international norms help to structure international order and cooperation; that the idea of 'compliance with international soft law' may blur and impair the very useful distinction that states traditionally have drawn between legally binding and non-legally binding normative techniques in constructing their normative arrangements; and that, in studies of the international normative order, our primary emphasis and objective should be helping nations cooperate rather than simply 'making them behave'.

The concept of compliance is a central focus of this study and is expressly discussed in the preceding contribution by Professor Haas. His analysis appears to take as a 'given' the prior existence of generally understood international norms, whether 'hard' or 'soft', embodying some kind of relatively determinable and authoritative normative prescriptions and obligations. Professor Haas then asks, *post hoc* and without regard to how and with what kind of expectations the norm or normative arrangement was established, why and how states under different circumstances choose or decide whether or not to comply with particular norms. To answer this question, he ably pulls together and analyzes a variety of factors and influences that he believes may affect a state's decision to comply. This model conforms, of course, to studies of compliance behavior regarding national laws, for example, studies of how individuals or firms decide to comply with drug, tax, or environmental laws. A principal objective of such studies is to learn more about why people fail to comply more fully with the applicable law, presumably so that we can then adopt corrective measures that will get them to behave. All such studies face the difficulty of satisfactorily defining and measuring 'compliance', a problem which those in this project note is particularly salient in the context of international normative behavior.

It is hardly news, however, that the international normative system is not identical to the typical national legal system. Most importantly, firmly-held notions of sovereignty and the broadly 'horizontal' character of the international system mean that international norms usually are developed and implemented primarily through consensual rather than authoritative centralized or coercive processes and there are often no compulsory procedures for deciding disputes as to what these norms mean. Consequently, because applicable norms are arrived at by largely voluntaristic and consensual means, a state's intention and decision about how willing or not willing it is to conform its behavior to the norm typically will be reached and manifested, not as a separate decision reached after the norm is formulated, but in the very process of the norm's formation. Not only are the initial compliance decision and intention usually inextricably intertwined with the formation and nature of the norm, as publicly expressed, rather than independent of them, but the content, form, and contextual elements of the norm generally will reflect and signal the participating states' broadly shared intentions and expectations regarding compliance. In short, 'compliance analysis' fits more comfortably into a discussion of imposed norms than it does into the kinds of consensually reached norms with which the international normative system is primarily concerned.[1] Of course, as Professor Haas and the other authors in this volume point out, many things can change between the time the norm is established and some subsequent time when a state's behavior is challenged as 'noncompliant'; as will be suggested, normative disputes frequently relate to such changing circumstances.

As a possible alternative model, let me suggest how I think those involved in making, implementing, interpreting, or evaluating foreign policy decisions typically take account of arguably relevant international norms and, in particular, how they think about issues of 'compliance'. As I have suggested elsewhere,[2] foreign office officials and other participants, including the public, in the foreign policy process view issues of compliance with and breach of international norms in much more murky, flexible, and unruly ways than conventional international law, international relations analysis, and other 'compliance' analysis based on analogies with national law seem to assume. The

---

[1] Of course, the international normative system has always embodied some coercive or imposed as well as consensually-reached norms, and many norms may reflect and combine both elements. The reach and importance of such community-imposed norms arguably is growing.

[2] See Bilder, R., 'Breach of Treaty and Response Thereto' (1967) 67 *Proc. Am. Soc. Intl. L.* 193 and Bilder, R., *Managing the Risks of International Agreement* (1981).

world of the foreign office official is dominated less by form and logic than by function, process, and accommodation. Obligation and no-obligation, compliance and breach, shade imperceptibly into one another and achieve operational definition only in the practical outcomes of deals between the states concerned. Issues of compliance and breach are frequently part of the ongoing game or process of international interaction rather than something subsequent to and apart from it.

Foreign office officials are likely, I believe, to approach so-called 'compliance' issues with certain attitudes, regardless of whether the norm allegedly involved is 'hard' or 'soft'. First, the primary concern of such officials will most likely be the integrity of the state's foreign policy position as a whole, both domestically and externally, with respect to the other state or states involved and to the world more generally, rather than the integrity of the norm itself. The norm typically will be viewed as only one element among complex components defining the overall pattern of foreign affairs interest, a pattern which, as is well brought out in Professor Haas' analysis, is constantly changing as dynamic internal and external factors play upon it. Moreover, officials typically will be less concerned with the past considerations that produced the consent to or acquiescence in formation of the norm than the present and future context in which it must be implemented.

Secondly, in making decisions about the formation, interpretation, or implementation of norms, officials will experience a continuing tension between their desire to maintain their own flexibility and freedom of maneuver to cope with changing circumstances and their desire for certainty and predictability on the part of relevant foreign officials and other international actors. International norms will often reflect, particularly in their relative 'hardness' and 'softness', an uneasy and uncertain compromise between these inconsistent objectives.

Thirdly, officials typically see international norms not simply as instruments for creating commitments and obligations, but rather as multi-purpose policy tools that may be used to accomplish broader objectives. Of course, in many cases officials are principally interested in establishing relatively firm and clear expectations as to other nations' or other international actors' behavior upon which they can justifiably rely and plan. The very purpose of norms is to affect human behavior. Unless norms are capable of having such effects, and of permitting at least some level of prediction as to how other individuals, groups, or political actors such as states will behave, there is little reason to bother adopting them. Thus, it seems clear that the unique normative pressures inherent in treaties and other clearly legal instruments and techniques can represent serious commitments that provide a firm base for long-range planning and greatly increase the probability that such expectations will be met. Indeed, as this project demonstrates, under some circumstances non-binding instruments produce similar results. However, in other cases the so-called 'norm' may be seen by some or all of the participants as intended, not primarily to control each other's behavior, but rather as a way to communicate foreign policy attitudes, encourage the growth of further cooperation or institutions, achieve propaganda objectives, lay the basis for future bargaining or further development of more elaborate norms, accomplish primarily internal political objectives, or so forth. I believe that some concept of what the norm was really intended to do, of why each party participated in its formation, and what EACH then understood it as requiring may have an important bearing on how seriously officials feel they should take the obligations it appears to contain.

Fourthly, I suggest that foreign office officials typically will approach a dispute about international norms not as an isolated transaction, but rather as an incident in the state's continuing relationship with the other state, states, or other international actors concerned—a relationship which will inevitably continue given our highly interdependent international system. As is often the case in continuing business disputes involving 'repeat players', pressing another state unduly to conform with the norm, over-legalizing the dispute, 'taking the other party to court', or 'winning' the dispute may be seen as less sensible than accommodation and compromise.

Finally, even where officials are deeply concerned about maintaining the integrity and reliability of the particular expectational framework established by the norm or particular complex of norms, they recognize that the norm usually constitutes only one stone in the arch of that expectational framework. There are usually many alternative, overlapping, and supplementary ways, apart from formal or informal norms, through which states acknowledge, define, and enforce their mutual expectations as to their future conduct. Indeed, as many commentators have pointed out, one of the most important functions of norms may be expressly to recognize, buttress, and coordinate the effective implementation of already existing non-normative pressures suggesting the mutual rationality and shared systemic advantages of particular behavior. Thus, officials will usually assess how they expect foreign office officials to behave on the basis of *all* the varied considerations and pressures which they see as acting on those officials, not simply on the basis of alleged 'hard' or 'soft' norms alone. Consequently, such officials' expectations may remain stable, even though a particular norm is not expressed in a legally binding form or even if they permit a violation of an apparent obligation in a particular case. Or officials may remain uncertain as to whether they can rely on another nation's future behavior even though a relevant norm is embodied in a legally binding treaty and they are able to secure 'compliance' in a particular case.

This is not to suggest that most foreign office officials do not take treaty and other normative obligations seriously. I believe the contrary is true. As indicated, most of these norms emerge only as a result of either expressly or

tacitly consensual processes and would not be approved by the major participants concerned unless they regard them as consistent with their national
interests. I suspect, however, that foreign office officials tend to look at such
normative commitments not simply in terms of the specific nature and scope
of the conduct covered or our more rigid legal concept of *pacta sunt servanda*,
but also in terms of what might be called the 'density of expectation' of their
observance—how strongly the parties really intended them to be counted or
relied on under different sets of conditions—conditions that may change over
time.

The important point is that officials may be willing to meet or 'comply'
with what they see as their actual commitment, but may see that commitment
as only one of meeting the fair and reasonable expectation they and others
had regarding how they would behave with reference to the norm. Thus, if
officials decide upon behavior by their state that only partially meets the standard of conduct ostensibly stated in the international norm, they still may
regard that as 'compliance' because, in their view, such partial or even occasional performance is all that the participants really expected of each other
when they formed or acquiesced in the norm. If this is in fact the case—if officials tend to regard failure to observe the norm under such circumstances as
not really breach or noncompliance at all, but rather as something tacitly
understood by all the participants as part of their joint expectational framework itself—then our attempts to analyze their behavior in terms of formal
notions of 'compliance' may be unsatisfactory indeed.

It is evident that such a broad concept of normative flexibility threatens
ideals of certainty and stability, and indeed our canons of interpretation. Yet
it seems also evident that if officials did not believe they retained such shared
expectations of flexibility, they might be even more reluctant than they are to
participate in the formation of the kind of dense and pervasive structure of
norms we have, given the risks inherent in our changeable and uncertain
world. And, as pointed out by many of the participants in this study, norms
can still be immensely valuable to foreign office officials in ordering their
interrelationships, even if the norms have varying densities of expectations
precluding complete reliance upon them. The important thing, as will be discussed, is to devise techniques and signals that allow officials to predict, with
some confidence, how seriously particular norms or normative arrangements
are meant to be taken and when and to what extent reliance is justified.

In this context, as Professor Haas indicates, the actual action and response
of states regarding claims of compliance or noncompliance with international
norms may be complex and uncertain. In many cases, normative, political,
and other considerations may substantially overlap and reinforce each other
and strongly influence officials' decisions either to comply with, strongly
protest, or sanction noncompliance with 'hard' or 'soft' norms. As this project demonstrates, in many—indeed probably most—situations, a decision to

behave in accordance with international norms will make most sense for states or other international actors involved. The consensual process of formulating the norms means that they must at least initially have reflected or crystallized some broad feeling by participants that they served their joint or several interests. In other cases, however, the norms may have less impact on official action or response. In the light of all relevant factors, it may serve one state's interest to violate a clear norm and it may serve another state's interest to ignore the most flagrant noncompliance, or conversely to allege noncompliance where none exists.

Other factors may contribute to the awkwardness of attempting to understand state behavior in response to norms in terms of usual concepts of compliance. First, both 'hard' and 'soft' norms are often ambiguous and subject to honest dispute. Further, as illustrated in a number of contributions to this project, a particular normative arrangement will frequently comprise an interrelated mixture of both 'hard' and 'soft' law elements. Indeed, a normative arrangement or understanding often reflects or embodies a complex web or 'package' of interrelated obligations, some more central and at the core of the norm or normative understanding, others more peripheral and subordinate, each of which may have different 'densities' of expectation, change over time, and be more or less open to flexible interpretation or implementation. In such cases, protesting or 'making a fuss' over alleged noncompliance often may not be worthwhile. Moreover, officials know that apparent disputes about compliance often mask what are really disputes over broader questions. Thus, conduct arguably contrary to norms or allegations of noncompliance frequently may be simply a tool in a bargaining process to achieve other political goals, create bargaining pressures, signal dissatisfaction with existing norms, bring pressure for tacit or express renegotiation of the norm, or even serve primarily internal political objectives. Finally, often there will be no procedural way in which an objective determination of compliance can be determined, even if the states concerned wish such a finding.

It is important to recognize that, after each noncompliance-potential situation has unfolded, the expectations of the parties may have a different 'density' and shape, and the norm as then understood and applied consequently may have a somewhat different meaning. Indeed, one of the most useful contributions of this project is to show the complex, dynamic, and evolving character of the interaction between states' expectations and behavior and international norms.

In sum, we should be aware that a compliance model may not fully reflect the attitudes and practice of officials and other international actors or observers towards international norms and behavior. In particular, it may not reflect their recognition of the legitimacy of tentative and incomplete obligation, of the possibility of varying 'densities' of commitment, of ranges of permissible flexibility around the 'core' obligations of the norm, and of the legitimate expectation-varying impact of events and pressures arising subsequent to the emergence of the norm. Equally important, we should recognize that the whole bias of the international normative system, particularly that comprising legally non-binding norms, is in practice more towards accommodation than 'legalistic' contention.

Let me briefly comment on several other aspects of the study. First, I join others in questioning the coherence and usefulness of the term 'soft international law', particularly as applied to legally non-binding norms and instruments. States, like all participants in continuing and complex social interactions, have developed a broad spectrum of normative techniques for managing and ordering their interrelations, capable of signaling a wide range of commitment, obligation, justifiable expectation, and reliance.[3] But, it is also clear that, from earliest times, states and other social actors have found it useful to draw a relatively sharp distinction between norms and normative arrangements that are meant to be binding, backed up by the organized community's authority, and those that are not. Indeed, it is considered sufficiently important that everyone know how seriously particular norms and normative arrangements are meant to be taken that all societies, including international society, have devised elaborate tests and rituals to distinguish between those norms and normative arrangements that are 'binding law', backed up by the community's authority and sanctions, and those that are not. Certainly, there has always been a strong presumption that anything that is 'law' *does* count and *is* meant to be taken seriously. Regimes of public legislation and regulation, contract and treaty, and, indeed, the conduct of personal affairs, rest in good part on maintaining the integrity of this law–nonlaw distinction. Much of the work of lawyers and judges in fact relates to administering and policing the law–nonlaw boundary and arguing or deciding on which side of it various alleged norms and conduct fall.

Obviously, this boundary is inexact and often disputed. Many norms and normative instruments, while concluded in ostensibly legal form and through legal procedures, nevertheless signal little genuine commitment or expectations of compliance; the term 'soft law' may be useful in calling attention to the low 'density of expectation' of such instruments and arrangements. And, as this study amply demonstrates, non-binding or nonlegal norms can and do play a very important part in structuring and ordering international relations—indeed, all social relations—and in some cases they may reflect such strong common interests, deeply embedded values, or effective nonlegal social sanctions that one can be highly confident of behavior in conformity with them. Nevertheless, there remains a widely-held and long understood assumption in all societies that there *is* a meaningful difference between

---

[3] See, *e.g.*, for a particularly useful discussion, Kingsbury, B., 'The Concept of Compliance as a Function of Competing Conceptions of International Law' (1998) 19 *Mich. J. Intl. L.* 345.

norms that are intended to be legally binding and those that are not, and that people may rely on this difference.

Consequently, it seems inappropriate and unhelpful to use the term soft *law* to describe norms and normative instruments which are clearly not in legal form, not intended to be legally binding, and thus not, in any of the usual senses in which we use the word, law at all. By blurring the traditional distinction between law and non-law, such usage threatens to damage a valuable normative tool which states have long used and relied on, and, in effect, 'depreciate the currency' of law. At the same time, it is important to make clear, as this book so well does, that we cannot hope to fully understand international relations if we fail to take account of the important role of non-binding norms. But, for this purpose, terms such as 'soft international norms' or 'nonbinding norms' seem preferable.[4]

The idea of compliance with such legally non-binding norms is also particularly awkward and incoherent. If the concept of 'compliance' fits uncomfortably in the analysis of disputes concerning legally-binding 'hard' international law norms, these difficulties are likely to be even greater as applied to the analysis of 'soft' norms, which are often—though not always—intended to reflect and signal only relatively low levels of commitment, expectations of performance, and reliance.

Secondly, I am concerned that an emphasis on compliance may point towards a backwards-looking and essentially legalistic approach focusing on state 'misbehavior', rather than towards a productive enquiry into devising and deploying better normative techniques and arrangements that facilitate more effective international dealings and cooperation. Thus, Professor Haas discusses various factors that he believes affect and predict the probability of compliance, such as technical and political capacity, national concern, domestic institutional constraints, the availability of monitoring and verification arrangements, and so forth. I suggest that it may be more useful to look at these factors, as I believe foreign office officials see them, primarily in terms of how they may affect the perceived risks of the proposed cooperative arrangements—risks that the potential cooperating parties must find a way to somehow overcome, or at least control, if they are to reach and successfully implement effective cooperation.[5] Indeed, I believe that the parties' choice between the use of legal and nonlegal normative techniques or some mixture of them reflects and is best understood in terms of just such risk management objectives. One of the most common and traditional ways of guarding against the risk of another party's nonperformance of a cooperative arrangement is

---

[4] See especially Weil, P., 'Toward Relative Normativity in International Law?' (1983) 77 *AJIL* 413. More generally see Johnson, D., *Consent and Commitment in the World Community* (1998).

[5] See Bilder, R., *Managing the Risks of International Agreement*, *supra* note 2, especially ch. 4 (discussing the various risks of nonperformance or inadequate performance involved in international agreements and techniques for dealing with them).

to make the arrangement legally binding. Conversely, one of the most accepted ways of protecting oneself against the risk that one may eventually not wish or be able to perform a proposed cooperative arrangement is to ensure that the arrangement is *not* legally binding.[6] Certainly, one of the most important tasks of international lawyers is to learn how better to craft hard and soft normative arrangements capable of enabling officials to overcome these perceived risks, thus helping their nations to cooperate.

Finally, the importance of this study suggests the usefulness of continued collective efforts to explore the relation between international norms and state behavior. I suggest, however, that further studies should not be limited to compliance alone, but should also include:

(1) a comprehensive exploration of the development, interaction, and relative advantages and disadvantages of different kinds of international normative techniques, particularly legally-binding and non-legal norms, and of how they can best be used, alone or in combination, to achieve higher, more useful, and more stable levels of cooperation;

(2) consideration of how to improve or expand the tool chest of such normative techniques, for example, by drawing on techniques employed in non-international, social, or business contexts;

(3) examining social psychological or behavioral science research for possible insights into international decision making processes and behavior affecting the reaching of international cooperative arrangements;

(4) studying ways of strengthening the deeper structures of social and international cooperation, including obtaining a better understanding of the pervasive role of trust as an undergirding resource for the development of an effective and efficient system of consensually-developed and implemented norms and cooperative arrangements.

---

[6] See, *ibid.*, at 24–36 (discussing various types of non-binding arrangements as risk management techniques).

Chapter 3
Challenges to the International Legal System

Interdependence, Globalization, and Sovereignty: The Role of Non-binding International Legal Accords

WOLFGANG H. REINICKE and JAN MARTIN WITTE

INTRODUCTION

The 'Asian financial crisis' of the mid-1990s not only had a global dimension in its causes and consequences but also, and ultimately more importantly, had long term implications for political and social dynamics around the world.[1] It fueled intense debate about the benefits and drawbacks of globalization and the ability of existing structures of governance, including international financial institutions, to prevent future crises. Yet the concept of globalization remains elusive, despite widespread use of the term and recognition of its growing importance not just in foreign but also domestic policy-making. Globalization often is simply asserted without being defined or it is described as a continuous increase of cross-border financial, economic, and social activities. If, however, globalization is understood as merely a *quantitative* change in the volume of cross-border activity, its full consequences are not fully captured.

Globalization instead represents a more fundamental change, a *qualitative* transformation of the international system with lasting implications for the public and private sectors alike, including changes in the nature of the legal processes and structures that shape the relationships and interactions among states. This qualitative transformation can be exposed by drawing an analytical distinction between the concept of economic interdependence, which characterized international relations for four decades after World War II, and globalization, which has come to dominate the debate during the last decade. Economic interdependence narrowed the distance between sovereign nations

---

[1] See Wolfensohn, J.D., *The Other Crisis*, Address to the Board of Governors, Washington, D.C., October 6, 1998; Goldstein, M., 'The Asian Financial Crisis: Causes, Cures, and Systemic Implications' [1998] *Policy Analyses in International Economics* 55; Lee, E., *The Asian Financial Crisis: The Challenge for Social Policy, International Labour Office* (1999); Wong, J., 'China's Economy and the Asian Financial Crisis' (1998) EAI Occasional Paper No. 4.

and necessitated closer macroeconomic coordination among public sector actors (governments). In contrast, the principal drivers of globalization are private sector firms that operate at the microeconomic level. This difference requires us to reconsider conventional forms of inter-state cooperation that were appropriate for the management of economic interdependence.

International law-making through treaties and custom is less appropriate to shape the relationships of the various actors that are an integral part of globalization. Indeed, scholars of international law and international relations recently have expressed doubt about the continued utility of traditional methods of international law-making in the new global environment.[2] Building on these criticisms and on the distinction between interdependence and globalization, this chapter sets forth a conceptual framework for the growing importance of non-binding international legal agreements (NBILAs) or so-called 'soft'[3] law. Following Koh's concept of the 'transnational legal process',[4] we understand soft law and its participating non-state actors as critical catalysts for and constituent elements of successful transnational cooperation and the creation of international norms that are crucial for a further development of a true international/transnational society.[5] Thus, NBILAs are not necessarily an alternative to international hard law or inter-state cooperation, but they can and often do represent the first important element in an evolutionary process that shapes legal relationships among and between multiple actors, facilitating and ultimately enhancing the effectiveness and efficiency of transnational policy-making. Both grand schools of international relations theory, (Neo-) Realism and (Neo-) Liberalism, would reject the suggested possibility of change in the interests and identity of nation-states. We argue, however, that globalization requires and induces such change, promoting greater cooperation. Indeed, short of a backlash against globalization, states will have little choice but to agree to pool their sovereignty to exercise public power in a global environment now mostly shaped by private actors.

[2] See Chayes, A., and Chayes, A. H., *The New Sovereignty: Compliance with International Regulatory Agreements* (1995); Ratner, S.R., 'International Law: The Trials of Global Norms' [1998] *Foreign Policy* 65–80; Weiss, E.B., 'The New International Legal System', in Jasentuliyana, N. (ed.), *Perspectives on International Law* (1993) 63–82; Reisman, M., 'Designing and Managing the Future of the State' (1993) 8 *Eur. J. Int'l L.* 410–20; Haas, P.M., *et al.*, *Institutions for the Earth: Sources of Effective International Environmental Protection* (1993).

[3] The term 'soft' law as used herein means normative agreements that are not legally binding. See Bernhardt, who denominates them 'rules, which are neither strictly binding nor completely void of any legal significance'. Bernhardt, R., 'Customary International Law' (1984) 7 *Ency. Pub. Intl. L.* 61, 62. NBILAs can take a wide variety of forms and, most importantly, are not subject to national ratification.

[4] Koh, H.H., 'Transnational Legal Process' (1996) 75 *Nebraska L. Rev.* 1; Koh, H.H., 'Why Do Nations Obey International Law?' (1997) 106 *Yale L.J.* 2599. See also Jessup, P.C., *Transnational Law* (1956).

[5] See Slaughter, A.M., *et al.*, 'International Law and International Relations Theory: A New Generation of Interdisciplinary Scholarship' (1998) 92 *Am. J. Int'l L.* 367, 383.

Finally, a purely structural perspective could conclude that under conditions of globalization a state's identity and interests are best served through transnational cooperation rather than territorial defense or even offense, while a focus on the process through which such cooperation is achieved might lead to a negative conclusion if the process fails to meet the most basic criteria of popular legitimacy and accountability.[6] The contribution concludes that NBILAs thus are important not only to facilitate cooperation in a world of globalization, but that the open and transparent integration of non-state actors in global cooperative venues is essential to enhance the legitimacy of transnational policy- and law-making processes, providing a crucial foundation for the emerging global civil society without which globalization cannot be sustained.

A. FROM INTERDEPENDENCE TO GLOBALIZATION

The concepts of interdependence and globalization often are used interchangeably; many studies characterize globalization as 'the intensification of economic, political, social, and cultural relations across borders'.[7] Such a broad quantitative characterization may seem appropriate at first because it embraces the features usually associated with the general concept of globalization while avoiding the details, yet the definition also could apply to the term interdependence. If globalization is merely an 'intensified version' of ever-increasing interdependence, how can globalization be responsible for the transformation processes, the 'epochal shift'[8] that scholars and policy makers claim is taking place? The central features of structural changes in the international system[9] demonstrate that the two concepts are not interchangeable. Richard Cooper was the first to offer a comprehensive theory of interdependence according to which liberalization of international trade and capital flows rendered nation-states increasingly vulnerable and sensitive to each other.[10] This process had two effects: first, interdependent countries were

---

[6] Kaiser, K., 'Transnational Relations as a Threat to the Democratic Process' (1971) 25 *Int. Org.* 706–20; Dahl, R.A., 'A Democratic Dilemma: System Effectiveness versus Citizen Participation' (1994) 109 *Pol. Sci. Q.* 23–34; Held, D., *Democracy and the Global Order: From the Modern State to Cosmopolitan Governance* (1995), Held, D., 'Democracy and Globalization' (1997) 3 *Global Governance* 251–68; McGrew, A., *The Transformation of Democracy? Globalization and Territorial Democracy* (1997); Habermas, J., 'Die postnationale Konstellation und die Zukunft der Demokratie' (1998) 7 *Blätter für deutsche und internationale Politik* 804–17.

[7] Holm, H.H., and Sorensen, G., *Whose World Order? Uneven Globalization and the End of the Cold War* (1995) 4.

[8] *Ibid.*, at 6.

[9] See Goldblatt, D., *et al.*, 'Economic Globalization and the Nation-State: Shifting Balances of Power' (1997) 20 *Alternatives* 269, 270.

[10] Cooper, R., *The Economics of Interdependence* (1968); see also Keohane, R.O., and Nye, J.S., Jr., *Interdependence in World Politics, in Power and Interdependence: World Politics in Transition* (1977).

obliged to adjust their domestic economies to the fact of openness and inter-dependence.[11] Secondly, they saw a need to create international institutions or regimes that provided a rule-based framework to manage their relations and generate a capacity for the joint management of macroeconomic policy, a systemic feature that became known as 'embedded liberalism'.[12]

Two aspects related to interdependence are significant for the present analysis. First, interdependence was structured and managed largely by func-tionally equivalent public entities (states) and often lacked the flexibility and dynamism that characterize today's global interactions among private actors.[13] Secondly, and related to discussions on the benefits of globalization and the degree to which this process is reversible, interdependence is not the product of some higher force, but the result of deliberate political choices of nation-states supported by broad segments of their constituents.[14]

In contrast to economic interdependence, globalization is a process mostly structured by private actors.[15] It is a corporate-level phenomenon that com-menced during the mid-1980s when companies responded to the heightened competition brought about by the deregulation and liberalization of cross-border economic activity. New and cheaper technologies, especially in the area of information, permitted individual companies to integrate a cross-national dimension into their organizational structure and strategic behavior.[16] The growing amount of cross-border movement of increasingly intangible capital and the ownership and control of assets have enhanced corporate competitive-ness and created a cross-border web of inter-connected nodes in which value and wealth are generated. Interdependence thus was an important causal pre-condition for globalization without being identical to it.[17]

Data on global private sector activity substantiate the emergence of global corporate networks and signal a qualitative transformation of the inter-

[11] Some even have argued that steadily increasing public expenditures for social security and other transfer payments became inevitable with growing openness. See Cameron, D., 'The Expansion of the Public Economy' (1978) 72 *Am. Pol. Sci. Rev.* 1243–61; Rodrik, D., *Has Globalization Gone Too Far?* (1997).

[12] Ruggie, J.G., 'International Regimes, Transactions, and Change: Embedded Liberalism in the Postwar Economic Order' (1982) 36 *Int. Org.* 195–231.

[13] Thus all major steps toward a more open world economy, such as the GATT negotiations, have been rather lengthy and full of setbacks. See WTO, *International Trade Trends and Statistics* (1995); Bairoch, P., *Economics and World History: Myths and Paradoxes* (1993) 40.

[14] Dombrowski, P., 'Haute Finance and High Theory: Recent Scholarship on Global Financial Relations' (1998) 42 *Mershon Int'l Studies Rev.* (Suppl. 1) 1–28; Helleiner, E., *States and the Reemergence of Global Finance: From Bretton Woods to the 1990s* (1994).

[15] Private actors not only comprise corporations, but also interest groups, NGOs, and know-ledge institutions that have begun to reorganize themselves on a transnational scale.

[16] OECD, 'Technology and Globalisation' in *Technology and the Economy: The Key Relationship* (1992); Chesnais, F., 'Technological Cooperation Agreements between Firms' (1988) 4 *STI Rev.* 52–119; Soete, L., *Technology in a Changing World: Policy Synthesis of the OECD Technology and Economy Program, MERIT/TEP* (1991).

[17] For a more detailed discussion, see Reinicke, W.H., *Global Public Policy: Governing with-out Government?* (1998).

national system. There is little doubt that foreign direct investment (FDI), international trade, and cross-border financial flows have increased during the last two decades. More significant, however, is that their nature and geography also have changed and that other transnational economic linkages have grown in importance. Foreign direct investment, for example, grew during the 1960s and 1970s in close correlation with tangibles such as world output and trade, but from 1985–95 it expanded at an annual average rate of 16 percent compared to 2 percent and 7 percent for output and trade, respectively. Controlling for the opening of both China and the former Soviet bloc, which attracted almost no investment prior to 1985, the share of foreign direct investment going to the developing world actually dropped. FDI in the developing world, generally focused on resource, labor-intensive and greenfield investments, remains an element in international economic activity, but it has been dwarfed by cross-investments in the OECD and a few emerging markets, concentrated on mergers and acquisitions in high value-added, knowledge, and R&D-intensive industries. The growing importance of corporate alliances and collaborative agreements, a variant of cross-border corporate organization adopted by companies that need cash or prefer arrangements of a less binding nature, confirms this shift.

These changes have qualitative implications for international trade, which increasingly is being structured by FDI and international alliances. The OECD estimates that about 70 percent of current world trade is accounted for by intra-industry and intra-firm trade, both closely tied to global corporate strategies and neither having much to do with the standard textbook case of comparative advantage.[18] The dramatic growth of cross-border capital flows during the last decade is a well-established fact, but here too the advent of securitization and the institutionalization of savings in the mid-1980s represent a qualitative transformation of financial intermediation and its risks, facilitating the implementation of global corporate strategies, while at the same time giving foreign entities access to domestic financial markets. The market for derivative instruments, in particular, has exploded and led to heightened volatility of cross-border capital flows, evidenced by the fact that the combined annual value of global trade and FDI in 1995 was equal to only six days of turnover on the global foreign exchange markets.[19]

Though incomplete, these data confirm that international economic activity during the last decade largely has reflected cross-border restructuring of corporate activities throughout a product's life cycle, enabling corporations

---

[18] Reasonable data for intra-firm trade exist only for the United States, but in 1995 approximately 40% of total U.S. trade comprised off-market trade. Governments continue to register these internal transfers because they cross borders, not because they are traded. The OECD reminds us that mergers and acquisitions, such investments 'may represent nothing more than a change of ownership, with no effect on resource allocation between the two countries'. OECD, *Globalization of Industry: Overview and Sector Reports* (1996) 46.

[19] *Ibid.*

to draw on and serve geographically expanding markets.[20] This is achieved either through the absorption of foreign capital stock into an already existing corporate structure and internalization of economic activities that were formerly conducted on the open market or through alliances such as long term supplier agreements, licensing or franchising contracts entailing transfers among legally-independent corporate entities without full exposure to market forces. The process of corporate restructuring has become an ongoing process with corporations now able to adjust quickly to changing political, social, and economic framework conditions. Globalization thus represents the emergence of a single integrated economic space cutting across political spaces and driven by the organizational logic of corporate industrial networks and their financial relationships.

To sum up, the widespread practice of equating globalization with interdependence can be misleading because globalization of corporate activity increasingly takes place in distinct institutional structures detached from the traditional economic relations among nation-states. In fact, although geographical differences in the effects of globalization remain[21] one can argue that global corporate networks are increasingly independent from nation-states.[22] Whether this implies that multinational, transnational, or global corporations should be characterized as 'footloose and stateless'[23] or even 'global corporate leviathans'[24] remains highly controversial. While a general definition of economic globalization is impossible because the data remain incomplete, clearly, reality is complex and the borders between interdependence and globalization are blurred. As will be shown, however, the key

---

[20] OECD, *Financial Market Trends* (1996) 15; Hatzichronoglou, T., 'Globalisation and Competitiveness: Relevant Indicators' (1996) STI Working Paper 5, OECD/GD (96).

[21] Some scholars argue that the term globalization is a misnomer; the best alternative has been proposed by Michael Zürn's concept of denationalization. Zürn, M., 'Does International Governance Meet Demand?', InIIS-Arbeitspapier Nr. 4–5 (1997). Obviously, the globalization of corporate activity depends on the specific sector. In addition, globalization until now largely has been limited to the OECD world. This is not to say that other regions will remain excluded; in fact, there is evidence that at least some non-industrialized countries are increasingly part of this process. Petrella, R., 'Globalization and Internationalization: The Dynamics of the Emerging World Order' in Boyer, R., and Drache, D. (eds.), *States against Markets: The Limits of Globalization* (1996) 62–83 at 77. In addition, some scholars have found, that '. . . the institutional and ideological legacies of distinctive national histories continue significantly to shape the core operations of multinational firms based in Germany, Japan, and the United States. . . . recognizable and patterned differences persist in the behavior of leading MNCs'. Pauly, L.W., and Reich, S., 'National Structures and Multinational Corporate Behavior: Enduring Differences in the Age of Globalization' (1997) 51 *Int. Org.* 3, 25.

[22] As Riccardo Petrella recently put it, 'the growing globalization of the economy is eroding one of the basic foundations of the nation-state, i.e. the national market . . . what is different today from thirty years ago is that the national economy is no longer the name of the game'. Petrella, *supra* note 21, at 67.

[23] Robert, W., 'Globalization and Its Limits: Reports of the Death of the National Economy are Greatly Exaggerated' in Berger, S., and Dore, R. (eds.), *Diversity and Global Capitalism* (1996) 60–88, at 79.

[24] Petrella, *supra* note 21 at 74.

features of globalization warrant examination for their impact on the sovereignty of nation-states and restructuring of the international system, including the role of international law.

B. GLOBALIZATION: A CHALLENGE TO SOVEREIGNTY?

Much has been written on the challenge that globalization poses to sovereignty,[25] but the fact that economic integration weakens the sovereignty of nation-states is nothing new. Two specifications of globalization and sovereignty provide useful foundations for this analysis.[26] First, neither globalization nor interdependence challenges the formal or legal sovereignty of a state—only other states can. Globalization instead challenges the *operational* sovereignty of a government, that is, its ability to exercise sovereignty in its conduct of public policy. Secondly, states live a 'double life'[27] according to John Hoffman, with sovereignty having two dimensions, an internal and an external. The *internal* dimension is the relationship between the state and civil society. Following Max Weber, a government is internally sovereign if it enjoys a territorial monopoly of legitimate power over a range of activities, including economic ones. That power is embodied in the domestic legal, administrative, and political structures and principles that guide public policies. Internal economic sovereignty takes effect when governments collect taxes or regulate private sector activities. The practice of sovereignty therefore can be described as 'the highest, original—as opposed to derivative—power within a territorial jurisdiction; this power is not subject to the executive, legislative or judicial jurisdiction of a foreign state or any foreign law other than public international law'.[28]

The *external* dimension of sovereignty refers to relationships among states in the international system, defined by the absence of a central authority. Countries exercise external economic sovereignty when, for example, they collect tariffs and alter their exchange rates. Economic interdependence poses

---

[25] See, *e.g.*, Ohmae, K., *The End of the Nation-State* (1995); Cable, V., 'The Diminished Nation-State: A Study in the Loss of Economic Power' (1995) 124 *Daedalus*, 23–54; Guehenno, J.-M., *The End of the Nation-State* (1995); Horsman, M., and Marshall, A., *After the Nation-State* (1994); Camilleri, J., and Falk, J., *The End of Sovereignty? The Politics of a Shrinking and Fragmenting World* (1992); Cerny, P.G., 'Globalization and the Changing Logic of Collective Action' (1995) 49 *Int. Org.* 595–625; Falk, R., 'Will Globalization Win Out?' (1997) 73 *Int. Aff.* 123–36; Held, *supra* note 6; Rodrik *supra* note 11.

[26] A comprehensive and broad discussion of the concept of sovereignty is not possible in this chapter and, indeed, two recent analyses argue that sovereignty in itself is not a coherent concept and therefore cannot be defined. See Bartelson, J., *A Genealogy of Sovereignty* (1995) and Weber, C., *Simulating Sovereignty: Intervention, the State and Symbolic Exchange* (1995). See also Hoffman, J., 'Blind Alleys. Can We Define Sovereignty?' (1997) 17 *Politics* 53.

[27] *Ibid.*, at 54.

[28] Lapidoth, R., 'Sovereignty in Transition' (1992) 45 *J. Int'l Aff.* 325, 327.

a challenge to this external dimension of sovereignty. Responding to the challenge, governments largely followed the principles of liberal economic internationalism, endorsing the incremental reduction of their external economic sovereignty by lowering tariff barriers and capital controls. The reductions were structured around a set of international norms and standards, generally including the principle of reciprocity, and embedded in international regimes such as the GATT, the IMF, and the OECD that formalized state adherence and assured compliance.[29]

External sovereignty loses much of its significance when examining the implications of globalization. Global corporate networks are posing challenges instead to a state's internal sovereignty by altering the spatial relationship between private and public sectors. The organizational logic of globalization induces corporations to seek the fusion of multiple, formerly segmented national markets into a single whole that subsumes multiple political geographies. As a result, governments no longer have a monopoly of the legitimate power over their territory, undermining the operability of internal sovereignty. The rising incidence of regulatory and tax arbitrage is a telling indicator that the monopoly has ended.

Globalization does not imply that private actors are always deliberately undermining internal sovereignty. Rather, they follow a fundamentally different organizational logic. Political systems, at least in their contemporary form as nation-states, are boundary maintaining systems[30] whose legitimization, internal and external, is derived from the ability to maintain their boundaries. Markets, although initially relying for their creation on political power, do not depend on the presence of boundaries. The spatial symmetry between the 'public' and the 'private' upon which internal sovereignty depends is disappearing. Governments, bound by territoriality, cannot project their power over the total space within which production and consumption organize themselves. Globalization thus integrates along the economic dimension and simultaneously fragments along the political.

The fact that political fragmentation threatens only the operational aspects of internal sovereignty in no way minimizes the challenge. The threat to a government's ability to exercise internal sovereignty implies a threat to the effectiveness of democracy. Individuals may continue to exercise their formal right to vote, but the power of that vote to shape public policy decreases with the decline in operational internal sovereignty. Persistent weakness in internal sovereignty will cast doubt on democratic institutions, ultimately challenging formal sovereignty. Governments have no choice but to respond.

[29] Krasner, S.D. (ed.), *International Regimes* (1983).

[30] Kratchowil, F., 'Of Systems, Boundaries, and Territoriality: An Inquiry into the Formation of the State System' (1986–7) 39 *World Politics* 27–52; Luhmann, N., 'Territorial Borders as System Boundaries', in Strassoldo, R., and delli Zoti, G. (eds.), *Cooperation and Conflict in Border Areas* (1982) 235–45.

C. POLICY RESPONSES

The responses of nation-states to the pressures of globalization largely fall into two broad categories. Some governments adopt essentially intervention-ist strategies that reemphasize the territorial nature of state jurisdiction, in the hope of regaining control over the economic and social environment. Alternatively, governments simply rely on existing structures and processes of international cooperation, including the use of international law, as practiced when managing external sovereignty. Neither of these responses is likely to generate the expected results.

1. Offensive and Defensive Intervention

Defensive intervention in response to globalization may involve the rein-statement of tariffs, non-tariff barriers, and capital controls, or may require companies to reorganize along national lines. If economic nationalism fails to arouse broad popular support, its political counterpart—territorial secession and partition—may do so.[31] Alternatively, governments may pursue an offensive strategy of predatory competition, subsidizing national champions and encouraging competitive deregulation. Such states may become 'global competitors', seeking to entice corporations to operate within their own ter-ritory. Offensive intervention has become popular as a political tool, as some countries attempt to broaden the reach of their internal sovereignty to match the economic geography of global corporate networks.[32]

Offensive intervention is commonly described as 'national competitive-ness', and in many industrialized countries it shapes the debate on important structural reforms in economic and social policy.[33] Nation-states seek to offer the best environment for FDI and production to generate economic growth and employment, or subsidize national corporations in their struggle for

[31] Increased calls for greater regional autonomy or even territorial secession and partition in the hope of regaining internal sovereignty is a political strategy that has become popular during the past decade.

[32] Two of the more prominent examples are California's attempt to tax resident companies on a global basis and the Helms-Burton Act. See Shamberger, D., 'The Helms-Burton Act: A Legal and Effective Vehicle for Redressing U.S. Property Claims in Cuba and Accelerating the Demise of the Castro Regime' (1998) 21 *B.C. Int't & Comp. L.R.* 497–537 and Novak, V., 'Tilting at Taxes: Foreign Governments are Screaming Bloody Murder over California's Insistence on its Right to Tax Multinational Corporations on a Share of their Global Income' (1993) 25 *Nat. J.* 1972–5.

[33] Zysman, J., and Tyson, L., *American Industry in International Competition: Government Policies and Corporate Strategies* (1983); Tyson, D'A., *Who's Bashing Whom: Trade Conflict in High-Technology Industries* (1992); Thurow, L.C., *Head to Head: The Coming Battle among Japan, Europe, and America* (1992); Luttwak, E.N., *The Endangered American Dream: How to Stop the United States from Becoming a Third World Country and How to Win the Geo-Economic Struggle for Industrial Supremacy* (1993).

international market shares. Although states are competitors, in rhetoric and political reality, the results of deregulation and subsidization for the sake of national competitiveness remain uncertain and unpromising.[34]

Neither defensive nor offensive intervention bodes well for the future of international relations. Protectionism invites retaliation and jeopardizes the path of deeper integration. Subsidizing an industry with the sole purpose of gaining (a temporary) competitive advantage also diverts scarce public funds from important public policy goals and competitive deregulation ultimately defeats the original purpose of the policy because a fully deregulated market further reduces a government's internal sovereignty.[35] Extraterritorial regulation also undermines deeper integration because other states usually retaliate against such dictates. Finally, redefining political geography through partition only gives the appearance of greater control of policy. Partitioning a country focuses exclusively on the external dimension of sovereignty and, rather than insulating governments from the challenges of globalization, may make them more vulnerable.

These approaches re-emphasize territoriality as an ordering principle of international relations, a condition that integration tried to overcome and the end of the Cold War appeared to have secured. At odds with globalization, they will succeed only if the achievements of interdependence are reversed. This possibility may seem remote, but the popularity of interventionist policies has increased considerably as political opportunists take advantage of the public's fear concerning declining internal sovereignty by advocating greater economic nationalism and/or closed regionalism. Unless an alternative can be found, governments may be forced to rely on interventions to halt the loss of internal sovereignty and further erosion of confidence in democratic institutions. A strategy to resolve the dilemma of 'fragmented sovereignty'[36] while preserving the benefits of globalization and interdependence must re-align the political with the economic geography, something which can only be achieved by overcoming public policy responses based purely on territory.

2. Traditional International Cooperation and International Law

If governments want to shape globalization, they must operationalize internal sovereignty in a non-territorial context. Forming a global government is

[34] As Paul Krugman has put it, 'it could result in the wasteful spending of government money supposedly to enhance U.S. competitiveness. Second, it could lead to protectionism and trade wars. Finally, and most important, it could result in bad public policy on a spectrum of important issues.' Krugman, P., 'Competitiveness: A Dangerous Obsession', in Krugman, P. (ed.), *Pop Internationalism* (1996) 18.

[35] Polanyi, K., *The Great Transformation. The Political and Economic Origins of Our Times* [1944] (1957).

[36] Streeck, W., 'Public Power Beyond the Nation-State: The Case of the European Community', in Boyer, R., and Drache, D. (eds.), *States against Markets in The Limits of Globalization* (1996) 299, 300.

one response, but it is unrealistic because it would require states to abdicate their formal sovereignty. It is also undesirable for reasons of accountability and legitimacy: there presently exists no 'transnational public space' where political discourse—one important pillar of a global civil society—could be organized, including mechanisms of public control over international policy-making.[37] Finally, while global government may be a technocrat's answer to the shortcomings of territorially-based approaches to public policy, it could not match the dynamism of transnational economic and social networks, legal and illegal alike, that have emerged with globalization; nor is there any reason to believe that a global government is better equipped to manage the technical complexities and speed of evolution of public policy at the beginning of the twenty-first century.

Thus, for many observers a better answer is to continue strengthening the structure of multilateralism, development of which is seen in the rising number of international institutions and organizations.[38] In this context, the present significance of international law is without doubt one of the preeminent achievements of the post-war international system.[39] These forms of inter-state cooperation have their roots and robustness in the management of external sovereignty, *i.e.* the management of interdependence. International law instruments have been the most important element in the cooperative processes.[40] State action has largely precipitated and structured the processes and the instruments, notwithstanding the growing importance of non-state actors and international organizations in inter-state negotiations and

[37] See Czempiel, E.O., 'Governance and Democratization', in Rosenau, J.N., and Czempiel, E.-O. (eds.), *Governance without Government: Order and Change in World Politics* (1992) 250–71; Rosenau, J.N., 'Governance in the Twenty-First Century' (1995) 1 *Global Governance* 13–43; Young, O.R., 'Anarchy and Social Choice. Reflections on the International Polity' (1978) 30 *World Politics* 241–63. Arguably, the investiture of a global government also would require a strong (hegemonic) power that no longer exists. At only one point recently was a single nation-state, the United States, strong enough to assume the role of a world government, *i.e.* by the installation of the Bretton Woods system that to a large extent reflected American visions of a post-war world. Today, even taking into account the U.S. hegemonic position on some issues, no nation-state can easily and generally dominate world politics. Therefore, a possible attempt to enlarge state power to implement a world government could be pursued only by force, an undesirable option.

[38] Zürn, M., Jacobson, H.K., *et al*, 'National Entanglements in International Governmental Organizations' (1986) 80 *Am.Pol.Sci.Rev.* 1.

[39] Although nearly all observers agree that there is growing international cooperation, the reasons for this development remain highly debated between (Neo-) Realists and (Neo-) Liberalists, as well as between social constructivist and reflectionist theorists. The present analysis does not engage the debate because of the existing vast literature on the question and, more importantly because, as it is argued below, the framework of interaction between nation-states is so rapidly and profoundly changing that much of the discussion of the 1980s and the early 1990s is outmoded. For a good overview see Baldwin, D.A. (ed.), *Neorealism and Neoliberalism* (1993).

[40] This does not imply that states utilize only hard law in cooperative processes, although treaties and custom are the preferred means. So-called international regimes could also rely on NBILAs as important instruments.

law-making.[41] The importance of international law can be seen not only in the number of international treaties and agreements, but also in the increasing impact of international law on people's lives.[42]

There remain major obstacles in the way of establishing a system of international law comparable to the legal systems of nation-states, in which all 'courts, agencies, and other formal organs of dispute settlement or rule application are all more or less coordinated in an integrated and hierarchical legal system'.[43] In fact, international law seems merely a patchwork. The uncoordinated division of labor among existing international institutions and organizations reflects this and uncovers the extensively-discussed gaps and loopholes in the system of multilateral international law.[44]

The advent of globalization has revived the issue of developing a system of global governance that is efficient, effective, and legitimate when compared to that of modern nation-states. If one accepts the notion of the diminishing importance and significance of individual nation-states, it becomes important to conceive of a system that acts as the principal institutional mechanism through which internal sovereignty can be applied and enforced at the global level. Some have proposed the emergence of a 'cosmopolitan democracy', an encompassing system of international law that includes individuals and groups, with fundamental individual rights guaranteed by supranational judicial authorities.[45]

This perspective, appealing as it is, appears overly broad and optimistic, given the historical evolution of the international system and international law, and it would take time to develop such an order.[46] In addition, several theoretical and operational concerns throw doubt on the ability of the traditional system to respond adequately to the growing demand for cooperation compelled by globalization.

First, the inter-governmental instruments, regimes, and organizations that were used to promote economic interdependence may not be appropriate to manage globalization. The issues for which cooperation is sought are likely to be more complex and highly contentious, embedded as they are in history and

---

[41] Weiss, *supra* note 2 at 65.

[42] David Held, among others, argues that individuals increasingly are affected by international law, in some cases appearing as subjects of international law. Held (1995), *supra* note 6 at 101. Hedley Bull noted as early as 1977 that 'opinion appears to have moved decisively against the doctrine of the nineteenth-century positivists that international law (in Oppenheim's words) is a "law between states only and exclusively"', but that '[i]t is widely held that individual human beings are subjects of international law'. Bull, H., *The Anarchical Society: A Study of Order in World Politics* (1977), 145; see also Levi, W., *Law and Politics in the International Society*, Sage Library of Social Research No. 32 (1976), 111–15.

[43] Janis, M.W., *An Introduction to International Law* (2nd edn. 1993) 7.

[44] Zürn, *supra* note 21 at 34.   [45] Held (1995), *supra* note 6.

[46] Held's work still serves an important purpose in rethinking classical theories of democracy that were designed for modern nation-states and that have come under increasing pressure with the internationalization and globalization of politics.

culture. Thus, in contrast to the management of interdependence, which promoted a widely accepted paradigm of free trade and reciprocal reduction of tariff barriers, globalization challenges policy makers to develop common standards on issues such as non-tariff barriers, heretofore the exclusive prerogative of nation-states,[47] in the face of national idiosyncracies and perceptions of the public good.

Secondly and relatedly, the management of interdependence and expansion of the international legal system was largely structured by functionally equivalent nation-states, while globalization has been driven primarily by non-state, especially corporate, actors. Given this development, the management of internal sovereignty in a non-territorial context is likely to require considerable interaction among functional opposites (nation-states and private actors) at the global level and may necessitate a reconsideration of conventional models of cooperation in light of the different modes and cultures of organization and communication that characterize the public and private sectors.

Thirdly, recent scholarship has argued convincingly, contrary to the assumptions of (Neo-) Realism and (Neo-) Liberalism, that states' interests as well as their identities are not static and exogenously created,[48] but are 'socially constructed products of learning, knowledge, cultural practices, and ideology'[49] shaped over a long period of time. This work acknowledges, in principle, the possibility of change in states' interests and identities, but also recognizes the obstacles, noting that 'notwithstanding the growing importance of non-state actors in world politics, states remain jealous of their sovereignty and so may resist collective identification more than other actors'.[50] It thus is not readily apparent that existing state-dominated structures and institutions of cooperation, including the formulation of treaties and custom, can easily respond to, let alone 'absorb', the set of issues involved in managing internal sovereignty in a manner that would resemble socially constructed outcomes.

The emergence of internal sovereignty as a global policy issue exposes existing shortcomings in negotiating, implementing, and monitoring international

---

[47] Cooperation on internal sovereignty can result in joint gains, but in general these gains will be much harder and take longer to achieve. A common set of labor standards, for example, can provide a joint gain, excluding as it does the possibility of regulatory arbitrage by multinational corporations, but complex considerations of political culture and history can pose obstacles to cooperation.

[48] Otherwise, it would be hard to explain peaceful change in the system. See Wendt, A., 'Anarchy is What States Make of It: The Social Construction of Power Politics' (1992) 46 *Int. Org.* 391–425; Wendt, A., 'Collective Identity Formation and the International State' (1994) 88 *Am. Pol. Sci. Rev.* 384–96.; Adler, E., 'Seizing the Middle Ground: Constructivism in World Politics' (1997) 3 *Eur. J. Int'l Rel.* 319–63.

[49] Koh (1996), *supra* note 4 at 20.

[50] Wendt (1994), *supra* note 48 at 385.

law.[51] First, legal and international relations scholars widely agree that treaty-making usually entails a slow and costly process, involving exhaustive negotiation processes between top levels of national bureaucracies. These processes are not effective and flexible enough to accommodate the public policy demands emanating from highly adaptive and responsive global corporate networks, which require a constant reassessment of the structures that govern them.[52]

Secondly, international treaties are based on negotiated consensus. Their content thus tends to reflect a narrow and often lowest common denominator not necessarily responsive to complex and interdisciplinary global challenges like environmental protection and labor market regulation. Moreover, most treaties classify states as either party or non-party. Such rigidity does not favor regime development, let alone success, because it excludes *a priori* those that are financially or technically unable to comply and those who disagree with the obligations.

Thirdly, the effectiveness of international cooperation through treaties is usually delayed because of the requirement of ratification, although states have adopted ameliorative techniques such as provisional treaty application and delegated law-making (to supranational regulatory authorities or agencies). While helpful, these techniques do not cure the problem and may create new ones. Provisional application does not resolve the need for a 'fast-track' device to manage a continuously changing policy landscape, while delegated law-making empowers institutions that lack the legitimacy and accountability of their national counterparts, results in a democratic deficit, and fosters the political resistance to globalization.

Fourthly, globalization fundamentally alters the prospects and possibilities of compliance, potentially leading to a higher incidence of defection from international agreements. In many cases it is no longer sufficient to ask whether states are willing, but if they are able, to comply. In some issue-areas nation-states cannot fulfill treaty obligations because the objects of regulation are highly mobile and act transnationally. According to Chayes and Chayes, '[t]he problem [of involuntary defection] is even more acute in contemporary regulatory treaties. Such treaties are formally among states, and the obligations are cast as state obligations. . . . The real object of the treaty, however, is not to affect state behavior, but to regulate the activities of individuals and private entities'.[53] Lack of capacity is not limited to developing countries; in some issue areas, *e.g.* banking regulation, money laundering, dual-use trade,

---

[51] For more extensive analysis see Sand, P.H., 'International Cooperation: The Environmental Experience', in Matthews, J.T. (ed.), *Preserving the Global Environment: The Challenge of Shared Leadership* (1991); Chayes and Chayes, *supra* note 2.

[52] Technological progress is so rapid in the international financial markets and banking that regulators find it difficult to keep pace with changes and the challenges they pose to existing regulatory frameworks. See Dombrowski, *supra* note 14 at 8; Reinicke *supra* note 17.

[53] Chayes and Chayes, *supra* note 2 at 14.

and terrorism, it affects members of the industrialized OECD world. Although Louis Henkin argues that 'almost all nations observe almost all principles of international law and almost all of their obligations almost all of the time',[54] this assertion may well be disproven by the advent of globalization and the challenges it creates, creating a new source of conflict between nations.

In sum, traditional international law and interstate cooperation to manage interdependence are unlikely to be effective, efficient, or legitimate instruments to respond to the challenges of globalization, although improvements have been made in hard law-making. Global environmental treaties often now include selective incentives, differential obligations or are regionalized to become more open and flexible,[55] although there may be good reason to reject a regionalized approach.[56] More importantly, it is doubtful whether these and other adjustments will be able to establish the degree of inclusiveness, support, and legitimacy that is required for the sustained and successful management of internal sovereignty. Treaty law usually does not offer the required 'process openness' many global policy issues need to achieve acceptance and compliance by all participants. Instead, successful global governance of internal sovereignty beyond the nation-state must transcend the governments and politics of nation-states to take on a much wider meaning in terms of participating actors and levels and structures of interaction.[57] Traditional international law and inter-state cooperation must be complemented by a more incremental and evolutionary approach that acknowledges and incorporates the qualitative differences between interdependence and globalization.

[54] Henkin, H., *How Nations Behave: Law and Foreign Policy* (2nd edn. 1979), 47.

[55] Sand, *supra* note 51 at 241–50.

[56] Labor standards, for example: 'from the ILO´s perspective, one thing is clear. We strongly feel that: (1) there should be a body of international labor standards (or social charter) agreed on by all parties concerned; and (2) at a time when the world economy becomes ever more integrated, a regionalization of standards (i.e., different minimum standards for different regions or cultures) must be avoided at all cost.' Maier, H., 'International Labor Standards and Economic Integration: The Perspective of the International Labor Organization', in Schoepfle, G.K., and Swinnerton, K.A. (eds.), *International Labor Standards and Global Economic Integration* (1994) 11.

[57] See Rosenau, Czempiel, *supra* note 37. There is no widely accepted definition of global governance, but the Commission on Global Governance describes it as 'the sum of the many ways individuals and institutions, public and private, manage their common affairs. It is a continuing process through which conflict or diverse interests may be accommodated and co-operative action may be taken. It includes formal institutions and regimes empowered to enforce compliance, as well as informal arrangements that people and institutions either have agreed to or perceive to be in their interests.' Commission on Global Governance, *Our Global Neighborhood* (1995), 5. James N. Rosenau adopts an even broader definition: 'global governance is conceived to include systems of rules at all levels of human activity—from the family to the international organization—in which the pursuit of goals through the exercise of control has transnational repercussions'. Rosenau, *supra* note 37 at 13.

Legal scholars sometimes distinguish the 'international law of coexistence' and the 'international law of cooperation'.[58] The latter, a pillar of interdependence, is understood as the 'development of an international law expressing the need for *states* to cooperate in order to attain objectives beneficial to all'.[59] Under conditions of globalization, the 'international law of cooperation' has gained in importance, but it can succeed only if international law can move beyond its narrow focus on states. It must adopt and employ broad and flexible legal structures and processes that facilitate the social construction of states' interests in order for them to establish and exercise internal sovereignty at the global level. As is shown in the following discussion, NBILAs make an important contribution to the emergence of such structures and processes.

D. GLOBAL PUBLIC POLICY AND THE ROLE OF NBILAS

There is growing, if scattered, evidence that state and non-state actors have begun to experiment with the idea of global public policy that aims, *inter alia*, at the active integration of non-state actors in all phases of the policy-making process. The evidence includes an increasing reliance on NBILAs, which provide a certain legal framework and sense of obligation for the multiple and functionally-different parties involved. This section proposes a more systematic involvement of non-state actors, highlights some of the challenges that are likely to arise if policy makers choose to rely on such an approach, and points to the crucial role that NBILAs will have to play in operationalizing the concept of global public policy.

1. Toward Global Public Policy

The concept of internal sovereignty and the perceived needs of national constituencies are in constant flux, depending on a wide variety of factors including overall economic conditions, changing external circumstances, and technological and scientific evolution, all of which serve to impact on the politics of public policy. What is perceived to be in the public interest varies not only across time but also across countries, reflecting differences in levels of economic development, historical experiences, and cultural norms and values.[60] As a result, implementing internal sovereignty globally cannot succeed

---

[58] Friedmann, W., *The Changing Structure of International Law* (1964).

[59] Leben, C., 'The Changing Structure of International Law Revisited' (1997) 8 *Eur. J. Int'l L.* 399, 401.

[60] Recent debates on human rights and labor standards provide a telling example. The classic economic debate on public goods is too narrow because public goods are not only items that are produced to internalize externalities and market inefficiencies but also reflect the political choice of regulation and redistribution of a society. '[T]he idea that state policy should or even can be

merely by ceding sovereignty to supranational authorities or by negotiating more sophisticated treaties. Global public policy is becoming a process of collective identity formation,[61] necessitating adaptation of the processes and forms of cooperation, critical elements through which actors interact to shape each other's identities and interests. The politics of global public policy must become more inclusive and participatory, a proposition that appears difficult to realize given the continuing importance of formal sovereignty and traditional emphasis on the principles of territoriality and non-interference.

This has created something of a paradox. On the one hand, states remain eager to preserve their formal sovereignty and thus are reluctant to cede formal power and sovereignty to other levels of governance, making the goal of sustained international law-making hard to achieve. On the other hand, states will be required to demonstrate a high degree of cooperation in order to maintain their internal sovereignty, that is to rationalize their very existence *vis-à-vis* their constituents. By elevating internal sovereignty to the rank of a global policy issue, globalization challenges the international system to manage and resolve this second, equally important determinant of states' overall identity. States can no longer afford to exhibit a singular systemic identity seen in the preservation of external sovereignty, but must rely on the international system to achieve internal sovereignty as well.

Cooperation, as advocated by (Neo-)Liberals, thus is no longer just a means to the end of managing external sovereignty but becomes an end in itself or, in other words, anarchy is no longer just the outcome of, but also the cause for, state interests in the international system. 'As the ability to meet corporate needs unilaterally declines, so does the incentive to hang onto the egoistic identities that generate such policies, and as the degree of common fate increases, so does the incentive to identify with others.'[62] Given this, the prospects for inter-state cooperation and compliance are better under conditions of globalization than under economic interdependence. This by no means eliminates the problem of free-riding but it can facilitate the establishment of incentive-based structures and rules to reduce it.

The social origins of state interests necessitates the systematic and sustained integration of private actors in the process of global public policy-and-law-making to facilitate the formation of collective transnational identities to sustain cooperation. Such an integration can be achieved by recognizing that governance, a social function crucial to the operation of any market

---

based on a single criterion of maximizing efficiency is demonstrably false . . . to maintain the loyalty of the majority of its citizens—a necessary condition for political security, legitimation, etc.—the state is called on to provide economic security.' Strange, S., 'Protectionism and World Politics' (1985) 39 *Int. Org.* 233, 236. On labor standards see Martin Witte, J., *Globalisierung, nationalstaatliche Handlungsfähigkeit und Demokratiedefizit: Globale demokratische Ordnungspolitik zur Regulierung internationale Arbeitsstandards*, Diplomarbeit, Faculty of Economics and Social Sciences at the University of Potsdam (1998).

[61] Wendt (1994), *supra* note 48 at 388–91.   [62] *Ibid.*, at 389.

economy, does not always have to be equated with government. Accordingly, a global public policy would de-link some operational elements of internal sovereignty (governance) from its territorial foundation (the nation-state) and hierarchical institutional environment (the government).

To implement such a strategy, policy-and-law-makers could invoke the principle of subsidiarity, but use the concept in a broader sense than it is used in the context of the European Union, the Tenth Amendment to the U.S. Constitution, and other federalist structures. The 'sub' in subsidiarity normally is used in a functional sense to refer to any actor or institution that is well positioned to support the operationalization of internal sovereignty. *Vertical* subsidiarity delegates policy-and-law-making to other public sector actors. As discussed above, however, these traditional forms of cooperation through inter-state bargaining, application of treaty law, and the establishment of intergovernmental organizations do not suffice. International bureaucratic structures cannot eliminate the organizational disparities between public territorial hierarchies and the private non-territorial networks that globalization has exposed. Global bureaucracies lack the dynamism, agility, and knowledge base that characterizes global economic and social networks. Adaptive and intelligent public policy systems to form the core of identity and interest formation in the context of globalization will only arise if policy makers are prepared to make extensive use of *horizontal* subsidiarity, that is, if they delegate or outsource some aspects of public policy-making to non-state actors such as business, NGOs, foundations, and other interested civil society participants.

There are numerous reasons why the integration of private actors can further global public policy-making. Five are listed here: *first*, it offers selective incentives for private actors. They have a direct stake not only in the outcome of global public policy, but also in the success of the network itself. By participating in the policy-making process, these actors can contribute to and influence global regulatory policy such as the setting of norms and standards, reducing transaction costs and simplifying the system itself for all involved. *Secondly*, the process of global public policy-making can be propelled and advanced by reducing information asymmetries between regulators and regulated. Already a problem at the national level, information asymmetries have increased in the wake of globalization. *Thirdly*, better information, knowledge, and understanding on the part of the non-state actors, with regard to increasingly complex, technology-driven, and fast changing public policy issues, will produce a more efficient and effective regulatory process. *Fourthly*, private sector participation will generate greater acceptability and legitimacy of global public policy and transnational law-making.[63] *Fifthly*,

[63] Participation alone is unlikely to solve the problem of the democratic deficit that is inherent in international as well as transnational relations. Research is urgently needed on the question of whether or not the integration of non-state actors can result in a more legitimate process

and relatedly, horizontal subsidiarity creates a real international community, a true global civil society, by encouraging mutual learning systems and openness to change among different systems of public policy, currently one of the biggest obstacles to establishing internal sovereignty at the global level.[64] It could therefore serve as a catalyst for collective identity formation, the most imminent precondition for an international society based on common norms and values.[65]

The wisdom of placing private and public interests under the direction of the same institution may be questioned. The public's interest could be neglected, as suggested by the limited experience with mixing public and private regulation at the national and regional levels. The deficiencies of mixed regulation should and can be addressed, however. Greater transparency can be achieved by establishing strict principles of disclosure-based regulation guaranteeing other groups sufficient access to ensure that their interests are adequately represented. Secondly, corporations must facilitate such public–private partnerships by improving their own internal control and management structures. The better these inside controls are, the lower the risk of market failure and the need for outside regulation.[66]

2. NBILAs and Global Public Policy

To garner credibility, trust, and eventual success, global public policy networks must be embedded in an international legal context. Here NBILAs can and do play a crucial role in establishing public–private partnerships. NBILAs are thus understood as tools that state and non-state actors choose to strengthen and sustain the operability of internal sovereignty in a

of transnational policy- and law-making. Arguably, the integration of private actors can lead to greater transparency and openness of international processes and establish forms of deliberative negotiation processes, providing elements of a participatory democracy in which all parties that have a stake in the issue can become involved. Cox argues that '[t]here is a meaning of democracy that could be built upon such a development of civil society—a "participative democracy", the organization of civic life upon the basis of a variety of self-governing groups that deal with the whole range of people's substantive concerns'. Cox, R., 'Globalization, Multilateralism and Democracy' (The John W. Holmes Memorial Lecture) Providence, Academic Council on the United Nations System Reports and Papers, 1992–2, 7. See Klein, A., and Schmalz-Bruns, R., 'Herausforderungen der Demokratie. Möglichkeiten und Grenzen der Demokratietheorie', in Klein, A., and Schmalz-Bruns, R. (eds.), *Politische Beteiligung und Bürgerengagement in Deutschland. Möglichkeiten und Grenzen* (1997) 35; see also our conclusion.

[64] Clark, A.M., 'Non-governmental Organizations and their Influence on International Society' (1995) 48 *J. Int'l Aff.* 507–25; Smith, J., 'Global Civil Society?' (1998) 42 *The American Behavioral Scientist* 93–107; Seagall, J.J., 'A First Step to Peaceful Cosmopolitan Democracy' (1997) 9 *Peace Rev.* 337–44; Boli, J., and Thomas, G.M., 'World Culture in the World Polity: A Century of International Non-Governmental Organizations' (1997) 62 *Am. Soc. Rev.* 171–90.

[65] Schachter, O., 'The Decline of the Nation-State and Its Implications for International Law', in Anton, D.K., *et al.* (eds.), *Politics, Values, and Functions: International Law in the 21st Century. Essays in Honor of Professor Louis Henkin* (1997) 11, 18–19.

[66] See Reinicke (1998), *supra* note 17.

non-territorial space. Compared to the structures and politics of traditional treaty-making, NBILAs have a major advantage in that they permit, in principle, the integration of all interested parties in a process of transnational law-making.[67] Moreover, NBILAs do not require the ceding of formal sovereignty. As such, they provide a potential answer to the paradox mentioned above. In fact, for the foreseeable future, most transnational legal arrangements that structure and facilitate the practice of internal sovereignty are likely to be of a non-binding nature, because the international system—with a few exceptions such as the global commons—continues to be 'fully determined', as far as external sovereignty is concerned, thus leaving little room for formal internal sovereignty to take hold.

The application of soft law measures, in contrast to traditional treaties or customary law, and the formal inclusion of non-state actors in the process of transnational law-making are highly controversial. Critics argue that the concept of international soft law itself is flawed and has no legal meaning. Others have charged that it contributes to a further blurring of the differences between policy and law, which leads to a 'trivialization' of the latter,[68] but 'today all but the most doctrinaire of scholars see a role for so-called soft law'.[69] In fact, as this volume demonstrates, NBILAs are used with increasing frequency, instilling, as Chinkin says, 'expectations about the future behavior and attitudes of international actors that provide some stability within the system while maintaining flexibility'.

NBILAs are necessarily an end in themselves, but also can be a helpful tool to initiate global public policy and a process of transnational law-making. While critics assert that soft law has no binding force and therefore no real impact, a perspective that considers NBILAs a part of an evolving process of interests and identity formation in the context of global public policy making comes to the opposite conclusion. Given the often contentious nature of the issues over which cooperation is sought, *anything other than* non-binding agreements would deter states and non-state actors from participating, precluding the possibility of informal and formal cooperation.

From a technical perspective, NBILAs display certain characteristics that overcome some of the drawbacks of international treaty and custom.[70] *First,*

---

[67] For detailed case-studies, see *ibid.* For a classical example of private–public partnership, the International Labor Organization provides an interesting model of international cooperation. See Johnson, J.L., 'Public–Private Convergence: How the Private Sector can Shape Public International Labor Standards' (1998) 24 *Brooklyn J. Int'l L.* 1; Kyloh, R., 'Governance of Globalization: ILO's Contribution' (1996) ACTRAV Working Paper; ILO (1997): ILO, *Standard Setting and Globalization: Report of the Director-General to the International Labor Conference, 85ᵗʰ Session* (1997).

[68] Levi, *supra* note 42 at 176.   [69] Ratner, *supra* note 2 at 67.

[70] See Weiss, *supra* note 2 at 71–3; Chinkin, C.M., 'The Challenge of Soft Law: Development and Change in International Law' (1989) 38 *Int'l & Comp. L.Q.*, 850–66; ASIL, 'A Hard Look at Soft Law: A Panel' (1988) 82 *Proc. Am. Soc. Int'l L.* 371–95; Riphagen, W., 'From Soft Law to Ius Cogens and Back' (1987) 17 *Vict. U. Wellington L. Rev.* 81–99.

NBILAs usually are flexible and therefore can adapt to a fast changing and technology driven environment that is characteristic of globalization. *Secondly*, they are open to all interested parties. Though important in the long run, inability to comply is not a critical barrier to entry, thus avoiding the fatal in-or-out mechanism of most legally binding agreements. *Thirdly*, NBILAs are open to transnational private actors that could not participate in the making, implementation, and enforcement of hard law because for the most part they are not recognized as participants of the global public space.[71] *Fourthly*, NBILAs in general exact lower transaction costs for all parties involved.[72] *Fifthly*, as was already mentioned above, NBILAs may well represent a first step on the path to legally binding agreements.[73] Their evolution into treaties or custom can lead to the very reconstruction of states' interests discussed above.

NBILAs are not a panacea to solve all the complex public policy challenges arising from globalization, but they do represent an important tool in bridging the growing divide between global private networks and public hierarchies constrained by territoriality. NBILAs will not always 'harden'; in some issue-areas, including international bank regulation and supervision, any agreements may well have to remain non-binding, assuming they can produce the expected results. Given the technology-driven nature of financial markets and their instruments, and the ease with which all participants cross territorial boundaries, it is unlikely that legally binding agreements can deliver on the commitments they entail. To the contrary, they may provide a false sense of security until a financial crisis erupts exposing their outmoded nature, further complicating and increasing the cost of resolution.[74] For other issue areas, as Dinah Shelton states in this volume, 'it may be that some of the norms will enter into the corpus of customary international law, as has happened with rights contained in the Universal Declaration of Human Rights'. Whatever the ultimate outcome, these norms and values associated with an emerging 'global civil society' cannot be imposed as part of a state's identity, but must evolve in an inclusive, participatory, and transparent manner for which NBILAs provide the appropriate starting point.

NBILAs and traditional hard law therefore are not mutually exclusive, but instead represent two cornerstones of the possible range of obligations chosen by multiple public and private parties in an effort to establish and

---

[71] To be sure, private actors participate to a large scale in agenda-setting and sometimes in the negotiation of multilateral treaties. Yet they are far away from having any formal and significant legal status. To date NBILAs offer the only way through which private actors can be included in the process of global public policy.

[72] Weiss, *supra* note 2 at 73.

[73] The use of such agreements 'whether termed, for example, recommendations, guidelines, codes of practice or standards, are significant in signaling the evolution and establishment of guidelines, which ultimately may be converted into legally binding rules'. Shaw, M.N., *International Law* (4th edn. 1997) 93.

[74] For a case study on financial markets, see Reinicke, *supra* note 17, ch. 3.

maintain internal sovereignty at the global level. Seen from this perspective, some NBILAs are a first step in an evolutionary process of cooperation that leads to more binding arrangements culminating in formal treaties.

3. Transnational Legal Process and Global Public Policy

Non-state actors play a transformative role regarding the interests, identities, and thus incentives of state actors, such that they are willing to enter more binding legal obligations. As Wendt has shown, 'when states interact, much more is going on than [IR schools such as] realism and rationalism admit'.[75] Harold Koh, along with Wendt and other constructivist IR scholars, argues that state behavior is conditioned not merely by rational self-interest, determined by the nature of the international system itself or narrow even nationalist domestic interests.[76] Rather, an explanation of why nations obey international law 'must . . . account for the importance of interaction within the transnational legal process, interpretation of international norms, and domestic internalization of those norms as determinants'.[77] Koh characterizes the transnational legal process as 'the theory and practice of how public and private actors including nation-states, international organizations, multinational enterprises, non-governmental organizations, and private individuals, interact in a variety of public and private, domestic and international fora to make, interpret, internalize, and enforce rules of transnational law'.[78]

Accordingly, international law-making and the observance of law itself are constructivist social activities, with feedback effects modifying domestic law, reshaping domestic bureaucracies, and changing the attitudes of domestic decision-makers, all of which influence the interests and identities of nation-states.[79] Linking horizontal subsidiarity and NBILAs appears to have all the major advantages and characteristics needed to initiate and sustain such a transnational legal process. It is nontraditional (there is no barrier between domestic and international, public and private international law), non-statist (not only nation-states are actors), dynamic (in terms of its evolution through different domains), and normative (law shapes and guides future interactions).[80] In addition, by integrating private actors, inter-societal links are established that over the long run can ease the complex negotiation processes where different cultural norms and values are involved and overcome national bureaucratic resistance and inertia that are likely to play an impor-

---

[75] Wendt, *supra* note 48 at 394.

[76] For a constructivist view of international relations and identity and interest formation see Wendt, *supra* note 48 and Adler, *supra* note 48.

[77] Koh (1997), *supra* note 4 at 2634.   [78] *Ibid.*, at 2626.

[79] With respect to participating actors, Koh's characterization of a transnational legal process is quite similar to the notion of global governance adopted by the Commission of Global Governance and quoted, *supra* note 57.

[80] Koh (1996), *supra* note 4 at 2.

tant part when internal sovereignty needs to establish a non-territorial context.[81] Global public policy also can have a normative character as it leads to new interpretations of existing rules and their internalization to shape future interactions between states and private actors. Going one step beyond Koh, transnational legal processes, in the context of global public policy, not only influence 'why nations obey', but also challenge private actors to do the same.

CONCLUSION

Global public policy and the application of NBILAs should not be seen as substitutes for hard law and more traditional forms of intergovernmental cooperation, but as supplements responding to a changing global environment. They also are catalysts for the development of a more inclusive and encompassing international society based on common norms and values. In the longer term, the critical challenge for NBILAs is to build a framework of law-and-policy-making whose effectiveness, efficiency, and legitimacy are comparable to the modern democratic nation-state. This can only be achieved, as Alex Wendt notes, if it induces collective identity formation in functional policy-areas, 'since without changes in identity, the most we can expect is behavioral cooperation, not community'.[82]

And yet the *process* by which internal sovereignty is sought at the global level may not encourage greater cooperation. More specifically, though not universally, internal sovereignty in most countries presumes popular sovereignty, *i.e.*, public policies that are legitimized at regular intervals through democratic elections and subsequently are accessible by interested parties. Decoupling the process and practice of internal sovereignty from its territorial base creates a risk of loss of accountability and legitimacy.[83] In some cases, this may be qualified when an international agreement is subjected to national ratification by the legislative branch, but evidence suggests that the pressure on national legislatures to acquiesce are often considerable.

Global public policy and the use of NBILAs present some democratic potential by offering direct channels of participation to private actors in policy-making and implementation. This, arguably, can enhance democratic principles and procedures as civil society actors have a direct stake in the process. Moreover, many of them interact across territorial borders, providing a 'transnational public space' through which political discourse can be

[81] Reinicke, W.H., *Deepening the Atlantic: Toward A New Transatlantic Marketplace?* (1996).

[82] Wendt, *supra* note 48.

[83] Recently there have been attempts to reconstruct democratic theory in the context of democracy beyond territorial borders. These theories are not fully developed and need further research. For critical evaluations and new approaches see Held, *supra* note 6; Habermas, J., 'Deliberative Politik—ein Verfahrensbegriff der Demokratie' [1998] *Faktizität und Geltung* 349–98; McGrew, *supra* note 6.

structured to shape the common interests and identities of nation-states and societies.[84] This further promotes the formation of a transnational civil society, in its roots already identifiable.[85] Finally, the process of interaction between civil society actors and their impact on public policy-making and implementation, lends legitimacy to the process and increases accountability and accessibility when compared to current international decision-making structures.[86]

Some important qualifications remain, however, regarding the use of horizontal subsidiarity and NBILAs to enhance democracy in new governance mechanisms. *First*, it must be ensured that all parties that have an interest in the issue at stake have access to the process to avoid a particular policy agenda being captured by a single powerful private interest group. *Secondly*, NGOs and other civil society organizations are not always accountable to a broader constituency.[87] Participation in a global public policy network may and should require that they adopt minimum standards of transparency and disclosure. Finally, many civil society actors, especially from developing countries, presently lack the resources to participate in global public policy networks. Multilateral institutions such as the World Bank should ensure their access to global networks and thus empower them through financial, technical, and knowledge assistance. In this context, capacity-building refers to non-state actors as well as nation-states.

The conceptual framework above presented NBILAs as an important element of all facets of global public policy from facilitating the initiation of cooperation to enhancing compliance by strengthening the possibilities of monitoring and prospects enforcement. Horizontal subsidiarity has been shown to be a starting point of the transnational legal process, a process of interaction, interpretation, and internalization of transnational norms, during which 'repeated compliance gradually becomes habitual obedience'.[88] As 'facilitators' of global governance, NBILAs first respond to the need for greater flexibility in a rapidly changing global environment; secondly, they lower the barriers for entry into cooperative arrangements, barriers that

---

[84] A related concept can be identified in Ernst-Otto Czempiel's notion of 'societal regimes' through which society can participate in foreign policy and which 'could fill the space between nations'. Cooperation among private organizations could establish patterns of a pluralistic society. Czempiel, *supra* note 37 at 268–69. The proposition that continued interaction can shape interests and identities of nation-states and societies is informed by Alexander Wendt's state-centered constructivist approach. Wendt, *supra* note 48. Of course, the idea of discourse and debate in a transnational space can also be traced back to Habermas' notion of deliberative democracy. Habermas, *supra* note 83.

[85] See Smith, *supra* note 64.

[86] Jackie Smith concludes in her study on global civil society that transnational social movements 'can generate social capital that is crucial to democratizing the global political process'. *Ibid.*, at 104.

[87] Mathews, J.T., 'Power Shift' (1997) 76 *For. Aff.* 50–66.

[88] Koh (1997), *supra* note 4 at 2603.

emerge from varying cultural norms and values as well as different percep-tions of what is and is not in the public interest; and thirdly, they provide for openness, accountability, and thus legitimacy.

Some scholars discussing globalization have focused on the growing rele-vance of non-state actors and international organizations in new structures of global governance, effectively breaking up the traditional policy monopoly of nation-states including on a formal/ legal basis.[89] Others disagree, arguing that the new world order does not imply 'a shift away from the state—up, down, and sideways—to supra-state, sub-state, and, above all, non-state actors'. Rather, states are increasingly disaggregated into their functional parts cooperating with their counterparts in other states, 'creating a dense web of relations that constitutes a new transgovernmental order'.[90] This essay argues for a synthesis of the two approaches. Few would doubt that for the foreseeable future nation-states and their bureaucracies will remain the most important actors in global governance, and, yet, it has been shown that enlarging and strengthening the traditional system of multilateralism and international hard law will not suffice as a response to the challenges posed by globalization. Instead, by engaging non-state actors through the establish-ment of global public policy networks and a reliance on NBILAs, states can enhance their ability to establish internal sovereignty at the global level. Whether these networks ultimately evolve into more traditional forms of international cooperation cannot and should not be determined *a priori*. To the contrary, it is the open ended nature of NBILAs that creates incentives for participation and interaction.[91]

Probing into the future, including the future of the nation-state itself, one must recognize that if globalization continues it will end the nation-states' monopoly over internal sovereignty, formerly guaranteed by territory. This result does not have to have the grave consequences that many predict. On the contrary, if internal sovereignty is to be realized through a global public pol-icy that requires political elites to dissociate themselves to some degree from territory and support the creation of public–private partnerships that can respond dynamically and responsively to the challenge of governance, glob-alization can become an opportunity to renew outmoded structures and insti-tutions. Whether and for how long this evolving hybrid is called a nation-state should be of little concern. As Martha Finnemore writes:

there is nothing inevitable or immutable about the state-as-actor that our theories have traditionally taken for granted. States are continually evolving. They take on

[89] Mathews, *supra* note 87.

[90] Slaughter, A.M., 'The Real New World Order' (1997) 76 *For. Aff.* 183, 197.

[91] Reinicke, W.H., 'Global Public Policy: A Vision for Multilateralism in the 21st Century', mimeo, World Bank (1998). In this context, multilateral institutions such as the World Bank can perform a crucial role in providing a platform for global public policy networks to convene. Notwithstanding the continued need to improve their openness and accountability, such institu-tions offer more overall legitimacy than the private sector, an NGO, or a single country.

new tasks and create new bureaucracies to carry out those tasks. Since, in an important sense, states *are* what they do, these changes in state function at some level change the nature of the state itself.[92]

The administration of sovereignty has changed many times over the centuries, and the nation-state is a relatively recent form of governance. It has no claim to perpetuity. While the territorial state may eventually become redundant, the principles and values that govern democracies should not. Steps should be taken to support the notion of global public policy so that society will be better equipped to respond to the demands of globalization. The international legal context will have to adapt to these changes, too, providing new venues for the organization of governance and civil society. In 1967, Wilfried Jenks gave remarks that today apply more than ever: '[a] legal system in which the judicial process is unresponsive to the groundswell of the world convulsion of our time cannot fulfill the primary function of providing an orderly framework for inevitable social change'.[93]

The Role of Soft Law in a Global Order

MARY ELLEN O'CONNELL

We are living at a time of cross-cutting trends[1] with the world simultaneously globalizing, localizing, and maintaining the status quo. This contribution considers the impact of those trends, particularly globalization, on recourse to soft law. Globalization, the expansion and acceleration of activities that span the globe, is a phenomenon that poses new challenges for humanity in ordering or controlling global activities so that they produce good and not ill. In particular, they must be regulated to provide goods, services, jobs, information, and ideas, without destroying the environment, crushing human rights, or generating armed conflict.[2]

   Humanity seeks to achieve an ordered world, moving in the direction of a norm-supporting stability. Current indications and conditions suggest that

---

[92] Finnemore, M., *National Interests in International Society* (1996) 13.

[93] Jenks, C.W., *Law in the World Community* (1967).

[1] See Rosenau, J. N., *The Dynamics of Globalization: Toward an Operational Formulation* (1996) 27 Sec. Dialogue 247.

[2] Regarding this agenda, see 'Secretary-General Proposes Global Compact on Human Rights, Labour, Environment', in *Address to World Economic Forum in Davos*, UN Doc. Press Release SG/SM/6881, Feb. 1, 1999; Rosenau, J.N., *Along the Domestic-Foreign Frontier: Exploring Governance in A Turbulent World* (1997) 182.

this search for order will be pursued through policy making at the global level that relies on law to achieve governance. Long history has taught, and we have apparently incorporated the lesson, that society under law is the optimal form of social organization. Law is the means to normative stability, which is in itself most normative and most stable. Legal techniques for global governance will be more varied than legal techniques of the past and will include a broader range of participants, but, at the core, the techniques will be identifiable as legal in nature. In the transition to a global society under law, the legal device of soft law is already playing a key role.

This analysis begins by looking at globalization and at the challenges it poses to world order. It then considers indications that these challenges are to some extent being met by international law. Finally, it looks at soft law's role in the transition to a world society under law.

A. GLOBALIZATION AND ITS CHALLENGES

The contemporary world scene is dynamic, comprising various, sometimes opposing, trends. Globalization is certainly a major trend, receiving vast attention from international affairs scholars.[3] It is not the only trend. In addition to globalization, which is marked by the decline of the nation-state, the diminution of sovereignty, and the rise of supra-national organizations, epistemic communities, the Internet, and global corporations, we see the opposite tendencies, toward localization or fragmentation and toward continuity. This section looks at globalization by first contrasting fragmentation and continuity.

Fragmentation describes the pull toward intense local orientations, renewed ethnicity, religious fundamentalism, and failed states.[4] Fragmentation means crises of authority at all levels, including loss of national authority. A Kosovar state means further break-up of Yugoslavia; a Kurdish state would break up Turkey, Iraq, Iran, and Azerbaijan. At time of writing, the Congo *is* a broken-up state and those who broke it up appear unable to form new states; indeed, much of Africa appears headed into a period mirroring Europe's Thirty Years' War.[5] As the state breaks down, so do the underpinnings of international law. International law grew up to respond to the state system; without it, international law loses its foundation. The breakdown to regions, provinces, ethnic groups, tribes, chaos, and conflict cannot support the creation and application of rules that require general acceptance out of a

[3] See, e.g., Mathews, J. T., 'Power Shift' (1997) 76 *For. Aff.* 50; Rosenau, *supra* note 1; Petrella, R., 'Globalization and Internationalization: The Dynamics of the Emerging World Order' in Boyer, R., and Drache, D. (eds.), *States Against Markets: The Limits of Globalization* (1996).

[4] Rosenau, *supra* note 2, at ch. 6.

[5] Kühne, W., 'Krieg in Zentral- und Ostafrika? Fuenf Szenarien', (1997) *SWP-Aktuell* No. 14, (1997), Stiftung Wissenschaft und Politik, Ebenhausen, 8.

sense of obligation, favoring neither secular, universal principles nor a culture of law obedience. The undermining of commitment to global law may be, in fact, the most pernicious current impact of fragmentation, presenting the opposite of multilateralism. It fosters the view that every region, nation, province, or ethnic group must be for itself and that respecting obligations derived from the authority of the international community is a fool's game.

Despite this trend, much also continues as it has for 400 years. The inter-state system endures, with the nation-state dominating. Indeed, in addition to the dozens of new states which have come on the international scene during the 1990s, a number of groups are pressing for the right to create new states, seeking to be recognized under international law. Each group pursues an ulti-mate quest to be a nation-state with all of the rights and privileges exercised by 190 or more nations at the end of the twentieth century: *e.g.*, equality with other states, the right to have territorial integrity respected, to be free of out-side intervention in internal affairs.[6] The continuing existence of states and the strong commitment to statehood and the status quo interstate system sup-port the continuation of traditional international law for the foreseeable future. In addition, important normative values realized through the tradi-tional order will attract support for the traditional order to continue, in turn, the support for those values. The prohibition on the use of force, arguably the highest norm of international relations, has found its concrete expression in the Charter of the United Nations and in customary international law. The same is true of human rights and principles of environmental protection.

Despite other trends toward fragmentation and toward continuity, global-ization appears most likely to shape our future to the greatest extent and, of all the present trends, it is having the greatest impact on the creation and implementation of international law. In particular, soft law is being recog-nized as a useful device for responding to the demands of globalization, espe-cially where traditional international law can only respond inadequately. With the increasing demand for regulation, globalization is driving the use of soft law. In turn soft law is aiding in the governance of globalization. This phenomenon warrants the special interest of international lawyers and is, therefore, the focus of this study.

McGrew, Lewis, and their colleagues provide the following description of globalization:

Globalization refers to the multiplicity of linkages and interconnections between the states and societies which make up the present world system. It describes the process by which events, decisions, and activities in one part of the world come to have signif-

---

[6] Much evidence exists of the robust nature of the state system. See, *e.g.*, Petrella, *supra* note 3, at 67; Rosenau, *supra* note 2, at ch. 11; Porter, M. E., *The Competitive Advantage of Nations* (1990). For a catalogue of the values of the state system supported by international law, see Henkin, L., 'International Law: Politics, Values and Functions' (1989–IV) 216 Recueil des Cours, revised and republished as Henkin, L., *International Law: Politics and Values* (1995).

icant consequences for individuals and communities in quite distant parts of the globe. Globalization has two distinct phenomena: scope (or stretching) and intensity (or deepening). On the one hand, it defines a set of processes which embrace most of the globe or which operate worldwide, the concept therefore has a spatial connotation. On the other hand, it also implies an intensification in the levels of interaction, interconnectedness or interdependence between the states and societies which constitute the world community. Accordingly, alongside the stretching goes a deepening of global processes.[7]

If the globalization trend continues as it has, we can expect an expansion in these types of processes and an increase in the speed with which they occur and the problems they cause, such as environmental damage, conflict, human suffering, and crime.

As Wolfgang Reinicke has demonstrated in the preceding part and elsewhere, globalization is not merely internationalization,[8] interdependence,[9] or transnationalism[10] writ large. Using the example of corporations, he has written, '[g]lobalization represents the integration of a cross-national dimension into the very nature of the organizational structure and strategic behavior of individual companies'.[11] The same can be said for other globalization processes. Information flow over the Internet can be added to Reinicke's model. Crime is another example. So while interdependence and transnational activities are related to or overlap the globalization process, globalization represents something distinctive. It is not just the presence of an issue in more than one state, it is the existence of the issue regardless of states.[12]

States have always been interdependent, engaging in international trade to obtain those things they cannot produce themselves. For the first time, however, we are seeing the development of a global market and global culture that has little to do with states. While corporations once engaged in trade to obtain commodities, say beef, people can now buy a Big Mac in most countries of the world, an example of globalization. Many will see this new development as positive because it results in more products for more people, more

---

[7] McGrew, A. G., *et al.*, *Globalization and the Nation States* (1992) 22, cited in Petrella, *supra* note 3, at 65–6. Cf. Rosenau: '[t]he notion . . . refers neither to values nor to structures, but to processes, to sequences that unfold either in the mind or in behavior, to interactions that evolve as people and organizations go about their daily tasks and seek to realize their particular goals. What distinguishes globalization processes is that they are not hindered or prevented by territorial or jurisdictional barriers'. Rosenau, *supra* note 2, at 80, 87.

[8] Petrella, *supra* note 3, at 63.

[9] The now-classic work on interdependence is Keohane, R.O., and Nye, J.S., *Power and Interdependence* (1977).

[10] Philip Jessup is credited with the first publication using the term 'transnational'. See *Transnational Law* (1956).

[11] Reinicke, W.H., 'Global Public Policy' (1997) 76 *For. Aff.* 127.

[12] See also Walker, G.R., *et al.*, 'The Concept of Globalization' (1996) 14 *Company and Security L.J.* 59.

jobs, and more information, as well as more understanding of and commitment to common norms.[13]

Globalization has negative aspects as well,[14] necessitating control measures and touching all four areas under consideration in this book. Globalization clearly has a profound impact on the environment.[15] The technological developments of one country migrate quickly throughout the world, introducing ozone-depleting chemicals and spreading fishing techniques that result in overfishing in all oceans. Nuclear power and its waste are found around the globe. The global market spews products to every corner of the earth without regard to their appropriateness or suitability. Dangerous pesticides and chemicals are sent to locations where consumers cannot read the labels, where national infrastructures do not support safe use or disposal, or where conditions may be wrong for their use.[16] The global market means more automobiles sold and used, increasing their impact on the climate. The demand for and ability to travel mean thousands of tons of jet fuel emissions and millions of tourists, spelling the end of wilderness and pressuring the habitats required by wild flora and fauna.

Among the most serious environmental problems is the collapse of world fisheries. Thirteen of the world's fifteen fisheries have collapsed, adding to the concern over ensuring adequate food supplies.[17] This emergency is a result of technological developments in ship-building and fish harvesting that mean better, faster, ships which can stay at sea longer, travel farther and find and catch more fish. The nets these technologically advanced ships are using are longer, stronger, and more efficient.

The international economy, another topic of the book, is probably most often associated with globalization.[18] As Reinicke and others have discussed, trade and finance have less and less to do with territorial states.[19] 'The forces shaping the legitimate global economy are also nourishing globally integrated crime, which UN officials peg at a staggering $750 billion a year, $400 billion to $500 billion of that in narcotics, according to U.S. Drug Enforcement

[13] See, *e.g.*, Fox, E.M., 'Globalization and Its Challenges for Law and Society' (1998) 29 *Loy. U. Chi. L.J.* 891 and Seita, A.Y., 'Globalization and the Convergence of Values' (1997) 30 *Cornell Int'l L.J.* 429.

[14] For a short comprehensive view of the evils of globalization, see Sanders, B., 'Globalization's the Issue', *The Nation* (September 28, 1998) 4–5.

[15] For an overview of world environmental problems, see Brown, L.R., *The State of the World* (1999).

[16] See, *e.g.*, Boardman, R., *Pesticides in World Agriculture: The Politics of International Regulation* (1986) 133, 135–6.

[17] 'Too Many Boats are in Pursuit of Too Few Fish, a Report Says', *N.Y. Times*, August 23, 1998, at 22; Stevens, W.K., 'After Drift Nets, a New Fishing Danger', *Int'l Herald Trib.*, November 7, 1996 at 12; Brown, L.R., *et al.*, *State of the World 1996* (1996) 5.

[18] See, *e.g.*, Reinicke, *supra* note 11 or Haas, R.N., and Litan, R.E., 'Globalization and Its Discontents' (1998) 77 *For. Aff.* 2.

[19] Reinicke, *supra* note 11 and Reinicke, p. 79 above; Mathews, *supra* note 3, at 56–8; Rosenau, *supra* note 1.

Agency estimates.'[20] Globalization has made it easier for firms to relocate to places where labor costs—and labor standards—are low.[21] These activities need regulation at the global level to ensure fairness, respect for human rights, and avoidance of criminal activity of all kinds. Globalization '[in] some quarters . . . is seen as having caused the rapid flows of investment that moved in and out of countries as investor sentiment changed and were behind the Mexican and Asian financial crises. In the United States it is blamed for job losses, increasing income inequality, and stagnant or deteriorating real wages.'[22]

The global market in goods, ideas, and skills has resulted in a weapons control problem of unprecedented proportions. The ability of Iran to attract Russian nuclear specialists, Chinese materials, and information from the Internet to build nuclear weapons is one end of the spectrum. Another end is represented by the vast number of conventional weapons available in Africa's unending conflicts. Landmines, Williamson writes, can be found for as little as $5.80.[23] The easy availability of weapons is linked to the high incidence of non-traditional conflict and crime seen the world over.

The communication flows of globalization have spread the word of human rights, the fourth topic of the book, but the inexorable transfer of capital to low-cost societies has also weakened respect for and realization of norms, at least in respect to economic and social rights.[24]

These challenges of globalization, whether in the area of environment, economics, arms control, or human rights, are not going unmet. Indeed, an unprecedented level of activity, by an unprecedented array of actors, is occurring to address the ills of globalization. Treaties, customary principles, understandings related to treaties, understandings unrelated to any treaty, understandings of states, understandings of states and international organizations (both intergovernmental and nongovernmental), understandings of banks and corporations, General Assembly resolutions, declarations of the Organization for Security and Cooperation in Europe (OSCE), statements of individuals, decisions of international and domestic tribunals, and so on are

---

[20] Mathews, *supra* note 3, at 57–8.   [21] Fox, *supra* note 13, at 897.

[22] Haas and Litan, *supra* note 18, at 2–3; see also Kahn, J., 'The Bear Draws Blood', *N.Y. Times*, August 30, 1998 at sec. 3, 1.

[23] Williamson, R., p. 506 below.

[24] '[G]lobalization engenders conflicts within and between nations over domestic norms and the social institutions that embody them. It threatens to change norms and rules, such as rules against child labor and bribery and norms for meaningful social safety nets. It induces firms to go abroad to evade their own norms, thus undercutting fundamental beliefs that form the fabric of society . . . [G]lobalization has made it exceedingly difficult for governments to provide social insurance—one of their central functions and one that has helped maintain social cohesion and domestic political support for ongoing liberalization throughout the postwar period.' Orford, A., 'Contesting Globalization: A Feminist Perspective on the Future of Human Rights' (1998) 8 *Transnat'l L. & Contemp. Problems* 171. See Fox, *supra* note 13, at 898, citing Rodrik, D., *Has Globalization Gone Too Far?* (1997) 5–6; see also Barber, B.R., *Jihad vs. McWorld: How Globalism and Tribalism are Reshaping the World* (1996) 7.

all being pressed into the job of regulating globalization.[25] Much of this is correctly labeled legal activity. In addition to resolving some of globalization's challenges, such activity also may be leading to a new international order. If the trend toward globalization turns out to be the dominant one, for the first time in human history we may be creating an international society under the rule of law.

Indications that the new order governing globalization will be a legal order are based on the view that the past is prologue and that human nature craves stability. Indications also can be found in the literature of scholars of globalization and in the chapters of this book. James Rosenau, who studies globalization closely, points out that the ability to achieve order may be undermined by the trends creating disorder—the trend toward fragmentation. Yet, I am inclined to agree with his ultimately optimistic view that the indications of our ability to create order and to govern will continue and ultimately triumph. I am also in agreement with Philip Allott's view that this triumph will take the form of a legal order.

Rosenau writes:

[T]he turbulence that seems destined to stir world affairs for the foreseeable future is to be welcomed. It offers the hope that humankind can eventually alter course and settle into forms of mutual adjustment through which governance can flourish effectively and bring a measure of tranquility to the politics of the [domestic-foreign] Frontier.[26]

Rosenau defines governance 'at a very abstract level as spheres of authority (SOAs) at all levels of human activity—from the household to the demanding public to the international organization—that amount to systems of rule in which goals are pursued through the exercise of control'.[27] He continues:

[I]t is possible to note an 'upsurge in the collective capacity to govern': despite the rapid pace of ever greater complexity and decentralization—and to some extent because of their exponential dynamics—the world is undergoing 'a remarkable expansion of collective power,' an expansion that is highly disaggregated and unfolds unevenly but that nevertheless amounts to a development of rules systems 'that have become 1) more intensive in their permeation of daily life, 2) more permanent over

---

[25] See, *e.g.*, Koh, H.H., 'Transnational Legal Process' (1996) 75 *Neb. L. Rev.* 181; Koh, H.H., 'A World Transformed' (1995) 20 *Yale J. Int'l L.* p. ix; Koh, H.H., 'Transnational Public Law Litigation' (1991) 100 *Yale L.J.* 2347, 2400.

[26] Rosenau, *supra* note 1, at 448.

[27] *Ibid.*, at 145. See also Rosenau, J.N., 'Governance and Democracy in a Globalizing World: Re-Imagining Political Community', in Archibugi, D., *et al.* (eds.), *Studies in Cosmopolitan Democracy* (1998)).

time, 3) more extensive over space, 4) larger in size, 5) wider in functional scope, 6) more constitutionally differentiated, and 7) more bureaucratic'.[28]

These rule systems already exist, and Rosenau wants them to go further to 'evolve techniques of cooperation that will bridge its multitude of disaggregated parts and achieve a measure of coherence which enable future generations to live in peace, achieve sustainable development, and maintain a modicum of creative order'.[29] He questions how this can be achieved and offers no model, merely the hope that it can be done.

Yet humanity probably will create an order out of the current turbulent conditions because human nature seems to demand order. Order has arisen from all other periods of intense human turbulence, most notably the Peace of Westphalia at the break-up of the Holy Roman Empire and the formation of the United Nations at the end of World War II. It seems especially likely that order will be found if globalization is the dominant trend. '[A] quest is under way for "a center," some body with the universally accepted authority medieval popes once claimed.'[30] That 'center' of authority in the world could be law.

After centuries of human progress, the development of society under law would appear to be our highest achievement and one that should be constructed for international society. Allott explains impressively and persuasively why law has worked only diffidently at the international level in the past, and suggests that the processes of globalization may well hold the key for successful development of international society under law in the future.

[S]ociety-under-law is thus a model of society as a three-tiered structure, a sandwich, with law in the center. Below the law is actual human life and behavior, the infrastructure of law. Above the law is the rest of the social process, the superstructure of law—religion, education, philosophy, society's ideas and ideals, the public realm in general, and what I call the *public mind*—social consciousness. Above all, the superstructure contains politics. Politics is the struggle to determine the common interest of society and the struggle to dominate society's public realm, especially its lawmaking and law-executing systems. Through politics we struggle about who shall dominate the law making process, about what the content of the law shall be about, how law shall be implemented.[31]

International society has lacked this politics, this struggle toward the *common* interest which is the missing piece to the effective functioning of

---

[28] Rosenau, *supra* note 2, at 151, quoting Hewson, M., 'The Media of Political Globalization', paper presented at the Annual Meeting of the International Studies Association, Washington, D.C. (March 1994) 2.

[29] Rosenau, *supra* note 2 at 449.

[30] Lewis, P., 'As Nations Shed Roles, Is Medieval the Future?', *N.Y. Times*, January 2, 1999, at A15.

[31] Allott, P., 'The True Function of Law in the International Community' (1998) 5 *Ind. J. Glob. L. Stud.* 391, 402.

international law. International law has been the coming together of governments to make arrangements with other governments for their own good and the good of their national societies, not the good of international society, or rarely for that good.

[L]aw will not perform its true function internationally until we have a conception of an international society of the whole human race, an international social system capable of processing conflicting interests and conflicting ideas about the future of the human world. . . . And it must be an international system capable of forming ideas about the common interest of all humanity and of each human being, and capable of disaggregating that common interest through legal relations, which condition the behavior of all human beings everywhere.[32]

Globalization is creating this conception of international society. It is creating global consciousness.[33] It is compelling policy makers to think globally. It is creating new policy makers with global writs, in particular international governmental organizations and nongovernmental organizations. They engage even now in policy struggles with states or global corporations that look very much like the politics of domestic societies. The outcomes of these struggles will increasingly be policy decisions that will be realized through law.

The chapters of this book provide vivid accounts of this process as it is already occurring. They describe the global actors taking up policy-making roles, working out responses to globalization's challenges.[34] They describe these efforts as creating soft law and often subsequent hard law instruments. They describe a nascent governance that is likely to mature. It is unlikely to reach the state of world government because the trend toward continuity is too strong for that,[35] but an optimism exists that the process can be shaped toward meeting globalization's challenges.[36] Through the efforts of multiple international actors, we can get governance of globalization that is comprehensive, democratic, and normative.

Shaping the future world order will challenge the pre-conceptions, creativity, and foresight of all involved in the process. For international lawyers, the challenge will be in the form of trying to navigate two legal systems—one emerging and one declining. International society under law is still in the future. First steps have been taken so that we are no longer wholly ensconced in the old international law, but clearly we are not yet in the new system. This time of transition presents us with jurisprudential problems. Traditional international law of the inter-governmental system has provided benefits to

---

[32] Allott, P., 'The True Function of Law in the International Community' (1998) 5 *Ind. J. Glob. L. Stud.* at 409.

[33] *Ibid.*, at 413.

[34] See Slaughter, A.M., 'The Real New World Order' (1997) 76 *For. Aff.* 183, 184.

[35] Reinicke, *supra* note 11, at 132.

[36] See Allott, *supra* note 31 at 413; Reinicke, *supra* note 11 at 136–8; Fox, *supra* note 13, at 904.

the world. It has created a certain orderliness in international relations, supported some important norms favoring human rights, peace, and environmental protection. International law has proven its ability to realize these desiderata to some extent. It has been able to do so because traditional international law achieved an authority, a legitimacy which can wither if its established processes and principles of law-making, application and enforcement are undermined.[37]

In the traditional system, nongovernmental organizations (NGOs) and corporations do not make law. That is why the new global policy makers turn to soft law (or process[38]) as an effective transitional tool to agree to and articulate non-binding rules and principles. Much evidence exists of global policy makers striving to keep the categories separate, because they understand what they will lose if hard law is undermined by the diluting effect of mixing it with soft law principles. Soft law thus is not given the same status in the legal order as hard law principles, but it is nonetheless within the legal order. As the transition proceeds and global policy makers gain the authority to represent the common interest, it would follow that their decisions would have the authority of law.

The chapters of this book provide a rich description of new actors with a new global consciousness engaged in policy-making at the international level. The studies describe how the outcomes of policy are being turned into law to guide the behavior of individuals, states, and non-state actors. In many cases, as described in the next section, governance follows the path from policy decision through soft law instrument to hard law agreement.

C. SOFT LAW IN THE LEGAL ORDER

The contributions to this book reveal much about the developing governance of globalization, in addition to testifying to the search for legal order in a globalizing world. Many actors can be seen searching for solutions to globalization's challenges and finding in soft law the quick, flexible answers needed. The chapters also show the tendency to begin with soft law responses but eventually develop hard law, demonstrating the understanding by global policy makers of the importance of the distinction in the present system in transition.

Upon examination, one quickly finds that it is completely understandable that soft law would be adopted as a tool of global governance. Soft law has many advantages in the regulation of globalization. Its instruments are flexible, being able to take almost any form global actors wish to use.

---

[37] See Weil, P., 'Towards Relative Normativity In International Law?' (1983) 77 *Am. J. Int'l L.* 413.

[38] See O'Connell, M.E., 'New International Legal Process' (1999) 93 *Am. J. Int'l L.* 334.

Soft law instruments thus can provide an experimental response to new challenges as they continually arise. Consider for example, what lies ahead in Internet regulation. Non-binding instruments can attract adherence to new and even detailed regimes because states or others accepting soft law norms may choose non-compliance if the approach turns out to be the wrong one, or they more easily may correct the errors rather than drop the approach altogether. Another attractive aspect of soft law for globalization is that it can regulate behavior of non-state actors from giant multinationals to NGOs and individuals. Soft law can fill the gaps of a hard law instrument without the need for entering into the laborious procedure of treaty amendment.

The problem of trade in pesticide and chemicals is illustrative. Ali Mekouar describes how the United Nations Food and Agriculture Agency (FAO) and the United Nations Environment Program developed non-binding standards to guide behavior and prevent some of the worst excesses of an unregulated global marketplace. Donald Rothwell describes the similar effort by NGOs, South Pacific states, and the United States, to get a ban on large driftnets used for fishing. Although South Pacific states have a treaty among themselves, they sought and sponsored United Nations General Assembly resolutions to prohibit the use of driftnets throughout the world.

The encroachment of people in Antarctica is paralleled by population pressure on habitats elsewhere.[39] Joyner's study on the Antarctic describes an active legal regime developing hard and soft principles to respond to the ever-increasing issues globalization has created for Antarctica. With technological development, pressure on Antarctica has increased—more scientific exploration, more tourism, fishing, and other commercial exploitation. Antarctic treaty states, NGOs, and others have pressed for the development of binding and non-binding instruments in response. Similarly, Clare Shine's contribution describes how a treaty to protect wetlands and its binding and non-binding side agreements preserve the habitats of migrating species. Shine describes how wetlands regulation was required to prevent the extinction of a species of Asian crane. The relevant states generally were not party to the treaty on migration, but nevertheless they undertook a non-binding commitment. The value of this approach is clear, allowing the crane to be saved through a faster, more streamlined process.

The global economy is being addressed by all manner of coalitions because the global marketplace requires common standards. Buyers and sellers in that market have thus developed them, as described by Roht-Arriaza. Keeping

---

[39] The primary cause of species decline in the world is loss of habitat; growing world population, climate change, and other pressures generally influenced by globalization are responsible. See, *e.g.*, Ehrlich, P.R., and Ehrlich, A.H., *Extinction: The Causes and Consequences of the Disappearance of Species* (1981) 128.

criminal elements from exploiting the globalized economy is addressed by Simmons' contribution on money laundering.

Several major treaties have been concluded to address the problem of arms trade, while other aspects of the issue are addressed by non-binding norms. The General Assembly adopted resolutions urging a ban on landmines, and the International Atomic Energy Agency regularly uses soft law to fill in the gaps of the hard law treaties it administers. Supplier states have formed three groups to develop non-binding guidelines to control the export of weapons-usable technology.

The human rights movement rings the globe. A major accomplishment of the movement occurred in the summer of 1998 with the Rome agreement to establish an international criminal court.[40] The Rome conference showed the face of the new globalized legal order, states, governmental and nongovernmental organizations, and individuals all creating a process for the development and application of human rights norms. The conferees responded to a deeply felt need to have a court where violations of cherished rights could be prosecuted and punished. They were motivated by the ethnic cleansing in the former Yugoslavia, the genocide in Rwanda, the dirty wars in Central and South America, the killings in Tiananmen Square, and other events made known through CNN, the Internet, and people-to-people contacts. The idea of human rights, that all human beings deserve to be treated with dignity, will be a fundamental orientation of the global age.[41] The challenge is to fulfill the demand for the enjoyment of human rights engendered by globalization. The contributions on human rights in this book testify to the very large amount of activity devoted to creating, developing, and gaining compliance with human rights norms. Labor unions, governments, and international organizations have produced binding and non-binding labor instruments with non-binding instruments being used with special success in technical fields.

The ability of scientists to participate, along with governments and international organizations, and to respond more quickly and flexibly to changing information makes soft law particularly appropriate for many areas of regulation, including environment, arms control, and labor. In the area of control of nuclear material, where many technical decisions need to be made and adopted uniformly, soft law has proven to be the appropriate mechanism.

Nevertheless, despite all of its utility, soft law is not confused with hard law; the aim of most in global governance is to get enforceable hard law obligations. Shelton points out that non-state actors in particular generally prefer hard law norms and strive to get non-binding principles transformed into hard law. Non-state actors want to be able to enforce the norms they champion. The book's various chapters are most consistent in revealing that hard

---

[40] See Wedgwood, R., 'Fiddling in Rome' (1998) 77 *For. Aff.* 20.
[41] Rosenau, *supra* note 2.

law, whether treaty or custom, continues to be at the top of the hierarchy of means of global governance.

Many of the chapters which follow provide evidence of this phenomenon. Mekouar's contribution, for example, outlines how the international trade in pesticides and chemicals was for years regulated through non-binding instruments developed by the FAO and the United Nations Environment Program, but in September 1998, ninety-five states adopted a treaty with binding principles to regulate this trade.[42] A similar story is told by Rothwell regarding driftnet fishing. The General Assembly adopted a ban on driftnets in the form of a non-binding resolution and the resolution has received widespread adherence; the resolution may well provide an example of a norm which has crystallized into binding, customary international law.

Joyner describes how the Antarctic Treaty Parties used the flexible instrument of the recommendation to get standards for environmental protection. This method worked better than classic, binding international law instruments, Joyner points out, because of the difficulty states have with moving a binding international law instrument through national legislatures. Nevertheless, in 1991, states adopted the binding Environmental Protection Protocol. The non-binding instruments played an important role because the recommendations provided guidance when it was difficult or time consuming to get treaties ratified. Precautionary measures could be outlined in those instances when scientific knowledge was not conclusive. The recommendations opened the way for hard norms.

The important, though non-binding, harmonizing standards for the global marketplace (again, the subject most often associated with globalization) developed by the International Standards Organization have become, in some measure, hard law in the form of the World Trade Organization's Agreement on Technical Barriers to Trade, according to Roht-Arriaza. The area of human rights also contains numerous examples of soft law agreements which became hard law treaties. Cassell describes generally the hardening as well as the growth of Inter-American human rights law. Schlager discusses the transformation of the Conference on Security and Cooperation in Europe into the Organization for Security and Cooperation in Europe. Labor unions, perhaps above all, are committed to binding commitments. Gualtieri suggests that the weapon and precursor supplier groups can increase their legitimacy by adopting more aspects of a legal regime. Non-binding guidelines can be improved with more institutionalization and improved procedures. Landmines present a recent and dramatic example of the move from very soft United Nations General Assembly resolutions to hard law treaty.

---

[42] Convention on the Prior Informed Consent Procedure for Certain Hazardous Chemicals and Pesticides in International Trade, September 11, 1998, (1999) 38 I.L.M. 1.

D. CONCLUSION

One of the present legal and political challenges is to take up the task of shaping global governance. This task will require energy, imagination, and vision,[43] avoiding the feelings of cynicism, helplessness, and confusion that can be engendered by the contradictions and chaos characterizing our times.[44] While it is very much a period of cross-cutting trends, of turbulence in Rosenau's terms, it appears that globalization is the dominant and dynamic trend, commanding the creative energy of our most able thinkers. International law came out of one period of chaos—Europe's Thirty Years' War. It was the medium through which a certain order was restored and through which some order has been maintained for 400 years. One can expect a new order out of a new period of turbulence. Like that earlier period, the new order is likely to build upon, rather than completely replace, the order which preceded it. Law worked in that earlier period; it works in our national societies, unitary or federal; it works in regional unions such as the European Union. It is likely to work and therefore likely to be chosen as the medium to govern globalization.

The first outlines of governance of globalization already can be seen. Global actors—corporations, international organizations, states, and individuals—are working in different issue areas to identify common interests and build legal regimes to realize those interests. We see them turning to soft law as a means of including all relevant actors, trying out solutions that are still experimental, regulating in greater detail than hard law would allow, and regulating more flexibly and quickly. Soft law thus meets many of the needs of global governance.

In the future, considerable soft law is likely to enter the realm of hard law where it will become binding. Soft law which is considered soft only because the participants in the regime are not all nation-states or inter-governmental organizations is likely to be the first to be re-categorized, when nongovernmental organizations, corporations, and others join the legal system as full members. The law made by international law's new actors will be hard law, not soft law. Traditional international law's doctrine of sources will have to continue to be modified to account for new developments.

Such change presents a risk that international law will be weakened, even mortally wounded, yet law that does not change and adapt to the times is sure to be ignored. The more likely scenario is that international law will be

---

[43] Fox, *supra* note 13, at 904–5.

[44] Allott describes the inability of Europe to cope with globalization. 'But the European public mind is in a sorry state at the present time—demoralized and confused in the face of a process often referred to anxiously in Europe as 'globalization', a process which seems to be beyond Europe's practical and theoretical control.' *Supra* note 31, at 410.

adapted to meet the challenges of globalization. New theories to support the changes in international law will provide a new jurisprudential basis for international law in a globalized world. This book provides some significant evidence of new law-making. Other examples could be found in the new law-making being done by international and national courts, tribunals and other legal processes. Evidence of change and development regarding law application and law enforcement also exists. Governance of international society is developing and it is developing into a legal order. No other order system, including the use of force or religion, can provide the stability humanity consistently craves while protecting the now universal norms of human rights, justice, environment, and peace.

In the words of Philip Allot:

For those of us who devote our lives to thinking about these things, the great task of the coming decades is to imagine a new kind of international social system, to imagine a new role for the United Nations in the new kind of world which is forming so rapidly, and to imagine at last a new kind of post-tribal international law, which extends to the level of all humanity the wonder-working capacity of law, when law is properly understood.

For those who would preserve the best of the human world as it is, the best form of defense is law—law in our local neighborhood, law cross the whole world. For those who suffer, in body or in spirit, from the imperfection of the human world as it is, the best way to make a better world is the way of law.[45]

Soft law most certainly has a place in Allot's post-tribal international law, law for an ever-more-globalized society. As we imagine his new kind of international social system, let us also imagine the role of soft law.

---

[45] *Supra* note 31, at 413. For other, not dissimilar views of the role of international law in the governance of globalization, see generally, 'Symposium: The Changing Structure of International Law Revisited' (1997) 8 *Eur. J. Int'l L.* 399; Delbrück, J., 'The Role of the United Nations in Dealing with Global Problems' (1997) 4 *Ind. J. Global Legal Stud.* 277

Chapter 4   Commentary

Compliance With International Soft Law

JONATHAN L. CHARNEY

This book enhances our understanding of compliance with so-called 'soft' international norms, but demonstrates that clear answers are not to be found. Considerable disagreement exists among experts regarding the meaning and even the concept of 'soft' international norms. Furthermore, few agree on how to calculate the rate of compliance with either 'hard' or 'soft' international norms. Nevertheless, this study was designed to identify those factors that appear to have relevance to the rate of compliance with non-binding international norms.

The international law doctrine of sources determines whether or not a norm is within the body of international law. Experts debate the details of the doctrine, its changes over time, and its application to specific norms, but for most norms there is little disagreement. In theory at least, a norm is either international law or it is not. If a 'soft' norm meets the requirements of the doctrine of sources of international law, it is 'hard law'. If it does not, it is not law; the choice is binary. This is indisputable in the areas of customary international law and general principles of law. More difficulty is presented in regard to international agreements. Certainly, the doctrine of sources distinguishes between those international agreements that are binding under international law and those that are not. Non-binding agreements are not within the realm of international law and might be classified as 'soft' norms.

Binding agreements under international law would appear, on the other hand, to create 'hard law' rights and obligations. Problems arise, however, in regard to specific provisions of such binding agreements. Some provisions may lack sufficient normativity to create definitive rights or obligations for the parties to such agreements. Thus within international agreements, one may find 'soft' provisions that may not amount to a right or obligation under international law. As Christine Chinkin indicates, these also may be included within the class of 'soft' norms. This may be the case even though the norm is found within a hard law instrument. Aside from treaty law, a judgement must be made under international law whether a norm has met the standards established by the doctrine of sources. Of course, within the doctrine of sources itself disputes exist and judgements must be made. A different kind of judgement is required in the case of a provision found within a binding international agreement that may lack the requisite degree of normativity. While the former has been the subject of considerable scholarly analysis the latter has not.

This leaves open the question of determining what a 'soft' international norm is, if it is not binding international law. In my opinion, such 'soft' norms are predetermined generalized norms of behavior that, while not binding as law, attract compliance by the targeted members of the international community. While I would draw a clear doctrinal division between law and non-law, this division has limited importance in regard to a study of compliance. Studies have shown that compliance with international law is substantial. I believe that if a norm acquires the status of international law the pull towards compliance with the norm is strengthened for multiple reasons. No study has determined, however, whether the rate of compliance with an international law norm is greater than that of non-legally binding international norms, 'soft' norms. It may not be possible to resolve this question one way or the other. One problem, of course, is that doctrine determines when a norm is within international law, but no definition exists for 'soft' norms. Secondly, a study of the influence of 'hard' and 'soft' norms on compliance requires that all the other potential variables be held constant. Such circumstances probably cannot be found.

More importantly, the relative rates of compliance with 'hard' and 'soft' international norms will remain unproven because the factors that influence compliance substantially overlap. Of course, it is true that in the case of 'hard international law' the legal system provides certain remedies to aggrieved parties, *e.g.*, countermeasures, third party dispute settlement procedures. Furthermore, denomination as 'law' has a certain cachet that independently motivates the subjects of the law to comply. International law remedies, however, are generally the last resort of aggrieved parties. Instead, they seek to exhaust non-legal remedies such as negotiation, or the use of political, economic, and other pressures to encourage compliance. Only in exceptional situations does an aggrieved party resort to law-based remedies and thus, although their use and availability have importance, resort to remedies for breaches of international law are relatively uncommon in the international legal system. In general, then, the remedies utilized are virtually the same whether the norm breached is 'hard' or 'soft'.

The international community has developed 'hard' and 'soft' norms to serve many of the same systemic functions, that is, to order relations among entities within a society and to satisfy the desire of groups within that society to promote their own value preferences. Often, no explicit, reasoned choice is made between 'hard' or 'soft' norm solutions; instead, the character of the norm may result from confluence of a variety of unforeseen and unplanned circumstances. Thus, while the status as law or non-law may be important to compliance in some respects, in most situations it is not. More important is the contribution that the norm provides to the ordering of relations within the international community.

As an ordering system, one must expect that compliance will not be perfect. In fact, the very reason for norms, be they 'hard' or 'soft', is to encourage those members of the society that may be motivated to behave differently to conform for the good of the larger group. They are, therefore, created to mold behavior in the face of the interests of some to do otherwise. Norms serve no useful purpose if all members of the target society would behave similarly even in the absence of the norm. Thus, the test of compliance is one of relative success within the society. This may be calculated on the basis of the rate of compliance at a specific time or on the basis of changes in the rate of compliance over time.

The rate of compliance is a function of a web of factors. It is unlikely that a specific formula can be discovered for all norms that would allow one to control the rate of compliance or allow one to fashion all norms to optimize compliance. The studies in the following chapters help to identify those factors that have influenced compliance with 'soft' norms. They also suggest how they may be manipulated to control the rate of compliance for international norms, generally. At best, in my opinion, the complexity of the international community means we may be able to identify some key factors that influence the rate of compliance of norms in many circumstances. If those factors were identified and their influence on compliance were understood, perhaps the international community might be able to use that knowledge to attain an optimum rate of compliance for specific norms, be they 'hard' or 'soft'.

The studies below present real situations in which 'soft' norms were applicable. By examining the context within which these norms operated, it is possible to identify factors that appear to be relevant to the rates of compliance with these norms. Thus, a better understanding of why some norms have attracted significant compliance and others have not may be gained by considering the varying contexts within which these norms were used. Certainly, the factors that influence compliance are infinite and no menu of definitive factors can be developed. Some significance should be given, however, to those factors that often are part of the environment in which these norms operate and can be linked to the rate of compliance. Based on the introductory chapters above, the studies below, and relevant contemporary literature, the factors that follow seem to be relevant to the rate of compliance in a variety of situations. Listed in no particular order, they include:

1. the linkage between the norm and hard law established by the international legal system or by domestic legal systems;
2. the linkage of the norm to other 'soft' norms;
3. the relationship of the norm to past practices;
4. the linkage of the norm to established international institutions;
5. the transparency of the norm and its implementation, including:
   a. the clarity of the obligation (be it is fixed or flexible),

    b. the ability of others to determine whether the target of the norm is in compliance or not, and

    c. the presence and nature of verification systems;

6. the degree of support for the norm among the affected members of the community (including how free rider problems and other disincentives created by non-supporters are addressed);

7. the degree of political, economic and/or military support for the norm;

8. the existence of epistemic communities, such as those of non-government organizations (including business organizations) and other interest groups;

9. the utilitarian interests of the targets of the norm;

10. the legitimacy of the process by which the norm was created;

11. the moral and ethical aspects of the norm and its perceived fairness among members of the relevant community;

12. the formality of acceptance by the affected members of the community;

13. the capability of the objects of the norm to conform to it, including their structural and economic capabilities and (if they are states) the nature of their domestic legal systems (*e.g.*, stability/war, liberal democracy/dictatorship);

14. the foreseeable consequences of non-compliance, including sanctions and dispute settlement procedures; and

15. the control that the norm's supporters have over the objects being regulated (*e.g.*, nuclear material, technology, financial and natural resources).

The case studies below may be fruitfully examined with the above factors in mind. These factors appear to be relevant to the rates of compliance discussed in the case studies. Certainly, all of the above factors will never be relevant to all norms, nor will all norms be similarly affected by these factors. On the other hand, they may very well be important to the success of an international norm. The value of this study is to contribute to our understanding of why members of the international community do or do not comply with international norms be they 'hard' or 'soft'. If one can then determine how certain factors might be used to influence the rates of compliance major progress will have been made. In the future, the effectiveness of international norms may be enhanced by designing the environment in which they operate with these factors in mind.

Part II
Perspectives on Compliance with Non-binding Norms

5
The Environment and Natural Resources

Environmental law is one of the most recent branches of international law. The first international treaties entirely devoted to nature protection and, in particular, to the protection of wild flora and fauna were adopted at the beginning of the twentieth century, but systematic elaboration of environmental norms began only at the end of the 1960s. Perhaps as a consequence of the newness of the topic and uncertainty about the effective response to environmental problems, legally non-binding instruments have been used very frequently to contribute directly to the development of legal obligations, either by originating or contributing to the development of customary law or by subsequent integration into treaties. Soft norms also have been implemented and complied with on their own merit. The case studies in this chapter and other international legal scholarship demonstrate the importance of soft norms in molding behavior of states and non-state actors. Studying compliance with international soft norms in the field of environmental protection thus contributes to understanding the nature and the functioning of present international law.

The General Assembly Ban on Driftnet Fishing

DONALD R. ROTHWELL

INTRODUCTION

International response to large-scale pelagic high seas driftnet fishing[1] occurred during the late 1980s and 1990s. At the domestic level, many coastal

---

[1] Driftnet fishing is described as being:
'a passive practice, by which the surface layer of the ocean is fished with nets allowed to drift with winds and currents. Drift-nets are held open in a vertical position by the tension exerted between numerous floats of the floatline and a weighted leadline. Marine organisms become gilled, entangled or enmeshed in the netting. Large mesh drift-nets can entangle large fish because they are loosely hung, lightly weighted and slightly buoyant. This type of gear is designed specifically to capture living marine organisms of a wide range of sizes and species, and is consequently less selective by species than gill-nets which have been staked to the seabed or tightly hung.'
Richards, A.H., 'Problems of Drift-Net Fisheries in the South Pacific' (1994) 29 *Marine Pollution Bulletin* 106.

states prohibited the use by their nationals of driftnets on the high seas.[2] Regional forums and organizations adopted declarations and statements and the South Pacific states concluded the 1989 Wellington Convention on the Prohibition of Driftnet Fishing in the South Pacific (Wellington Convention).[3] The global response is perhaps the most interesting because of the attempts to regulate driftnet fishing through the use of United Nations General Assembly Resolutions rather than the traditional response of a convention imposing clear, legally binding obligations. This study will review the history of international responses to driftnet fishing before undertaking a detailed assessment of the mechanisms established pursuant to UNGA resolutions, the role of various parties in that process, and compliance with the United Nations' initiatives.

A. BACKGROUND

Driftnets originally developed as gillnets[4] for inshore waters. Not until the 1950s were new synthetic fibers developed that allowed successful deployment of very long nets, extending from 50 to 60km.[5] Driftnet fishing has several important consequences for both the marine environment and marine living resources. Miller has identified the following six characteristics of driftnets:

1. they are non-selective, in that they capture or ensnare a wide range of fish and marine wildlife;
2. they are wasteful because the use of a driftnet results in drop-out and wastage of a significant proportion of catch of up to 40 percent;
3. they can be lost or discarded and continue to 'ghost fish' by drifting without control while continuing to entangle fish and other marine wildlife;
4. they can be a hazard to navigation because of their length;
5. they can be economic even when species are not abundant;
6. assessing the impact of large scale driftnets on non-target species is particularly difficult and expensive.[6]

---

[2] See the discussion in Hewison, G.J., 'The Legally Binding Nature of the Moratorium on Large-Scale High Seas Driftnet Fishing' (1994) 25 *Journal of Maritime Law and Commerce* 557 at 576–8.   [3] (1990) 29 I.L.M. 1454.

[4] Richards, *supra* note 1 at 106, describes gillnets as being 'made of either multi-filament twine or mono-filament nylon, woven into netting designed to lock behind the gill covers of bony fish or the gill slits of sharks'.

[5] The FAO has noted that driftnets have been used in the Mediterranean since 177 B.C.: FAO General Fisheries Council for the Mediterranean and International Commission for the Conservation of Atlantic Tunas: Expert Consultation (Bari, Italy, June 21–27, 1990: FAO Fisheries Report No. 449) reproduced in United Nations, *The Law of the Sea: Annual Report of Ocean Affairs Law and Policy—Main Documents 1990* (1993) 233–4.

[6] Miller, B., 'Combating Drift-Net Fishing in the Pacific' in Crawford, J., and Rothwell, D.R. (eds.), *The Law of the Sea in the Asian Pacific Region* (1995) 155 at 155–6.

Global concern over the use of driftnets (also referred to as gillnets) began to emerge during the late 1980s. At that time driftnets had become popular in various fisheries.[7] In the Indian Ocean, Taiwan commenced large-scale pelagic driftnet fishing in November 1983.[8] In the North Pacific, Japan had conducted large scale driftnet fishing for salmon since the 1950s under agreements with the USSR, Canada, and U.S. A driftnet fishery for albacore tuna also developed in coastal waters adjacent to Japan and expanded to the North Pacific in the mid 1970s.[9] In the South Pacific, the practice of driftnet fishing spread across more fish species, with Taiwanese vessels fishing for shark, Spanish mackerel, and long-tail tuna from 1974. In the Arafura Sea, Taiwanese fishermen began driftnetting for shark in the Gulf of Papua in 1976, and for squid in New Zealand waters in 1981.[10] The most extensive form of driftnetting in the South Pacific, however, was for Albacore tuna, after Japan commenced an exploratory fishery in 1982. The fishery reached a high point during the 1988–9 season when as many as 198 vessels (mainly Japanese and Taiwanese) operated in high seas waters south of Tonga, French Polynesia, and the Cook Islands, and west of New Zealand in the Tasman Sea.[11]

B. INTERNATIONAL RESPONSE TO DRIFTNET FISHING

The United Nations responded to concerns over driftnet fishing in 1989, preceded by regional and subregional action throughout the world. The latter initiatives, including the adoption by the South Pacific countries of a legally binding convention to prohibit the use of driftnets, had undoubted impact upon the eventual response of the United Nations.

1. The South Pacific Forum

One of the first international organizations to express concern over the effects of driftnet fishing was the South Pacific Forum. The Forum's members, comprising nearly all of the small island states of the South Pacific and Australia

---

[7] Richards, *supra* note 1 at 107.

[8] The main catches took place in the region between 30°S and 45°S. In addition, artisanal or semi-artisanal fleets were operating in waters adjacent to Bangladesh, India, Indonesia, Iran, Malaysia, Oman, Pakistan, Sri Lanka, Thailand, and Yemen. FAO Indian Ocean Fishery Commission: Committee for Management of Indian Ocean Tuna, Eleventh Session (Bangkok, July 9–12, 1990) reproduced in *The Law of the Sea, Annual Review of Ocean Affairs Law and Policy: Main Documents 1990*, *supra* note 5 at 236.

[9] Report of the Secretary General, *Large-scale Pelagic Driftnet Fishing and its Impact on the Living Marine Resources of the World's Oceans and Seas*, UNGA Doc. A/45/663, October 26, 1990, para. 30.

[10] Richards, *supra* note 1 at 107–8.

[11] Richards, *supra* note 1 at 108; see also the discussion in Miller, *supra* note 6 at 157.

and New Zealand,[12] were particularly troubled by the increasing use of drift-nets within the region and evidence of the damage they caused.[13] Scientific apprehension preceded the political interest; a meeting of the South Pacific Albacore Research (SPAR) Working Group noted in June 1989 that the total surface catch of juvenile albacore tuna at 1988–9 levels was unsustainable.[14]

The Forum's concern was quickly reflected at the political level when it adopted the Tarawa Declaration a month later (July 1989).[15] The Declaration specifically addressed the problem of driftnet fishing and resolved to develop a Convention to address the issue. It also provided that:

individual member States of the South Pacific Forum will take all possible measures in the interim to prevent drift-net fishing within their waters, and otherwise actively to discourage the operations of drift-net fishers;
. . . member States, acting individually and collectively, will take what action they can within relevant international organizations to contribute to the cessation of this harmful form of fishing.[16]

The Declaration commended the Republic of Korea for its decision to suspend driftnet fishing and specifically called upon Japan and Taiwan to follow this example and immediately abandon their driftnet operations.[17] Japan responded in September 1989 by outlining steps it intended to take in the conservation of albacore tuna stocks, including a reduction in the size of its driftnet fleet for the 1989–90 season.[18]

Members of the Forum Fisheries Agency soon acted upon the Tarawa Declaration. A working group met in the Solomon Islands in October 1989 to

[12] Members of the South Pacific Forum include Australia, Cook Islands, Federated States of Micronesia, Fiji, Kiribati, Marshall Islands, Nauru, New Zealand, Niue, Papua New Guinea, Solomon Islands, Samoa, Tonga, Tuvalu, and Vanuatu.
[13] Miller, *supra* note 6 at 157 notes that the development of the driftnet fishery in the South Pacific was prompted by the closure of U.S. waters to Japanese driftnet fishermen and a desire to operate year-round driftnet fishing operations in the Pacific Ocean which alternated between the North and South Pacific depending on the season.
[14] Richards, *supra* note 1 at 109. Miller, *supra* note 6 at 160 comments that following this meeting, representatives of SPAR met with representatives of the driftnet fishers to discuss possible measures to address driftnet fishing, with Japan and Taiwan offering to freeze their level of fishing activity at 1988/9 levels.
[15] A further reason for the political concern in the South Pacific was the economic importance of tuna throughout the region to many of the small island states of the Southwest Pacific and the impact that the loss of the tuna fishery would have upon those economies; for further background see Tsamenyi, B.M., and Mfodwo, K., 'South Pacific Island States and the New Regime of Fisheries: Issues of Law, Economy and Diplomacy' in Crawford and Rothwell, *supra* note 6 at 121–53.
[16] Tarawa Declaration—Final Communiqué of the Twentieth South Pacific Forum, held at Tarawa, Kiribati, on July 10 and 11, 1989, reproduced in United Nations, *The Law of the Sea—Annual Review of Ocean Affairs: Law and Policy—Main Documents 1989* (1993) 118–89; also found in 5 *International Organizations and the Law of the Sea Documentary Yearbook 1989* (1991) 692–3.
[17] Richards, *supra* note 1 at 110 records only one Korean fishery survey vessel engaging in driftnet fishing in the South Pacific during the period 1985/6 to 1991/2.
[18] Richards, *supra* note 1 at 110.

prepare a draft convention that prohibited the use of driftnets in the region, followed by a further series of meetings eventually resulting in the adoption in Wellington, New Zealand, on 24 November 1989 of the Convention for the Prohibition of Fishing with Long Drift Nets in the South Pacific.[19] The Convention was drafted and opened for acceptance by the members of the South Pacific Forum, but two Protocols were added to enable distant water fishing nations and other nations seeking to prohibit driftnet fishing to adhere to the measures provided for in the Convention.[20] The Convention entered into force in 1991.[21]

The members of the South Pacific Forum quickly endorsed the Convention, with the final communiqué from the Forum's 1990 meeting calling upon interested parties to accede to the Convention, and welcoming Japan's decision to cease driftnetting. Particular reference also was made to the need to find a means to involve Taiwan in negotiations for a management regime for South Pacific albacore tuna.[22]

2. The Organization of Eastern Caribbean States

Another initiative issued from a meeting of the Organization of Eastern Caribbean States (OECS) in November 1989 at Castries, Saint Lucia. The meeting adopted a Declaration which directly addressed the members' concerns over driftnet fishing. The 'Castries Declaration' recognized the importance of marine fisheries to peoples of the OECS region and expressed concern at the damage being caused to the marine environment by the use of driftnets. It resolved:

to seek to establish a regional régime for the regulation and management of the pelagic resources in the Lesser Antilles region that would outlaw the use of drift nets and other

[19] (1990) 29 I.L.M. 1454; the Convention entered into force on May 17, 1991. For discussion of this Convention see Hewison, G.J., 'The Convention for the Prohibition of Fishing With Long Driftnets in the South Pacific' (1993) 25 *Case Western Reserve J. Int' L.* 449–530; Miller, *supra* note 7; Islam, M.R., 'The Proposed "Driftnet-Free Zone" in the South Pacific and the Law of the Sea Convention' (1991) 40 *Int'& Comp. L.Q.* 184–98; Shearer, I.A., 'High Seas: Drift Gillnets, Highly Migratory Species and Marine Mammals' in Kuribayashi, T., and Miles, E.L. (eds.), *The Law of the Sea in the 1990s: A Framework for Further International Cooperation* (1992) 237 at 246–55.

[20] The U.S. signed Protocol 1 on February 26, 1991 and ratified it on February 28, 1992, Canada signed Protocol 2 on September 24, 1991, and Chile signed Protocol 2 on November 1, 1991.

[21] Art. 1(a) of the Convention defines the 'Convention Area' as being:

'(i) Subject to subparagraph (ii) of this paragraph, shall be the area lying within 10 degrees North latitude and 50 degrees South latitude and 130 degrees East longitude and 120 degrees West longitude, and shall also include all waters under the fisheries jurisdiction of any Party to this Convention;

(ii) In the case of a State or Territory which is Party to the Convention by virtue of paragraph 1(b) of 1(c) of article 10, it shall include only waters under the fisheries jurisdiction of that Party, adjacent to the Territory referred to in paragraph 1(b) of 1(c) of article 10.'

[22] Final communiqué of the 21st South Pacific Forum, held at Port Vila, Vanuatu, from July 31 to August 1, 1990, reproduced in (December 1990) No 16 *Law of the Sea Bulletin* 75 at 76.

disruptive fishing methods by commercial fishing vessels, and call upon other States in the region to co-operate in this regard;

. . . that all member States of OECS will take all possible measures in the interim to prevent the use of indiscriminate fishing methods in their exclusive economic zones;

. . . that member States, acting individually and collectively, will take whatever action possible within relevant regional and international organizations that would contribute towards the global restriction of harmful fishing practices.[23]

3. United Nations Response

The United Nations first addressed the issue of driftnet fishing in 1989 at the 44th Session of the General Assembly. Throughout 1989, UN agencies such as the FAO and UNDP had been investigating the effects of driftnet fishing.[24] The Secretary-General also raised the issue in his annual report on the Law of the Sea. The report noted that over 1,000 Japanese, South Korean, and Taiwanese vessels had been using driftnets to catch mainly squid, tuna, and billfish in North Pacific high seas, and that there had recently been a 'massive expansion' of driftnet operations in the South Pacific.[25] The matter was raised for discussion in the Second Committee of the General Assembly in late 1989 when the U.S., supported by seventeen other states, introduced a draft resolution addressing driftnet fishing and its impact on marine living resources. The resolution went forward to the General Assembly and was adopted as UNGA Resolution 44/225 on December 22, 1989.

An important component of UNGA Resolution 44/225 was the request to the Secretary-General to submit a report to the next session of the UNGA, ensuring that the issue remained on the agenda for consideration at the 45th session. Throughout 1990 a number of UN agencies gave detailed consideration to the driftnet issue, in particular the FAO because of its concerns over the impact of driftnets upon fisheries and stock management.[26] The 1990

---

[23] The Castries Declaration (November 24, 1989) reproduced in 5 *International Organizations and the Law of the Sea Documentary Yearbook 1989, supra* note 16 at 686; *The Law of the Sea—Annual Review of Ocean Affairs: Law and Policy—Main Documents 1989, supra* note 16 at 119.

[24] See FAO/UNDP, FFA, SPC Consultations on Southern Albacore Fisheries Interaction (Fiji, March 2–3, 1989) (Forum Fisheries Agency Report No:18/89) reproduced in *The Law of the Sea—Annual Review of Ocean Affairs: Law and Policy—Main Documents 1989, supra* note 16 at 115.

[25] United Nations Secretary-General, *Law of the Sea: Report of the Secretary-General* (UN Doc A/44/650, November 1, 1989) para. 114, reproduced in *The Law of the Sea—Annual Review of Ocean Affairs: Law and Policy—Main Documents 1989, supra* note 16 at 49.

[26] See FAO Indian Ocean Fishery Commission, Committee for the Management of Indian Ocean Tuna, Eleventh Session (Bangkok, July 12, 1990) reproduced in *The Law of the Sea—Annual Review of Ocean Affairs: Law and Policy—Main Documents 1990, supra* note 5 at 236–8; FAO Western Central Atlantic Fishery Commission, Committee for the Development and Management of Fisheries in the Lesser Antilles, Fourth Session (Saint Vincent and the Grenadines, October 31–November 7, 1990) reproduced in *The Law of the Sea—Annual Review of Ocean Affairs: Law and Policy—Main Documents 1990, supra* note 5 at 241–2.

Secretary-General's Report provided a thorough review of the state of drift-net fishing throughout the world, concluding that the effects of driftnet fish-ing upon fish stocks were most keenly being felt in the North and South Pacific, and the Mediterranean Sea.[27] The Report noted with respect to implementation of UNGA Res 44/225:

the complete implementation of the provisions of the resolution requires further mea-sures in the form of national legislation governing activities of the flag State's vessels on the high seas, international agreements and the adoption of internationally agreed practices, which may be subregional, regional or global in character.[28]

The General Assembly responded by adopting UNGA Res. 45/197 on December 21, 1990. The Resolution noted the continuing international expressions of concern over the impact of driftnet fishing, such as the mea-sures taken by the South Pacific Forum and the Castries Declaration of the OECS, reaffirmed the intent of UNGA Resolution 44/225, and called upon the Secretary-General to submit another report on the issue to the following session of the General Assembly.

The Secretary-General duly prepared a further report on the matter for presentation to the 1991 General Assembly session. It resulted in the adop-tion of UNGA Resolution 46/215, the most substantive resolution on this matter, which called for the complete cessation of high seas driftnet fishing operations by December 31, 1992. Subsequent decisions and resolutions adopted by the UNGA on the topic of driftnet fishing have endorsed and reaffirmed UNGA 46/215, while also requesting the Secretary-General to continue to assess the level of international acceptance of the action taken by the General Assembly.

C. THE UN GENERAL ASSEMBLY RESOLUTIONS

Three primary resolutions were adopted by the General Assembly during the period 1989–91, followed by three decisions (1992–94), and more recently a further four resolutions (1995–98). Each of the resolutions and decisions was adopted without a vote.

[27] The Mediterranean Sea driftnet fishery was developed from traditional fishing practices in the region and had developed throughout the 1980s to include large fleets of small vessels with driftnets varying in length from 2 to 40km, the average being 12km: Report of the Secretary-General, *Large-scale Pelagic Driftnet Fishing and its Impact on the Living Marine Resources of the World's Oceans and Seas* (UN General Assembly, 45th Session; UN Doc A/45/663: October 26, 1990) paras. 146–7, reproduced in *The Law of the Sea—Annual Review of Ocean Affairs: Law and Policy—Main Documents 1990*, *supra* note 5, 242 at 261.

[28] Report of the Secretary-General, *Large-scale Pelagic Driftnet Fishing and its Impact on the Living Marine Resources of the World's Oceans and Seas* (UN General Assembly, 45th Session; UN Doc A/45/663, October 26, 1990) para. 153, reproduced in *The Law of the Sea—Annual Review of Ocean Affairs: Law and Policy—Main Documents 1990*, *supra* note 5, 242 at 263.

The first initiative came with UNGA Resolution 44/225 in 1989. The preamble placed emphasis on international concerns over the use of high seas driftnets because it was considered to be 'a highly indiscriminate and wasteful fishing method that is widely considered to threaten the effective conservation of living marine resources, such as highly migratory and anadromous species of fish, birds and marine mammals'.[29] The main terms of the Resolution called upon the international community to cooperate in conservation and management of marine living resources (paragraph 1) and to collect and assess the best available scientific data on the impact of driftnet fishing (paragraphs 2 and 3). The Resolution also recommended that the international community agree that:

(a) Moratoria should be imposed on all large-scale pelagic driftnet fishing on the high seas by June 30, 1992, with the understanding that such a measure will not be imposed in a region or, if implemented, can be lifted, should effective conservation and management measures be taken based upon statistically sound analysis to be jointly made by concerned parties of the international community with an interest in the fishery resources of the region, to prevent unacceptable impact of such fishing practices on that region and to ensure the conservation of the living marine resources of that region;

(b) Immediate action should be taken to reduce progressively large-scale pelagic driftnet fishing activities in the South Pacific region with a view to the cessation of such activities by July 1, 1991, as an interim measure, until appropriate conservation and management arrangements for South Pacific albacore tuna resources are entered into by the parties concerned;

(c) Further expansion of large-scale driftnet fishing on the high seas of the North Pacific and all other high seas outside the Pacific Ocean should cease immediately, with the understanding that this measure would be reviewed subject to the conditions in paragraph 4(a) of the resolution.

The Resolution also requested the Secretary-General to bring the terms of the Resolution to the attention of all members of the international community (paragraph 7) and that the Secretary-General submit a report to the next session of the UNGA regarding implementation (paragraph 8).

The second resolution, UNGA 45/197 of 1990, essentially reaffirmed UNGA 44/225 and did not substantially advance the movement towards a prohibition on driftnet fishing. The resolution does, however, make reference to the importance of implementation. The General Assembly noted that it:

---

[29] UNGA Res. 44/225, Preamble.

2. Reaffirms its resolution 44/225, and calls for its full implementation by all members of the international community, in accordance with the measures and time-frame elaborated in paragraph 4 of that resolution concerning large-scale pelagic driftnet fishing on the high seas of all the world's oceans and seas, including enclosed and semi-enclosed seas.

Reference is also made to the need for continuing study of driftnet fishing, for the Secretary-General to bring the resolution to the attention of the international community, and for the Secretary-General to report on the matter at the following General Assembly session.

The principal UNGA Resolution concerning the threat posed by driftnet fishing is UNGA Resolution 46/215 adopted on December 20, 1991, which followed the Secretary-General's second and most comprehensive report assessing the impact of driftnet fishing on marine living resources. The report particularly assessed the impact of high seas driftnet fishing on the viability of certain fish stocks and the consequences resulting from excessive by-catch upon other marine living resources, especially marine mammals.[30]

The resolution reviewed the progress in addressing the issue of driftnet fishing, and made particular reference to the continuing efforts to collect statistically sound data on the effects of the activity, particularly in the North Pacific Ocean. The central component of UNGA 46/215 was as follows:

The General Assembly

. . .

3. Calls upon all members of the international community to implement resolutions 44/225 and 45/197 by, inter alia, taking the following actions:
(a) Beginning on 1 January 1992, reduce fishing effort in existing large-scale pelagic high seas drift-net fisheries, by, inter alia, reducing the number of vessels involved, the length of the nets and the area of operation, so as to achieve, by 30 June 1992, a 50 per cent reduction in fishing effort;
(b) Continue to ensure that the areas of operation of large-scale pelagic high seas drift-net fishing are not expanded and, beginning on 1 January 1992, are further reduced in accordance with paragraph 3 (a) of the present resolution;
(c) Ensure that a global moratorium on all large-scale pelagic drift-net fishing is fully implemented on the high seas of the world's oceans and seas, including seas and semi-enclosed seas, by 31 December 1992.

In addition, UNGA 46/215 referred to the importance of compliance. Not only did it request the Secretary-General to bring the resolution to the attention of the international community,[31] the General Assembly also:

---

[30] Report of the Secretary-General, *Large-scale Pelagic Driftnet Fishing and its Impact on the Living Marine Resources of the World's Oceans and Seas* (UN Doc No 45/615 + Corr.1 + Add.1, November 8, 1991) reproduced in 7 *International Organizations and the Law of the Sea Documentary Yearbook 1991* (1993) 63–87.

[31] UNGA Res. 46/215, para. 5.

4. Reaffirm[ed] the importance it attaches to compliance with the present resolution and encourages all members of the international community to take measures, individually and collectively, to prevent large-scale pelagic drift-net fishing operations on the high seas of the world's oceans and seas, including enclosed seas and semi-enclosed seas.

. . .

6. Request[ed] the members and organizations referred to above to submit to the Secretary-General information concerning activities or conduct inconsistent with the terms of the present resolution.[32]

The Secretary-General was also requested to report on the implementation of the resolution at the following session.

Between 1992 and 1998 the UNGA reviewed the implementation of UNGA Resolution 46/215 in response to a series of annual reports conducted by the Secretary-General on the degree of international acceptance and implementation of the driftnet fishing moratorium. In 1992, the UNGA merely noted the Secretary-General's report and requested that a further report be prepared for the following session.[33] The 1993 response by the UNGA requested a further report, while reaffirming the importance it attached to compliance with UNGA Resolution 46/215.[34] The 1994 response by the UNGA had more substance. In addition to reaffirming the importance it attached to compliance and acknowledging efforts to implement the moratorium, it decided:

(c) To express further serious concern that, despite the measures taken and the progress made, there are reports of continuing conduct and activities inconsistent with the terms of its resolution 46/215, and to urge authorities of members of the international community to take greater enforcement responsibility to ensure full compliance with resolution 46/215 and to impose appropriate sanctions, consistent with international law, against acts contrary to the terms of the resolution.[35]

Since 1995, the General Assembly has given increasingly more attention to the need for compliance with the driftnet moratorium. The General Assembly's response has been bolstered by other developments in international fisheries management, including the adoption of the following instruments:

---

[32] The members and organizations referred to in para. 6 were those noted in para. 5 as including members of the international community, intergovernmental and non-governmental organizations, and scientific institutions with expertise in relation to marine living resources.

[33] Decision adopted by the General Assembly, *Large-scale Pelagic Driftnet Fishing and its Impact on the Living Marine Resources of the World's Oceans and Seas*, UN Doc A/Dec.47/443: December 22, 1992.

[34] Decision adopted by the General Assembly, *Large-scale Pelagic Driftnet Fishing and its Impact on the Living Marine Resources of the World's Oceans and Seas*, UN Doc A/Dec.48/445: December 21, 1993.

[35] UNGA Decision on Large-scale Pelagic Driftnet Fishing and its Impact on the Living Marine Resources of the World's Oceans and Seas, UN Doc A/Dec.49/436, December 19, 1994.

- 1993 FAO Agreement to Promote Compliance with International Conservation and Management Measures by Fishing Vessels on the High Seas;
- 1995 Agreement for the Implementation of the Provisions of the United Nations Convention on the Law of the Sea of December 10, 1982 relating to the Conservation and Management of Straddling Fish Stocks and Highly Migratory Fish Stocks;[36]
- 1995 FAO Code of Conduct for Responsible Fisheries;

The UNGA has emphasized, in its resolutions, the need for greater enforcement responsibility to ensure full compliance and the imposition of appropriate sanctions against acts that are contrary to the terms of the resolution.[37] Of some significance, the UNGA Resolutions adopted since 1995 have also included within their scope the question of unauthorized fishing in zones of national jurisdiction and on the high seas, and fisheries by-catch and discards.

D. INSTITUTIONAL FRAMEWORK OR SUPERVISORY MECHANISMS

One of the problems with the implementation of any resolution adopted by the General Assembly is enforcement. If member states believe that they have an obligation to give effect to the resolution, then initially it is for those member states to implement the resolution and ensure domestic compliance. In the case of UNGA Resolution 46/215, however, this was made difficult because of the limited jurisdictional competence of all states over the high seas. The high seas have been recognized as an area beyond the reach of national sovereignty, within which states may exercise jurisdiction only over their nation-

---

[36] (1995) 34 I.L.M. 1542.
[37] The Resolutions are as follows:
   UNGA Resolution on Large-scale pelagic drift-net fishing and its impact on the living marine resources of the world's oceans and seas; unauthorized fishing in zones of national jurisdiction and its impact on the living marine resources of the world's oceans and seas; and fisheries by-catch and discards and their impact on the sustainable use of the world's living marine resources, UN Doc A/Res/50/25, December 5, 1995;
   UNGA Resolution on Large-scale pelagic drift-net fishing; unauthorized fishing in zones of national jurisdiction; and fisheries by-catch and discards, UN Doc A/Res/51/36, December 9, 1996;
   UNGA Resolution on Large-scale pelagic drift-net fishing; unauthorized fishing in zones of national jurisdiction and on the high seas; fisheries by-catch and discards; and other developments, UN Doc A/Res/52/29, November 26, 1997;
   UNGA Resolution on Large-scale pelagic drift-net fishing, unauthorized fishing in zones of national jurisdiction and on the high seas, fisheries by-catch and discards, and other developments, UN Doc A/RES/53/33, January 6, 1999.

als or flagged vessels.[38] The exercise by flag states of jurisdiction over their vessels has been variable throughout the twentieth century, with some so-called 'flag of convenience' states exercising minimal control over their flagged vessels, whether within the high seas or coastal waters. A further difficulty, especially in response to matters on the high seas, is capacity for enforcement. In many instances the offending vessel engages in an activity on the high seas at a place far distant from the flag state's territory, making contemporaneous enforcement and policing virtually impossible. Flag states often are unable to take action until an offending vessel has returned to its home port, though fishing vessels are more prone to return to home ports than other commercial vessels. The implementation of UNGA Resolution 46/215 therefore presented additional difficulties to those normally associated with giving effect to a UNGA Resolution. The Resolution provided, however, for continual monitoring of driftnet fishing by the UN Secretary-General, and requested member states to provide information regarding activities or conduct inconsistent with the Resolution. In addition, the Resolution encouraged the international community to take both individual and collective measures to prevent driftnet fishing.

Since 1991, the UN system has engaged in continual monitoring of high seas driftnet fishing. This has been achieved formally between 1992 and 1998 by way of reports from the Secretary-General to the General Assembly, in which state practice giving effect to UNGA Resolution 46/215 has been reviewed. The General Assembly thus has been able to annually assess implementation of its resolution and adopt additional responses as necessary.

The Secretary-General's reports are based upon information and data supplied by member states, UN agencies, other international organizations, and NGOs. International organizations have assisted the Secretary-General with both the FAO and, to a lesser extent, UNEP, continuing to monitor the status of high seas driftnet fishing throughout the 1990s. The Secretary-General also has been able to gather responses from other international organizations with a specific interest in fishing, including:

- Commission for the Conservation of Antarctic Marine Living Resources (CCAMLR);
- Commission for the Conservation of Southern Bluefin Tuna (CCSBT);
- Council of Europe;
- European Community (EC);
- Food and Agricultural Organization of the United Nations (FAO);
- General Fisheries Commission for the Mediterranean (GFCM);
- Indo-Pacific Tuna Programme (IPTP);

---

[38] See the discussion in Brown, E.D., *The International Law of the Sea I* (1994) 277–335; one important exception is where the right of hot pursuit is being exercised on the high seas in response to the infringement of coastal state laws and regulations committed within the territorial sea of EEZ of the coastal state.

- Inter-American Tropical Tuna Commission (I-ATTC);
- International Commission for the Conservation of Atlantic Tunas (ICCAT);
- Latin American Fishing Development Organization (OLDEPESCA);
- North Atlantic Salmon Conservation Organization (NASCO);
- North Pacific Anadromous Fish Commission (NPAFC);
- Northeast Atlantic Fisheries Commission (NEAFC);
- North Atlantic Fisheries Organization (NAFO);
- Organization for Economic Co-operation and Development (OECD) Commission for Fisheries;
- South Pacific Commission (SPC);
- South Pacific Forum Fisheries Agency (FFA);
- United Nations Economic Commission for Latin America and the Caribbean (ECLAC);
- Western Central Atlantic Fishery Commission (WECAFC).[39]

Responses from UN member states to requests for information from the Secretary-General have been variable. The U.S. has provided annual extensive comments, and Canada, New Zealand, and Japan have also responded frequently to requests for information. The Secretary-General's reports do not comment on the level of compliance with the driftnet moratorium, although occasionally extracts from information provided address the issue. Another aspect of the reports has been the inclusion of information provided by NGOs, either directly to the Secretary-General or via other organizations. This information often highlights problems with enforcement and compliance.

At times, NGOs contest the claims made by states as to their implementation of the UNGA Resolution. The UN does not have the capacity to verify the information that it receives and is therefore reliant upon the goodwill of member states and the competence of bodies such as the FAO in compiling data regarding compliance. Ultimately, the capacity of the UN to monitor implementation of its Resolutions depends upon the information supplied.

A factor assisting the institutional framework is the legal obligations created through other initiatives to prohibit driftnet fishing, legal obligations both international and national. Regional initiatives such as the Wellington Convention proved to be particularly important in giving effect to the provisions of the moratorium in the Southwest Pacific. Likewise, the Convention for the Conservation of Anadromous Stocks in the North Pacific Ocean between Canada, Japan, Russia, and the U.S. was important in limiting

---

[39] See the various Reports of the Secretary-General from 1991–8.

driftnet fishing in the North Pacific.⁴⁰ Recent E.C. initiatives to give effect to the moratorium in the Mediterranean have been significant in creating an impetus for the eventual cessation of driftnet fishing in that region. Various states also have prohibited driftnet fishing by their nationals, their flagged vessels, and within their waters. A sample of these initiatives is included in Table 5.1. Some states have taken a particularly proactive approach towards implementing the moratorium in their domestic law, with the U.S. perhaps the most prominent. These initiatives are discussed in more detail below.

E. THE ROLE OF NGOS AND OTHER INTEREST GROUPS IN PROMOTING COMPLIANCE

The role played by environmental NGOs and the scientific community in raising concerns over the unsustainable nature of the fishing practice was an important feature of the debate over driftnet fishing. Evidence also suggests, however, that other groups had strong interests in ensuring the elimination of driftnet fishing on both the high seas and also within the EEZ. U.S. and Canadian fishermen were particularly concerned about the impact of North Pacific driftnet fishing upon the West Coast salmon and tuna fishery. Burke, Freeberg, and Miles have suggested that these commercial interests were influential in swaying U.S. policy makers against driftnet fishing:

Interests of the Alaskan and other U.S. salmon fishery industries in the driftnetting issue are clear. They have as their basis a desire to remove both the Japanese land-based gillnet salmon fleet and the squid driftnet fleet from the high seas. The same interests applied vis-a-vis the Korean and Taiwanese squid driftnet fleets, especially since Taiwanese vessels were clearly involved in illegal salmon fishing operations. Congressional delegations of U.S. West Coast states were simply falling into line behind a group of significant constituencies against foreign transgressors. As such, the politics of the issue were easy since they did not involve major internal conflicts between different groups of fishermen. For the environmentalists, whether or not the alarming claims about driftnets were true, the issue proved to be a potent force for mobilizing both financial and political support.⁴¹

NGOs have continued to play an important role in monitoring implementation and compliance with the UNGA Resolutions. Each Secretary-General's report has noted NGO submissions. Greenpeace International has

⁴⁰ For a discussion of this and other initiatives dealing with driftnet fishing in the North Pacific, see Davis, L.A., 'North Pacific Pelagic Driftnetting: Untangling the High Seas Controversy' (1991) 64 *So. Cal. L. Rev.* 1057–102; also see Mirovitskaya, N.S., and Haney, J.C., 'Fisheries Exploitation as a Threat to Environmental Security: The North Pacific Ocean' (1992) 16 *Marine Policy* 243–58.

⁴¹ Burke, W.T., Freeberg, M., and Miles, E.L. 'United Nations Resolutions on Driftnet Fishing: An Unsustainable Precedent for High Seas and Coastal Fisheries Management' (1994) 25 *Ocean Development and International Law* 127 at 139.

been very active, and has continued to provide information to the Secretary-General and other international organizations on activities in breach of the Resolution.[42] The Humane Society of the United States has taken a particular interest in driftnetting in the Mediterranean, going to the extent of filing suit in the Court of International Trade in an attempt to force the U.S. government to take action against Italy under U.S. domestic laws.[43] Eventually, in *Humane Society of the United States* v. *Brown*, the Court ruled that the United States Commerce and State Departments were required under U.S. law to declare that Italy was violating the UNGA Resolution on driftnet fishing.[44] The scientific community, either independently or in conjunction with international organizations, also has played an important role in gathering together data on the effects of unregulated high seas driftnet fishing during the late 1980s and early 1990s. There is little evidence, however, that the scientific community has continued independently to monitor the situation.[45]

F. THE INCENTIVES AND DISINCENTIVES TO COMPLIANCE

The prominent role taken in the debate over driftnet fishing by the United States has been an important incentive for compliance. Not only did the U.S. lead the debate in the General Assembly, but it has taken influential actions domestically to enforce the Resolutions against U.S. fishermen and those operating in U.S. waters and on the high seas. In particular, the threat of trade sanctions against fishing nations that continue to engage in high seas driftnet fishing, in which potential loss of access to the U.S. market was one outcome, most likely proved to be a major incentive for states such as Japan, Korea, and Taiwan to eventually scale down and cease driftnet fishing.[46] More recently, the threat of U.S. sanctions against Italy may have been decisive in Italy eventually agreeing to adopt policies to phase out driftnet fishing

[42] Other NGOs to have made submissions include the Cousteau Society, Federation of Japan Tuna Fisheries Cooperative Associations, and the World Wildlife Fund.

[43] See the discussion in Blackwell, A., 'The Humane Society and Italian Driftnetters: Environmental Activists and Unilateral Action in International Environmental Law' (1998) 23 *North Carolina J. Int' L. & Comm. Reg.* 313–40.

[44] See *Humane Society of the United States* v. *Brown*, 920 F. Supp. 178 (Court of International Trade 1996); and discussion in Blackwell, *supra* note 43 at 334–7; and Report of the Secretary-General, Oceans and the law of the sea: Large-scale pelagic drift-net fishing, unauthorized fishing in zones of national jurisdiction and fisheries by-catch and discards ((UN Doc A/52/557, October 31, 1997) (http://www.un.org/Depts/los/a_52_557) (hereafter UN Secretary-General Report 1997) para. 40.

[45] Note, however, should be made of the interest of the International Oceanographic Commission (IOC) in the IOC–FAO Ocean Science in relation to Living Resources (OSLR) program.

[46] For a detailed review of this U.S. action see Hewison, G.J., 'Trade and the Environment: PPMS Issues and the Case of Driftnet Fishing' (unpublished: paper prepared for OECD Conference on Trade and Environment, Helsinki, Finland, 1994: on file).

Table 5.1: * A selection of states responses to prohibiting driftnet fishing*

Country	Prohibition of driftnet fishing in Territorial Sea/EEZ	Prohibition of High Seas diftnet fishing by Nationals/Ships	Other Responses
Australia	Yes	Yes	
Argentina	Yes	Yes	
Bahrain	Territorial waters		
China	Yes	Yes	
Cook Islands	Yes	Yes	
Croatia	Yes	Yes	
Ecuador	Yes		No permits granted
Fiji	Yes		
Guyana		Yes	
Italy	Yes, driftnets 2.5km+		
Japan	Yes	Yes, enforced in 1993	No permits granted
Latvia		Yes	
Malaysia	Yes		
Monaco	Yes	Yes	
Mexico			No permits for shark and marlin driftnets over 2.5km
Maldives	Yes		
Mauritius	Yes		Bans transship-ment of fish caught by driftnets
Namibia	Declared FZ and EEZ	Yes	
Netherlands	Yes	Yes, driftnets 2.5km+	
New Zealand	Yes	Yes	
Norway		Yes	
Pakistan	Yes		
Panama			Refuses registra-tion to driftnet fishers
Peru			Prohibits non-handcrafted driftnets
Republic of Korea	Yes from 31/12/92	Yes from 30/11/92	
Russia	No Driftnets 3.7km+	No Driftnets 3.7km+	
South Africa	Yes	Yes	
Spain		Yes	

Country	Prohibition of driftnet fishing in Territorial Sea/EEZ	Prohibition of High Seas diftnet fishing by Nationals/Ships	Other Responses
Sri Lanka			Fish caught with long lines only permitted by foreign fishermen
Taiwan		Yes	Ban on building of new driftnet vessels
Tunisia	Yes, driftnets 2.5km+		
Turkey	Yes	Yes	
Ukraine			Observes UNGA 46/215 on HS
United Arab Emirates	Yes		
USA	Yes	Yes	
Uruguay	Yes	Yes	
Venezuela	Yes, driftnets 14m+	Yes, driftnets 14m+	

* Sources: Hewison, G.J., 'The Legally Binding Nature of the Moratorium on Large-Scale High Seas Driftnet Fishing' (1994) 25 *J. Maritime L. & Comm.* 557–79; Report of the Secretary-General, *Large-scale Pelagic Driftnet Fishing and its Impact on the Living Marine Resources of the World's Oceans and Seas*, UN Doc A/47/487, October 6, 1992; Report of the UN Secretary-General, *Large-scale Pelagic Driftnet Fishing and Its Impact on the Living Marine Resources of the World's Oceans and Seas*, UN Doc A/48/451 & Corr 1, October 11, 1993; Report of the UN Secretary-General, *Large-scale Pelagic Driftnet Fishing and its Impact on the Living Marine Resources of the World's Oceans and Seas*, UN Doc A/49/469, October 5, 1994; Report of the Secretary-General, *Large-scale Pelagic Drift-net Fishing and its Impact on the Living Marine Resources of the World's Oceans and Seas*, UN Doc A/50/553, October 12, 1995; Report of the Secretary-General, *Law of the Sea: Large-scale Pelagic Drift-Net Fishing and its Impact on the Living Marine Resources of the World's Oceans and Seas*; *Unauthorized Fishing in Zones of National Jurisdiction and its Impact on the Living Marine Resources of the World's Oceans and Seas*; and *Fisheries By-Catch and Discards and their Impact on the Sustainable Use of the World's Living Marine Resources*, UN Doc A/51/404: September 25 1996; Report of the Secretary-General, *Oceans and the Law of the Sea: Large-scale Pelagic Drift-net Fishing, Unauthorized Fishing in Zones of National Jurisdiction and Fisheries By-catch and Discards*, UN Doc A/52/557, October 31, 1997; Report of the Secretary-General, *Large-scale Pelagic Drift-net Fishing, Unauthorized Fishing in Zones of National Jurisdiction and on the High Seas, Fisheries By-catch and Discards, and Other Developments*, UN Doc A/53/33, October 8, 1998.

amongst its fleet.[47] The U.S. response was not merely one of issuing threats, however. It also participated in a driftnet conversion plan, which in 1998 resulted in 419 of the 678 vessels in the Italian driftnet fleet applying for compensation.[48] In addition, significant constraints began to be imposed upon

[47] UN Secretary-General's Report, 1997, para. 40.
[48] UN Secretary-General's Report, 1998, para. 48.

driftnet fishing nations through a combination of coastal states' enactment of laws and regulations prohibiting driftnet fishing within their EEZ and their threats to enact laws dealing with transhipment of driftnet catches within areas under their jurisdiction.[49] Continuing review of the driftnet issue by the UNGA also indicated the degree of seriousness with which the international community viewed the adoption of the moratorium. To that end, the wording of UNGA Decision 49/436 in 1994 and UNGA Resolutions 50/25, 51/36, 52/29 and 53/33 has been significant: all of them called upon the international community to take greater enforcement responsibility to ensure full compliance with resolution 46/215 and to impose appropriate sanctions, consistent with international law, against acts contrary to the resolution.

The disincentives for compliance with the UNGA Resolution clearly center on its non-binding nature.[50] States that distinguish between UN non-binding actions and those of the UN and other international organizations which are binding can clearly justify non-compliance with the UNGA Resolution. In addition, implementation of the Resolution by states engaged in driftnet fishing results in significant economic loss not only because of the inability to exploit a particular fishery, but also through failure to use fishing gear. This has been borne out in the costs associated with the conversion of the Italian driftnet fleet.[51] For some states such as Italy, a prohibition on driftnet fishing has not only an important economic impact, but also a cultural one, given the history of the use of driftnets in parts of the Mediterranean and the heavy reliance upon the fishing technique by a large group of fishermen.

G. IMPLEMENTATION AND COMPLIANCE

The acceptance by the international community of the moratorium by both fishing and non-fishing nations has been a significant consequence of the actions taken by the UNGA against driftnet fishing. As Table 5.1 shows, on the basis of evidence collected by the Secretary-General, a number of states have prohibited driftnet fishing within their territorial seas and EEZ, and also have taken action to prohibit either their fishing vessels or their nationals from engaging in driftnet fishing on the high seas. Additionally, a number of other states openly support the moratorium, but have not implemented any laws or policies to regulate the activity either because their fishermen have never used driftnets, or because driftnet fishing has never taken place within

---

[49] On the issue of transhipment, see Shearer, *supra* note 19 at 253.

[50] Cf. Hewison, *supra* note 19 arguing that UNGA Res. 46/215 has become a part of customary international law.

[51] Italy has estimated that under its recently adopted program providing for the phasing out of driftnet fishing vessels, 676 vessels will be retrenched at a cost of 200 billion lire during the first phase of implementation: UN Secretary-General's Report 1997, paras. 18, 23.

their national waters. It is particularly useful to review the actions taken to give effect to the moratorium by the U.S., European Union, driftnet fishing states, and states in the Southwest Pacific.

1. United States Response

The United States has been particularly active in responding to the moratorium. It has done so domestically through the adoption of laws and regulations controlling driftnet fishing,[52] and also at a bilateral and regional level where it has concluded several agreements seeking to regulate the activity.

Five legislative acts impose obligations upon U.S. nationals to not engage in driftnet fishing, and provide for monitoring of high seas driftnet fishing by the nationals and vessels of those states which had previously engaged in the activity.[53] Of all the legislative initiatives, the High Seas Driftnet Fisheries Enforcement Act 1992 and the High Seas Driftnet Fishing Moratorium Protection Act 1995 are perhaps the most directly related to the concerns raised by the UNGA Resolutions. The first Act provides for denial of port privileges for high seas driftnet fishing vessels, prohibition of the import of fish and fish products from driftnet fishing nations, high seas fisheries enforcement in the Central Bering Sea, and consequential provisions dealing with fishing in the U.S. EEZ.[54] The second prohibits the U.S., or any agency or official acting on behalf of the U.S., from entering into an international agreement with respect to conservation and management of marine living resources of the sea or the use of the high seas by fishing vessels that would prevent the full implementation of UNGA Resolution 46/215. The Act additionally provides that the U.S. is to detect, monitor, and prevent violations of the driftnet moratorium for all fisheries under U.S. jurisdiction, and in all other cases to the fullest extent possible under international law.[55]

In an effort to give effect to these Acts and also to the UNGA Resolutions, the U.S. has engaged in an active program of monitoring and surveillance of driftnet fishing activity through agencies such as the U.S. Coast Guard and National Marine Fisheries Service.[56] In 1993, patrols against driftnet fishing

[52] Principal US legislation regulating driftnet fishing and related activities include:
Driftnet Impact Monitoring, Assessment, and Control Act 1987;
Driftnet Act Amendments of 1990 (Public Law 101–627);
Fishery Conservation Amendments Act 1990;
Dolphin Protection Consumer Information Act 1990;
High Seas Driftnet Fisheries Enforcement Act 1992 (Public Law 102–582);
High Seas Driftnet Fishing Moratorium Protection Act 1995 (Public Law 104–43).
[53] For review of these U.S. laws, see Hewison, *supra* note 46.
[54] High Seas Driftnet Fisheries Enforcement Act, Public Law 102–582 (November 2, 1992), reprinted in (1993) 32 I.L.M. 530.
[55] UN Secretary-General's Report 1997, para. 16.
[56] This program of surveillance has been formalized through a Memorandum of Understanding between the United States Departments of Transportation, Commerce and

were upgraded to include the use of Coast Guard aircraft and cutter patrols in areas of former high seas driftnet fishing activity.[57] As part of that process, plans were announced on March 8, 1993 to promote observance of the moratorium through a series of procedures which were to become operative when U.S. authorities had reasonable grounds to believe that a foreign vessel was engaging in driftnet fishing on the high seas.[58] This program was continued through to 1994.[59] The U.S. Coast Guard also issued a Notice to Mariners in 1996, which sought reports of vessels suspected of using high seas driftnets in the North Pacific Ocean.[60] Between 1996 and 1998, Coast Guard vessels and aircraft also patrolled sectors of the North Pacific Ocean and undertook operations in conjunction with Japan, Canada, and Russia.[61]

The U.S. also has undertaken bilateral and regional initiatives including high seas enforcement action in conjunction with several driftnet fishing nations by way of a series of agreements with Japan, Korea, and Taiwan in the North Pacific.[62] In late 1993, the U.S. and China signed a Memorandum of Understanding providing for reciprocal high seas enforcement against vessels flying the Chinese or U.S. flag equipped for, or engaging in, high seas driftnet fishing.[63] This arrangement was continued in 1997 and 1998. A further U.S. initiative is the U.S.–Italy Driftnet Agreement, under which compensation is paid for the conversion of vessels in the Italian driftnet fleet. Central to this plan is the decommissioning of driftnet vessels and/or their conversion to other types of gear including longlining. The plan, to be financed on a 50/50 cost-sharing basis at a cost of US$235 million, was expected to involve the retrenchment of 676 driftnet vessels by 2000.[64] In

---

Defense signed on October 11, 1993: Report of the Secretary-General, *Large-scale Pelagic Drift-net Fishing and its Impact on the Living Marine Resources of the World's Oceans and Seas*, UN Doc A/50/553, October 12 1995; UN Secretary-General's Report, 1995, para. 11.

[57] Report of the Secretary-General, *Large-scale Pelagic Driftnet Fishing and its Impact on the Living Marine Resources of the World's Oceans and Seas*, UN Doc A/48/451 & Corr. 1, reprinted in 9 *International Organizations and the Law of the Sea Documentary Yearbook 1993* (1993) 75–91; UN Secretary-General's Report, 1995, para. 31.

[58] UN Secretary-General's Report, 1993, para. 35.

[59] The U.S. response to the UN Secretary-General's 1994 report noted that in 1993 the USCG had used a total of 148 cutter patrol days and 829 aircraft patrol days to monitor areas formerly used for high seas driftnet fishing, and that in 1994 a cutter had been maintained full time for 56 days during the peak of the previous driftnet fishing season: Report of the Secretary-General, *Large-scale Pelagic Driftnet Fishing and Its Impact on the Living Marine Resources of the World's Oceans*, UN Doc A/49/469, October 5, 1994, reprinted in 10 *International Organizations and the Law of the Sea Documentary Yearbook 1994* (1996) 128–45; UN Secretary-General's Report, 1994, para. 18.

[60] UN Secretary-General's Report 1997, para. 50.

[61] UN Secretary General's Report 1997, paras. 47–48.

[62] UN Secretary-General's Report 1992, para. 23. The U.S. has indicated that in July 1996 it had cooperated with authorities from Taiwan in taking action against a Taiwanese flag fishing vessel conducting high seas driftnet fishing: UN Secretary-General's Report 1997, para. 46.

[63] UN Secretary-General's Report 1994, para. 46.

[64] UN Secretary-General's Report 1997, para. 23.

addition, the U.S. has also monitored driftnet fishing in the Mediterranean and provided information to Italian officials of driftnet vessel sightings.[65]

2. European Union Response

The response by members of the E.C. to driftnet fishing has varied, no doubt due to the divergent practices and views amongst E.C. members on the question of driftnet fishing. For some E.C. members such as Norway and Sweden, the moratorium had little consequence, as their fishermen did not use driftnets on the high seas. For others such as Italy, which had a longstanding driftnet fishery in the Mediterranean, the matter was of greater importance. The response by the E.C. to the action taken by the UNGA in 1991 was to adopt in 1992 Resolution 345/92, which prohibited the use of driftnets longer than 2.5km by E.C. vessels within both E.C. waters and on the high seas. An exception was established for vessels fishing for albacore tuna in the North Atlantic until December 3, 1993. In a further response, EEC Regulation No 3094/86 provided that from January 1, 1994 all E.C. vessels, with the exception of those operating in the Baltic Sea, the Belts and the Sound, were prohibited from using driftnets which exceeded 2.5km. In the case of the Baltic, the E.C. accepted a recommendation from the International Baltic Sea Fishery Commission which permitted vessels to use driftnets of up to 21km for salmon and sea trout fishing.

The E.C. responses created problems for two fishing areas: the Bay of Biscay and the Mediterranean. In the case of the Bay of Biscay, France initially requested an extension of the exception for the French tuna fishery; however, at the end of 1993 the E.C. Council of Fisheries Ministers refused the request. France subsequently announced that it would respect the E.C.'s 2.5km limit on driftnets and now enforces that limit.[66] In the Mediterranean, Italy pressed for acceptance of a 9km limit on driftnets and proposed that the phase out of all driftnet gear be postponed from 1997 to 2004.[67] This proposal met with resistance within the E.C., while Italian fishermen continued to engage driftnets in the Mediterranean.[68] The continued reluctance of Italian

---

[65] UN Secretary-General's Report 1998, paras. 49–50; Report of the Secretary-General, *Law of the Sea: Large-Scale Pelagic Driftnet Fishing and its Impact on the Living Marine Resources of the World's Oceans and Seas; Unauthorized Fishing in Zones of National Jurisdiction and Its Impact on the Living Marine Resources of the World's Oceans and Seas; and Fisheries By-Catch and Discards and their Impact on the Sustainable Use of the World's Living Marine Resources*, UN Doc A/51/404, September 25, 1996; UN Secretary-General's Report 1996, para. 33; UN Secretary-General's Report 1997, para. 36.

[66] Hayes, M.F., 'Fisheries/Maine Mammals' (1994) 5 *YBIEL* 260 at 262; UN Secretary-General's Report 1996, para. 20.

[67] UN Secretary-General's Report, 1994, para 9.

[68] The FAO reported to the Secretary-General in 1996:
  'Italy's fleet of large-scale pelagic driftnet vessels, totalling about 650 vessels, remains in existence and has commenced fishing for the 1996 season. The fleet targets swordfish in the

authorities to give effect to the UN Resolution and E.C. regulations was the subject of continued comment in the UN Secretary-General's Reports of 1995–7 by international organizations such as the FAO and by NGOs.[69]

The E.C. took a major step in 1998 when the Council of Fisheries Ministers agreed to ban driftnet fishing on the high seas by all vessels flying the flags of E.U. states as of January 1, 2002. This decision was based on two major considerations. First, the use of driftnet gear was proving unselective. Secondly, the previous E.U. regulation permitting driftnets of up to 2.5km was impossible to enforce.[70] Upon the implementation of this ban, driftnetting will be prohibited on the high seas adjacent to all European waters excepting the Baltic Sea.

3. Driftnet Fishing States Responses

The principal large-scale driftnet fishing nations have been Japan, Korea, and Taiwan. All have adopted initiatives to control driftnet fishing in response to the UNGA Resolutions. In the case of the South Pacific, Japanese vessels withdrew from the area not long after the adoption of the Wellington Convention, while there were no Korean vessels engaged in driftnet fishing during the 1990–1 southern albacore tuna season. Japan began to limit driftnet fishing in the North Pacific from January 1992, reducing the permitted fishing area by approximately 40 percent, and also reducing the number of licenses granted to engage in the fishery.[71] Japan subsequently elected to not issue any licenses for large-scale pelagic driftnet fishing from January 1, 1993; in addition, it announced an enforcement plan utilizing six patrol vessels for a total of 495 days.[72] Korea also began to reduce its driftnet fishing activity in 1992, decreasing the number of vessels permitted to operate, reducing the area permitted for high seas driftnet fishing, and also reducing the length of driftnets. Korea also announced in 1992 that it intended to impose a complete moratorium on all large-scale pelagic driftnet fishing from December 31, 1992. Necessary legislative changes were made to give effect to this decision.[73]

Mediterranean sea on a seasonal basis. The Italian fishermen maintain that operating in this fishery is not viable unless they can utilize large-scale pelagic driftnets of at least 9 km in length. The fishermen have therefore asked the Government to authorize the use of such nets or to compensate fishermen if they are required to abandon the fishery.'
UN Secretary-General's Report 1996, para. 20.

[69] See UN Secretary-General's Report 1995, paras. 13, 28, 36; UN Secretary-General's Report 1996, para. 20; UN Secretary-General's Report 1997, para. 40.

[70] Report of the Secretary-General 1998, paras. 34–35.

[71] Report of the Secretary-General, *Large-scale Pelagic Driftnet Fishing and its Impact on the Living Marine Resources of the World's Oceans and Seas*, UN Doc A/47/487, October 6, 1992, reprinted in 8 *International Organizations and the Law of the Sea Documentary Yearbook 1992* (1993) 106–16; UN Secretary-General's Report 1992, para. 30.

[72] UN Secretary General's Report 1993, para. 29.

[73] UN Secretary General's Report 1993, para. 27.

In the case of Taiwan, measures were progressively introduced from 1990, which culminated in 1993 with a decision to not issue any further fishing licenses for large-scale pelagic driftnet fishing vessels.[74]

4. Southwest Pacific Responses

Given the existence of the Wellington Convention imposing a prohibition upon the use of driftnets in the Southwest Pacific, it comes as no surprise that states in the region have been particularly strong supporters of the UN moratorium and that this support is reflected in the domestic implementation of initiatives to prohibit driftnet fishing.[75] Australia and New Zealand have been especially active in giving effect to the Wellington Convention and to the UN moratorium. They provided the UN Secretary-General with extensive reports on their efforts in 1992–4. There is no evidence, however, that any South Pacific states have taken any action against high seas driftnet fishing by foreign fishing vessels.

In respect to compliance, apart from isolated incidents in some regions and a reluctance by a small number of states to fully implement the UNGA Resolutions, the degree of global acceptance of the UNGA Resolution prohibiting the use of driftnets on the high seas appears to have been high. There have been some problem areas, with the Mediterranean and parts of the North Pacific being the most prominent. In 1994, for example, it was reported by the General Fisheries Council for the Mediterranean that violations of the driftnet moratorium were still occurring, especially in those areas where monitoring, control, and surveillance was lacking. The FAO noted in 1994 a claim made by Greenpeace International that a French fleet of sixty vessels continued to engage in driftnet fishing for tuna in the North-East Atlantic.[76] The 1994 UN Secretary-General's Report to the General Assembly on Driftnet Fishing noted the following instances of reported fishing activity in violation of the UNGA Resolution:

- French vessels and one Irish vessel engaged in tuna fishing in the North Atlantic;
- Italian vessels (estimated at 600) and some vessels from Morocco and Spain using driftnets in excess of the EC specific limit of 2.5km;
- an Indonesian vessel was prosecuted for driftnet fishing in the Australian EEZ;
- a Taiwanese vessel was sighted engaging in driftnet fishing in Solomon Islands waters.[77]

[74] UN Secretary-General's Report 1994, para. 19.
[75] See the discussion of the response by Southwest Pacific states in Hewison, *supra* note 2 at 576–7, and Hewison, *supra* note 19 at 457–64.
[76] UN Secretary-General's Report 1994, para. 9.
[77] UN Secretary-General's Report 1994.

Significantly, there were no reports of large-scale driftnet fishing by prominent driftnet fishing nations such as Japan, Korea, or Taiwan, though isolated incidents have been reported.[78] However, these 1994 reports also
conceded that difficulties existed with verification. The FAO report to the
Secretary-General in 1994 noted:

> Little information is available concerning the use of large-scale pelagic drift-net ves-
> sels in the Atlantic Ocean. According to industry sources, vessels with a drift-net fish-
> ing capacity continue to be based in the region, and such vessels could be operating
> seasonally in the Atlantic Ocean. Monitoring of their activities is difficult.[79]

Reports of the Secretary-General for the period 1996–8, while containing
continued evidence of small-scale violation of the UNGA Resolution, do not
highlight any major breach, with the exception of Italy's driftnet fleet operating in the Mediterranean. During that period, the following 'violations' were
noted:

- a Spanish fleet with driftnets of about seven km in length operated in
  the Alboran sea in the Mediterranean in 1996;
- Greenpeace reports of vessels from Italy, Japan, South Korea,
  Morocco, Tunisia, Turkey, Algeria, Malta, and Albania operating in
  the Mediterranean;
- concerns expressed by the World Wildlife Fund over the continued use
  of driftnets by fishing vessels from China, Italy, France, Ireland;
- a small number of Chinese and Taiwanese registered vessels operating
  in the North Pacific.[80]

H. CONCLUSION

The response by the international community to concerns over high seas
pelagic driftnet fishing makes for an interesting study of the impact of non-
binding international norms. While driftnet fishing had been an ongoing issue
throughout the 1980s, the impetus for a global response to the practice arose
only in the late 1980s, following the particular concerns of a small group of
states and a region in which high seas driftnets were prominently being used.
Notwithstanding the arguments over the true environmental impact of drift-

---

[78] In 1995, the U.S. Coast Guard pursued a stateless vessel found to be engaging in driftnet
fishing in the Pacific. The *Luyan Bu 6006* was eventually subject to investigation by Taiwanese
authorities who concluded that the vessel had been most recently flagged as Honduran and carried mainly a Taiwanese crew. Following capture, Taiwan revoked the captain and crew's
licenses for two years: Areias, A., 'Fisheries/Marine Mammals' (1995) 6 *Yearbook of
International Environmental Law* 333 at 334.

[79] UN Secretary-General's Report 1994, para. 27.

[80] UN Secretary-General's Report 1996, paras. 20, 42; UN Secretary-General's Report 1997,
para. 47.

net fishing[81] and the relatively few areas in the world where extensive high seas driftnet fishing was being conducted, the international community in the period 1989–91 moved towards a position where a global moratorium was approved. In addition, states in the Southwest Pacific also were prepared to adopt a legally binding moratorium. This has been reinforced by the E.U. decision to ban high seas driftnets.

Given the essentially non-binding nature of the global moratorium, how has this been achieved? First, it should be noted that the response to driftnet fishing was not an isolated attempt to deal with fishing issues. Rather it was part of a much larger global effort to address concerns over the environmental and resource implications of fishing practices in the late 1980s and early 1990s at a time when 'sustainable development' was becoming influential.[82] Recall that the year following the adoption of UNGA 46/215 the international community came together for the 1992 United Nations Conference on Environment and Development at Rio de Janeiro. Secondly, the continued monitoring by the United Nations of the implementation of the global moratorium has had the effect of making states aware that a close watch is being maintained on state practice. In that respect, the annual Secretary-General's reports have contained not only contributions by individual states, but also reports from international organizations and NGOs, ensuring a degree of independence in the monitoring that would not have been possible if only states had contributed to the process. Thirdly, the role of the U.S. should not be underestimated. Prior to the adoption of the UN Resolutions, the three major areas of driftnet activity were the North Pacific, South Pacific, and the Mediterranean. Through U.S. monitoring and surveillance in the North Pacific, a close check could be maintained on driftnet fishing in that region. In the Mediterranean, the U.S. was able to exert leverage against Italy, with the result that the Italian government has implemented a program of retrenching driftnet vessels. U.S. laws prohibiting the landing of driftnet catch and also providing for trade sanctions against states acting in violation of the global moratorium also have been influential. The U.S. therefore has played an important role in 'enforcing' the UNGA Resolution. Finally, the global moratorium has been given legal effect through not only the individual domestic laws and policies of U.N. member states, but also at a regional level through the Wellington Convention and, most recently, through E.U. initiatives.

Ultimately, the campaign to control high seas pelagic driftnet fishing through non-binding legal means seems to have succeeded. In the background, however, states have employed a variety of legal measures at both the

---

[81] A critique of these arguments is found in Burke, Freeberg and Miles, *supra* note 41.

[82] See the discussion in Goydon, K.B., 'Destructive Fishing Practices and Conflicting International Agendas: Inadequate Structures and Possible Solutions' (1992) 13 *N.Y.U. J. Int'l & Comp. L.* 359–79.

individual and regional level to give the UNGA resolution more 'teeth'. The control of high seas pelagic driftnet fishing has therefore been achieved through an interesting mix of both hard and soft law and global, regional and national initiatives.

Pesticides and Chemicals

The Requirement of Prior Informed Consent

MOHAMED ALI MEKOUAR

INTRODUCTION

International trade in highly dangerous chemicals and pesticides became the subject of a global treaty in September 1998 when senior representatives of nearly 100 nations participating in a Conference of Plenipotentiaries in Rotterdam adopted the Convention on the Prior Informed Consent Procedure for Certain Hazardous Chemicals and Pesticides in International Trade. Upon entry into force, the Convention will provide a firm international legal foundation for the prior informed consent (PIC) procedure, making it illegal for states parties to export banned or severely restricted pesticides and chemicals without the explicit agreement of the importing countries.[1] Previously, the PIC system was grounded primarily on two legally non-binding instruments: (1) the 1985 FAO International Code of Conduct on the Distribution and Use of Pesticides (the 'Code')[2]; and (2) the 1987 UNEP London Guidelines for the Exchange of Information on Chemicals in International Trade (the 'Guidelines').[3] In 1989, both the FAO Code and the UNEP Guidelines were amended to include specific provisions on PIC.

The PIC concept is defined in almost identical terms by the two instruments, the only difference being the reference to 'pesticides' in the Code (Article 2), and to 'chemicals' in the Guidelines (Paragraphs 1(g), (h)). For the purposes of the Code and the Guidelines alike, PIC is used as a principle and as a procedure. PIC refers 'to the principle that international shipment of

---

[1] The Convention was signed by 61 country representatives. (1998) 15 *Earth Negotiations Bulletin*, September 14, 1998. It remained open for signature until September 1999 and enters into force after receipt of the 50th instrument of ratification.

[2] The FAO Conference adopted the Code at its 23rd Session, Res. 10/85 of November 28, 1985.

[3] UNEP's Governing Council adopted the Guidelines by Decision 14/27 of June 17, 1987.

a pesticide [or] a chemical that is banned or severely restricted in order to protect human health or the environment should not proceed without the agreement, where such agreement exists, or contrary to the decision of the designated national authority in the participating importing country'. PIC procedure 'means the procedure for formally obtaining and disseminating the decisions of importing countries as to whether they wish to receive future shipments of pesticides [or] chemicals that have been banned or severely restricted. A specific procedure was established for selecting pesticides [or] chemicals for initial implementation of the PIC procedures. These include pesticides [or] chemicals that have been previously banned or severely restricted as well as certain pesticide formulations which are acutely toxic.'

This study reviews the PIC provisions of the Code and the Guidelines and discusses their implementation, with a view to assessing the degree of compliance with these two non-binding instruments by states concerned. It will address, successively, the drafting history of the two texts, their substantive content, their institutional arrangements, the role of interest groups in promoting them, incentives and disincentives to comply with them, and their normative impact.

A. DRAFTING HISTORY

Originally, both instruments contained provisions dealing with information exchange and export notification in respect of pesticides and chemicals in international trade, without any particular clause formally requiring PIC. Information exchange was the main thrust of the initial version of the Guidelines, as indicated by the title.[4] 'Information exchange' was also the title of the original version of Article 9 of the Code.[5] According to these provisions, in order to protect health and the environment, as well as to increase chemical safety, governments are expected to inform each other of control actions taken to ban or severely restrict pesticides and chemicals, and the reasons therefore, to provide additional related information upon request, and to notify importing states regarding the first export of pesticides or chemicals following a control action.

Although helpful, the information/notification measures were not sufficient in practice, especially with respect to third world nations' interests.[6] As the World Commission on Environment and Development recognized, third world importers 'have no way to effectively control trade in chemicals that have been banned or severely restricted in exporting countries'. It therefore recommended

---

[4] UNEP, 'Exchange of Information on Chemicals in International Trade', in *Environmental Law Guidelines and Principles* (1987) 10.

[5] FAO, Report of the Conference of FAO, 23rd Session, Rome, November 9–28, 1985 (1985) 75.

[6] Wodageneh, A., 'Trouble in Store' (1997) 8 *Our Planet* 6, 12–14.

that governments of major chemical-producing countries 'should strictly regulate the export to developing countries of those chemicals for which authorization for domestic sale has not been sought or given, by extending requirements for prior notification and information exchange to them'.[7]

The FAO Conference voiced a similar concern in 1987 about the serious consequences of export to developing countries of pesticides that have been banned or severely restricted in industrialized countries. Lack of adequate manpower and infrastructure to regulate and control the use of such pesticides in those countries was particularly stressed. The Conference felt that a requirement of PIC from importing countries would represent a valuable tool to address such problems,[8] and the Conference thus decided that PIC should be incorporated in the Code.[9]

Subsequent action taken to implement that decision included an Expert Consultation (March 1988) and a Government Consultation (January 1989), where agreement was reached on the amendments required for including PIC in the Code, and on the operation of the PIC procedure.[10] The following session of the FAO Conference endorsed the proposed revisions.[11] As a result, the PIC system was introduced in the Code through substantive changes to Article 2 (definitions) and Article 9 (procedure), in addition to more detailed 'Guidelines on the Operation of PIC' appended to Resolution 6/89.[12]

A parallel process to revise the Guidelines for PIC purposes took place within UNEP. Even prior to preparing the Guidelines themselves, UNEP had developed a 'Provisional Notification Scheme for Banned and Severely Restricted Chemicals', which Governing Council Decision 12/14 of May 28, 1984 adopted. Coordinated by UNEP's International Register of Potentially Toxic Chemicals (IRPTC), the scheme provided for information exchange on control actions to prohibit or restrict the use of chemicals. The working group considered development of broader guidelines on this matter at its second session in 1985, and finalized the Guidelines in London in 1987, during its third session. Decision 14/27 (1987) adopted the Guidelines, replacing the provisional scheme.[13]

In accordance with the same Decision 14/27, UNEP created a working group of experts to develop the concept of PIC and methods for its inclusion

[7] WCED, *Our Common Future* (1987), 225–6.

[8] FAO, Report of the Conference of FAO, 24th Session, Rome, November 7–27, 1987, 30.

[9] Resolution 5/87 of November 26, 1987, *ibid.* at 32.

[10] FAO, Report of the Tenth Session of the Committee on Agriculture (COAG), CL 95/5 June 1989 (1989), 19.

[11] Resolution 6/89 of November 29, 1989 FAO, Report of the Conference of FAO, 25th Session, Rome, November 11–29, 1989, 33.

[12] *Ibid.*, Appendix E; FAO, International Code of Conduct on the Distribution and Use of Pesticides (Amended to include Prior Informed Consent) (1990).

[13] Rummel-Bulska, I., 'United Nations Environment Programme' (1990) 1 *YBIEL* 369–96, 380.

in the Guidelines. In the course of several working group meetings, the proposal for incorporating the PIC requirement in the Guidelines was discussed and finalized.[14] Soon thereafter, by Decision 15/30 of May 25, 1989, the 'Amended London Guidelines for the Exchange of Information on Chemicals in International Trade' were formally adopted by UNEP's Governing Council.[15]

As the sequence of events makes clear, the two processes that led to the incorporation of PIC in the Code and the Guidelines were approximately concomitant. Though conducted separately, both took place between 1987 and 1989. Both also involved technical debates and building political consensus, which required lengthy discussions through experts' meetings and government consultations. Ultimately, the end-result was virtually the same: an identical concept of PIC and a similar procedure for its implementation. The corresponding provisions were embodied in an existing soft-law instrument, as opposed to creating a new binding or non-binding text.

This convergence of approaches was not inadvertent. Although the two processes were carried out independently by FAO and UNEP, the two organizations closely consulted each other and coordinated their efforts.[16] Such a full collaboration not only yielded a conceptual synergy in the design of the PIC procedure, but also allowed the creation of a joint mechanism for its operation under both instruments. Furthermore, since each organization had previously adopted a non-binding text on pesticides/chemicals and put it into operation, not surprisingly both of them favored the soft-law option regarding the related PIC clauses, at a time when it would have been extremely laborious to reach political consensus on the need for a treaty.

B. SUBSTANTIVE CONTENT OF THE INSTRUMENTS

The Code and the Guidelines differ significantly in their respective scope and objectives. The Code deals with pesticides only, but broadly covers all aspects of pesticide management: manufacture, testing, use, control, labeling, packaging, advertising, distribution, trade, storage, disposal, etc., including information exchange. The Guidelines in contrast deal with all chemicals, both

---

[14] *Ibid.*

[15] UNEP, London Guidelines for the Exchange of Information on Chemicals in International Trade, Amended 1989 (1989).

[16] This is illustrated, for instance, in Resolution 6/89 of FAO's Conference on the inclusion of PIC in the Code, where note is taken of 'the decisions of the Governing Council of UNEP to amend the "London Guidelines" . . . to include Prior Informed Consent, and the emphasis placed . . . on the necessity of cooperation between UNEP and FAO on the implementation of Prior Informed Consent'. FAO, *supra* note 11 at 33. Similarly, para. 7 of the 'Introduction to the Guidelines', as amended in 1989, stresses the complementarity of the Guidelines and the Code, characterizing the latter as 'the primary guidance for the management on pesticides internationally'. UNEP, *supra* note 15 at 1.

industrial and pesticides, but are more particularly aimed at controlling international trade in hazardous chemicals by means of appropriate exchange of information. These variations do not affect the PIC requirement. The only relevant difference is the type of substances subject to PIC: only pesticides under the Code, all chemicals under the Guidelines.

The original pre-PIC information exchange and export notification procedures provided participating countries with a 'one-way flow' of information about regulatory measures taken in other countries to reduce the risk of damage from certain pesticides/chemicals. To this effect: (1) states received notification of control actions taken to ban or to restrict severely pesticides/chemicals so that their competent authorities were given the opportunity to assess the environmental and health dangers associated with those products, and could make informed decisions about their importation and use (Article 9.1–2 of the Code; Paragraph 6 of the Guidelines); (2) when a pesticide/chemical that had been banned or severely restricted in a country was to be exported for the first time, relevant information thereon was to be provided by the country of export to the country of destination in order to alert the latter to the fact that the export was about to occur (Article 9.3–6 of the Code; Paragraph 8 of the Guidelines).

The PIC requirement goes beyond this system of information exchange: importing countries are expected to react to such notifications and make a formal decision regarding future import and use of the pesticide/chemical in their country. Upon receipt of notification of a control action, states willing to participate in PIC as importing countries must decide whether: (i) they will not allow the import of such pesticide/chemical in the future; (ii) they will allow it under specified conditions; or (iii) they will allow it generally. The decision may be a final or an interim one. If a state chooses not to accept the import of a pesticide/chemical, the ban should equally apply to the domestic production of the same substance (Article 9.7–11 of the Code and the FAO 'Guidelines on the Operation of PIC'; Paragraph 7 and Annex II of the Guidelines).

The PIC procedure consists of various steps involving triangular collaboration among countries of export, countries of import, and FAO (under the Code) or UNEP's IRPCT (under the Guidelines). These steps may be briefly described as follows:[17]

- notification to FAO/UNEP by the country concerned of final regulatory actions to ban or severely restrict the use of a pesticide/chemical;
- review of the notification by FAO/UNEP to ensure compliance with the definitions contained in the Code/Guidelines;

---

[17] For a detailed description of these steps, see FAO/UNEP, *Guidelines for Governments— Operation of the Prior Informed Consent Procedure for Banned or Severely Restricted Chemicals in International Trade, Joint FAO/UNEP Programme for the Operation of the Prior Informed Consent* (1991).

- transmittal by FAO/UNEP of the notification and any additional related information to the competent national authorities for their consideration;
- within the ninety following days, decision of potential importing countries on future acceptability of a pesticide/chemical;
- communication of such importation decisions to FAO/UNEP for their further dissemination to all participating countries;
- communication by exporting countries to their export industry of importation decisions;
- measures by exporting countries to ensure that no shipments are made by their export industry contrary to importing countries' decisions.

Thus, responsibilities for the regular shipment of PIC pesticides/chemicals are shared between exporting and importing countries, with FAO and UNEP acting as intermediaries and advisers. The country of export is required to notify any control actions, thereby informing other countries of the hazards connected with the substances concerned. Having had prior notice of the risks, importing countries are in a position to decide on possible regulatory measures. In turn, when notified of importation decisions, the exporting country must be sure that unwanted pesticides/chemicals are not exported to the objecting countries. Participating countries should not use PIC as a trade barrier, inconsistently with the relevant provisions of GATT/WTO (Article 9.10.3 of the Code; Paragraph 2(c) of the Guidelines). Likewise, they should take into account proprietary rights over technical data provided for the purposes of PIC operation (Article 9.6 of the Code; Paragraph 11 of the Guidelines).

Pesticides and chemicals[18] are subject to PIC if their use has been entirely prohibited or severely restricted (virtually all uses banned nationally), refused approval for first time use, or withdrawn from the market because of environmental or health reasons, as a result of a final government regulatory action. The PIC procedure normally applies to any such pesticide or chemical upon notification to, and further listing by, FAO or UNEP. An earlier system required agreement on a priority list of PIC pesticides/chemicals before the PIC procedure could start and the Code and the Guidelines foresaw the listing of an initial set of those pesticides/chemicals previously banned or severely restricted in at least five countries. As of January 1, 1992, however, any notification of a government regulatory action regarding a pesticide/

---

[18] Under the Code, a 'pesticide' is 'any substance or mixture of substances intended for preventing, destroying or controlling any pest' (Art. 2). For the purposes of the Guidelines, a chemical means 'a chemical substance whether by itself or in a mixture or preparation, whether manufactured or obtained from nature and includes such substances used as industrial chemicals and pesticides' (Para. 1). Pharmaceuticals, radioactive materials, food additives, as well as small quantities of chemicals imported for research purposes or as personal effects are not, as a matter of principle, under the purview of the Guidelines (Para. 3).

chemical should automatically qualify the latter for inclusion in the PIC pro-cedure.[19] Based on these notifications, the list of PIC pesticides/chemicals must be regularly updated by FAO/UNEP. For each new pesticide/chemical that is banned or severely restricted, a Decision Guidance Document (DGD), providing relevant information thereon, must be prepared by FAO/UNEP and sent, together with the notification, to all participating countries, either for action by countries of import or for information to other countries.

C. INSTITUTIONAL ARRANGEMENTS

Implementation of the PIC provisions of the Code and the Guidelines involves national bodies from the participating countries as well as inter-national action by FAO and UNEP. This is clearly stated in the Code (Article 9) and in the Guidelines (Paragraph 5), where the respective roles of these entities are delineated.

At the national level, states deciding to be part of the PIC system must des-ignate a governmental authority with appropriate powers to perform admin-istrative functions regarding information exchange and importation decisions in respect of PIC pesticides/chemicals. A Designated National Authority (DNA) may have been nominated earlier under the ordinary information exchange procedure. In such case, its designation may be reconfirmed, with a specific indication that such a DNA is vested with PIC-related responsibili-ties.[20] States may also appoint more than one DNA if they are needed for distinct purposes. States may designate, for example, separate DNAs for dif-ferent categories of products (pesticides, chemicals) or types of procedures (information exchange, PIC). Designation of DNAs is important even in those countries not participating in PIC, for purposes of receiving and dis-seminating information on hazardous pesticides/chemicals.

DNAs are the official national focal points of PIC participating countries for international communications. As such, DNAs should be empowered to communicate with each other and with international organizations con-cerned, directly or through other appropriate channels, in order to exchange information and to convey decisions concerning PIC pesticides/chemicals. They also should be authorized to submit reports in this regard, on their own initiative, to other DNAs or to international organizations. States should ensure that DNAs are adequately equipped with the necessary resources to allow them to assume their PIC responsibilities. As soon as a DNA is desig-nated or changed, the state concerned must provide its name and address to FAO/UNEP for registration. This allows a Register of DNAs to be main-tained, updated and disseminated.

---

[19] FAO/UNEP, *supra* note 17 at 5.   [20] *Ibid.*

Internationally, implementation of the PIC procedure provides a good example of operational arrangements involving two international organizations. As the Code and the Guidelines were developed in different fora, FAO and UNEP could have opted for entirely self-reliant implementing mechanisms, one for pesticides and the other for chemicals. Instead, they favored a system to manage jointly the PIC procedure, not only to avoid duplication of efforts and waste of resources, but also to benefit from their combined expertise in the field of chemicals.[21] Based on their respective mandates, the lead agency on technical matters may be one or the other organization: FAO for pesticides, UNEP for other chemicals.

Such an institutional cooperative effort is clearly echoed in both instruments.[22] Under the Guidelines, for instance, UNEP is called upon: (i) to develop with FAO a system for information exchange; (ii) to share with FAO the operational responsibility for PIC and jointly manage common elements; (iii) to collaborate with FAO in reviewing the implementation of the PIC procedure. These provisions were further specified in the 'Guidance for Governments', an operational document which was jointly developed by the two organizations.

In order to facilitate the joint implementation, the organizations created a Joint FAO/UNEP Group of Experts on PIC to advise the secretariats of both organizations on matters pertaining to the operation of PIC.[23] FAO and UNEP also agreed to maintain a current register of PIC decisions reported by importing countries, which 'can be made available to exporters unsure of the status of a particular chemical in a specific country'.[24] It was decided that the database containing PIC-related information will be kept by UNEP's International Register of Potentially Toxic Chemicals (IRPTC), in view of its specific mandate on chemical data gathering and dissemination. The two organizations agreed to deal with the other operational aspects of the PIC procedure jointly. These include, in particular, the review of notifications of control actions, the preparation of Decision Guidance Documents, the listing of PIC pesticides/chemicals, the development of reporting criteria, and the preparation and dissemination of joint publications.

D. THE ROLE OF INTEREST GROUPS

Interest groups from civil society are not very visible in the PIC provisions of the Code, and even less so in those of the Guidelines. With the exception of

[21] In this respect, para. 7 of the 'Introduction' to the Guidelines explicitly states that they 'should be implemented in a non-duplicative manner for the different classes of chemicals'. A similar provision is found in FAO's Guidelines, *supra* note 11, Appendix E.
[22] Art. 9 of the Code and Para. 5 of the FAO Guidelines.
[23] Pallemaerts, M., 'Regulation of Chemicals' (1990) 1 *YBIEL* 163–6, 163.
[24] FAO/UNEP, *supra* note 17 at 14.

industry, groups representing the interests of the public at large; consumer, health, and environmental associations; and grassroots organizations appear to have been marginalized. This may not be evident on a first reading of the Code, because the standards of conduct for the distribution and use of pesticides set out in the Code are generally meant to govern both public and private entities. In addition to agencies several segments of society are addressed: 'industry, including manufacturers, trade associations, formulators and distributors; users; and public-sector organizations such as environmental groups, consumer groups and trade unions'.[25]

Nevertheless, the overall responsibility for most aspects of pesticide management remains in governmental institutions, acting in collaboration with the pesticide/chemical industry. This is explicitly stated in various parts of the Code, including the PIC clauses (Articles 3.1, 9, and *passim*). This also may be implicit in the Guidelines' silence on the role of non-governmental organizations generally. Such a marginalization of NGOs in the PIC provisions of the two instruments is probably partly due to the fact that during the period over which they were developed (1987–9), inter-governmental fora were far less open to civil society than they are today.

The pesticide/chemical industry has remained the main non-public actor under the PIC system, which is understandable given its prominent economic and professional interest in this field. Other interest groups have occasionally made contributions to the promotion of PIC. This may be illustrated by the interesting example of an industry-oriented undertaking: the 'Code of Ethics on the International Trade in Chemicals' (the 'Code of Ethics'), adopted on August 9, 1994. The instrument is one of voluntary self-regulation and was largely developed by and for the industry and NGO parties concerned under the auspices of UNEP acting as a 'facilitator'.[26]

UNEP initiated the process by mandating a working group of experts to advise it on further regulatory action in the field of chemical management to ensure full attainment of the objectives set out in the Guidelines. Two main options were then under consideration: a convention or a soft law document. The second approach prevailed in the working group, provoking strong criticism from several developing countries and NGOs. The lack of consensus apparently caused UNEP to reduce its commitment to the exercise and to place 'primary responsibility for it on industry'.[27] The eventual Code of

---

[25] Art. 1.4. For the purposes of the Code: (i) 'industry' means 'all those organizations and individuals engaged in manufacturing, formulating or marketing pesticides and pesticide products'; (ii) 'public sector groups' means, but is not limited to, 'scientific associations; farmer groups; citizen's organizations; environmental, consumer and health organizations; and labor unions' (Art. 2).

[26] Pallemaerts, M., 'International Transfer of Restricted or Prohibited Substances, Regulation of Chemicals' (1994) 5 *YBIEL* 209–18, 213.

[27] Pallemaerts, M., 'International Transfer of Restricted or Prohibited Substances, Regulation of Chemicals' (1991) 2 *YBIEL* 170–5, 171.

Ethics thus was not formally approved by UNEP, but it is the result of four 'informal consultations' which took place between 1992 and 1994.[28] Hence, such a product may be viewed as a 'soft-soft' text: soft because of its non-binding nature, and soft in view of its informal preparation/adoption process.

The Code of Ethics consists of a number of guiding principles and standards dealing with the production and management of chemicals in international trade, taking into account their entire life cycle (Paragraph 1). Its scope is broader than that of the London Guidelines, whose focus is on PIC and information exchange. Also, while the Guidelines are mainly addressed to governments, the Code of Ethics is basically intended for private-sector parties.[29] In this respect, it is different from the FAO Code of Conduct as well, the latter being predominately aimed at governmental institutions. Nevertheless, the two Codes are similar in their substantive coverage. All three instruments have the PIC requirement as a common denominator. Making explicit reference to the Code and to the Guidelines, the Code of Ethics calls upon chemical producers, formulators, and traders to cooperate with importing countries and comply with their PIC decisions, ensuring 'implementation of the export notifications procedures for banned or severely restricted chemicals' (Paragraph 19).[30]

E. INCENTIVES AND DISINCENTIVES TO COMPLIANCE

In addition to obtaining critical information on hazardous pesticides and chemicals through the PIC system, technical assistance and financial aid are surely the major motivations for compliance with the PIC procedure.[31] Specific provisions in this respect were included both in the Code (Article 1.5) and in the Guidelines (Paragraph 15). The latter, as amended in 1989 for the purposes of the PIC requirement, provide for various incentives, such as: technical and financial assistance by funding agencies and bilateral donors for institutional strengthening and specialized training; technical and financial

---

[28] UNEP, Mid-Term Report on the Implementation of the Programme for the Development and Periodic Review of Environmental Law for the 1990s (1993–1996) (1996) 40.

[29] 'Private sector parties' is meant to cover industry as well as 'workers and their representatives, environmental and consumer groups and other non-governmental organizations, and the public' (Para. h 2(d)).

[30] Following its adoption, the Code of Ethics was distributed to 185 industry associations and 77 NGOs around the world. By July 1996, organizations that had expressed their intention to apply it included the European Chemical Industry Council, the European Fertilizer Manufacturers' Association, the International Union of Pure and Applied Chemistry, the Japan Responsible Care Council (75 member companies), and the Spanish Chemical Industry Federation. UNEP, *supra* note 28 at 40.

[31] Saunders, P., 'Development Cooperation and Compliance with International Environmental Law, Panel on Are International Institutions Doing Their Job?' [1996] *Proc. A.S.I.L.*, 360.

assistance by states with advanced chemical programmes to developing countries in order to improve their capacity and infrastructure; interchange of
experts among participating countries with a view to sharing experiences and
assisting one another.

Technical and financial support are particularly critical in those countries
that lack the basic infrastructure and necessary expertise to evaluate, manage,
and reduce pesticide/chemical risks under local conditions.[32] Concern about
the use of such products is widespread because some of the more toxic chemical compounds have come into increasing use after most of the older
organochlorines were banned or severely restricted in many countries.[33]
Hence, the continuous need for external aid to help those countries
strengthen their capabilities effectively to operate their pesticide/chemical
control schemes.

Disincentives for compliance with the PIC provisions of the Code and the
Guidelines stem from two main sources. First, the non-binding nature of
these instruments and the correlated absence of enforcement measures, sanctions for non-compliance, and mechanisms for dispute resolution are obviously not conducive to firm and regular commitments. Secondly, economic
loss resulting from inhibited trade in PIC pesticides/chemicals is likely to
discourage compliance with the PIC requirement, especially on the part of
producing/exporting countries. In this context, a further disincentive to compliance may be the fear of possible inconsistencies between the PIC procedure
and the WTO trade provisions.[34]

F. IMPLEMENTATION AND COMPLIANCE

Under the Code and the Guidelines, states are required to take appropriate
measures, including regulatory systems and institutional arrangements, to
implement the PIC procedure (Article 6 of the Code; Paragraph 4 of the
Guidelines). Paragraph 2 of the Guidelines provides examples of possible
implementing actions, including the development of model legislation to
improve chemical control; the creation of national registers of toxic chemicals
and pesticides; and the preparation of manuals for better information collec-

---

[32] FAO, *Analysis of Government Responses to the Second Questionnaire on the State of Implementation of the International Code of Conduct on the Distribution and Use of Pesticides* (1996), 4–6.

[33] It is estimated that there currently are more than 100,000 tons of obsolete pesticides in developing countries, including large amounts of highly persistent and toxic compounds. These are regarded as hazardous waste, as they can no longer be used because they have been banned while still in store or have deteriorated through prolonged storage. In Africa alone, the cost of cleaning up of obsolete stocks is about $80 to $100 million. The donor community is called upon to provide assistance to help solve this problem. Wodageneh, *supra* note 6 at 12–14.

[34] In this regard, note that the trade-related provisions of the PIC Convention were eventually placed in its Preamble, after lengthy and inconclusive debates during the negotiations.

tion and dissemination. The institutional mechanisms (designation of DNAs) and reporting requirements for banned or severely restricted chemicals (notification of regulatory actions and importation decisions) also directly pertain to implementation of PIC.

In accordance with these provisions, PIC participating countries have taken numerous actions. As of December 31, 1997, no fewer than 154 states had elected to participate in the PIC procedure and had officially appointed their Designated National Authorities.[35] On the same date, 219 DNAs had been registered by FAO and UNEP.[36] Decisions on imports have been regularly communicated and disseminated among parties, while updated compilations of such import responses are also periodically published and distributed.[37] Notably, for most PIC pesticides/chemicals, a large number of import decisions consist of 'no consent' responses. In those instances where 'consent' decisions were made, a justification was generally given, and permitted or banned uses were always specified.[38]

As part of the implementing measures, many countries adopted or amended legislation or regulations to accommodate control actions.[39] In this regard, the adoption by the European Union of E.C. Regulation 2455 of July 23, 1992, concerning Community exports and imports of certain dangerous chemicals, was an important legal development. Replacing a previous Regulation that had provided for a mandatory export notification scheme, the new Regulation introduced a formal PIC procedure in line with the FAO/UNEP-sponsored PIC system. Annex II of the Regulation, which specifies PIC chemicals, was originally left blank.[40] In 1994, an amendment to the Regulation inserted in that Annex a list of pesticides/chemicals subject to the

---

[35] The number of PIC participating countries increased over the years, but was high right from the beginning: 109 in 1991; 116 in 1992. Pallemaerts, *supra* note 27 at 170; Pallemaerts, M., 'International Transfer of Restricted or Prohibited Substances, Regulation of Chemicals' (1992) 3 *YBIEL* 281–7, 284.

[36] A complete list of DNAs, as updated in June 1997, is contained in FAO/UNEP, PIC Circular VII—July 1997, FAO/UNEP Joint Programme for the Operation of the Prior Informed Consent (1997).

[37] FAO/UNEP, Update of PIC Circular VII—January 1998, FAO/UNEP Joint Programme for the Operation of the Prior Informed Consent (1998). A recent compilation of import responses can be found in PIC Circular VII, *supra* note 36.

[38] Following are some examples of consent decisions that were reported in the Update of PIC Circular VII, *ibid.*: (i) Brazil gave an interim consent response to the import of Aldrin pending final decision, with all agricultural uses banned; (ii) Australia gave a consent response to the import of EDB (1,2-dibromoethane), indicating that it would ban the use of EDB on June 30, 1999.

[39] For instance, by a Decree of November 30, 1993, Madagascar discontinued the use of DDT-based products for agricultural practices, allowing it only for malaria vector control; in Kuwait, Decree 95/1995 prohibited the importation of Hexachlorobenzene and Lindane; in Colombia, Dieldrin's importation, production and use were banned by Res. 10255 of 1993; and there are numerous other examples of similar regulatory actions taken in countries worldwide. FAO/UNEP, *ibid.*

[40] Pallemaerts (1992), *supra* note 35 at 285.

FAO/UNEP PIC procedure,[41] making this procedure enforceable in E.U. countries as part of European Community law and imposing legal obligations directly on E.U. exporters of PIC chemicals, thereby crystallizing in hard law provisions what had been previously voluntary practices. In 1996, the E.U. PIC Regulation was further amended so that more detailed information would be supplied in the notifications, with a view to improving control of PIC chemicals' shipments by importing countries.[42]

In order to gather reliable information on the implementation of the Code, a questionnaire was sent to FAO member nations in 1993. The basic purpose was to monitor the extent of observance of the Code by governments, industry, and other parties involved in pesticide management and use, in addition to identifying deficiencies that require priority attention.[43] Out of the 177 addressees, ninety-nine countries completed and returned the questionnaire by October 31, 1994. The information received through the responses was computerized and analyzed. The results of that investigation provide interesting information about compliance with the PIC system, although some of the analysis now may be outdated in part. The main general conclusions drawn from the study can be summarized as follows:[44]

- all countries reported that they had found the Code 'useful', and several developing countries specifically indicated that they were relying on its provisions for guidance in controlling the introduction and use of pesticides;
- there was evidence of significant progress towards compliance with various provisions of the Code, particularly in the Asia and Pacific region, but deficiencies in pesticide control continued in many countries, notably in Africa and Latin America;
- numerous countries used relevant provisions of the Code, together with the recommended standards in the corresponding technical guidelines, as the basis for promoting enforcement procedures;
- several countries were able to increase their infrastructural and technical capabilities in pesticide management through enforcement of improved regulations and participation in the PIC procedure.

As to more specific questions regarding the degree of compliance with the PIC procedure as set out in Article 9 of the Code, PIC participating countries reported the following:[45]

---

[41] Pallemaerts, *supra* note 26 at 217.

[42] Pallemaerts, M., 'International Transfer of Restricted or Prohibited Substances' (1996) 7 *YBIEL* 176–82, 182.

[43] FAO, *Analysis of Government Responses to the First Questionnaire on the State of Implementation of the International Code of Conduct on the Distribution and Use of Pesticides* (1993).

[44] *Ibid.*, at 3–6.   [45] *Ibid.*, at 82–9.

- most countries (94 percent) found the PIC procedure 'useful'; the rest (6 percent) thought it was of 'little value', but none of the reporting countries felt that it was 'not useful';
- on the question of control actions taken to ban or severely restrict the use of a pesticide, 34 percent of responding developing countries reported that they did not notify FAO of such actions;
- globally, 27 percent of reporting, PIC-participating, pesticide-importing countries had not yet established internal procedures for the receipt and handling of PIC information (this percentage was 40 percent in Latin America, 33 percent in Africa, 20 percent in the Near-East, 20 percent in Europe, and 0 percent in Asia);
- 56 percent of developed, pesticide-exporting countries responded that they had not been able to use effectively, or they had been able to use only partly effectively, the procedures for advising their pesticide exporters and industry of the decisions of importing countries;
- 8 percent of responding countries reported that there had been difficulties in ensuring that measures or actions taken were not more restrictive on imported pesticides than those applied to the same substances produced domestically;
- 8 percent of responding countries said that such measures were used inconsistently with the trade-related provisions of GATT/WTO.

In the performance of their PIC-related tasks, FAO and UNEP have played a key role in promoting and implementing the procedure, both as technical advisers and as institutional intermediaries.[46] Individually and jointly, they have been instrumental at the initial phase of the PIC system, then at later stages of its operation and development. Among the various tasks they have accomplished, the listing of PIC pesticides/chemicals was a crucial one, one without which the procedure would have remained ineffective.

Today, twenty-seven banned or severely restricted substances, most of which are pesticides, are subject to the PIC procedure. Based on participating countries' notifications, these pesticides/chemicals have been identified at different times over a period of about six years by the FAO/UNEP Joint Group of Experts on the Prior Informed Consent. In turn, the corresponding Decision Guidance Documents (DGDs) providing relevant information on each listed chemical have been prepared and distributed by the FAO/UNEP Joint Secretariat, between 1991 and 1997, as follows:

- DGDs for banned or severely restricted pesticides (seventeen): first set in September 1991, second set in November 1992, third set in January 1997;

[46] By doing so, the two organizations acted in accordance with the relevant provisions of the Code and the Guidelines, in particular those requiring them to develop programmes and measures to make the PIC procedure effective, and to keep the latter under review.

- DGDs for pesticides included because of their acute hazard under conditions of use in developing countries (five): first set in August 1997;[47]
- DGDs for industrial chemicals (five): first set in March 1993.

As of the end of 1997, the PIC list included twenty-two pesticides[48] and five industrial chemicals.[49] These are deemed to be among the most dangerous existing chemical substances to health, safety, and the environment. Their listing for international trade monitoring purposes represents, therefore, a significant achievement under the PIC system. However, it is estimated that more than fifty chemical substances could probably enter the PIC list in future.

A further important contribution of the FAO/UNEP Joint Secretariat to the implementation of the PIC procedure was the collection, generation, and dissemination of the information and data that were needed to establish and operate the system. A yearly publication, the *PIC Circular*, has been jointly produced by the two organizations since 1993. It usually contains updated information on the status of PIC's implementation, compilations of import responses for PIC pesticides/chemicals and follow-up actions expected from participating countries, as well as new developments and recent activities of interest to PIC, such as notifications from DNAs, reports on PIC-related meetings, training, and capacity building activities linked to PIC.[50]

More recently, the two organizations have developed PIC's information base through computerization. Under the FAO/UNEP Joint Program, most documents regarding the PIC procedure, including those related to its implementation, have been made available on the Internet through two websites.[51] Furthermore, in order to facilitate access to PIC-related information, the Joint Secretariat has developed a database containing relevant information on DNAs, as well as on notification of control actions and import decisions on PIC substances.[52] The database facilitates the identification of PIC pesti-

---

[47] Acutely hazardous pesticide/chemical formulations are those which pose particular handling problems in developing countries mainly due to precarious conditions of use. Their listing as PIC substances is envisaged by the Code and the Guidelines, upon the advice of an FAO/UNEP/WHO Expert Group.

[48] These are: 2,4,5–T, Aldrin, Captafol, Chlordane, Chlordimeform, Chlorbenzilate, DDT, Dieldrin, Dinoseb, 1,2-dibromoethane (EDB), Fluoroacetamide, HCH, Heptachlor, Hexachlorobenzene, Lindane, Mercury compounds, certain formulations of Monocrotophos, Methamidophos, Phosphamidon, Methyl-parathion, Parathion.

[49] These are: Crocidolite, Polybrominated Biphenyls (PBB), Polychlorinated Biphenyls (PCB), Polychlorinated Terphenyls (PCT), Tris (2,3 dibromopropyl) phosphate.

[50] Between 1993 and 1998, 7 *PIC Circulars* were published (July 1993, February 1994, July 1994, March 1995, July 1995, July 1996, and July 1997), with semi-annual updates for Circulars V (January 1996), VI (January 1997), and VII (January 1998).

[51] The sites are: <http://www.fao.waicent/FaoInfo/Agricult/AGP/AGPP/Pesticid> and <http://irptc.unep.ch/pic/>.

[52] Parts of this database have been made available to interested users on CD-ROM and over the Internet at <http://faowfs0a.fao.org/PICD/> or through the links mentioned in the previous note.

cides/chemicals, either through a substance or a country query, thereby providing public and private entities involved in the trade of chemicals with the latest information required for the implementation of the PIC procedure.[53]

Soon after its emergence in 1989, the PIC concept found its way into a treaty: the Convention concerning Safety in the Use of Chemicals at Work, adopted by the General Conference of ILO on June 6, 1990. Focused primarily on the work environment, the Convention applies to industrial employment and to the use of pesticides by farm workers.[54] Under the Convention, competent authorities are generally empowered to require 'advance notification and authorization' of hazardous chemicals before they are used (Article 5). More specifically, reference is made to PIC in a provision calling for communication by exporting states to importing countries of regulatory actions to ban the use of hazardous chemicals for reasons of safety and health at work (Article 19).

A further acknowledgment of the PIC procedure at the global level may be found in UNCED's Agenda 21 of 1992,[55] whose Chapter 19 set the international policy framework for chemicals.[56] Referring repeatedly to the FAO/UNEP PIC system, the Chapter calls for 'full participation in and implementation of the PIC procedure' by the year 2000. Governments are urged to develop 'regulatory and non-regulatory measures and procedures aimed at preventing the export of chemicals that are banned, severely restricted, withdrawn or not approved for health or environmental reasons, except when such export has received prior written consent from the importing country or is otherwise in accordance with the PIC procedure' (paragraphs 19.38 and 19.52).

Clearly, this provision is a 'mirror-image' of the PIC clauses of the Code and the Guidelines. Therefore, while corroborating the existing PIC system, Agenda 21 did not develop it further because attempts to 'harden' the PIC principle were unsuccessful. UNCED did address the desirability of elaborating a legally binding international instrument on PIC, but the political debate on this matter was not conclusive. This persistent disagreement is reflected in Agenda 21. In what was termed 'cryptic language',[57] Chapter 19 merely envisioned 'possible mandatory applications' of the PIC procedure through 'legally binding instruments' (paragraph 19.38).

Political consensus on this issue could not be reached, in fact, until November 1994 when the FAO Council agreed that the organization should proceed with the preparation, in collaboration with UNEP, of a draft legally-

---

[53] FAO/UNEP, *supra* note 37 at 3.   [54] Pallemaerts, *supra* note 23 at 165.

[55] Agenda 21, UNCED, A/Conf.151/4 (1992).

[56] Entitled 'Environmentally Sound Management of Toxic Chemicals, Including Prevention of Illegal International Traffic in Toxic and Dangerous Products', this Chapter identifies six programme areas requiring priority attention, including information exchange on toxic chemicals and chemical risks.

[57] Pallemaerts (1992), *supra* note 35 at 282.

binding instrument on PIC.[58] In May 1995, UNEP was in turn authorized by its Governing Council to convene, together with FAO, an intergovernmental negotiating committee (INC) with a mandate to prepare an instrument for the application of the PIC procedure for certain hazardous chemicals and pesticides in international trade.[59]

The first session of the INC was held in March 1996 in Brussels,[60] followed by four other sessions.[61] The final draft text of the PIC Convention was agreed upon at Brussels session of the INC, almost two years to the day after the first INC.[62] A few months later the Convention was formally adopted at a Diplomatic Conference which took place in September 1998 in Rotterdam.

Overall, the Convention is modeled on the existing voluntary PIC procedure. During the negotiations, several countries, particularly those from the G77, sought to enlarge the scope of the convention to cover all aspects of chemical management, but these attempts were strongly opposed by a number of large chemical producing and exporting nations. In the end, the consensus among negotiators in the INC was that the convention's scope should not extend beyond the existing PIC system.[63] Accordingly, the agreed text of the Convention faithfully mirrors the FAO/UNEP PIC clauses and the future treaty will apply to the same list of PIC pesticides/chemicals, under nearly identical procedural requirements.

---

[58] FAO, *Report of the Progress of Negotiations of an International Legally-Binding Instruments for the Application of the Prior Informed Consent (PIC) Procedure for Certain Hazardous Chemicals and Pesticides in International Trade*, C 97/6 July 1997 (1997).

[59] Pallemaerts, M., and Heyvaert, V., 'International Transfer of Restricted or Prohibited Substances, Regulation of Chemicals' (1995) 6 *YBIEL* 278–86; UNEP, *supra* note 28.

[60] UNEP/FAO, *Report of the Intergovernmental Negotiating Committee for an International Legally-Binding Instruments for the Application of the Prior Informed Consent Procedure for Certain Hazardous Chemicals and Pesticides in International Trade on the Work of its First Session*, UNEP/FAO/PIC/INC.1/10 (1996).

[61] The reports of these sessions may be found in UNEP/FAO, *Report of the Intergovernmental Negotiating Committee for an International Legally-Binding Instruments for the Application of the Prior Informed Consent Procedure for Certain Hazardous Chemicals and Pesticides in International Trade on the Work of its Second Session*, UNEP/FAO/PIC/INC.2/7 (1996); UNEP/FAO, *Report of the Intergovernmental Negotiating Committee for an International Legally-Binding Instrument for the Application of the Prior Informed Consent Procedure for Certain Hazardous Chemicals and Pesticides in International Trade on the Work of its Fourth Session*, UNEP/FAO/PIC/INC.4/2 (1997); UNEP/FAO, *Report of the Intergovernmental Negotiating Committee for an International Legally-Binding Instruments for the Application of the Prior Informed Consent Procedure for Certain Hazardous Chemicals and Pesticides in International Trade on the Work of its Third Session*, UNEP/FAO/PIC/INC.3/2 26 (1997) and UNEP/FAO, *Report of the Intergovernmental Negotiating Committee for an International Legally-Binding Instruments for the Application of the Prior Informed Consent Procedure for Certain Hazardous Chemicals and Pesticides in International Trade on the Work of its Fifth Session*, UNEP/FAO/PIC/INC.5/3 (1998).

[62] Ivers, L., *et al.*, 'Report of the Fifth Session of the INC for an International Legally-Binding Instruments for the Application of the Prior Informed Consent Procedure for Certain Hazardous Chemicals and Pesticides in International Trade' (1998) 15 *Earth Negotiations Bulletin* 4.

[63] Pallemaerts, *supra* note 42 at 176–8.

Once in force, the Convention will furnish a legally-binding foundation for the PIC procedure. Its primary accomplishment will be one of 'hardening' the PIC provisions of the two soft law instruments already in place, the Code and the Guidelines. In itself, this represents a meaningful achievement in terms of treaty-law development. By transforming voluntary practices into legal obligations, the Convention drafters have significantly contributed to the codification of pre-existing soft law norms.[64] At the same time, the soft norms themselves were a substantial achievement and over time were widely accepted and implemented. Without them it is unlikely that the treaty could have been achieved. The added value of the treaty is its legally binding character.

The Legal Status and Effect of Antarctic Recommended Measures

CHRISTOPHER C. JOYNER

INTRODUCTION

The legal regime governing the Antarctic region is a synthesis of treaty-based international law and non-binding norms, whose core instrument is the 1959 Antarctic Treaty (AT).[1] The AT provides that 'recommended measures' may

---

[64] A similar process occurred in the last decade with respect to a soft law instrument on hazardous wastes, the 1985/1987 Cairo Guidelines and Principles for the Environmentally Sound Management of Hazardous Wastes, which led up to the 1989 Basel Convention on the Control of Transboundary Movements of Hazardous Wastes and Their Disposal.

[1] The Antarctic Treaty System consists of the Antarctic Treaty, done December 1, 1959, 12 U.S.T. 794, T.I.A.S. No. 4780, 402 U.N.T.S. 71, and four other related instruments: The Agreed Measures on the Conservation of Fauna and Flora, Recommendation III–VIII, done in Brussels, June 2–13, 1964, 17 U.S.T. 996, 998, T.I.A.S. No. 6058, modified in 24 U.S.T. 1802, T.I.A.S. No. 7693 (1973) (hereinafter the Agreed Measures); the Convention on the Conservation of Antarctic Seals, done in London, June 1, 1972, entered into force March 11, 1978, 27 U.S.T. 441, T.I.A.S. No. 8826; the Convention on the Conservation of Antarctic Marine Living Resources, done May 20, 1980, entered into force April 7, 1982, 33 U.S.T. 3476, T.I.A.S. No. 10,240; and the Protocol on Environmental Protection to the Antarctic Treaty, XIth Special Consultative Meeting in Madrid, Doc. XI ATSCM/2, June 21, 1991, adopted October 4, 1991, entered into force January 14, 1998 (hereinafter Madrid Environmental Protection Protocol). An Antarctic minerals treaty, the Convention on the Regulation of Antarctic Minerals Resource Activities, Doc. AMR/SCM/88/78 (June 2, 1988), was negotiated in 1988, but in effect has been superseded by the Madrid Protocol. Similarly, provisions in the Agreed Measures will be consolidated and superseded by the Protocol once it enters into force. All these documents are reprinted in Heap, J. (ed.), *Handbook of the Antarctic Treaty System* (8th edn. 1994). For a current list of measures adopted by the Antarctic Treaty Consultative Parties, see ATCM Archive, List of Recommendations, Measures, Decisions and Resolutions, at web site <Antartica-rcta.com.pe/archi-rcta01b.htm#22>

be adopted and approved by the Antarctic Treaty Consultative Party (ATCP) states[2] participating in the annual Antarctic Treaty Consultative Meetings (ATCMs). Over time, the Treaty obligations have expanded through the process of adopting and approving recommended measures, without amending the Treaty. Recommended measures in effect become AT policies that are affirmed by the practice of states parties following a rigorous double-approval procedure that makes a recommended measure 'effective'. By 1999, twenty-two ATCMs had adopted 202 recommended measures and fifty-four associated instruments, supplying a corpus of binding and non-binding international norms that are intended to regulate and guide the activities of ATCP nationals in the Antarctic region.

Three difficulties complicate any conclusions about the form and substance of the recommended measures. First, the degree to which recommended measures are legally binding is unclear, and the legal value attached to recommendations remains subject to varied interpretation by AT states parties. Recommended measures may be viewed as non-binding norms, or they may be seen to constitute hard law, or they may be considered as something in between. Secondly, it is not clear whether the recommendations are addressed only to the ATCPs or whether they address all AT parties, non-party states, or non-state actors. Thirdly, no uniform procedure exists to approve, integrate, and enforce recommendations as binding acts within the domestic legal systems of ATCP governments.

Partly to remedy this confusion, the character of ATCM recommendations was formally transformed in 1995. Three separate categories were denominated: (1) *measures* are intended to be legally binding after approval by all ATCPs in conformity with AT Article IX(4); (2) *decisions* relate to internal ATCP organizational matters and become operative immediately following the ATCM at which they are adopted; (3) *resolutions* are hortatory texts adopted at an ATCM, and are not binding on states.[3] These categories do much to clarify the legal nature of recommended measures under contemporary AT law. Even so, they do little to clarify the status of those recommendations adopted before 1995.

This study examines whether the recommended measures adopted prior to 1995 are merely non-binding exhortations, generating limited, voluntary

---

[2] As of 1998, the Antarctic Treaty Consultative Parties comprise the 12 original parties to the Antarctic Treaty (Argentina, Australia, Belgium, Chile, France, Japan, New Zealand, Norway, South Africa, the Soviet Union (Russia), the United Kingdom, and the United States) and the following additional states: Brazil, Bulgaria, China, Ecuador, Finland, Germany, India, Italy, South Korea, Netherlands, Peru, Poland, Spain, Sweden, and Uruguay. Consultative Party status can be conferred on states that have qualified by 'demonstrating scientific research activity' in and around the continent. The Antarctic Treaty, Art. IX, para. 2. The ATCPs convene in annual meetings to discuss and set recommended policy for the Antarctic.

[3] Final Report of the Nineteenth Antarctic Treaty Consultative Meeting (Seoul, May 8–19, 1995), at 19, paras. 69–70.

effects, or whether they constitute legal instruments that create binding rights and duties for states. In the latter case, compliance determines the legal reach and relevance of ATCM recommendations for state policy. An examination of the process by which ATCM recommended measures are created, the status of these instruments under international law, and the implementation record by AT governments since 1961 leads to a number of conclusions about compliance with Antarctic recommendations.

A. ADOPTION OF ATCM RECOMMENDATIONS

The Antarctic Treaty Article IX, paragraph 1, affirms that representatives[4] of the contracting states must meet regularly in order to recommend to the governments 'measures' in the furtherance of the principles and objectives of the Treaty.[5] Paragraph 4 adds that recommended measures shall 'become effective' after approval by all Consultative Parties, thus requiring their adoption by the unanimous vote of all ATCPs attending an ATCM.[6] Only the Consultative Parties approve measures, thereby excluding states parties that have not obtained Consultative Party status[7] and observers and experts from international organizations.[8]

Since 1961, a multi-phase process has evolved for producing and adopting recommended measures. First, a proposal is discussed informally and its substance is negotiated among various ATCPs. After agreement on the text is reached, the measure is formally submitted to the ATCM for consideration. ATCM decision-making is 'on the basis of consensus informally arrived at'.[9] Concerns about various measures thus can be discussed, negotiated, and compromised to ensure that the measures will be acceptable, precluding diplomatic strains and political friction that might arise from divided voting.

---

[4] AT Art. IX, para. 1 provides that participants at ATCMs represent the Consultative Parties' Governments and are not experts or private persons. Representatives speak as government agents, negotiate as government officials, and determine policy based on government instructions. The actions of official representatives are clearly attributable to the ATCP governments.

[5] The test for whether a matter may be considered a measure under Art. IX is whether it is 'in furtherance of the principles and objectives of the Treaty'. In fact, the Treaty does not specify what are its principles and objectives, a situation that must be inferred from the instrument's preamble and provisions. See AT, *supra* note 1, at Art. IX.

[6] This rule is not expressed in the AT, but was established in practice at the First ATCM in 1961, and subsequently was codified in Rule 24 of the Rules of Procedure of the ATCM. See Guyer, R.E., 'The Antarctic System' (1973-II) 139 *Recueil des Cours de l'Académie de Droit International* 184–92, at 186. The Rules have been amended twice, in 1983 and 1987. See *Handbook of the Antarctic Treaty System, supra* note 1 at 271–84.

[7] *Ibid.*, Rule 1.

[8] *Ibid.*, Rule 2. This rule permits attendance by representatives from the Commission for the Conservation of Antarctic Marine Living Resources and the Scientific Committee on Antarctic Research (SCAR).

[9] Watts, A., *International Law and the Antarctic Treaty System* (1992) 29.

After adoption, the representatives recommend to their respective governments acceptance of the adopted measure, acceptance that takes place according to municipal legal and political processes. The final phase is that of approval by each ATCP government,[10] which must then implement the measure in its municipal law.

During the period between the adoption of a recommended measure and its subsequent approval, a period when the ATCP governments prepare for integrating the measure into their domestic law and policy, there should be no efforts to defeat the object and purpose of a recommended measure, or actions to dissuade other governments from approving it. There is also a fundamental expectation that all ATCP governments will make appropriate efforts to ensure that no one engages in any activity in Antarctica contrary to the principles and purposes of the Treaty. Thus, once a recommendation has been adopted, it is implicit that governments will strive not to subvert it in contravention of the approval process and the Treaty objective that Antarctica not become a source of international discord.[11]

On balance, the process of recommended measures prior to 1995 worked well, in part because nearly all Antarctic activities have been directed and supported by governments and therefore can be government-regulated. The non-binding form has been advantageous for governments with serious domestic constitutional or legislative barriers to adopting a measure as a legally binding obligation. This flexibility remains a strength of the Antarctic Treaty arrangement, so long as governments implement in practice what they have agreed to accept in principle.[12]

B. APPROVAL

Governments usually have approved recommendations adopted after they attain ATCP status. They need not disapprove or reject a recommendation, but can simply refrain from giving approval, in effect preventing it from becoming effective. This is the 'legislative price' paid for the Antarctic

[10] See generally Focarelli, C., 'The Legal Nature of the Acts Adopted under Article IX of the Antarctic Treaty and Their Implementation in Italy', in Francioni, F., and Scovazzi, T. (eds.), *International Law for Antarctica* (2nd edn., 1996) 505–80.

[11] This duty flows from Art. 18 of the Vienna Convention on the Law of Treaties, which affirms that states are obligated not to defeat the object or purpose of a treaty prior to its entry into force until it has 'made its intention clear not to become a party to the treaty'. Vienna Convention on the Law of Treaties, Art. 18, done May 23, 1969, U.N. Doc. A/CONF.39/27, entered into force January 27, 1980, reprinted in (1969) 8 I.L.M. 679.

[12] More recently, resort to hortatory measures has been viewed as inadequate in regulating conduct due to the increasing numbers of private parties and commercial tourists in the Antarctic. Proposals emerged in the early 1990s to draft a legally-binding annex to the Environmental Protection Protocol in order to regulate tourism. See Vidas, D., 'The Legitimacy of the Antarctic Tourism Regime', in Stokke, O.S., and Vidas, D. (eds.), *Governing the Antarctic: The Effectiveness and Legitimacy of the Antarctic Treaty System* (1996) 294–322.

Treaty's consensus system of adoption and subsequent approval of ATCP recommendations. When a recommendation is approved, the instrument of approval has generally been an executive declaration addressed to the other ATCPs and deposited with the United States as the AT depository.[13] The depository government has the responsibility to 'inform all signatory and acceding States when any recommendation has been approved in accordance with Article IX, paragraph 4, of the Treaty by all the contracting parties'.[14]

A survey of recommendations that various governments have failed to approve over the 40-year history of the AT suggests some interesting findings. It is often difficult, however, to determine which recommended measures are fully effective, because of the erratic pattern of the ATCPs' depositing notification of their approval with the United States. As indicated in Appendix A, several governments have been neither punctual nor consistent in performing this responsibility.[15] As a result, no recommendation adopted after 1987 has become 'effective' in accordance with Article IX of the AT. Nonetheless, ATCPs have agreed to apply recommendations they have accepted for themselves, pending the full deposit of required notifications. At the same time, while not all ATCP governments have deposited their decisions on recommended measures since 1992, analysis of the available data yields insights into actions taken regarding recommended measures. Appendices B and C inventory those recommended measures adopted by each ATCM since 1961 that have not received universal approval.

During the 1960s, seventy-four ATCM recommended measures were adopted, mostly dealing with functional issues pertaining to the AT system, viz., scheduling meetings, exchanging information and facilitating scientific cooperation. With a few exceptions, all ATCPs approved all recommendations (see Appendix B). During the 1970s, the fifty-three adopted recommendations focused on exchange of information, facilitation of international scientific cooperation, and various issues concerning environmental protection and conservation, especially as regards the protection and management of specific Antarctic areas. During this decade, the most notable objection to a recommended measure came in the VIIth ATCM in 1972. Four states (Brazil, China, Germany, and Italy) failed to approve the recommendation

---

[13] As provided in para. 4 of Recommendation I–XIV (Administrative Arrangements).

[14] Recommendation I–XIV, para. 5, reprinted in *Handbook of the Antarctic Treaty System*, *supra* note 1, at 22.

[15] The following ATCP governments, showing the ATCM year of required submission, have been delinquent in submitting notifications to the Depository State: India (all since 1983); Italy (for 1987, 1989, 1991, 1992, and 1996); Peru (all since 1989); Japan (in 1989, 1991, 1992, and 1995); Russia (all since 1989); Chile (all since 1992); Argentina and China (all since 1992); and Korea (for the 1989 ATCM). Since 1994, Australia, New Zealand, and Uruguay have not deposited any approvals, nor did Norway for 1994 or 1995. Of the 27 ATCPs, only Finland and Korea have deposited notification for the 1995 and 1996 ATCMs; only Norway has deposited its notification for the 1997 ATCM.

pertaining to importation of laboratory animals and plants taken from the Antarctic.

Overall, between 1964 and 1994, Germany was the ATCP that most persistently did not approve recommended measures. Germany opted not to approve forty-five measures of the 178 recommendations adopted. Twenty-four of the measures not approved concerned area protection and management. The Republic of Korea, with sixteen non-approvals, ranked second (six of its rejected recommendations concerned area protection and management).

The United States failed to approve fourteen measures coming from the XVth and XVIth ATCMs. The measures cover a wide range of issues: international scientific cooperation, the regulation of Antarctic mineral resource activities, environmental impact, waste disposal and waste management, prevention of marine pollution, area protection and management, and environmental monitoring. Eight measures not approved concern area protection and management.

The 1989 ATCM meeting in Paris was the most contentious in regard to resultant recommendation approvals. Of twenty-two recommended measures adopted at the XVth ATCM, only six (Recommendations XV–12, 13, 15, 17, 20, and 21) have secured the necessary approval from all ATCPs to become effective. Ten of the fourteen recommendations the U.S. has not approved are measures adopted in Paris. The 1991 ATCM in Bonn also produced recommendations that met with significant negative reactions. Of the thirteen recommendations adopted at Bonn, only six have gained unanimous approval from ATCP governments (Recommendations XVI–1, 2, 3, 5, 11, and 13).[16]

India, Italy, and Spain agreed in rejecting two specific recommendations at the Xth ATCM in 1978, one concerning the regulation of Antarctic mineral resources activities and the second regarding postal services. There are also single rejections of recommendations by various states: Brazil and China, two populous developing countries, have each approved all but Recommendation VI–10 (1970) on area protection and management. Argentina has not yet approved one adopted measure, Recommendation XVI–10, which also concerns area protection and management. Given the well-known intensity of Argentina's position toward its sovereignty claim in the Antarctic, this record of near total acceptance is striking.

There are a total of about sixty non-approvals in response to the 211 recommendations adopted from 1961 to 1996. They concern a wide variety of

---

[16] While problems clearly existed for governments over the substance of the recommendations, the political atmosphere during 1989–91 was particularly tense and confrontational. Friction erupted over the fate of the Antarctic minerals accord that had been negotiated from 1981 to 1988, and its precipitous demise when Australia and France refused to sign or ratify the agreement, thereby causing it to be abandoned in place of negotiating a protocol to protect the Antarctic environment. See Joyner, Ch. C., 'CRAMRA: The Ugly Duckling of the Antarctic Treaty System?', in Jorgensen-Dahl, A., and Ostreng, W. (eds.), *The Antarctic Treaty System in World Politics* (1991) 161–85.

issues as diverse as the facilitation of scientific cooperation, postal services, conservation of fauna and flora, waste disposal and management, marine protection, and environmental monitoring. The largest concentration of recommended measures that has failed to secure ATCP approval is that dealing with area protection and management. Twenty-four of the non-approvals, more than one-third of the total, have pertained to this topic.

Subsequent legal developments in the Antarctic Treaty system indicate why this last issue has failed to generate approvals. Annex V of the 1991 Antarctic Environmental Protection Protocol has superceded many of the measures, especially with its new designations of Specially Reserved Areas and Multiple-Use Planning Areas. This appears to be the case for Recommendations XV–8, 10, and 11. The United Kingdom, Germany, and the U.S. apparently were concerned about implementing recommendations through domestic legislation that would need amendment after the entry into force of the Madrid Protocol. This concern was raised in particular with regard to the creation of new Sites of Special Scientific Interest (SSSIs) and Specially Protected Areas (SPAs), which the Protocol consolidates under a new designation, Antarctic Specially Protected Areas (ASPAs). In sum, the management plans addressed in Recommendations XVI–4, 6, 8, and 9 became moot, and were so nearly from the time of their adoption.[17]

C. IMPLEMENTATION

The Antarctic Treaty gives ATCP governments virtually complete autonomy regarding domestic implementation of recommended measures. Some governments, for example those of Finland and Korea, consider ATCM recommendations legally binding and hence automatically effective in their domestic legal systems from the time that they are unanimously approved.[18] Many other ATCPs, including Argentina, Australia, Belgium, Brazil, Germany, New Zealand, Peru, Russia, Spain, the United States, and Uruguay, consider approved recommendations binding, but not directly applicable until an implementing measure has been adopted through specific procedures including executive decree, modification of existing legislation, revision of agency regulations, or parliamentary law. Two ATCP states, France and Japan, do not recognize the binding nature of recommendations, and thus require special implementation to make specific measures binding in their domestic law.[19]

---

[17] Dr. M.G. Richardson, Head, Polar Regions Section, South Atlantic and Antarctic Department, British Foreign & Commonwealth Office, 'ATCM Recommendations: UK Approval', September 12, 1997 (letter to the author).

[18] Colella, A., 'The Legal Nature of Antarctic Recommendations and Their Implementation in the Domestic Legal Systems', in Francioni, F. (ed.), *Environmental Law for Antarctica*, 207 (1992) 218.

[19] See Focarelli, *supra* note 10, at 572–3, n. 531.

Several examples indicate the variety of state practice. The United States generally treats recommended measures as executive agreements, though in some circumstances, *e.g.*, the 1964 Agreed Measures, they have been transmitted to the Senate for advice and consent to ratification as treaties.[20] The United States considers recommended measures legally binding after they are adopted by all ATCPs at an ATCM, upon which time notice of approval is communicated by the depositary. For Australia, in contrast, measures adopted by the ATCPs 'are regarded by the Australian Government as binding once necessary changes to domestic legislation have been carried out'.[21] Thus, for an approved recommended measure to become legally binding on an Australian citizen, a law needs to be passed. Australian citizens are notified by the publication of such legislation, or the government may issue an official press release or special guidelines.[22]

The United Kingdom publishes the outcome of each ATCM in a Government Command Paper that sets out recommendations adopted by ATCPs. Subsequent approval of measures is demonstrated by passing either primary legislation, *e.g.*, The Antarctic Treaty Act of 1964, which implemented the Agreed Measures (Recommendation III–VIII), or secondary legislation (Orders in Council), which has been used to make effective designations of Specially Protected Areas.[23]

D. LEGAL STATUS OF ATCM RECOMMENDATIONS

In the Antarctic Treaty system, the key query is whether Antarctic Treaty recommendations are merely hortatory assertions or whether they impose legal obligations. Determination of the legal status of Antarctic Treaty recommendations requires interpretation of paragraphs 1 and 4 of Article IX according

---

[20] Letter to the author from Harlan K. Cohen, Office of Oceans Affairs, U.S. Department of State, September 24, 1997. Notice that a measure has been implemented in U.S. law as reported in the Federal Register.

[21] Timothy Kane, Antarctic Desk Officer, Department of Foreign Affairs and Trade, Government of Australia, 'Information Relating to Article XI of the Antarctic Treaty', August 21, 1997 (communication with the author).

[22] *Ibid.*

[23] M.G. Richardson, Head, Polar Regions Section, South Atlantic and Antarctic Department, British Foreign and Commonwealth Office, 'Article IX of the Antarctic Treaty Responses: United Kingdom', August 12, 1997 (communication to the author), at 1. The British government uses three procedures to implement approved measures. For non-mandatory recommendations, 'administrative or executive action' is taken. For mandatory recommendations, domestic legislation must be introduced before formal approval can be given. Since entry into force of the Antarctic Act of 1994, which implements the 1991 Antarctic Environmental Protection Protocol, protected area management plans adopted by the ATCPs in the Protocol's Annex V were incorporated into Schedule 1 of the Antarctic Regulations (1995), thus giving legal effect to these protected areas in British law.

to the traditional criteria used in international practice and codified in the 1969 Vienna Convention of the Law of Treaties.[24]

It appears that ATCM measures begin as mere recommendations made by the states' representatives to their governments. All ATCP governments must approve a recommendation through their domestic decision-making processes before the recommendation may be considered binding, but even then the legal nature of the recommendation remains questionable. After being adopted unanimously by an ATCM, a recommended measure appears to enjoy a status analogous to that of an international agreement following signature by governments, but before ratification. It is 'in limbo', in that governments are not legally bound to the duties in the measure, but remain obliged in spirit, if not in law, not to defeat the object or purpose of the measure.

This process resembles procedures concerning treaties: the text of an instrument is negotiated and adopted by representatives of the attending governments. In order to enter into force, however, the instrument is subject to formal approval, usually through ratification, by each individual government according to the latter's own municipal processes. A critical distinction, however, is that in the case of Antarctic Treaty recommendations, unanimous consent by all ATCPs is required, a stipulation rarely imposed for international agreements outside the Antarctic Treaty System.

After all the states approve the measure, one might infer that the term 'shall become effective' (Article IX paragraph 4) means 'shall enter into force'. If so, the act would seem to generate rights and duties;[25] however, the meaning of the phase to 'become effective' is ambiguous and subject to wide interpretation. While 'effective' might suggest notions of producing desired results or actually becoming operative, it should not be considered synonymous with either 'to become legally binding' or 'to impart legal obligations', but neither does it exclude that meaning. The obligatory depth attached to a recommendation's 'effectiveness' remains open to interpretation.

The double unanimity rule required for adoption, first by the ATCM representatives present at the meeting and later by the ATCP governments, strongly suggests that the recommended measures ultimately have a binding nature under the Antarctic Treaty. After unanimous approval twice, 'recommended' measures are no longer just recommendations, but are 'effective' ones. It seems logical that the result of this double approval process would be construed as carrying some legal obligation.

While Consultative Parties are bound by effective measures, it is less clear what impact recommendations have on other states. It seems reasonable that recommendations obligate non-consultative states party to the Antarctic

---

[24] Done May 23, 1969, U.N. Doc. A/CONF. 39/27, entered into force January 27, 1980, Arts. 31–33 (Interpretation of Treaties).

[25] Colella, *supra* note 18.

Treaty because non-ATCP governments are obligated to abide by the Treaty provisions. Adopting an approved measure is a function of the Treaty, producing legal effects for all Treaty parties, even though some of them are removed from making that decision.

A number of governments have acceded to the Antarctic Treaty since 1961, after certain measures became effective. State practice suggests that acceding governments are bound to recommended measures that were adopted prior to their entry into the AT relationship despite the fact that these governments had no voice in adopting the earlier measures.[26] The measures can be construed as integral parts of the Antarctic Treaty regime, thus constituting an Antarctic Treaty package deal to which a government accedes in full, with the implicit obligation to accept adopted measures as Treaty policy.

The ATCPs have adopted texts explicitly calling for adherence to all recommendations stemming from Article IX of the Treaty. Recommendation III–VI asserts that recommendations approved by the contracting parties are 'so much a part of the overall structure of cooperation established by the Treaty' that any new Consultative Party is 'urged to accept these recommendations and to inform other Contracting Parties of its intention to apply and be bound by them'.[27] Further, Non-Consultative Parties should be invited to adhere to these measures as well. The logic of the ATCPs affirms that the underlying Antarctic Treaty is the source of the obligation. At the IVth ATCM in 1966, the parties revealed the considerations that lead to demands for acceptance of approved recommendations:

1. In becoming parties to the Antarctic Treaty, states bind themselves to carry out the Treaty's purposes and principles;
2. Recommendations that become effective in accordance with Article IX of the Treaty are 'measures in furtherance of the principles and objectives of the Treaty';
3. Approved recommendations are thus an essential part of the overall structure of co-operation established by the Treaty;
4. In pursuance of the principles and objectives of the Treaty there should be uniformity of practice in the activity of all parties active in Antarctica; and
5. Approved recommendations are to be viewed in light of the obligations assumed by Contracting Parties under the Treaty and in particular Article X.[28]

---

[26] Since 1977, when Poland joined as the first new member of the Consultative Party group, the practice has been for governments applying for ATCP status to give assurances that they will approve and comply with measures previously adopted as recommendations. See Watts, *supra* note 9, at 32.

[27] Recommendation III–VII, reprinted in *Handbook of the Antarctic Treaty System*, *supra* note 1, at 23.

[28] *Ibid.*, at 285 ('Annex D: Status of Antarctic Treaty Recommendations'). In full, Art. X of the Antarctic Treaty provides that '[e]ach of the Contracting Parties undertakes to exert

To the extent that recommendations further the purposes, principles, and objectives of the Treaty, they enhance the legal mandate in Article X.

It appears, then, that recommendations, once approved unanimously by the ATCPs, are intended by those governments to have certain qualities of obligation. A different question is whether each AT recommendation is equally binding or whether some are only hortatory or declarative of existing principles of AT law, *i.e.*, whether each recommendation is co-equal in legal status. The process of adopting each ATCP recommendation under Article IX of the Antarctic Treaty could suggest uniformity, but each recommendation may also stand on its own as a separate instrument to be judged according to its contents.

Given the wide-ranging nature of ATCM recommended measures, the prudent approach to the issue is to appraise each measure individually. Where a measure is drafted in terms that are unmistakably hortatory, approval by all the respective ATCP governments would not alter its legal status. Its 'effectiveness' on obtaining approval from all governments concerned will remain that of an exhortation and the measure remains an appeal for action.

On the other hand, when a measure is composed in language that clearly aims to convey legal obligations and that measure becomes effective, the effect is to impose the legal obligations explicitly contained in that measure. Both the content of the measure and the process of its approval by all ATCP governments are necessary and may be sufficient to confer legally binding status on norms contained in the measure.[29]

Various recommendations are phrased to convey an intent that they be binding. In Recommendation VII–2 (Review of Specially Protected Areas), the ATCPs observe that 'Recommendation VI–8 has notably increased the protection afforded to Specially Protected Areas by *prohibiting entry [into them]*, except in accordance with a permit'.[30] Prohibition ostensibly conveys the connotation not to do something because it would contravene a norm or violate a law, suggesting a legal obligation.

There may be temptation to accord each recommendation individual, separate treaty status.[31] While the 1964 Agreed Measures on the Conservation of Antarctic Fauna and Flora clearly possesses the requisite elements to qualify as a treaty, it is difficult to accept that status for recommendations in general,

appropriate efforts, consistent with the Charter of the United Nations, to the end that no one engages in any activity in Antarctica contrary to the principles or purposes of the present Treaty'. Antarctic Treaty, *supra* note 1, at Art. X.

[29] A government that is entitled to be represented at an ATCM, but which in fact did not attend when some measure was adopted must nonetheless give its approval to that measure for it to 'become effective' under the requirements of Art. IX. Antarctic Treaty, *supra* note 1, at Art. IX, para. 4.

[30] *Handbook of the Antarctic Treaty System, supra* note 1, at 2086.

[31] Bush, W.M. (ed.), *Antarctica and International Law: A Collection of Inter-State and National Documents* I (1982) 97.

or other recommendations in particular. Article 2(1)(a) of the Vienna Convention on the Law of Treaties defines a treaty as 'an international agreement concluded between states in written form and governed by international law, whether embodied in a single instrument or in two or more related instruments and whatever its particular designation'. According to this definition, the essential requirement is that the instrument be intended by the parties to create international legal rights and obligations. By name and formalities, recommendations do not appear intended to create international legal rights and obligations; therefore, they are not treaties.

Acts adopted and approved as recommended measures under the Antarctic Treaty also do not enjoy the same legal status as acts adopted by international organizations.[32] While both types of decisions are anticipated, authorized, and regulated by treaty and both share the common terminology of 'recommendation', 'resolution', 'decision', and 'measure', the Antarctic Treaty does not establish an international organization. There is no charter or constitution granting competence to issue acts, no autonomous organs with specific powers, no headquarters, and no secretariat. The Antarctic Treaty does not anticipate such an organization being established. Nor does it anticipate any body having the power to declare acts unlawful, meaning that the ATCPs are left to agree amongst themselves by consensus that certain acts are permissible or impermissible.

Another view is that some measures can be considered as binding when adopted under AT Article IX in order to extend or adjust the Treaty, expanding or limiting its regulatory scope. Such acts may be viewed as actual agreements independent of AT provisions, presumably prevailing over the Treaty by virtue of their subsequent adoption. They are legally sustained by an observable fact: the unanimous will exercised by the ATCPs to approve such an act, demonstrated twice by their own vote.

In contrast and finally, ATCM recommended measures can be seen as 'soft' normative instruments providing a mid-way stage in the law-creating process. Recommendations do not entail law in the sense of the legal sources enumerated in Article 38 of the Statute of the International Court of Justice. In process and content, however, recommendations convey some binding obligation upon all AT governments, carrying a certain measure of legal authority. Consultative Parties hold strong expectations that norms contained in adopted recommendations will command respect by all ATCP governments, as well as by other Antarctic Treaty parties, and that these norms will be adhered to over the long term.

The variable legal effects of ATCM recommendations in different countries and internationally over the years led to confusion. The problems finally resulted in the decision by the ATCPs previously discussed to shift from the

---

[32] See Bush, W.M. (ed.), *Antarctica and International Law: A Collection of Inter-State and National Documents* I (1982) at 97–8; Colella, *supra* note 18, at 210–11.

past practice of adopting 'Recommendations' as Measures under Article IX of the Treaty to decision-making through (1) Measures, which are legally binding, subject to unanimous ATCP approval; (2) Decisions, which become binding immediately after the ATCM of adoption; and (3) Resolutions, which are hortatory.

The main intent behind this change in ATCM decision making 'was to introduce greater selectivity over which decisions of the Treaty parties should [be] require[d] to undergo the Article IX procedures'.[33] The aim was to eliminate disadvantages of the previous practice, in particular: (1) to minimize the considerable delay between the adoption of recommendations and when they became effective; and (2) to lessen the prospect that 'innocuous' recommendations (e.g., those mandating that SCAR undertake some task before the next ATCM) would not be needlessly subjected to the governmental approval process. In great part, these aims appear to have been met.

The four ATCMs since this new schema was adopted in 1995 have generated fifty-four new policy instruments: fifteen measures have been approved, ten decisions have been effected, and twenty-nine resolutions have been adopted. The ultimate test for determining whether this new categorization clarifies and enhances legal effects will lie in how the ATCPs treat the new forms of recommendations once they have been adopted, and whether making explicit the legal obligation to comply with 'measures' will in any way impair adoption of new instruments.

Governments retain ultimate control over the level of commitment attached to a recommendation. Not all recommendations necessarily become normative or legally binding; not all of them are intended to do so. Some ATCP recommendations have been more procedural rather than legally substantive, for example, measures that call for scheduling the next ATCM, or facilitating postal, telecommunication, or meteorological services. Still, the very fact that such an instrument has been approved by the ATCPs would seem to foster hardening the normative content of that recommendation.

E. COMPLIANCE AND ENFORCEMENT

Non-binding norms generally escape the protracted ratification process to which treaties are subjected, and agreement on soft norms is usually obtained more readily than in the case of treaty law. AT recommended measures, adopted as soft normative instruments, allow for great flexibility. ATCP governments often are more willing to be innovative when the adopted instrument is not legally binding. New notions or approaches can be tested and refined in a non-binding situation, providing immediate benefits while laying the

---

[33] Richardson, *supra* note 23 at 2.

structural foundation for negotiating binding agreements at a later time. This was the experience in the 1960s and 1970s, when the ATCPs laid the international legal foundation for wide-ranging obligations to conserve living and nonliving resources and to protect the environment in the Antarctic; the measures taken evolved into the 1991 Antarctic Environmental Protection Protocol.

As non-binding norms, Antarctic Treaty recommendations generally assume two main roles: (1) they appear as strands in a web of explicit agreements comprising a general code of conduct for national activities in the Antarctic; and (2) they serve as non-binding principles to guide the behavior of ATCP governments in the region.

When processed as part of the code to regulate activities in the Antarctic, recommendations can be constructed in ways that mimic the terms of binding agreements or cooperative practices of treaty agreements. Alternatively, they may promote the convergence of national standards or practices, which in turn can facilitate subsequent treaty negotiations or remove the need for a treaty altogether. A code-of-conduct approach for Antarctic Treaty recommended measures, such as that fostered by recommendations dealing with tourism, environmental protection, meteorology, or telecommunications, permits governments to participate in a cooperative arrangement based on their ability to do so. It can also engender the participation of governments that might avoid binding international agreements, either because of competing national interests, or the lack of technical or fiscal means to participate. As codes for conduct, ATCP recommendations can supply constructive, if only temporary, mechanisms or precursors to treaty commitments.

Soft principles not only furnish a conceptual frame of reference for future agreements, they also facilitate the crystallization process that gives rise to customary law. Undergirding the body of recommended measures is the principle of 'common concern of humankind' that advocates protection of resources and the environment beyond the limits of national jurisdiction. The Antarctic Treaty in general and the recommended measures in particular reflect a realization by governments that state responsibility extends to protecting and conserving the polar environment as a global commons in the general interest of the international community, not only in the present, but for future generations as well. The need to protect the Antarctic commons suggests the recognition that ATCP governments are bound by rules of common interest, and, more significantly, that each ATCP government, even if not directly affected, is legally entitled to demand compliance. These attitudes provide additional pull for compliance by all ATCP governments with recommendations that have been made 'effective'.

Recommended measures also may inculcate the precautionary principle to fill the temporal gap in customary law for the Antarctic commons. That is, the measures recommended, adopted, and approved by the ATCPs under Article

IX signal certain problems and activities that might adversely affect the Antarctic. These measures are taken to address those problems or regulate those activities before they become deleterious.

The Antarctic Treaty provides no specific criteria by which to measure states' compliance, nor any monitoring programs to determine the recommendations' effectiveness or the extent to which they are enforced. Article VII of the Treaty does, however, provide for unannounced, on-site inspections by any Consultative Party of any of other ATCP government's station in the Treaty area. While originally intended as a means to enforce demilitarization provisions in the Treaty, these ATCP inspections have taken on added significance as means for encouraging adherence to environmental measures approved by the ATCPs. At least thirty-one inspection missions of more than 130 research stations have been carried out since 1961, during which not a single violation of any Treaty agreement has been formally reported. To the extent that it is possible to determine compliance through ATCP on-site inspections, it appears that the obligations in ATCM recommended measures have been generally upheld by ATCP governments while operating in the Antarctic Treaty area.[34]

Inspections under the Antarctic Treaty do not escape criticism, however. Inspection procedures are limited, and only Consultative Parties may conduct inspections. No collective inspection or independent inspectorate is available. While the Antarctic Treaty asserts that all areas of Antarctica, including all stations, installations, and equipment, as well as all ships and aircraft that are discharging cargoes and personnel, are subject at all times to open inspection, the Treaty does not furnish any guidance on what sanctions or procedures should be followed if an inspection should reveal violations of the Treaty.[35]

Environmental groups have detected some violations by ATCP nationals of AT measures and have been ignored by ATCP governments. Perhaps the most egregious episode occurred during 1983–5 at Dumont d'Urville on Point Geologie, along the coast in the French sector. Point Geologie is one of Antarctica's richest areas in birds and seals, and an attractive area for

---

[34] There is, in addition, an inspection and monitoring system set up under the Convention for the Conservation of Antarctic Marine Living Resources, through which national governments can inspect fishing vessels to ensure compliance with national laws regulating fishery activities in the Southern Ocean. See Joyner, C., *Antarctica and the Law of the Sea* (1992) 245–8.

[35] See generally, Giuliani, P., 'Inspections under the Antarctic Treaty', in *International Law for Antarctica, supra* note 10 at 459–74. An inspection system has also been implemented under the Convention on the Conservation of Antarctic Marine Living Resources, which deals with conserving resources in the circumpolar Southern Ocean. Implemented in 1990, CCAMLR inspectors are authorized to stop vessels from Antarctic Treaty party states that are fishing in the Southern Ocean, and report their findings to their own governments, who then report to the CCAMLR's Commission. Prosecutions and sanctions for violations are the responsibility of the flag state of the offending vessel. Inspections are brief (less than two hours), and involve only one or two inspectors. See Joyner, *supra* note 34 at 245–8, 273–4.

scientists and environmentalists to study. It was here that in 1983 the French began constructing an airfield by leveling a series of small islands offshore and connecting them with archipelagic fill. No environmental impact study was done prior to beginning construction, and apparently no alternatives to the airstrip were seriously considered.

Environmentalists reported in 1985 that penguins were killed when land areas were dynamited and other penguin rookeries were damaged or destroyed. Although it was known that the French Point Geologie airstrip project was having deleterious environmental impacts upon indigenous wildlife, no action was taken by other ATCPs to pressure the French to abandon their efforts. The attitude of the ATCPs apparently was to avoid stirring up public controversy. In that sense, compliance by France with the 1964 Agreed Measures failed, enforcement by the other ATCPs was set aside, and maintenance of a non-conflictive AT Consultative process was given priority over concern for compliance with environmental norms.[36]

It might appear that the regulation of activities in the Antarctic entails a weak regulatory system, one premised more on exhortation than legal obligation. This conclusion misses the mark, however. Nearly all recommendations adopted at ATCMs have secured approval from ATCP governments within three years of their adoption, perhaps an expected result when initial approval is by consensus. In addition, though, most ATCP governments generally act in accord with recommended measures, even before the measures receive formal approval from all ATCPs and become effective as obligations. This practice may be attributed to good faith on behalf of the ATCPs to one another. It may also signal that the ATCPs view the recommended measures as essentially obligatory and therefore binding even before they are formally in effect. If so, it is reasonable to expect that governments will conduct interim policies such that they do not defeat the object and purpose of a recommendation.

Long delays have sometimes stalled recommendations becoming effective, either because of the requirement of unanimous agreement or due to the need for parties to implement legislation that gives effect to recommendations, or to changed practices at various stations and national expeditions.[37] F. M. Auburn charges that this is 'a serious defect in a system which claims to be the legitimate decision-maker for a whole continent'.[38] Subsequent approval of recommendations by the ATCPs, however, suggests that recommendations are not mere proposals for action—that in fact once they become effective, they are considered to be legally binding.

---

[36] For elaboration see Joyner, C., 'Protection of the Antarctic Environment: Rethinking the Problems and Prospects' (1986) 19 *Cornell Int'l L.J.* 259, 268–80; ASOC, 'Background Paper on the French Airfield at Point Geologie, Antarctica', March 1, 1985; Antarctica Briefing No. 9, 'The French-Airstrip—A Breach of Antarctic Treaty Rules?', July 30, 1986.

[37] See Rothwell, D., *The Polar Regions and the Development of International Law* (1996) 96–100.

[38] Auburn, F.M., *Antarctic Law and Politics* (1982) 204.

F. THE BALANCE SHEET

International instruments may be placed on a continuum according to various criteria, among them normative quality. On one end, there are norm-creating instruments carrying legally-binding content and obligatory pull. On the other end of the continuum are non-binding instruments, or non-law. Somewhere in between lie so-called instruments of 'soft law', a term that is more of a misnomer than an accurate reflection of legal quality. Antarctic Treaty recommendations lie somewhere within these realms.

The Antarctic Treaty establishes a regime governed through a series of interconnected, legally-binding international agreements among the ATCPs. Recommended measures contribute to the Antarctic regime system as policy links among the ATCP governments themselves, as well as between the various treaties. A review of the language of the Antarctic Treaty and of many recommendations, and of state practice, suggests that 'decisions taken unanimously or by consensus by the Consultative parties . . . may amount to an agreement binding in international law',[39] hence imparting to recommended measures a certain obligatory status.

In the Antarctic legal regime, difficulty may reside in determining the relative softness or hardness of international norms. International agreements such as recommended measures under the AT may be binding or not. To the extent that an agreed measure among ATCPs is binding, it can be soft or hard depending upon its substance and whether it has been unanimously approved, although where that distinction lies may not always be easy to locate with precision or confidence. The normative softness of a recommended measure, then, does not connote the degree of legalistic content so much as it signifies the extent of binding quality, and hence legal obligation, of that agreement.

Some Antarctic Treaty recommendations are soft norms for predetermined specified conduct that, though not legally binding, engender compliance by Antarctic Treaty Consultative Parties. The softness of such norms varies according to the tug and pull of compliance evidenced by the affected governments. There is, regrettably, no exact means available for determining precisely the extent to which governments feel obligated to comply with these 'soft' norms, save for the degree of compliance that they demonstrate through state practice. In this regard, while attaining consensus approval has eluded every ATCM measure adopted since 1987, perceived noncompliance has not risen to the point where any serious objections have been lodged by any ATCP against another. At the very least these recommendations serve as an

[39] Explanatory Note concerning Measures Adopted under Art. IX of the Antarctic Treaty, Draft Final Report of XIX ATCM, Doc. ATCM/WP 35, May 19, 1995, at para. 16.

'ordering system' for policy priorities recognized and agreed upon, though perhaps not formally adopted as legally binding, for various activities in the Antarctic.

Certain factors influence the rate of compliance by ATCPs with various agreed measures. Among these are a recommended measure's perceived links to other international norms recognized in international law; its links to state practice, or links to practices by the Antarctic scientific community; the legitimacy of the adoptive process of a recommended measure; the perceived fairness and legitimacy of the recommended practice by the international community; and the control that ATCP governments have over national agents who are targets for an agreed measure.

Although as soft norms ATCM recommendations may not be binding *per se*, they can indicate the likely direction in which formally binding legal obligations will develop. They also can contribute to international law by establishing informal norms of behavior and by reflecting and possibly even codifying rules of customary law or the need for new hard treaty law. Such indeed was the process through which the Madrid Environmental Protection Protocol evolved to replace and strengthen the 1964 Agreed Measures and the panoply of recommendations related to conservation and protection of the Antarctic environment that had been subsequently adopted.

In 1964, the ATCPs negotiated and approved Recommendation III–VIII, the Agreed Measures for the Conservation of Antarctic Fauna and Flora. The Agreed Measures became the legal catalyst for the body of environmental norms that evolved for protecting and conserving living and nonliving resources in the Antarctic including the adoption between 1964 and 1992 of at least ninety-seven relevant measures, although not all were formally approved by the ATCPs.

The Agreed Measures became hard law for the ATCPs. Recommendations relating to the Agreed Measures were not hard law, however. They were adopted as soft norms, subject to the process of formal consensus adoption and unanimous approval by ATCPs that is necessary and sufficient to qualify them as hard law. As a result, some recommended measures pertaining to the Antarctic environment became hard, binding norms, while many others did not. This latter group of unapproved measures could be considered soft, non-binding normative instruments. Such a confusing array of binding and non-binding instruments underscored the need for a comprehensive environmental protection and conservation instrument grounded in hard treaty law.

The Environmental Protection Protocol, with its four original annexes, culminated in Madrid as the legal product of that need for hard law consolidation. While the thrust of the Protocol derives from and contributes to general principles of environmental law, its annexes more particularly have their roots in the Agreed Measures and the related ATCM recommendations adopted since 1961. The Protocol itself drew from five previous recommended measures concerning human impact on the Antarctic environment and the need to protect it from interference,[40] as well as the express realization of the necessity of elaborating and implementing a comprehensive regime for the protection of the Antarctic environment and its dependent and associated ecosystems.[41]

Similarly, the substance of the annexes built directly upon the wording and principles of previous ATCM recommended measures. Annex I, which concerns environmental impact assessment, originated in three earlier recommended measures and hortatory guidelines on the need for environmental impact analysis.[42] Annex II deals with the conservation of fauna and flora and is essentially extrapolated from Articles II, V, VI, IX, and XII in the 1964 Agreed Measures. Concern over waste disposal and waste management is the subject of Annex III, a concern expressed in four earlier recommended measures going back to 1975.[43] The fourth annex deals with the prevention of marine pollution, which can be traced to a special recommended measure adopted by the ATCPs in 1989, but never formally approved.[44] In late 1991 a fifth annex on area protection and management was adopted by the ATCPs. Annex V consolidates into a more manageable system at least fifty-five previous recommended measures adopted between 1961 and 1991. They had created an unwieldy, complicated arrangement for protecting historic sites, historic monuments, sites of special scientific interest, specially protected areas, specially reserved areas, and multiple use planning areas.[45]

In sum, soft Antarctic recommendations gave rise to new, hard law that is legally binding on all ATCPs to protect and preserve the Antarctic environment. Essential concepts, language, normative principles and directives were extrapolated from previously adopted recommended measures and incorporated to form the substantive basis for the new environmental protocol and its annexes.

---

[40] See Recommendations VI–4 (Man's Impact on the Antarctic Environment); VII–1 (Man's Impact on the Antarctic Environment); VII–11 (Man's Impact on the Antarctic Environment); VIII–13 (The Antarctic Environment); and IX–5 (Man's Impact on the Antarctic Environment).

[41] See Recommendation XV–1 (Comprehensive Measures for the Protection of the Antarctic Environment and Dependent and Associated Ecosystems).

[42] See Recommendations VIII–11 (Man's Impact on the Antarctic Environment: Annex. Code of Conduct for Antarctic Expeditions and Station Activities, para. 4); XII–3 (Man's Impact on the Antarctic Environment); and XIV–2 (Man's Impact on the Antarctic Environment: Environmental Impact Assessment).

[43] Namely, Recommendations VIII–11 (Man's Impact on the Antarctic Environment: Annex. Code of Conduct for Antarctic Expeditions and Station Activities, para. 1); XII–4 (Man's Impact on the Antarctic Environment: Code of Conduct for Antarctic Expeditions and Station Activities); XIII–4 (Man's Impact on the Antarctic Environment: Code of Conduct for Antarctic Expeditions and Station Activities: Waste Disposal) and XV–3 (Human Impact on the Antarctic Environment: Waste Disposal).

[44] Recommendation XV–4 (Human Impact on the Antarctic Environment: Prevention, Control and Response to Marine Pollution).

[45] See *Handbook of the Antarctic Treaty System, supra* n. 1 at 2081–2123 and Annex C.

CONCLUSION

Questions may persist over the legal nature and effect of ATCM recommendations, but it seems clear that they assume a quasi-legislative character. Article IX requires that measures be formulated, adopted, and recommended to governments, and their repeated consent to the measures suggests that the recommendations are more than merely exhortation. Yet, concern over the perceived status of recommendations as legal instruments has fostered the tendency among ATCPs to rely less on hortatory and more on legally-binding measures. This has become obvious as environmental protection and resource conservation have acquired greater prominence as ATCP policy objectives.[46] It is also apparent in the Decision made at the 1995 ATCM in Seoul.

ATCM recommendations provide norm-setting, norm-applying, and norm-monitoring opportunities for governments in the polar South. While guidelines for governments and their nationals in the Antarctic are hardened and usually codified by formal international agreements, the evolutionary process toward that end is furthered by the cumulative effects of measures recommended, adopted, and approved by ATCP governments. As normative instruments, ATCP recommendations provide a principal means for articulating and effectuating international norms.

Recommendations are a unique international instrument designed to foster cooperation on specific issues affecting activities of ATCP governments in the Antarctic. Recommended measures enunciate norms still in the process of becoming distilled into legal principles. By taking the non-binding form of soft norms, resort to recommended measures permits the ATCPs to address serious problems collectively while refusing to hamstring their ability to act. This has been especially significant in recommendations pertaining to environmental matters, when scientific evidence is wanting or inconclusive, but precautionary measures are still deemed necessary.

Antarctic recommended measures, even if not fully approved, contain emergent normative qualities and can exert a tug in the direction of obligation and the need for compliance. Thus they operate as soft norms, but the degree and authority of these measures' normative qualities remain uncertain. As 'soft' instruments, recommended measures are not hard law; they lack the definitive status of legally binding agreements that contain the full measure of

---

[46] For example, in Recommendation XV–1, para. 3(b)(iii), the requirements for a more comprehensive environmental protection system include the need to 'consider the nature of legal obligations contained in existing measures and the need, as necessary, to state those obligations with greater precision'. Para. 3(c) underscores this point as it calls for the need to consider 'the form or forms of the legal or other measures needed to ensure the maintenance, integration, consistency, and comprehensiveness of the system for protecting the Antarctic environment'. *Handbook of the Antarctic Treaty System, supra* note 1 at 2007.

normative obligation inherent in the treaty doctrine of *pacta sunt servanda*. Moreover, the status of these non-binding normative instruments may be in flux. Yet, while many Antarctic Treaty recommendations may not be legally binding or normatively obligatory, they are in the process of evolving into a higher, more authoritative normative status.

By treating recommendations as soft normative instruments, the ATCPs retain the advantage assuming obligations that they might not be able to assume otherwise. Many recommendations embody norms that have been distilled and harmonized by the ATCPs so that they can be promulgated as common aims and standards. As non-binding norms, the obligations contained in recommendations can be formulated in a more precise, distinct, and restrictive manner than is acceptable in a formally binding international agreement. These recommendations are not susceptible to formal municipal approval by ratification, as are international treaty agreements.

Recommended measures adopted and implemented by the ATCPs are significant. Principles in these recommendations provide ingredients and channels for international cooperation throughout the Antarctic Treaty System, and their acceptance and activation can foster the evolution from soft international norms to hard legal principles. Likewise, recommended measures suggest where there is need for new hard law to regulate activities in the Antarctic. These are important contributions that substantially add to strengthening the Antarctic Treaty regime. No less important, recommended measures help to expand the breadth and robustness of law in that regime. In these ways, recommended measures facilitate and undergird the rule of law in the polar South.

APPENDIX A—APPROVAL, AS NOTIFIED TO THE GOVERNMENT OF THE
UNITED STATES OF AMERICA, OF MEASURES RELATING TO THE
FURTHERANCE OF THE PRINCIPLES AND OBJECTIVES OF THE ANTARCTIC
TREATY

(Printed on pp. 185–188)

	16 Recommendations adopted at First Meeting (Canberra 1961) Approved	10 Recommendations adopted at Second Meeting (Buenos Aires 1962) Approved	11 Recommendations adopted at Third Meeting (Brussels 1964) Approved	28 Recommendations adopted at Fourth Meeting (Santiago 1966) Approved	9 Recommendations adopted at Fifth Meeting (Paris 1968) Approved	15 Recommendations adopted at Sixth Meeting (Tokyo 1970) Approved
Argentina	ALL	ALL	ALL	ALL	ALL	ALL
Australia	ALL	ALL	ALL	ALL	ALL	ALL
Belgium	ALL	ALL	ALL	ALL	ALL	ALL
Brazil (1983)+	ALL	ALL	ALL	ALL	ALL	ALL (except 10)
Chile	ALL	ALL	ALL	ALL	ALL	ALL
China (1985)+	ALL	ALL	ALL	ALL	ALL	ALL (except 10)
Ecuador (1990)+						
Finland (1989)+						
France	ALL	ALL	ALL	ALL	ALL	ALL
Germany (1981)+	ALL	ALL	ALL (except 8)	ALL (except 1–11 and 13–19)	ALL (except 5* and 6)	ALL (except 9 and 10)
India (1983)+	ALL	ALL	ALL (except 8***)	ALL (except 18)	ALL	ALL (except 9 and 10)
Italy (1987)+	ALL	ALL	ALL	ALL	ALL	ALL
Japan	ALL	ALL	ALL	ALL	ALL	ALL
Korea, Rep. (1989)+	ALL	ALL	ALL	ALL	ALL	ALL
Netherlands (1990)+	ALL	ALL	ALL	ALL	ALL	ALL
New Zealand	ALL	ALL	ALL	ALL	ALL	ALL
Norway	ALL	ALL	ALL	ALL	ALL	ALL
Peru (1989)+	ALL	ALL	ALL	ALL	ALL	ALL
Poland (1977)+	ALL	ALL	ALL	ALL	ALL	ALL
Russia	ALL	ALL	ALL	ALL	ALL	ALL
South Africa	ALL	ALL	ALL	ALL	ALL	ALL
Spain (1988)+	ALL	ALL	ALL	ALL	ALL	ALL
Sweden (1988)+	ALL	ALL	ALL	ALL	ALL	ALL
U.K.	ALL	ALL	ALL	ALL	ALL	ALL
Uruguay (1985)+	ALL	ALL	ALL	ALL	ALL	ALL
U.S.A.	ALL	ALL	ALL	ALL	ALL	ALL

*IV-6, IV-10, IV-12, and V-5 terminated by VIII-2.

***Accepted as interim guideline.

+Year attained Consultative Status. Acceptance by that State required to bring into force Recommendations or Measures of meetings from that year forward.

Country	9 Recommendations adopted at Seventh Meeting (Wellington 1972) Approved	14 Recommendations adopted at Eighth Meeting (Oslo 1975) Approved	6 Recommendations adopted at Ninth Meeting (London 1977) Approved	9 Recommendations adopted at Tenth Meeting (Washington 1977) Approved	3 Recommendations adopted at Eleventh Meeting (Buenos Aires 1981) Approved	8 Recommendations adopted at Twelfth Meeting (Canberra 1983) Approved
Argentina	ALL	ALL	ALL	ALL	ALL	ALL
Australia	ALL	ALL	ALL	ALL	ALL	ALL
Belgium	ALL	ALL	ALL	ALL	ALL	ALL
Brazil (1983)+	ALL (except 5)	ALL	ALL	ALL	ALL	ALL
Chile	ALL	ALL	ALL	ALL	ALL	ALL
China (1985)+	ALL (except 5)	ALL	ALL	ALL	ALL	ALL
Ecuador (1990)+						
Finland (1989)+						
France	ALL	ALL	ALL	ALL	ALL	ALL
Germany (1981)+	ALL (except 5)	ALL (except 1, 2, 5)	ALL	ALL	ALL	ALL
India (1983)+	ALL (except 5)	ALL	ALL	ALL (except 1 and 9)	ALL	ALL
Italy (1987)+	ALL (except 5)	ALL	ALL	ALL (except 1 and 9)	ALL	ALL
Japan	ALL	ALL	ALL	ALL	ALL	ALL
Korea, Rep. (1989)+	ALL	ALL	ALL	ALL	ALL	ALL
Netherlands (1990)+						
New Zealand	ALL	ALL	ALL	ALL	ALL	ALL
Norway	ALL	ALL	ALL	ALL	ALL	ALL
Peru (1989)+	ALL	ALL	ALL	ALL	ALL	ALL
Poland (1977)+	ALL	ALL	ALL	ALL	ALL	ALL
Russia	ALL	ALL	ALL	ALL	ALL	ALL
South Africa	ALL	ALL	ALL	ALL	ALL	ALL
Spain (1988)+	ALL	ALL	ALL	ALL (except 1 and 9)	ALL (except 1)	ALL
Sweden (1988)+	ALL	ALL	ALL	ALL	ALL	ALL
U.K.	ALL	ALL	ALL	ALL	ALL	ALL
Uruguay (1985)+	ALL	ALL	ALL	ALL	ALL	ALL
U.S.A.	ALL	ALL	ALL	ALL	ALL	ALL

	16 Recommendations adopted at Thirteenth Meeting (Brussels 1985) Approved	10 Recommendations adopted at Fourteenth Meeting (Rio de Janeiro 1987) Approved	22 Recommendations adopted at Fifteenth Meeting (Paris 1989) Approved	13 Recommendations adopted at Sixteenth Meeting (Bonn 1991) Approved	4 Recommendations adopted at Seventeenth Meeting (Venice 1992) Approved	1 Recommendation adopted at Eighteenth Meeting (Kyoto 1994) Approved
Argentina	ALL	ALL	ALL	ALL except XVI-10	ALL	
Australia	ALL	ALL	ALL	ALL	ALL	ALL
Belgium	ALL	ALL	ALL		ALL	ALL
Brazil (1983)+	ALL	ALL	ALL	ALL	ALL	
Chile (1985)+	ALL	ALL	ALL			
China (1985)+	ALL	ALL	ALL	ALL		
Ecuador (1990)+						
Finland (1989)+		ALL	ALL	ALL	ALL	ALL
France	ALL	ALL	ALL	ALL	ALL	ALL
Germany (1981)+	(except 10 to 13)	ALL	(except 3, 4, 8, 10, 11, 22)	(except 4, 6, 7, 8, 9, 10)	(except 2 and 3)	ALL
India (1983)+		ALL	ALL	ALL	ALL	
Italy (1987)+		ALL	ALL	ALL	ALL	ALL
Japan	ALL	ALL	ALL	ALL	ALL	ALL
Korea, Rep. (1989)+	ALL	ALL	(except 1–11, 16, 18, 19)	(except 12)	(except 1)	ALL
Netherlands (1990)+						
New Zealand	ALL	ALL	ALL	ALL	ALL	ALL
Norway	ALL	ALL	ALL	ALL	ALL	
Peru (1989)+		ALL	ALL	ALL	ALL	
Poland (1977)+	ALL	ALL	ALL			
Russia	ALL	ALL	ALL	ALL	ALL	
South Africa	ALL	ALL	ALL	ALL	ALL	ALL
Spain 1988						
Sweden (1988)+		ALL	ALL	ALL	ALL	ALL
U.K.	ALL	(except 2)	(except 3, 4, 8, 10, 11)	(except 4, 6, 8, 9)	ALL	ALL
Uruguay (1985)+	ALL	ALL	(except 1–5, 8–11, 14)	ALL	ALL	ALL
U.S.A.	ALL	ALL	(except 1–5, 8–11, 14)	(except 10)	ALL	ALL

*IV–6, IV–10, IV–12, and V–5 terminated by VIII–2.
+Year attained Consultative Status. Acceptance by that State required to bring into force Recommendations or Measures of meetings from that year forward.

	5 measures adopted at Nineteenth Meeting (Seoul 1995) Approved	2 Measures adopted at Twentieth Meeting (Utrecht 1996) Approved	Measures adopted at Twenty-first Meeting (Christchurch 1997) Approved	Measures adopted at Twenty-second Meeting Approved	Measures adopted at Twenty-third Meeting Approved
Argentina					
Australia					
Belgium					
Brazil (1983)+	ALL				
Chile					
China (1985)+					
Ecuador (1990)+					
Finland (1989)+	ALL				
France					
Germany (1981)+					
India (1983)+					
Italy (1987)+	ALL	ALL			
Japan	ALL				
Korea, Rep. (1989)+	ALL				
Netherlands (1990)+					
New Zealand	ALL	ALL	ALL		
Norway					
Peru (1989)+					
Poland (1977)+					
Russia					
South Africa					
Spain (1988)					
Sweden (1988)+					
U.K.					
Uruguay (1985)+					
U.S.A.					

+Year attained Consultative Status. Acceptance by that State required to bring into force Recommendations or Measures of meetings from that year forward.

Office of the Assistant Legal Adviser for Treaty Affairs
Department of State
Washington, D.C.

APPENDIX B—ATCP RECOMMENDED MEASURES ACCORDING TO AREAS
OF CONCERN, 1961–1992

The following taxonomy breaks down ATCP Recommended Measures by issue area. It also indicates the number of measures recommended in parentheses, and which governments have yet to approve any specific measure. Beginning with the XVIIIth Meeting, ATCPs have been lax in reporting their adoption of recommended measures to the depository state. Therefore, this list only includes information on recommendations through the XVII Meeting in 1992.

Operation of the Antarctic Treaty System: Meetings (7)

I–XIV	III–VII
I–XVI	IV–24
II–IX	XIII–15[a]
III–VI	

Operation of the Antarctic Treaty System: Information (9)

I–IV	XII–8[a]
I–V	XIII–1[a]
I–VIII	XIII–2[a]
V–3	XIV–1[a]
XII–6[a]	

Operation of the Antarctic Treaty System: Exchange of Information (22)

I–I	II–IV	VI–7
I–III	II–VI	VI–12
I–VI	III–I	VI–13
I–VII	III–II	VIII–6
I–VIII	IV–23	XIII–3[a]
I–XIII	IV–27	XVI–1[ab]
II–I	VI–2	
	VI–3	

Facilitation of International Scientific Cooperation (30)

I–II	VIII–5 (not approved by Germany)
I–X	VIII–7
I–XI	IX–3
II–III	IX–4
II–V	X–3
II–VII	XIV–9[a]
III–III	XIV–10[a]

III–V	XV–14 (not approved by the US)[ac]
IV–25	XV–15[ac]
IV–26	XV–16 (not approved by Korea)[ac]
V–2	XV–18 (not approved by Korea)[ac]
VI–1	XV–19 (not approved by Korea)[ac]
VI–3	XV–20[ac]
VII–7	XVI–12 (not approved by Korea)[ac]
VII–8	XVII–4[abcd]

Postal Services (4)
I–XII
V–I
X–9 (not approved by India, Italy, or Spain)
XV–22 (not approved by Germany)[ac]

Activities of Non-Consultative Parties (1)
VIII–8

International Conventions:
    Seals (5)

III–XI	IV–22
IV–21	V–7
	V–8

    Antarctic Marine Living Resources (4)

VIII–10	XI–2[a]
IX–2	
X–2	

    Regulation of Antarctic Mineral Resource Activities (6)
    VII–6
    VIII–14
    IX–1
    X–1 (not approved by India, Italy, or Spain)
    XI–1 (not approved by Spain)[a]
    XV–2 (not approved by Korea or US)[ac]

The Antarctic Environment: Protection and Conservation
    Man's Impact on the Environment (6)

VI–4	VIII–13
VII–1	IX–5
VIII–11	XV–1 (not approved by Korea or US)[ac]

Environmental Impact Assessment (3)
VIII–11
XII–3[a]
XIV–2 (not approved by United Kingdom)[a]

Conservation of Fauna and Flora (9)
I–VIII
II–II
III–VIII (not approved by Germany or India)
III–IX
III–X
IV–18 (not approved by Germany or India)
IV–19 (not approved by Germany)
IV–20
VI–9 (not approved by Germany or India)

Waste Disposal and Waste Management (4)
VIII–11
XII–4[a]
XIII–4[a]
XV–3 (not approved by Germany, Korea, United Kingdom, or U.S.)[ac]

The Antarctic Environment: Prevention of Marine Pollution (1)

XV–4 (not approved by Germany, Korea, United Kingdom, or U.S.)[ac]

The Antarctic Environment: Area Protection and Management (55)

I–IX	VIII–4
IV–1 (not approved by Germany)	VIII–5 (not approved by Germany)
IV–10 (not approved by Germany)[e]	X–5
IV–12[e]	X–6
IV–15 (not approved by Germany)	XI–3[a]
V–4	XII–5[a]
V–5 (not approved by Germany)[e]	XII–7[a]
VI–8	XIII–5[a]
VI–10 (not approved by Brazil, China, Germany or India)	XIII–7[a]
VI–14	XIII–8[a]
VII–2	XIII–9[a]
VII–3	XIII–10 (not approved by Germany)[a]
VII–9	XIII–11 (not approved by Germany)[a]
VIII–1 (not approved by Germany)	XIII–12 (not approved by Germany)[a]
VIII–2 (not approved by Germany)	XIII–13 (not approved by Germany)[a]
VIII–3	XIII–16[a]
	XIV–4[a]

XIV–5[a]
XIV–6[a]
XIV–8[a]
XV–6 (not approved by Korea)[ac]
XV–7 (not approved by Korea)[ac]
XV–8 (not approved by Germany, Korea, United Kingdom, or U.S.)[ac]
XV–9 (not approved by Korea)[ac]
XV–10 (not approved by Germany, Korea, United Kingdom, or U.S.)[ac]
XV–11 (not approved by Germany, Korea, United Kingdom, or U.S.)[ac]
XV–12[ac]
XV–13[ac]
XVI–2[abc]
XVI–3[abc] XVI–4 (not approved by Germany, United Kingdom, or U.S.)[abc]
XVI–5[abc]
XVI–6 (not approved by Germany, United Kingdom or U.S.)[abc]
XVI–7 (not approved by Germany)[abc]

XVI–8 (not approved by Germany, United Kingdom, or U.S.)[abc]
XVI–9 (not approved by Germany)[abc]
XVI–10 (not approved by Argentina, Germany, United States)[abc]
XVI–11[abc]
XVII–3 (not approved by Germany)[abcd]

The Antarctic Environment: Environmental Monitoring (2)
XV–5 (not approved by Korea or US)[ac]
XVII–1 (not approved by Korea)[abcd]

Siting of Antarctic Scientific Stations (2)
XIII–6[a]
XV–17[ac]

Oil Contamination (2)
IX–6
X–7

Disposal of Radioactive Wastes (1)
VIII–12

Use of Radio Isotopes (2)
VI–5
VI–6

Scientific Drilling (1)
XIV–3[a]

Use of Antarctic Ice (1)
XV–21[ac]

New Islands (1)
VI–11

Tourism and Non-Governmental Activities (7)

IV–27	VIII–9
VI–7	X–8
VII–4	XI–3[a]
	XVI–13[abc]

Notes
a. No information is available on India's or Italy's approval of recommendations from the 11th Meeting onward.
b. No information is available on Chile's or Poland's approval of recommendations from the 16th Meeting onward.
c. No information is available on Belgium's, Brazil's, Japan's, or Russia's approval of recommendations from the 15th Meeting onward.
d. No information is available on Argentina's or China's approval of recommendations from the 17th Meeting onward.
e. IV–6, IV–10, IV–12, and V–5 terminated by VIII–2.

APPENDIX C—STATES NOT APPROVING ATCP RECOMMENDATIONS,
1961–1994

Germany

Facilitation of International
Scientific Cooperation
    VII–5
Postal Services
    XV–22
Conservation of Fauna and Flora
    III–VIII
    IV–18
    IV–19
    VI–9
Waste Disposal and Waste
Management
    XV–3

United States

Facilitation of International
Scientific Cooperation
    XV–14
Regulation of Antarctic Mineral
Resource Activities
    XV–2
Man's Impact on the Environment
    XV–1
Waste Disposal and Waste
Management
    XV–3
Prevention of Marine Pollution
    XV–4

Germany

Prevention of Marine Pollution
    XV–4
Area Protection and Management
    IV–1
    IV–10
    IV–15
    V–5
    VI–10
    VIII–1
    VIII–2
    VIII–5
    XIII–10
    XIII–11
    XIII–12
    XIII–13
    XV–8
    XV–10
    XV–11
    XVI–4
    XVI–6
    XVI–7
    XVI–8
    XVI–10
    XVII–3

United States

Area Protection and Management
    XV–8
    XV–9
    XV–10
    XV–11
    XVI–4
    XVI–6
    XVI–8
    XVI–10
Environmental Monitoring
    XV–5

Republic of Korea

Facilitation of International
Scientific Cooperation
    XV–16
    XV–18
    XV–19
    XVI–12
Regulation of Antarctic Mineral
Resource Activities
    XV–2
Man's Impact on the Environment
    XV–1
Waste Disposal and Waste
Management
    XV–3

India

Postal Services
    X–9
Regulation of Antarctic Mineral
Resource Activities
    X–1
Conservation of Fauna and Flora
    III–VIII
    IV–18
    VI–9
    VI–10

Italy

Postal Services
    X–9

Prevention of Marine Pollution
    XV–4
Area Management and Protection
    XV–6
    XV–7
    XV–8
    XV–9
    XV–10
    XV–11
Environmental Monitoring
    XV–5
    XVII–1

United Kingdom

Environmental Impact Assessment
    XIV–2
Waste Disposal and Waste
Management
    XV–3
Prevention of Marine Pollution
    XV–4
Area Protection and Management
    XV–8
    XV–10
    XV–11
    XVI–4
    XV–6
    XVI–8

Regulation of Antarctic Mineral
Resource Activities
    X–1

Spain

Postal Services
    X–9
Regulation of Antarctic Mineral
Resource Activities
    X–1
    XI–1

Brazil and China

Area Protection and Management
    VI–10

Argentina

Area Protection and Management
    XVI–10

APPENDIX D—ATCM MEASURES, DECISIONS AND RESOLUTIONS,
1995–1999

Year	Measures[1]	Decisions[2]	Resolutions[3]
1995	5	2	9
1996	2	—	5
1997	5	2	3
1998	2	4	6
1999	1	2	6
TOTAL	15	10	29

Source: http://www.tromso.npolar.no/atcm/AtcmInfo/consrecs.htm, 1998

[1] All Measures adopted since 1995 have pertained to establishing and modifying the Antarctic Protected Area System. Measures must be approved by all ATCPs to be binding.

[2] Decisions have included acts adopting the rules of procedure for ATCMs, the notion of marine protected areas, the need for liability, and acknowledging Bulgaria as an ATCP (1998). Once adopted, Decisions are immediately binding on ATCPs.

[3] Resolutions vary widely in issue-area, from concerns over nuclear waste disposal, tourism, fuel storage, Antarctic inspections, environmental impact assessment and management plans to emergency response and contingency planning, comprehensive environmental evaluation, Antarctic data management and the need for a safety code for polar navigation. Resolutions are merely hortatory on ATCPs.

Selected Agreements Concluded Pursuant to the Convention on the Conservation of Migratory Species of Wild Animals

CLARE SHINE

This report compares the formal and less formal conservation Agreements[1] developed pursuant to the 1979 Convention on the Conservation of Migratory Species of Wild Animals[2] ('CMS'). It outlines the provisions of CMS that set forth a legal basis for such Agreements before presenting a structured comparison of two formal Agreements and two Memoranda of

[1] In keeping with the established practice of the UNEP/CMS Secretariat, 'Agreement' is used here to denote all types of accord which are possible under CMS, namely AGREEMENTS under Art. IV.3, agreements in the form of treaties concluded pursuant to Art. IV.4, and memoranda of understanding or informal agreements which are also adopted under that Art.

[2] Bonn, June 23, 1979, in force November 1, 1983, reprinted in (1980) 19 I.L.M. 15.

Understanding. The article seeks to evaluate whether and how the choice of instrument affected the drafting process, substantive content, institutional arrangements, implementation, and compliance in each case.

A. THE CONVENTION ON THE CONSERVATION OF MIGRATORY SPECIES OF WILD ANIMALS (CMS)

CMS is the only global convention for the conservation and management of all migratory terrestrial and marine species. Its Preamble recognizes that 'wild animals are an irreplaceable part of the earth's natural system which must be conserved for the good of mankind' and that 'each generation of man holds the resources of the earth for future generations and has an obligation to ensure that this legacy is conserved and, when utilized, is used wisely'.

CMS provides a legal framework within which states that exercise jurisdiction over any part of the range of a particular migratory species[3] can take concerted action for scientific research, habitat and species conservation. The legal mechanisms laid down for this purpose vary significantly according to the Appendix in which a species is listed:[4] Appendix I lists migratory species in danger of extinction throughout all or a significant portion of their range. Article III requires parties to take specific measures for the conservation of these species and their habitats and to prohibit the taking of such species, subject to limited exceptions (Article III(5)).

Appendix II lists migratory species that have an 'unfavorable conservation status' requiring international agreements for their conservation and management and species whose conservation status would significantly benefit from international cooperation (Article IV(1)).[5] The Range States Parties of Appendix II species must endeavor to conclude AGREEMENTS[6] where these would benefit the species, giving priority to those species in an unfavorable conservation status (Article IV.3). Article V sets forth guidelines for AGREEMENTS, including substantive conservation measures and procedural elements such as the establishment of institutional machinery and procedures for dispute settlement.

The Convention also provides for the adoption of a second kind of conservation accord. Article IV.4 encourages parties 'to take action with a view to concluding agreements for any population or geographically separate part of

[3] The definition of 'migratory' in Art. I.1.a has been the subject of an interpretative resolution of the Conference of the Parties, but the topic is outside the scope of this paper.

[4] Note that a migratory species may be listed in both Appendices (Art. IV.2).

[5] Appendix II lists several entire families of birds and the number of migratory bird species that could be covered by Agreements under CMS probably exceeds 1,000. See de Klemm, C., 'Migratory Species in International Law' (1989) 29 *Nat. Res. J.* 935–78.

[6] The use of upper case letters for Art. IV.3 instruments is intentional, to distinguish them from Article IV.4 agreements, described below, pp. 201–4.

the population of any species or lower taxon of wild animals, members of which periodically cross one or more national jurisdictional boundaries'. No guidance is provided concerning the legal nature or content of such agreements.[7]

The coexistence of two types of conservation accord under Article IV has understandably led to confusion and has been the subject of much debate by the Conference of the Parties to CMS, as discussed below. The text of the Convention does make clear that regional accords were intended to be key components of CMS implementation. The ultimate effectiveness of the Treaty thus depends on wide participation in the conclusion and implementation of such accords.[8]

The negotiation of CMS agreements was significantly hampered in the early years by the low number of parties,[9] uncertainty over substantive and procedural aspects of Agreements and chronic underfunding of the CMS Secretariat. In 1984, CMS was dubbed a 'sleeping convention'.[10] It took seven years from its entry into force before the first Agreement was concluded. The position has now improved with eight Agreements concluded between 1990 and 1999 and others being well advanced.

1. Implementing Agreements Concluded to Date

Five of the eight Agreements concluded to date are in the form of treaties, and three are less formal Memoranda of Understanding (MoU). In chronological order, these Agreements are:

- Agreement on the Conservation of Seals in the Wadden Sea (October 16, 1990, in force October 1, 1991). Denmark, Germany, and the Netherlands, the three parties to this Article IV.4 agreement, have undertaken to provide for the development of a conservation and management plan for harbor seals in the Wadden Sea. The agreement

---

[7] One commentator has suggested that this provision is intended to promote the conclusion of agreements for species which have not yet been listed in Appendix II or which cannot be so listed because they do not meet the definition of 'migratory' in Art. I.1.a. See Lyster, S., *International Wildlife Law* (1985) 291.

[8] Birnie, P.W., and Boyle, A.E., *International Law and the Environment* (1992) 457.

[9] Unfortunately, CMS has traditionally lacked enough parties to cover the majority of species included in the Appendices, making the inclusion of endangered migratory species in Appendix I largely symbolic. The distribution of parties by region is also uneven: parties are concentrated in Europe and Africa, with coverage being weaker in Asia and the Americas. Countries of major importance for migratory birds, such as the Russian Federation where the great majority of Eurasian waterfowl nest, the United States, Canada, many Latin American countries, China, and Japan are still not parties. The position is now improving: by August 1999, CMS had 60 parties which compares very positively to the 1991 tally of 38. However, this is still only half or less of the membership of the other global conventions such as Ramsar, World Heritage, CITES, and CBD.

[10] Lyster, *supra* note 7.

also requires parties to take habitat protection and pollution reduction measures, to prohibit most forms of taking and to coordinate research and monitoring.

- Agreement on the Conservation of Bats in Europe (September 10, 1991, in force January 16, 1994), an Article IV.3 AGREEMENT discussed below.
- Agreement on the Conservation of Small Cetaceans of the Baltic and North Seas (ASCOBANS) (New York, September 13, 1991, in force March 29, 1994). This Article IV.4 agreement has seven parties, who are required to apply the conservation, research, and management measures prescribed in an Annex and encouraged to cooperate on habitat conservation and management, surveys, research, and public information. Parties must 'endeavor' to prohibit the intentional taking and killing of small cetaceans and require the immediate release of any animals caught alive and in good health. The agreement provides for institutional and financial arrangements.
- Memorandum of Understanding concerning Conservation Measures for the Siberian Crane (June 16, 1993, superseded by a revised MoU concluded in Ramsar, Islamic Republic of Iran on December 13, 1998 and in force for signatories from January 1, 2000), an Article IV.4 agreement, discussed below.
- Memorandum of Understanding concerning Conservation Measures for the Slender-billed Curlew, *Numenius tenuirostris* (signed and in force September 10, 1994), an Article IV.4 agreement, discussed below.
- Agreement on the Conservation of African-Eurasian Migratory Waterbirds (The Hague, August 15, 1995, entered into force on November 1, 1999), an Article IV.3 AGREEMENT, discussed below.
- Agreement on the Conservation of Cetaceans of the Black Sea, Mediterranean Sea, and Contiguous Atlantic Area (ACCOBAMS) (Monaco, November 24, 1996, not in force as of September 1999), an Article IV.4 agreement, signed by 12 Range States. The agreement and the annexed legally binding Conservation Plan require states parties to cooperate to create and maintain a network of specially protected areas to conserve cetaceans; generally to prohibit any deliberate taking of them; to regulate fisheries activities; to require environmental impact assessments for specified activities; and to take specified measures for research, monitoring, training, and emergency planning. General reservations are not permitted. The agreement provides for a Meeting of the Parties and a secretariat and for the designation of a coordination unit in each subregion within an existing institution. The MOP is required to elect a small Bureau and to entrust the functions of the Scientific Committee 'to an existing organization assuring geographically-balanced representation' (Articles IV–VII).

- Memorandum of Understanding concerning Conservation Measures for Marine Turtles of the Atlantic Coast of Africa (Abidjan, May 29, 1999, in force for signatories from July 1, 1999). Signed by seven Range States, it sets out conservation measures for six species of marine turtle at all stages of their life cycle and their habitats, including nesting beaches. A conservation plan outlining measures to be undertaken in the short- and medium-term is under development.

Other formal Agreements and less formal undertakings are now being prepared with the assistance of the UNEP/CMS Secretariat and IUCN Environmental Law Centre in Bonn.[11]

2. Relationships between CMS, Agreements, and other instruments and institutions

The broad scope of CMS means that although the UNEP/CMS Secretariat is the only United Nations-based global organization to focus exclusively on migratory species, several other international institutions have interests in the protection of one or more of the species covered, including the European Commission, the International Whaling Commission established under the 1946 International Convention for the Regulation of Whaling,[12] and the 1979 Convention on the Conservation of European Wildlife and Natural Habitats ('the Bern Convention').[13] The overlapping mandates could impede the development of Agreements under the Convention.[14]

---

[11] The two formal agreements are: (1) draft Agreement for the Conservation of the Asian Houbara Bustard (*Chlamydotis undulata macqueeni*), under discussion since November 1990 and sponsored by the Government of Saudi Arabia. The revised Agreement and its action plan are expected to be negotiated and adopted during 1999. (2) draft Agreement on Sahelo-Saharan Ungulates. See Djerba Declaration by participants in the Seminar on the Conservation and Restoration of Sahelo-Saharan Ungulates (Tunisia, February 1998). Many less formal instruments are also under active discussion, including: draft Memorandum of Understanding for the conservation of the population of the Great Bustard (*Otis tarda*) in Central Europe, submitted to competent authorities of Range States as well as relevant governmental and non-governmental organizations; draft Memorandum of Understanding for the Conservation of Wild Ungulates in the Arabian Peninsula, currently being developed to provide a legal basis for the coordinated strict protection of a number of desert mammals and their habitats; draft Memorandum of Understanding on the Ruddy-headed Goose (*Chloephaga rubidiceps*), between Argentina and Chile which share the migratory population of this Appendix I-listed species. This would actively involve Wetlands International and local non-governmental organizations; draft Memorandum of Understanding for the conservation and sustainable use of the Sandgrouse (family: *Pteroclidae*), being developed by Namibia, South Africa, and Botswana. National species action plans are now being prepared. See *CMS Bulletin* No. 5.

[12] The Commission was established under the 1946 International Convention for the Regulation of Whaling. Washington, in force November 10, 1948, 161 U.N.T.S. 72; U.K.T.S. 5 (1949) Cmd.7604. CMS tacitly acknowledges the potential overlap with other marine mammal treaty regimes in a specific provision relating to Agreements on cetaceans.

[13] Bern, in force June 1, 1982, U.K.T.S. 56 (1982), Cmd. 8738; E.T.S. 104.

[14] Birnie and Boyle, *supra* note 8 at 473.

Where a draft Agreement relates to matters covered even partially by more than one treaty regime or institution, the competent institutions need a common understanding on the most appropriate framework for the proposed instrument.[15] The UNEP/CMS Secretariat makes constructive use of other international processes to develop or strengthen Agreements. The meeting to finalize the original Memorandum of Understanding on the Siberian Crane, for example, was organized during the 1993 Ramsar Convention Conference of the Parties in Kushiro, Japan. Some informal initiatives under Agreements have been integrated into wider political and strategic processes, such as the Pan European Biological and Landscape Diversity Strategy (Action Theme 11 on Threatened Species).[16] Since 1996, the secretariats of CMS and the Bern Convention have held regular meetings to explore common fields of cooperation, as the early Agreements developed pursuant to CMS apply in large measure to Europe.

Finally, in the last two years the UNEP/CMS Secretariat has concluded memoranda of cooperation with the Secretariats of CBD and Ramsar to promote institutional coordination and joint or harmonised work programs. Whilst the CBD establishes strictly country-related measures,[17] its designated financial mechanism (the Global Environmental Facility or 'GEF') offers new perspectives for financing international cooperative actions under CMS where the Range States concerned are eligible for GEF funds.

B. THE NATURE AND SCOPE OF AGREEMENTS UNDER CMS

As mentioned above, CMS provides for two types of accord: AGREEMENTS under Article IV.3 and Agreements under Article IV.4. The draft Convention presented by the former Federal Republic of Germany to the 1979 Diplomatic Conference that adopted the text of CMS referred to only one category of accord (AGREEMENTS covered by Article IV.3 and concerning species listed in Appendix II). Following a proposal by the United States,[18] however, the Conference decided to create a second category of accord and consequently inserted Article IV.4. The Conference documentation does not

[15] This issue arose with regard to the proposed Agreements on African-Eurasian waterbirds and cetaceans of the Black and Mediterranean Seas. The Bern Convention confers extensive protection on many of the species concerned but has a geographically limited mandate and does not have the means to cooperate on matters related to conservation throughout Africa. CMS was thus considered to be the most appropriate framework for coordination of matters concerning conservation of the migratory species concerned. See Seminar on African-European Cooperation in Nature Conservation (Dakar, Senegal, June 21–24, 1993), *CMS Bulletin* no. 4, July 21, 1993.

[16] Two Chiroptera action plans are being prepared under the Bern Convention, whilst projects developed under the 1991 Agreement on the Conservation of Bats in Europe have been included in the Pan-European Strategy.

[17] See UNEP/CMS.Conf.4.16, at 3.   [18] Document PL 11 of the Bonn Conference.

explain the reasons for the amendment, making it difficult to ascertain its exact purpose.[19]

The institutions created under CMS (Conference of the Parties or COP, Standing Committee, and Scientific Council) have grappled for years with the differences between the two categories of Agreements. Discussion of the legal nature and/or content of proposed Agreements has featured on the agenda of each COP meeting held to date with debate tending to focus on the need for flexibility and minimizing cumbersome ratification procedures.

In 1988, the Second Meeting of the COP[20] acknowledged disappointing progress in the conclusion of Agreements. Concern was expressed about the complex administrative arrangements proposed in some of the draft AGREEMENTS and the need to develop a simplified formula if such instruments were to be implemented by as many Range States as possible.[21] The Scientific Committee reported that draft Agreements in preparation might be delayed if too many new ones were initiated.[22] Several members supported the drafting of open-ended AGREEMENTS initially including only a small list of species, and thus making it possible to move more quickly towards implementation. Simple procedures then would be put in place to negotiate subsequent extensions in scope, embodied in annexes to the original texts, to accommodate new developments and local circumstances.[23]

In response to such concerns, the COP has approved the use of very diverse instruments under Article IV.4 and has sought to streamline procedural aspects thereof. COP2 adopted two important decisions in this respect. First, Resolution 2.6 (Implementation of Articles IV and V of the Convention) recommends that parties implement Article IV.4 within the spirit of the Convention through the use of instruments other than AGREEMENTS: 'such instruments, whenever appropriate and feasible, may take the shape of . . . resolutions adopted by the Conference of the Parties on proposals submitted by the Party Range States, administrative agreements or memoranda of understanding'. This non-exhaustive list expressly brings instruments other than treaties within the scope of Agreements under CMS. The Resolution also suggests that Article V.2 should apply to this type of instru-

---

[19] De Klemm, C., *Elements for the Formulation of Guidelines for the Harmonization of Future Agreements*, UNEP/CMS/Conf.4.9 of May 20, 1994.

[20] Geneva, Switzerland, October 11–14, 1988.

[21] France, *e.g.*, emphasized that the form of the proposed regional AGREEMENTS should be flexible: 'they should not require ratification; otherwise France would . . . be confronted with procedural problems': UNEP/CMS.Conf.2.16 at 8–13.

[22] *Ibid.* at 37. More recently, the Scientific Council report to COP4 discussed how to establish priorities for the development of future Agreements. It developed criteria, on the basis of which it proposed a list of about 30 possible future Agreements. It emphasized the difficulty of simultaneously drafting so many potential new Agreements and also that creating the Agreements tended to be hampered by the lack of knowledge on the migration of the targeted species. Annex 4, UNEP/CMS/Conf.4.11.

[23] Conf. 2, supra n. 21, at 37–8, Agenda item 5.

ment, which should thus 'cover the whole of the range of the migratory species concerned and should be open to accession by all Range States of that species, whether or not they are Parties to this Convention'. Resolution 2.7 (Administration of Agreements) provides that reference to Agreements shall be interpreted inclusively to cover both AGREEMENTS under Article IV.3 and agreements under Article IV.4 and establishes common rules for 'administrative arrangements' for all Agreements.

The third meeting of the COP in 1991[24] continued this streamlining process by adopting Resolution 3.5, which extends certain provisions of CMS on AGREEMENTS to Article IV.4 agreements. Noting that the draft Agreements then under discussion varied in their treatment of legal aspects, it expressed support for a study on harmonization of future Agreements, including memoranda of understanding.[25]

The first expert's report on this subject, presenting Guidelines for the Harmonization of Future Agreements, was submitted to COP4 in 1994[26] and a revised version was submitted to COP5 in 1997.[27] COP5 Resolution 5.2 expressed the desire to 'avoid unnecessary and unintended divergence in form and effect, with its consequent uncertainty'. It recognized the non-binding legal nature of international guidelines but considered the draft Guidelines to be 'a valuable compendium of Agreement practices which will enable parties to make considered choices in framing future Agreements'. The Resolution also acknowledged 'that treaty practice is subject to some variance between Parties, that some flexibility is desirable and that the range and type of possible Agreements, the best and most achievable means of conservation and management under the framework of CMS, and other circumstances may not render a single form of Agreement optimal for all cases'. The Guidelines are currently undergoing further revision in close consultation with parties. Other matters related to Agreements were clarified by the Strategy for the Future Development of the Convention[28] as revised and updated by Resolution 5.4 and its Annex, Objectives and Action Points for the 1998–2000 Triennium.[29]

---

[24] Geneva, Switzerland, September 9–13, 1991.

[25] Statement by the Netherlands on behalf of European Community Parties, UNEP/CMS/Conf.3.21, 7.

[26] Nairobi, Kenya, June 7–11, 1994. See de Klemm, *supra* note 19.

[27] De Klemm, C., and Shine, C., *Guidelines on the Harmonisation of Agreements*. Geneva, Switzerland, April 10–16, 1997. See UNEP/CMS/Conf. 5, paras.114–120.

[28] Adopted in principle by the COP in 1994 (Res. 4.4).

[29] Objective 4.1 supported the intensification of activities to lay the basis for the identification and development of new Agreements, as far as resources are available. Parties, including regional economic integration organizations ('REIOs'), were encouraged to take the lead in developing and/or sponsoring Agreements and in hosting interim secretariats. Developed party states were encouraged to facilitate initiatives of developing countries by providing technical, scientific, and financial assistance on request. The Objective also called for strengthening the Secretariat's capacity to assist in the development of new Agreements.

1. Legal Characteristics of Formal Agreements[30]

AGREEMENTS adopted under Article IV.3 are restricted to species listed in Appendix II and their substantive content is largely governed by Article V. The object of the AGREEMENT must be to restore the migratory species concerned to a favorable conservation status or maintain it in such a status (Article V.1). It should cover the whole of the range of the migratory species concerned and be open to accession by all Range States of that species whether parties to CMS or not (Article V.2). The Guidelines for such instruments are non-binding but an accord that departed significantly from them might not legally constitute an AGREEMENT. AGREEMENTS usually must take the form of legally-binding treaties, as the Guidelines provide for the creation of institutions and financial arrangements which will generally require ratification by the state concerned. Certain procedural rules are laid down by CMS Article V, while others may be inferred from the list of powers conferred on the COP (Article VII).

Article IV.4 agreements also may be concluded in the form of treaties.[31] They normally should be restricted to species or populations which are not listed in Appendix II to avoid overlap with Article IV.3 AGREEMENTS,[32] but there is nothing to prevent Range States from following the Article V Guidelines. These agreements may have a territorial scope narrower than the range of the species concerned and be closed to certain Range States. Procedural differences between AGREEMENTS and agreements have been largely removed by Resolutions 2.7 and 3.5, but certain institutional differences remain.

2. Legal Characteristics of Memoranda of Understanding

As noted above, the Convention does not lay down any particular rules for the form or content of Article IV.4 agreements. The COP has responded to concerns for flexibility and simplicity by recommending the conclusion of instruments such as Conference Resolutions,[33] administrative agreements, or

---

[30] See also the revised Guidelines on the Harmonisation of Agreements, *supra* note 29.

[31] Covering, as mentioned above, any population or any geographically separate part of the population of any species or lower taxon of wild animals, members of which periodically cross one or more national jurisdictional boundaries. This provision clearly departs from the definition of 'migratory species' given in Art. I.1.a of the Convention. Note that there is no obligation to cover the whole of the range of the migratory species concerned, cf. Art.V.2 and Res. 2.6 on less formal Art. IV.4 agreements.

[32] Once a species is listed in this Appendix, it counts as a migratory species as defined by Art. I.1.a and should therefore form the subject of an Art. IV.3. AGREEMENT in accordance with the spirit of CMS.

[33] It is open to question whether an ordinary resolution of the COP could really be considered as an agreement under Art. IV.4 in the absence of concrete proof evidenced by signatures that the parties concerned wish to commit themselves. See de Klemm, C., *supra* note 19.

memoranda of understanding, to which the procedural provisions of Resolutions 2.7 and 3.5 should apply. Existing instruments in this category are all memoranda of understanding, dealing respectively with the Siberian crane, the slender-billed curlew, and African marine turtles.

The abovementioned Resolutions do not define the legal character of such instruments by reference to terminology such as 'formal/informal' or 'legally-binding/non-binding', raising the question of the legal character of a MoU under CMS. The issue is under debate within CMS circles. Existing MoUs constitute official undertakings signed by high-level government representatives. At the very least, they should be seen as politically binding, creating a moral obligation on signatory states to carry out undertakings. Beyond this, however, CMS states parties have markedly different views on the legal effects of these undertakings.

One view holds that a MoU creating obligations for its signatories is as legally binding as any other international agreement. Its content and the intention of its signatories determine whether it has an international law character, irrespective of the instrument's designation. Another view is that a MoU is an agreement at the implementation level which can be concluded by any government office and does not require formal government credentials. A signatory can withdraw from or cease to participate in a MoU without legal consequences. According to this view, it is inappropriate for a MoU to contain terminology or provisions characteristic of formal legally-binding treaties such as AGREEMENTS.[34]

CMS institutions seem to support the legally non-binding nature of MoUs. The CMS Secretariat, in its official information sheet on the results of COP4, affirms that international cooperative Agreements under CMS may range from 'legally-binding treaties to less formal memoranda of understanding'. COP Resolution 4.4, adopting in principle the Strategy for the Future Development of the Convention, provides a useful indicator of how MoU instruments are perceived. Priority 15 provides that 'Agreements should continue to be developed as legally binding instruments. Recommendations and memoranda of understanding should be used where necessary to conserve species through non-binding instruments linked to the Convention.'

Based on the proceedings and resolutions of the COP and the MoU concluded to date, it appears that memoranda of understanding are not intended to be developed as quasi-treaties, but instead as short-term practical mechanisms characterized by certain features:

- MoU are intended to initiate and co-ordinate short-term administrative and scientific measures by Range States in collaboration with specialised NGOs;

[34] This view is supported by commentators such as Birnie and Boyle, who classify the MoU and administrative agreements referred to in Resolution 2.6 as 'informal agreements'. Birnie and Boyle, *supra* note 8 at 472.

- They should cover the whole range of the migratory species concerned and be open to accession by all Range States (Resolutions 2.6 and 3.5). However, this is not mandatory and there could be biological or political reasons why it would be useful for an informal agreement to cover only a subgroup of Range States;
- MoU may be couched in simple language and establish individual tasks for each of their signatories in an annexed action plan;
- To the extent that MoU are essentially administrative agreements, they should contain only undertakings which can be implemented under existing national legislation or by administrative decision;
- They may enter rapidly into force for a fixed period and be easily amended;
- States cannot be required to make financial contributions under MoUs, but there is nothing to prevent a MoU from requiring signatories to use their best endeavours to secure technical and financial support on a purely voluntary basis.

3. Relationship of Memoranda of Understanding to Formal Agreements

Memoranda of understanding can be transitory in character or form standalone accords.[35] They offer the important advantage of speed, enabling action to be taken quickly and the most urgent issues to be addressed first, possibly while Range States are negotiating more comprehensive legally binding Agreements. In such cases, a MoU could be incorporated at a later date into an action plan under such an Agreement.

The MoUs on Siberian cranes and slender-billed curlews refer specifically to the conclusion of longer term conservation or action plans for possible inclusion under the Asian-Pacific Waterbird Agreement ('APWA') and the African-Eurasian Waterbird Agreement, respectively. The MoU concerning conservation measures for the Siberian crane would probably become redundant if the APWA were to be concluded as a treaty in the future.

C. DRAFTING HISTORY OF SELECTED AGREEMENTS

1. 1991 Agreement on the Conservation of Bats in Europe

In 1985, the CMS Scientific Committee's Working Group on Bats[36] submitted an outline proposal for a European Agreement for bats to the first meet-

---

[35] Resolution 3.5 recognizes that whilst administrative agreements or MoU may be established as a first step towards the conclusion of a legally-binding AGREEMENT, this may not be appropriate in all cases.
[36] CMS/COM.I/1.

ing of the COP, linked to a German proposal to include European bats on Appendix II. A background document provided justification for the conclusion of an Agreement.[37] The Working Group recommended that immediate steps be taken to conclude an Agreement, a proposal approved by the COP in Resolution 1.6. The United Kingdom sponsored further work on the draft, but stated at the second meeting of the COP that the draft AGREEMENT could not be finalized 'until the fundamental issues regarding the nature of such AGREEMENTS had been resolved'.[38] Other legal questions arose concerning the possible coverage of non-migratory species and possible duplication with the protection afforded to bats under the Bern Convention on the Conservation of European Wildlife and Natural Habitats. COP1's inclusion of all the species covered by the draft AGREEMENT in Appendix II answered the first question, because they were thus by definition migratory.

The draft was designed to achieve international coordination of the differing national measures in accordance with the Guidelines of Article V of CMS[39] with which Article IV.3 AGREEMENTS must comply. The Article IV.3 AGREEMENT was opened for signature on December 4, 1991, more than six years after the first proposal, and came into force on January 16, 1994. As of August 20, 1998, fourteen states parties to CMS were parties to the Agreement, out of forty-three Range States.

2. 1993 Memorandum of Understanding on the Siberian Crane

In December 1991, recommendations for an agreement concerning Siberian cranes[40] were drawn up by a working group of crane specialists who met during the Symposium on Wetland and Waterfowl Conservation in South and West Asia (Karachi, Pakistan),[41] at which the UNEP/CMS Secretariat was represented. A specialist NGO, the International Crane Foundation, prepared the first draft of an agreement early in 1992 but consensus was reached that 'a less formal Memorandum of Understanding among the Range States ... would be a more practical way of promoting short term actions'.[42] During the May 1993 fourth meeting of the CMS Scientific Council in Bonn, a small working group, supported by the UNEP/CMS Secretariat, developed a draft MoU on conservation measures for the Siberian crane. The draft MoU was

---

[37] CMS/COM.I/1/Add.1.　　　　　　　　　[38] UNEP/CMS.Conf.2.16, 13.

[39] UNEP/CMS.Conf.2.16, 36.

[40] The Siberian crane *Grus leucogeranus* has the longest migration route of all cranes, ranging from breeding areas in the far north of Asia to wintering grounds some 5,500 km further south. Western and central Asian populations are on the brink of extinction, believed to be due primarily to hunting and loss of wetlands. *CMS Bulletin* 4, July 21, 1993 and *Bulletin* 5, July 1996.

[41] Convened by the National Council for the Conservation of Wildlife (Pakistan), the Asian Wetlands Bureau, and the former IWRB. The Symposium also produced an action plan to address the degradation and loss of South East Asian wetlands on which the cranes heavily rely for their survival.

[42] *CMS Bulletin* 4 (July 21, 1993), 5.

further discussed and revised in Kushiro, Japan, in June 1993; in another example of streamlining of international meetings, the UNEP/CMS Secretariat used the occasion of the fifth meeting of the Conference of the Parties to the Ramsar Convention to convene a series of meetings for government representatives and interested NGOs.

The original MoU was signed on June 16, 1993 and came into force on July 1, 1993 for an initial period of three years. It was the first informal instrument to be considered an agreement under Article IV.4 of CMS and also the first instrument to be signed by a state not yet party to the parent Convention (the Russian Federation). Its rapid development and signature indicated the consensus on the urgency of the actions to be taken. The MoU was wholly revised on December 13, 1998 at the third meeting of the signatories (Ramsar, Islamic Republic of Iran) and became effective for signatories on January 1, 1999: for Range States that sign at a future date, the MoU will become effective on the first day of the first month following signature. The revised MoU was immediately signed by seven Range States (Azerbaijan, Pakistan, Kazakhstan, India, Turkmenistan, Uzbekistan, and Islamic Republic of Iran) and by China in April 1999. Signatures on behalf of Afghanistan and the Russian Federation (a signatory to the original MoU) are still awaited. The revised MoU has also been signed by two 'cooperating organisations': the International Crane Foundation and the UNEP/CMS Secretariat. The latter, which *de facto* acts as depositary and provides administrative support and strategic guidance to Range States, is also a signatory in its own right to substantive provisions of the Conservation Plan annexed to the MoU.

3. 1994 Memorandum of Understanding Concerning Conservation Measures for the Slender-billed Curlew, *Numenius Tenuirostris*

This severely endangered species is listed in Appendix I; in 1996, there were thought to be only 100–300 individuals still in existence. Their breeding, wintering, and migrating range covers twenty-seven states in south-west Asia, southern Europe, and northern Africa. Birdlife International published an extensive report and action plan in 1991[43] and the following year a workshop organized by the *Fondazione Il Nibbio* was held in Arosio, Italy, with participants from national and regional authorities, conservation and hunter organizations, and research institutes. Discussions in the Scientific Council in 1993 in cooperation with BirdLife International and the scientific advisors of the European Community led to the proposal to develop a MoU under CMS. It was considered by the Secretariat to be 'a last effort to save the species, which had been on Appendix I for a long time without any visible conservation improvement'.[44]

---

[43] Formerly the International Council for Bird Preservation (ICBP).
[44] UNEP/CMS/Conf.4.16, para.37.

The Secretariat coordinated preparation of the draft MoU and circulated a draft to all Range States, whose comments and amendments were incorporated into a revised draft submitted to the fifth meeting of the Scientific Council in 1994.[45] Following further consultation, the draft was sent after COP4 to the relevant national authorities of all Range States with an action plan for each state annexed to the MoU. The first signatures were submitted on September 10, 1994, the date on which the MoU became effective for the Range States concerned. By August 1999, sixteen Range States out of thirty had signed the MoU, only six of these being party to CMS. The MoU has also been signed by three cooperating organisations: UNEP/CMS Secretariat, BirdLife International, and the International Council for Game and Wildlife Conservation (CIC).

4. 1995 Agreement on the Conservation of African-Eurasian Migratory Waterbirds

This Article IV.3 AGREEMENT had a long gestation. Elements of an Agreement on the Conservation of Western Palearctic Migratory Species of Wild Animals[46] were prepared in the early 1980s even before CMS had entered into force.

The Scientific Committee's Working Group on Ducks and Geese supported conclusion of such an agreement in principle during COP1 in 1985.[47] It considered that proper protection and management on a biological basis would necessitate cooperation with hunters, hunting organizations, and nature conservation organizations as well as education and confidence-building measures. Any agreement should be flexible and, at least at the beginning, should not define its goals too strictly in the form of rules, regulations, and prohibitions. Close links should be established with the Ramsar Convention and relevant non-governmental organizations (NGOs) such as CIC, the Fédération Européenne des Associations de Chasseurs (FACE), Wetlands International, and BirdLife International.

The Government of the Netherlands further elaborated the draft Western Palearctic Waterfowl Agreement between 1988 and June 1991. The text was originally intended to be negotiated and adopted under the sponsorship of the E.C.,[48] but little progress was made and consultations were therefore undertaken in autumn 1992 between scientific councillors, other experts, and the Chairman of the Standing Committee. At the latter's request, the E.C. Commissioner for the Environment suggested in February 1993 that the

---

[45] UNEP/CMS/Inf.4.5 and Corr.1.
[46] IUCN Environmental Policy and Law paper no. 21, 1983.   [47] CMS/COM.I/6.
[48] *CMS Bulletin* 1, January 1992. A text was to be adopted by the European Commission and formally presented to the E.C. Council of Ministers in order to obtain a mandate for the E.C. to negotiate with other Range States, the procedure being completed by mid-1992.

UNEP/CMS Secretariat take the lead to develop a draft agreement and promised financial support.

Much of the negotiation focused on the species and geographic area to be covered. The Secretariat took a strategic decision to develop a small number of comprehensive waterbird Agreements, rather than 100 or more separate Agreements,[49] to cover the entire range of Western Palearctic anatidae,[50] as required under Article V.2 for Article IV.3 AGREEMENTS, and to develop subsequently AGREEMENTS for migratory waterbirds of the Asia-Pacific region and possibly the Americas.

Non-governmental organizations were actively involved in revising and developing the draft African-Eurasian Agreement ('AEWA'). In January 1993, UNEP/CMS Wetlands International was requested to update the text to ensure harmonization with the draft Asia-Pacific Waterbird Agreement and consistency with the principal conclusions of the 1992 U.N. Conference on Environment and Development. The Royal Society for the Protection of Birds sponsored an updating of the management and action plan. A new action plan for African storks, ibises, and spoonbills was elaborated by April 1993.

For the draft AEWA to have the status of an Article IV.3 AGREEMENT it was necessary for COP4 to approve the listing in Appendix II of many additional species of migratory waterbirds with an unfavourable conservation status. The first intergovernmental meeting to discuss the draft AEWA was held immediately after COP4 in Nairobi in 1994.

The AEWA finally was adopted in The Hague on August 15, 1995, but was not opened for signature until August 15, 1996 due to difficulties in the preparation of the Arabic and Russian versions of the text. With 117 Range States, AEWA is the most ambitious Agreement concluded to date under the auspices of CMS. It entered into force November 1, 1999.

D. CONTENT AND EVOLUTION OF SELECTED AGREEMENTS

1. 1991 Agreement on the Conservation of Bats in Europe

This binding instrument provides for the conservation of European populations of Chiroptera (*Rhinolophidae* and *Vespertilionidae*) occurring in Europe and non-European Range States. Article III (Fundamental Obligations) requires parties to prohibit the deliberate capture, keeping, or killing of bats except under permit, to identify and protect sites of importance for their conservation, to promote research programs and public awareness initiatives, and to designate

---

[49] UNEP/CMS.Conf.4.16, at 15.

[50] From western Siberia and the arctic regions of Scandinavia, Greenland, Iceland, and northeast Canada through the whole of Europe and Africa.

an appropriate body for advice on bat conservation and management. Parties are to exchange information on their experiences in this matter. Article IV (National Implementation) requires parties to adopt and enforce such legislative and administrative measures as may be necessary for the purpose of giving effect to the Agreement. The Agreement also provides for institutional arrangements. Article II.2 specifies that the provisions of the Agreement shall not relieve parties of their obligations under any existing treaty, convention, or agreement. Unlike the more recent AEWA,[51] there is no provision in the Bats Agreement on the adoption of management plans, but the Meeting of the Parties has adopted and updated a Conservation and Management Plan.

2. 1998 Memorandum of Understanding on the Siberian Crane Superseding the 1993 MoU

This revised MoU is addressed to the Heads of Environment Ministries of signatory Range States. The Preamble acknowledges 'their shared responsibility for the conservation and wise management of the Siberian crane and the wetland habitats on which the species depends, and the desirability of involving all Range States of the western, central and eastern populations of the species in common initiatives'. It affirms that signatories will work closely together to improve the species' conservation status throughout its breeding, wintering, and migration range.

The obligations of the MoU are formulated in mandatory terms. The signatories 'shall' provide strict protection for Siberian cranes and their wetland habitats, implement the relevant provisions of the conservation plan in their respective countries subject to availability of resources, facilitate the exchange of scientific, technical, and legal information needed to coordinate conservation measures, cooperate with recognized scientists of international organizations and other Range States, and designate a competent authority to serve as a contact point for other parties and the UNEP/CMS Secretariat (paragraphs 1–4). The procedural provisions broadly equating to the final clauses of a treaty are listed at the end of the text, under the puzzling heading of 'Basic Principles'. These cover the issues of entry into force, duration, amendment of the MoU, including the Conservation Plan, and working language. As this is not a formal treaty, there are no provisions on reservations, ratification, or accession, nor does the MoU designate a depositary or contain institutional or financial provisions.

The annexed Conservation Plan is presented in annotated tabular form with separate measures laid down for the Western and Central Asian Siberian crane populations. The three basic objectives are to reduce mortality in remaining populations; increase numbers and genetic diversity; and enhance

---

[51] And the 1996 ACCOBAMS.

cooperation among the Range States and other concerned agencies. Primary responsibility for implementation of each activity is assigned to one government, all governments (generic activities), or to a cooperating organization. The table indicates progress and results achieved from 1997 to 1999 and specific follow-up activities to be undertaken in 1999 and 2000. These specific actions are also listed in a separate table, divided into two parts. The first group of actions applies to all Range States of a given population. The second sets out country-specific conservation actions.

Three points are of particular interest. First, the actions are precisely targeted at each Range State's role in the species' migration (breeding, wintering, etc.) and are capable of verification. Secondly, a section is devoted to each Range State, whether or not it has signed the MoU. Non-signatory Range States therefore know in advance what would be required if they were to participate in the MoU. Thirdly, specific actions are also required from each of the three cooperating organizations, relating to administrative and technical aspects of implementation as appropriate.

A small number of actions fit somewhat awkwardly within this non-binding instrument. For example, the Russian Federation is required to expand the network of protected areas for central populations, realize a new hunting law at federal level, and adapt it to the level of a named region. The adoption of such legislation depends on the exercise of political power which falls outside the remit of the signatory administrative authorities and is qualitatively different from actions such as exchanges of information, submission of reports, research, and monitoring, which may unquestionably be implemented by authorities responsible for negotiating and signing the MoU.

3. 1994 Memorandum of Understanding Concerning Conservation Measures for the Slender-billed Curlew

This MoU is addressed to the Environment Ministries of signatory Range States. The Preamble affirms agreement by signatories to work closely together to improve the species' conservation status throughout its range.

The MoU has a similar format to the Siberian crane MoU described above, being divided between generally applicable provisions and conservation measures specific to each signatory state and to the three cooperating organizations. The substantive provisions are qualified: signatories 'shall . . . endeavor' to provide strict protection for the slender-billed curlew, identify and conserve the wetlands and other essential habitats, implement the applicable provisions of the action plan as a basis for the conservation of the whole population of the species, and facilitate information exchange and cooperation (paragraphs 1–3).[52] In contrast, the requirements in the first part of the action

---

[52] They must also designate a competent authority or authorized scientist to serve as a contact point and submit annual reports to the UNEP/CMS Secretariat.

plan are mandatory: all Range States shall, *inter alia*, enact or improve legislation to protect the slender-billed curlew and the wetlands that are critical to
their survival, and take necessary measures to enforce such legislation: 'the
most urgent measure would be to completely ban the shooting, other taking
and significant disturbance of this species'. Once again, this type of action is
conditional upon the exercise of political power and is hard to reconcile with
the concept of an informal instrument.

The second part of the action plan sets out measures to be taken by the individual Range States and cooperating organizations subject to availability of
resources and to any amendments made at the time of signature and communicated to all Range States by the UNEP/CMS Secretariat. Although such an
amendment sounds like a reservation by another name, its scope is restricted
to country-specific actions and does not extend to generally applicable
requirements under the MoU. In addition, Basic Principle 2 of the MoU,
described below, permits a Range State unilaterally to amend its section of
the action plan at any time, subject to notification of such changes to the
UNEP/CMS Secretariat. In other words, a signatory can choose at any time
not to be 'bound' by its undertakings.

Some country-specific provisions contained in the action plan fall outside
the remit of the administrative authorities responsible for signing and implementing the MoU. For example, the European Commission is required to
propose certain amendments to Appendix II/2 of the 1979 E.C. Wild Birds
Directive and to 'ensure that the use of the EU Development Fund concerning farming and other commercial activities does not adversely affect those
wetlands that are important to *Numenius tenuirostris*'.

The MoU requires signatories to cooperate with the UNEP/CMS
Secretariat in developing a longer-term conservation or action plan within
two years after the entry into force of the MoU, for possible inclusion in the
AEWA. The MoU provides that such a plan 'shall include, inter alia . . .
appropriate legal regulations to protect the birds from significant disturbance
or killing through hunting or other activities'.

The MoU does not establish institutional machinery, but does provide
that, after entry into force of what is now the AEWA, 'all those functions
listed in this Memorandum concerning the coordination, the receipt and further distribution of reports, as well as the development of further actions, may
be transferred to the Secretariat'. Although the different measures taken by
the individual 'Parties' are to be financed on a national basis, 'efforts should
also be made to gain financial support for key points of the Action Plan from
other sources'.

The final clauses, again described as 'Basic Principles', cover *inter alia* the
issue of entry into force, duration, automatic renewal, termination of
participation, and working language. Once again, there are no provisions
on finance, reservations, ratification, or accession and no depositary is

designated. The amendment provision (Basic Principle 2) is significantly different from the equivalent provision in the Siberian crane MoU. This MoU may be amended by 'a consensus of the majority of the signatory States', consensus that would have to be obtained by correspondence as the MoU does not provide for meetings of Range States.

4. 1995 Agreement on the Conservation of African-Eurasian Migratory Waterbirds

This legally binding Article IV.3 AGREEMENT applies to waterbirds that are ecologically dependent on wetlands in Africa and in Eurasia, including the Middle-East, Greenland, and parts of Canada. It consists of an Agreement and, for the first time in an international environmental agreement, a legally binding action plan which forms an integral part of the Agreement.[53] Parties are required to take coordinated measures to maintain migratory waterbirds in a favorable conservation status or to restore them to such a status. Taking account of the precautionary principle, they must apply both the General Conservation Measures in Article III and the specific actions in the action plan contained in Annex 3.

The action plan contains detailed obligations for species conservation, habitat conservation, management of human activities, research and monitoring, education and information, and implementation. The legal measures to be taken vary according to the conservation status of the species concerned, as laid down in a scientific table in Annex 3. Article 2.2 of the plan requires parties to cooperate with a view to developing and implementing international single species action plans for two categories of species, those which are endangered[54] and those for which hunting may continue on a sustainable use basis where hunting of such populations is a long-established cultural practice. The action plan must be reviewed at each ordinary session of the Meeting of the Parties, taking into account conservation guidelines,[55] and may be amended by the MOP according to a simplified procedure set out in Article X.5.[56] This should enable parties to adopt binding measures in

[53] The AEWA is not subject to general reservations, but a Range State or REIO may enter a specific reservation with regard to any species or provision of the action plan at the time of ratification.

[54] Listed in Appendix I or the 1994 IUCN Red List Categories.

[55] Para.7.3 of the action plan requires the AEWA Secretariat, in coordination with the Technical Committee and with the assistance of experts from Range States, to coordinate the development of conservation guidelines in accordance with Art. IV.4 of the Agreement to assist the parties in the implementation of this action plan. The Agreement secretariat shall ensure, where possible, coherence with guidelines approved under other international instruments. These conservation guidelines shall aim at introducing the principle of sustainable use.

[56] 'Any additional annexes and any amendment to an annex shall be adopted by a two-thirds majority of the Parties present and voting and shall enter into force for all Parties on the ninetieth day after the date of its adoption by the Meeting of the Parties, except for Parties which have entered a reservation in accordance with paragraph 6 of this Article.'

response to changing priorities and circumstances much more rapidly than if such amendments had to go through the full ratification process.

1. 1991 Agreement on the Conservation of Bats in Europe

Parties must designate a national authority or authorities responsible for implementation of the Agreement (Article II.3). Article V establishes a Meeting of the Parties ('MOP'), whose only specific powers cover the adoption of rules of procedure and financial rules (including budget provisions and the scale of contributions) and the establishment of such scientific and other working groups as it sees fit.

The primary mechanism to supervise compliance with the Agreement is the requirement for parties to submit national reports on implementation, to be circulated to the parties not less than ninety days before ordinary meetings of the MOP (Article VI). The content of these reports may be discussed by the MOP, which adopted a standardized format for reports at its second session in July 1998.

Under Article V.3, Range States or REIOs (regional economic integration organizations) not party to the Agreement, the UNEP/CMS Secretariat, the Secretariat to the Bern Convention and 'similar intergovernmental organizations', which presumably includes treaty institutions competent in the field of wild fauna,[57] may attend MOP sessions as observers. In addition, any agency or body technically qualified in bat conservation and management may send observers unless at least one-third of the parties present object.

The MOP has held two sessions (Bristol, UK, July 18–20, 1995; Bonn, July 1–3, 1998). At its first session, it approved the establishment of a permanent secretariat which is now co-located with the UNEP/CMS Secretariat in Bonn, as well as a scientific Advisory Committee. Resolutions adopted at MOP2 concerned *inter alia* transboundary programmes on species and habitat conservation, terms of reference for the Advisory Committee and the establishment of a prioritized action plan for 1998–2001. The Advisory Committee has met on four occasions, with central European venues being selected to facilitate attendance by a greater number and diversity of Range States. The Bern Convention works closely with the Agreement Secretariat and has attended meetings of the Advisory Committee as an observer.

---

[57] MOP2 in 1998 was attended *inter alia* by the interim Secretariat to the AEWA and the Secretariat of ASCOBANS.

2. 1998 Memorandum of Understanding on the Siberian Crane Superseding the 1993 MoU

Implementation of the memorandum, including the conservation plan, must be assessed at regular meetings attended by representatives of each of the governments concerned and persons or agencies technically qualified in the conservation of Siberian cranes. These meetings are to be convened by the UNEP/CMS Secretariat but hosted and organized by one of the Range States or cooperating organizations (paragraph 2).

Each meeting reviews implementation of the MoU by considering national reports and technical and other data. Each signatory Range State must provide the UNEP/CMS Secretariat with a report on its implementation by March 31 of each year. In consultation with the Range States concerned, it then updates the conservation plan under the MoU for all Range States, even those which are not signatories. The effect of these provisions is that signatories to the MoU submit reports and meet together probably much more frequently than do parties to formal Agreements, where the frequency of reporting is tied to bi- or tri-ennial sessions of the Meeting of the Parties.

The current annotated Conservation Plan, covering the period 1999–2000, was adopted in Ramsar in 1998. The CMS Scientific Council has praised the conservation plan as clear, realistic, simple, and easy to use, showing very clearly who the different players are.[58] COP5 in 1997 noted the 'success of the work undertaken under the Memorandum in terms of communication and cooperation of the Range States' governmental and scientific bodies, specialised international non-governmental organizations and internationally reputable experts'.[59]

3. 1994 Memorandum of Understanding concerning Conservation Measures for the Slender-billed Curlew

This MoU does not establish its own institution or a regular supervisory mechanism in the form of meetings of the Range States. Instead, implementation of the Memorandum, including the action plan, must be assessed 'by correspondence or personal contacts with the Secretariat and the Scientific Council of the Bonn Convention' (paragraph 3). Range States must submit annual reports on the implementation of the MoU to the Secretariat, which not only transmits these reports to other Range States but must also provide an overview report compiled on the basis of information at its disposal. Supervision of the MoU is thus heavily dependent on the resources and per-

---

[58] Report on Seventh Meeting of the Scientific Council, Geneva, April 7–8, 1997, 136.
[59] Report on the Fifth Meeting of the Conference of the Parties, para. 100.

sonnel in the UNEP/CMS Secretariat,[60] which in turn liaises closely with competent organizations, scientific institutions, and national authorities.

In 1996, the Secretariat produced the first overview report which was distributed to Range States, interested scientific institutions, and NGOs. A seminar on the identification of breeding locations of the slender-billed curlew was held in Moscow in 1997, during which year twelve Range States submitted reports for circulation and information on migration routes. This information was entered into a database in cooperation with BirdLife International,[61] which also prepared the draft long-term action plan required under the MoU. A Slender-billed Curlew Working Group (SbCWG) was officially established under CMS in 1998. Financial assistance has been provided by the E.C. to make it possible to carry out research monitoring and habitat conservation measures.

4. 1995 Agreement on the Conservation of African-Eurasian Migratory Waterbirds

The AEWA establishes a MOP with detailed powers to adopt legally binding annexes or amendments to annexes, a Secretariat,[62] and a Technical Committee. The latter, established at the first session of the MOP in November 1999, consists of regional experts, representatives of three NGOs (the International Union for Conservation of Nature and Natural Resources (IUCN), Wetlands International, and CIC, and experts on rural economics, game management, and environmental law. Financial contributions to the budget are to be made in accordance with the United Nations scale of assessment, up to a maximum of 25 percent for any given Range State.

As under the European Bats Agreement, the primary mechanism to supervise compliance is the requirement for parties to submit national reports on implementation. Supervision of AEWA's implementation is actively supported by the Bureau to the 1971 Ramsar Convention, pursuant to a memorandum of understanding signed on February 18, 1997 between the CMS Secretariat and the Ramsar bureau to intensify co-operation in the fields of implementation covered by both conventions and by Agreements concluded under CMS. This MoU establishes a formal basis for future collaboration and concerted action to facilitate implementation of the AEWA. The

---

[60] The MoU makes no provision for secretariat services but basic services for this purpose are provided by the UNEP/CMS Secretariat.

[61] Report on Seventh Meeting of the Scientific Council, Geneva, April 7–8, 1997, para. 34; see also UNEP/CMS (ed.), *Conservation Measures for the Siberian Crane* (1999), CMS Technical Series Publication No. 1, UNEP/CMS Secretariat, Bonn, Germany.

[62] The interim secretariat, now fully operational, is provided by the Government of the Netherlands at its own expense until the first meeting of the parties (provisionally scheduled for late 1999) and for a transitional period thereafter. The permanent Secretariat is to be established by the MOP at its first meeting.

electronic Ramsar Forum is one of the channels used to publicize and distribute the AEWA newsletter published by the Interim Secretariat, four editions of which have appeared to date.

5. Institutional Relationship Between Agreements and the Parent Convention

The nexus between the parent Convention and an Agreement differs significantly depending on whether it is a formal Agreement providing for the creation of its own institutions or whether it takes the form of a memorandum of understanding. The Convention establishes formal links between its own institutions and bodies established pursuant to Article IV.3 AGREE-MENTS. Some of these provisions have been extended to bodies established under Article IV.4 agreements.[63] Other provisions are technically still restricted to Article IV.3 AGREEMENTS, namely the power of the COP to review progress made under AGREEMENTS, the power of the Scientific Council to provide scientific advice to bodies set up under AGREEMENTS, and the admission of such bodies as of right at meetings of the COP. Such distinctions are now of little practical consequence because bodies established under Article IV.4 agreements (e.g. ASCOBANS) are routinely admitted as observers.

In contrast, memoranda of understanding do not provide for the creation of institutions and thus have no separate representation at meetings of the COP. This does not mean that their implementation is not supported by CMS institutions. The Standing Committee,[64] for example, reviews the progress of all Agreements at each of its meetings and reports on this to the COP. The COP can adopt recommendations addressed to any type of Agreements: COP5 urged all Range States to sign and implement the MoU on the slender-billed curlew (Recommendation 5.1).

The number of Agreements under CMS and the fact that not all parties/signatories are party to the parent Convention obviously has the potential to cause administrative and financial complexity and arguably to dilute supervision of compliance. The CMS Secretariat therefore has sought ways to rationalize institutional arrangements by promoting collaboration in the implementation of Agreements, as well as cost-effective provision of administrative services and support. Acknowledging the need 'to maintain the mutually independent and autonomous functioning of each secretariat according to the instructions of their relevant bodies',[65] COP5 approved a

---

[63] *e.g.* Art. IV.5 (copy of each Agreement to be provided to the Secretariat), Art. VII.5.d (the COP may examine reports presented by bodies established pursuant to Agreements), and Art. IX.4.b (CMS Secretariat to maintain liaison with such bodies); see Res. 2.7 (Administration of Agreements) and Res. 3.5.

[64] Which comprises one representative from each of 6 geographic regions plus the Depositary (Germany).

[65] Res. 5.5 (Co-location of Agreement Secretariats).

model for the co-location of Europe-based Agreement secretariats in a special Agreements Unit with the Secretariat of the Convention.

With regard to funding, the COP has determined that secretariats for individual Agreements should be financed entirely by their parties, except where membership is such that financial support from the Convention is essential in the early stages of development.[66] In addition, parties to the respective Agreements should provide substantial voluntary support 'to facilitate the administration and effective implementation of the Agreement'. No specific reference is made to funding memoranda of understanding.

F. ROLE OF NON-GOVERNMENTAL ORGANIZATIONS IN PROMOTING COMPLIANCE

Non-governmental organizations have played a major role in the negotiation and/or implementation of many Agreements under CMS. The 1991 Agreement on the Conservation of Bats in Europe does not confer a formal role on any NGO, but any agency or body technically qualified in bat conservation and management may be represented at sessions of the MOP by observers unless at least one-third of the parties present object (Article V.3). In 1998, MOP2 was attended by six NGOs as observers.

The other three instruments under consideration all make specific provision for NGO involvement. Article VII of the AEWA provides for representation of three specific NGOs on its Technical Committee. BirdLife International drafted the Single Species Action Plans to be considered for adoption by the first meeting of the MOP to AEWA (Recommendation 5.1). The two MoU have gone further in their inclusion of NGOs as quasi-institutional partners in implementation, under the title of 'cooperating organizations'. The NGOs have accepted specific undertakings under the respective action or conservation plans, primarily linked to administrative and technical support for Range States. BirdLife International, for example, was responsible for drafting the long-term action plan under the MoU on the slender-billed curlew. NGO involvement in the AEWA Technical Committee and the MoU on the slender-billed curlew may also facilitate systematic consideration of the conservation and hunting issues associated with the species in question. Like the AEWA, this MoU brings together a conservation NGO (BirdLife International) with an international hunters' organization (CIC).

Over the last few years, the UNEP/CMS Secretariat has developed more permanent support systems with major specialized NGOs to strengthen implementation and strategic development of the Convention. In 1996, it concluded a MoU with the IUCN Environmental Law Centre concerning its

---

[66] Res. 5.4 (Objectives and Action Points for the 1998–2000 Triennium), Objective 7.

provision of legal advice. A similar memorandum is now envisaged with Wetlands International for the provision of scientific advice and more intensive assistance in waterbird conservation issues.

The COP to CMS has strongly endorsed the role of non-governmental organizations in the implementation of informal Agreements. Recommendation 5.1 encourages the NGOs which signed the MoU on the slenderbilled curlew actively to support the UNEP/CMS Secretariat's efforts in organizing the implementation on an international level. The COP has also systematically supported the catalyst role of appropriately qualified NGOs. In 1994, it encouraged parties 'to consult NGOs, provide them with relevant information and offer them ample opportunities to contribute to the formulation and implementation of governmental policy on migratory species conservation' and recommended that parties to Agreements 'invite appropriate representatives of NGOs to participate in meetings held to discuss the development or implementation of such Agreements'.[67] In 1997, the COP called on the Secretariat to hold at least one intersessional meeting with NGOs, and urged individual parties to consult and, where appropriate, make use of NGOs in implementing the Convention. NGOs are specifically encouraged to target their project work *inter alia* towards the implementation of CMS and Agreements.[68]

G. INCENTIVES AND DISINCENTIVES TO COMPLIANCE

As all of the Agreements under consideration are so recent that little or no information is available on the practical aspects of compliance, it is not possible to say from the relevant reports how far states have adopted the respective norms in their laws or regulations. However, certain observations can be made on the basis of the texts and progress to date and, specifically, the fact that there have been no complaints of non-compliance.

The Bats and AEWA Agreements are formal legally-binding instruments which contain fairly standard provisions on dispute settlement and denunciation and termination. In contrast, the MoU are silent on such matters although, as mentioned above, they emphasize the requirement to submit reports annually to the UNEP/CMS Secretariat. For the MoU, there appear to be few disincentives to compliance other than opposition by vested interests and lack of adequate financial and human resources. The main incentives for compliance, other than favorable publicity, appears to be the provision of

---

[67] Recommendation 4.6 (the role of Non-Governmental Organizations in CMS), paras. 2 and 3.

[68] Res. 5.4 (Objectives and Action Points for the 1998–2000 Triennium), Objective 8.3.

financial, scientific, or technical assistance by CMS institutions, other states, or relevant NGOs.[69]

Under the MoU on the Siberian crane, the CMS Scientific Council has approved the allocation of funds to a project, developed by the International Crane Foundation, that will transform the 1997–9 Conservation Plan into a five-year project suitable for funding by GEF.[70] With regard to the MoU on the slender-billed curlew, funds have been allocated from the CMS Trust Fund to support a project developed by the Belgian Royal Institute of Natural Science and German Federal Agency for Nature Conservation for conservation measures in several Range States.[71] CIC, the NGO, has made financial contributions to help identify the birds' Siberian breeding grounds, and conservation measures are also being funded under an E.C. LIFE project.[72]

The CMS Trust Fund is generally empowered to finance activities in support of the Convention, including the development of Agreements, particularly in developing countries and in areas where the coverage was inadequate. The Standing Committee determines proposals made by the Secretariat. Funding can be allocated for regional workshops that may lead to the initiative for a formal or less formal Agreement.

CONCLUSION

The number of ratifications or signatures by Range States has increased steadily, if slowly, for the Agreements discussed above. Under each of the three instruments that are already in force, there has been positive progress evidenced by the adoption of detailed action or conservation plans. Mechanisms are in place to assess compliance, although there are no applicable unilateral or multilateral enforcement systems. To update the actions required of parties or signatories, CMS' in-house publications are used to report progress and publicize individual or collective successes by Range States.

The memoranda of understanding concluded under CMS raise very interesting issues, both legal and practical. These less formal instruments have had a shorter negotiating period and been signed by a significantly higher

---

[69] This is recognized by CMS: one of the priorities identified by COP5 was to encourage developed states parties, whether or not they are Range States, to facilitate initiatives of developing countries by providing technical, scientific, and financial assistance on request, Res. 5.4 and its Annex (Objectives and Action Points for the 1998–2000 Triennium).

[70] Report on Seventh Meeting of the Scientific Council, Geneva, April 7–8, 1997, 136.

[71] *CMS Bulletin* 5.

[72] The E.C. has financed a project in Greece for two and a half years on migration routes and wintering sites (see Report on Seventh Meeting of the Scientific Council, Geneva, April 7–8, 1997, para. 34).

proportion of Range States than is the case for any formal CMS Agreement concluded to date. The MoU on the Siberian crane, for example, has an enviable 'critical mass' with all Range States attending the most recent meetings: it has already been fully revised and updated. Signatories to these MoU have to report on their implementation measures more frequently than is required under almost any international environmental law agreement.

Whilst the binding/non-binding debate is obviously an important one, it needs to be set in context. Global and regional treaties related to nature conservation and biological diversity often consist of qualified obligations whereby parties' undertakings are subject to formulae such as 'available resources', 'wherever practical and appropriate', or 'best endeavors'. Supervision and enforcement of these binding but open-ended provisions is notoriously difficult. Seen in this light, MoUs have the advantage of setting out extremely specific actions which are targeted and capable of verification, even if supervision stops short of enforcement. The contribution of neighboring Range States to shared conservation objectives can be compared with relative ease. Negotiators may feel able to take a more aspirational approach and include more innovative or demanding provisions.

The choice of instrument depends partly on the geographic and scientific characteristics of the issue under consideration and partly on the intentions of the Range States concerned. AEWA and ACCOBAMS were too complex, involved too many Range States, and affected too many economic sectors to be comprehensively negotiated through informal channels. On the other hand, each took many years to be concluded and neither is yet in force. Memoranda of understanding can provide swift coordinated international action for very highly endangered species.

Memoranda can also play a role in involving states which are not party to CMS. There are often political, legal, and administrative constraints that impede countries from acceding to or implementing international and regional conventions. Regional or species-specific workshops to consider the possibility of Agreements can provide an avenue to bring officials and scientists into contact with the CMS framework. Work on individual Agreements can be developed even with non-party states: international interest in CMS can thus be strengthened through its Agreements and memoranda of understanding.

Memoranda are not equipped with separate institutions but are directly administered by the UNEP/CMS Secretariat. They also lack financial autonomy. This presumably imposes some strain on an under-resourced Secretariat and might constrain future activities under the respective MoU unless additional finance is mobilized in some way on a voluntary basis. In this respect, the quasi-institutional role of NGOs under existing MoU is particularly interesting.

In conclusion, memoranda of understanding and equivalent instruments offer essential flexibility for the rapid negotiation of conservation and management instruments under CMS. They do not require ratification and can enter into force immediately. They may be used in isolation or as a preliminary step (species-specific action plan) towards the negotiation of a formal treaty. On the basis of experience gained in the last five years from the two memoranda of understanding in force, this innovative type of legal mechanism appears promising and should play a catalyst role in global migratory species conservation and management.

Commentary and Conclusions

ALEXANDRE KISS

The problem of compliance with non-binding international environmental norms must be approached on both the international and the domestic levels. It implies two preliminary stages: first, the definition of soft law norms in international environmental law and, secondly, the identification of the authors of such norms, with special attention given to the issue of compliance with norms developed by non-state actors. An inquiry into the causes of compliance and non-compliance concludes the present section.

A. THE CREATION OF SOFT LAW NORMS IN INTERNATIONAL ENVIRONMENTAL LAW

There is a strong link between the method of creating soft law norms and the identification of soft law authors. States may choose to create legal norms in binding or in non-binding form. Non-state actors, including most international institutions, cannot choose the form of instruments they adopt because their legal status allows them to adopt only non-binding rules. In general, then, the participation of non-state actors on an equal footing in the adoption of an international instrument automatically confers a non-binding character upon the text, whatever its normative content.

1. Creation of Non-binding Norms by States

The drafting of non-binding norms by states meeting in conferences is particularly important in the field of environmental protection. First, global conferences like the 1972 Stockholm Conference on Human Environment and the 1992 Rio de Janeiro Conference on Environment and Development (UNCED) adopted declarations that articulated new values emerging from growing environmental awareness. Secondly, states parties to international treaties, meeting in conferences of the parties, must often develop norms to guide compliance with the obligations contained in the treaties. In general, such norms have a non-binding character, because conferences of the parties are not invested with the power to impose hard obligations on the contracting parties. Regulations adopted for Antarctica pursuant to the Antarctic Treaty are long-standing examples. However, provisions of legally non-binding instruments can be formulated in mandatory terms, as shown by certain memoranda of understanding concluded pursuant to the Convention on the Conservation of Migratory Species of Wild Animals.

Conferences may stimulate joint action by states outside a formal framework. While the 1979 Montreal Protocol on Substances that Deplete the Ozone Layer provided for CFC reductions of 50 percent by 1999,[1] the March 1989 London Conference of the European Community pledged a reduction of 85 percent as soon as possible and 100 percent by the year 2000. This led eventually to the Helsinki Declaration in May 1989 with eighty-two countries calling for a complete CFC phase-out by the end of the century.[2] Subsequent amendments to the Montreal Protocol phased out most ozone-depleting substances by 1996.[3] Such interaction between hard law instruments and soft law can create a process which leads from hard law to the creation of soft law and from there to new hard law standards.

2. Creation of Soft Law by International Institutions

Soft law development by international institutions, both global and regional, is important qualitatively and quantitatively. The constituting instruments of international organizations generally do not confer on those organizations the power to impose binding obligations on member states, except in respect to internal organizational matters. Most recommendations, however, do not concern internal matters, but are intended to orient the conduct of states, even non-member states in some instances, and sometimes non-state actors. It is this group of recommendations that is relevant for the present study.

The content of normative resolutions can either call on member states to order their conduct in a specific manner or can declare principles of a general scope.[4] The case study on driftnet fishing shows the power of the UN General

---

[1] Opened for signature September 16, 1987, (1987) 26 I.L.M. 1550, Art. 2, para. 4.

[2] Sand, P.H., 'Lessons Learned in Global Environmental Governance' (1990) 18 *B.C. Envt'l Aff. L. Rev.* 213, at 233.

[3] Gehring, T., and Oberthür, S., 'Montreal Protocol, The Copenhagen Meeting' (1993) 23 *E.P.L.*

[4] Res. 37/7, 37 U.N.G.A.O.R. Supp. (No 51) at 17, U.N. Doc. A/37/51 (1982), C (74)224, (1975) 14 I.L.M. 234. The latter is exemplified by the World Charter for Nature, adopted by the

Assembly (UNGA) in this regard, and also its limits. The first resolution on this topic, adopted in 1989, called upon the international community to cooperate in conservation and management of marine living resources and recommended moratoria on all large-scale pelagic driftnet fishing on the high seas by 1992. It also called for a progressive reduction of such activities in the South Pacific region and a halt to the expansion of such techniques on all high seas outside the Pacific ocean. In 1991, a new resolution reinforced the first. Since then, the UN system has continually monitored high seas driftnet fishing through reports prepared by the Secretary General and presented to the General Assembly. Despite the absence from membership of Taiwan, a key driftnet fishing entity, the UNGA clearly expressed its intent that no one engage in the prohibited behavior. The urgent common interest led to an approximation of legislation in content, albeit in non-binding form, and pulled states towards implementation, enforcement, and compliance.

Elaboration of soft law is an important method by which the UNEP Governing Council has contributed to the development of international environmental law. Since 1978, UNEP has drafted a series of guidelines and principles. Once adopted by *ad hoc* groups of experts nominated by governments, these provisions normally are approved by the UNEP Governing Council for submission to the UN General Assembly, which either incorporates them in a resolution or recommends them to states for use in the formulation of international agreements or national legislation.[5] The FAO/UNEP legally non-binding instruments on pesticides and chemicals show the possibility of cooperation between different institutions in the creation and the management of such instruments. Moreover, under the leadership of UNEP, non-binding regimes in several fields have evolved into binding treaties, reflecting a belief that legal form does make a difference and that non-binding instruments can facilitate the achievement of consensus on hard law content.[6]

Specialized intergovernmental bodies also frequently elaborate technical standards that generally function satisfactorily without being obligatory. The Statute of the International Atomic Energy Agency specifically charges the

UNGA on October 28, 1982, and the OECD Principles Concerning Transfrontier Pollution, adopted on November 14, 1974.

[5] See the 1982 Conclusions of the Study of Legal Aspects Concerning the Environment Related to Offshore Mining and Drilling Within the Limits of National Jurisdiction, UNGA Res. 37/217 (1982).

[6] Three examples are the following: (1) even while in the process of adopting the 1987 Cairo Guidelines and Principles for the Environmentally Sound Management of Hazardous Wastes, UNEP established a working group to prepare a global convention which was signed in 1989 as the Basel Convention on the Control of Transboundary Movement of Hazardous Wastes and their Disposal; (2) in 1995, Decision 18–32 of the Governing Council identified 12 persistent organic pollutants (POPs) for assessment, and subsequent recommendations facilitated progress in the direction of a binding treaty in the field; (3) elements of the Goals and Principles of Environmental Impact Assessment, adopted by the UNEP Governing Council in 1987, have been integrated in some of the regional seas agreements and provided a basis for negotiating the 1991 Espoo Convention on Environmental Impact Assessment in a Transboundary Context.

Agency, which has no legislative powers, to establish standards of safety for protection of health and minimization of danger to life and property. Its safety standards thus constitute recommendations only; there is no statutory obligation to take these standards into account or to report on compliance with them.[7] Other examples are the 'international health regulations' of the World Health Organization, the 'standard meteorological practices and procedures' of the World Meteorological Organization, the standards for facilitating international maritime traffic of the International Maritime Organization and the international food standards of the Codex Aliment-arius Commission, a joint technical body of WHO and the Food and Agriculture Organization of the U.N. (FAO).

3. Texts Elaborated by Non-state Actors

Non-state actors also produce soft normative instruments. Declarations by non-governmental expert groups may attain reference status, even without approval by governments. The Helsinki Rules on the use of the waters of international rivers, drafted in 1966 by the International Law Association,[8] have often been referred to as guidelines for state practice. In some cases, they were even incorporated into bilateral agreements.[9] The International Law Commission recognized their importance during its efforts to codify the inter-national law applicable to the non-navigational uses of international water-courses. Similarly, guidelines for drinking water quality and ambient air quality published under the auspices of the World Health Organization, though drafted by *ad hoc* expert groups and never adopted by governments, became a reference source for national standard-setting and a yardstick for comparative evaluation of environmental quality.[10]

Governmental agencies or officials who lack the capacity to represent their states in negotiating treaties also may engage in transnational negotiations and conclude informal agreements of considerable importance. The maritime administrative authorities of different countries, for example, have agreed upon memoranda of understanding on Port State Control to eliminate mar-itime transportation by substandard vessels. By the end of 1996 four MoUs on Port State Control were adopted for different areas of the world, follow-ing the pattern of the oldest, the 1982 Paris MoU.[11] While such agreements

---

[7] See Szàsz, P., 'The IAEA and Nuclear Safety' (1992) 1 *RECIEL* 165 at 169.

[8] International Law Association, 1966 Report of the 52nd Conference in Helsinki (1967) at 484.

[9] For instance, in the 1992 Namibia–South Africa Agreement on the Establishment of a Permanent Water Commission, September 14, 1992 (1993) 32 I.L.M. 1147.

[10] See Sand, *supra* note 2, at 241.

[11] The first MoU was adopted in the Hague in 1978 by 8 maritime administrations from Western and Northern Europe. In 1982 the Paris MoU superseded this agreement with the participation of 17 maritime authorities. Following the 1991 Resolution of the Assembly of the

do not constitute international treaties and do not legally oblige states,[12] the objective of these memoranda of understanding is the enforcement of international treaties, such as the 1973 MARPOL Convention.[13]

Two agreements adopted under the 1979 Bonn Convention on the Conservation of Migratory Species of Wild Animals,[14] dealing respectively with the Siberian crane and the slender-billed curlew, also qualify as memoranda of understanding or administrative arrangements. Intended to initiate and co-ordinate short-term administrative and scientific measures to be taken by Range States in collaboration with specialized NGOs, they constitute official undertakings signed by high-level government representatives and should be seen, at the very least, 'as politically binding, creating a moral obligation on signatory states to carry out undertakings'.[15] They have been signed by states that are not parties to the main Convention, as well as by intergovernmental and non-governmental bodies.

Non-governmental industrial, environmental, and consumer protection associations can also conclude agreements considered as international soft law. Sometimes they are empowered by the public authorities to exercise functions which generally belong to the latter.[16] A number of worldwide technical standards related to the environment have been adopted and updated by the International Organization for Standardization (ISO). Similarly, industry associations, such as the Chemical Manufacturers Association (CMA) and the American Petroleum Institute (API), have developed codes of conduct which multilateral corporations and other business entities must accept as a condition of membership. The codes apply to the members' operations worldwide. In Europe, the European Chemical Industries Federation (CEFIC), representing fifteen national chemical federations that account for approximately 30 percent of the world's chemical production, published *Guidelines for the Protection of the Environment* to assist chemical companies.[17]

International Maritime Organization, Regional Co-operation in the Control of Ships and Discharges (A.682(17)), a Latin American Agreement on Port State Control (Vina del Mar Agreement) was adopted in 1992 by 10 maritime authorities; an Asia-Pacific MoU on Port State Control was adopted in Tokyo in 1993 by 18 maritime authorities; and a MoU on Port State Control was adopted for the Caribbean Region in 1996 by 21 authorities. See Sand, *supra* n. 2, 241–2.

[12] According to one author, 'the form of a memorandum of understanding, the non-mandatory style of its wording, its conclusion between Maritime Authorities and not states, the absence of registration with the UN, and the apparent absence of a disagreement between its participants about the status of the instrument give a strong presumption of something less than a treaty'. E. Molenaar, 'The EC Directive on Port State Control in Context' (1996) 11 *Int'l J. Marine & Coastal L.* 241 at 246.

[13] See Mitchell, R.B., *From Paper to Practice: Improving Environmental Treaty Compliance*, Ph.D. Dissertation, Harvard (1992), at 239–47.　　　　[14] June 23, 1979, (1980) 19 I.L.M. 15.

[15] See Shine, C., *Selected Agreements Concluded Pursuant to the Convention on the Conservation of Migratory Species of Wild Animals*, above, at p. 205.

[16] See Sand, *supra* note 2, at 259.

[17] See Naish, C.P., 'The Policy of Waste Disposal in the Chemical Industry', in Kiss, A., and Shelton, D. (eds.), *Manual of European Environmental Law* (2nd edn., 1997), 486.

The adoption of non-binding normative instruments by international organizations and non-state actors reflects the growing complexity of the international legal system, in which states no longer have an exclusive role, but have yet to relinquish full law-making functions to other entities. The result is normative content in non-binding form. This may be a point of transition, leading to the eventual conferring of legislative powers on international organizations and other non-state actors, or it may be a long-term method of managing the line between binding obligations states are willing to accept and non-binding exhortations they agree are useful and to which they politically commit.

B. HOW IS COMPLIANCE ENSURED?

It is useful to distinguish three types of compliance: (1) compliance at the international level; (2) compliance within domestic legal orders; and (3) compliance with norms created by non-governmental actors. Such distinction allows account to be taken of the different legal techniques of compliance.

1. Compliance at the International Level

State compliance with soft law instruments can consist in agreeing to be guided by soft law rules in international relations. The situation is exemplified by negotiations between Uganda and other Nile basin countries, beginning in 1983, on a proposed water use project for Lake Victoria. The government of Uganda referred, *inter alia*, to the 1978 UNEP Principles of Conduct in the Field of the Environment for the Guidance of States in the Conservation and Harmonious Utilization of Natural Resources Shared by Two or More States. The governments of Egypt and Sudan in turn, in their replies, referred to the guidelines as 'jointly honored principles'.[18]

Non-binding norms also can be applied internationally after their domestic adoption of them by a state. For example, Japan applies the OECD principles related to environmental impact assessment to its major overseas development projects. The Japan International Co-operation Agency and the Overseas Economic Co-operation Fund formulated internal guidelines for Japanese development assistance projects and strengthened the systematic assessment of their environmental effects.[19] Similarly, the FAO/UNEP instruments requiring prior informed consent for the international shipment

---

[18] See Sand, *supra* note 2, at 240.

[19] See Japan, OECD, Environmental Performance in OECD Countries, Progress in the 1990s, 172 (hereinafter OECD Reports). See also OECD Series of Environmental Performance Reviews.

of pesticides or chemicals involve applying their standards to activities that take place outside the concerned countries.

International instruments often omit specific criteria or procedures by which to measure states' compliance on the international level. As the study by Christopher Joyner shows, however, Article VII of the Antarctic Treaty provides for unannounced on-site inspections by any consultative party to any ATCP government's station in the Treaty area. Obligations in recommended measures generally have been honored by ATCP governments while operating in the Antarctic Treaty area.

Although soft norms may not be binding *per se*, they can indicate the likely direction in which formally binding legal obligations will develop. Compliance can lead to the formation of 'hard law' rules through the inclusion of soft law rules in binding international texts, or through the creation of customary international law on the basis of soft law norms. Two of the case studies show that soft law instruments may serve as forerunners of treaty law. The annexes to the Protocol on Environmental Protection to the Antarctic Treaty of October 4, 1991[20] have their roots in the Agreed Measures and the sundry related ATCM recommendations adopted since 1961, as Joyner notes. Similarly, Mekouar indicates that the FAO International Code of Conduct on the Distribution and Use of Pesticides and the UNEP London Guidelines for the Exchange of Information on Chemicals in International Trade paved the road for the preparation of a legally binding instrument on Prior Informed Consent. Further, the 1985–7 Cairo Guidelines and Principles for the Environmentally Sound Management of Hazardous Wastes drafted by UNEP[21] led to the 1989 Basel Convention on the Control of Transboundary Movements of Hazardous Wastes and Their Disposal.[22] One or more legal principles formulated in the 1992 Rio Declaration appear in all the most important conventions adopted since the Rio Conference.

The case study on Antarctica demonstrates that soft principles not only can furnish a conceptual frame of reference for future agreements, but they 'facilitate the crystallization process that gives rise to customary law'.[23] The transformation of soft law norms into customary ones can follow different tracks. First, the repetition of the same norm in successive soft law instruments can give rise to, and then express, the '*opinio juris*' of the international community. International rules concerning transboundary environmental relations, for example, first were formulated in soft law instruments but now can be considered as constituting customary law. Recent 'dicta' of the International

---

[20] Protocol on Environmental Protection to the Antarctic Treaty (Madrid) (1991) 30 I.L.M.1455.

[21] U.N. Doc. UNEP/GC14/30 (1987).

[22] Basel Convention on the Control of Transboundary Movements of Hazardous Wastes and Their Disposal (1989) 28 I.L.M. 657.

[23] Joyner, C., *The Legal Status and Effects of Antarctica Recommended Measures*, above, at p. 176.

Court of Justice recognized a binding norm stemming in part from Principle 21 of the Stockholm and Principle 2 of the Rio Declarations: '[t]he existence of the general obligation of States to ensure that activities within their jurisdiction and control respect the environment of other States or of areas beyond national control is now part of the corpus of international law relating to the environment'.[24] In his dissenting opinion, Judge Weeramantry stressed that customary international law today prohibits actions that cause transfrontier environmental damage.[25] Other international environmental norms regularly repeated in soft law instruments also have been accepted as customary law, such as the obligation to cooperate with other states for the protection of the environment.

Soft law norms are also frequently introduced into binding international instruments. This raises the question of whether the incorporation of a soft law rule in a long series of treaties can be deemed to create a new customary law norm. Several principles proclaimed by the 1992 UNCED Declaration in Rio de Janeiro have been reproduced and detailed in a large number of treaties, in particular Principle 10 on public participation, Principle 18 on notifying other states of natural disasters or other emergencies that are likely to produce sudden harmful effects on their environment, Principle 19 requiring prior and timely notification and provision of relevant information to potentially affected states about activities that may have a significant transboundary effect. Arguably, the answer depends on the nature of the treaties in which a non-binding norm is introduced. Non-binding norms repeated in widely ratified global conventions such as the Convention on the Law of the Sea, the Framework Convention on Climate Change, and the Convention on Biological Diversity, may be considered as having been accepted as customary law, applicable even outside the scope of such conventions.[26]

In all these instances, theoretically, the soft law disappears as such, being replaced by an identical binding rule. In practice, however, such a situation exists only when the relevant treaty is signed and ratified by all the states that originally adopted the soft law rule, an infrequent occurrence at best. More often soft law rules are 'hardened' for the states that become parties to the relevant treaty, while for other states they either become customary law or they remain soft law. In such situations the question of compliance with such norms becomes one of compliance with binding obligations.

---

[24] International Court of Justice, *Legality of the Threat or Use of Nuclear Weapons*, Advisory Opinion of July 1995 (1996) 35 I.L.M. 809 at 821.

[25] Dissenting Opinion, *ibid.*, at 905.

[26] See *e.g.* International Court of Justice, *The North Sea Continental Shelf Cases (Federal Republic of Germany* v. *Denmark; Federal Republic of Germany* v. *Netherlands)*, 1969 I.C.J. 2.

2. Compliance within Domestic Legal Orders

Within states, compliance means performing the measures flowing from non-binding norms. In principle, the transcription of soft law rules into national law constitutes their implementation, and does not necessarily ensure compliance with their prescriptions. It is tempting to conclude that real compliance is effectuated through administrative or judicial decisions, unless it can be shown that the behavior of actors is influenced by internationally agreed soft laws, rules, and norms without such enforcement. Such hypothesis supposes far-reaching investigation into the everyday life of societies and has not thus far been conducted on a systematic basis. Nonetheless, some information could be collected concerning the implementation of provisions contained in non-binding instruments. The question asked in the case study on Antarctica is well-founded: in which states are measures approved under Article IX paragraph 4 of the Antarctic Treaty enforceable?

Generally speaking, national governments have complete autonomy regarding the means of domestic implementation of international norms. Full ratification of soft law instruments is of course impossible, but national endorsement can be required for agreed upon international standards. This can involve affirmative acceptance by governments.[27] Some information is known about such acceptance with respect to several major environmental soft law instruments; the Rio Declaration, Agenda 21, OECD recommendations, and FAO/UNEP guidelines.

Two series of studies give indications about domestic compliance with soft law texts adopted at the 1992 Rio de Janeiro Conference on Environment and Development (UNCED). First, as part of the preparation for an International Environment Conference on Codifying Rio Principles in National Legislation, organized by the Netherlands Ministry of Housing, Spatial Planning, and the Environment,[28] participants from twenty-four countries answered a questionnaire on the implementation of and compliance with non-binding texts adopted by the 1992 Rio Conference.[29] Secondly, between 1993 and 1998 the OECD conducted an in-depth study on environmental performance by twenty-six countries, including information on compliance with UNCED texts.[30]

[27] An example is the Codex Alimentarius Commission which has published a set of non-binding guidelines for pesticide residues on food (*i.e.*, product standards) that nations may apply both domestically and also to imported food. Many advanced industrial and developing countries have adopted Codex standards, while others have adopted even stricter standards. See 'Toxic Chemicals and Hazardous Wastes; An Overview of National and International Regulatory Programs' (1988) 12 *Int'l Envtl L. Rep.* 687.

[28] The Conference took place at the Hague on May 22–24, 1996. Its documents have not been officially published.

[29] References to answers to the questionnaire are made in the present study as CCRP followed by the name of the concerned state.

[30] OECD Reports, *supra* note 19.

Several answers to the Dutch questionnaire recognized the normative importance of the principles of the Rio Declaration, but emphasized that national authorities and the public in general feel more concerned with and committed to compliance with obligatory and mandatory legislation.[31] Even when such principles are codified as direct rights conferred upon individuals, they often need secondary legislation.[32] Nevertheless, some legal arguments and actions have proven effective to obtaining compliance.[33]

Some Rio principles have been incorporated so as to constitute direct obligations for citizens and enterprises or rules to be applied by administrative bodies.[34] The 1993 Constitution of the Russian Federation largely restates the Rio principles, although a 1991 comprehensive law on the Protection of the Natural Environment already generally conformed to them. In France, administrative bodies and public interest groups may invoke principles in discussions prior to activities being permitted that may have an impact on the environment.[35] On September 25, 1998, the highest French administrative jurisdiction decided to suspend a decision of the Minister for Agriculture authorizing the use of genetically modified material, considering that the precautionary principle, as incorporated in the French Law of February 2, 1995, had to be applied.[36]

For some states, the entire Declaration is a source of law and policy. According to the OECD Report, New Zealand recognizes and supports the Rio Declaration, having incorporated most of the principles which have a legal character into New Zealand legislation or policies. The Environment 2010 Strategy expressly refers to the polluter pays principle and the precautionary principle as elements of the government approach to modifying the market in order to protect the environment. New Zealand also has sought to avoid unsustainable production patterns, in accordance with Rio Principle 8, by removing subsidies and internalizing administrative and transaction costs.[37] The Republic of Korea similarly claims to support the Rio Declaration and considers it a description of guiding principles. In Hungary the Rio principles do not appear in the national legislation verbatim, but their essence is incorporated. While the principles do not create direct obligations for citizens, they are regarded as instructions to administrative authorities, especially applicable when interpreting the meaning of a given regulation. Similarly, the Finnish Government did not incorporate principles proclaimed by the Rio Declaration as such in a comprehensive national environmental law, but they are applied in sectoral laws.

---

[31] CCRP Peru.   [32] *Ibid.*

[33] For instance, in a case regarding the conservation of a mangrove swamp in northern Peru endangered by shrimp farming activities those involved invoked the principle of the right to a healthy environment in the face of reluctance by public officials to execute a legal mandate. *Ibid.*

[34] CCRP Russia.   [35] CCRP France.

[36] Conseil d'Etat, Association Greenpeace France, no. 194348.

[37] OECD Reports, New Zealand, *supra* note 19, 165.

Several Rio principles have had a particularly pronounced impact. In the Flemish Region of Belgium, a Decree of April 5, 1995 states that the Flemish environmental policy rests, *inter alia*, on the precautionary principle and the polluter pays principle. The Decree's explanatory memorandum declares that the insertion of principles in a binding legal document means that government authorities must take them into account when establishing their policies.[38] Korea has introduced the polluter pays principle in many domestic laws and formally adopted the precautionary principle in 1996.[39] The information submitted particularly stresses the role of Rio Principle 10 concerning public information, participation, and remedies.[40] Principle 17 of the Rio Declaration, which advocates the introduction of the environmental impact assessment procedure into national legislation, also has been widely implemented according to the response.

Administrative measures, such as the 1993 creation of a Ministry for Environment in Colombia, are sometimes considered a consequence of the Rio Declaration.[41] Implementing Rio Principle 13, Nepal issued National Impact Assessment Guidelines (1993) and created a Ministry of Environment and Population to pay particular attention to environmental problems of the country.[42] In Belgium, different organizations have been established to ensure adequate follow-up to UNCED, in particular a Federal Council for Sustainable Development consisting of fifty members from administration and civil society. For the Flemish Region of Belgium, a Royal Decision of October 12, 1993 established a 'National Council for Sustainable Development' with explicit reference to the Rio Declaration and Agenda 21.[43] In 1995, Wallonia adopted an Environment Plan for Sustainable Development and created a Walloon Committee for Environment and Sustainable Development. France also has created a Commission on Sustainable Development, consisting of fourteen members selected for their expertise and three *ex officio* members, including one environmental NGO representative. The Commission's task is to formulate sustainable development policy guidelines and to advise a national sustainable development strategy.[44]

---

[38] CCRP Belgium, Flemish Region.   [39] OECD Reports, Korea, *supra* note 19, 173.

[40] In Nepal, NGOs and pressure groups invoked Rio Principle 10 and asked for a more thorough analysis of a multi-billion dollar hydro-electric power plant. They also brought a case before the Supreme Court asking respect for their right to information. The Court endorsed the demand in a 1994 judgment and directed the government to ensure that the people have access to information regarding, *inter alia*, development projects likely to affect the environment of the country. CCRP Nepal, *supra* note 19. Other countries, like the Netherlands, also mentioned the importance of public information, participation and right to remedies, although relevant legislation does not refer to Principle 10, partly because some of it was adopted before the Rio Conference. CCRP Netherlands, *supra* note 19.

[41] CCRP Colombia, *supra* note 19.   [42] CCRP Nepal, *supra* note 19.

[43] CCRP Belgium, Flemish Region, *supra* note 19.

[44] OECD Reports, France, *supra* note 19, at 205.

A 1996 judgment of the Supreme Court of India constitutes an important application of principles proclaimed by the Rio Declaration.[45] A petition filed by a public interest group protested soil and the groundwater pollution caused by enormous discharges of untreated effluent by tanneries and other industries in the State of Tamil Nadu. After holding that the precautionary principle and the polluter pays principle have been accepted as part of the law of India, the judgment ordered the government to constitute an authority and to confer upon it all the powers necessary to deal with the situation, implementing the two principles. The polluting industries were ordered to pay compensation and threatened with closure if they evaded or refused to pay. Schemes were framed to reverse the environmental damage and a protected area was created within which no new listed industries could be established.

The implementation of Agenda 21 also has led governments to take administrative measures. In 1993, the New Zealand Government established an UNCED implementation officers' group, consisting of representatives of eleven ministries and convened by the Ministry for Environment. The Government identified a number of areas where domestic performance was not consistent with Agenda 21 and issued guidelines to raise awareness of this.[46] In 1994 Spain created an Environment Advisory Council to advise the minister in charge of environment regarding co-ordination of activities to implement Agenda 21. The Council's members are mostly representatives of business, trade unions, consumers, and environmental NGOs.[47] Switzerland similarly created a Council for Sustainable Development composed of twelve independent persons from civil society, whose task is to assess sustainable development policy of the country.[48]

Some governments adopted national or regional programs in order to implement Agenda 21. The United Kingdom published a national strategy for sustainable development for the implementation of Agenda 21,[49] and Mexico adopted a 1995–2000 National Plan for Sustainable Development, as well as supporting plans and assessments to be implemented at the national, state, and municipal levels.[50] The Swiss Federal Government integrated the requirements of sustainable development in sectoral policies, such as agriculture, transportation, and energy, and in 1997 approved a report on Sustainable Development in Switzerland.[51] Spain has promoted activities by the autonomous regions to draft their own Agenda 21 programs. In response, Andalusia and Madrid prepared environmental action plans on the basis of

---

[45] *Vellore Citizens' Welfare Forum* v. *Union of India and Others* (1996) 5 Supreme Court Cases 647.
[46] OECD Reports, New Zealand, *supra* note 19, at 164.
[47] OECD Reports, Spain, *supra* note 19, at 167–8.
[48] OECD Reports, Switzerland, *supra* note 19.
[49] OECD Reports, United Kingdom, *supra* note 19, at 168.
[50] OECD Reports, Mexico (not yet published).
[51] OECD Reports, Switzerland, *supra* note 19.

Agenda 21.[52] The Swedish Government also has encouraged local authorities to draw up local action plans for sustainable development in the twenty-first century. In 1993 it organized seven regional conferences to spread information about local Agenda 21 programs and provided subsidies to encourage work in this field. Over 200 out of 288 municipal authorities decided to implement such programs in a process based on dialogue with citizens, local organizations, and private enterprise covering all sectors and involving long-term objectives.[53] In New Zealand, the Ministry for Environment has assisted a number of local authorities to initiate pilot local Agenda 21 projects. Many regional councils have also started Agenda 21 projects. A workshop for local authorities was organized so that they could share their experiences.[54]

Recommendations issued by OECD also are implemented in domestic legal orders, such as the Japanese Government's application of recommendations related to environmental impact assessment.[55] Germany introduced a procedure for the notification of public authorities concerning the export of banned and severely restricted chemicals, implementing the 1984 OECD Recommendation on Information Exchange Related to Export of Banned or Severely Restricted Chemicals[56] and the UNEP London Guidelines for the Exchange of Information on Chemicals in International Trade.[57]

Finally, as noted in Ali Mekouar's study, FAO/UNEP non-legally binding instruments have to be implemented with appropriate regulatory measures and institutional arrangements. The overall responsibility for most aspects of pesticide management has been in governmental institutions, acting in collaboration with the pesticide/chemical industry. As part of the implementing measures, many passed or amended legislation or regulations to accommodate control actions. Relevant provisions of the International Code of Conduct, together with the recommended standards in the corresponding technical guidelines, also have been used as the basis for promoting numerous enforcement procedures.

3. Compliance with Norms Created by Non-state Actors

Pursuant to the memoranda of understanding related to Port State Control,[58] maritime authorities have undertaken to ensure that ships entering their ports comply with standards laid down in international instruments related to safety at sea, living and working conditions, and pollution prevention. They inspect ships, irrespective of whether the flag states are party to the relevant instrument. The 1982 Paris memorandum of understanding requires

---

[52] OECD Reports, Spain, *supra* note 19, at 168.
[53] OECD Reports, Sweden, *supra* note 19, at 166.
[54] OECD Reports, Australia (not yet published).
[55] OECD Reports, Japan, *supra* note 19, at 172.
[56] Res. C(84)37 Final.
[57] OECD Reports, Germany, *supra* note 19, at 192.
[58] See *supra* note 11.

inspections of at least 25 percent of ships entering port for compliance with international treaties related to marine pollution control. In recent years, Norwegian authorities controlled some 33 percent of ships in national ports,[59] the Netherlands more than 25 percent,[60] and the British 30 percent. Altogether, 85 percent of ships operating in European waters were inspected by European authorities in at least one port.[61] Inspection results show that the number of deficiencies, the number of delays and detentions, and the percentage of delays and detentions of the individual ships inspected have increased.[62] The rate of compliance also was high with the 1994 memorandum of understanding on Port State Control in the Asia Pacific Region. In 1994–5, over 250 ships were inspected in Korean ports and a third of them were deemed deficient and the deficiencies quickly rectified. Many of these ships came from flag-of-convenience countries. The rate of inspections was to be increased to reach half of all foreign vessels by 2000.[63] In 1994, New Zealand Maritime Safety Authorities inspected all tankers, vessels that had not visited the country before or been inspected in the last six months, and those that had previously reported deficiencies. In 1994, 447 ships were found to have deficiencies and eight were detained.[64]

As Clare Shine's report indicates, both memoranda of understanding drafted pursuant to the 1979 Bonn Convention on the Conservation of Migratory Species of Wild Animals[65] raise specific problems of implementation. The MoU on the Siberian cranes requires signatories to enact legislation to protect Siberian cranes and the wetlands that are critical for their survival, and to take such measures as may be necessary to enforce such legislation. This obligation does not seem to account for the fact that the signatory administrative authorities do not have the power to enact legislation. Similarly, the MoU concerning Conservation Measures for the Slender-billed Curlew includes non-state actors among its signatories, but requires enactment or improvement of legislation and that measures be taken to enforce such legislation. While the two memoranda of understanding do not provide for the creation of institutions to monitor compliance, they include NGOs as quasi-institutional partners in implementation. They also emphasize the requirement to submit reports annually to the Secretariat of the Bonn Convention.

Compliance with ISO 14001 standards is monitored at the corporate and, indeed, at the facility level by corporate self-audits. ISO displays two serious

---

[59] OECD Reports, Norway, *supra* note 19, at 124.
[60] OECD Reports, The Netherlands, *supra* note 19, at 181.
[61] OECD Reports, United Kingdom, *supra* note 19, at 159.
[62] See Molenaar, *supra* note 12 at 255–7.
[63] OECD Reports, Korea, *supra* note 19, at 168.
[64] OECD Reports, New Zealand, *supra* note 19, at 158.
[65] Bonn Convention on the Conservation of Migratory Species of Wild Animals (1980) 19 I.L.M. 15.

deficiencies at the compliance oversight stage. First, under heavy pressure from U.S. industry, 14001 has been stripped of any requirement for verification that a company's environmental performance conforms to national or international laws, regulations, and standards. Secondly, the ISO standard has no requirement to publicly report environmental impacts and/or compliance with applicable standards.[66]

ISO standards have considerable influence, although their legal implications, however, vary from country to country. In the U.S., federal officials are encouraged to participate in establishing voluntary consensus standards, which may then become binding regulatory requirements. A good example is the National Technology and Advancement Act of 1995,[67] which specifies that 'all Federal Agencies and departments shall use technical standards that are developed or adopted by voluntary consensus standards bodies, using such technical standards as a means to carry out policy objectives or activities determined by the agencies and departments'.[68]

Finally, although compliance with codes of conduct developed by industry associations such as the Chemical Manufacturers' Association and the American Petroleum Institute is a condition of membership, less than 20 percent of the surveyed firms said they followed the CMA guidelines. These findings confirm that non-binding accords adopted at the international level must be made binding on domestic non-state actors in order to be effective. They also undermine the assertions of multinational corporations that their overseas operations meet the same environmental standards as the facilities in the home country.

C. CONCLUSIONS: USE OF SOFT LAW AND CAUSES OF COMPLIANCE AND OF NON-COMPLIANCE

1. Why are Soft Law Rules Used?

International practice reveals a variety of reasons why non-binding norms are used in international environmental law instead of mandatory rules:

(1) States sometimes decide to forgo treaty-making to avoid serious domestic constitutional or legislative barriers, instead adopting

---

[66] The European Eco-Management and Audit Scheme (EMAS)—the European version of ISO—requires such disclosure. Parker, R., *Choosing Norms to Promote Compliance and Effectiveness: The Case for International Environmental Benchmark Standards*, unpublished.

[67] National Technology and Advancement Act of 1995, §12(d), Pub. L No. 104–113, 110 Stat. 775.

[68] *Ibid.*, at 783; See also Wirth, D., 'International Trade Agreements: Vehicles for Regulatory Reform?' [1997] *The University of Chicago Legal Forum* 331, at 348 ('[f]ederal agencies and departments shall consult with voluntary, private sector, consensus standards bodies and shall participate with such bodies in the development of technical standards').

recommendations, joint declarations, or common rules of conduct. The negotiating period of such instruments can be shorter and they can take instant effect because they are not subject to national ratification.

(2) States may accept soft law norms more readily than hard law obligations[69] and feel able to ensure compliance because they retain the ultimate control over the level of commitment attached to the instrument.

(3) Non-legally binding instruments may be more appropriate to the nature of the subject matter than formal agreements in some circumstances, *e.g.*, action plans outlining desirable approaches or orientations, rather than commitments that may be difficult to negotiate and fulfil when contracting parties are at different stages of development. Soft law texts also can be more apt for incorporating country-specific actions than traditional legally binding instruments, which still presume sovereignty, equality, and reciprocity in rights and duties.

(4) In certain instances, soft law instruments can allow international institutions and non-state actors to participate in the processes of creating and ensuring compliance with environmental rules. For example, IUCN prepared the first draft of the World Charter of Nature, which the UN General Assembly sent to the member states for comments and later adopted and solemnly proclaimed on October 28, 1982.[70] NGOs also participated in the adoption and the monitoring of memoranda of understanding complementing the 1979 Bonn Convention on the Conservation of Species of Wild Animals.[71]

(5) Soft law norms make it easier to tackle new problems where scientific knowledge and its evolution can be the major factors. The codes of good practices and guides relating to safety of nuclear facilities adopted by the International Atomic Energy Agency show how soft law regulations can reflect the development of knowledge. The case study on Antarctica notes that governments are more willing to be innovative when the product is not explicitly legally binding; 'as new notions or approaches can be tested and refined in a non binding situation, thus providing immediate benefits while laying the structural

---

[69] See 'International Atomic Energy Agency, Regulation of Nuclear Activities' (1986) 13 *Legal Collection* 13–19.

[70] G.A. Res. 37/7, 37 U.N.G.A.O.R., Supp (No 51) at 17, U.N. Doc. A/37/51 (1982).

[71] See Shine, *supra* note 15, at p. 219. On the participation of NGOs in the negotiation of environmental treaties see Mathews, J., 'Power Shift' (1997) 76 *Foreign Affairs* 50, 55; Spiro, P., 'New Global Communities: Nongovernmental Organizations in International Decision-Making Institutions' (1995) 18 *Washington Quarterly* 45, 50.

foundations for negotiating binding requirements at a later time'.[72] Non-binding instruments, because they are easily adjusted and do not require strict legal compliance, allow for learning through experimentation.

In sum, soft law rules have the necessary flexibility to enable the international community to progress and address problems new to international co-operation, such as the conservation of biological diversity or control of the movements of hazardous substances.

2. Compliance at the International Level

The causes of compliance and non-compliance with international non-binding agreements can differ at the international level from in domestic legal orders. One of the factors affecting compliance with a non-binding instrument is the authority of the text that is its legal foundation. In becoming parties to the Antarctic Treaty, states bind themselves to carry out the Treaty's purposes and principles. Recommendations that become effective in accordance with Article IX of the Treaty are 'measures in furtherance of the principles and objectives of the Treaty'. A certain legitimacy can also be conferred on non-binding texts because they have been adopted by an intergovernmental institution or under the aegis of such a body.

Another factor is the content of the non-binding instrument. Its language may clearly convey legal obligations which can be translated into domestic measures. The case study on Antarctica points out that the rate of compliance by Antarctic Treaty Contracting Parties can be influenced by a recommended measure's perceived links to other international norms recognized in international law, links to practices by the Antarctic scientific community, the legitimacy of the adoptive process of a recommended measure as an emergent norm, or the perceived fairness and legitimacy of the recommended practice by the international community. The case study on driftnet fishing reinforces this conclusion: the adoption of the 1989 Convention for the Prohibition of Fishing with Long Driftnets in the South Pacific was a major incentive to extend such prohibition to the other oceans. Further, the response of UNGA to driftnet fishing was not an isolated attempt to deal with fishing issues, but was part of a larger global effort to address concerns over the environment and resources at a time when the concept of sustainable development became influential.

The 1987 Montreal Protocol on Substances that Deplete the Ozone Layer was revised by successive adjustments adopted by meetings of the parties that accelerated the phasing out of ozone-depleting substances. This upward revision was the consequence of a declaration adopted in Helsinki in May 1989

---

[72] See Joyner, *supra* note 23, at pp. 175–6.

with eighty-two countries calling for a complete CFC phase-out by the end of the century. The declaration itself was motivated partly by new scientific evidence of the ozone hole, but media coverage and the world-wide publicity also proved influential.

The case study on the FAO/UNEP non-legally binding instruments stresses the importance of incentives such as scientific, technical, and financial assistance for institutional strengthening and specialized training, improving the capacity and infrastructure of developing countries and the sharing of experience. Information on the status of PIC's implementation and the creation of a database which helps provide public and private entities with the latest information also furthered the implementation of the PIC procedure.

On the negative side, the absence of enforcement measures, sanctions for non-compliance, and mechanisms for dispute resolution are not conducive to regular compliance. In the face of non-compliance by a state, other states involved in the adoption of a non-binding text may prefer to maintain a non-adversarial process rather than to express their concern over the violation of the text. The case study on driftnet fishing shows that monitoring compliance with non-binding texts constitutes a useful tool for exercising pressure upon states that are inclined to ignore them, especially when monitoring is ensured not only by individual states but by intergovernmental organizations and NGOs which guarantee a degree of independence. This is a general trend in present international relations that also applies to treaty obligations, but whether it really encourages compliance is unclear.[73]

3. Compliance within the Domestic Legal Order

The incorporation of soft law principles in national legislation or practice can be an important incentive to compliance. While such incorporation may be possible only if the concerned principle has a legal character,[74] the case study on the memoranda of understanding related to migratory species shows that such non-binding texts can suggest the adoption of necessary implementing legislation.

At first glance, compliance with, or at least the acceptance of, environmental soft law rules and norms is naturally easiest in countries whose legislation already contains the same rules and norms. Sometimes, though, existing legislation can be an obstacle to compliance with soft law. Poland agreed to implement the Rio Declaration on environment and development, even though it would require amendment of Polish law, which was drafted when information was more strictly controlled and democracy less developed. The new law eliminates confidentiality regarding emissions of pollutants and

---

[73] See Farer, T., 'New Players in the Old Game' (1995) 38 *American Behavioral Scientist* 841, 855.
[74] OECD Reports, New Zealand, *supra* note 19, at 165.

inventories of toxic substances from industrial plants, whether publicly or privately owned or being privatized.[75] Another important factor in compliance is the control that governments have over national agents who are the targets of a non-binding norm.

A non-binding text can encourage sanctions for non-compliance. UNGA Resolution 46/216 on driftnet fishing urged authorities and members of the international community to take greater enforcement responsibility to ensure full compliance with the former resolution asking for the prohibition of driftnets and to impose appropriate sanctions, consistent with international law, against acts contrary to the terms of the resolution. As the case study on driftnet fishing shows, monitoring of implementation and compliance with the UNGA Resolutions by NGOs can be extremely useful. The involvement of regional and local authorities in ensuring compliance with international soft law instruments can also be a major factor of effectiveness. National authorities should foster awareness at all the levels involving regional and local authorities as well as different sectors of the civil society.

Compliance with international environmental norms clearly depends on the capacity of the concerned states to enforce them. The case study on the MOUs related to the Bonn Convention on Migratory Species shows that implementation is subject to availability of human and financial resources. This stresses the importance of capacity building in numerous developing countries.[76] The case study on the FAO/UNEP instruments notes that economic loss resulting from inhibited trade in PIC pesticides/chemicals is likely to discourage compliance with the PIC requirement. The Portuguese Government mentioned its difficulty in assuring full implementation of the polluter pays principle because of the sometimes precarious situation of certain polluting industries.[77] Opposition by vested interests also may constitute a disincentive to compliance. Many developing countries, and even a number of OECD countries, have small, technically unsophisticated, and relatively powerless environmental ministries, with under-trained and under-paid staff. Still, the examples of Nepal[78] and of India[79] show that in such countries courts can nonetheless apply Rio principles.

At the same time, the experience of the International Atomic Energy Agency reveals that states that generally are not able to develop their own nuclear safety norms seek to incorporate IAEA standards into their national legislation or regulations, in the absence of internationally endorsed legally binding norms.[80]

---

[75] OECD Reports, Poland, *supra* note 19, at 149.
[76] See Gündling, L., 'Compliance Assistance in International Environmental Law: Capacity Building through Financial and Technology Transfer' (1999) 56 *ZaöRV* 796 at 802–4.
[77] OECD Reports, Portugal, *supra* note 19, at 113.   [78] See *supra* note 48.
[79] See *supra* note 51.   [80] See Szàsz, *supra* note 7.

Members of epistemic communities[81] can focus the attention of government policy makers on the risks and harms arising from pollution, and thereby mobilize international consensus for action. As well as sharing an acceptance of a common body of facts, their members share common interpretative frameworks from which they convert such facts or observations to policy-relevant conclusions. They identify problems in the same manner and process information similarly. They also share a common vocabulary, common political objectives, and a common network in which findings are exchanged and shared concerns are formulated. Although members of a community may be drawn from different scientific disciplines, all share a common world view and concern about the same subject matter.

Examples from the field of international environmental law show the fundamental importance of non-binding instruments. They also demonstrate the variety of such instruments, and of the situations in which they are or should be implemented. The consequence is a general uncertainty as to their effectiveness. Still, considerations drawn from international and domestic practice show that in specific cases such uncertainty can be prevented or reduced by assessing the general context and using the right incentives in the drafting and adopting of the instrument, taking into account and, as far as possible, avoiding the disincentives. Generally, states that have voluntarily negotiated, drafted, and adopted an international instrument comply with the agreement which is the final product of their efforts. Thus functionally, such instruments often approximate international treaties.

---

[81] An epistemic community can be defined as a professional group that believes in the same cause-and-effect relationship, truth tests to assess them, and shares common values.

Chapter 6 Trade and Finance

INTRODUCTION

Transborder trade is as old as civilization, and states have long fluctuated in their policies between advocating free trade and protecting domestic enterprises. International law governing trade and the more recent problems of transboundary flows of money remains a patchwork of bilateral and multilateral arrangements seemingly without a coherent set of underlying principles. The arrangements that exist appear to have as much in common with private law as with public regulation. Like the subject of multilateral arms control, but unlike human rights and environmental matters, trade appears to utilize agreements containing bargained-for benefits and burdens. Consequently, sanctions for non-compliance through the withdrawal of benefits seems easier than in the other fields; if one side breaches an agreement by raising tariffs, the other side may retaliate with tariffs of its own. In theory, therefore, enforcement should be easier than in 'unilateral' regimes like human rights. In practice, however, the interdependence of markets, financial institutions, and competing political interests within states may make the theoretical ease of enforcement difficult to implement in practice. Despite the WTO/GATT regime, international trade and finance are not governed by detailed international agreements. Thus, unlike the other areas of law studied in this volume, non-binding norms more often substitute for binding agreements than act as a precursor to or gap-filler in an existing treaty. The absence of political will to accept binding obligations may indicate a lack of consensus that undermines compliance. The lack of will or lack of capacity may be due in part to the fact that the targets of its economic regulation are frequently non-state actors, be they banks or multilateral companies. As Barry Kellman notes in his study of multilateral arms control, states frequently are unwilling to accept binding norms where the targets of the regulation are their domestic commercial enterprises.

Trade agreements are usually explicitly constructed as 'deals' to increase market access or limit barriers to trade. As David Wirth has noted, they may be considered more in the nature of generic dispute settlement arrangements. The Sanitary and Phytosanitary Agreement in the Uruguay Round, for example, was first and foremost designed to resolve the U.S.–E.C. beef hormone dispute. In such a context the binding format may be necessary to create a reasonable enforcement mechanism to give meaningful effect to, and widespread confidence in, a negotiated deal. This may suggest why the non-binding format of APEC, discussed in this chapter, has been halting in its advances.

International Efforts against Money Laundering

BETH SIMMONS

INTRODUCTION

The explosion of international financial activity over the last decade has been a central fact of international economic life. Balance of payments statistics indicate that cross-border transactions in bonds and equities for the G-7 states rose from less that 10 percent of gross domestic product in 1980 to over 140 percent in 1995.[1] International bond markets have reached staggering proportions: by the end of 1995, some US$ 2.803 trillion of international debt securities were outstanding worldwide. Capital flows to developing countries and countries in transition grew from US$ 57 billion in 1990 to over US$ 211 billion in 1995.[2] Foreign lending in the form of international syndicated credit facilities has surged since the 1980s, to over US$ 320 billion at the end of 1995. Foreign exchange transactions—which represent the world's largest market—reached an estimated average *daily* turnover of nearly US$1.2 trillion in 1995 compared to US$590 billion daily turnover in 1989.[3]

The growth of international capital markets has been a boon to economic efficiency and growth for many countries, but enlarges the opportunities for resources raised from illicit financial activities to cross borders undetected and make their way into the legitimate stream of capital, increasing the opportunity to use international markets for illicit activities. Money laundering—or the transferring of illegally obtained money or investments through an outside party to conceal the true nature of the source—has exploded as a

Research was accomplished while on leave from Duke University to take up a Foreign Affairs Fellowship sponsored by the Council on Foreign Relations, during which time the author worked in the Capital Markets and Financial Studies Division of the International Monetary Fund. Support from these institutions is gratefully acknowledged. Views expressed here are those of the author and not of the institutions named above.

[1] Figures exclude the U.K. Cited by White, W., *International Agreements in the Area of Banking and Finance: Accomplishments and Outstanding Issues*, paper presented at the conference Monetary and Financial Integration in an Expanding (N)AFTA: Organization and Consequences, organized by the Center for International Studies at the University of Toronto, Toronto, May 15–17, 1996, 3.

[2] International Monetary Fund, World Economic Outlook Database.

[3] Bank for International Settlements, *Central Bank Survey of Foreign Exchange and Derivative Market Activity* (1996) 5.

result. The Financial Action Task Force (FATF), created by the major industrial countries in 1989, estimated that by 1990 about US$ 122 billion was
being laundered annually in Europe and the United States (or about US$85
billion net after 'expenses')[4]. By some estimates, one billion dollars of criminal profits finds its way into the world's financial markets *every day*.[5] Lifting
capital controls has made laundering easier by reducing the scrutiny given to
international transactions.[6] Money laundering has become a global phenomenon: as North American and European regulators have stepped up enforcement efforts, sometimes with notable success, illicit funds have moved on to
eastern Europe, the former Soviet Republics, the Middle East, and parts of
Southeast Asia.[7]

Since the late 1980s national decision makers, regulators, standard setters,
and law enforcers have stitched together standards to address the problem of
money laundering in increasingly globalized financial markets. This effort has
been hampered by disagreements among states as to whether money laundering itself should be illegal; the relative responsibilities of the banking sector
versus law enforcement bodies; and, most importantly, the best way to
address the problem without jeopardizing legitimate financial activities. Non-
binding legal accords have been used extensively among states to coordinate
their rules and procedures and to strengthen cooperation for purposes of
prosecution. This essay will discuss why it is that compliance has been difficult to obtain in this issue area, and will examine in some depth the role of the
Financial Action Task Force (FATF) and its 'Forty Recommendations' in
securing a measure of coordination, at least among the most industrialized
countries, with respect to rules to detect and discourage money laundering.
The rub for compliance has been the strong political resistance in a number
of important financial centers to highly demanding financial disclosure rules,
as well as deeper resistance in a number of jurisdictions to close scrutiny of
foreign capital that might aid in development. Despite their non-binding
nature, however, the FATF standards do have significant influence: peer
review and pressure have helped to bring some countries into line with the
most significant of the recommendations. Globally, however, compliance

---

[4] Harrington, H., 'Go East—or Bust' (1993) 143 *The Banker* 15–17. The Task Force included
the G-7 plus Austria, Australia, Belgium, Luxembourg, the Netherlands, Spain, Sweden, and
Switzerland.

[5] Estimate given by Eduardo Vetere, head of the Crime Prevention and Criminal Justice
Branch at the opening sitting of the European Regional Preparatory Meeting for the 9th UN
Congress on Crime Prevention and the Treatment of Offenders (1995) February 28, 1994,
Vienna.

[6] See testimony in April 1989 of the Governor of the Bank of Italy, quoted in Gurwin, L.,
'1992 Means a Single Market for Crime, Too' (1990) 4 *Global Finance* 46–50 at 48. See also Tanzi,
V., *Money Laundering and the International Financial System*, International Monetary Fund:
Fiscal Affairs Department, Working Paper 96/55, May 1996.

[7] Harrington, *supra* note 4 at 15; Colitt, R., 'Survey of Ecuador', *Financial Times*, July 27,
1995, 28.

remains minimal, as the financial rewards for a 'don't ask, don't tell' approach to financial transactions have to date largely exceeded the benefits of cooperation for many jurisdictions.

A. BACKGROUND TO INTERNATIONAL EFFORTS AGAINST MONEY LAUNDERING

International initiatives to control money laundering have come primarily from the United States, in alliance with the United Kingdom, France, and increasingly Australia. In 1986, the United States was the only country to have criminalized money laundering, and it remains by far the leader in prosecutions.[8] Relatively few prosecutions have taken place in Europe, although regulations have tightened significantly as a result of an E.U. directive on money laundering. Australia has begun to take on a crucial leadership role with one of the most technologically sophisticated methods for detecting financial patterns associated with illicit activities. Australian authorities have used forfeiture funds to establish a secretariat for the FATF in Asia.[9]

1. The Nature of the Problem

Money laundering cannot be handled effectively on a unilateral or bilateral basis. Significantly different rules across jurisdictions invite 'forum shopping', the shifting of business to countries with weaker controls.[10] When the United States passed the Bank Secrecy Act of 1970, tightening reporting requirements for cash transactions over US$10,000, illicit money moved to Europe, where most banks were not required to collect information on large cash deposits.[11] As the rules have tightened in Western Europe, illegal-source money is increasingly directed towards jurisdictions where regulations are more lax (Eastern Europe and the former Soviet Republics, the Gulf and Mediterranean regions, and the emerging economies of Asia[12]) or to non-bank institutions, where stockbrokers are much less likely than bankers to know their customers.[13] One Bank of England official has reportedly said

---

[8] Between 1991 and 1993 the number of cases filed and tried under Title 18 U.S.C. 1956 or 1957 approximately quintupled. In 1993, 822 cases were filed and 106 tried. Justice Department figures, reported in Courtney, A., 'The Buck Never Stops' (1994) 144 *The Banker* 82–5.

[9] Discussion with officials from the US Treasury and FINCEN, August 5 and 8, 1996.

[10] Ron Noble, immediate past president of the FATF.

[11] Switzerland, Andorra, the Channel Islands, and Luxembourg, with their strict bank secrecy rules, and Austria where anonymous numbered accounts are permitted, probably absorbed a significant share of these funds. Gurwin, *supra* note 6.

[12] Burns, J., 'MPs Urge Money Laundering Crackdown', *Financial Times*, July 26, 1995, 8. Harrington, *supra* note 4 at 16–17;. MacDonald, S.B., 'Asia-Pacific Money Laundering' (1993) 22 *International Currency Review* 30–4.

[13] Courtney, *supra* note 8.

fighting money-laundering is like squeezing a balloon—you simply displace the activity to wherever there is the least resistance.[14] To yield significant benefits, near-global cooperation is a virtual necessity.

Despite the need for cooperative efforts, individual jurisdictions have incentives to resist international agreements to control money laundering. First, banking secrecy is often considered essential in attracting legitimate business; extensive inquiry into the source of funds is likely to push funds offshore.[15] Private banking, as it has been practiced in Switzerland, Liechtenstein, and Luxembourg, for example, has established a lucrative financial niche. The business of managing the funds of wealthy clients provides a third of the Swiss Bank Corporation's very stable profits.[16] These funds also provide the basis for the country's relatively large capital and securities market. Swiss officials have long recognized that bank secrecy has contributed significantly to the high standard of living and thus 'at least indirectly concerns substantial economic interests of the state'.[17] In Liechtenstein, even mild rules regarding 'due diligence', which require bankers to report suspicious activities to authorities, 'pose a direct threat to Liechtenstein's basic competitiveness', according to bankers in Vaduz.[18]

Banking secrecy combined with loose supervision may be an attractive policy for a large number of resource-poor who hope to augment national revenues. Some jurisdictions have instituted easy rules of incorporation, eschewed recording requirements for large cash transactions, and have a limited or non-existent capacity for asset seizure or confiscation.[19] Especially

[14] *Ibid.*, 88–9; Dumbacher, J., 'The Fight Against Money Laundering' (1995) 30 *Intereconomics* 177–86.

[15] Troshinsky, L., 'Ex-NatWest Lawyer Fears "Know Your Customer" Fallout' (1996) 96–31 *International Banking Regulator* 1 and 6.

[16] Some estimates suggest that private assets managed in Switzerland total SFr 20,000bn, or about a third of all money placed by wealthy individuals in banks outside their home countries. Roger, I., 'Survey of Swiss Banking', *Financial Times*, October 26, 1995, London, III.

[17] This statement is a translation of official Swiss Federal Government policy, quoted in Aubert, M., *et al.*, *Das Schweizerische Bankgeheimnis* (1978) 59 (translation provided in a summary generously supplied by an official of the International Monetary Fund). Recent changes in Swiss bank secrecy law now give banks the *right*—but *not the obligation*—to report suspicious clients. The current Swiss Federal Attorney General is now pressing for Switzerland to adopt obligatory reporting, in line with the rest of the E.U. But her attempt to introduce such an obligation in a bill last year was defeated by ferocious lobbying by the financial community, which claimed that such a rule would have turned bankers into policemen, and would have resulted in the whole detection process becoming buried in a blizzard of insignificant cases. See articles by Williams, F., and Roger, I., 'Survey of the Swiss Banking System', *Financial Times*, October 26, 1995, IV and V. See also Clarke, Th., and Tigue, J.J., *Dirty Money: Swiss Banks, the Mafia, Money Laundering, and White Collar Crime* (1975).

[18] Liechtenstein offers a level of banking secrecy that is even tighter than that of Switzerland; bankers there are not required to know the identity of the account's ultimate beneficiary as would be required in Switzerland. 'So Far but no Further' (July 1996) *Euromoney* 151.

[19] Not all offshore centers can be characterized by these priorities. Bermuda, for example, has shunned an influx of foreign banks because of fears of money laundering. Saul, D., 'Survey of Bermuda', *Financial Times*, November 7, 1995, V. Malta, which is attempting to establish itself

where banks and other financial institutions allow dollar deposits, these practices often unintendedly attract drug money.[20] 'The core of the dilemma is
that not all the money that needs to be laundered necessarily stems from criminal activity. Dirty money is hot money, but the reverse is not [always] true.'[21]

Another motive to decline cooperative initiatives may be the costs
involved, because extensive financial reporting systems are expensive.[22]
Tradition and idiosyncratic domestic political constraints in some countries
also may be a factor. Austria's unwillingness to give up its anonymous savings accounts provoked a dispute with the E.U. about whether Austria has
fulfilled its obligations under the 1991 directive on money laundering.[23]
Unlike the interest financial institutions may have in developing a reputation
for safety, 'it is not necessarily in the direct financial interest of financial institutions to adopt anti-laundering behavior'.[24] Anti-money laundering efforts
provide no clear economic payoff, and may in fact exact immediate costs.

2. Major International Anti-money Laundering Efforts

International political pressure, largely from the United States, has been the
driving force behind harmonization of national money laundering rules to
date.[25] The earliest and clumsiest initiatives came when the U.S. Congress

as a financial center, has closely followed British regulatory practice and has enacted a range of
laws, including the Prevention of Money Laundering Act. Graham, R., 'Survey of Malta',
Financial Times, September 22, 1995, III. The British Virgin Islands have developed strict rules
and a clean reputation as an offshore center. 'British Virgin Islands: International Financial
Center', *Asia Money Supplement*, July/August 1996, 2.

[20] MacDonald, S., *supra* note 12 at 32.
[21] Bosworth-Davies, R., 'Money Laundering—Cleaning Up', *Banking World* vol. 11, no. 3,
March 1993, 28.
[22] In the U.S., approximately 10 million Currency Transaction Reports for cash transactions
exceeding US$10,000 were filled out in 1993. Estimated costs for the financial institutions per
report were between US$15–17. Additional costs include training, recording, and storing the
data. Dumbacher, *supra* note 14 at 181. Some industry sources place the cost of CTR preparation alone as high as US$136 annually. Powis, R., 'Money Laundering: Problems and Solutions'
(1992) 175 *The Banker Magazine* 52–6.
[23] Anonymous accounts were introduced in the 19th century to protect savers against arbitrary taxation by the authorities and now number some 26 million passbooks with a total value
of about 1,400 billion shillings (about US$140 billion). Discussions with an official of the
International Monetary Fund, August 2, 1996.
[24] Quirk, P.J., *Macroeconomic Implications of Money Laundering*, IMF Working Paper 96/66,
Monetary and Exchange Affairs Department (1996) 24.
[25] For general reference to such pressure, see Dumbacher, *supra* note 14 at 180–1; see also
'Falling Out with Uncle Sam' (1996) 338 *The Economist* No. 7957. Firms subject to more stringent regulations of course very much support strict enforcement of the rules for their competitors, including penalties such as banning disreputable institutions from payments systems such
as CHIPS and SWIFT, or legislation calling for suspension of banking licenses in cases of gross
negligence, see the comments of Fullerton, R.D., Chairman and CEO, Canadien Imperial Bank
of Commerce, Toronto, Canada, *Clearing Out the Money Launderers*, portions of a speech made
before the Bankers Association for Foreign Trade Conference, reprinted in (1990) 9 *The World
of Banking* 5–7.

passed the 'Kerry Amendment',[26] that required the Treasury to negotiate with foreign countries with the objective of having foreign banks record all U.S. cash deposits over US$ 10,000 and provide information to U.S. authorities in the event of a narcotics related investigation. Should a bank fail to agree, the amendment gave the President the power to deny that bank access to the U.S.'s clearinghouse system, in an effort to isolate it from world trade. For a number of reasons (including the universal nature of the problem, opposition from Treasury,[27] the fear of stimulating foreign alternatives to U.S. clearing facilities, and the fear of retaliation against U.S. banks) this unilateral approach had few tangible results.

Since 1988, political efforts have had a broad regional or multilateral focus, as shown in Table 6.1. The United States' role was central to the drafting of the 1988 Vienna Convention Against Illicit Traffic in Narcotic Drugs and Psychotropic Substances,[28] which calls 'intentionally' laundering drug profits a criminal activity.[29] Such a designation is meant to assist information-sharing, since mutual legal assistance agreements usually specify that an activity under investigation must be a crime in both the requesting and the receiving country.[30] The U.S. Federal Reserve also brought the issue of money laundering to the initially unenthusiastic G-10 banking supervisors. There was some suspicion that congressional pressure underlay the Federal Reserve's interest in the matter. Nevertheless, as the wrongdoing at BCCI began to unfold, both the Swiss and Italian regulators were won over to the idea that the Basel banking committee should issue some kind of statement that financial systems must not be allowed to be used to aid criminal activity.[31] In December 1988 the G-10 bank supervisors came up with a 'statement of principles'. It recommended that banks cooperate with investigators and limit their dealings with customers if they believed the funds were either derived from illegal activity or to be used for illegal purposes, but the agreement noted explicitly that bank supervisors in the G-10 had very different roles and responsibilities in this area, that this was *not* a legal document and *not* in any way intended to supersede national legal approaches.

---

[26] S. 4702 of the 1988 Omnibus Drug Bill. See also Crocker, T., 'Bankers, Police Yourselves' (1990) 9 *International Financial Law Review* 10–11.

[27] Treasury's lack of enthusiasm for this approach is described in *Drug Money Laundering, Banks, and Foreign Policy: A Report to the Committee on Foreign Relations*, United States Senate, by the Subcommittee on Narcotics, Terrorism, and International Operations (USGPO), 101st Congress 2d session, February 1990, 28. This opposition was also confirmed in an interview with a Treasury official, August 7, 1996, Washington, D.C.

[28] The Vienna Convention (December 20, 1988). 20 ratifications were needed for it to enter into force, which it did in 1990; 100 ratifications had been deposited by the end of 1994 .

[29] Art. 3, s. 1, (b)(i) and (ii).   [30] Crocker, *supra* note 26.

[31] Telephone interview with a Federal Reserve Official who was involved in the drafting and negotiation of the 1988 agreement, Washington, D.C., August 8, 1996.

Table 6.1: Major international anti-money laundering initiatives

Sponsoring Organization:	Agreement:	Binding?	Major Provisions
Group of Ten Committee on Banking Regulation and Supervisory Practices.[1]	Basle Statement of Principles; Prevention of Criminal Use of the Banking System for the Purpose of Money Laundering (December 1988)	NO	—establishes a minimum set of operating standards and management principles by which all banks in the IMF member countries should operate. —includes standards on customer identification, and adherence to national laws and policies intended to prevent money laundering.
United Nations International Drug Control Program	UN Convention Against Illicit Traffic in Narcotic Drugs and Psychotropic Substances (Vienna Convention; December 1988)	YES	—treaty ratified by 115 nations, attempts to coordinate international efforts to control illicit drugs. —requires signatories to criminalize the laundering of drug money.
United Nations International Drug Control Program	Legal Assistance Money Laundering Model Law (November 1993)	NO	—outlines model prevention measures, including limitations on the amount of cash deposits, reporting of international transfers of funds and securities, creating standards of vigilance required of financial institutions. —outlines detection procedures, including requirements for reporting suspected launderers; recommends that banking secrecy not be legally invoked as a reason for not doing so.
United Nations Commission on Narcotic Drugs	Encouraging the Reporting of Suspicious or Unusual Transactions . . . to Facilitate the Investigation and Prosecution of Money Laundering Activities. (March 1995)	NO	—urges states to encourage reporting of suspicious or unusual transactions, and to collect national data on these; and to share this information with the 'competent authorities' —recommends states with experience in financial investigations lend technical assistance, at their request, to

Sponsoring Organization:	Agreement:	Binding?	Major Provisions
			states whose financial systems make them especially vulnerable to money laundering.
OECD Financial Action Task Force (FATF).[2]	Financial Action Task Force on Money Laundering Report: Forty Recommendations (February 1990)	NO	—establishes a framework of comprehensive programs to address money laundering and facilitate greater cooperation in international investigations, prosecutions, and confiscations. —calls for each country to define money laundering and make it a criminal offense; recommends that countries extend the definition to 'knowingly' having laundered, and to the proceeds from all illegal activities, not just drug proceeds. —recommends that financial institutions not keep anonymous accounts or accounts in fictitious names; financial institutions should establish the principal owners and beneficiaries of all accounts. —financial institutions should be permitted or required to report suspicious activity to the competent authorities.
Caribbean Financial Action Task Force (CFATC)[3]	19 Aruba Recommendations (June 1990)	NO	—countries need to establish competent authorities and provide resources for combating financial crimes. —calls for countries to make money laundering a crime. —endorses many aspects of FATF's 40 Recommendations. —each country ought to decide for itself what counts as a 'predicate offense' in determining whether money has been laundered, and should decide for itself

Table 6.1: cont.

Sponsoring Organization:	Agreement:	Binding?	Major Provisions
			whether laundering was done 'knowingly' or whether objective facts establish that the offender ought to have known this was the case. —establishes a series of recommendations on confiscation measures, record keeping, and currency reporting.
Caribbean Financial Action Task Force (CFATC)	Kingston Declaration on Money Laundering (November 1992)	NO	—declaration that member governments should sign and ratify the 1988 Vienna Convention, and endorse and implement the 40 FATF recommendations and the 19 Aruba recommendations, and adopt as soon as possible the OAS Model Regulations concerning money laundering offenses. —creates a secretariat for the CFATF —creates a 'forfeiture fund' to dispose of illegally obtained property. —says that individual governments should choose between voluntary and mandatory reporting of suspicious activities.
Council of Europe[4]	Convention on Laundering, Search, Seizure, and Confiscation of the Proceeds of Crime (Strasbourg Convention) (November 1990)	YES	—effort to coordinate policies with respect to investigation of suspected money laundering and confiscation of the property and proceeds associated with illegal activities. —creates an obligation to assist other parties with the 'widest possible measure of assistance in the identification and tracing' of property and proceeds, including providing and securing evidence to establish its existence, location, nature, etc.

Sponsoring Organization:	Agreement:	Binding?	Major Provisions
European Union	Directive on Prevention of the Use of Financial System for the Purpose of Money Laundering. (June 1991)	YES	—obliges credit and financial institutions to require proper identification for all their customers when beginning a business relationship, when a single transaction or linked transactions are conducted exceeding 15,000 ECUs, or when money laundering is suspected. —allows member states to put stricter rules in place than those provided in the directive (these should be coordinated by and communicated to a 'contact committee' to be established by the European Commission).
Organization of American States (OAS)[5]	Model Regulations Concerning Laundering Offenses Connected to Illicit Drug Trafficking and Related Offenses (May 1992)	NO	—in conformity with the 1988 Vienna Convention, criminalizing money laundering related to drug proceeds, preventing the use of financial systems for laundering, strengthening national seizure and forfeiture laws, and changing legal and regulatory systems to ensure that bank secrecy laws do not impede effective law enforcement and mutual legal assistance. —bar anonymous accounts. —reporting of large transactions involving domestic or foreign currency exceeding an amount specified by the competent authority; regardless of amounts involved, financial institutions shall report suspicious transactions to the competent authorities. —provide for international cooperation with competent foreign authorities.

Table 6.1: cont.

Sponsoring Organization:	Agreement:	Binding?	Major Provisions
Summit of the Americas[6]	Buenos Aires Ministerial Communiqué; Ministerial Conference Concerning the Laundering of Proceeds and Instrumentalities of Crime (December 1995)		—calls on all countries in the hemisphere to declare money laundering a crime but allows each to define the 'predicate offenses' that give rise to laundering in national legislation. —calls on each government to come into compliance with the 1988 Vienna Convention, and recommends the adoption of OAS/CICAD Model Regulations. —recommends the thorough review and strengthening of national capabilities and procedures with respect to reporting, seizure and forfeiture, and law enforcement.
INTERPOL[7]	Anti-Money Laundering Resolution (draft, October 1995)	NO	Recommends that INTERPOL members: —provide for the criminal prosecution of persons who knowingly participate in the laundering proceeds derived from serious criminal activity. —allow for legal authority for seizure of assets derived from illicit activities. —allow for reporting of unusual or suspect currency or other transactions to competent authorities. —require financial institutions to maintain records of transactions for at least five years. —allow for expeditious extradition of individuals charged with money laundering offenses.

[1] G-7 countries plus Austria, Switzerland, Sweden, and Luxembourg.

[2] The original FATF consisted of the G-7 members, eight other industrialized nations, and the European Commission.

[3] Members: Anguilla, Antigua and Barbuda, Aruba, Bahamas, Barbados, Bermuda, British Virgin Islands, Cayman Islands, Colombia, Costa Rica, Dominica, Dominican Republic, Grenada, Guyana, Jamaica, Mexico, Monserrat, Netherlands Antilles, Panama, St. Kitts, St. Lucia, St. Vincent and the Grenadines, Suriname, Trinidad and Tobago, Turks and Caicos Islands, and Venezuela.

[4] Membership currently includes 25 nations from Western Europe, Scandinavia, and several Central and Eastern European nations.

[5] Members include 35 countries from North, Central, and South America, plus 31 states with 'observer status' from around the world. Anti-money laundering efforts are centered in the Intern-American Drug Abuse Control Commission (CICAD), which was created by the OAS General Assembly in 1986.

[6] Involving heads of state of 34 nations in the Western Hemisphere.

[7] 176 members. General purpose is to establish information network for seeking foreign investigative assistance and for alerting foreign authorities to criminal threats.

B. FATF'S FORTY RECOMMENDATIONS

1. Major Provisions

The center of multilateral political pressure to secure rules against money laundering is the headquarters of FATF in Paris. The FATF has given more sustained attention to the problem of capital from illicit activities than any other organization. It is comprised of experts from government ministries, law enforcement authorities, and bank supervisory and regulatory agencies from twenty-six industrialized countries. To induce compliance with its 'Forty Recommendations' promulgated in 1990,[32] it regularly employs peer pressure and potentially a graduated set of sanctions to review and influence the policies of its members and those of non-members.

The Forty Recommendations are addressed to state authorities (financial regulators) and to financial institutions. Section B addresses ways in which national legal systems can be improved to combat money laundering. In addition to Recommendation 1 that states ratify the 1988 Vienna Convention, it urges countries to define money laundering to include at least the proceeds of criminal drug activities, where such laundering was knowingly undertaken or such knowledge could be inferred from objective factual circumstances (Recommendations 4–6). The FATF recommended that states adopt effective seizure and forfeiture laws, including in them authority to identify and trace property subject to confiscation, to freeze or seize assets to prevent their

---

[32] The Financial Action Task Force has only recently involved private actors in its rule making process. Private actors were excluded from the formation of the original 40 recommendations, but in September 1995, the FATF met with leading banking and securities federations in order to involve them in its review and update its 40 guidelines.

disposal or transfer, and to undertake any appropriate investigative measures (Recommendation 8).

Section C makes specific recommendations to enhance the role of the financial system in cracking down on money laundering. These recommendations are supposed to apply not only to banks but also to non-bank financial institutions. A key provision recommends the prohibition of anonymous accounts (Recommendation 12) and thus effectively endorses the Basel group's 'know your customer' guidelines. Recommendation 12 suggests that financial institutions be required 'by law, by regulations, by agreements between supervisory authorities and financial institutions or by self-regulatory agreements among financial institutions' to identify and record the identity of their clients when establishing business relations or conducting transactions. Recommendation 13 further suggests that in case of doubt about a client's identity, financial institutions should take reasonable measures to obtain information about the true identity of the persons on whose behalf an account is being opened or a transaction conducted. If financial institutions suspect that funds stem from a criminal activity, they should be permitted or required to report promptly their suspicions to the competent domestic regulatory authorities (Recommendation 16). In the absence of such an obligation, such suspicions should at least lead the institution to sever relations with the customer and close the account (Recommendation 19).

Many of the specific recommendations of the FATF indicate that there is still noticeable disagreement among members over how stringent reporting efforts ought to be and how to handle the sensitive issue of branches and subsidiaries located abroad. While the U.S. has a strict reporting standard for all cash transactions over US$10,000, the FATF only recommends that countries study the feasibility of creating such a system within their jurisdictions (Recommendation 24). Moreover, extraterritorial enforcement is precluded, despite the desirability of strengthening the ability of the financial system to detect money laundering globally, '[w]hen local applicable law and regulations prohibit this implementation, competent authorities in the country of the mother institution should be informed by the financial institutions that they cannot apply these Recommendations' (Recommendation 22).

Finally, Section D addresses the problem of strengthening international cooperation among regulatory and law enforcement authorities, including the exchange of information, cooperation in confiscation, mutual assistance and extradition, and improving asset forfeiture capabilities.

2. FATF Compliance Supervision

The FATF employs a system of mutual review in which each member's laws and efforts are scrutinized by an FATF team and then assessed by the full membership. Implementation of the Forty Recommendations by each member is monitored through an annual self-assessment exercise, as well as a more detailed mutual evaluation process under which each member is subject to an on-site examination. In addition, the FATF carries out cross-country reviews of measures taken by its members to implement specific Recommendations.

Each member provides information for the self-assessment, which is then compiled and analyzed to evaluate the extent to which the Forty Recommendations have been implemented. Through this process, the FATF has determined that there has been a steady improvement in compliance over the past few years, with noticeable improvements, for example, in New Zealand, where major anti-money laundering legislation was adopted over the past year.[33] Turkey is the only country in the FATF that has failed to date to make money laundering a crime;[34] nineteen members have criminalized laundering of money beyond that gained from illicit drug trafficking. Still, as of 1996 only seventeen members had ratified the Vienna Convention, the basic international legal commitment to make money laundering a crime.

All members but one had put into place measures to facilitate mutual legal assistance in investigations. However, with respect to the freezing, seizure, and confiscation of assets pursuant to mutual legal assistance, sixteen members were deemed to be in full compliance, four were expected to be within the year, and another four were determined to be in partial compliance. While almost all members comply fully with customer identification and record-keeping recommendations of the FATF, the organization considered it a 'matter for serious concern' that Austria and Turkey still permit anonymous accounts.[35] All but three members require banks to look into unusually large, complex transactions; all but two require banks to develop specific programs to combat money laundering; and twenty-three members require banks to report suspicious transactions.[36]

Monitoring is also done through mutual evaluation, in which members are examined by a select team of experts from among the FATF countries. These reports generally are not made public; they are for internal discussion only. For this reason, it is difficult to cull systematic information from the mutual evaluation process. Information was available on two of FATF's 'model members', France and Sweden. In France's case, mutual review indicated super-compliance: France regularly went beyond the text of the recommendations, by extending the definition of laundering, widening reporting requirements,[37] and creating a new specialized unit within the Ministry of

[33] Financial Action Task Force on Money Laundering, Annual Report, 1995–6, June 28, 1996 (hereafter FATF Annual Report).

[34] Interview with a Treasury Official, August 5, 1996, Washington, D.C.

[35] FATF Annual Report, *supra* note 33 at para. 44.   [36] *Ibid.*, para. 45.

[37] In France new rules will force all banks with a presence in France, including French branches of foreign banks, to collect detailed information on all transfers of clients' funds of above FF100,000 to other countries, similar to the U.S.$10,000 rule in the U.S. The move is opposed in French banking circles, where concerns include confidentiality and the cost of

Justice to focus on combating money laundering. Sweden also was cited for general compliance with the Forty Recommendations, although laws relating to asset tracing and confiscation were seen as needing better enforcement.[38]

Members can be sanctioned for making no effort to implement the Forty Recommendations. The mildest sanction is a letter from the president to the country indicating the shortcomings; the harshest sanction is expulsion. Turkey is now being sanctioned, the sole country singled out in the 1995–6 Annual Report as being seriously deficient in overall compliance. The sanctioning began with a letter from the FATF president to the relevant Turkish ministers about lack of progress in compliance. A high-level mission then met with several members of the Turkish government in April 1996, in order to encourage Turkey to expedite the enactment of its anti-money laundering bill. In the absence of any progress, the FATF Plenary likely will take more serious steps. Sanctioning is therefore a graduated system of embarrassment through peer pressure.

The FATF also encourages non-member countries to adopt its recommendations. The purpose of maintaining nonmember contacts is explicitly to encourage adoption of the Forty Recommendations and to monitor and 'reinforce' this process rather than merely to provide technical assistance.[39] The FATF also sanctions non-cooperative non-members. Recommendation 21 suggests that members publicize flagrantly uncooperative behavior and warn businesses and financial institutions to be careful in their business dealings in non-cooperative countries.[40] The Seychelles has recently been on the receiving end of a Recommendation 21 sanction. In February 1996, the FATF vigorously and publicly opposed provisions of the country's Economic Development Act (EDA) that guaranteed anonymity, immunity from criminal prosecution, and protection of all assets to anyone who invested more than US$ 10 million in approved investment schemes in the Seychelles. The American FATF president, Ron Nobles, termed the EDA 'an incitement to criminals throughout the world to use the Seychelles as a clearing bank for their illegally acquired gains with full immunity'. France, the U.K., the U.S., and the British Commonwealth Secretariat all urged the Seychelles to repeal the EDA. The FATF used Recommendation 21 to warn financial institutions worldwide 'to scrutinize closely business relations' having to do with the

implementation. A. Jack, 'France Might Force Banks to Disclose Transfers', *Financial Times*, December 23, 1995, 18.

[38] FATF Annual Report, *supra* note 33 at para. 58.   [39] *Ibid.*, para. 64.

[40] Recommendation 21 reads: '[f]inancial institutions should give special attention to business relations and transactions with persons, including companies and financial institutions, from countries which do not or insufficiently apply these Recommendations. Whenever these transactions have no apparent economic or visible lawful purpose, their background and purpose should, as far as possible, be examined, the findings established in writing, and be available to help supervisors, auditors, and law enforcement agencies.' FATF, Forty Recommendations, <http://www.oecd.org/fatf/recommendations.htm>.

Seychelles, and called on all OECD members to 'bring all pressure to bear on the government of the Seychelles to repeal the EDA',[41] so far with only limited effects.[42]

3. Extra-FATF Sources of Pressure to Comply

The FATF is not the only international organization that is concerned with money laundering, although it is one of the most specialized and visible. A number of regional groupings also have tried to address flows of illegal money through their financial systems, with varying degrees of zeal. It is clear that the efforts of the FATF are strengthened by regional authorities which have taken money laundering seriously. Some of these have cooperated explicitly with the FATF; others have well-established mechanisms for achieving their anti-money laundering goals.

The European Community, for example, is a significant source of pressure to control money laundering, along lines very similar to those advocated by the FATF. Removal of capital controls, with the concomitant potential danger of importing criminal activity from Eastern Europe, has helped to forge a strong consensus that money laundering rules must be stringent and harmonized across the market. The E.U. Directive on the Prevention of the Use of the Financial System for the Purposes of Money Laundering (1991) applies to all credit and financial institutions, including insurance companies. The rules require the identification of customers, data recording and storage, an obligation to report suspicious transactions, and internal control mechanisms and staff training.[43] The rules have entailed costly adjustments, for example in Luxembourg,[44] and influenced a major 1995 overhaul of the Spanish penal code, encompassing money laundering and corruption.[45] But the most contentious case has been that of Austria, which, despite significant reforms,[46] is on a collision course with the Commission over anonymous bank accounts.

---

[41] Quotations reported by AP, Worldstream, International News, dateline Paris, February 1, 1996; and in 'We Love the EDA' 705 *The Indian Ocean Newsletter*, February 10, 1996. Seychelles' defense of the law is reported by Litchen, M., 'Storm Rages over Proposed Seychelles Investor Legislation', *International Money Marketing*, February 16, 1996, 17.

[42] An anti-money laundering law was passed in March 1996, but the dialog is continuing at this writing over the immunity provisions of the EDA, which is not yet in force. 'FATF Says "Wait and See"', 726 *Indian Ocean Newsletter*, July 6, 1996, 5.

[43] Dumbacher, *supra* note 14 at 183.

[44] Financial services account for an estimated 20% of Luxembourg's GDP, four times the proportion in most other European countries. It hosts 220 banks, almost twice as many as a decade ago. Treasury Minister Ive Mersch lamented the loss of some of this business with the E.U. reforms: 'I've never seen private banking in the absence of confidentiality agreements. Why should we leave this business to non-European countries?' quoted by Eade, P., 'Facing Up to Harder Times', *Euromoney*, May 1996, 132–43 at 133.

[45] White, D., 'Spain Overhauls Penal Code', *Financial Times*, November 9, 1995, 3.

[46] In Austria, the 1994 Banking Act revisions had put in place a strong set of measures, including an obligation to report any 'suspicious' dealing or clients. Austria's anonymous numbered

Trade and Finance

The FATF has made efforts to work systematically with other international forums in regions around the world to secure better compliance. In Latin America, a major initiative was undertaken through the Summit of the Americas Ministerial Conference on Money Laundering, which took place in Buenos Aires in November and December 1995. Though much more limited in scope, the ministerial communiqué added weight to the FATF's external efforts by informally committing each of the thirty-four governments to enact laws to criminalize money laundering of drugs and other serious crimes;[47] to modify bank secrecy laws;[48] and to establish an ongoing assessment of the progress of each country in implementing these steps. Though limited to self-assessment, the OAS' Inter-American Drug Abuse Control Commission (CICAD) was given an important role in the monitoring process.[49]

In the Caribbean, the FATF has continued to support its regional counterpart, the CFATF, rather than launch any independent initiatives. The regional group undertakes systematic self-assessment, though it has not moved to mutual assessment. Regional institutions have only begun to develop in Asia, and little has been done to tackle the problem systematically in eastern Europe and the former Soviet Union, beyond the organization of a money laundering seminar in cooperation with the countries of the Black Sea Economic Cooperation.[50]

CONCLUSIONS

The convergence across national jurisdictions since 1986 has been significant but hard fought and hardly complete. Almost all industrialized countries would agree that money laundering should be considered a crime, although there is continuing disagreement on the 'precedent offensives' that produce illicit gains. Furthermore, few countries have embraced the American approach of comprehensive reporting of all cash transactions above US$ 10,000 and extensive record keeping for all international wire transactions. Indeed, most banks have lobbied their governments hard to reject U.S.-style record keeping and reporting,[51] although recent rules in France bring that

bank accounts remain (though foreigners are not allowed to use them). 'Survey of Austria', *Financial Times*, December 12, 1995, III.

[47] Summit of the Americas, Ministerial Conference Concerning the Laundering of Proceeds and Instrumentalities of Crime (Buenos Aires, Argentina, December 2, 1995), Ministerial Communiqué, para. Al.

[48] *Ibid.*, paras. C2, C9.   [49] *Ibid.*, para. F1.

[50] FATF Annual Report, *supra* note 34 at para. 81.

[51] Opposition to extensive reporting schemes was common from non-U.S. international banks which criticize the vastness of the scheme and the meagerness of its payoffs: *e.g.*, international bankers have criticized the U.S. reporting system for cash transactions over U.S.$10,000, which in 1989 resulted in about 7 million submissions to the IRS and generated virtually no evidence which led to money-laundering cases. Fullerton, *supra* note 25 at 5–7.

jurisdiction closer to the American approach. The traditional European approach of leaving it to the banks to know their customers and to report suspicious activities has found much more favor worldwide and is currently the basis of the FATF recommendations.

Tightening money laundering rules continues to meet with significant resistance in much of the financially-influential world. Outside of Japan, Singapore, and Hong Kong, money laundering is not a crime in much of Asia. Nor have these three powerful financial centers taken a leadership position on money laundering in their region. Although the United States and Australia tried to put the issue on APEC's agenda, no other APEC participant has shown any interest in contributing funds to the Asian FATF secretariat in Sydney.[52] Cooperation in the Western Hemisphere provides an interesting contrast: here, sustained U.S. leadership during the Summit of the Americas kept the pressure on and laggards in the international spot-light. Many more central and south American countries have made money laundering a crime, and have even agreed to 'self-assessment' in their own regional grouping, the Caribbean Financial Action Task Force (CFATF).

Though non-binding, the FATF's Forty Recommendations have provided the substantive core for developing international rules with respect to anti-money laundering efforts. Among the most advanced industrialized countries, the degree of compliance has been fairly high, with a few notable exceptions. Only one country within the FATF, Turkey, has been the subject of group censure for falling far short of the standards set by the recommendations. A larger group that cannot be quantified precisely but probably amounts to some four or five members, seems likely to have failed to comply with a significant number of recommendations, while making progress in other areas. Outside of the FATF, the most progress seems to have taken place in the Western Hemisphere (Latin America and the Caribbean) where the FATF model is used to coordinate regional efforts.

The key to FATF's success seems to flow from the serious and sustained attention the organization gives to monitoring and assessment. FATF has succeeded in providing a larger and more credible pool of information regarding the fate of money laundering efforts across countries. It has also shown a spotlight on countries that do not live up to its standards. The formal consequences have been slight; violations as flagrant as those of Turkey are not punished, but have been reprimanded in formal letters from the organization's president. Bids for illicit money as indiscreet as those of the Seychelles have met with strong disapproval, though no material sanctions.

[52] Interview with a Treasury official, Washington, D.C., August 5, 1996. In December 1995 the FATF held a conference in Tokyo to encourage Asian countries to implement similar guidelines (Japan, Hong Kong, and Singapore already belong to the Task Force) but the response was meager.

Still, it is clear that such negative publicity has been the basis for bringing national laws and rules in closer accord with those of the FATF membership.

It should be recognized that the FATF tests compliance by the extent to which national rules reflect FATF recommendations (implementation). A tougher standard yet would be the extent to which the crime of money-laundering is actually prosecuted and punished. Such a measure of compliance is still a long way off: even the most highly compliant European countries do not begin to approach U.S. rates of prosecution. Moreover, as in other cases where domestic practice parallels international norms, it remains difficult to infer significant behavioral changes based on the adoption into national law of the international standard.

The choice of a non-binding legal accord in the area of money laundering was a significant step toward harmonizing national rules to fight money laundering. The reason the FATF has given for using recommended principles for action rather than binding legal accords is straightforward: its members have diverse legal frameworks and financial systems, and so are in no position to take identical measures. Guidelines in the form of recommendations permit countries to implement them according to their particular circumstances, in contrast to mandatory detailed obligations in a binding document.[53] This nod to practicality is easy to understand and has likely contributed to a more influential agreement as a result. First, the use of non-binding legal accords may be the most appropriate way to deal with rapidly changing financial practices and market conditions. Like other financial issues, anti-money laundering efforts are subject to rapid changes in the appropriate 'state of the art'. It is much easier to amend non-binding recommendations, as the FATF did in 1996, than agreements that require formal ratification.

Secondly, it is less likely that mechanisms for mutual monitoring and surveillance would have been agreed to in a binding legal context. Such supervisory mechanisms have proved crucial to the FATF's effectiveness. It is hard to imagine any significant progress in this area without consistent, informed pressure for change. Thirdly, the cooperation of the financial sector and financial regulators is central to the effectiveness of this regime. It is difficult to imagine gaining the cooperation of private financiers with a binding international agreement that forces change in the way they conduct much legitimate business and alters, for many, their fundamental relationship with their clients. In most of the countries where money laundering has become a significant concern, the financial sector is an important political actor. Many have long been successful in convincing their government that what is good for the financial sector is good for the economy as a whole. Stringent legal requirements instead of non-binding recommendations would have made

---

[53] Background paper by the FATF Secretariat, *Combatting Money Laundering: The Role of the Financial Action Task Force*, para. 8. (no date; faxed to the author July 24, 1996).

international accord much less likely, especially given the close alliance in many cases between the regulatory authorities and the financial sector.

The Forty Recommendations hardly stand isolated from more formal commitments states have made to combat money laundering. The top priority of the FATF is to get a legally binding commitment from states on the broadest possible principle—that money laundering should be considered a crime, however each jurisdiction defines the 'precedent offenses' and whatever the particular technique for nabbing offenders. The first Recommendation of the FATF is that countries should sign and ratify the Vienna Convention committing them legally to this principle. Virtually every other non-binding agreement signed over the past decade has similarly called for states to make a legally binding commitment. This suggests that while the means may be flexible, a legal commitment to the most basic principle of the regime is viewed as a prerequisite to its success.

'Soft Law' in a 'Hybrid' Organization: The International Organization for Standardization

NAOMI ROHT-ARRIAZA

INTRODUCTION

Most non-binding norms are made by and for states. The voluntary international standards of the International Organization for Standardization (ISO) are different. Created through a process involving both state agencies and private entities, they are intended for use by private actors in the market place. They consist of a range of technical guidelines and standards aimed at facilitating the flow of goods worldwide through standardization of such specifications, such as screw widths or air filter capacity.

A few ISO standards, especially the environmental management standards (EMS) series that is the subject of this study, have broad policy implications for business, governments, civil society, and the international legal system as a whole. First, technical rules and guidelines play an increasingly important role in international commerce. Although formally voluntary, these rules and guidelines may acquire a force equivalent to legally-binding rules through acceptance as market requirements. Conformance[1] with the environmental management system standard, in particular, may be less significant as an environmental measure than as a condition for participation in global markets; to that extent, at least, the standards are trade-focused rather than environment-focused. Secondly, the hybrid nature of the rule-making process illustrates another facet of the complexity of international law-making, which has moved well beyond formal treaty processes to encompass myriad efforts and institutions.

Finally, although technical rules and guidelines may not be 'law' *per se*, they are related to national and international rule-making processes in both a proactive and reactive sense. Like other forms of soft law, they may be and often are adopted into national laws and regulations, stimulating further legal developments. ISO standards now have a privileged place in international trade agreements, as explained below. At the same time, such standards can play a defensive role, allowing business to avoid more intrusive national or international regulation. Part of the debates around the ISO 14000 environmental management systems series revolves around its possible use to advance a deregulatory environmental agenda nationally and to forestall substantive industrial regulation internationally.

This study looks generally at the ISO and specifically at the process of drafting and implementing the ISO 14001 environmental management systems standard, to explore the role of ISO standards as 'soft law'. To summarize, the ISO 14000 series extends the management systems approach first pioneered in ISO 9000's quality control series to environmental management. ISO 14001 is the centerpiece of the 14000 series.[2] To conform to the standard, company management must first define the organization's environmental policy and ensure that it is appropriate to the nature, scale, and environmental impacts of the organization's activities. Each organization must commit to continual improvement, to compliance with relevant laws and other requirements to which the organization subscribes, and to prevention of pollution. The environmental policy must be publicly available, and must contain a documented framework for setting and reviewing environmental objectives and targets; assessments of environmental impacts need not be published.

---

[1] Within ISO, one speaks of 'conformance' with a standard, to distinguish that action from 'compliance' with a public regulatory standard.

[2] While the 14,001 EMS is the only 'auditable' standard to which an organization may be 'certified', the ISO 14000 series includes a 'guidance document' providing more detailed information on EMS. It also contains environmental auditing standards that set out a methodology for audits and qualifications for auditors, labeling standards covering goals and criteria for environmental labeling, and specific methods and criteria for manufacturer's self-declaration claims (for product attributes like recyclability) and for 'seal of approval' programs like Green Seal or Blue Angel. Other related guidelines will deal with life-cycle assessment and with environmental performance indicators. The EMS standard and guidance document and the auditing standards became final in 1996.

Once plans, objectives, and timetables are in place, management must designate responsibility for achieving targets, provide necessary resources and train appropriate personnel, and prepare an emergency response plan. These activities must be periodically monitored and corrective action taken in cases of noncompliance. Periodic audits of the system, whether internal or external, are required. Such audits may be used by third party certification bodies to verify compliance with the EMS. In addition, periodic management reviews must evaluate the system's continuing effectiveness. The existence of an adequate system may be self-certified or a firm may seek third party verification to 'certify' that it conforms to the standard.

The discussion below describes the ISO decision making process and the drafting of ISO 14001, then explores potential ramifications of the standard in domestic and international law. It then looks at implementation, compliance, and effectiveness issues before attempting to draw some conclusions.

A. THE INTERNATIONAL ORGANIZATION FOR STANDARDIZATION

The ISO was founded in 1946 to promote voluntary international standards that would facilitate global trade. It is a federation of some 120 national standards bodies, each of which is the body 'most representative of standardization in its country'.[3] Standardization bodies vary and each standards body determines its own composition. In some countries, government officials predominate, while in others the standards institute is essentially a private organization dominated by industry and industry consultants. A number of countries, including the U.S., have hybrid organizations staffed mostly by trade association and industry officials, but with government staff experts as members. The member organizations provide most of the financing, staffing, and administrative and technical services for the committees. A small Geneva-based secretariat serves largely as coordinator, and a Technical Management Board made up of active national secretariats oversees the process of initiating a given standard-setting exercise. Thus, the ISO is a hybrid, both IGO and NGO.[4]

The ISO's structure is based on technical committees, which may establish their own subcommittees and working groups. Each national group selects its

---

[3] There are three types of members: (1) full members, who can participate in technical committees; (2) correspondent members, usually standards-related organizations in a developing country that does not yet have its own national standards body, who can receive correspondence and observe at meetings; and (3) subscriber members, who are standards-related organizations from 'countries with a very small economy'. In addition, consumer and other groups may become liaison members, able to receive documentation and, in some cases, attend meetings, but unable to vote. Krut, R., and Gleckman, H., *ISO 14001: A Missed Opportunity for Sustainable Global Industrial Development* (1998) 43, 46.

[4] See also Clapp, J., *International Environmental Standard-Setting: ISO 14000 and the Developing World* (1998).

own members and decides the positions they will take in the technical committees and subcommittees. For the most part, ISO standards are highly technical and of little interest outside a particular industry. The ISO's recent
forays into softer management sciences have not to date resulted in changes
in its internal decision making, although calls for reform are growing.

The process of creating a standard commences with the formation of a
technical committee. The members of the technical committee (TC), volun-
teers representing the interested national groups, organize the work into its
component parts, assigning tasks to subcommittees and working groups.
Participants negotiate and discuss the drafts in the various subcommittees
and working groups as well as in national advisory groups. These groups may
meet simultaneously and often hundreds of groups will be meeting as part of
different TCs at any one time. The working groups, unlike subcommittees,
are composed of individual experts who are not supposed to represent their
national positions. The subcommittee and working group drafts are eventually integrated into a committee draft that must be approved by 'consensus',
following the ISO's definition of the term.[5] After the technical committee
approves the draft, it becomes a 'draft international standard', and is circulated to the entire ISO membership for a vote. A substantial majority must
approve the standard for it to be published as an official international standard.

ISO began considering environmental management standards in a preparatory committee known as SAGE, set up at the time of the 1992 U.N.
Conference on Environment and Development to provide ISO input into 'the
concept of sustainable industrial development'. A technical committee, TC
207, was officially launched in October 1992. The mandate of TC 207 was to
create standards in the areas of environmental management systems, environmental auditing, environmental performance evaluation, labeling, life-
cycle analysis, and environmental aspects of product standards.

The drafting process within TC 207 was dominated by officials from
transnational industrial producers, industry associations, and industry consultants. Developing countries, small businesses, and consumer or environmental groups were conspicuously absent. The heads of the sub-committees
and working groups almost invariably came from large industrial countries
and concerns; over half the working group chairs came from transnational
corporations and all came from developed countries. Although each national
standards association is supposed to seek a balance of the relevant interest

[5] Consensus means 'general agreement, characterized by the absence of sustained opposition
to substantial issues by any important part of the concerned interests and by a process that
involves seeking to take into account the views of all parties concerned and to reconcile any conflicting arguments. Note—consensus need not imply unanimity.' ISO/IEC Guide 2, 1991, cited
in Krut and Gleckman, *supra* note 3 at 56. In practice, consensus means at least two-thirds of permanent members in favor. *Ibid.*

groups, transnational corporate and consultant interests dominated the crucial early stages when the architecture of the standards was put in place. In part, lack of broad participation was due to the cost of attending meetings, which must be borne by the participants.[6] Recent meetings have been held in the U.S., Japan, Brazil, Australia, France, Korea, Norway, and South Africa. The intent is to distribute the costs of travel evenly, but the result is that only those who can afford to pay huge travel costs can consistently attend meetings. Moreover, effective participation requires knowledge of English, an ability to be at all meetings, to follow several meetings simultaneously, and to wade through a large number of technical documents in a short period of time. Developing country delegations often complain that they do not receive documents or receive them late.[7]

The presence of government, NGO, and small business interests in TC 207 improved over time. Government agencies like the U.S. EPA began to take an active role, as did large NGOs like the Environmental Defense Fund and Worldwide Fund for Nature. By the time these actors became engaged in the process, however, most of the basic decisions on ISO 14001 and other EMS documents had already been made, and their role was limited largely to damage control.

Transnational corporate domination of the drafting process raises a number of issues regarding the ISO rules. First, the largely non-state nature of the process does not necessarily guarantee adequate representation of societal interests. Indeed, compared to one-country, one-vote intergovernmental processes where NGOs are present and able to address delegates, the ISO process is a step backwards. Secondly, the lack of developing country, small business, and NGO participation drains legitimacy from the resulting standards, creating a risk that they will be implemented solely if and only to the extent they are forced by market pressures, rather than for purposes of real environmental improvement.

B. THE CONTENT OF THE EMS STANDARD

The debates during the drafting of ISO 14001 centered on the extent to which the EMS standard would contain substantive, performance-based obligations, or would be only a set of prescribed procedures and management techniques. A purely procedural approach allows maximum flexibility for

---

[6] The Netherlands provided some funding to bring developing country participants to later TC 207 meetings, as did the ISO Developing Country Committee; nonetheless, funding was insufficient to ensure adequate developing country participation. Only 26% of developing countries have institutions that are members of TC 207 and only 17% can vote. Krut and Gleckman, *supra* note 3, at 45.

[7] See *e.g.* 'Small- and Medium-Size Businesses, Along With Developing Nations, Face Challenges', Quality Systems Update, July 1995, at SR–10.

management, but does not guarantee optimal environmental outcomes. It has the advantage of forcing organizations to engage in internal discussion before establishing goals and priorities, making it perhaps more likely that organizations will take the resulting plans seriously rather than seek minimal compliance with externally-imposed regulations. The danger is that because the goals and priorities are entirely self-chosen, they will be implemented only until changes no longer result in short-term cost avoidance or savings.

The EMS series 'does not establish absolute requirements for environmental performance beyond commitment, in the policy, to compliance with applicable legislation and regulation and to "continual improvement"'. An annex elaborates: 'the rate and extent of [continual improvement] will be determined by the organization in the light of economic and other circumstances. The establishment of an EMS will not necessarily result in an immediate reduction of adverse environmental impact.'[8] Companies that set and meet extremely lenient goals will conform to the standard to a greater extent than those companies that set more ambitious, difficult to attain objectives.

The definition of 'continual improvement' in the ISO 14001 standard and the question of whether the EMS evaluation would assess only improvements in the system itself, or include its actual results as well, were major sources of controversy during the drafting process. The United States and some other participants pushed for a definition of 'continual improvement' that did not impose minimum rates of reduction of emissions or toxics. European delegates sought language directly linking continual improvement with improvement in *performance*, not simply of the system's operation. The delegates' respective positions reflected the greater preponderance of large industrial interests on the United States' delegation, compared to the more government-heavy European delegations, as well as their different legal and regulatory climates. The final document specifies that continual improvement merely refers to the 'process for enhancing the EMS to achieve improvements in overall environmental performance, in line with the organization's environmental policy'. Notably, the process need not take place in all areas simultaneously.[9]

The United States and other non-European delegations also wished to limit evaluation of performance to the management system itself, rather than the actual environmental performance of the organization. They argued that an international standard could not be dominated by the requirements of one region, and environmental performance should be assessed by other regulatory agencies and other parts of the standard-setting process. The final standard contains a compromise—the EMS standard covers objectives and targets, and continual improvement refers not only to refinements in the system itself, but to improvement of objectives and targets. While an improvement over prior drafts, the standard still leaves no way to judge whether the

⁸ ISO 14001, Introduction and Annex A, A.4.0.   ⁹ *Ibid.*, at 3.1.

improvements are sufficient, and permits a company starting from a very low baseline to 'improve' without ever meeting any international benchmark for adequate performance.

European delegates pressed as well for a specific level of pollution control technology, *i.e.*, 'viable and achievable best available technology'. U.S. participants worried that this standard would change substantive legal requirements in the United States and would result in enormous civil and/or criminal liability. As a result, the standard's Introduction merely provides that 'the EMS should encourage organizations to consider implementation of best available technology where appropriate and where economically viable. In addition, the cost effectiveness of such technology should be fully taken into account'. It also specifies that the standards 'are not intended to be used to . . . increase or change an organization's legal obligations'.

Another subject of debate was the specificity and public nature of requirements for evaluating environmental impacts. The original British standard which served as a model for the ISO draft contained a requirement for an 'environmental effects register' to identify areas for improvement. U.S. participants worried that in the U.S. legal and regulatory culture a document listing a corporation's detrimental environmental impacts could be requisitioned by regulators or discovered in litigation. The U.S. position prevailed, and the ISO standard does not require an environmental register; rather, the organization need merely consider the significant environmental aspects over which it has control in setting objectives and targets. There is no mandatory requirement to consider air emissions, releases to water, or the like.

The U.S. also succeeded in preventing a requirement that the results of the procedure be made public. The United States argued that such a requirement would discourage companies from setting ambitious, meaningful objectives. European delegates countered that credibility depended on making at least basic information publicly available. The final standard requires only that the organization's environmental policies be publicly available; data on environmental impacts need not be published. Rather, the 'organization shall consider processes for external communication on significant environmental aspects of its activities and record its decision'.[10]

A final area of controversy concerned the relationship between the EMS and environmental audits. European participants favored a system of audits that included independent audit verification and publication of at least a summary of results, including data on environmental performance. The United States and other delegations objected, finding the costs of third party verification excessive and often unnecessary. The U.S. position prevailed, and the final standard requires only an *internal* audit of the management system itself to determine whether it conforms to the standard and has been properly

---

[10] *Ibid.*, at 4.3.3.

implemented and maintained. There is no obligation to make the results public.

To summarize, differences among the drafters over the content of the standard resulted, in almost every instance, in weakening the language and making the obligations less stringent and more subject to management discretion. In part, this is inevitable in a consensus-based, voluntary drafting exercise, where it is not possible to bind those who are unwilling to assume more stringent commitments. Also in part, it reflected the composition of the drafters and the lack of transparency and accessibility of the drafting process.

C. ISO 14001 IN DOMESTIC AND INTERNATIONAL LAW

One hypothesis for the use of non-binding norms is that they act as gap-fillers for 'harder' forms of law. ISO standards, including ISO 14001, appear in part to fulfill this role. At the same time, the EMS standard also may be designed to deflect attempts to create stronger domestic and international law norms and to reinforce the primacy of trade liberalization over environmental concerns.

One gap-filling function involves harmonization of national technical standards within the European Union. In 1985 the E.C. developed a new approach to product standards, under which the Commission establishes the 'essential requirements' for a product to be sold freely throughout the E.C., but the technical specifics are left to voluntary standards developed by private bodies, especially the regional ISO affiliate. Compliance with the harmonized private standards creates a presumption that the essential requirements of the regulation have been met.[11] On occasion, U.S. regulatory agencies have employed a similar approach, for example, using private standards to fill in gaps in the case of interim OSHA standards.[12]

Gap-filling can apply to other soft law instruments as well. For example, many corporate or sectoral codes of conduct prescribe more detailed or extensive obligations than those an organization undertakes through compliance with ISO 14001. The chemical industry's Responsible Care initiative, for example, includes creation of a community review board to oversee health, safety, and environment issues. Conformance with this obligation, not verifiable through the industry code's own mechanisms, can be audited through ISO 14001's requirement of an environmental policy that includes a commitment to comply with 'other requirements to which the organization

---

[11] See, *e.g.*, Hunter, R.D., 'Standardization and the Environment' (1993) 16 *International Environment Reporter* 185.

[12] See Hamilton, R.W., 'The Role of Nongovernmental Standards in the Development of Mandatory Federal Standards Affecting Safety or Health' (1978) 56 *Texas L. Rev.* 1329.

subscribes'. Thus, within limits, one 'soft' instrument may provide the verification mechanism of another, equally 'soft' one, thus making it 'harder'.

Another major gap-filling function for ISO standards comes from the 1994 changes to the World Trade Organization's rules on technical standards. Since 1974, international trade agreements have shown a preference for harmonized global standards. With the signing of the Final Act of the Uruguay Round (GATT 1994), this preference has strengthened considerably. The Agreement on Technical Barriers to Trade (TBT), part of GATT 1994, covers both government regulations and private voluntary product standards like those relating to size, quality, or emissions levels. It creates a preference for international standards, and a presumption that ISO-created international rules are consistent with GATT. The TBT Agreement for the first time encompasses non-governmental standardizing bodies like ISO, and commits central governments to ensure that their standardizing bodies comply with GATT's national treatment and least trade-restrictive requirements, as well as with an annexed 'Code of Good Practice for the Preparation, Adoption, and Application of Standards'. That Code generally requires that standardizing bodies use existing international standards as a basis for their own. An equivalent set of non-discrimination rules applies to governments instituting conformity assessment procedures to ensure that suppliers actually conform to standards.

Thus, rules created by ISO and its sister bodies have privileged status in trade law, a status not conferred on voluntary standards created by intergovernmental technical bodies.[13] ISO standards help define what is meant by a 'standard' in any given area, providing an impetus to create such standards and allowing the trade regime access to a great number of potential supplemental rules. States that impose or allow standards differing from existing (or draft) ISO ones on the same topic bear the burden of justifying the departure. In the case of ISO 14001 and related standards, if a state adopted into its regulatory or procurement policies an environmental management or eco-labeling requirement that differed from the ISO version, that decision might be challenged by another state that felt its industries disadvantaged.[14] This provides an incentive for states to actively participate in ISO drafting processes that may outweigh the costs involved and creates a strong pull towards using these standards.

This link with the international trade regime also facilitates the preemptive role of the ISO 14000 series, supporting those who seek to avoid or replace

---

[13] See Krut and Gleckman, *supra* note 3, at 70.

[14] Presumably, WTO disciplines would be inapplicable if the standard were used only as a market requirement and not adopted by states. Also, it is unclear to what extent a requirement for an environmental management system—either tied to a specific product or in general—constitutes a process and production measure (PPM) under the TBT. See Roht-Arriaza, N., (1996) 5 *YBIEL* 107, 154; Krut and Gleckman, *supra* note 3, at 70–1.

potentially more intrusive forms of environmental control. A soft law instrument like ISO 14001 can forestall more demanding 'soft' rules and harder ones, and operates on both a national and international level. Confronted with declining regulatory budgets and decreasing returns from existing emissions limits, states are relying to an increasing extent on voluntary standards.

A European predecessor to ISO 14001 that included several more demanding requirements illustrates the preemptive nature of the ISO standard. The Eco-Management and Audit Scheme (EMAS), European Council Regulation 1836/93, established a system for using management and auditing systems to achieve continuous improvement in environmental performance. Although inter-government regulation was the source of EMAS, compliance is voluntary and it relies on public pressure and market mechanisms for effectiveness. EMAS differs from ISO 14001 in a number of respects: EMAS has a clearer tie to actual environmental performance outcomes; it requires a periodic public statement of emissions, waste generation, use of raw materials, and the like, whereas ISO 14001 requires only a public statement of policy but no publication of actual data; and it requires the use of a third-party verifier. EMAS itself applies only to sites located within the European Union, and the European Commission now accepts ISO 14001 conformance as partial satisfaction of EMAS requirements.[15] Non-European manufacturers initially expressed fears that their products would be disadvantaged in environment-conscious European markets due to their inability to receive EMAS registration. One solution has been to develop an alternative, less demanding standard with global reach, which can be promoted on the ground that it is accepted globally, not just in Europe. Initial reports indicate that this strategy is working, as European manufacturers turn away from EMAS in favor of ISO 14001.[16]

More generally, the use of voluntary systems allows industry to argue that it is capable of sufficient self-regulation for environmental improvement, and that mandatory, or even substantive, international guidelines or regulations are unnecessary. If the existence of a voluntary environmental management standard retards the development of a greater regulatory capability internationally, whether through a global environment agency or through multilateral agreements on specific sectors and/or substances, it will fit within a long tradition of soft law instruments serving to preempt harder law.[17]

---

[15] ISO 14001 satisfies EMAS requirements for an environmental management system, but not for a public statement, initial analysis, or verification. Differences between the two are spelled out in a 'bridging' document. (1997) 20 *International Environmental Reporter* 911.

[16] 'Businesses in Number of European Countries Favoring ISO 14000 Over EMAS, FoE Report Finds' (1997) 20 *International Environmental Reporter* 1016. The study found that the EMAS requirement of a public environmental statement was the main stumbling block to greater industry.

[17] See Roht-Arriaza, N., 'Shifting the Point of Regulation' (1995) 22 *Ecology L.Q.* 479, 532–4 (giving examples from marine oil pollution and pesticide control contexts).

The ISO 14000 series standards also may preempt other soft law instruments, representing a step backward to the extent that other standards are more ambitious in requiring improved environmental performance, public reporting, uniform standards throughout a company, or oversight of suppliers. ISO 14001 is a floor that, if it became the preferred mark of corporate environmental probity, would become a ceiling. To give one example of potential weakening of standards, the International Chamber of Commerce's Business Charter for Sustainable Development requires signatory companies to apply the same criteria internationally, while ISO 14001 requires only a commitment to comply with local laws and regulations. Thus ISO 14001 reverses the trend towards requiring transnational corporations to meet a single standard in their global operations.

The most important potential use of the ISO voluntary standards may be their potential to reduce domestic regulatory obligations. ISO 14001 fits within an emerging paradigm shift in environmental law, from a media-specific, 'command-and-control' approach to controlling emissions and wastes to one more focused on voluntary, incentive-based, market-based, and information-based approaches. Manifestations of the new approach range from the voluntary covenants and sectoral plans being developed in Europe to state and federal efforts in the U.S. to create incentives for industries to move 'beyond compliance'. Heavier reliance on voluntary approaches also reflects prevailing deregulatory and decentralizing agendas in the U.S. and Europe.

Although the standard is voluntary, it may, through a link to domestic environmental law, assume binding characteristics. To date, few jurisdictions have said they will require ISO 14001 for national companies, although Chinese, Japanese, and Korean officials have made some statements to that effect. A requirement for companies to adopt the standard would be the clearest sign of a transition from soft to hard law. More likely is the creation of incentives, rather than mandates. Such incentives could take the form of procurement preferences or requirements, or of regulatory relief. While ISO's sister quality control standard, ISO 9000, has become a requirement for many government contracts, the same is not yet true of ISO 14001.

Incentives may be indirect as well. For instance, a regulatory structure that results in high waste disposal costs will prove a powerful indirect incentive to firms to seek forms of waste minimization, including the implementation of environmental management systems. A regulatory requirement that firms provide certain information on environmental releases will similarly stimulate internal procedures to track such information. This reverse causal chain—from 'hard' domestic law to a 'soft' instrument that facilitates compliance with hard law—may be hard to trace, but is no doubt part of the explanation for the growth of tools like ISO 14000.

Early on, proponents of the ISO 14001 standard predicted that its greatest impact would come in the form of regulatory relief. A showing of self-regulation would, in this view, lead to reduced inspections, less regulatory oversight, and greater flexibility on the part of environmental authorities. To date, this promise has been largely unrealized. Several federal-level experiments in the U.S. require use of an EMS, but both federal and state regulators are largely waiting to specify the standard's role in regulatory schemes until more data on the actual environmental effectiveness of ISO 14001 are available; a Multi-state Working Group is designing research protocols to obtain the data. Nonetheless, a number of courts have required installation and verification of an ISO 14001-based environmental management system as part of the settlement in cases of environmental law violations, and agencies have agreed to similar settlements with polluters.[18] Indonesia has said it will use ISO 14001 certification as one element in ranking a company as 'green' in its PROPER company rating system.[19] Eventually, some form of regulatory encouragement for ISO 14001 implementation may become more widespread.

D. IMPLEMENTATION, COMPLIANCE, AND EFFECTIVENESS

ISO implementation either may be through regulation, as discussed above, or ISO simply may be transposed into an accepted national voluntary standard and thereby acquire a privileged status under national law. The latter process is greatly facilitated by the presence of national standards bodies in the Technical Committees that create the standards. Once a standard is agreed on, each national body takes it home and is in charge of transposing and promoting it nationally. Such transposition has occurred quickly and without too much difficulty in the case of ISO 14001, at least in those countries that have been active in the drafting process.

There is, however, a much more complex aspect to implementation which overlaps with issues of compliance. Under ISO 14001, an organization may choose to make a self-declaration of conformance without third-party verifi-

[18] U.S. EPA once allowed companies to use the creation of audited EMSs to reduce fines applicable for violations of the environmental laws, but as of May 1998 no longer explicitly allowed such deals. EMS might still be part of a larger package resulting in penalty reductions. 'U.S. TAG Hosts TC 207 Plenary Amid Mixed Signals from Government, Industry' [1998] *Business & the Env't's ISO 14000 Update*, Vol. IV, No. 6. A Canadian court has required ISO 14001 certification as part of the penalty for excess sulfur emissions. [1996] *Business & the Env't* 2.

[19] The PROPER rating scheme, run by the National Pollution Control Agency of Indonesia (BAPEDAL) attempts to use public disclosure and reputation incentives to induce better environmental performance. The scheme uses water pollution data to rate large enterprises based on five color performance categories, from black for total noncompliance, through red, blue for bare-bones compliance, green for effort beyond compliance, to gold for extraordinarily high standards and clean technology. ISO 14001 conformance would be part of the determination of whether a company deserved a green rating. The ratings are periodically published. World Bank, PROPER-PROKASIH Team, BAPEDAL, and PRDEI, *What is PROPER? Reputational Incentives for Pollution Control in Indonesia* (1995), unpublished manuscript.

cation. Some outside verification will probably be necessary, however; the inherent credibility limits to self-certification will probably make markets and regulators reluctant to accept such declarations. Under the ISO scheme, 'conformity assurance' is carried out by private entities for a fee. Indeed, one of the advantages of the scheme from a regulator's point of view is that it transfers a significant part of the costs of monitoring and enforcement to the private sector through a third-party verification system.

Private or public sector ISO certifiers may be accredited by any national accreditation body. As the ISO 14000 standards have become better known, many countries, especially in Asia, have rushed to set up or expand their own national accreditation body. Accreditation bodies set the professional requirements for firms which then hire themselves out to companies to perform certifications. No single international body is charged with drafting internationally acceptable mutual recognition standards or national accreditation/certification procedures for environmental management standards. The International Accreditation Forum (IAF) and ISO's Conformity Assessment Committee (CASCO), as well as other regional bodies such as Europe's European Accreditation of Certification (EAC), are working to develop international guidelines for accreditation bodies and certifiers, which should eventually allow for mutual recognition of accreditations.[20]

To date, however, accreditation of certifiers in one country does not guarantee worldwide acceptance of the certification. Industries have voiced concern that some states will only recognize certifications from locally-accredited organizations, as was the case with the ISO 9000 quality control standard, thus undermining the goal of an internationally recognized and accepted standard. Similarly, if buyers require a verifier to be accredited in the buyer's home market a *de facto* trade barrier can result. The trade barrier issue is of special concern to developing countries, because the costs of certification multiply if certifiers must be brought in from Europe or the United States. In addition, those firms that have already certified to the ISO 9000 quality control standard, and those that already have environmental management systems in place, will find conformance and certification less expensive—again, these will tend to be developed country firms.

Lack of an international mutual recognition process raises these market concerns; however, at the other extreme, too automatic recognition raises credibility concerns. Some accreditation as well as certification bodies are government-operated and are closely tied to ministries of commerce and

---

[20] The IAF as of 1999 was still preparing an international multilateral agreement to establish confidence in members/bodies accredited by the ISO/IAF standards. Accreditation bodies are encouraged to meet the non-binding international guidelines in order to obtain mutual recognition. Organizations must agree to participate in a peer review process, whereby they allow other regional or national bodies to examine their procedures, and, alternatively, agree to perform an internal audit on their reviewer in order to ensure harmonization and provide some guarantee of the integrity of the process.

trade, particularly within Asia, one of the regions that is most quickly
embracing ISO standards. Thus, they have an economic incentive to be lax in
their oversight of certifiers. It is easy to envision a 'race to the bottom' in the
certification industry, with the 'easiest' certifiers receiving the most business.
Over time, this dynamic can be expected to undermine the value of certification.

Beyond these for-profit, third-party certification schemes, non-governmental
representatives will play a minimal watchdog role. Until recently, environmental NGOs paid little attention to the ISO process, in part because ISO as
an institution was little known and the full implications of a private standard-
setting exercise were not clear. Most NGOs had neither time, money, nor
technical expertise sufficient to influence the drafting process. Now, however,
a U.S.-based NGO initiative has been established primarily to police whether
companies are using the standards to 'greenwash' their activities, as well as to
influence the revision of the standards. European NGOs are involved in monitoring as well as trying to influence the process of revision of the EMAS regulation.

It is presently difficult to gauge the extent to which the industry targets of
the standards are taking them on board. Most large transnational corporations already have their own environmental management systems, many of
them more demanding than ISO 14001. In some cases, EMS implementation
has resulted from internally-generated needs for regulatory compliance track-
ing or a conviction that greater efficiencies can result. Cost savings could
come from possible process or waste reduction technique changes, lower litigation costs, and improved public relations. Lucent Technologies, a U.S.-
based company, recently obtained ISO certification at a cost of $30,000 per
site, but stated, 'the investment has already returned dividends through the
efficiency of having a business-wide, disciplined approach to environmental
management'.[21]

A major disincentive to ISO implementation and third-party certification is
cost, which can be prohibitive, particularly for small businesses. Internal
development costs required to create a company-wide EMS policy, as well as
the costs of third party certification, may prevent companies from adopting
the standards, or may encourage companies to create their own environmental management systems. The U.S.-based Procter & Gamble Corporation
opted to implement its own EMS policy, and did not declare conformity to
ISO 14000, primarily because it estimated the cost of full ISO 14001 implementation and certification at $100,000 per site, or roughly $15 million per
year.[22] Justifying this level of costs is difficult for environmental managers
and may be impossible for small businesses. Additionally, many companies
view the ISO process as yet another 'paper trail' lacking any identifiable asso-

[21] 'ISO 14000 Update' [1997] *Business & the Environment*'s, July, 3.   [22] *Ibid.*, at 1.

ciated benefits. Thus many corporations, especially in the U.S., are taking a 'wait-and-see' attitude toward ISO conformance.

Nonetheless, some 7,000 companies have become certified to ISO 14001, with more saying their environmental management systems conform to the standard.[23] Japan leads in certifications, as do the electronics and auto industries. The U.K. and Germany have the largest number of companies among Europe's nearly 4,000 certifications.[24] Where companies seem to be embracing the standards more wholeheartedly, as in Asia, neither regulatory benefits nor internal uses seem to be the paramount reason. Rather, by far the greatest incentive comes from the promise of improved market access to European (and secondarily, other developed country) markets, or, conversely, from the fear of being squeezed out of these markets for lack of adequate assurances of corporate environmental probity. Indeed, stories of lost contracts and dropped suppliers abound,[25] fanned no doubt by an environmental consultant industry seeking a new market niche. In addition, many Asian suppliers lost business when they were late in implementing and certifying to the ISO 9000 quality control scheme, and are determined not to repeat past mistakes.

In theory, such market-chain, market-driven pressure could be a powerful positive force for environmental change. One of the potential advantages of ISO 14001 over traditional regulation is precisely that it harnesses business self-interest to environmental improvement without the mediation of state enforcement. If large global businesses begin preferring certified entities or requiring proof of certification to ISO 14001 or another EMS standard from their suppliers, demand for certification could grow. As global business transforms itself into dense networks of large and small suppliers and contractors, the leverage exercised by large transnational businesses over other firms in their supply chain is potentially quite powerful. Government procurement policies incorporating a preference or requirement could have similar effects, as could the policies of banks and insurers. Such pressure emanating down the supply chain would encompass a wide range and size of producers, potentially multiplying the initial impulse towards certification manyfold.

ISO 14001 itself contains only weak provisions regarding suppliers' adherence to environmental management systems. Rather than an explicit requirement for evaluation of suppliers, like that contained in both EMAS and ISO 9000, ISO 14001 requires only the establishment of 'procedures related to the identifiable significant environmental aspects of goods and services used by the organization and communicating relevant procedures to suppliers and contractors'.[26]

[23] [1999] *Business & the Environment*, January, 13.   [24] *Ibid.*
[25] B & Q, a large British home improvement corporation, reportedly dropped one of its tropical timber suppliers because of failure to conform to ISO 14001. 'Japan: Environment Agency Program to Encourage Small Entities, Public Sector to Use ISO 14000' (1996) 19 *International Environment Reporter* 930.
[26] ISO 14001, sec. 4.3.6(c).

It is as yet unclear, however, whether and under what circumstances large global industries will see a business advantage in either complying with ISO 14001 themselves or in encouraging conformance in their suppliers. Unlike ISO 9000, no immediate impact on product quality or usability is associated with better environmental management. Certification requirements may be limited to high-profile companies or sectors, where a major accident or discharge would reflect badly on the entire industry, or to sectors heavily dependent on exports.

The little bit of existing evidence shows that many global corporations are indeed looking into the environmental performance of their suppliers, but that this concern does not necessarily translate into a requirement for ISO 14001 certification. A survey by Business for Social Responsibility of twenty environmental 'leaders'[27] found that all were undertaking efforts to improve the environmental performance of their suppliers, although the efforts varied from comprehensive programs expecting 'beyond compliance' activity to development of industry-wide screens. While the existence of an EMS was the single most widely-shared criterion for environmental responsibility, this did not translate into adoption of ISO 14001 as a screening device. Most suppliers engaged in more direct reviews of a supplier's environmental performance, through questionnaires, interviews, on-site visits, or the like. Other studies in both Asia and the U.S. also failed to show that companies intended to make use of ISO 14001 a supplier condition.[28]

Thus, for some companies, it may be the EMS and actual performance, not the certification, that matters. If this is the case, large global enterprises based in developed countries may end up serving as transmission belts not for ISO 14001 certification, but for real performance improvement among their suppliers. If so, such enterprises may be instrumental also in providing the training and capacity-building to enable suppliers to meet their requirements, through product stewardship or similar programs. It is unclear, however, if under this scenario one could trace a causal connection between the existence of the ISO standard and the multiplier effect: probably the most reasonable hypothesis is that some amount of supply-chain 'greening' would have happened anyway, but that the ISO standard's existence catalyzed some discussions of each company's most appropriate response.

Moreover, the success of ISO 14001-centered supply chain pressure might have perverse consequences: favoring large companies over small, developed country-industry over developing country industry, or ISO 9000-certified companies over those who must start from scratch in developing procedures

[27] Business for Social Responsibility, *Greening the Supply Chain: Environmental Considerations in Worldwide Purchasing* (1997) (unpublished paper on file with author).

[28] Krut, R., and Drummond, C., *Global Environmental Management: Candid Views of Fortune 500 Companies, U.S.-Asia Environmental Partnership* (1997); Krut and Gleckman, *supra* note 3, at 80.

and paper trails. It might defer or replace more effective investments in environmental improvement. Finally, as discussed above, supply chain pressure that takes the form of preferences or requirements for public procurement may well raise concerns that, even though the standard is ostensibly international, it still constitutes a non-tariff barrier.

CONCLUSIONS

Of the factors that impelled the use of a non-binding instrument, the relationship to existing domestic laws and policy and the transnational dimension stand out. Existing domestic regulation and regional law (EMAS) created both a need for action—to forestall further regulation, as well as to take advantage of the regulatory reinvention trend—and a template. A binding instrument would have had neither the flexibility nor the backing needed within a reasonable period of time. Moreover, the trade, not the environmental, implications of the standard predominated, so that concern with facilitating trade and avoiding trade barriers pushed towards a single global standard. In addition, many of the initial drafters, familiar with the ISO 9000 quality control process, believed this was a technical, non-political effort that could best be left to standards professionals.

Institutional and contextual factors include the existence of a third party certification system, well-known in related contexts, that could potentially lend credibility to claims of conformance. ISO 9000 and EMAS were precedents that could be followed, although doing so has proven problematic. Industry domination of the standard-setting process gave some confidence to the target audience that the results would be both useful and achievable. On the other hand, the lack of transparency and adequate representation of a range of interests within the drafting process has undermined the degree of acceptance from other constituencies, especially NGOs and regulators. The ISO's perceived lack of suitability and credibility for developing rules with public policy implications also worked against acceptance by these constituencies.

By far the strongest factor leading to success in terms of the actors involved in creating the standard was the participation of the targets of the norm in the standard-setting and implementation processes. While European government representatives were instrumental in getting the drafting process started and tried to strengthen and make more precise the requirements to be imposed by ISO 14001, they ultimately accepted a weaker version. The U.S. government became involved late in the process and was unable to wrest control of the U.S. delegation from representatives of regulated industries.

Those actors concerned with public knowledge and interest in the drafting and implementation process were, in contrast, unimportant. Few members of the media, NGOs, or even other IGOs were involved in or aware of the drafting process. International lawyers generally took a secondary role compared to engineers and standards professionals. ISO in general remains only tenuously connected to public law environmental institutions, although it does have an ongoing relationship to the WTO Secretariat. While all these factors made agreement easier to reach, they may in the long run mean a standard that is less credible and of less value to industry.

What does the development of ISO 14001 tell us about soft law? First, the soft law form was used here for fairly straightforward reasons. Non-state (or in this case hybrid) actors cannot create binding treaty instruments. While private interests can surely influence the conclusion of such treaties, the process would necessarily be much more cumbersome and time-consuming. Moreover, a treaty is not needed to get the benefit of trade facilitation through harmonization of differing practices and indicators. Nor would a treaty on acceptable corporate environmental practices or performance likely be feasible at this time, beyond agreement to phase out a few highly dangerous or polluting substances.

An instrument aimed directly at non-state actors, moreover, may be more effective if it requires voluntary action—that is, if it is deliberately 'soft'. Voluntary assumption of the obligations may imply more 'buy-in' by those expected to put the standard into practice, which may mean less perfunctory and more dedicated translation of the standard to company reality. On the other hand, the very voluntariness of the standard may leave a margin of managerial discretion that makes meaningful comparisons of performance difficult.

Secondly, ISO standards were chosen for this study in part because they impact on, and are impacted by, the actions of states. Some of ISO 14001's proponents as well as critics insist that it is not meant to become incorporated into law at all but to serve as a stand-alone business management system, complementing but not replacing national and international public regulation. If in the long run the standard is not incorporated into law at all, does that mean it loses its character as 'soft law' as defined in this study? At the least, these non-regulatory private standards seem to indicate that eventual adoption as law may not be the sole purpose of a soft law instrument. In other words, norm-creation and effectiveness as a trade facilitator may both be independent of formal law-making processes, whether defined as 'soft' or 'hard'.

Thirdly, and relatedly, the ISO case indicates that there are multiple pathways from 'soft' to 'hard' law and back again. A 'soft' obligation may harden because of the requirements of big-market countries, or of private companies with big-market purchasing power, as well as through incorporation into law. These requirements may be defined in private contractual obligations, or in softer purchasing 'preferences'. In either case, the transformation of soft law into hard occurs through markets, not through the state. This may be the case for an increasing number of technical guidelines and the like.

Finally, the ISO case illustrates the possibility of simultaneous preclusive, complementary, and foreshadowing roles for soft law. In some cases, the ISO 14001 standard may replace other standards, codes, or even rules, while in others it complements existing patterns of regulation. It may also foreshadow other harder approaches, for example, by showing that companies can generate certain environmental indicators on a voluntary basis, which may lead to a decision to require generation of such indicators.

In short, ISO standards seem to be emblematic of the increasing complexity of what we call 'law'—on a continuum between state and private, between norm and regulation, between precursor and holding action. As use of the standards develops, their place along any axis of these continuums may change as well.

Policy Guidance and Compliance: The World Bank Operational Standards

LAURENCE BOISSON DE CHAZOURNES

In discussions of compliance with and the role of non-binding norms in the international legal system, it initially might appear curious to consider the Operational Standards developed by the World Bank.[1] They appear to be quasi-administrative in nature, for internal use by the Bank to guide its staff in their activities. However, they also are applied in the framework of financing development projects through loan and credit agreements negotiated between the Bank and borrowing countries. As such, they gain an external dimension, potentially affecting the behavior of the borrower.

The author would like to thank Andres Rigo, Acting Vice President and General Counsel, the World Bank, for his comments and observations.

[1] The terms 'World Bank' and 'Bank' refer to the International Bank for Reconstruction and Development (IBRD) and the International Development Association (IDA) established in 1960, the latter providing concessional funding for less economically developed countries. A more encompassing term, 'World Bank Group', refers to the IBRD and IDA, plus the International Finance Corporation (IFC) established in 1956 to engage in private sector financing, the Multilateral Investment Guarantee Agency (MIGA), established in 1988 to provide guarantees against various types of noncommercial risks faced by foreign private investors in developing countries, and the International Centre for Settlement of Investment Disputes (ICSID), established in 1966 to provide conciliation and arbitration facilities for the settlement of disputes related to transnational investments.

The Operational Standards are atypical of international policy and legal instruments. Their purpose is to assist individuals working for an international organization to fulfill their tasks pursuant to the mandate of the organization. As policy instruments they do not have legal status *per se* in the international legal system. They may enter the legal order, however, and be regulated by the law of treaties by being incorporated into a loan or credit agreement.[2] The Operational Standards also may play a crucial role in fostering the emergence of new international practices that seek to promote sustainable development and in facilitating respect for international legal instruments negotiated and adopted in other arenas. Finally they play an important role in assessing the quality of the World Bank's activities.[3]

The World Bank Operational Standards reveal the multifaceted, complex nature of the compliance issue. The Bank has developed an array of procedures and mechanisms to ensure compliance with the Standards during an operational activity, taking into account their policy nature, as well as their contractual character when incorporated into a loan or credit agreement. In addition, the Standards promote compliance with international conventions and nonlegally binding instruments. Last but not least, by favoring the participation of non-state actors the Standards make such actors the 'guardians' of respect for the Bank's norms and procedures. The establishment of the World Bank Inspection Panel has significantly reinforced this last element.[4]

The present study begins by discussing the notion of Operational Standards, describing various environmental and social standards. This is followed by an assessment of the role of procedures and mechanisms in promoting compliance with Operational Standards and the role of Operational Standards in fostering compliance with other international law. Links are drawn between public participation in the Bank's activities and compliance. The conclusion comments on the linkages between Operational Standards, compliance issues, and the international legal system.

A. OPERATIONAL STANDARDS IN THE WORLD BANK'S ACTIVITIES

Operational Standards, also termed 'operational policies and procedures',[5] consist of numerous instructions from the Bank management to its staff.

---

[2] The expression 'loan or credit agreements' encompasses guarantee agreements, grant agreements, such as Global Environment Facility grants, as well as other legal documentation entered into by the World Bank and others for the purposes of financing specific operations.

[3] See Wirth, D, 'Economic Assistance, The World Bank and Nonbinding Instruments', in Brown Weiss, E. (ed.), *International Compliance with Non-binding Accords* (1997) 219, 227–32.

[4] Res. No. IBRD 93–10, Res. No. IDA 93–6, 'The World Bank Inspection Panel' (1995) 34 I.L.M. 503.

[5] The Res. establishing the Inspection Panel calls for reviewing complaints regarding 'operational policies and procedures'. This term is given a specific meaning in the context of the Res. and

They encompass a wide array of topics intended to assist the Bank staff in its work concerning financed activities falling within the mandate of the Bank, such as specific investment activities or activities aimed at facilitating investments for productive purposes.[6] The operational policies and procedures have been elaborated around general themes, some of them designed to avoid or mitigate detrimental impacts of financial activities on certain groups of people and on the environment.

Operational Standards encompass documents entitled 'Operational Policies', 'Bank Procedures', and 'Operational Directives', as well as various other documents including operational statements and *ad hoc* circulars embodying the Bank policies and procedures. The various titles reflect the evolution of the policy documents towards codification of prescriptive conduct.[7] Originally, Operational Standards were conceived as aspirational targets drawn from practice and enshrined in policy documents. Over time, the Standards increasingly have been considered to express mandatory processes and prescriptions and have been more strictly and literally interpreted. Various events taking place in the early 1990s contributed to the change of perception, especially the release of two reports commissioned by the Bank: the 'Morse Report',[8] an independent review of highly-criticized projects known as the 'Narmada projects', and the 'Wapenhans Report',[9] an internal review of Bank operations commissioned by its President in the wake of the Morse Report. The latter assessed the implications of Bank financed projects to draw some lessons and recommendations on how to improve their effectiveness. The Morse and Wapenhans Reports both highlighted a need to strengthen quality control in the Bank's operations and to enhance transparency and accountability in the implementation of projects. Compliance with Operational Standards was identified as an important tool for achieving such objectives. Subsequent shifts in the role of the Operational Standards occurred in 1992, when the Bank's management clarified the extent to which

consists 'of the Bank's Operational Policies, Bank Procedures and Operational Directives and similar documents issued before these series were started. It does not include Guidelines and Best Practices and similar documents of statements'. *Ibid.*, para. 12.

[6] Art. I(i) of the Articles of Agreement establishes that the primary purpose of the Bank is to 'assist in the reconstruction and development of territories of its members by facilitating the investment of capital for productive purposes'. Articles of Agreement, 2 U.N.T.S. 134, as amended 606 U.N.T.S., 294. See 'Project and Non-Project Financing under the IBRD Articles', Legal Opinion of the Senior Vice-President and General Counsel, December 21, 1984.

[7] For most of the Bank's history, operational policies and procedures have been codified in a reference document called *The Operational Manual*. A system of Operational Manual Statements (OMS) and Operational Policy Notes (OPN) was used in the 1970s and 1980s. After 1987, they were consolidated into Operational Directives (OD); see World Bank Operational Policies: Lessons of Experience and Future Directions, CODE97–73 (November 20, 1997).

[8] Morse, B., and Berger, T.R., *Sardor Sarovar: The Report of the Independent Review* (1992). See also Berger, T., 'The World Bank's Independent Review of India's Sardor Sarovar Projects' (1993) 9 *Am. U. J. Int'l L. & Pol'y* 33–48.

[9] Effective Implementation: Key to Development Impact (R92–125), November 3, 1992.

the Operational Standards are binding, and in 1993 when the World Bank Inspection Panel was established.

Operational Standards are now looked upon as normative and procedural benchmarks for assessing the Bank's activities. This evolution was supplemented by a change in the Bank's disclosure policy. Originally, operational policies and procedures were not accessible to the public at large, as their purpose was solely to guide Bank staff in the conduct of its operational activities. The process of making them publicly accessible began at the end of the 1980s and was strengthened, as discussed below, by the 1993 adoption of a general disclosure policy[10] concerning Bank documents.

1. Adoption and Binding Nature of Operational Standards

The adoption process for Operational Standards is not a systematic internal legislative process that covers every topic of relevance for the operational work of the organization. Instead, the process is *ad hoc*: a topic emerges and eventually becomes sufficiently important and relevant to justify the adoption of an operational policy or procedure.[11] When the Bank feels that an issue should be dealt with this way, its staff and management prepare draft documents. Consultations are held at different stages with external partners, including non-governmental organizations (NGOs). These partners may make comments and observations before the drafting process starts and thereafter on draft documents. There are no formal requirements for the consultation process, which may take place by electronic means or other written modes, or orally when NGOs and other partners are invited to round tables. When finalized, operational policies and procedures are issued by the management.

The Board, the Bank's executive body composed of representatives of member states, is involved in the elaboration of Operational Standards. The Board's Executive Directors may approve policy papers, to which are attached draft operational policies submitted for their consideration. The Board is thereby given an opportunity to discuss the proposed policy.[12] When not attached to a policy paper, draft operational policies are circulated to the Board for comment. In addition, all policies and procedures must be consistent with the Bank's constituent agreement, *i.e.*, the Articles of Agreement. The Articles are interpreted by the Board, which is responsible for determin-

---

[10] A policy on disclosure of operational information was formally adopted in 1993. See Shihata, I.F.I., 'The World Bank and Non-Governmental Organizations', in F. Tschofen and A. Parra (eds.), *The World Bank in a Changing World* (1995), 265–6.

[11] For example, in 1982 the Bank issued an Operational Manual Statement on 'Tribal People in Bank-financed Projects' (OMS 2.4) whose objective was to protect the interests of relatively isolated and non-acculturated tribal groups. The adoption of this policy had been prompted by criticisms against projects financed by the Bank and dealing with the Amazonian forest.

[12] Shihata, I.F.I., *The World Bank Inspection Panel* (1994), 43.

ing matters of policy for the Bank. Operational Standards constitute one of the channels by which the mandate of the organization is translated into practice.

Some Operational Standards are mandatory for Bank staff, while others are merely of persuasive value. The mandatory character of a policy determines the jurisdiction of the World Bank Inspection Panel to receive complaints. The management of the Bank issued a decision in 1992 that specified the extent of the binding nature of Operational Standards. The objective of the decision was to ensure greater clarity of, and compliance with, Operational Standards. Within the Bank, there had been discussions about the need to clarify the limits of flexibility in applying a series of Operational Standards known as 'Operational Directives' to simplify the Bank's business practices and to better monitor the performance of Bank operations.[13] The Bank decided to replace the 'Operational Directives' (ODs) with statements termed 'Operational Policies' (OPs), 'Bank Procedures' (BPs), and 'Good Practices' (GPs). OPs are 'short statements (usually one or two pages) of policy'. BPs 'spell out the required documentation and common set of procedures needed to ensure operational consistency and quality'.[14] GPs are intended to disseminate knowledge and indicate successful examples.

OPs and BPs are binding on the staff of the Bank within the limits of flexibility provided, while GPs are not binding. The issue is complicated, however, by the fact that not all ODs and other earlier documents have been converted to OPs, BPs, and GPs. The situation may be a source of legal controversy because ODs include procedures and practices that are not all binding on the staff of the Bank. An assessment of the binding nature of the provisions of ODs depends on the wording of each standard.[15]

2. Environmental and Social Operational Standards

The Bank's operational policies and procedures cover a number of social and environmental considerations, ranging from the protection of specific vulnerable groups of people to water resources management issues. Some of the instruments are of general application, others are more specific. All contain provisions that are process-oriented, requiring respect for certain procedural steps and actions, while others add normative clauses, prescribing certain patterns of behavior. These policies and procedures not only provide guidelines for the Bank staff, they also indicate what requirements the borrower must fulfill before the Bank will finance an operation. The 'pillar' policies[16] for

---

[13] *Ibid.*, at 44–5.   [14] *World Bank Policy on Disclosure of Information* (1994).

[15] Shihata, *supra* note 12 at 45.

[16] The operational policies and procedures are available on the Bank's Internet website <http://www.worldbank.org>. As of June 1, 1999, the Environment Assessment policy has been issued as OP 4.01 (January 1999). The Indigenous Peoples policy and the Involuntary

integrating social and environmental considerations into the financial activities of the Bank[17] are found in the Environment Assessment policy, the Indigenous Peoples policy, and the Involuntary Resettlement policy, as well as the policies dealing with the Involvement of Non-governmental Organizations (NGOs) in Bank-supported Activities, and Disclosure of Operational Information.

The Policy on Economic Evaluation of Investment Operations also plays an important role, integrating environmental concerns in the cost-benefit analysis conducted for Bank-financed projects. The Bank analyzes every proposed project in order 'to determine whether the project creates more net benefits to the economy than other mutually exclusive options for the use of the resources in question',[18] including the option of not undertaking the project at all. Assessment of project sustainability requires taking into account economic, financial, and institutional risks, as well as environmental risks on the territory of the borrower, on neighboring countries, and on the global environment.[19] This policy is complemented by other requirements, notably the Environment Assessment (EA) requirement.

The Bank's EA operational policy is the cornerstone for evaluating project activities with potential environmental impacts.[20] It lays down standards and procedures for conducting environmental assessment and aims at improving decision-making by ensuring that the project options are environmentally sound and sustainable. The Bank screens all projects for classification into one of three categories that determine the appropriate level of environment assessment.[21] The most rigorous assessment is required for Category A pro-

Resettlement policy are still in the OD format. GP 14.70 on Involvement of Nongovernmental Organizations in Bank-supported Activities was issued in March 1997 and BP 17.50 on Disclosure of Operational Information was issued in September 1993. The Environment Assessment policy, the Indigenous Peoples policy and the Involuntary Resettlement policy are part of a group of policies entitled 'Safeguard Policies'. Their common feature is that they concern actions which may adversely impact people, environment and third countries. See Di Leva, C.E., 'International Environmental Law and Development' (1998) 10 *Georgetown Int'l Envtl L. Rev.* 501, 518–42.

[17] Most of the requests so far made to the Inspection Panel allege that the Bank has not followed its environmental and social policies and procedures. See Bissel, R.E., 'An Environmental Inspection Mechanism for World Bank Projects' [1997] *Ecodecision* 47–50. For an analysis of the Planned Arun III Hydroelectric Project in Nepal (1994) see Bradlow, D.D., 'A Test Case for the World Bank' (1996) 11 *Am. U. J. Int'l L. & Pol'y* 247–94.

[18] OP 10.04 on Economic Evaluation of Investment Projects (April 1994).

[19] Impacts on the global environment are considered when (a) payments related to a project are made under an international agreement, or (b) projects or project components are financed by the Global Environment Facility. *Ibid.*

[20] In fiscal year 1997, 18 projects totalling $2.9 billion of Bank lending underwent full EA and a further 82 projects totalling about $6.1 billion in Bank lending underwent some measure of EA appropriate to their potential environmental impact. The World Bank, *Annual Report* 1997 (1997), 25.

[21] OP 4.01 on Environmental Assessment includes a fourth category, 'Category F1'. According to the Bank, '[a] proposed project is classified as Category F1 if it involves investment of Bank funds, through a financial intermediary, in sub-projects that may result in environmental

jects, those which are likely to have a significant adverse environmental impact, such as impacts that are sensitive, diverse, or unprecedented or that affect an area beyond the sites or facilities subject to physical works.[22] Category B projects are those whose environmental impacts are less serious and thus require a less exhaustive form of environment assessment.[23] No environmental impact assessment is required where the project has no, or only minimal, adverse environmental impacts (Category C projects).[24]

The borrower must conduct the assessment to ensure that development options under consideration are environmentally sound and sustainable, and that possible environmental impacts are recognized early in the project cycle and taken into account in the project design. Environmental assessments identify ways to improve projects to minimize, mitigate, or compensate the adverse impacts. The environment assessment also should ensure that the project is consistent with domestic law and that it does not contravene any international treaties to which the borrowing country is a party.

Meaningful consultations with project-affected groups and local NGOs must be held during the environment assessment process and should be initiated as early as possible. For Category A projects, public participation must begin shortly after classification of the project and before the terms of reference for the EA are finalized. Public participation is required again once a draft EA is prepared, and throughout project implementation.

Dam and reservoir projects receive special EA treatment in order to avoid, minimize, or compensate for adverse environmental impacts wherever possible, using design features and other measures implemented as part of the project. Environmental specialists help identify potential project impacts at an early stage. Even before the project is categorized, the Bank must ensure that the borrower selects independent, recognized experts to carry out environmental reconnaissance to identify the project impacts, ascertain the scope of the EA, assess the borrower's capacity to manage an EA process, and advise on the need for an independent advisory panel, which would normally be set up for large dam projects.

Indigenous Peoples

The Bank has a specific policy to address the concerns of indigenous peoples, defined as social groups whose social and cultural identity is distinct from that

---

impacts'. Sub-projects under a financial intermediary project would have to be categorized individually as category A, B, or C projects. OP 4.01 also specifies that in the context of evaluating a proposed project, the analysis of alternatives should include a 'without project' option.

[22] OP 4.01 in relevant part provides, '[a] proposed project is classified as category A if it is likely to have significant adverse environmental impacts that are sensitive, diverse or unprecedented'. A potential impact is considered sensitive if it may be irreversible or raise issues covered by operational policies and procedures on Indigenous Peoples, Natural Habitats, Management of Cultural Property or Involuntary Resettlement. *Ibid.*

[23] *Ibid.*   [24] *Ibid.*

of the dominant society and who are vulnerable to being disadvantaged in the development process. The notion includes, but is not limited to, 'indigenous ethnic groups', 'tribal groups', and 'scheduled tribes'. The definitional criteria focus on the issues of vulnerability and distinctiveness, but other criteria have a role to play: close attachment to ancestral territories, indigenous language, self-identification, presence of customary, social, and political institutions, and the existence of subsistence-oriented production. The purpose of the policy is to ensure that these groups benefit from development projects and that potentially adverse effects are avoided or mitigated. The policy requires the 'informed participation' of indigenous peoples in projects and programs that affect them. The borrowing country must prepare an indigenous peoples' development plan to provide the framework for their participation in project activities and to ensure that they receive socially and culturally appropriate benefits. The policy requires that development plans assess: (i) the legal status of groups covered by the policy, as reflected in the country's constitution and legislation; and (ii) the ability of such groups to obtain access to and effective use of the legal system to defend their rights.

Involuntary Resettlement

The Bank's policy states as a basic objective that involuntary resettlement should be avoided or minimized where feasible and that all viable alternative project designs should be reviewed. The Bank studies any operation that involves involuntary land acquisition for potential resettlement requirements early in the project cycle. The objective of the policy is to assist displaced people who have lost their land, houses, or both, or their means of livelihood, in their efforts to restore or improve former living standards and earning capacity.

Where displacement is unavoidable, the borrowing country must prepare resettlement plans or development programs that indicate compensatory measures and an implementation scheme, including a grievance mechanism permitting affected peoples to bring complaints, as well as a timetable and a budget. Bank policy standards state that compensation for displaced people should (i) evaluate their losses through methods such as a land-for-land approach, a market value approach, or a mixture of land-based and non-land-based strategies, (ii) assist with their move and support them during their transition to the resettlement site, and (iii) assist them to improve their former living standards and the income earning capacity that they would have had without the proposed Bank project.

Like the policy on indigenous peoples, the policy on resettlement requires informed participation and consultation with the affected people during the preparation of the resettlement plan. Community participation in planning and implementing resettlement should be encouraged as well. The policy stresses the need to pay particular attention to the needs of the poorest and to give appropriate attention to indigenous peoples, ethnic minorities and 'pastoralists' who may have customary rights to the land or other resources taken for the project.

NGOs and Disclosure of Information

The policies and procedures on environmental impact assessment, indigenous peoples, and involuntary resettlement also contain specific provisions requiring the involvement of NGOs. In addition, a 'Good Practices' policy sets out a framework for involving NGOs in Bank-supported activities and provides staff with guidance for working with them.

The policy on disclosure of operational information[25] sets out procedures to be followed for making environmental assessments and environmental action plans accessible to affected groups and local NGOs in borrowing countries. This policy, and the one on the involvement of NGOs, complements the other policies. Legally, these policy requirements are important vehicles for 'operationalizing' or implementing broader international standards on access to information, public awareness, and participation in decision making.[26] As such they acknowledge the role of the beneficiaries of development assistance activities in ensuring the sustainability of such activities.

3. Incorporating Operational Standards in Loan and Credit Agreements

Although Bank practice can make Operational Standards binding on the Bank's staff, it is also important to consider their status under international law. In terms of compliance, Operational Standards create normative and procedural expectations for the staff and partners of the Bank and contribute in many ways to forging and developing accepted practices under international law. In addition, their incorporation in loan and credit agreements negotiated between the Bank and the borrowers enables them to become binding under international treaty law. By entering into an agreement with the World Bank, a borrowing state is placed under an obligation to take the measures necessary to comply with its contractual obligations. These obligations may in some cases include references to policy requirements, causing the latter to become part of the contractual terms. This practice progressively has gained acceptance with respect to environmental and social policy requirements.

[25] The Bank has established a Public Information Center, called the 'Infoshop', through which much of the material covered by the policy is available. It is located at the Bank Headquarters and serves the public in member countries through the Internet and through Bank field offices.
[26] See the Convention on Access to Information, Public Participation and Access to Justice in Environmental Matters (Aarhus, June 25, 1998), 998 EmuT. 48

A number of legal techniques have been devised to ensure that the Operational Standards reflected in loan and credit agreements are accompanied by safeguards against non-compliance. The policy requirements thus become enforceable under international law like any other provision of a loan or credit agreement.[27] The various contractual techniques used for integrating such measures and commitments into loan and credit agreements include, *inter alia,* drafting a stipulated prior condition, meaning that the loan or credit agreement only comes into force when the condition has been met,[28] or including a stipulated condition with respect to the disbursement of the loan or credit. Another technique is to include a covenant committing the borrower to execute specific measures by a certain date. These obligations may be complemented by detailed requirements in project agreements concluded with the project executing agencies. Loan and credit agreements thus may include detailed provisions on resettlement and rehabilitation should these issues be relevant to the project, making compliance a condition of effectiveness for a loan or a credit. The government then is required to take all necessary action to adopt and implement a resettlement action plan designed in accordance with the Bank policy on Involuntary Resettlement, before the agreement would be declared effective. Alternatively, an implementation program or plan of action may be attached as a schedule to the loan or credit agreement. Such a program or plan of action specifies the borrower's obligations with respect to policy requirements.[29]

The relevant policy on environmental assessment expressly requires the staff of the Bank to ensure that mitigation measures identified in an Environmental Management Plan[30] are fully integrated in the implementation and operation of a project. References to such measures in project legal documents, for example in the project description, are part of the measures taken for pursuing such an objective.

B. COMPLIANCE WITH OPERATIONAL POLICIES AND PROCEDURES

Various mechanisms play a role in promoting compliance with Operational Standards, and more particularly with environmental and social operational

---

[27] For a discussion of principles and rules of international law as applicable law to loan and credit agreements between the Bank and borrowing countries, see Broches, A., 'International Legal Aspects of the Operations of the World Bank' (1959 III) 98 *R.C.A.D.I.* 297.

[28] The effectiveness deadline is normally 90 calendar days from signing the loan or credit agreement.

[29] On the use of legal techniques for environmental protection purposes, see Shihata, I.F.I., 'The World Bank and the Environment: Legal Instruments for Achieving Environmental Objectives', in F. Tschofen and A. Parra (eds.), *The World Bank in a Changing World* (1995), 183.

[30] An Environmental Management Plan (EMP) is 'an instrument that details (a) the measures to be taken during the implementation and operation of a project to eliminate and offset adverse environmental impacts, or to reduce them to acceptable levels; and (b) the actions needed to implement these measures'. See OP 4.01—Annex A on Environment Assessment.

policies and procedures. Some mechanisms are rule-oriented, while others are more institutionally oriented.

1. Rule-oriented and Quality Insurance Mechanisms

Rule-oriented mechanisms promote respect for policy requirements in a number of ways. The legal techniques mentioned in the prior section, for example, have been developed to ensure that policy requirements are reflected in loan and credit agreements. The borrower should resort to all necessary means and measures to comply with these contractual commitments. For its part, the Bank should exercise compliance supervision with due diligence. If the Bank is not satisfied with the borrower's performance, it may suspend disbursement of a loan or credit, cancel it, or accelerate its maturity.[31] This kind of action is rather exceptional[32] because dialogue with the borrowing country is usually persuasive,[33] allowing compliance to be readjusted before the extreme stage is reached. The interruption of a contractual relationship is disfavored because it impedes the continuation of a dialogue that may find ways to correct the non-complying situation and does nothing to foster the environmental and social policies.

In addition to legal techniques that aim to ensure implementation of and compliance with project legal documents, there are operational mechanisms and procedures that have been established within the organization to guarantee the quality of the Bank's activities. One of the parameters of evaluation is compliance with operational policies and procedures. Internal review processes during the preparation of a project and random audits during the course of its preparation and implementation are among the quality insurance mechanisms put in place to ensure compliance. Eventually, disciplinary measures may be imposed.

The Operations Evaluation Department (OED), an independent evaluation unit within the Bank, plays an important role in the process, conducting a post-project evaluation that looks, *inter alia*, at the environmental and social aspects of completed operations, draws lessons from past practices, and suggests further roles to be played by operational policies and procedures. It rates the development impact and performance of the Bank's operations, reporting its results and recommendations to the Board. By doing so, it promotes the good practices contained in operational policies and procedures

[31] See General Conditions Applicable to Loan and Guarantee Agreements, Art. 6.02, January 1, 1985. See also Shihata, *supra* note 29 at 199–208.

[32] For an example of suspension of the proceeds of a grant agreement, see Boisson de Chazournes, L., 'The Global Environment Facility Galaxy: On Linkages Among Institutions' (1999) 3 *Max Planck Y.B.U.N. Law* 26.

[33] Shihata, I.F.I., 'Implementation, Enforcement, and Compliance with International Environmental Agreements—Practical Suggestions in Light of the World Bank's Experience' (1996) 9 *Georgetown Intl. Envtl. L. Rev.* 37, 50.

and highlights the problems encountered in implementing such standards. This assessment activity is supported by the publication of reports that provide recommendations and 'best practices' guidelines drawn from the Bank's development experience. To summarize, this post-project evaluation creates incentives for stricter and more effective compliance with Operational Standards.

2. The World Bank Inspection Panel

The World Bank Inspection Panel was created in 1993 to improve quality control in the Bank's operations during project preparation and implementation. The Panel also was expected to increase accountability of the Bank's management and staff *vis-à-vis* the Bank's Board and to ensure transparency in the Bank's operations,[34] and thus was established as an independent and permanent organ within the Bank's organizational structure. It was granted the competence to receive and, subject to the approval of the Bank's Board, investigate complaints from groups of individuals whose rights or interests have been or are likely to be directly and adversely affected by the Bank's failure to comply with operational policies and procedures.[35] An Executive Director in the Bank or the Bank's Board also may instruct the Panel to conduct an investigation, even though affected people have not introduced a request.

Individuals or any affected group of people[36] who share common concerns or interests in the country where the project is located may submit a request on condition that it is possible to demonstrate that their 'rights or interests have been or are likely to be directly affected by an action or an omission of the Bank'. The affected party may present its request directly or through local representatives acting as an agent. NGOs based in the country can take on this representation role and international NGOs may assume representation in exceptional cases where the party submitting the request asserts that appropriate local representation is not available. In those circumstances, the Executive Directors have to agree to such representation when they consider the request for inspection.

---

[34] On the motives for the establishment of the Inspection Panel, see Shihata, *supra* note 12 at 5–13.

[35] The mandate of the Inspection Panel covers projects financed by the International Bank for Reconstruction and Development (IBRD) and the International Development Association (IDA).

[36] The Resolution provides in a non-restrictive manner that the 'Panel shall receive requests for inspection presented to it by an affected party in the territory of the borrower which is not a single individual (i.e., a community of persons such as an organization, association, society or other grouping of individuals)'. The Clarifications endorsed by the Executive Directors on October 17, 1996 (hereinafter Clarifications–I) specify that a group of individuals alleging to be affected should be understood as meaning 'any two or more individuals with common interests or concerns'.

Outside scrutiny of the Bank's compliance with Operational Standards, through requests to the Inspection Panel, is a new means of promoting compliance with Bank Standards. Compliance concerns are institutionalized, in fact, by establishment of this specific entity to conduct investigations, offering the possibility of remedial action by the Bank if a violation is found. Moreover, establishment of the Inspection Panel has encouraged a Bank-wide process that can help clarify for the staff and management the content of operational policies and procedures and increase their awareness of the need for compliance with them.

Complaints must satisfy admissibility criteria. A complainant must allege a violation of operational policies and procedures[37] and demonstrate that the violation is due to an omission or action of the Bank with respect to the design, appraisal, and implementation phases of a Bank-financed project, *i.e.*, from the time of the project design until its substantial completion.[38] Complainants must allege that such failure has had, or threatens to have, a material adverse effect on them. The notion of 'project' is wide and encompasses all developmental activities eligible to be financed by the Bank.[39] The terms design, appraisal, and implementation are understood in light of the Bank's concept of 'project cycle', in each phase of which the Bank has a role and different responsibilities.[40]

---

[37] Res. No. IBRD 93–10, Res. No. IDA 93–6, 'The World Bank Inspection Panel' (1995) 34 I.L.M. 503.

[38] Para. 12 of the Res. establishing the Inspection Panel refers to the 'failure of the Bank to follow its operational policies and procedures with respect to the design, appraisal and/or implementation of a project financed by the Bank (including situations where the Bank is alleged to have failed in its follow-up on the borrower's obligations under loan agreements with respect to such policies and procedures), provided in all cases that such failure has had, or threatens to have, a material effect'. The Panel's *ratione materiae* competence should be ascertained in the light of four requirements: (1) an alleged failure of the Bank to follow its operational policies and procedures in the design, appraisal, and/or implementation of a project financed by the Bank; (2) the alleged failure must be of a certain gravity; (3) the alleged failure must relate to the Bank's own policies and procedures; and (4) the alleged failure must be such as to have or to be likely to have an adverse material effect on the complainant. See 'Role of the Inspection Panel in the Preliminary Assessment of Whether to Recommend Inspection—A Memorandum of the Senior Vice President and General Counsel, January 3, 1995' (1995) 34 *I.L.M.* 503, 525–34.

[39] Clarifications–I made clear that the word 'project' as used in the Res. 'has the same meaning as in the Bank's practice, and includes projects under consideration by Bank management as well as projects already approved by the Executive Directors'. The notion of project is not limited to specific investments. It includes programs or activities other than specific physical works. See Decision No. 2 of the Executive Directors, *Scope of the Panel's Mandate—Compensation for Expropriation and Extension of IDA Credits to Ethiopia under OMS 1.28*, The Inspection Panel, Report, August 1, 1994 to July 31, 1996, 57. See generally 'Project and Non-project Financing under the IBRD Articles', Legal Opinion of the Senior Vice-President and General Counsel, December 21, 1984.

[40] The Bank's project cycle covers the life of a project from identification of needs and priorities until the final completion of work and evaluation of results. See. Braum, W.C., *The Project Cycle* (1982); The World Bank, *The World Bank's Partnership with Non-governmental Organizations* (1996), 7.

The request for inspection by the Panel may relate either to a project in the design, preparation, pre-appraisal, or appraisal stage, or to a project already approved by the Board and financed by the Bank. With respect to the implementation phase, the Panel has the mandate to investigate whether the Bank has properly ensured that the borrower carried out its obligations under a loan or credit agreement.[41]

The Inspection Panel is not vested with general law-making powers and thus lacks the competence to enact new standards or amend existing operational policies and procedures. It may only adopt rules for 'procedural matters relating to the work of the Panel'.[42] The Panel adopted such rules on August 19, 1994 (hereinafter the 'Operational Procedures') based on the Resolution establishing the Inspection Panel.[43]

The Panel possesses limited investigatory powers with respect to complaints alleging a failure by the Bank to follow its policies and procedures in specific operational activities. By implication, the Panel is not entitled to review the consistency of the Bank's practice with *all* of its policies and procedures,[44] nor is the Panel entitled to decide on a general basis the adequacy of a particular policy or procedure.[45] Within the limits of its mandate, however, the Panel plays an important role in promoting compliance with Operational Standards.

The Panel exercises its investigatory and quasi-investigatory powers[46] on a case-by-case basis. In so doing, the Panel decides on the applicability of

[41] The Res. specifies that a complaint can be lodged for 'situations where the Bank is alleged to have failed in its follow-up on the borrower's obligations under loan agreements' with respect to operational policies and procedures. The Res. also states as a principle that no requests will be declared eligible regarding a project after the project's loan 'closing date' or after 95% or more of the loan proceeds have been disbursed. For an interpretation of this requirement, see *Time-Limits on the Eligibility of Complaints Submitted to the Inspection Panel*, Legal Opinion of the Senior Vice President and General Counsel, July 28, 1997.

[42] See Para. 24 of the Res.

[43] See World Bank, 'Introduction to the Operating Procedures', in The Inspection Panel, *Operating Procedures* (1994), 4.

[44] See 'Clarifications (Eligibility and Access)' in The Inspection Panel, *Annual Report*, August 1, 1996 to July 31, 1997, 30.

[45] See Forget, L., 'Le Panel d'inspection de la Banque mondiale' (1996) 42 *A.F.D.I.* 643, 654–5.

[46] The practice developed so far is described by Shihata, I.F.I., *The World Bank Inspection Panel—A Background Paper on its Historical, Legal and Operational Aspects*, The World Bank Inspection Panel (forthcoming). The first set of Clarifications issued by the Bank's Executive Directors stated, in fact, the practice that has been followed by the Panel by providing that 'where the Inspection Panel believes that it would be appropriate to undertake a 'preliminary assessment' of the damages alleged by the requester (in particular when such preliminary assessment could lead to a resolution of the matter without the need for a full investigation), the Panel may undertake the preliminary assessment and indicate to the Board the date on which it would present its findings and recommendations as to the need, if any, for a full investigation'. The second set of Clarifications, entitled 'Conclusions of the Board's Second Review of the Inspection Panel' (hereinafter Clarifications–II), approved April 20, 1999 and with immediate effect, states, however, that '[t]he "preliminary assessment" concept, as described in the October 1996 Clarification, is no longer needed. The paragraph entitled "The Panel's Function" in the October 1996 "Clarifications" is thus deleted' (para. 11).

relevant policies and procedures, interprets their content in deciding whether or not the Bank failed to comply with them, and clarifies their content through interpretation.[47] The Inspection Panel also has the opportunity to highlight best practices in applying Bank policy instruments. Most importantly, the Inspection Panel can publicize the inadequate practices that gave rise to the complaint before it, and reveal possible failures and inconsistencies in compliance with Operational Standards.

The dynamics attached to such an interpretative function should be considered in the broader institutional context as well. The Panel engages in a dialogue with the Bank's management when discussing an alleged failure of the Bank to follow its operational policies and procedures. The Executive Directors play a pivotal role when exercising their powers to decide whether or not to authorize an investigation and what action to take following an investigation. The end result of the process may contribute to a clarification of the content of policies and procedures, as well as to remedying the problems through the adoption of action plans. The Executive Directors also may adopt decisions on general matters relating to the Inspection Panel and have done so to define the scope of the Panel's mandate. Exchanges of views on issues related to the institutional aspects of the Panel may contribute incidentally to clarifying some operational policies and procedural requirements.[48]

The Inspection Panel contributes generally to improving the quality of Bank operations by signaling possible failures in following operational policies and procedures and increasing awareness among the Bank's staff of the importance of implementing them. Most of the requests brought to the attention of the Panel so far have dealt with environmental and social standards. The ensuing recommendations and findings of the Inspection Panel have stressed the need for devoting greater attention to compliance. They have in fact contributed to the establishment of abovementioned mechanisms, such as internal review processes and random audits, for quality insurance purposes.

---

[47] This interpretative function of operational policies and procedures is exercised under the overall review of the Bank's Board, and to the extent that it does not involve the Bank's legal rights and obligations. For matters related to the 'Bank's rights and obligations with respect to a request under consideration', the advice of the Bank's Legal Department should be sought (para. 15 of the Res.). As of the end of 1998, the General Counsel had given two legal opinions. The first one was issued on January 3, 1995 and dealt with the 'Role of the Inspection Panel in the Preliminary Assessment of Whether to Recommend Inspection'. The second one dealt with the question of 'Time-Limits on the Eligibility of Complaints Submitted to the Inspection Panel' and was issued on July 24, 1997.

[48] The Decision of the Executive Directors on the Scope of the Inspection Panel's Mandate— Compensation for Expropriation and Extension of IDA Credits to Ethiopia under OMS 1.28 may provide an example of a nurturing process or 'constructive dialogue'. Although the main issue was the scope of the Inspection Panel's mandate, the exchange of views that took place provided some guidance as to the interpretation of OMS 1.28 (now OP 7.40 on Disputes over Defaults on External Debt, Expropriation, and Breach of Contract). See The Inspection Panel, Report, August 1, 1994 to July 31, 1996, 56–8.

The contribution of the Panel to promoting compliance with operational policies and procedures is enhanced through making public all documents related to the Inspection Panel's activities, as provided in the Resolution establishing the Inspection Panel, Clarifications-I, and the Operating Rules. The public can access the request itself, the management's response to it, the Panel's recommendation on the eligibility of the request, the Board's decision to authorize or deny an investigation, the Panel's findings, the management's comments, and the final Board decision.[49] This contributes to the role of the Panel in raising awareness of and respect for operational policies and procedures, but the impact could be enhanced by a decision to systematically publish the sets of documents issued at the different stages of each complaint, *e.g.*, by setting up an official Bank collection or series.[50] In addition, more extensive use could be made of electronic technology, simplifying access to and dissemination of information, and helping 'make the Inspection Panel better known in borrowing countries'.[51] At present, the information is publicly available but not easily accessible.

Making all the documents publicly available helps 'objectivize' the issues at stake, providing a record of the decisions taken by different organs (Inspection Panel, management, the Executive Directors) involved at the various steps of the procedure. Such transparency contributes to fairness and accountability at all procedural stages. These aspects could be strengthened if the process could be further formalized, keeping in mind that the procedure is non-judicial in nature. Formalization means greater resort to comparative jurisprudence and to legal interpretative methods, both of which have a role to play in the process of decision-making on the admissibility of a complaint, interpretation of the policies and procedures, and drafting of recommendations to the Executive Directors. Such changes would not only facilitate improvement of the decision-making process, but also favor consistency and predictability in the decisions and recommendations of the various organs.[52]

[49] See paras. 25 and 26 of the Res. and paras. 41, 56, and 65 of the Operating Rules. See also the first set of Clarifications (Outreach) which state that 'management will make its response to requests for inspection available to the public within three days after the Board has decided on whether to authorize the inspection. Management will also make available to the public opinions of the General Counsel related to the Inspection Panel matters promptly after the Executive Directors have dealt with the issues involved, unless the Board decides otherwise in a specific case.' The Inspection Panel, Annual Report, August 1, 1996 to July 31, 1997, 30. The Clarifications–II emphasize the importance of prompt disclosure of information to claimants and to the public (para. 18). They also require that 'such information be provided by Management to the claimant in their language, to the extent possible'.

[50] The publication of Umaña, A. (ed.), *The World Bank Inspection Panel—The First Four Years (1994–1998)* (1998) constitutes a first step in this direction. It contains the Panel reports of the most significant cases.

[51] See Clarifications–I (Outreach). The second set of Clarifications restate this concern (para. 17).

[52] The issues of consistency and predictability are also important should requests concerning a co-financed project be brought before the inspection mechanisms of several financial institutions. As

The Inspection Panel, the management of the Bank, and the Executive Directors could take this into consideration when exercising their respective powers, notably in selecting the members of the Panel.[53] The composition of the Panel deserves close attention as it has direct relevance to the way activities are conducted.

C. DEVELOPMENT OF AND COMPLIANCE WITH INTERNATIONAL LAW

The World Bank does not operate in isolation. Its environmental and social operational policies and procedures reflect concerns related to the promotion of sustainable development as expressed in many other fora. Operational Standards are in fact vehicles for achieving this objective, although they are not necessarily exhaustive in covering the issues. The relationship between these policies and international law standards highlights their mutually reinforcing contribution to the promotion of sustainable development and the rule of law. In particular, the policies' references to international law promote respect for best practices. Although some policy statements make precise reference to various international treaties, they do not exclude the possibility of taking into account treaties not explicitly mentioned. Operational policies and procedures also refer to soft law instruments, and in so doing promote respect for them. Both types of instruments are taken into account because they are intrinsically linked to the Bank's activities.

As noted earlier, the policies on environmental assessment, indigenous populations, and involuntary resettlement require that Bank-financed projects take into account the domestic legal order of the borrowing country. The Bank should exercise due diligence and good faith in assessing the legal situation prevailing in a borrowing country, including the international commitments the country has undertaken. Clearly, various means exist for integrating international commitments into domestic legal orders, including enabling legislation, direct incorporation, or executive order. Such requirements then may be taken into consideration when implementing the relevant Operational Standards. While the Bank's Standards normally will correspond to the domestic legal order, in some cases the Bank's mandatory policy standards may call for the application of higher standards than those contained in national law.

---

an example, the Yacerita hydroelectric project gave rise to two complaints, one brought before the Inspection Panel of the Bank, the other before the Independent Investigation Mechanism of the Inter-American Development Bank. See Umaña, *supra* note 50 at 327.

[53] It has been suggested that at least one of the members of the Inspection Panel should have legal expertise. See Bradlow, D., 'International Organizations and Private Complaints: The Case of the World Bank Inspection Panel' (1994) 34 *Va. J. Int'l L.* 553, 573.

As a general requirement, first stated in a policy adopted in 1984,[54] the Bank has committed itself *not* to finance projects that contravene international environmental agreements to which the concerned member country is a party. This commitment was reiterated in the OP on forestry[55] and in the OP on environment assessment.[56] It not only shapes the conduct of the Bank with respect to international environmental agreements, but also increases the awareness of borrowing countries of the need to implement and comply with international environmental law.

Operational policies and procedures also may expressly refer to international principles and rules as a means of identifying the good and best practices to be followed, helping identify the minimum standards applicable to a Bank project. The binding nature of these international instruments may vary, but the main reason for referring to them is their wide acceptance and usefulness for development activities. The OP on 'management of cultural property in Bank-financed projects', for example, makes explicit reference to country obligations under international treaties concerning cultural property, such as the 1972 Convention Concerning the Protection of the World Cultural and Natural Heritage.[57] The OP on pest management refers to international instruments as an indication of minimum standards to be followed in the area covered by the policy,[58] with the FAO Guidelines for Packaging and Storage of Pesticides[59] and the Guidelines on Good Labeling Practice for Pesticides[60] playing a technical role in providing detailed standards and norms. Other international instruments, even though not referred to explicitly, may play a similar role, at least for interpretation purposes. The UN

---

[54] See OMS 2.36 on Environmental Aspects of Bank Work (1984). The provision reads: '[t]he Bank will not finance projects that contravene any international environmental agreement to which the member country concerned is a party'.

[55] Operational Policy (OP) 4.36 on Forestry. The provision reads: '[g]overnments must also commit to adhere to their obligations as set forth in relevant international instruments to which they are a party'.

[56] Operational Policy (OP) 4.01 on Environmental Assessment. The relevant part of the policy reads: '[E]A . . . takes into account the obligations of the country, pertaining to project activities, under relevant international environmental treaties and agreements. The Bank does not finance project activities that would contravene such country obligations, as identified during the EA.'

[57] The 1972 Convention Concerning the Protection of the World Cultural and Natural Heritage is given as a reference for defining the notion of cultural property. See OP 4.11, para. 2(a) (forthcoming).

[58] For the purpose of the policy (OP 4.09), minimum standards are defined with reference to the FAO's Guidelines for Packaging and Storage of Pesticides (1985), Guidelines on Good Labeling Practice for Pesticides (1985), and Guidelines for the Disposal of Waste Pesticide and Pesticide Containers on the Farm (1985). See also the forthcoming policy on application of EA to projects involving pest management (BP 4.01–Annex C) which refers to the WHO Classification of Pesticides by Hazard and Guidelines to Classification (1994–5) and to the UN Consolidated List of Products Whose Consumption and/or Sale have been Banned, Withdrawn, Severely Restricted or not Approved by Governments (1994).

[59] See *ibid.*   [60] See *ibid.*

Convention on Biological Diversity,[61] for example, may be considered in the context of the policy on indigenous peoples. Programmatic instruments may similarly provide guidance, including Agenda 21[62] and the 1995 Global Program of Action for the Protection of the Marine Environment from Land-based Activities.[63] The interactions between these international instruments and Operational Standards underline the pragmatic nature of the Operational Standards, which aim to identify and implement the best practices to promote sustainable development. They also highlight the flexibility of international law in general, allowing for practices to be codified in both hard law and soft law instruments. The general recognition of such practices in appropriate international fora serves as a useful tool for promoting sustainable development.

Operational policies and procedures constitute a means by which new patterns of behavior are encouraged in borrowing countries. As such, they favor the emergence or consolidation of international practices which may acquire the status of customary norms. This has been the case notably with the Environmental Assessment policy. Since it was first introduced in 1989, it has served as a model for the legislation of many countries and for multilateral development banks, including the Inter-American Development Bank, the Asian Development Bank, and the European Bank for Reconstruction and Development, for bilateral donors and for the private sector in providing assistance and investment activities.[64] In addition, it helped pave the way for inclusion in the Rio Declaration on Environment and Development of an 'Environment Impact Assessment' requirement as a national instrument.[65]

Such cross-fertilization also can be seen in respect of the requirement that riparian countries of an international watercourse be notified in cases of planned measures or projects financed by the Bank. The application of the Bank policy on international waterways[66] has contributed significantly to the

---

[61] The text of the convention is reprinted in Sands, P., *et al.*, *Documents in International Environmental Law* (1994), 845.

[62] UN Conference on Environment and Development: Agenda 21, UN Doc. A/CONF.151/4 (1992).

[63] Global Program of Action for the Protection of the Marine Environment from Land-based Activities and the Washington Declaration on the Protection of the Marine Environment from Land-based Activities, November 3, 1995. See Nolkaemper, A., 'Marine Pollution' (1995) 6 *YBIEL* 244–5.

[64] In this context, co-financing of investment operations is one way to promote such practices. For an assessment of the Bank's policies towards other actors, see Mahony, S., 'World Bank's Policies and Practice in Environmental Impact Assessment' (1995) 12 *Envtl & Plan. L.J.* 97–115; Guyett, S., 'Environment & Lending, Lessons of the World Bank, Hope for the European Bank for Reconstruction and Development' (1992) 24 *N.Y.U. J. Int'l L. & Pol.* 896.

[65] Principle 17 of the Rio Declaration on Environment and Development reads as follows: '[e]nvironmental impact assessment, as a national instrument, shall be undertaken for proposed activities that are likely to have a significant adverse impact on the environment and are subject to a decision of a competent national authority'. Sands *et al.*, *supra* note 612 at 53.

[66] OP 7.50 International Waterways (October 1994).

recognition of this procedural requirement in general international law and to its codification in the UN Convention on the Law of the Non-Navigational Uses of International Watercourses.[67] Such a practice highlights the composite nature of the norm-creating process whereby non-legally binding instruments and policy instruments, such as the Bank Operational Standards, play a role in the formation and development of an international customary norm, enabling *lex ferenda* to become *lex lata*.

While operational policies and procedures promote respect for progressive and process-oriented standards, their application on the ground may face resistance or there may be uncertainty about how to soundly implement them. The requirement of public participation and/or meaningful consultations provides a good example of the challenges and difficulties. It is one thing to establish the sequencing of actions to be conducted and the timing of public participation, but quite another to put in place a real and meaningful participation process. Cultural traditions, the need for public space for debate, the existence or lack thereof of an institutional framework, the rate of literacy, etc. all play a significant role in implementing the principle and have to be taken into account within the flexibility provided by the relevant operational policies and procedures. The borrowing country is required to expend its best efforts to take the appropriate measures for implementing the policy requirements,[68] while the Bank should exercise due diligence during the preparation and the implementation of the project to make sure that the borrower complies with the policy requirements. The emergence of patterns of behavior for promoting public participation takes place in a rather experimental context whereby the Bank and the borrowers engage in a dialogue on how best to implement public participation requirements and both share responsibility in shaping such practices.

The fact that the international instruments to which a borrowing country has committed itself should be taken into consideration or should be considered as reflecting agreed international good and best practices, shows the close relationship of the Operational Standards with international law principles and standards in areas covered by them. It also demonstrates the virtues of operational policies and procedures in promoting the implementation of international law instruments, be they of a binding or non-binding, normative or technical nature. Another important compliance feature is the

---

[67] See Salman, S., and Boisson de Chazournes, L., 'International Watercourses—Enhancing Cooperation and Managing Conflict', World Bank Technical Paper No 414 (1998), 169.

[68] Parallels can be drawn with international law notions for interpreting the concept of best efforts, *e.g.*, with the obligation to undertake to take steps with a view to achieving progressively the full realization of economic, social, and cultural rights, as spelled out in Art. 2, para. 1 of the International Covenant on Economic, Social and Cultural Rights. See the General Comment of the UN Committee on Economic, Social and Cultural Rights, Compilation of General Comments and General Recommendations adopted by Human Rights Treaty Bodies, HRI/GEN/1/Rev. 3, para. 1–14.

role played by Operational Standards in contributing to the development of new international practices. They create normative expectations and pave the way for the consolidation of patterns of behavior. In addition, they lead to the emergence of principles and rules and may contribute to their recognition as *lex lata* under international law.

D. PUBLIC PARTICIPATION AND COMPLIANCE WITH OPERATIONAL STANDARDS

Prior to and during the 1992 Rio Conference on Environment and Development, the practice of permitting representatives of civil society to participate in decision-making processes and granting them the right of access to remedies for ensuring sustainable management of resources gained legitimacy.[69] This evolution reveals the possible integrative nature of development efforts and environmental protection and highlights the close interrelationships between the fields of development, environment, and human rights in promoting sustainable development.

With the possibility that non-state actors may participate in the elaboration and implementation of projects, the Bank is acknowledging that public participation is central to ensuring the sustainability of developmental activities. The Bank's calls for public participation are numerous, including public consultation of affected people and local NGOs about a project's environmental aspects,[70] community participation and consultations with people affected by a resettlement,[71] informed participation of indigenous populations,[72] and involvement of local groups in the planning, designing, implementing, and monitoring of projects related to the protection of natural habitats,[73] or in forestry and conservation management activities.[74] There is no doubt that these policy prescriptions, which are operationalized in the Bank's activities, contribute to a large extent to the development of international rules and standards. Furthermore, the measures that have been taken to strengthen information disclosure have promoted transparency and access to information. In doing so, the policy prescriptions have contributed to the empowerment of non-state actors, and more especially local populations, by giving them the possibility to be more effectively involved in the decision-making process.

[69] See Principle 10 of the Rio Declaration on Environment and Development, Sands *et al.*, *supra* note 61 at 52. See also Program for the Further Implementation of Agenda 21, adopted by the Special Session of the General Assembly, June 23–7, 1997 (A/S–19/33), (1997) 27(5) EPL, 428. On the notion of sustainable development, its content and the challenges for implementing it, see Ginther, K., Denters, E., and de Waart, P.J.I.M. (eds.), *Sustainable Development and Good Governance* (1995), 483.

[70] See OP 4.01 on Environment Assessment, para. 15.

[71] See OP 4.30 on Involuntary Resettlement, paras. 7–10.

[72] See OD 4.20 on Indigenous Peoples, para. 8.

[73] See OP 4.04 on Natural Habitats, para. 10.   [74] See OP 4.36 on Forestry, para. 1(c).

In establishing the Inspection Panel, the Bank created a new path for public participation: it allowed individuals to bring complaints before a newly established organ if they believed that their interests protected under the Bank's Operational Standards had been impaired. Also noteworthy is the fact that during an investigation representatives of the public-at-large may provide the Panel with supplemental information if they believe that it is relevant to a request.[75] The Inspection Panel in fact provides a new venue for dialogue on compliance issues between a lending institution and the direct beneficiaries of its developmental activities, and in doing so significantly complements initiatives and actions aimed at ensuring compliance with Operational Standards.

CONCLUSIONS

A few paradoxical comments help underline the hybrid but nonetheless rich nature of the World Bank Operational Standards. Originally designed to provide guidance to the staff of the Bank in its operational work, the role played by Operational Standards has evolved over time, as they have been increasingly perceived as quality assessment tools in Bank operations as well as means for ensuring transparency and accountability. This has contributed to focusing attention on the need to strengthen the means for ensuring compliance. A wide array of mechanisms and procedures has been established, strengthened, or revitalized so as to meet this objective. Checks and balances of an operational nature have been created to ensure that Operational Standards are complied with during the entire cycle of a project from inception to completion. Increased attention is put on the role of the Operations Evaluation Department (OED) to identify non-compliance problems in its post-project evaluations and for drawing lessons. Legal tools have been attracting increasing attention, with a view to ensuring that when policy terms are transformed into legal terms through their incorporation in loan or credit agreements, they acquire a more established status under international law, *i.e.*, treaty law status, and they therefore benefit from the legal remedies that can be taken in the event of a breach. Lastly, the need was felt to institutionalize compliance concerns in establishing an independent and permanent organ within the Bank's structure which investigates complaints brought by groups of individuals whose rights or interests would have been adversely affected by the Bank's failure to comply with Operational Standards in the context of a project. The establishment of the Inspection Panel also con-

---

[75] See Operational Procedures of the Inspection Panel. Under this basis, NGOs in Switzerland and in the United States submitted memoranda in the Indian NTPC Power Generation Project. See Bissell, R.E., 'Recent Practice of the Inspection Panel of the World Bank' [1997] *Am. J. Int'l L.* 743.

tributed to increase the Bank management's accountability towards the Board with respect to the implementation of Operational Standards.

The Operational Standards are the product of the particular institutional setting of the World Bank and are designed for internal purposes. They nevertheless entertain multiple relationships with the international legal system, whether through their elaboration or their implementation. External actors, such as NGOs, play a role in their elaboration. Local NGOs are involved in the design and implementation of projects, as they are granted a voice through participation and consultation processes. Furthermore, environmental and social Operational Standards take into account international good practices as reflected in other international instruments. A process of cross-fertilization is noticeable, which can lead to the emergence of principles and norms of general international law. All these elements reveal the composite nature of the law-making process in the international legal system. Policy instruments and the attention given to their compliance contribute in many ways to this process. They reveal that porosity and interactions are core aspects of the contemporary legal system, where a plurality of actors is engaged in activities at the local, national, and international levels. Although states retain a pre-eminent role in the making and implementation of international law, international organizations, NGOs, and individuals play an increasingly important role in shaping new practices and ensuring their respect.

Environmental Norms in the Asia-Pacific Economic Cooperation Forum

LYUBA ZARSKY

INTRODUCTION

The Asia-Pacific Economic Cooperation forum (APEC) is quintessentially a soft law organization.[1] Made up of twenty-one Pacific Rim nations, APEC operates on the principle of consensus. Eschewing binding agreements, its

---

[1] As of February 1999, APEC's members are: Australia, Brunei, Canada, Chile, China, Chinese Taipei, Hong Kong, Indonesia, Japan, Malaysia, Mexico, New Zealand, Papua New Guinea, Peru, Philippines, Russia, Singapore, South Korea, Thailand, Vietnam, and the United States.

broad purpose is to build a sense of trans-Pacific community through discussion and non-binding, voluntary accords.

Between 1993 and 1998, APEC's agenda was dominated by the politics of trade liberalization. Under the banner of regional cooperation, the U.S. and its Western allies utilized APEC to press East Asian elites to abandon mercantilist policies in favor of neo-liberal trade and investment rules. The strategy apparently worked: in 1994, APEC economies agreed to create 'free and open' trade and investment in the Asia-Pacific region by 2020.[2]

Starting in the early 1990s, under the leadership primarily of Canada and the U.S., APEC heads of state and environment ministers undertook a process of developing legally non-binding regional environmental norms to govern market behavior. In 1994, APEC countries adopted a *Framework of Principles for Integrating Economy and Environment in APEC,* and in 1996, an *Action Programme on Sustainable Development.* The effort gathered considerable momentum, with two Environment Ministerial Meetings, a symposium, and a host of workshops and seminars. By mid-1997, however, it was moribund, with neither governments nor non-governmental environmental advocates pressing for implementation or compliance.

This study describes and evaluates APEC's generation of regional environmental soft law norms from 1993 to 1997. It first briefly describes the regional context and most pressing environmental problems, and then sketches a conceptual framework analyzing the requirements of regional environmental market governance in the context of economic integration. It follows with a description of the history and politics leading to the drafting of the *Framework of Principles* and the *Action Programme.*

Part C examines the institutional and political context of APEC and what factors impeded the development of environmental norms and compliance with them. Most important were APEC's failures to integrate its environmental program with its trade diplomacy, the reluctance of the U.S. and other rich countries to offer side payments, and the lack of mechanisms for non-governmental groups to participate. Absent the scrutiny and passion of civil society and cut off from linkages to aid and trade, there were virtually no compliance mechanisms. Moreover, with the hard knocks of the financial and economic crises which hit the region in late 1997, APEC's soft law approach to furthering neo-liberal economic norms was itself overshadowed by the 'big stick' of the IMF. Unable to fashion a meaningful response to the crisis, APEC lost momentum making its future as an effective regional institution murky. The conclusion reflects on what the APEC experience suggests for the efficacy of soft law approaches to enhancing environmental protection in a global economy.

---

[2] The formulation was that developed countries would create free and open trade and investment by 2010, the developing countries by 2020.

A. ASIA-PACIFIC REGIONALISM AND THE ENVIRONMENT

East Asian and trans-Pacific politics were delineated by the Cold War for most of the second half of the twentieth century. With the transformations that began in 1991, new imperatives to cooperate in building regional institutions were unleashed, not the least of which has been the need to manage the changing regional power balance between China, Japan, and the U.S.[3] The primary driving force behind the founding and evolution of APEC, however, was the increasing market-driven integration of APEC economies. Nearly 70 percent of total APEC trade was intra-regional in 1994.[4] Capital flows are also highly concentrated in APEC, with about 65 percent of Japan's foreign direct investment outflows, for example, going to APEC countries in 1990, some 46 percent to the U.S. alone.[5] Within APEC, North America and East Asia form two highly integrated economic sub-regions.[6]

For the last two and a half decades, the development strategies pursued by most East Asian nations have had two overarching features: (1) they have been based on promoting exports to and capital flows from developed countries, while retaining national control over imports and foreign investment ('linkage led' growth); and (2) they have utilized an economic paradigm that excludes environmental and social concerns, including ecosystem sustainability, human health and economic equity.

Until the financial crisis of 1997, linkage-led growth made East Asia a burgeoning world economic power.[7] Rapid growth raised the standard of living for millions of people,[8] but the rapid rise in exports strained political ties with trade partners, especially the U.S., as trade surpluses mounted in East Asia. Socially and environmentally blind growth also exacerbated poverty in the countryside and created severe problems of ecological degradation.[9] Well before the financial crisis, a World Bank study warned that 'the pace of environmental damage from pollution and over extraction of renewable resources

---

[3] Bonnor, J., 'APEC's Contribution to Regional Security', in Soesastro, H., and Bergin, A. (eds.), *The Role of Security and Economic Cooperation Structures in the Asia Pacific Region, Indonesian and Australian Views* (1996) 45–56.

[4] International Monetary Fund, *Direction of Trade Statistics* (1995).

[5] United Nations, *World Investment Directory*, Vol. III 'Developed Countries' (1993).

[6] In 1990, about 40% of total East Asian trade was to other East Asian countries; within North America, intra-regional trade was roughly 37% of total trade. Yamazawa, I., 'On Pacific Integration', in Garnaut, R., and Drysdale, P. (eds.), *Asia Pacific Regionalism, Readings in International Economic Relations* (1994) 201–11; Table 16.4.

[7] In most Southeast Asian nations, GNP grew more than 5% per year throughout the 1980s and early 1990s. In China, GNP has been growing at an annual rate of about 10% or more for nearly two decades. World Resources Institute, *World Resources 1994–1995* (1994).

[8] UNDP, *Human Development Report* (1995).

[9] Anuja, V., *et al.*, *Everyone's Miracle? Revisiting Poverty and Inequality in East Asia* (1997).

threatens to compromise the welfare gains in East Asia from higher incomes'.[10]

While environmental woes are many, three broad areas are most relevant to regional environmental norms: air, atmospheric, and water pollution, especially stemming from energy production and use; natural resource depletion and degradation; and demographic shifts, including rural out-migration, food security, and urbanization. Issues related to energy production and use, including air and atmospheric pollution, are among the most pressing problems for the developed and developing countries of APEC.[11] Prior to the financial crisis, commercial energy demand in East Asia was projected to double by 2010, propelled by high rates of economic growth. Economic recession will cut into that demand, but energy needs continue to grow.[12] If future investment decisions resemble those of the past, power sector development will be based heavily on fossil fuels, including 'dirty' high-sulfur- and/or carbon-emitting coal.

Energy-related air pollution is already among the most severe regional environmental problems in Northeast Asia.[13] In 1990, sulfur dioxide emissions in Northeast Asia totaled 14.7 million tons. Under a 'business-as-usual' scenario, sulfur dioxide emissions will more than double by 2010 and nearly triple by 2020; emissions of nitrogen oxide (NOx) will more than triple between 1990 and 2020. Even under a 'higher efficiency forecast', in which governments make targeted efforts to increase energy efficiency and institute reasonable fuel substitution measures, sulfur dioxide emissions would double in the next thirty years.[14] The lion's share of the emissions will emanate from China and could double the levels of acid rain in neighboring countries. The politics of acid rain are tense and of high priority in Northeast Asia.

Rapid growth in coal-based energy, as well as motorized urban transport, is also responsible for projected large increases in greenhouse gas emissions in Asia, especially carbon dioxide, with related impacts on climate change. Between 1990 and 2000, the growth of carbon dioxide emissions in Asia will

[10] Hammer, J.S., and Shetty, S., 'East Asia's Environment, Principles and Priorities for Action', World Bank Discussion Paper #287 (1995), 4.

[11] In addition to environmental impacts, there are security implications to energy development choices in Northeast Asia, including potential conflicts erupting over insecurity of supply; and the potential for nuclear weapons proliferation arising from the widespread development of nuclear power. See Calder, K.E., 'Fueling the Rising Sun, Asia's Energy Needs and Global Security' [1997] *Harvard International Review* (Summer) 24–31.

[12] In China alone, electricity-generating capacity is expected to quadruple. Fereidun, F., Banaszak, S., and Kang, W., *Energy Supply and Demand in Northeast Asia*, paper to the Seventh Meeting of the Northeast Asia Economic Forum, Ulan Bator, Mongolia, August 17–21, 1997.

[13] Zarsky, L., 'Energy and the Environment', in Chasek, P. (ed.), *Asia-Pacific: Regional Cooperation and Market Governance* (1999).

[14] Streets, D.G., *Energy and Acid Rain Projections for Northeast Asia, Energy, Security and Environment Project*, Nautilus Institute for Security and Sustainable Development (1997).

more than triple that of the rest of the world.[15] As a whole, Asia accounted for about 20 percent of worldwide greenhouse gas emitted in 1985; by 2000, its share will be 30 percent. By the year 2025, China is projected to be the world's largest annual emitter of greenhouse gases.[16] Problems of energy demand and use are not restricted to the East Asian members of APEC, however; the United States, Canada, and Australia, are among the world's highest *per capita* carbon emitters.[17]

Rapid industrial development is also an important source of both air and water pollution. The pollution intensity of industry has increased rapidly in all the 'emerging economies' of East Asia.[18] Water pollution, generated especially by high organic pollution loads, is a serious problem throughout the region.[19] The increase in pollution intensity is a result both of an overall increase in manufacturing and the sectoral growth of pollution-intensive industries within manufacturing. In Thailand, for example, hazardous waste-generating industries accounted for 58 percent of industrial GDP in 1989, up from only 29 percent in 1979.[20] In Indonesia, manufacturing output doubled in volume every six to seven years during the 1970s and 1980s. Before the crisis, it was projected by the World Bank to expand another thirteen-fold by the year 2020.[21]

APEC economies also suffer high rates of resource depletion and degradation. East Asia has the world's highest rate of deforestation and loss of original habitat. According to the Asian Development Bank, the region's remaining timber reserves will be depleted in less than forty years.[22] The forest fires that have repeatedly ravaged Borneo and East Kalimantan since the early 1980s have depleted the forest resource and cast a large pall of thick smoke over much of Southeast Asia.[23]

The marine environment and fisheries are also under severe stress in many APEC countries, both in East Asia and North America. In Canada,

[15] Brandon, C., and Ramankutty, R., 'Toward an Environment Strategy for Asia', World Bank Discussion Papers No. 224 (1993), 25, Fig. 1.3.

[16] China is also the world's most populous country. Historically, it has been the rich, relatively unpopulated countries which have been the primary emitters. For a discussion of the ethical and historical dimensions of allocating responsibility for greenhouse gas emissions, see Hayes, P., and Smith, K., *Global Greenhouse Regime: Who Pays?* (1994).

[17] World Resources Institute, *supra* note 7 at Table 11.7.

[18] Wangwacharakul, V., *Trade, Investment and Sustained Development*, paper to ESCAP/ADB Expert Meeting on Trade, Economic and Environmental Sustainability, October 23–27, 1989.

[19] Rock, M.T., *Industry and the Environment in Ten Asian Countries: Synthesis Report of US–AEP Country Assessment*, USAID, October 9, 1996.

[20] Reed, D., *Structural Adjustment and the Environment* (1992).

[21] World Bank, *Indonesia Environment and Development: Challenges for the Future* (unpublished World Bank Confidential Report No. 12083–IND, 1993) 68.

[22] Asian Development Bank, *The Environment Program of the Asian Development Bank, Past Present and Future* (1994).

[23] See Integrated Forest Fire Management Project Indonesia, <http://smd.mega.net.id/iffm/>.

misguided fishery policies that aimed to maintain commercial fishing at the expense of preserving stocks precipitated a collapse of Northeastern fisheries. In Northeast Asia, the Sea of Japan suffers a high level of marine pollution stemming from oil exploration and transport, radioactive waste disposal, and shipping and industrial waste dumping.[24] Throughout East Asia, coastal zones are threatened by flows of urban, industrial, port, and riverine wastes. Intensive shrimp aquaculture ponds have damaged significant areas of coastal mangrove forests throughout China and Southeast Asia. A marked increase in fishing effort has resulted in the over-exploitation of several important species in Southeast Asian seas, one of the world's most productive fisheries.[25]

Interwoven into the society–nature interface are demographic factors, including population growth, rural–urban migration, and urbanization. The population of Asia was about 3.4 billion in 1995 and is projected to rise to 4.9 billion in 2025. About one of three Asians live in cities, up from one in five in 1965.[26] In APEC as a whole, nearly two-thirds of the population will be urban-dwellers by 2015.[27] The environmental infrastructure is not keeping pace with the rapid rise in the urbanized population. Problems of air pollution in many East Asian cities are severe, generated by high levels of particulates, lead from leaded gasoline, and emissions from households, vehicles, and small industry. In the Western countries of APEC, widely dispersed cities, coupled with lack of public transport, make automobile dependence high, with associated problems of local and atmospheric pollution.[28]

Interrelationships between natural resource degradation and demographic change are not well charted,[29] but there is ample evidence that unplanned and large jumps in the number of people living in a given area can increase ecological degradation.[30] Throughout Asia, rural–urban migration has been

[24] Nautilus Institute for Security and Sustainable Development, ESENA, Papers to Conference on Marine Pollution, Energy and Security in Northeast Asia (1998).

[25] Soegiarto, A., *Sustainable Fisheries, Environment and the Prospects of Regional Cooperation in Southeast Asia*, paper to Workshop on Trade and Environment in Asia Pacific: Prospects for Regional Cooperation, Nautilus Institute, East–West Center, Honolulu, September 22–4, 1994.

[26] World Resources Institute, *supra* note 7.

[27] Gilbert, R., *Reducing Urban Air Pollution in APEC Economies*, paper for Workshop on Toward Sustainable Cities in APEC, National Roundtable on the Environment and the Economy, Vancouver, May 5–6, 1997. The definition of 'urban' and 'rural' differs among nations, making cross-national comparisons problematic. This estimate is based on UN data, which total the figures submitted by governments.

[28] Kenworthy, J. and Laube, F., 'Indicators of Transportation Efficiency in Global Cities and Their Implications for Urban Sustainability,' Workshop on Toward Sustainable Cities in APEC, National Roundtable on the Environment and Economy, Vancouver, Can., May 5–6, 1997.

[29] One detailed study concluded: '[p]opulation density and natural resource degradation cannot be correlated in any fixed way since factors such as poverty and land-tenure policies mediate what happens to the resource base'. Comparing Costa Rica and the Philippines, the study showed *inter alia* that, despite much lower population density, Costa Rican soils were relatively more damaged due to large-scale conversion of forest to cattle pasture. See Cruz, M.C., *et al.*, *Population Growth, Poverty and Environmental Stress* (1992), p. vii ff.

[30] See papers of the Project on Environment, Population, and Security, a collaboration of the Peace and Conflict Studies Program, University of Toronto, Canada, and the Population and

driven by the prospect of employment and higher incomes on the one hand, and by the demise of traditional sources of livelihood in rural areas due to marketization and resource depletion, on the other hand.[31] Migration across borders has created ethnic and national tensions, especially in the wake of the financial crisis. The shift from agricultural production and rural living to industrial work and urban habitation has been a feature of all countries in the process of industrialization. In Asia the shift is occurring at great speed, stimulated by 'structural adjustment' economic policies.[32]

It is likely that environment-blind development not only has severe human and ecological consequences, but is far more costly than environmentally-sensitive development. According to the World Bank, the annual health costs from air pollution in Bangkok, Jakarta, and Kuala Lumpur total $5 billion—about 10 percent of city income. In Jakarta, unsafe drinking water generates health costs of $300 million per year. A study in Vancouver found that traffic congestion cost the city $200 million per year.[33] Given the projected large increases in energy and industrial growth, one of the central environmental management issues for the next twenty years will be the creation of incentives for the 'greening' of investment and 'innovative financing' for the provision of public goods.

B. APEC ENVIRONMENTAL NORMS

1. Environmental Governance and Regional Economic Integration

Environmental and resource management is largely the unilateral preserve of nation-states, but there are three cases when cooperation between two or more nations is needed: first, when ecosystems or resources straddle national borders (transboundary); secondly, when a resource is wholly or partially outside the jurisdiction of any state (common property resource); and thirdly, when two or more nations are highly integrated economically (globalization).

It is commonly understood that the management of transboundary and common resources requires international collective action. APEC could potentially serve this function by acting as an umbrella under which Asia-Pacific nations develop regimes to manage common resources, especially the Western Pacific Ocean and fisheries. However, APEC is highly dispersed geographically and weak institutionally. With land masses on four continents,

Sustainable Project of the American Association for the Advancement of Science, Washington. Papers are available from the AAAS, 1200 New York Ave NW, Washington DC 20005.

[31] World Resources Institute, *World Resources 1996–97, The Urban Environment* (1996).

[32] Cruz, W., and Repetto, R., *The Environmental Effects of Stabilization and Structural Adjustment Programs: The Philippines Case* (1992).

[33] Michael Harcourt, Presentation to Sustainable Cities Workshop, National Round Table on the Environment and the Economy, Vancouver, March 4–6, 1997.

few resources are truly regional. APEC could help to catalyze or support cooperation on sub-regional transboundary issues, such as acid rain in Northeast Asia or fisheries in Southeast Asia. However, given its character as an economic organization, APEC's primary 'value-added' is more likely to lie in promoting better governance of the environment–economy interface in the context of globalization. There are four key tasks: (1) vision: developing common norms and a sense of long term goals for integrating environmental and economic objectives into the region's trade and investment regime; (2) capacity-building: developing capacities for environmental and resource management by closing national gaps between richer and poorer countries and by creating new, regional capacities to monitor and raise environmental performance; (3) policy coordination: undertaking common policies aimed at creating market incentives to improve environmental performance ('upward harmonization'); and (4) institutional strengthening: developing regional institutional mechanisms to coordinate, evaluate, and stimulate environmental initiatives and to provide avenues for public information and input.

The rationale for focusing on regional economy–environment cooperation stems from the high level of Asia-Pacific economic integration. Under conditions of globalization, the environmental policies and commitments of nations are highly conditioned by those of major trade and investment partners and competitors. Environmental degradation as well as good environmental management imposes costs. Unless specific measures are taken, these costs are not reflected in market prices but are borne socially, today or in the future.[34] An individual country or business that takes significant measures to internalize its own local or global environmental costs could be priced out of export markets or lose attractiveness as a production site for domestic or foreign investors. Even if the actual change in relative costs is negligible, the fear of such an effect can politically paralyze policy makers, especially if there are implications for jobs and campaign contributions.[35]

There are thus strong market-driven incentives for nations and firms to adopt environmental policies and standards that converge toward those of their primary competitors.[36] For traded goods, product standards tend to be

---

[34] While gains in eco-efficiency can offer 'win-win' solutions on the micro level, deeper problems stemming from too large a total ecological load and poor land use planning require more costly, macro measures.

[35] Hoerner, J.A., and Muller, F., *Carbon Taxes for Climate Protection in a Competitive World*, Environmental Tax Program, Center for Global Change, University of Maryland at College Park, June 12, 1996.

[36] More subtly, there is a tendency for the total costs to business of meeting environmental management requirements to converge. Total costs include compliance costs, as well as information, regulatory, and other transactions costs. More efficient regulatory regimes may generate a higher level of environmental performance for the same cost. See Anderson, C.L., and Kagan, R.A., *Adversarial Legalism, Transaction Costs, and the Industrial Flight Hypothesis*, draft, Carleton University, Ottawa, Canada, October 1996.

drawn toward large-market countries such as the United States and Japan.[37] In the absence of regulation, process standards within particular industries are likely to converge toward those of market leaders. Beyond market forces, policy makers have a further incentive to harmonize environmental policies in order to facilitate trade and investment by reducing transactions costs, *i.e.*, the costs to business of getting information about and meeting different environmental requirements. APEC refers to this as trade facilitation.

Policy convergence pressures for environmental performance lead, on the one hand, to improved product standards of the worst performers, perhaps toward an OECD average and, on the other hand, to either strengthened or relaxed production and process standards, depending on the structure of global competition in the particular sector or industry.[38] Many environmentalists worry that globalization will lower standards and they provide case studies justifying their fears. Other studies suggest that globalization, especially foreign direct investment, may improve the environmental performance of developing countries, at least incrementally, even where regulation is weak. Assuming that cases of both short-term positive and negative impacts can be found, the overall trend might be positive in the long term as a result of better technology, management, and resource allocation.

The central issue linking globalization and the environment revolves around the effect of intense competition on the rate of change of environmental improvement—and what is lost in the meantime. Due to intense competition from investment and markets, national governments tend to be looking over their shoulders and are reluctant to take bold measures to raise standards domestically.[39] Without international cooperation to raise standards, markets are likely to promote harmonization without fully incorporating specific environmental goals. To 'lift the game', governments must make a commitment to upward harmonization and set common policy frameworks that create incentives for better environmental performance. An example is a common commitment to reduce or eliminate environmentally damaging financial subsidies.[40] While countries could reduce subsidies

[37] Vogel, D., *Trading Up: Consumer and Environmental Regulation in a Global Economy* (1995). For the rich countries of the OECD, primary competitors and export markets are typically other OECD countries. The Newly Industrializing Countries (NICs) typically compete with other NICs for foreign investment and export opportunities, while at the same time they are drawn towards the product standards of the large-market countries. There is thus likely to be more than one 'equilibrium' convergence point at a global level at any given time.

[38] Some analysts have argued that the process of policy convergence will be a 'race to the bottom' in terms of environmental performance standards. For an exposition and critique see Revesz, R., 'Rehabilitating Inter-State Competition: Rethinking the "Race to the Bottom"' (1992) 67 *New York U.L. Rev.* 1210.

[39] A similar argument is made by Esty, D., 'Environmental Regulation and Competitiveness: Theory and Practice', Tay, S.C., and Esty, D. (eds.), in *Asian Dragons and Green Trade* (1996) 33–48.

[40] Porter, G., 'Natural Resource Subsidies and International Policy: A Role for APEC' (1997) 6 *Journal of Environment and Development*, 279–82.

unilaterally, the sectoral impacts on competitiveness create powerful domestic lobbies in opposition. A recent OECD workshop concluded that '[o]vercoming opposition to subsidy reform will be substantially easier if countries can be convinced to react *together,* rather than *separately,* in reducing subsidies/tax concessions to particular industries or sectors'.[41]

2. APEC's Development of Environmental Norms

Environmental issues have been on APEC's radar screen virtually since its inception. At APEC's founding conference in 1989, ministers agreed to examine national issues related to energy, fisheries, and marine pollution. In 1991, the Seoul Declaration defined equity and sustainable growth to be within the scope of APEC, and two years later, with the launching of the 'Sustainable Development Dialogue', APEC explicitly addressed the task of developing regional environmental norms.

APEC itself underwent pivotal changes in 1993, from a low level consultative forum focused primarily on technical aspects of economic cooperation to an organization concerned with rules and compliance with them. When the 'Uruguay Round' global trade talks stalled, the Clinton Administration seized on APEC as a vehicle to uphold and extend principles of economic openness and convoked the first APEC 'Leaders' Meeting' in November 1993. The participants agreed to create, long term, free trade throughout the Asia-Pacific region. In doing so, they subtly shifted APEC's purpose from mutual assistance to rule-making, albeit a soft form of rule-making based on the consensual embrace of broad liberalization goals and voluntary initiatives in achieving them.

In parallel with the move toward rule-making on trade, APEC undertook 'from the top' a process of developing regional environmental norms. In November 1993, Canadian Prime Minister Chretien promised to 'green' APEC and offered to host APEC's first Environment Ministerial meeting. Held in March, 1994, the session produced an *Environmental Vision Statement* and a *Framework of Principles for Integrating Economy and Environment* (see Appendix 1).[42]

The *Vision Statement* established APEC's goal to be the pursuit of sustainable development. 'We are committed to develop policies that are sound economically and environmentally', the *Vision Statement* proclaimed and called on senior officials of member states to 'develop a strategic approach, based on sustainable development principles, for environment considerations to be

---

[41] Runge, C.F., and Jones, T., 'Subsidies, Tax Disincentives and the Environment: An Overview and Synthesis', in OECD *Subsidies and Environment: Exploring the Linkages* (1996) 7–22.

[42] APEC Environmental Vision Statement (1994), <http://www.apecsec.org.sg>, also available from the Nautilus Institute <http://www.nautilus.org>.

fully integrated into the program of each APEC working group and policy committee'.[43] Like the Rio Declaration, the *Vision Statement* assumed that the region's trade and investment regimes are governed by or are pointed in the direction of principles of economic openness. Environmental norms were thus grafted onto the region's pursuit of free trade.

To help implement the *Vision Statement*, the Environment Ministers generated a *Framework of Principles for Integrating the Environment and Economy in APEC.* The nine principles included the precautionary principle and the principle of making trade and environment policies mutually supportive. According to APEC protocol, the *Vision Statement* and *Framework* were sent to the APEC foreign ministers and leaders for approval. After approval, they were forwarded to senior officials for implementation. In a crucial initiative, the senior officials in 1995 directed APEC's ten working groups and three committees to include environmental issues in their annual reporting process.

The Principles were to be implemented solely through existing institutional mechanisms. In line with its consensual, non-binding character, there is a resistance within APEC to institutionalization and bureaucratization. As a result, no new, dedicated mechanism for policy development, coordination, or oversight was put in place and no oversight function was assigned to an existing mechanism. The explicit aim was to integrate environmental issues fully and fundamentally within existing working groups and committees.

Problems arose in implementation because existing working groups and committees had virtually no substantive expertise on environmental issues. When the working groups, which focus on promoting commerce and are made up largely of trade-oriented bureaucrats, began to grapple with implementation of the senior officials' directive, it became apparent that they did not know what to do. Another problem was that crucial issues of sustainable resource and environmental management cut across sectors. At their 1995 Osaka meeting, APEC leaders directed the Economic Committee to consider cross-cutting issues in an initiative called 'FEEEP': Food, Energy, Environment, Economic Growth, and Population. A FEEEP symposium held in September broke new ground in including both governmental and non-governmental participants, but it failed to produce a useful conceptual or policy framework and generated no substantive initiatives.

Recognizing the need for more guidance, environment ministers sought to implement the Principles through the development of a regional work program. In July 1996, the Philippines hosted a second APEC ministerial conference on sustainable development at which consensus was reached on developing an 'action programme' in three priority areas: sustainable cities; clean production/clean technology; and sustainability of the marine

[43] *Ibid.*

environment.[44] Over the following year, 'action strategies' were developed for the clean technology and the marine environment priority areas, largely at the initiative of the U.S.[45] Shepherded by the Industrial Science and Technology Working Group, the Clean Production Strategy focused on building capacities for better environmental management through, first, the adoption by industry sectors of cleaner technologies, policies, and practices, including ISO 14,000 and environmental performance indicators; and secondly, cross-cutting institutional, professional, and private sector partnerships, including the facilitation of demonstration projects and mechanisms to diffuse best practices. The Strategy for the Sustainability of the Marine Environment, developed and shepherded by the Marine Resource Conservation Working Group, settled on APEC cooperation on three issues: integrated approaches to coastal management; the reduction of marine pollution; and sustainable management of marine resources. The primary 'tools' are the familiar APEC litany of information and technology exchange; training, and education; and public–private sector participation and partnership.

APEC's third meeting of environment ministers, held in Toronto in June 1997, adopted the three action strategies. The working groups and other existing mechanisms were placed in charge of implementation. With Canada as APEC chair in 1997, environmentalists had hoped that the ministerial would propel a 'great leap forward' in the adoption of regional environmental norms. Instead, ministers took a few baby steps and developed very weak programs based largely on information exchange. The problem lay not in the content but in the weak implementation of the work programs. The Clean Technology Strategy *could* offer a way out of the North–South conundrum over technology transfer. The Sustainable Cities Program *could* point APEC toward an integrative, cross-cutting approach to sustainable urban-industrial development. The Marine Strategy *could* point towards a Pacific-wide regime of sustainable coastal and ocean management. Few are optimistic, however, about the fulfillment of this potential.

The three initiatives garnered little passion or enthusiasm as they moved forward in 1997 and 1998. The meetings typically were attended by a handful of line bureaucrats and true believers. In early 1998, Malaysia assumed the chairmanship of APEC. Fatigued with the number of ministerial-level meetings in 1997—Canada had six—and caught up in financial crisis, Malaysia announced it would focus only on trade and finance. Even the trade agenda became stalled when Japan refused to offer concessions to liberalize its

---

[44] APEC Declaration, APEC Ministerial Meeting on Sustainable Development, Manila, July 1996, available from the Nautilus Institute <http://www.nautilus.org>.

[45] For the full text of both strategies, see <http://www.nautilus.org/aprenet/library>.

forestry sector, one of fourteen selected for 'early voluntary sector liberalization', and insisted that the matter be taken to the WTO.[46]

3. Implementation: The Role of the Working Groups

While the leaders and environment ministers were the architects of regional environmental norms, the working groups and three committees were given the burden of implementing them. The most active became the working group on regional energy cooperation, whose objective is to maximize 'the energy sector's contribution to the region's economic and social well being', including through regional discussion on how to respond to 'energy related issues such as the greenhouse effect'.[47] The regional energy cooperation working group has focused its environment-oriented work primarily on developing an information base and stimulating regional discussion, but it undertook a foray into policy development with its proposed 'Joint Regional Action on Appliance Efficiency Improvement and Harmonization of Standards'. It also expanded its regional capacity-building efforts by establishing an Asia Pacific Energy Research Centre in Tokyo.

Other working groups whose outputs could be seen as implementing the *Framework of Principles* include Tourism, which developed regional 'Sustainable Tourism' guidelines; Human Resources Development, which promotes environmental training; Marine Resources Conservation, which spearheaded the regional action programme component on sustainability of the marine environment; and Industrial Science and Technology, which spearheaded the 'clean technology' component of the regional action program. While the sheer number of meetings is impressive, the working groups suffer from lack of technical expertise and resistance to the discussion of policy issues. Moreover, environmental initiatives are only part of what working groups do. They also pursue agendas that may have negative impacts on the environment, such as liberalization of resource-intensive trade and harmonization of vehicle emissions standards.

Finally, the overall orientation and technical capacities of working groups reflect their original *raison d'être*, to promote trade and investment liberalization and facilitation on a sectoral basis. Often, the working groups themselves are captured by specific country or commercial interests. The Regional

[46] Standing in for President Bill Clinton, U.S. Vice President Al Gore further deflated regional enthusiasm for APEC when he publicly criticized Malaysian President Mahathir on human rights grounds.
[47] The Regional Energy Cooperation Working Group has expert groups focused on five key themes: (1) energy supply and demand; (2) energy and the environment, which aims to promote clean coal technologies; (3) energy efficiency and conservation; (4) energy research and development and technology transfer, with a priority on new and renewable energy technologies; and (5) minerals and energy exploration and development. See Regional Energy Cooperation Working Group, Internet Home Page.

Energy Cooperation Working Group, for example, is dominated by Australia and Japan and heavily focused on promoting regional energy trade, including Australian coal exports to East Asia.

4. NGOs: Outside the Gate

As long as APEC remained primarily a forum for broad regional economic consultation, it captured little public imagination or concern. With APEC's turn toward trade activism in 1993, non-governmental and private sector groups throughout the region began to consider how to engage APEC on issues of environment, human rights, and equitable development. The business-oriented Pacific Basin Economic Council, for example, organized a task force on the environment in May 1996. Environmental advocacy has been strongest among non-governmental and quasi-governmental think tanks. Between 1994 and 1996, a series of NGO workshops and seminars aimed to understand the parameters and articulate an agenda for regional trade–environmental cooperation.[48] In addition, activist NGOs targeted specific initiatives and working groups.[49]

Civil society efforts to engage APEC in developing and implementing environmental norms were somewhat successful in countries where there are established institutional mechanisms for regular contact between NGOs and government, like the Philippines Council for Sustainable Development. Such mechanisms, however, are few and far between. Even the United States has no regular avenue for environmental groups to consult with policy makers on issues related to U.S. policy on APEC.[50]

The *Framework of Principles* was thus drafted by government bureaucrats and discussed and approved by government ministers with virtually no NGOs or business consultations. With little sense of ownership and no openings for consultation or monitoring, Asia-Pacific NGO activists were skeptical about the ability of the 'environment track' to deliver anything but rhetoric. NGOs themselves articulated no clear political demands, such as greater transparency or NGO inclusion, but focused primarily on APEC's

[48] These include workshops organized by the Canadian National Round Table on the Environment and Economy in March 1996; and by the Nautilus Institute for Security and Sustainable Development, held at the East–West Center in Honolulu in September 1994. ASEAN also held a series of conferences during 1995.

[49] In Australia, for example, a coalition of environment and development groups challenged a meeting of APEC Energy Ministers in July 1996 to focus on social and environmental, rather than purely commercial, aspects of energy development. Even more specifically, an NGO has formed to target the minerals-oriented work of the Regional Energy Committee. See Danny Kennedy <dannyk@moles.org> Project Underground, at the International Rivers Network, Berkeley, California.

[50] The Office of the U.S. Trade Representative established a Trade and Environment Policy Advisory Committee in 1994. However, the agenda has been tightly focused on narrow issues relating to trade-environment conflicts at the World Trade Organization.

'free trade' push, which they flatly opposed on grounds including environment, human rights, North–South equity, and anti-U.S. sentiment.

In 1995, an NGO 'parallel conference' to the official APEC November ministerial conference was held in Kyoto and became a feature of the APEC political landscape.[51] In 1996, five separate NGO conferences were held, including the Manila People's Forum which drew over 500 people from a wide range of groups working on human rights, environment, women's empowerment, and economic development. United in their rejection of (unregulated) free trade, APEC-based NGOs were less sure about their posture toward APEC itself. A debate over whether to 'engage or oppose' APEC emerged in Kyoto in 1995, raged in Manila in 1996, and was politely pushed under the table in Vancouver in 1997. The central argument of the opposers was that there is 'no *there* there', that APEC is mostly a figment of instrumental American imagination. Attempts to engage it on any issue, including environment, would simply lend legitimacy to the U.S.-imposed free trade thrust.

Those seeking to engage APEC argued that NGOs should support the principle of regional cooperation which is, after all, better than regional hostility. They also stressed that NGOs must not only oppose, but propose. APEC provides a vehicle, they suggested, by which to challenge and to generate alternatives to the free trade orthodoxy, including by pressing for regional environmental norms. The opponents held sway.

NGOs thus were left standing 'outside the gate' in the process of generating and complying with regional environmental norms. On the one hand, they were excluded by APEC governments at home. On the other hand, they were excluded by the difficulty of working with APEC itself, due to its particularly opaque nature and non-institutional structure. There were allies within governments, individuals who wanted to see environmental norms fundamentally integrated with trade diplomacy rather than developing under its shadow, but it was not easy for NGOs to identify them. Asia-Pacific NGOs also had little experience of working regionally or grappling with global issues because of their mostly local focus. With its peculiar institutional structure and non-binding approach to rule-making, APEC was especially difficult to comprehend and lack of experience made it difficult for many Asia-Pacific NGOs to identify or seize openings to press a social agenda within APEC.

C. INSTITUTIONAL AND POLITICAL CONTEXT

APEC's ability to effectively undertake the tasks of regional environmental market governance depends on politics and leadership. During its first six years,

[51] The first NGO parallel conference was slated for Indonesia in 1994. However, Indonesia refused to grant permission or visas for the gathering and it was hastily relocated to Bangkok. In 1995, an NGO conference held in Kyoto drew over 150 participants from throughout the region to discuss the environmental and social costs of 'free trade'.

environmental politics at APEC were intimately bound up with the regional politics of trade diplomacy and the global politics of environmental diplomacy. Externally, APEC's defining political feature was initially the attractiveness of membership. Throughout the 1990s, APEC was a 'club of winners'. It embraces two of the world's three largest industrial economies, Japan and the United States; two of the world's most populous nations, China and Indonesia; and a clutch of the most successful newly industrialized economies, including South Korea, Singapore, Chinese Taipei, Chile, Thailand, and Malaysia. APEC membership grew rapidly from twelve in 1989 to eighteen by 1997 and twenty-one in 1998.[52] The membership issue is a recurrent and contentious theme centering on whether APEC should continue to expand to include big, powerful developing countries like India, possibly changing substantially the organization's *modus operandi* and even *raison d'être*.

Market-driven economic integration and the gaps in economic capacities have shaped the 'two legs' of APEC diplomacy. The first leg is trade and investment liberalization and facilitation, primarily the lowering of tariff and non-tariff trade barriers in East Asia, the creation of a non-discriminatory investment regime, and measures to reduce regulatory and procedural barriers to trade. The other leg is economic and technical cooperation, dubbed 'eco-tech', primarily promoting economic and human resource development in APEC's poorer economies, environmental norm-building included. APEC diplomacy has been characterized by differences in the priority the members accord to the two legs. On the surface, APEC developed a broad consensus on the desirability of free trade and investment. Below the surface, however, are tensions among Western and Asian elites over the scope and pace of liberalization. In Asian countries hit hard by the financial crisis in late 1997 and early 1998, these tensions were exacerbated by the structural adjustment policies imposed by the IMF as a condition of assistance.

There is also contention and some confusion about APEC's role in trade diplomacy. It is unclear whether APEC should act primarily to implement commitments made under the GATT/World Trade Organization or move beyond them to be a leader in the push toward global free trade. On the one hand, APEC's broad vision of 'free trade by 2020' is much more sweeping than any free trade goals yet embraced by the WTO. On the other hand, the actual 'action plans' for trade liberalization are meager and few new 'GATT-plus' commitments have been offered.[53]

---

[52] Russia, Peru, and Vietnam became full members in November 1998. Hong Kong will retain its separate membership in APEC, as in all international fora, for 50 years after reunification with China in July 1997.

[53] APEC's utility as a leader in the global push toward free trade is constrained by the differences in diplomatic styles between the WTO and APEC. In the WTO, tariff reductions and other market access offers are made on a 'tit-for-tat' reciprocal basis. APEC, by contrast, is not a negotiating forum. Trade liberalization is presumed to be in the self-interest of all members and any actions to increase market access are offered unilaterally. WTO negotiators are reluctant, therefore, to give up bargaining chips at APEC which they could use in Geneva.

Despite its lackluster performance, the free trade track dominated APEC diplomacy throughout the 1990s. The environment track ran parallel to it, but under its shadow. While environmental diplomats considered how environmental norms would support rather than impede free trade, trade diplomats simply ignored considerations of how trade rules could promote rather than undermine environmental health. An egregious example of this failure at APEC was the designation of two resource-intensive sectors (forest and wood products and fisheries) as targets for 'early sector voluntary liberalization' with virtually no consideration of their environmental impacts. Environmental groups protested loudly about the absence of environmental impact assessment, including an evaluation of whether existing policies, such as financial and environmental subsidies and management capacities, would be adequate or appropriate under a changed trade regime.[54]

Three factors within APEC inhibited more substantive environmental cooperation: cultural and economic differences among APEC members; the complex and confused politics of regional leadership, especially the preponderant but non-hegemonic power of the United States; and APEC's particular resistance to institutionalization.

1. A Motley Crew

A high degree of cultural diversity and economic disparity exists within APEC. Income *per capita*, for example, is about thirty times greater in Japan, APEC's richest country, than in the Philippines, one of its poorest.[55] Northeast Asia is predominantly Confucian, while Southeast Asia is a mixture of Buddhist, Moslem, Christian, and others. Western countries have strong legal, juridical traditions, while East Asian and Latin APEC countries generally do not. Western countries also have strong democratic traditions, with noisy civil society groups which press their governments to act on social and environmental issues. In much of East Asia, strong advocacy-oriented organizations are young or nascent.

A 'North–South' political dividing line could be drawn in APEC between developed and developing/newly industrialized countries, another line could be set between East and West, and a third between ASEAN and the rest. The first of the primary fault lines stems from different models of development. Over the past twenty years, rapid growth and industrialization in several East Asian countries, including South Korea, have come as a result of strong 'developmental' state policies, including import protection and export promotion,[56] generating large and persistent trade deficits with the United States.

---

[54] The campaign to raise environmental concerns about liberalization was led by the Pacific Environment Resource Center in Sausalito, California (perc@pop.igc.org).

[55] World Resources Institute, *supra* note 31.

[56] Evans, P., *Embedded Autonomy: States and Industrial Transformation* (1995).

U.S. bilateral and regional relations with East Asia since the early 1980s have been dominated by U.S. threats accompanied by some restrictions on domestic market access to pressure Asian countries to expand the import of American goods, services and investment.

The broad East–West differences in development strategies and political-economic cultures, as well as a new-found sense of power and identity, have fueled an East Asian nationalism within APEC, centered especially in ASEAN.[57] ASEAN initially blocked the formation of APEC in the 1980s, and a decade later Prime Minister Mahathir of Malaysia called for the creation of an 'East Asian Economic Organization' which would exclude Western nations. The proposal failed due largely to the overriding economic interests of ASEAN in Western capital and export markets and security concerns about Japan and China. Nonetheless, an APEC East Asian Caucus was established.

APEC nations have very different capacities for environmental and resource management and compliance with international norms. For APEC's Western nations and Japan, environmental regulation and legislation began in earnest in the late 1960s or early 1970s. For most of East Asia, environmental awareness and regulation were sparked only in the early 1990s. While there is some potential for fast-growing Asian economies to 'leapfrog' Western technology and avoid the West's ecological sins, environmental managers in both the public and private sectors generally are playing 'catch up' with the West. Economic managers, in turn, resist the rapid imposition of environmental requirements that they fear could impose costs and slow growth.

The gaps in management/compliance capacities and development priorities have generated tension in APEC, as in other international environmental fora, over the weight given to the 'development' and 'environment' agendas. At first, it appeared that the tension would not deadlock progress toward environmental cooperation and, indeed, that APEC could be an example of finding a way around debilitating North–South conflict. It became apparent by 1997, however, that the tension slowed and complicated the articulation of a common vision. Within APEC, frank discussion of differences in environmental and development priorities has been muted, with general consensus on the need to focus on non-controversial issues such as information exchange and capacity-building.

---

[57] Some Southeast Asian analysts argue that it is important for industrializing countries in Asia to retain flexibility in trade policy, that is, to retain the option to undertake import protection/export promotion strategies in particular sectors. See Bello, W., Presentation to Forum on APEC and Its Implications for Asia and the Pacific. Washington, D.C., School of Advanced International Studies, Johns Hopkins University, October 1996. However, reliance on external market access limits the political viability of developmental state policies: U.S. threats to limit market access carry political weight.

2. The Politics of Leadership

The second feature of internal politics at APEC is the preponderant power of the United States. With the largest economic and military capability, the United States has been called the '800-pound gorilla' of APEC.[58] While the United States remains APEC's largest and most powerful economy, East Asia is highly dynamic. Between 1980 and 1995, Japan's share of APEC's GDP increased from about 22 percent to about 33 percent.[59] If China continues its current growth rates of 9–12 percent per year, it will emerge as a significant economic player over the next fifteen years. Until the crisis, ASEAN too had become an increasingly important political player in Asia.

The U.S. tends to take leadership in APEC on all important issues. Indeed, U.S. policymakers are inclined to view APEC as a way to quietly strong-arm Asian governments on trade issues. The success of unilateral U.S. initiatives is not assured, however, especially in the gap between acquiescence and compliance. To be truly successful, initiatives require skillful leadership to tease out a sense of perceived common self-interest and/or to build supporting coalitions. The support of ASEAN is especially important. Many U.S. diplomats, however, do not operate effectively as coalition-builders, and since the end of the Cold War work implicitly under an assumption of American unilateralism.

Environmental cooperation at APEC in the 1990s was promoted primarily by the U.S. and by Canada, which promised in 1993 to 'green APEC'.[60] The North American push has been driven primarily by the need to maintain domestic support for free trade following bruising domestic battles over NAFTA; and the sense that the 'environment track' reinforces the goals of trade liberalization. In addition, there is an increasing recognition of the intrinsic importance of good environmental management, stemming both from changes in norms and rising costs of environmental degradation. Finally, American and Canadian, as well as Japanese and Australian, governments and businesses see commercial opportunity in the export of environment management products and services, as well as cleaner, leading-edge technologies.

There are also security incentives for regional environmental cooperation. Japan, for example, has taken leadership on energy issues largely out of concern for security of energy supplies, as well as export opportunities. U.S. State Department diplomats have increasingly come to view environmental cooperation as a 'second crop' of seedlings to nurture broader U.S. security

---

[58] *Ibid.*   [59] World Bank, *World Development Indicators* (1997) 134–6, Table 4.2.
[60] The analysis in this section is based largely on interviews with a variety of government officials in the United States and Canada.

interests in Pacific regionalism.[61] When the Labor Party was in government, Australia promoted the notion that environmental cooperation enhanced Australia's trade interests and vice versa.[62]

The leadership of the United States and Canada was short of brilliant. The U.S. pursuit of narrow, sectoral trade interests often trumped efforts to articulate and implement an overarching strategic vision of long-term U.S. economic, environmental, and security interests in Asia-Pacific. There has been confusion over U.S. commercial versus strategic priorities in APEC and little articulation of how environmental objectives fit in with other U.S. strategic interests or are important in their own right. This confusion continues to play itself out in the different signals the U.S. gives APEC. On the one hand, the U.S. has taken the lead to promote specific environmental initiatives, including clean technology and marine conservation. On the other hand, the U.S. has promoted rapid liberalization without regard to environmental impacts or management capacities. Moreover, environmental issues tend to get swallowed in the framework of trade expansion in the coordinating office of the U.S. Ambassador to APEC.[63] When Asian governments press for 'development cooperation', U.S. diplomats recite the mantra that technology transfer will be on a commercial basis only.

Eschewing development aid, the United States pressed for 'public–private partnerships', which increase the role of markets in virtually every APEC initiative including environment. The U.S. was reluctant to offer any side payments, in the form of aid or concessional financing, to help build capacities to comply with environmental norms. Side payments are an important compliance mechanism, especially in the context of regional economic disparity. Instead, the United States—in APEC and elsewhere—has sought environmental leadership 'on the cheap'.

In 1994, Canada catalyzed environmental cooperation at APEC when it organized and hosted APEC's first meeting of environment ministers. In 1997, shortly after taking the helm as APEC chair, the Canadian government announced it would make environment the 'key theme' for the year's activity. As the months unfolded, however, Canada produced no bold initiatives and diluted the focus on environment by adding other, vote-attracting themes like women and youth. Like the United States, Canada is highly trade depen-

[61] Joseph Hayes, Interview with Author. Office of Economic Policy: U.S. State Department, June 1996. In April 1996, U.S. Secretary of State Warren Christopher made a widely publicized speech about integrating environmental issues into U.S. foreign policy. Since then, the State Department has announced the creation of six regional 'environmental hubs', including in Bangkok for Southeast Asia. See Environmental Diplomacy, U.S. Department of State, <http://www.state.gov/www/global/oes/earth.html>.

[62] Keating, P., Prime Minister of Australia, Foreign Policy Speech. Singapore National University, February 6, 1996.

[63] Zarsky, L., Report from Sustainable Development Ministerial, Manila, Nautilus Institute, July 1996 <http://www.nautilus.org.aprenet>.

dent—exports comprised about 37 percent of its GDP in 1990—and faces a trade deficit with East Asia.[64] Moreover, although its diplomats often display a high level of diplomatic skill, Canada found it difficult to articulate specific environmental initiatives and was unable to design an institutional process to pursue its priority issue, sustainable cities. Canada's environmental push was hampered by conflicts with its own trade bureaucracy and by a domestic fiscal crisis which undercut financial support for APEC-oriented officials, even as Canada pursued a plethora of initiatives. Faced with proliferating demands, Canada's APEC supporters were too constrained and overextended to generate and guide an environmental agenda.

Japan also attempted to affirm an environmental agenda at APEC. While Canada waved the banner of integration of environment and economy, Japan steered toward development goals, especially energy. In 1995, it successfully proposed a program on the '3Es' (environment, economy, and energy) and the APEC Leaders meeting called for a consideration of issues related to the interrelationship of food, energy, environment, economy, and population issues. Japan also established and funded a central fund for APEC projects and was instrumental in establishing the APEC Energy Resource Center (APERC), based in Tokyo.

Japan's focus on development has been welcomed by many Asian governments, although both Western and Asian APEC countries are wary because of Japan's strong self-interest in ensuring security of energy supply and promoting its energy technologies. Japan's proposals for developing–developed country partnerships often include a 'tied aid' component which Western countries consider contrary to the push for trade liberalization and Asian countries consider a constraint on national sovereignty.

Other Asian voices on environmental issues include the Philippines which, as the 1996 chair of APEC, strongly promoted a new focus on 'sustainable development'; and Chinese Taipei, which collaborated with the U.S. in designing APEC's clean technology initiative. For East Asian NICs and developing countries, incentives for compliance stem from the desire to enhance domestic management capacities, both technological and managerial, maintain market access in developed country markets, and encourage 'green' foreign investment. Taiwan, for example, faces enormous problems of water and soil pollution, and is eager to embrace market-oriented approaches to environmental management like ISO 14,000.

3. 'Soft Law' or Soft Spine?

The third defining feature of APEC politics is a consensus-building, non-bureaucratic institutional style which has been dubbed the 'APEC way'.[65] By

---

[64] World Bank, *supra* note 59.
[65] Funabashi, Y., *Asia Pacific Fusion, Japan's Role in APEC* (1995) 142–4.

design, APEC is not a forum in which binding regional agreements are negotiated on trade, environment, or any other issue.[66] Moreover, APEC members are generally keen to limit bureaucracy and constrain formal institutional development. APEC is primarily task-oriented and aims to promote private sector initiatives. The chair of APEC rotates every year, the Secretariat is purposefully kept very small, the ten working groups and three committees do most of the work, and coordinating mechanisms, if they exist, are built into existing Committees. Indeed, APEC may be seen as the virtual embodiment of the 'soft law' approach to regulation in a global economy or at least one variant of it.

The consensus-building approach was important in gaining East Asian participation in APEC as a whole and the environmental norm-building process in particular. It helped to avoid a paralyzing North–South conflict over issues of market access, which gridlocked trade-environment discussions at the World Trade Organization. Yet, the requirement to move ahead only in ways and on issues in which there is unanimity or no strong objection derails discussion and the resistance to formal institutional development undermines effective coordination of APEC's various initiatives, clouds the transparency of APEC processes, and inhibits public input.

One characteristic of APEC's cartilage-like institutional structure is that it is easy for a variety of players in different countries and bureaucracies to take initiatives to fill issue vacuums. As a result, a proliferation of seminars, workshops, etc. on a wide spectrum of issues has erupted under the APEC umbrella. APEC bureaucrats complain of being swamped by demands to participate in gatherings with little sense of priority among them. This approach also allows the annual chair to raise the profile of specific areas of interest, as seen in Canada's initial environment ministerial. Another example is the Philippine push in 1996 for a 'sustainable development' paradigm that resulted in specific language in the ministerial statement. A shortcoming of this approach is that initiatives held dear by one APEC Country Chair can be completely dropped by the next. The lack of continuity encourages grandstanding and impedes the building of a momentum sufficient to actually change the normative environment or foster compliance.

While it is relatively disorganized in relation to making rules or setting priorities, APEC is almost seamless when it comes to civil society groups. With a tiny secretariat in Singapore, APEC barely has a public face. For most of the 1990s, its activities were largely opaque. Throughout Asia, advocacy and professional NGOs are blossoming and seeking to engage governments as both critics and partners. The principle of stakeholder participation, how-

---

[66] 'The value of APEC is not that we are going to do trade agreements in APEC', claimed a U.S. trade official in 1995. 'I mean, if that's all APEC were, we could do it in Geneva. We don't need it. The value of APEC is that it will help create the conditions for commercial and economic integration.' Quoted in *ibid.*, at 146.

ever, has not yet been embraced either within most member economies or APEC as an organization. Only business groups are courted and receive a hearing and only a few APEC members, including Canada, the U.S., the Philippines, and Indonesia, have included NGOs in official delegations to environment or other ministerials.[67] Even this meager attempt at transparency and inclusion drew criticism from other APEC members.

Without institutional mechanisms for stakeholder participation in the creation of common norms and in pressing governments to be accountable for compliance with them, the effectiveness of the 'soft law' approach in actually changing behavior is limited. The sustainable development push by the Philippines in 1996, for example, ignited little governmental discussion outside Manila and a spate of ridicule inside it. Without pressure at home to hold their feet to the fire, the embrace by APEC leaders of 'sustainable development' reflected more a rhetorical than a political commitment.

CONCLUSION

In the mid-1990s, APEC's approach to setting environmental norms in the global economy looked promising. By adopting a consensual, soft law approach, APEC held out the promise of avoiding the paralysis of the WTO approach to trade and environment. By the late 1990s, however, the APEC effort to adopt and promote compliance with norms 'from the top' had largely dissipated. Low level workshops and working group efforts continued, but the idea of widespread compliance with a coherent set of norms fell off the agenda. While this effort could conceivably revive, the financial and economic crises which hit East Asia at the end of 1997 have dramatically changed the political context in which APEC operates. Given its inability to forge a hardhitting and relevant response to the crises, the future efficacy of APEC itself is in question.

APEC's lackluster experience offers important insights about the effectiveness of soft law approaches to environmental regulation in a global economy. It would be facile to conclude that the APEC experience shows the ineffectiveness of soft law approaches, although other attempts at global market environmental regulation, including those of the WTO and the broader Agenda 21 process, have also stalled. More useful is to consider the particular institutional context in which the environmental norms were seeded and to examine what factors contributed to their failure to germinate. At the

[67] The organizations that participated in the 1996 Ministerial on Sustainable Development in Manila were the Philippine Commission on Sustainable Development, the National Round Table on the Environment and Economy (Canada), and the Nautilus Institute for Security and Sustainable Development (U.S.). These three organizations also participated in the 1997 Environment Ministerial in Toronto. In addition, a representative from a women's organization in Indonesia participated.

broadest level, the APEC effort failed because of the failure to create a fertile institutional context in which norms could take root. Beyond a simple notion of compliance, APEC attempted to develop environmental norms by deeply internalizing them, but it did not create the institutional processes by which norms could be jointly developed, promoted, or monitored. In essence, there were no compliance mechanisms.

The APEC experience suggests that the likelihood that non-binding environmental norms will be complied with or internalized depends on the following conditions:[68] (1) self-interest: when the targets of the norm, whether governments or businesses, see the norms in their self-interest, they follow them—an important way to overcome gaps in benefits is to offer side payments to absolute or relative losers; (2) common goals: when governments have common overarching foreign policy and commercial goals, they are more likely to adopt and enforce common environmental norms; (3) institutional mechanisms: good mechanisms to provide oversight, coordination, and strategic direction, as well as to integrate new scientific information, are crucial in deepening compliance with environmental norms—also important are good discursive mechanisms in which parties can continually engage each other in understanding the issues involved in compliance; and (4) citizen watchdogs: the norms and the institutions involved in promoting them need to be transparent and stakeholder mechanisms need to be put in place in order to hold governments and corporations accountable.

The APEC effort was less than stellar on all four counts. The *Framework of Principles* was designed rapidly and modeled on the Rio process without an attempt to broadly engage Asia-Pacific governments to define their own self-interest. Given the diversity of economic and social conditions in the region, mechanisms to define self-interest are crucial to the political success of any attempt at regional cooperation. Moreover, the environmental agenda was new and controversial. To firmly plant environmental norms, it would have been important to engage economic, finance, and foreign ministers from East Asian and Western countries, not only environment ministers. It was easy for governments to sign onto a set of norms when no clear commitments were implied. By short-circuiting the process of building consensus and a sense of self-interest, the norm-setting attempt stayed within the realm of rhetoric. Further, by eschewing side payments, the richer countries of APEC were not able to change the calculus of self-interest of many of the East Asian governments, for whom serious environmental commitments appeared primarily to be a drag on rapid growth.

The internalization of regional environmental norms was also thwarted by the conflicts over the pace and scope of trade liberalization. The members of APEC did not have clear common goals. Even though Asian elites increas-

---

[68] See Weiss, E.B. (ed.), *International Compliance with Nonbinding Accords* (1997).

ingly embraced trade liberalization through the 1990s, they keenly felt U.S. and other Western pressure to do so. This caused resistance to environmental norms, while at the same time, the U.S. and other APEC members refused to link the environment and trade tracks, that is, to consider how trade rules themselves should be shaped by environmental objectives. The Western countries, in short, refused to consider changes to *their own* trade and economic policies in order to enhance environmental performance.

Even with these failures, APEC's efforts might have borne more fruit if better institutional mechanisms had been put in place. The failure to create an oversight mechanism, either an Environment Commission or even the Environmental Eminent Persons Group called for by some environmental groups, robbed the effort of a sense of momentum and direction. Such a mechanism could also have provided an interface with scientific, professional, and advocacy groups, which could have provided not only 'watchdog' services but proactive, agenda-setting, policy and project ideas. The creation of an NGO interface at APEC also would have encouraged Asia-Pacific NGOs to develop a more regional perspective and enhanced their efforts to be propositional rather than only oppositional. As it was, the APEC effort was almost solely driven 'from the top', that is, by government leaders and bureaucrats. Moreover, it was driven by only a handful of the relevant governments in the region. There was a failure to develop the discursive, institutional mechanisms that would encourage 'buy-in' and other compliance mechanisms. In the end, compliance is a matter of political will. How and why political will changes are the fundamental questions to be answered in designing effective soft law approaches to environmental and other social governance in a global economy.

What the APEC experience suggests, finally, is that compliance with nonbinding environmental norms requires effective institutional mechanisms to promote more open-ended, creative discussions among governments, as well as to provide effective channels for citizen input, both domestically and at the level of the international institution.

APPENDIX I—FRAMEWORK OF PRINCIPLES FOR
INTEGRATING ECONOMY AND ENVIRONMENT IN APEC

Preamble

The challenge of sustainable development requires integration of economy and environment in all sectors and at all levels.

The experience of APEC members is that a market economy can be a very efficient and flexible means of allocating resources to meet individual preferences. Competitive market economies make for a dynamic and innovative society.

But the market will not necessarily deliver other objectives that society may have, such as meeting the basic needs of all citizens, environmental quality, and access to resources for future generations.

In seeking to reconcile the objectives of economic growth and efficiency with improved environmental outcomes, the following principles could be taken into consideration by member economies to achieve sustainable development.

Principle: Sustainable Development

Member economies should promote sustainable development and a higher quality of life for all people. All the possible measures should be seriously considered to bring about a society where 'environmental protection shall constitute an integral part of the development process and cannot be considered in isolation from it' (from Principle 4, Rio Declaration on Environment and Development).

Member economies should promote the complementary principles of reduction of poverty and improvement of the environment, consistent with Principle 5 of the Rio Declaration.

Principle: Internalization

Members should 'endeavor to promote the internalization of environmental costs and the use of economic instruments, taking into account the approach that the polluter should, in principle, bear the cost of pollution, with due regard to the public interest and without distorting international trade and investment'. (Principle 16, Rio Declaration)

Principle: Science and Research

Scientific research should be fostered to increase the community's understanding of ecological systems, and their interactions with the economy, employment and human communities.

Principle: Technology Transfer

Member economies should cooperate to strengthen capacity-building for sustainable development through exchanges of scientific and technical knowledge. They should enhance the development and transfer of technologies, including new and innovative technologies, consistent with Chapter 34 of Agenda 21.

Principle: The Precautionary Approach

Member economies should, according to their capabilities, widely apply the precautionary approach in accordance with Principle 15 of the Rio Declaration: 'Where there are threats of serious or irreversible damage, lack of full scientific certainty shall not be used as a reason for postponing cost-effective measures to prevent environmental degradation.'

Principle: Trade and the Environment

Member economies should support multilateral efforts to make trade and environment policies mutually supportive, consistent with Principle 12 and other relevant principles of the Rio Declaration.

Principle: Environmental Education and Information

Member economies, industry, consumer groups and environmental groups should provide to all citizens information and educational opportunities that will enhance informed choices that affect the environment.

Principle: Financing for Sustainable Development

Member economies should cooperate to meet the goal of mobilizing financial resources for sustainable development, including the exploration of innovative approaches to fund raising schemes and mechanisms, taking into account conditions and priorities of APEC members.

Principle: Role of APEC

APEC members should, in promoting regional cooperation, make the best use of existing multilateral and bilateral fora, and activities of APEC to attain sustainable development. These fora and activities have contributed to the implementation of Agenda 21 in the fields of environmental priority setting, accumulation of scientific knowledge, and enhancement of capacity building. APEC members should seek appropriate ways and means by which APEC can add concrete value to these ongoing activities, avoiding duplication of functions.

Meetings of APEC ministers responsible for the environment should be held on an ad hoc basis as the necessity arises.

APEC members should consider ways to better incorporate sustainable development into the work of APEC Working Groups and Committees, where relevant, including consideration of these issues at the levels of Senior Officials Meetings and APEC Ministerial Meetings.

APEC members should achieve the integration of economy and environment considerations through conscious efforts to incorporate environmental concerns into decision making for sustainable development at all levels.

APEC Ministers Responsible for the Environment
Vancouver, Canada
March 25, 1994

Compliance with Non-Binding Norms of Trade and Finance

DAVID A. WIRTH

The studies collected in this chapter are emblematic of the wider universe of non-binding instruments, illustrating the flexibility in substantive content and procedural context that is a principal hallmark of non-binding undertakings. Taken as a group, the studies reveal cleavages characteristic of the legal and policy dynamics surrounding non-binding instruments, as they vary in: (1) choice of non-binding rather than binding format; (2) institutional setting; (3) relationship to binding international law; (4) identity of norm-creating entities; (5) identity of parties addressed; (6) processes for adoption and implementation; (7) impact on domestic policy and law; and (8) the role of the public in norm formulation, implementation, and compliance.

Beth Simmons' analysis highlights many attributes of a 'classical' or 'traditional' non-binding vehicle, to the extent such a model can be identified among the extraordinarily diverse examples assembled in this volume. Her study consequently is useful as a benchmark, providing a reference point against which the others can be compared. The Forty Recommendations of the Financial Action Task Force (FATF) are a policy response to an archetypal collective action problem: how to overcome the incentives inherent in the decentralized and consent-based international system, which often rewards holdouts, scofflaws, free riders, and laggards. As described by Professor Simmons, the efforts of the United States to encourage or, indeed, leverage higher standards of performance on the part of other states—to 'harmonize up'—was a principal motivating factor explaining the nature of the FATF's activities generally and the Forty Recommendations in particular.

Professor Simmons identifies characteristics frequently cited as benefits of a non-binding approach, which might be described as the 'choice of instrument' question. The commitment of states other than the United States is described as tentative or equivocal. In such a context, states might commit to binding obligations only of a modest character, if at all, while a non-binding 'soft' instrument can allow them to gain experience with more ambitious, aspirational goals in a less risky milieu. non-binding instruments also may be appropriate for circumstances in which consensus is elusive or illusory. Thus, they may be attractive alternatives to an inertial downward spiral towards the 'least common denominator' characteristic of many multilateral efforts. For these reasons, among others, non-binding instruments are often phrased, as are the Forty Recommendations, in hortatory 'shoulds' rather than obligatory 'shalls'. Perhaps somewhat unexpectedly, a non-binding format characterized by a sense that less is at stake in a legal sense may also facilitate more vigorous compliance mechanisms than might be expected in a binding international agreement. The FATF's mutual evaluation mechanism described by Professor Simmons clearly falls into this category. The monitoring process accompanying the Forty Recommendations capitalizes on the non-binding format's flexibility, facilitating transparency as to the activities of participating states, helping to ensure compliance, and allowing elaboration of general principles for particular situations.

The Forty Recommendations, while adopted by states, also are addressed directly to private actors, primarily financial institutions. The character and status of non-state actors makes the binding international agreement a considerably less-well suited form of regulatory instrument. In formal terms, treaties and other international agreements are concluded only among states or other subjects of international law, not with or among private actors. Acting as desirable or necessary intermediaries, states parties to a treaty may undertake to regulate the behavior of private actors within their jurisdiction. In the area of trade and finance, where the private sector predominates and is the primary targets of norms, non-binding instruments, despite their nonbinding character, become appealing vehicles through which states can establish expectations. The latter are often phrased as 'good practice standards' and are transmitted directly to nonstate actors without the necessity for government regulatory action.

The ease of amendment identified by Professor Simmons is another advantage frequently attributed to a non-binding format. The Forty Recommendations were adopted originally in 1990 and 'revised in 1996 to reflect changes in money laundering trends',[1] apparently with a minimum of procedural complexity. The use of the nontechnical description 'revised' is telling, as the analogue in treaty practice would be an amendment to a binding multilateral agreement. Under customary international law, an amendment to a multilateral treaty is in effect a new agreement, binding only those states that indicate their affirmative intent to accept the new obligations.[2] States ordinarily

---

[1] Financial Action Task Force on Money Laundering, *Annual Report 1997–1998*, O.E.C.D. Doc. FATF-IX 6 (June 1998) (<http://www.oecd.org//news_and_events/release/FATF98. PDF>). The 1996 revision of the Recommendations can be found at Financial Action Task Force on Money Laundering, *Annual Report 1995–1996*, Annex 1 (June 28, 1996) (<http://www.oecd.org//fatf/pdf/96ar-e.pdf>).
[2] See Vienna Convention on the Law of Treaties, May 22, 1969, Art. 40, 1155 U.N.T.S. 331, reprinted in (1969) 8 I.L.M. 679. The Vienna Convention is ordinarily considered a codification of most customary international law concerning treaties. For example, this instrument, although not in force for the United States, has been accepted there as an authoritative source regarding the customary law of international agreements. See S. Exec. Doc. L, 92d Cong., 1st Sess. 1 (1971); Restatement (Third) of the Foreign Relations Law of the United States pt. III, introductory note (1987).

indicate their assent to an amendment through the often time-consuming and cumbersome processes of signature, ratification, and acceptance.[3] One obvious consequence of this rule is the potential to create classes of parties with different obligations, an undesirable situation in multilateral surroundings whose principal purpose is to encourage concerted action by states.

Another aspect of Professor Simmons's subject that makes it a typical nonbinding initiative is the 'choice of forum', the fact that the efforts were undertaken in connection with the Organization for Economic Cooperation and Development (OECD). The decision to treat the subject matter of money laundering in this institutional setting appears far from coincidental. One senses that the OECD, often described as a 'club' of wealthy developed market-oriented economies, was a desirable venue precisely because of its limited membership of like-minded states characterized by a sense of shared outlook and purpose. In such a framework, the identification of common goals may well be easier than in an organization with universal membership, such as a specialized agency or program of the United Nations. As a corollary to this principle, once a grouping such as the OECD has overcome the impediments to joint action among its own members, it is in a position to exert significantly enhanced leverage over outsiders. Professor Simmons' description of the treatment of nonmembers by the FATF is a classic example of this phenomenon.

The OECD's constituent multilateral treaty anticipates the adoption of non-binding recommendations and binding decisions.[4] The FATF instead started as an OECD 'project' but subsequently evolved into an *ad hoc* nonbinding undertaking involving OECD members and nonmembers. As described by Professor Simmons, the FATF now has its own secretariat specifically crafted to meet the substantive and institutional demands presented by the subject matter and identified by the participating states. The Forty Recommendations do not have the character of, and arguably have less binding force than, formal recommendations within the meaning of the OECD treaty. But as Professor Simmons points out, such legal distinctions are largely irrelevant to the efficacy of the FATF's work, which is more determined by the participating states' collective political will than by the niceties of legal form.

---

[3] A particular agreement may specify another procedure. *E.g.*, Montreal Protocol on Substances That Deplete the Ozone Layer, September 16, 1987, art. 2, para. 9, S. Treaty Doc. No. 10, 100th Cong., 1st Sess. (1987), reprinted in (1987) 26 I.L.M. 1550, adjusted and amended, June 29, 1990, S. Treaty Doc. No. 4, 102d Cong., 1st Sess. (1991), reprinted in (1991) 30 I.L.M. 539, adjusted and amended, November 25, 1992, S. Treaty Doc. No. 9, 103d Cong., 1st Sess. (1993), reprinted in (1993) 32 I.L.M. 875 (adjustments binding on all parties adopted by two-thirds majority of parties to parent instrument).

[4] Convention on the Organization for Economic Cooperation and Development, December 14, 1960, art. 5, paras. (a) and (b), 12 U.S.T. 1728, T.I.A.S. No. 4891, 888 U.N.T.S. 179. See, *e.g.*, Organization for Economic Co-operation and Development, *OECD and the Environment* (1986) (collecting OECD decisions and recommendations on environment).

The FATF's work, like many non-binding efforts, is embedded in a complex web of binding agreements, such as the Vienna Convention Against Illicit Traffic in Narcotic Drugs and Psychotropic Substances and other non-binding instruments and initiatives. The FATF thus performs another oft-cited function of non-binding initiatives: filling gaps and holes in binding regimes. The less formal venue of the FATF provides an alternative channel for treating money laundering against a background of few ratifications of the binding Vienna Convention.

Read against the baseline of the FATF study, Laurence Boisson de Chazournes' analysis of the World Bank's policies is a useful study in contrasts. Perhaps most obviously, where the FATF's Forty Recommendations identify a specific subject matter characterized by relatively straightforward problems and goals, the World Bank's operational policies are a quite conscious attempt to integrate and balance competing themes in the Bank's functional mission, which historically has been defined primarily in economic terms. Until roughly a decade ago, the Bank was resistant to incorporating social welfare concerns such as human rights, environment, the interests of indigenous peoples, and labor standards[5] into its work. In the FATF a non-binding approach is employed directly to advance readily identifiable policy goals through an *ad hoc*, freestanding structure. The Bank's operational policies described by Professor Boisson de Chazournes are intended instead to encourage the penetration of exogenous social policy factors into the operations of an existing international institution by modulating, regulating, and constraining what might be described as the natural institutional momentum of the Bank.

The situation described by Professor Boisson de Chazournes is not set out in the World Bank's constituent treaties,[6] but instead has been crafted in a less formal context to occupy interstices in the Bank's institutional structure. No explicit provision in the Bank's constitutional instruments governs the generic sort of policies that guide the Bank's discretion in approving particular proposals for loans and credits, nor is there any indication of a procedure by which those instruments can or must be adopted. Likewise, there is no express legal authorization for the Inspection Panel, which was created by resolution of the Bank's Board of Executive Directors.[7] To that extent, these

---

[5] See *e.g.*, (1988) 82 *Proc. Am. Soc'y Int'l L.* 41, 42 (remarks of Ibrahim Shihata, Vice President and General Counsel, World Bank, noting that '[i]n the case of the World Bank, its Articles of Agreement entrust the organization with specific functions and responsibilities—all of them related to economic growth, reconstruction, and development').

[6] See Articles of Agreement of the International Development Association, January 26, 1960, 11 U.S.T. 2284, T.I.A.S. No. 4607, 439 U.N.T.S. 249; Articles of Agreement of the International Bank for Reconstruction and Development, December 27, 1945, 60 Stat. 1440, T.I.A.S. No. 1502, 2 U.N.T.S. 134, amended August 25, 1965, 16 U.S.T. 1942, T.I.A.S. No. 5929.

[7] See I.B.R.D. Res. No. 93–10; I.D.A. Res. No. 93–6 (September 22, 1993), reprinted in (1995) 34 I.L.M. 503 . See generally Shihata, I.F.I., *The World Bank Inspection Panel* (1994).

vehicles can be viewed as performing a gap-filling function similar to that of the Forty Recommendations. The analogy is limited, however, because in the World Bank the lacunae arise in the structural framework of an existing international institution with a continuing operational mission; the interstices in the international system occupied by the FATF, given the existence of a reasonably comprehensive binding instrument, are instead more plausibly described as ones of political will expressed as the failure of targeted states to ratify and implement the agreements.

That the World Bank's constituent treaties do not expressly anticipate an approach of the kind described by Professor Boisson de Chazournes does not suggest that such a strategy is necessarily ineffective. On the contrary, the Inspection Panel is the first instance in which any multilateral institution has submitted the question of the adequacy of its own operations to external review. At least in principle, the interlocking system of the Bank's operational standards and its Inspection Panel provides a comprehensive structure for application and implementation of a system of good practice standards in the Bank's day-to-day work. Indeed, given the Bank's institutional structure and the opportunities in the project cycle at which internal decision making might be amenable to external input, it would be difficult to identify a different or a better approach.

The World Bank study presents an interesting permutation on the categorization of non-binding or 'soft' norms and binding or 'hard' law, and of the relationship between them. First, it would probably be a mistake to characterize the Bank's operational standards as 'soft' or non-binding as a categorical matter. As Professor Boisson de Chazournes points out, certain categories of these instruments, including the Bank's 'Good Practices', are no more than precatory by their own terms. Others, such as the new 'Operational Policies' and 'Bank Procedures', are more often phrased in obligatory language. The Bank staff clearly views the application of the latter instruments as nondiscretionary and private parties can enforce the policies and procedures through the mechanism of the Inspection Panel.

The Bank's operational standards, whether mandatory or discretionary, apply to the institution's professional staff, not to borrowing countries, and consequently cannot bind the latter as a formal matter. World Bank loan agreements, however, have a status in international law similar to that of binding treaties[8] and are enforceable by the Bank against the borrower. To the extent that the covenants in the loan agreement explicitly or implicitly incorporate the Bank's operational standards, those standards become transformed or 'hardened' into binding legal obligations. While the Inspection Panel mechanism as a formal matter does not apply to allegations made

---

[8] See Nurick, L., 'Certain Aspects of the Law and Practice of the International Bank for Reconstruction and Development', in Stephen M. Schwebel (Ed.), *The Effectiveness of International Decisions* (1971) 100, 127 (statement by World Bank Deputy General Counsel).

against borrowing country governments directly, through that channel private parties can scrutinize the adequacy of Bank staff's performance at two major junctures: (1) in the design and appraisal of individual loans; and (2) in Bank staff's oversight of borrowers' contractual obligations. The Bank's internal standards are relevant and, at least when phrased in those terms, binding in both these settings. Consequently, although not formally binding on borrowing country governments, the Bank's operational standards are likely to have significant legal and practical implications for borrowers, both internationally and domestically.

A revealing dynamic arises in the application of standards external to the Bank in the design and appraisal of loans. As noted by Professor Boisson de Chazournes, the Bank makes use of a number of non-binding normative instruments of external origin, such as the FAO Code of Conduct on the Distribution and Use of Pesticides, in its operations. The good practice standards contained in such instruments may inform or be incorporated by reference in internal policies, such as the Bank's Operational Policy on Pest Management, which expressly cites the FAO Code. References such as this to external standards may perform a useful legitimating function within the Bank, while legally, through a process similar to that characteristic of the Bank's internal standards, these advisory instruments may be transformed into binding loan covenants.

The Bank's policies specify that the institution 'will not finance projects that contravene an international environmental agreement *to which the member country concerned* [*i.e.*, borrowing country] *is a party*'.[9] In other words, in the case of binding obligations the Bank will insist that borrowers comply only with those they have already undertaken, at least in the environmental field. This limitation presumably is motivated by a recognition that, unlike non-binding instruments, international agreements have identifiable parties and that the borrower concerned should not be held to obligations it has shown itself unwilling to accept.

It is clear that this reluctance to rely on multilateral agreements to which a borrower is not party as a standard of good practice arises from policy sensitivities and not legal impediments. The key factor distinguishing a loan agreement with the Bank from an unratified multilateral agreement is that in every instance the consent of the borrowing country government to the terms of a loan agreement with the Bank is a necessary condition precedent to the conclusion of that agreement. If the borrower agrees to the terms on which the loan is offered, then the loan agreement with the Bank operates *per se* as a consensual derogation of sovereignty that is no different from any other international agreement to which the borrowing country is party. If, on the

---

[9] World Bank Operational Manual Statement No. 2.36: Environmental Aspects of Bank Work 9(e) (May 1984), reprinted in Shihata, *supra* note 7, at 137 (emphasis supplied).

other hand, the borrower rejects the terms proposed by the Bank, there are no international legal consequences because the borrower has no right to the loan and has voluntarily declined to enter into the agreement.

The principle as stated in the Bank's policy, moreover, is belied by the institution's own practice. Barber Conable, President of the Bank at the time of the adoption of the Basel Convention on Transboundary Movements of Hazardous Wastes, is reported to have directed Bank staff to refrain from financing projects involving international shipments of toxic detritus.[10] The Bank's policy thus appears to be more stringent than the obligations contained in the relevant international instrument. While borrowers may not appreciate such an approach, the Bank has both the authority and responsibility to determine loan conditionality according to its own standards, regardless of whether those policies arise strictly from within the institution or are informed by 'soft' or 'hard' sources of external origin. Additionally, promoting wider ratification of multilateral environmental agreements is both a desirable and a legitimate element of the Bank's operational mandate.

The Bank's practice is less clear about customary international law. The Bank 'will not finance projects that could significantly harm the environment of a neighboring country without the consent of that country'.[11] This requirement closely tracks a customary standard prohibiting transboundary pollution as found, for instance, in Principle 21 of the Stockholm Declaration. Otherwise, customary international legal standards do not appear to operate as a constraint on the Bank's operations, either as a matter of principle or of practice. On the other hand, the Bank's policy on international waterways mirrors customary norms in this area, presumably as a policy consideration not compelled by international law, as least from the Bank's point of view.

The resolution creating the Inspection Panel contains some potentially significant limitations on its authority that are of particular interest in the instant context. The Panel, pursuant to the resolution creating it, is confined to considering 'a failure of the Bank to follow its operational policies and procedures with respect to the design, appraisal and/or implementation of a project financed by the Bank'. The Bank's 'operational policies and procedures' referred to in the resolution creating the panel do not necessarily reflect binding customary norms even in such areas as human rights, let alone the good practice standards contained in non-binding multilateral instruments. Just as there is no legal impediment to reliance on non-binding instruments or treaties to which the borrower is not a party in crafting loan conditions and covenants, there is similarly no legal reason why Bank policies and practices

---

[10] See, *e.g.*, Land, T., 'Managing Toxic Waste: International Regulation of Hazardous Waste Materials', *The New Leader*, November 27, 1989, at 4 (available in Lexis, News file) ('the World Bank . . . has announced that it will refuse to finance any development project and [sic] involves the disposal of another country's toxic waste').

[11] World Bank Operational Manual Statement No. 2.36, *supra* note 9, ¶ 9(f).

cannot incorporate customary norms, subsequently to be enforced through the Inspection Panel process.

In the case of customary legal obligations, there is a compelling argument precisely to the contrary. As a public, multilateral, intergovernmental organization, the Bank is considerably more than just an agent of borrowing country governments. Instead, the Bank, whose membership is now nearly universal, is accountable to the international community as a whole and is consequently under an obligation not to act inconsistently with international law. In other words, the Bank's Articles of Agreement ought to be read in light of customary international law binding on the Bank's member states and the Bank itself as subjects of public international law.[12] One might well argue that international law precludes the Panel from taking action contrary to customary norms and that the Inspection Panel would be a natural forum for enforcing such customary norms. In the case of a non-binding instrument, these legal arguments admittedly do not have the same force. It would nonetheless appear to be only natural, and certainly appropriate, to assume that widespread, generally accepted multilateral standards contained in non-binding instruments would presumptively apply in the Bank's lending operations.

As described in Lyuba Zarsky's contribution, the Asia-Pacific Economic Cooperation Forum (APEC) is an example of an organization whose entire existence rests on 'soft' or non-binding instruments. APEC, unlike the OECD and the World Bank, has not been established by a binding multilateral agreement. Although instruments such as the 1994 Framework of Principles address APEC's states as 'members', one hesitates to use the term 'organization', let alone 'international organization', in characterizing such a loosely structured arrangement. The most obvious comparison is with the World Trade Organization (WTO), which, even in its earlier incarnation as the General Agreement on Tariffs and Trade, evinced a considerably more sophisticated institutional structure than does APEC. In recent years, the GATT/WTO regime has evolved a more formal and rule-based institutional structure, while APEC has consciously and purposefully chosen an alternative, more loosely textured path to trade liberalization and economic integration. As Ms Zarsky suggests, one consequence of APEC's relatively informal institutional structure may well be flexibility and speed, attributes characteristic more generally of non-binding undertakings.

Naomi Roht-Arriaza's study of the International Organization for Standardization (ISO) rings a further set of changes on these themes. In the case studies of the FATF, the World Bank, and APEC, the entities

---

[12] See International Agreements on Environment and Natural Resources: Relevance and Application in Environmental Assessment (March 1996) (publication of Environment Department of World Bank updating Environmental Assessment Sourcebook) (stating that '[t]he World Bank, an organization created and governed by public international law, undertakes its operations in compliance with applicable public international law principles and rules').

adopting the relevant non-binding standards are subjects of international law, vehicles through which sovereign states act collectively to express their will. ISO is different; it is not an intergovernmental organization.[13] Moreover, in the three previous case studies the non-binding norms are directed either at states alone or at states and private parties. FATF's Forty Recommendations target both states and private parties. The World Bank's policies apply to its own professional staff, with indirect but palpable collateral effects on borrowers. The member states of APEC coordinate policies for and among themselves, although certainly with significant effects on private transactions and nongovernmental actors. In contrast, ISO voluntary standards deal solely with the behavior of private parties, generally industry. At least as far as the United States is concerned,[14] ISO standards are a somewhat curious example of international non-binding instruments adopted by and directed to private entities, amounting to a system of voluntary self-regulation by the principal stakeholders. To that extent, ISO presents a fundamentally different setting for private parties from that identified in the APEC case study, which concerns attempts by nonstate actors to influence a quintessentially intergovernmental process.

The municipal legal and policy implications of ISO standards necessarily vary from country to country. Some observers have expressed concern that countries with poorly developed regulatory infrastructures may eschew national regulation, instead adopting wholesale the ISO 14000 series of standards without regard for the fundamentally process-oriented approach of this voluntary instrument. For example, by the express terms of the standard a company may be ISO 140001 certified notwithstanding outstanding regulatory violations. Even proponents of the new ISO standards admit that they are at most complements to, and not substitutes for, performance-based criteria such as emission limitations for air and water pollutants. In the United States, federal officials are encouraged to participate in the establishment of voluntary consensus standards, including ISO efforts, which then may be appropriate candidates for application through binding regulatory require-

---

[13] ISO is an international federation of standardizing bodies from 118 countries and is not an intergovernmental organization, typically established by multilateral agreement, whose members are states represented by governmental authorities. ISO's work product consists of voluntary standards, which are addressed directly to private parties and are not binding under international law.

[14] Some countries are represented in ISO by national standardizing bodies that are governmental entities. The United States member of ISO, however, is the American National Standards Institute (ANSI), a private entity. For the United States, the primary, although not sole, participants in ISO processes are representatives of private industry. At least for the United States, the private, voluntary character of international standards adopted by ISO mirrors similar undertakings with respect to standards on the national level. See, *e.g.*, Hamilton, R.W., The Role of Nongovernmental Standards in the Development of Mandatory Federal Standards Affecting Safety or Health', in *Administrative Conference of the United States, Recommendations and Reports* (1978) 247, reprinted in (1978) 56 *Tex. L. Rev.* 1329.

ments.[15] But federal agencies may use governmental standards adopted by a nongovernmental entity like ISO only as hortatory guidance for agency regulatory activities, which must be reevaluated by reference to appropriate statutory standards.[16]

The relationship of ISO standards to 'hard' international law, as well as to domestic law, has recently become complex, in large measure due to the Uruguay Round of Multilateral Trade Negotiations. As a result of the relatively obvious trade benefits from harmonized standards such as those promulgated by ISO, the new Agreement on Technical Barriers to Trade (TBT Agreement), expressly references voluntary international standards. The TBT agreement establishes that 'standards', as that term is used in that text, may include voluntary guidelines adopted by an 'international standardizing body', a term which appears intended to include ISO. Although standards adopted by ISO are non-binding instruments addressed directly to private entities, the TBT agreement then goes on to specify that governmentally established requirements or 'technical regulations' shall be based on those standards. Governmental regulations that conform to the standards adopted by an international standardizing body are presumptively legitimate.[17] Many regulatory requirements that have environmental or public health implications, including specifications for consumer products such as children's toys, appliance efficiency criteria, and vehicle fuel efficiency standards, are potentially covered by the Uruguay Round TBT agreement.

Professor Roht-Arriaza describes the status of ISO standards under the TBT Agreement as 'privileged'. It may also be asserted that the TBT Agreement 'hardens' ISO standards into binding law, at least under some circumstances. In the structure of the TBT agreement, those national regulatory requirements that are not based on the output of an international standardizing body are particularly vulnerable to challenge as unnecessary obstacles to international trade. The governmental requirements that are most likely to create impediments to international trade are those that are more rigorous than the international requirements, which may well be the product of a least-common-denominator consensus in an industry-dominated forum. The result is that, through a trade agreement, the expectations of what, at least from the point of view of the United States, is a *private* standardizing organization are

[15] *E.g.*, National Technology Transfer and Advancement Act of 1995, § 12(d), Pub. L. No. 104–113, 110 Stat. 775 (1996); Office of Management and Budget Circular No. A-119, ¶ 6(a) & (b), 58 Fed. Reg. 57,643 (October 26, 1993); 61 Fed. Reg. 68,312 (December 27, 1996) (proposed revisions to OMB Circular A–119).

[16] See, *e.g.*, Office of Management and Budget Circular No. A–119, *supra* note 15, ¶ 7(a)(6); 61 Fed. Reg. 68,312 (December 27, 1996).

[17] An analogous passage in NAFTA sets out a similar approach. North American Free Trade Agreement, December 8, 11, 14 and 17, 1992, U.S.–Can.-Mex, arts. 905 and 915, reprinted in 32 I.L.M. 296, 612 (1993) (use of international standards, defined as 'a document, approved by a recognized body, that provides, for common and repeated use, rules, guidelines or characteristics . . . with which compliance is not mandatory').

transformed into an outer limit of rigor—a ceiling—for *public* regulation to protect health and environment in the United States. Like the vast bulk of international trade agreements, the Uruguay Round TBT agreement is asymmetric,
in that it establishes no analogous minimum standards of performance.

The requirements of the Uruguay Round TBT Agreement and other trade
agreements initially may appear similar to those in the United States, such as
OMB Circular A–119, which counsel reliance on ISO standards to the extent
consistent with statutory mandates. In actuality, however, the two cases are
very different. The OMB Circular authorizes consistency where possible with
ISO standards as non-binding advisory guidelines, but it reasserts the primacy of Congressionally-enacted legislative requirements. In a domestic pro-
ceeding for judicial review, a court in principle should apply the statutory test
without regard to a privately agreed standard in a forum such as ISO. By way
of contrast, the recent trade agreements establish the *private* standard as a reference point and require *public* authorities to justify departures, especially
those tending in the direction of more rigorous requirements. This situation
in effect bootstraps a nongovernmental standard into one with binding significance for governmentally-established regulatory requirements, at least as
a matter of international law. Departures from the benchmark standard can
then be challenged by foreign governments through the efficacious trade
agreement dispute settlement process. In other words, operating through the
TBT agreement, non-binding ISO standards may acquire international legal
significance, may be transformed from minimum standards of performance
into regulatory ceilings from which governments must justify departure in
terms of greater rigor, and, at least from the U.S. point of view, may meta-
morphose from strictly private, non-binding instruments to standards with
significance under public law.

The impact within the United States may be considerable. Adverse reports
of trade agreement dispute settlement panels, like the agreements themselves,
are binding on the United States as a matter of international law. While those
same reports are without domestic legal effect and as a formal matter cannot
alter domestic statutory standards, the reports as a practical matter may have
significant legal impact in domestic administrative and judicial proceedings.[18]
Moreover, through their implementing legislation, the trade agreements are
given the effect of binding domestic law and may preempt state law.

Professor Roht-Arriaza highlights an important issue that pervades the other
three case studies as well, either expressly or by implication: public participation
in international processes. An ever-increasing demand for mechanisms responding to the interests, needs, and inputs of a variety of private parties is characteristic of many international processes, both 'hard' and 'soft'. In general, one can
identify at least two critical points in the life of an international 'soft law' instru-

---

[18] See generally Wirth, D.A., 'International Trade Agreements: Vehicles for Regulatory
Reform?' (1997) *U. Chi. Legal F.* 331, 355–63.

ment at which the public, broadly defined to include all private parties such as business and industry, experts such as scientists, the press, public interest organizations, and individuals, might have an interest: in the formulation of non-binding expectations on the one hand and in encouraging compliance with and implementation of a non-binding instrument on the other.

While Ms Zarsky notes in the case of APEC that 'both research and advocacy NGOs were left standing outside the gate' of intergovernmental consultations and deliberations, such a result is not a necessary consequence of the informal, non-binding character of APEC. Indeed, there are few generalizations that can be made linking the binding or non-binding nature of an international setting to the question of transparency and accountability to nonstate actors or the public generally. The text of a major, binding multilateral agreement on the protection of endangered species entrenched rights of participation for nongovernmental organizations more than twenty-five years ago[19] while the formally-established WTO, which adopts binding rules, has declined to take analogous steps.[20]

In contrast with APEC, the process for adopting ISO standards, as described by Professor Roht-Arriaza, is prescribed with exquisite precision and is anything but *ad hoc*. She is more than justified in pointing out that the participation of environmental groups and other members of the public, though expanding, remains small, at least in United States practice in ISO. The practical reality is that few representatives of stakeholders from sectors other than business and industry have the resources of time or money to participate effectively in ISO processes. The result is that independent voices contribute little to consensus on the national level and, perhaps more importantly, have insufficient leverage to impede or frustrate consensus as that term is defined in the ISO context. The implementation phase consists largely of accrediting certifiers who then certify individual companies to the ISO 14001 standard, during which there is little if any opportunity for meaningful public participation.[21]

[19] Art. XI, para. 7 of the Convention on International Trade in Endangered Species of Wild Flora and Fauna, March 3, 1973, art. XI(7), 27 U.S.T. 1087, T.I.A.S. No. 8249, 993 U.N.T.S. 243, reprinted in (1973) 12 I.L.M. 1035, specifically provides for participation by non-voting observers in meetings of the parties to that agreement.

[20] See Guidelines for Arrangements on Relations With Non-Governmental Organizations, W.T.O. Dec. No. WT/L/162 (July 18, 1996) (available at website <http://www.wto.org/ngo/guide.htm>) ('As a result of extensive discussions, there is currently a broadly held view that it would not be possible for NGOs to be directly involved in the work of the WTO or its meetings. Closer consultation and cooperation with NGOs can also be met constructively through appropriate processes at the national level where lies primary responsibility for taking into account the different elements of public interest which are brought to bear on trade policy-making.'). Cf. United States—Import Prohibition of Certain Shrimp and Shrimp Products, WTO Doc. WT/DS58/AB/R, para. 110 (October 12, 1998), (1999) reprinted in 38 I.L.M. 118 (1999) (available at website <http://www.wto.org/wto/dispute/distab.htm>) (WTO dispute settlement panel report concluding that panels have authority to accept unsolicited submissions from nongovernmental actors).

[21] Since 1997 the author has served, first, as a representative of environmental group stakeholders and currently as an at-large member, on the Management Committee for the

This theme of untapped potential for public participation echoes through the other cases as well. Professor Simmons describes an evolution in the involvement of affected business communities in the FATF's work. The World Bank's quasi-adjudicatory Inspection Panel process can be initiated by private parties meeting the Bank's eligibility requirements, and is in many respects a high water mark for public participation in implementation and compliance. Public participation can be expected to increase the perception of legitimacy, as well as enhancing efficacy in at least some circumstances.[22]

Despite obvious benefits under certain circumstances, the flexibility and *ad hoc* character of many non-binding undertakings do not necessarily facilitate participation or direct accountability at either the international or the domestic levels. As Ms Zarsky's case study implies, it may well be that the fluidity of an institution such as APEC makes it easier to exclude nonstate actors by default, without an articulated policy or formal decision, than it might be in a more highly structured context such as the WTO. In general there are two principal, and far from mutually exclusive, points for nonstate actors in multilateral processes, both 'hard' and 'soft' to enter directly into the international consultations, or indirectly, through participating national governments. The efficacy of either or both of these approaches may be attenuated because of the non-binding character of a particular international undertaking.

In the United States, international agreements that are treaties in the Constitutional sense require that the Senate give advice and consent to ratification. The process often includes scheduled hearings and other less formal consultations with nongovernmental actors, presenting an obvious occasion for participation by concerned members of the public. In anticipation of this process, the Executive Branch may well find it advantageous to grant those constituencies access to the negotiating process in the first instance. In the case of non-binding instruments, there often is no notice of governments' intent to initiate discussions and the process may not be open to participation by nongovernmental observers. On the other hand, the very attribute of informality that characterizes most, if not all, non-binding international efforts may also facilitate the creation of entry points for nonstate actors in a low-profile manner that would be perhaps somewhat less likely in an established intergovernmental organization or in the negotiation of a binding international agreement.

Although the implications for compliance with non-binding norms of the elements discussed above are not entirely evident, it is nonetheless possible to make some general observations. Among the case studies presented in this

Environmental Management System (EMS) component of National Accreditation Program (NAP), a joint undertaking of the American National Standards Institute (ANSI) and the Registrar Accreditation Board (RAB).

[22] See generally Wirth, D.A., 'Reexamining Decision-Making Processes in International Environmental Law' (1994) 79 *Iowa L. Rev.* 769.

section, APEC probably comes closest to what is customarily regarded as a purely non-binding scheme. This impression is particularly strong when APEC's structural and institutional attributes are juxtaposed with the GATT/WTO regime, whose progress toward a system of enforceable rules based on the rule of law has been noteworthy in recent years. By contrast with the WTO, undertakings in APEC obviously have a nonbinding, voluntary character. Of the four case studies in this section, APEC environmental standards, which largely represent the agenda of a small number of states and clash with other perceived interests of the member states, consequently are set in an institutional context in which the impact on actual state behavior would be expected to be the least. In addition, the norms are not only soft in form, they are soft in content.

The case study of the World Bank can be elucidated most readily as creating enforcement mechanisms to implement binding standards. After the creation of the Inspection Panel, the Bank's internal standards are clearly segmented into binding and non-binding categories, with the former amenable to enforcement through the Inspection Panel mechanism and the latter not. It is probably no coincidence that the 'reformatting' of the Bank's internal standards into neatly-defined categories roughly coincided with the creation of the Inspection Panel; prior to that development there was considerably less need for this conceptual distinction. While the Inspection Panel may have contributed to improving compliance by both Bank staff and borrowing countries with binding internal norms, one could hardly reach that conclusion with respect to non-binding instruments, which are not amenable to application through the Inspection Panel process. Indeed, the Panel's capacity to apply even binding standards exogenous to the Bank is highly circumscribed. Somewhat perversely, the creation of the Inspection Panel may actually reduce compliance with certain standards. When the reformatting process was initiated on a systematic basis, a number of observers alleged that some of the Bank's standards were purposefully being 'downgraded' to nonbinding status. Whether that is so or not has been difficult to document, but the potential for this kind of 'negative feedback' is clear.

Particularly when viewed against the baseline of the other two analyses, the case studies of the FATF and ISO are perhaps most notable for their potential, notwithstanding the non-binding format, to encourage performance or compliance by third parties whose commitment is reluctant or equivocal. The leverage possible and the strong financial incentives behind the FATF and similar efforts to combat money laundering may induce some states to comply that otherwise would not and may stimulate some states to pressure others to comply. Although ISO standards are described as adopted by consensus, 'consensus' in ISO is defined not as unanimity, as in most intergovernmental organizations, but supermajority. Once adopted, ISO standards are often sufficiently widely implemented that even objectors have little realistic choice but to comply. That attribute is the whole point of the Organization's existence and the obvious key to the success of its initiatives, notwithstanding their nonbinding, extragovernmental character. When applied in social policy areas such as environment, the approach can be a weakness as well, especially if the distribution of interest group representation is perceived as less than adequate and the work product therefore lacking in fundamental indicia of legitimacy.

With the notable exception of the World Bank, one might well observe that a hard law form of the norms discussed in this section would not have brought greater compliance and certainly would not have been more effective. The norms were drafted in non-binding form for strong reasons that make it unlikely, or in the case of ISO impossible, to envisage binding obligations in their place. The choice appears to have been between non-binding norms and no norms, not between non-binding norms and binding ones. Even if a binding text could have been agreed, it seems probable that the contents of the norms would have been weaker than the agreements that were reached. If these conclusions are correct, they suggest that legal form does make a difference, that states take seriously their legal obligations, but that in resolving problems of international concern, formal legal obligation is not always the most efficacious means to achieve the goals of international cooperation.

Chapter 7   Human Rights

The international protection of human rights, elaborated in agreements and non-binding texts, is largely a development of the second half of the twentieth century, although the International Labour Organization (ILO) took up human rights issues long before the United Nations was created and continues to do so. Concern for human rights in the immediate post-World War II period is reflected in human rights standard-setting activities that most international organizations initiated soon after they were created. The results of five decades of effort are evident today in a complex network of human rights norms and institutions.

Most organs and agencies of the United Nations confront human rights problems in carrying out their mandates. The General Assembly and, increasingly, the Security Council, address human rights through standard-setting, investigations, and quasi-judicial decisions in response to allegations of human rights violations. UN organs with direct responsibility for human rights matters, especially the Commission on Human Rights and the Sub-Commission on Prevention of Discrimination and Protection of Minorities, elaborate human rights standards and monitor compliance with them to particular human rights topics. Special rapporteurs have studied such issues as extra-judicial, summary, and arbitrary executions, disappearances, administration of justice, religious intolerance, and human rights and the environment. These studies and their conclusions provide a rich source of non-binding normative instruments.

Numerous treaty bodies created by human rights instruments are devoted exclusively to human rights, including the Committees established for the United Nations Covenants, on Civil and Political Rights (CCPR), and on Economic, Social and Cultural Rights (ICESCR). Committees of experts also monitor state compliance with the Convention on Elimination of Racial Discrimination, the Convention on Elimination of Discrimination against Women, the Convention on the Rights of the Child, and the Torture Convention. The various treaty bodies adopt recommendations and guidelines on human rights issues relevant to the specific treaty which created each of them.

Among regional organizations, the Council of Europe, the Organization of American States (OAS), the Organization for Security and Cooperation in Europe (OSCE), and the Organization of Africa Unity (OAU) have established human rights systems of norms, institutions, and procedures. The recently adopted Arab Charter of Human Rights could lead to the emergence of yet another regional system. Although regional human rights systems are largely founded on treaty law, the Inter-American system has made considerable use of the American Declaration of the Rights and Duties of Man and the OSCE is based entirely on soft law. The Council of Europe institutions, particularly the Committee of Ministers and Parliamentary Assembly, have issued significant non-binding recommendations setting forth human rights norms on issues such as conscientious objection and the rights of the mentally ill.

Among the obvious wealth of human rights law, the studies in this chapter analyze the use of non-binding norms in four contexts. The institutional settings range from the global (the ILO) and regional (OSCE and OAS) to human rights non-governmental organizations within a single state. Erika Schlager first presents the case of the OSCE, whose participating states deliberately have chosen not to conclude treaties, but instead have adopted a series of legally non-binding normative instruments. Francis Maupin considers the use of recommendations and similar non-binding instruments in the ILO, which also concludes treaties, and the extent to which compliance differs with the nature of the instrument. A similar dual normative structure is found in the OAS, as described by Douglass Cassel. Finally, Christopher McCrudden compares the McBride and Sullivan Principles, examples of increasingly-frequent codes of conduct for transnational corporations.

A Hard Look at Compliance with 'Soft' Law: The Case of the OSCE

ERIKA B. SCHLAGER

INTRODUCTION

The Conference on Security and Cooperation in Europe (CSCE), or Helsinki process, began with the signing of the Helsinki Final Act (HFA) in 1975.[1] It has been a dynamic, multilateral diplomatic process that is perceived to have played a role in ending the Cold War, in large part by fostering compliance by Communist countries with international human rights norms. Because of

---

[1] Major CSCE and OSCE documents are available, along with other information about OSCE activities, at: <*http://www.osce.org./*>. For further reading on the CSCE and OSCE, see Maresca, J.J., *To Helsinki—The Conference on Security and Cooperation in Europe, 1973–1975* (1985); Bloed. A. (ed.), *The Conference on Security and Cooperation in Europe: Analysis and Basic Documents* (1993); Buergenthal, T., 'The CSCE Rights System' (1991) 25 *George Washington J. Int. L. and Econ.* 333; Buergenthal, T. (ed.), *Human Rights, International Law and the Helsinki Accord* (1978); Korey, W., *The Promises We Keep: Human Rights, The Helsinki Process, and American Foreign Policy* (1993); Russell, H.S., 'The Helsinki Declaration: Brobdingnag or Lilliput' (1976) 70 *Am. J. Int. L.* 242; Schlager, E.B., 'The Procedural Framework of the

this role, the CSCE was designated in 1990 as the forum-of-choice for grounding North Atlantic–Eurasian relations for the foreseeable future. In 1994, participating states re-christened the Conference the *Organization for Security and Cooperation in Europe* (OSCE), formalizing an institutional transition that began with the end of the Cold War and the signing of the CSCE Charter of Paris for a New Europe in 1990. The OSCE today is fundamentally different from the CSCE. Examining this transformation may indicate what factors previously made the Helsinki process successful in promoting compliance with its human rights norms and what recent factors arguably have made the OSCE more limited in this regard.

A. THE CSCE (1975–1990)

1. Background

The origins of the Helsinki process are sometimes traced to 1945, when World War II ended without a peace treaty. Stalin and his immediate successors in the Soviet Union used mass murder, torture, and political intimidation on an unprecedented scale to control a vast territory spanning eleven time zones, while Communist regimes used force and coercion to consolidate power in half a dozen East European countries. Occupying armies divided Germany and remained for five decades; even Austria was occupied by the victors of World War II. Albania entered a state of self-imposed isolation, virtually impenetrable by outsiders.

In this unlikely setting, in 1954, the Soviet Union launched the first of many proposals for a pan-European security conference, designed to legitimize the post-World War II division of Europe. Although Western countries initially were skeptical, neutral countries showed a keen interest. Over time, a number of significant developments in East–West relations paved the way for such a gathering. The first and most important factor was the evolution of detente in general and *Ostpolitik* in particular. The slight thaw in the East–West dialogue made it possible to resolve several problems symptomatic of the generally strained relations between the Cold War blocs.[2] It then became politically

---

CSCE: From the Helsinki Consultations to the Paris Charter, 1972–1990' (1991) 12 *Human Rights Law Journal* 221–37. Regular reporting on the Helsinki process is also available from the U.S. Commission on Security and Cooperation in Europe, Washington, D.C. (<http://www.house.gov./csce/>) and in the Helsinki Monitor, a quarterly journal on OSCE-related issues, published in The Hague.

[2] The Federal Republic of Germany and its Eastern neighbors successfully negotiated several bilateral treaties that some have portrayed as substitute peace treaties. The adoption of the Quadripartite Agreement on Berlin brought what in those times passed for some degree of normalization to the divided city. Finally, it was agreed that Mutual and Balanced Force Reductions negotiations, *i.e.*, arms control negotiations, would commence in Geneva upon opening the conference in Helsinki.

feasible for the West to agree to Moscow's initiative, setting the stage for preliminary talks for a pan-European security conference in Helsinki, Finland, in 1972. Thirty-five countries attended for the CSCE: the Soviet Union, Canada, the United States, and all of Europe except Albania, Andorra, and the then still occupied Baltic States. Permitting East Germany to attend at a time when it was struggling for international recognition was viewed by many as evidence of the West's capitulation to Moscow.

The signing of the HFA in 1975 was greeted with suspicion in many quarters, especially in Washington, where Members of Congress established a special bi-partisan commission to monitor its implementation. It took fifteen years and the fall of the Berlin wall before critics would grudgingly acknowledge the positive role played by the Helsinki process in ending the Cold War and improving human rights.[3]

During the preliminary discussions, two main tensions threaded the debates. The first concerned the agenda for the conference. The Warsaw Pact countries generally sought to minimize or block discussion and negotiation of commitments on the human dimension,[4] wanting instead to focus primarily on security issues, and, secondarily, on enhanced trade relations with the West. This generated debate among Western countries between those who believed that reducing the threat of military confrontation was too important to be linked to human rights and those who believed that compliance with human rights commitments is a barometer of country's willingness to comply with international obligations generally.

The second point of divergence in Helsinki centered on the form of the conference and its results. Some of the earliest proposals, for example, conceived of an international organization staffed by a secretariat and woven together by a web of treaties. Such grandiose visions were apparently abandoned during the negotiations on the negotiations, which culminated in the conference rule book in 1973, and the subsequent negotiations on a substantive concluding document. Each side ultimately sought to achieve its objectives in the context of the Helsinki Final Act, which became an end in itself. Accordingly, the states participating in the Conference on Security on Cooperation in Europe (CSCE) opted against having a standing body of representatives, a fixed meeting place, or an independent support staff.

Almost as an afterthought, the participating states agreed to convene a series of diplomatic follow-up meetings that would meet in a different city for each new meeting, with the secretariat for each meeting provided by the host

---

[3] Safire, W., 'Bring on CSCE', *N.Y. Times* (October 15, 1990). Says Safire, 'I accept the C.S.C.E. My 18-year battle against the Conference on Security and Cooperation in Europe is over.'

[4] The term 'human dimension' was first used in the Helsinki process in the 1989 Vienna Concluding Document. It generally refers to the human rights and humanitarian concerns included in the Helsinki documents.

country. Most importantly, the rules provided that no meeting could end until consensus had been reached on the date and location of the next meeting. As a consequence, the Helsinki process developed into an amorphous process of diplomatic brinkmanship moving from city to city, with no fixed beginning and no fixed end. There were moments when this tenuous exercise in public diplomacy all but fell apart.[5] Nevertheless, both sides had considerable political investment in the process and neither wanted to appear as a spoiler.

2. Scope of the Commitments

The substantive scope of the HFA embraced everything from military-security issues, economic and environmental cooperation, and human rights and humanitarian concerns. Western European countries sought language on 'humanitarian concerns' as a means of ameliorating the harsh conditions of the East–West divide. The United States joined later as a fervent convert to the cause. The goals of this part of the HFA, known as Basket III because the drafting texts reportedly were placed in 'the third basket' on the table during the negotiations, included the improvement of working conditions for foreign journalists, an increase in educational exchanges among the participating states, and facilitation of family reunification across borders. The obligations fell exclusively to state actors.

HFA Basket I covered military security and set forth ten 'principles guiding relations among States', sometimes known as the decalogue or the ten commandments of the Helsinki process. Principle VII contained a general commitment to protect human rights and fundamental freedoms; Principle X committed the participating states to fulfill, in good faith, the international legal obligations to which they are bound. For the most part, the HFA did not make dramatic leaps in substance, although later CSCE texts certainly would do so.

Significantly, human rights are explicitly linked to consideration of other issues. The HFA states that, '[a]ll the principles set forth above are of primary significance and, accordingly, they will be equally and unreservedly applied, each of them being interpreted taking into account the others'. Human rights were thus linked to security issues and to economic and environmental issues, to process and substance. In practice, the integration of and balance of all the 'baskets' of the Helsinki Accords were a cornerstone of the process and helped ensure that human rights were not subordinated to other issues.

The linkage was an especially important feature during the early phase of the Helsinki process. If the Soviets wanted to talk about arms reductions, they

---

[5] During the Madrid Follow-up Meeting (1980–3), for example, the introduction of martial law in Poland brought the meeting to a standstill between March and November in 1992, while negotiations were suspended.

also had to talk about human rights; if they wanted a follow-up meeting on economic cooperation, they had to agree to a meeting on human contacts and freedom of movement. In short, linkage between issues of interest to Eastern countries (arms negotiations and, to a lesser degree, economic cooperation) and issues of interest to Western countries (human rights and humanitarian concerns) kept both sides engaged in these issues in the face of strong centrifugal forces that could have easily pulled one or the other away from the negotiating table. Today, without the linkages of the Cold War period, the incentives for some states to comply are much weaker. The 'newly admitted participating States', principally the Central Asian states that joined the CSCE when the Soviet Union collapsed, come to hear their respective human rights records criticized at OSCE meetings today because their attendance is paid for by the Western states which seek to reform them.

3. Binding Status of the Commitments

Some of the original proposals for the CSCE envisioned the conclusion of legally-binding agreements, but this approach was rejected during the drafting of the HFA and, indeed, considerable effort was made to ensure that the document itself would convey its political, rather than legal, orientation. This concern, held particularly but not exclusively by the Americans, was driven largely by a desire to control interpretations of the military-security agreements within the HFA and avoid any appearance that the HFA might require Senate approval.

The agreements are politically binding, a character strengthened by the fact that all decisions taken in the Helsinki process are reached by consensus. Unanimous approval means that all agreements are equally and universally binding on all participating states. Although the rules of the OSCE permit a participating state to submit 'reservations' or 'interpretive statements', a reservation in the Helsinki process does not have the same meaning as when that term is used in the legal context. A reservation in the Helsinki process may not conflict with or even limit commitments or agreements which have achieved consensus, in contrast to the concept of 'reservation' under treaty law, which, within limits, permits a country to withdraw its consent at ratification after it has been given during negotiations.[6]

The significance and meaning of the 'politically binding' status of the Helsinki process have been best explained by Peter van Dijk:

The conclusion that the Final Act is not a legally binding agreement does not mean that the matters agreed upon between the participating states, and laid down in the Final Act, should not be binding. A commitment does not have to be legally binding

---

[6] Cf. Vienna Convention on the Law of Treaties, opened for signature May 23, 1969, Art. 19.

in order to have binding force; the distinction between legal and non-legal binding force resides in the legal consequences attached to the binding force.[7]

Put another way, violations of legal agreements have legal consequences; violations of political agreements have political consequences. In reality, many legal agreements, particularly those in the human rights field, provide for few if any meaningful consequences in the event of non-compliance.

This distinction is illustrated by events in 1990, when East Germans began to flee to freedom through Hungary. Although Hungary had a bilateral agreement with East Germany requiring Hungary to return the East Germans, Hungary refused to implement this legally binding accord, choosing instead to uphold its CSCE political commitments respecting the right to leave and return.[8] In effect, the legal agreement had non-existent legal 'consequences', while the CSCE political agreements which obligated Hungary to permit East Germans to transit through Hungary had the potential to subject Hungary to significant political consequences at a time when Hungary was working to demonstrate its reformist credentials.

Some countries expressed a preference for grounding the CSCE on a legal foundation. Treaties not only have a legal authority that political agreements lack but a certain prestige deriving from their formal status. However, many of the subjects included in the HFA could not be easily incorporated into a hard law format, such as the agreement to expedite the issuing of travel documents in the event of 'urgent necessity', such as serious illness or death, and many participating states would have been reluctant or unwilling to accept such provisions if cast as inflexible hard law. In fact, at different times in the OSCE's history, there have been proposals to convert some agreements into treaty law. These proposals consistently failed to secure consensus. Opponents have argued that placing some norms in a legally binding framework but not others would create an undesirable hierarchy, inevitably diminishing the status and credibility of those provisions relegated to the category of 'merely politically binding'.

In recent years, proposals to make OSCE provisions legally binding have surfaced in connection with two particular concerns. First, beginning around 1990, there were renewed efforts to establish a CSCE mechanism for the peaceful settlement of disputes (PSD).[9] Some countries, notably Switzerland, favored highly legalistic and structured PSD mechanisms. Hungary supported the Swiss approach and argued that a political process would be less

---

[7] Van Dijk, P., 'The Implementation of the Final Act of Helsinki: The Creation of New Structures or the Involvement of Existing Ones?' (1989) 10 *Mich. J. Int. L.* 110, 114.

[8] Bureau of Public Affairs, U.S. Dept. of State, Special Rep. No. 183, Twenty-seventh Semiannual Report by the President to the Commission on Security and Cooperation in Europe on the Implementation of the Helsinki Final Act 16 (April 1–September 30, 1989).

[9] Principle V of the HFA sets out the obligation to resolve disputes peacefully; efforts to elaborate further this concept were unsuccessful during the Cold War.

desirable because, by definition, it could not result in a legally binding outcome. For Hungary, the prospect of a country being held 'in violation of the
law' was such a strong sanction that it would surely result in compliance.
Other countries, including the United States and Great Britain, preferred a
political mechanism, reasoning that political pressure, not legal formalities,
changes behavior. Eventually, both sides prevailed: the Swiss approach, formulated in a French proposal, emerged as the treaty-based OSCE Court on
Arbitration and Conciliation, a treaty ratified by only some OSCE participating states. The American-British concept survived as a 'directed conciliation' mechanism. Neither has been used to mid-1999.

The second issue concerns the status of the OSCE itself. The OSCE continues to field proposals that would cast it as an international organization
with legal character. Adherents claim the proposals are designed to regulate
questions such as diplomatic immunity and tax status for the ever growing
OSCE staff.

4. Strengthening the Commitments

During the CSCE meetings, new agreements were negotiated and adopted
because of shortcomings in the implementation of existing agreements.
Western countries formulated proposals for new agreements to strengthen
compliance with existing agreements in areas where they felt non-compliance
was the most egregious. For the most part, the new commitments resulted in
relatively modest expansions of existing language on human rights, with the
most dramatic progress achieved in 1989–91.[10] Nevertheless, many observers
believed that each successive CSCE meeting helped increase the pressure on
Communist regimes to undertake more sweeping reforms in human rights
and other areas.

During the Madrid Follow-up Meeting (1980–3), for example, Western
countries responded to the Polish imposition of martial law to crack down on
the Solidarity Trade Union by proposing new commitments that would
explicitly permit independent trade union activity. Although the proposed
language was adopted in a weakened form, the process of negotiating the text
served to underscore the inconsistency between Eastern bloc practices and the
proposed new agreements. Moreover, the newly expanded commitment
added to the arsenal that trade unionists and other non-governmental organizations could use in their struggle with national governments.

Another example concerns freedom of information. Participating states
had agreed, in the HFA, to facilitate the freer and wider dissemination of

---

[10] For the evolution of various commitments, see *Human Rights Commitments within the
CSCE Process: Nature, Contents and Application in Finland* (2nd edn., 1994), a publication of the
Advisory Board for International Human Rights Affairs. The book includes a chart of human
rights commitments compiled from CSCE documents.

information of all kinds, but the Communist practice of jamming foreign broadcasts persisted, as did Western criticism of this practice. The issue of radio jamming became a mainstay at CSCE meetings. At the Madrid Follow-up Meeting (1980–3), a Swiss-Austrian proposal sought to give foreign broadcasting an official seal of approval, but Soviet negotiators predictably opposed their draft. The issue reemerged at the next major CSCE gathering, the Vienna Follow-up Meeting (1986–9). The Soviet position appeared intractable and there was little hope that Western efforts to reach an agreement to ban jamming would succeed, until speaking at a meeting of the U.N. General Assembly in December 1988, Soviet leader Mikhail Gorbachev signaled his intent to end jamming 'within the context of the Helsinki process'.[11] The practice of jamming foreign radio transmissions, which had begun in the Soviet Union in the 1950s, ended for all of the Warsaw Pact countries within weeks of this announcement. The Vienna Concluding Document, adopted in January 1989, pronounced that the participating states 'will ensure that individuals can freely choose their sources of information. In this context they will ensure that radio services operating in accordance with the ITU Radio Regulations can be directly and normally received in their States.'

In a third example, at the 1989 Paris Meeting of the CSCE Conference on the Human Dimension, the United States proposed language calling for free and fair elections in all participating states in an effort to create greater pressure on Eastern European countries where Communist control was beginning to unravel. Commitments on free and fair elections were adopted a year later, in the 1990 Copenhagen Document of the Conference on the Human Dimension.

The fact that Helsinki agreements were not cast in the form of legally binding treaties ultimately permitted more ambitious norms to be adopted, best illustrated by the 1990 Copenhagen Document. By 1990, when the second meeting of the CSCE Conference on the Human Dimension was held in Copenhagen, Europe had begun its extraordinary transformation. Semi-free elections had been held in Poland, free elections had been held in Hungary, and free elections were being held in Czechoslovakia during the Copenhagen meeting. Within a few months of the meeting, Germany would unify and, a little more than a year later, the Soviet Union would collapse. At the moment the Copenhagen meeting began, however, the fall of Gorbachev and his liberalizing policies of *glasnost* and *perestroika* seemed more likely than the fall of the Berlin Wall. The Copenhagen meeting thus opened with a sense of historic importance and urgency. Representatives from Central European countries were anxious to make the human rights progress being achieved in their countries irreversible.

Against this backdrop, the countries of the European Community introduced a proposal to incorporate into a CSCE document many of the rights

---

[11] Korey, *supra* note 1 at 266.

contained in the European Convention on Human Rights and Fundamental Freedoms. While well intended, the proposal lacked both ambition and vision, as most of those standards were already directly or indirectly part of CSCE standards. Thomas Buergenthal, a member of the U.S. delegation, recognized that a window of opportunity existed to reach agreement on substantially higher standards. He injected concepts of democracy, separation of powers, accountability of the military to civilian authorities, and the rule of law. In the space of four weeks of very long days, the Copenhagen meeting produced a document that catapulted human rights norms to a level unmatched in other international human rights instruments.

In this instance, the 'softness' of the Helsinki process was an asset, as was the tight, pre-set, four-week time frame for negotiations. The Copenhagen Document probably would never have seen the light of day if it had been vetted by lawyers from capitals. Many of the significant provisions of the Copenhagen Document would have been unacceptable to legal advisors as *treaty obligations* without clearer definitions of key terms or phrases and the elaboration of exceptions, limitations, and derogation provisions customary in human rights treaties. American legal advisors were dismayed, during the final days of negotiations, to find the word 'legislation' used in several paragraphs of the Copenhagen Document where the word 'law' would have been more in keeping with the meaning of the drafters. While this drafting oversight was not a deal breaker for a document that was merely politically binding, treaty drafting probably would have required ironing out kinks to reach agreement.

The translation of the document into all six official CSCE languages also might have proven a stumbling block if all six versions were to be equally authentic treaties. It had been the U.S. practice, prior to Copenhagen, to have the Russian text of all CSCE documents reviewed by an interpreter specializing in treaty affairs prior to giving consent to them. Time limitations made this impossible in Copenhagen. CSCE secretariat interpreters and Russian-speaking members of the U.S. delegation were left to guess at an appropriate translation of 'rule of law' into Russian, because the concept simply did not exist under Soviet or even Czarist law.

The four-week time frame for the Copenhagen meeting created a set of artificial constraints and, in theory, efforts to produce a comparable hard-law instrument might have succeeded given more time. As a practical matter, however, the political momentum that made the adoption of these standards possible in Copenhagen in 1990 diminished markedly and rapidly as the Soviet, Yugoslav, and Czechoslovak federations broke apart.

5. Enforcement of the Commitments

The HFA requirements to hold periodic implementation review meetings and to publicize the HFA had unanticipated but far-reaching effects in promoting compliance with the commitments. First, the HFA obligated the participating states to 'continue the multilateral process initiated by the Conference' by meeting again for 'thorough exchange of views both on the implementation of the provisions of the Final Act and of the tasks defined by the Conference'. Between 1975 and approximately 1990, the periodic follow-up and intersessional meetings evolved, over time, into a forum where Western governments could raise the cases of beleaguered human rights activists in Communist countries. Thus, the Helsinki Final Act set in motion a process devoted to the review of actual implementation of Helsinki agreements by the participating states.[12]

Secondly, the HFA required that the 'text of this Final Act will be published in each participating State, which will disseminate it and make it known as widely as possible'. The HFA was in fact widely distributed throughout Eastern Europe and the Soviet Union, in some instances even published on the front page of the Communist propaganda newspapers. The effect of this cynical gesture on the part of the Eastern regimes was dramatic and unexpected. Emerging human rights movements in these countries, including Charter 77 in Czechoslovakia, the Committee to Defend Workers in Poland (KOR, the predecessor to Solidarity), and the Moscow Helsinki Watch in the Soviet Union, seized the HFA as a manifesto for their campaigns and made specific and repeated reference to the Helsinki accords in appeals to their governments and to the international community.

The articulation of human rights and humanitarian norms in Helsinki-process documents legitimated the efforts of human rights groups in Communist countries by giving them a highly publicized yardstick by which to measure their governments' performance. The signing of the HFA and the emergence of these groups was coincidental, but of historic importance: but for the non-governmental interest in the Helsinki process, the CSCE might not have amounted to anything. The HFA included many of the same human rights norms by which most Warsaw Pact countries were already bound through acceptance of the International Covenant on Civil and Political Rights, but those documents had not been widely publicized in Eastern Europe. Much more importantly, the adoption of the Covenant preceded the emergence of grass roots movements to build civil society in the region. It should also be noted that the Eastern countries party to the Covenant did not

[12] Cf. Beth A. Simmons' observation, above, at p. 261: '[t]he key to FATF's success seems to flow not from the legal nature of the instrument spelling out standards for anti-money laundering efforts, but from the serious and sustained attention the organization gives to monitoring and assessment'.

accept the Optional Protocol providing for the right of individual petition until after 1990.

In practice, human rights monitors from Eastern countries and groups working on their behalf in the West, such as Helsinki Watch, played a critical role at implementation review meetings held between 1976 and 1990 by regularly providing highly specific and reliable documentation of human rights violations. Of equal importance, Western governments had the political will to raise the cases and situations brought to their attention by human rights monitoring groups. Accordingly, CSCE meetings became a bully pulpit where governments risked being shamed for behavior in violation of their CSCE obligations.[13]

For the most part, Western countries raised cases and situations that were symptomatic of the repressive Communist regimes in Europe: political prisoner cases, denial of religious liberties and freedom of association, repression of the rights of persons belonging to national minorities, restrictions on freedom of movement, denial of trade union freedoms. In doing so, these governments used information provided by non-governmental organizations. Widespread human rights problems in NATO allies like Turkey or neutral countries like Yugoslavia tended to be overlooked in this framework.

Much of the CSCE dialogue focused on the fate of individual political prisoners, the reunification of divided families, cases of individuals denied the right to leave their country, restrictions on religious liberties, and restrictions on minorities. The United States systematically raised such cases, presenting lists of political prisoners or divided families to Soviet and Romanian officials, in particular, with a view to securing their release or right to leave. A small number of other Western states followed suit, but less methodically than the United States. The perception that the Helsinki process was successful during this early period was enhanced by its ability to secure the freedom of real people, some of whom, like Lech Walesa and Vaclav Havel, later rose to power in post-Communist governments.

Initially, Eastern countries tended to respond to Western queries on human rights matters by claiming this was interference in their internal affairs. Over time, however, Warsaw Pact countries began to raise concerns about alleged human rights violations in Western countries, thereby legitimating the practice of raising human rights concerns in the context of the Helsinki process. Communist governments generally raised issues which they cast as violations of social and economic rights, *e.g.*, problems of homelessness or poverty. More rarely, they raised race-relation problems in the United States or the Northern Ireland conflict, but without much effect because they rarely offered concrete

---

[13] See Korey, *supra* note 1, for a detailed and comprehensive description of the way in which non-governmental organizations used the Helsinki process as a vehicle to press their causes.

or viable solutions to the real problems they raised.[14] In any case, such interventions became less frequent in the late 1980s as the economic bankruptcy of European Communism became increasingly apparent. In the end, only the Ceausescu regime was left as the champion of economic and social rights, even as Romanian economic devastation was increasingly grave and evident.

Human rights groups concerned with problems in Western countries rarely sought to use the CSCE as a forum, probably because they preferred the political and legal machinery available at the national level in Western countries and that available for member states of the European Convention on Fundamental Freedoms and Human Rights. In their view, perhaps, the 'legal consequences' that could be imposed by a national court or by the Council of Europe would be more significant than the 'political consequences' that could be imposed through the Helsinki process.

In general, countries did not raise human rights cases or situations casually, since any country which did so expended some political capital in the process. Moreover, countries raising human rights cases to try them before the court of public opinion bore the burden of persuasion in the process. Raising frivolous cases or specious arguments would undermine that goal.

While Communist countries ultimately reciprocated the Western practice of raising human rights concerns, they never ceased arguing that, at least in some instances, the Western practice constituted interference in their internal affairs.[15] Western countries, in turn, argued that by incorporating human rights norms into international instruments, the subject matter had been 'internationalized', and was no longer purely an internal affair. More to the point, implementation review in the Helsinki process was founded upon an agreement to discuss these issues.

Two CSCE decisions ended the tired Communist argument against raising human rights concerns. First, the 1989 Vienna Concluding Document established a so-called 'human dimension mechanism' that explicitly permitted states to raise such concerns on a bilateral or multilateral basis. Then, in the 1991 Moscow Document, the participating states 'categorically and irrevocably declare[d] that the commitments undertaken in the field of the human dimension of the CSCE are matters of direct and legitimate concern to all participating States and do not belong exclusively to the internal affairs of the State concerned'.[16]

---

[14] An exception was Soviet criticism of McCarthy-era visa restrictions; after hearings on the subject in 1986 by Congress' CSCE watch-dog commission, the act was repealed. See The 1952 McCarren-Walter Act (Hearing Before the Commission on Security and Cooperation in Europe) (Feb. 6, 1986) (examination of restrictive U.S. visa policies and legislation).

[15] Principle IV of the HFA requires 'non-*intervention* in the internal affairs' of other states. Designed as a rejoinder to the Brezhnev Doctrine—the *ex post facto* rationale offered by the Soviet Union and its allies to justify their 1968 invasion of Czechoslovakia—East bloc representatives sought to corrupt this into something more self-serving.

[16] Preamble, Document of the Moscow Meeting of the Conference on the Human Dimension.

Another important factor in 'enforcing' the commitments was linking human rights concerns to negotiations on the timing, location, and subject matter of future CSCE meetings. During the Vienna Follow-up Meeting (1986–9), for example, Czechoslovakia proposed holding a follow-up meeting on economic issues in Prague and invested considerable political capital in its effort to secure this goal. After the hard-line Czechoslovak regime broke up a non-governmental meeting in Prague, jailing its organizers including Vaclav Havel, Warren Zimmermann, the U.S. Ambassador to the Vienna meeting, stated:

[T]he pattern of repression in Czechoslovakia, together with the persistent efforts of the Czechoslovak delegation to secure approval for Prague as host for an economic follow-up, lead me to state for the record the U.S. position on the candidacy of Czechoslovakia . . . [A] prospective host should reflect the commitment to openness and access, for its visitors and for its own citizens, that has been so well exemplified by the government of Austria at the Vienna meeting. By this simple and reasonable standard, the government of Czechoslovakia fails—and fails abysmally. For that reason, the United States will not join any consensus to any proposal that any post-Vienna follow-up meeting be held in Czechoslovakia. That decision is irrevocable; it will not be subject to review or change during the life of the Vienna Follow-up Meeting.

Other countries in Vienna quickly associated themselves with this position.

Similarly, consensus on a controversial proposal to hold a human dimension meeting in Moscow was reached in 1989 only after human rights concessions were made by the Soviet Union, such as the release of more than 600 political prisoners, including all those sentenced under the political or religious clauses of the Russian Criminal Code.[17] The choice of Prague in 1990 as the location of one of the CSCE's new offices and the site for post-1990 economic meetings was a sign of approval for the democratic leadership of Vaclav Havel, although Liechtenstein delayed giving its consensus because of outstanding property claims against Czechoslovakia based on post-World War II confiscations.

6. Did the CSCE Make a Difference?

From 1975 to 1990, the CSCE meetings became a vehicle for 'public diplomacy', the use of diplomatic dialogue *in public* as a tool for managing Cold War tensions and raising and resolving human rights concerns. Any countries that used this forum to raise specious concerns not only depleted limited political capital, they failed to compete successfully in a marketplace of ideas. The willingness of Western countries to use the CSCE as a forum for raising and resolving human rights problems reflected genuine revulsion at the

---

[17] Preamble, Document of the Moscow Meeting of the Conference on the Human Dimension, at 251.

human rights repression of Communist regimes. It was equally, if not more, driven by the view of the Warsaw Pact as a threat to military security.

Between 1975 and 1990, any number of events could have undermined the credibility of the entire process: the 1979 Soviet invasion of Afghanistan; the 1981 imposition of martial law in Poland; the mass expulsion of ethnic Turks from Bulgaria in 1989. In the face of such persistent violations of the most basic provisions of the Helsinki accords, some argued that continued negotiations in the Helsinki process lent a veneer of legitimacy to repressive regimes and even created an incentive for such regimes to exploit political prisoners and divided families as political hostages. From this perspective, the West did not so much get Moscow to release political prisoners in exchange for agreeing to convene a meeting there in 1991, as Moscow was able to force the West to agreement by putting innocent people in prison. Criticism of the CSCE was sufficiently pronounced that, in 1985, the U.S. CSCE Commission held hearings on whether the United States should simply withdraw from the process.[18] In the end, however, public opinion turned in favor of the CSCE, as one Communist regime after another toppled in relatively bloodless and seemingly miraculous revolutions. Testimonials from political prisoners-turned-statesmen like Lech Walesa and Vaclav Havel bolstered this shining vision of the Helsinki process. In retrospect, the CSCE made *a* difference, but it is only one of many things that made a difference. It happened to be in the right place at the right time.

To be successful, the Helsinki process needed to coincide with three other elements. First, it needed the human rights groups, east and west, to serve as its engine. They were the ones who turned it into a catalyst for change and kept it from merely validating the status quo. They examined every agreement and compared it to the reality they saw; when reality was found wanting, they sought to change reality to make it more closely mirror the rights and freedoms pronounced in Helsinki agreements. Secondly, the Helsinki process required the political will of a community of states to articulate a common view of right and wrong, to interpret Helsinki agreements in a way that advanced human rights and deprived human rights violators of a cloak of legitimacy. U.S. leadership was necessary in this but not sufficient. Had the United States spoken alone, its voice probably would not have carried. The perception of the Warsaw Pact as inherently threatening fostered alliance solidarity among Western countries and contributed to their willingness to raise human rights issues. Thirdly, the Helsinki process required leaderships that were capable of being shamed.[19] The emergence of reformist leaders in

[18] Human Rights and the CSCE Process (Hearing Before the Commission on Security and Cooperation in Europe) (October 3, 1985).
[19] Mikhail Gorbachev, Wojciech Jaruzelski, and Imre Poszgay were capable of being shamed; Nicolae Ceausescu and Milos Jakes were not.

Central and Eastern Europe in the late 1980s made it possible for compliance with the Helsinki process to become a measure of their progress.

Clearly, timing has been a critical component of the Helsinki process' success. A similar process in the 1940s or 1950s or 1960s would not have coincided with the emergence of a grass roots, populist movement in Poland nor with a Gorbachev in the Soviet Union. The economic desperation of Communist regimes would not have been as pronounced, nor the widespread disaffection with the ideology they espoused. Together, the factors that contributed to the success of the CSCE shed light on why the OSCE functions so differently and help explain why the CSCE has not become a model that can be transferred intact to other regions.

B. THE OSCE

1. From a Process to an Organization

In November 1990, the CSCE heads of state or government held their first summit since the signing of the HFA in 1975. They met to acknowledge and acclaim the watershed events that set the stage for their gathering. The Summit also had a second, overarching purpose. CSCE leaders wanted to commend to Europe a new framework in which the long-term democratization of Eastern Europe would be assured, in which the emerging democracies' 'return to Europe' would take place, and in which North American–European political relations would be conducted for the foreseeable future. That framework would be a new, improved, and institutionalized CSCE. The choice of the CSCE for this role stemmed from the widely shared perception that the Helsinki process had played a pivotal role in bridging the East–West divide, a view bolstered by many of the national leaders who came to power as Communism fell. Thus, although the *Conference on* Security and Cooperation in Europe was not formally rechristened the *Organization for* Security and Cooperation in Europe until 1994, the transformation from a process to an institution began in 1990 with the signing of the Charter of Paris. Since then, the organizational framework of the Helsinki process has continued to evolve.

Since 1990, the OSCE has developed a regular schedule of meetings of participating states: weekly meetings of a Permanent Council; periodic meetings of a Senior Council; annual meetings of a Ministerial Council; and biannual summits of heads of state or government. These meetings are augmented by ceaseless military security negotiations; periodic specialized meetings relating to environmental and economic cooperation or the human dimension; and annual meetings to review the implementation of all OSCE commitments in all areas. With the establishment of a regular schedule of meetings, the opportunity to link human rights performance to proposals for future meetings has diminished, although it is not completely gone. A proposal by Turkey to host a summit meeting in Istanbul in 1999 met with resistance because of its widespread human rights problems.

The OSCE is also now supported by various permanent offices, notably a secretariat in Vienna headed by a Secretary General and an Office for Democratic Institutions and Human Rights (ODIHR) in Warsaw headed by a Director. The position of Chair-in-Office is held by a different OSCE participating state for a one-year period on a rotating basis.[20] These offices have come to provide support for the OSCE's numerous field missions.

2. The Fate of Implementation Review

In the past, participating states raised compliance with human rights norms in the Helsinki process because of the view that widespread and systematic violations of human rights in the Communist countries were manifestations of the very characteristics that made those countries military security threats. Accordingly, human rights cases were not necessarily raised because of a deep and altruistic commitment to human rights compliance *per se*, but because human rights violations were symptomatic of undemocratic regimes, and undemocratic regimes—especially Communist regimes with nuclear weapons— were dangerous threats to international security.

Today, the OSCE participating states that were traditional champions of human rights are relatively reluctant to raise cases and situations of non-compliance. Several factors have contributed to this. First, many human rights violations of the past, such as political imprisonment, have dramatically decreased and there are fewer complaints to be made. Secondly, human rights problems in the post-Cold War context may be harder to identify specifically as human rights problems as opposed to, for instance, intra- or inter-state political conflict. A marked degree of confusion has characterized governmental responses to many post-1990 human rights problems relating to claims of self-determination, minority rights, and citizenship in the context of state succession. In earlier years, many OSCE participating states strongly agreed on the key human rights norms and what constituted an actual human rights violation. Thus, there was wide agreement that Natan Sharansky, Lech Walesa, and Vaclav Havel were political prisoners.

Thirdly, there is a widespread perception among OSCE participating states that governments now generally possess the political will to comply with human rights obligations. Non-complying countries need technical expertise, time, patience, and support to make the transition to democracy. Many

---

[20] For a list of OSCE offices and institutions and the evolution of their nomenclature, see 'An Overview of the OSCE', in *The OSCE After the Lisbon Summit*, A Report Prepared by the Staff of the Commission on Security and Cooperation in Europe (August 1997) 35–39.

governments also appear reluctant to criticize countries where human rights problems defy an easy answer or immediate solution. Post-Communist countries, for instance, almost universally lack qualified judges which, in turn, has a negative impact on those countries' abilities to fulfill OSCE standards relating to the rule of law. The OSCE 'answer' to ameliorating this problem has been to support democracy training programs through the ODIHR.

Fourthly, many countries view the practice of criticizing other countries, even at closed-door OSCE meetings, as a vestige of the confrontational Cold War period. This view is especially widespread among European Union member states, a club with an ever increasing membership.[21] Finally, there appears to have been an unwritten assumption that with the advent of democracy, evidenced by free and fair elections, human rights problems automatically diminish. Those participating in the OSCE only now may be coming to grips with the idea that free and fair elections can install anti-democratic dictators in office.

In sum, while implementation review was the principal means through which the Helsinki process fostered human rights compliance during the period running from roughly 1975 to 1990, the political dynamic in the OSCE has changed in the post-Cold War period. There is vastly diminished willingness on the part of the participating states to utilize the OSCE as a forum to engage in public review of non-compliance.

3. Human Rights and Conflict Resolution

The signing of the 1990 Paris Charter was accompanied by euphoria, but the joy that greeted the end of the Cold War was short-lived. By the summer of 1991, the crisis in Yugoslavia had taken a violent turn and stories of atrocities began circulating throughout European capitals. The OSCE participants, for the most part, were ill-equipped to respond and, in classic understatement, the 1992 Helsinki Summit Declaration asserted that '[t]he CSCE has been instrumental in promoting changes; now it must adapt to the task of managing them'.[22]

The OSCE mission thereafter shifted from fostering human rights compliance, in order to lessen the military threats stemming from undemocratic regimes, to 'preventive diplomacy' aimed at preventing, managing, and resolving conflicts. Just as the perception of military security threats ultimately drew attention to human rights violations in the CSCE community, so conflict prevention draws attention to underlying human rights problems in the OSCE today.

---

[21] Significantly, the unwillingness of countries to raise human rights concerns on a state-to-state basis has been one of the most compelling arguments for the right to individual petition under treaty-based human rights systems.

[22] CSCE Helsinki Document 1992: The Challenges of Change (1992), para. 18.

The High Commissioner on National Minorities

The OSCE High Commissioner on National Minorities (HCNM) currently personifies the OSCE preoccupation with conflict prevention and resolution. The outbreak of hostilities in Yugoslavia provided the impetus for the creation of this post in 1992.[23] Designed to prevent future similar conflicts, it was one of the OSCE's first efforts to institutionalize conflict prevention. The HCNM is defined as an independent, unbiased individual of high stature whose mandate is to investigate problems relating to national minorities confidentially, before they reach crisis proportions. The title of the position, High Commission ON National Minorities, not FOR National Minorities, indicates that the HCNM is not an advocate for minorities, but a mediator tasked with finding common ground between differing ethnic groups, one of which usually controls the government, and facilitating a resolution of their differences. The mandate has three restrictions of note: (1) at the insistence of the United Kingdom and Turkey, the HCNM is barred from communicating with 'any individual or organization which practices or publicly condones terrorism or violence';[24] (2) engagement is restricted to issues that have not yet developed 'beyond an early warning stage',[25] precluding involvement in conflicts which have already degenerated into violence; (3) he is not to become engaged in minority or inter-ethnic disputes that do not have inter-state implications, but is limited to those that 'have the potential to develop into a conflict requiring the attention of the OSCE Council of Ministers or Permanent Council or which have the potential to affect peace and stability'.[26] Thus far, the only discernible value of these limitations is that it makes it easier for the HCNM to narrow down an otherwise potentially overwhelming list of places for engagement.

Since its creation, the post has been held by former Dutch foreign minister Max van der Stoel, who has engaged more than a dozen countries and has taken up a broad range of issues including citizenship; language laws, particularly minority-language use in government and education; censuses; political autonomy; voting and other privileges for non-citizens; and political autonomy. Estonia and Latvia were the first countries in which the HCNM was involved; they illustrate the way in which human rights norms can be applied through conflict prevention.

After Estonia and Latvia regained their independence from the Soviet Union, they re-established the citizenship laws that had been in effect at the time of the Soviet invasion and occupation in 1940. This decision deprived large numbers of Soviet-era immigrants of Estonian or Latvian citizenship

---

[23] The mandate for this office is in *ibid.*, Ch. II.
[24] *Ibid.*, Ch. II, para. 25. The restriction is clearly intended to preclude involvement in Northern Ireland or Kurdish issues.
[25] *Ibid.*, Ch. II, para. 3. [26] *Ibid.*, Ch. II, para. 3.

which prompted complaints from the Russian Government about violations of the rights of the predominantly Russian-speaking minorities. The HCNM was able to rebut Russian allegations of wide-spread violations of the immigrants' human rights while impressing on Tallinn and Riga the need to regularize the status of their legal non-citizen residents. The simultaneous actions by the HCNM contributed to a lessening of tension between Russia and the Baltic states and helped pave the way for the resolution of other bilateral problems. In addition, placing these two countries under a microscope may have prevented understandable anti-Soviet sentiments from degenerating into inter-ethnic violence or other human rights abuses.

The HCNM identified a number of areas where human rights issues were implicated in the Baltic states. He sought to ensure reasonable and well-published citizenship requirements for Soviet-era immigrants to Estonia and Latvia; elimination of force or pressure on non-citizens in Estonia and Latvia to be involuntarily made citizens; regularization of the status of non-citizen resident aliens; and the grant of 'resident alien' papers to non-citizens, papers that are recognized as valid travel documents by OSCE participating states, thereby facilitating the freedom of movement of the holders. Most recently, the HCNM has sought to ensure that the children of non-citizen resident aliens in Estonia who would otherwise be stateless are granted Estonian citizenship.

A number of factors probably have contributed to the success of the HCNM in the Baltic states, not the least of which is the skill with which Max van der Stoel has plied his craft. In addition, the strong desire of Estonia and Latvia to 'prove' themselves to the international community, in part out of fear that their newly regained independence might still be at risk, created an incentive for the governments to provide unprecedented access to the OSCE to examine a very broad range of issues. The participating states of the OSCE were also prepared to invest time and energy in monitoring the situation because of their concerns over regional stability in the Baltic region. To this end, the participating states were prepared to leverage political pressure to support the 'non-binding' recommendations of van der Stoel. Financial inducements, such as EU funding to provide language training for Russian speakers, has also helped back up the HCNM recommendations.

Mechanisms and Missions

Beginning in 1989, the OSCE participating states began crafting tools usually designated as 'mechanisms' specifically designed to facilitate the resolution of inter-state disputes; in some instances, these tools addressed human rights concerns; in other instances they were meant to address more generic inter-state differences.[27] The mechanisms generally establish rigid procedures and

---

[27] These tools include the 1989 Vienna Human Dimension Mechanism; the 1990 Unusual Military Activities Mechanism; the 1991 Emergency Meeting Mechanism; the 1991 Moscow

lack flexibility; they have rarely been used and often are dismissed as failures. They may nonetheless have fostered a willingness on the part of the participating states to adopt *ad hoc*, relatively innovative responses to crises with human dimension consequences. These are usually cast as 'missions'.

Although the OSCE's *ad hoc* missions do not fit neatly into an organizational chart or form a nice paradigm, they have played a significant role in conflict prevention and resolution. As it now stands, there are OSCE 'missions of long duration'[28] and an 'OSCE Presence' in Albania, an 'Assistance Group to Chechnya', a 'Minsk Conference' which deals with the Nagorno–Karabakh conflict, a 'Personal Representative' of the OSCE Chair-in-Office dealing with issues relating to Estonia, Latvia, and Russia, and an 'OSCE Advisory and Monitoring Group' in Belarus. Each of these entities has a tailor-made mandate and title designed to ensure that it can get into the country in question and address the underlying issues that have generated international concern. This kind of flexibility stands in sharp contrast to the one-legal-procedure-fits-all approach of the as yet unsuccessful PSD paradigm.

The consistent impetus for OSCE engagement has been a desire to prevent conflict from escalating or to engage in some form of collective 'concerted action', or conflict management or resolution. Human rights compliance has not been a primary motivation in these endeavors, but it has often been a fortuitous by-product. There is constant pressure to ensure that human rights concerns are not brushed aside in the name of other OSCE objectives, such as achieving a cessation of hostilities. The OSCE appears to be more transparent than the Council of Europe or United Nations; the access of non-governmental organizations to the OSCE makes them better able to hold the OSCE participating states accountable for their activities, including the reconciliation of various priorities.

The ODIHR

After 1990, participating states generally agreed that the days of standard setting in the OSCE had passed and that they should focus attention on achieving compliance with already agreed norms. To use the jargon preferred by many OSCE representatives, the human dimension should be 'operationalized'. The Office for Free Elections (OFE), established in 1990 by the Charter of Paris, would contribute to that goal. Renamed 'the Office for Democratic Institutions and Human Rights' (ODIHR) in 1992, its main activities include

---

Mechanism (human dimension); the 1991 Valletta Mechanism (peaceful settlements of disputes); the 1992 procedures for Directed Conciliation; the 1992 Convention on Arbitration and Conciliation. See 'An Overview of the OSCE,' *supra* note 20, at 35–9.

[28] Such missions exist in Croatia, Georgia, Estonia, Latvia, Macedonia, Moldova, Tajikistan, and Ukraine; the mission to Bosnia-Herzegovina is the OSCE's most well-known and largest scale mission to date.

hosting a biennial implementation review of human dimension commitments by the participating states; coordinating election monitoring; conducting rule of law training programs for constitutional court judges, law enforcement officials, or other legal professionals; convening human dimension seminars on subjects mandated by the participating states; and organizing round-tables or workshops on specific human dimension issues.

Thus far, the OSCE has assisted with more than forty elections in sixteen participating states. Intriguingly, the OSCE also may begin to observe elections in North African countries which are linked to the OSCE as 'Mediterranean partners for cooperation'. In addition to fielding observer or monitor teams on the day or days of the elections, OSCE presence often has extended over several months prior to the elections, during which time advice may be given regarding the general conduct of the campaign, conformity of media laws with OSCE commitments, adequacy or deficiency of the election law, procedures for registering voters, etc. Where there is already an OSCE mission in place, the ODIHR coordinates its efforts with the mission. In the case of Bosnia-Herzegovina, the OSCE not only monitored the elections, it actually supervised their administration.

OSCE election observation remains a work in progress and it has become more sophisticated and professional over time. It is one of the rare instances in the post-1990 process where the participating states have remained deeply engaged in seeking the full implementation of human rights norms, in this instance those from the 1990 Copenhagen Document on free and fair elections. As suggested earlier, this reflects a strong conviction that the promotion of democracy, evidenced by free and fair elections, ultimately advances other human rights.

It is difficult to gauge the success of the OSCE's election observation, although the presence of large numbers of monitors may have deterred some voter fraud that might have otherwise taken place. In some instances, the OSCE's election observation process has itself come under fire. In Bosnia-Herzegovina, for example, there was a perception in some quarters that the desire to certify that conditions were ready for elections in 1996 led the OSCE mission in Bosnia to down-play human rights problems.[29] Similarly, the initial statement of the OSCE's Special Representative after the March 1993 Armenian presidential elections appeared surprisingly mild, leading to speculation that the statement had been watered down out of fear for upsetting

---

[29] In this same vein, Judge Louise Arbour, Chief Prosecutor of the International Criminal Tribunal for the Former Yugoslavia, complained that the OSCE Mission to Bosnia-Herzegovina had, inadvertently or otherwise, telegraphed the idea that holding elections is more important than holding war criminals responsible when it announced that there would be no arrests of indicted criminals on the day of the elections. Statement of Judge Louise Arbour, made at a briefing organized by the International Helsinki Federation at the OSCE Implementation Meeting on Human Dimension Issues, Warsaw, Poland, November 19, 1997.

the delicate negotiations on the status of Nagorno-Karabakh.[30] These examples reflect on-going tension over the appropriate hierarchy of goals within the human dimension, as well as between the human dimension and other conflict-management goals.

In other respects, the mission of the ODIHR continues to evolve[31] and, behind the scenes, the participating states debate a number of questions related to the OSCE institutions. There are at least two schools of thought regarding how to enhance the OSCE's operational activity. One school sees the ODIHR itself as a human rights advocate and would give increasing responsibility to the ODIHR Director for reporting on emerging problems within the region; this reporting function, it is argued, would lead to greater attention on the part of the OSCE participating states and prompt governments to undertake desired reforms. Critics argue, however, that there is an inherent conflict of interest when governments delegate to international civil servants the task of criticizing the very countries which pay their salaries and approve their budgets.

The second school of thought emphasizes the ODIHR's potential in the field of democracy building and would have the ODIHR concentrate on those places where it receives some government cooperation. During 1996, for example, the ODIHR conducted training programs at the request of Belarus, Georgia, Russia, Tajikistan, and Turkmenistan. By building on a demonstrated interest, the OSCE can spend its limited resources where they are likely to be well received and effectively utilized.

The Pact on Stability in Europe

The Pact on Stability in Europe,[32] a political agreement adopted in Paris, March 20–21, 1995, designed a loose framework to pressure European Union aspirants with inter-state minority issues to resolve their differences as an implicit prerequisite to European Union membership. The OSCE was entrusted 'with following its implementation';[33] the decision to entrust the OSCE with this responsibility seems to stem from a belief that the OSCE not only generates political pressure, but can have a multiplier effect.

The 1996 Vienna Review Conference has been the sole meeting to date where OSCE participating states set aside time to review implementation of the Stability Pact. It is thus premature to draw conclusions regarding its effectiveness. Nevertheless, the existence of the Pact appears to have moved some countries to take some actions, in particular, to conclude bilateral agreements with the stated goal of complying with the Pact. Some of these treaties, e.g.,

---

[30] A final report of the ODIHR was more pointed in its conclusions and criticisms.
[31] See ODIHR Status Report, prepared by the ODIHR for the OSCE Human Dimension Implementation Meeting, November 1997.
[32] Also known as the Baladur plan, after its French architect.
[33] The Pact on Stability in Europe (March 21, 1995), para. 13.

the Treaty on Good Neighbourliness and Friendly Cooperation between the Slovak Republic and the Republic of Hungary, specifically incorporate OSCE norms, turning them into 'hard law'. The OSCE thus oversees the Stability Pact and a web of bilateral treaties and agreements, some of which incorporate agreed OSCE texts, the implementation of which the OSCE already is mandated to review.

Representative on Freedom of the Media

The success of the HCNM led the OSCE to establish, in November 1997, the post of Representative on Freedom of the Media (RFM). Although inspired by the work of the HCNM, the media representative is more of a human rights advocate than conflict mediator. The mandate specifically provides that the RFM 'will address serious problems caused by, *inter alia*, obstruction of media activities and unfavorable working conditions for journalists'.[34] It appears that there was implicit linkage during the negotiation of the mandate for the RFM to parallel negotiations for a mandate on OSCE Economic and Environmental Activities.

In the case of the HCNM, a mediator was believed necessary because inter-ethnic tension does not always involve human rights violations and the *absence* of international norms governing many of the issues addressed by the HCNM makes a mediator crucial. In contrast, the media issues of concern in the OSCE context generally involve violations of established norms. Accordingly, the RFM is not intended to 'mediate' with governments to secure the rights to free expression and free media, but to act as an advocate on behalf of those whose rights have been violated.

4. The Limits of the OSCE Approach

The recent overriding concern of the OSCE participating states with conflict prevention, management, and resolution generally has facilitated the partici-pating states' involvement with human rights issues and, ultimately, fostered human rights compliance: when the OSCE becomes engaged in conflict set-tings, usually in the form of the HCNM or some kind of mission, human rights issues become part of the dialogue with the host country. In some cases, such as the missions to Bosnia-Herzegovina and Albania, the OSCE has devoted considerable resources specifically to human dimension activities. While some critics have complained that these missions do not foster human rights compliance *enough*, there seems to be some agreement that the missions do foster human rights compliance.

From a human rights perspective, the obvious and serious deficiency in the OSCE's approach is that, absent a conflict or potential conflict that rises to

---

[34] Mandate of the OSCE Representative on Freedom of the Media (November 5, 1997), PC Journal No. 137, Decision No. 193, para. 2.

the level of mobilizing international attention, human rights problems are unlikely to make it onto the agenda. This problem is well illustrated by the different emphasis given to citizenship problems where, arguably, a double standard has emerged. In the Baltic states, OSCE actors (principally the HCNM) determined that Russian-speakers had no *right* to automatic citizenship; similarly, OSCE actors concluded that Crimean Tatars who had been deported from their homeland (now a part of Ukraine) during the Stalinist era and were therefore not on the territory of Ukraine at the time Ukraine became independent do not have an automatic *right* to return to Crimea and to obtain Ukrainian citizenship. At the same time, the OSCE has actively sought to ensure that Russian-speakers in Estonia and Latvia have, in practice, a fair and attainable *option* of citizenship, and the OSCE mission in Ukraine has actively sought to facilitate the acquisition of Ukrainian citizenship by deported Tatars. In both cases, the OSCE community was not motivated by a desire to protect a right to citizenship (in these cases, there was no right to citizenship), but to ameliorate tension and avoid inter-state conflict.

In the case of the Czech Republic, in contrast, the OSCE has been conspicuous by its absence. A number of people were left stateless under the citizenship regime adopted after the break-up of the Czechoslovak Federation; the Czech Government has admitted that there are at least 8,000 such people and non-governmental organizations believe the figure is much higher. All of the former Czechoslovaks left without Czech citizenship are Roma, the Czech Republic's largest minority. The law, both as drafted and as implemented, gives every indication that it was designed to exclude the members of this particular minority. Reporting by the Council of Europe, the UNHCR, and others has concluded that the Czech citizenship law violates international standards.[35] The problems identified by the Council of Europe and the UNHCR have remained unresolved and the OSCE participating states have been unwilling to engage in any systematic efforts to pressure the Czech Republic to bring its citizenship law and practices into line with international commitments. In short, while the Czech citizenship law is, in terms of compliance with international human rights norms, far more egregious than the Estonian, Latvian, or Ukrainian citizenship laws, the OSCE community has made no efforts on behalf of the Czech Romani minority. The denial of citizenship to Roma in the Czech Republic may be the largest single act of

---

[35] See Office of the United Nations High Commissioner for Refugees, Regional Bureau for Europe, Division of International Protection, The Czech and Slovak Citizenship Laws and the Problem of Statelessness, Document (February 1996) paras. 6, 15, 74, and 84 (made public in April 1996 and published along with the Position of the Czech Republic on the UNHCR Regional Bureau for Europe Document: The Czech and Slovak Citizenship Laws and the Problem of Statelessness); and Report of the Experts of the Council of Europe on the Citizenship Laws of the Czech Republic and Slovakia and Their Implementation and Replies of the Governments of the Czech Republic and Slovakia (April 2, 1996) paras. 54 and 116.

denaturalization since World War II, but unless and until it creates a danger of inter-state conflict, the OSCE participating states may remain unmoved.

CONCLUSION

The end of the Cold War sparked new hopes that the softness of the OSCE's human rights system might be replaced by an expanded Council of Europe that would deal with many of the same concerns embraced by the OSCE, but in a stronger, treaty-based framework. In fact, the difficulties faced by the Council in this endeavor illustrate some of the continued restraints on the development of and compliance with hard law. The rapid eastward expansion of the Council of Europe, although of debatable wisdom, was not difficult to achieve: between 1990 and 1996, the Council of Europe admitted sixteen post-Communist countries from Central and Eastern Europe. In April 1998, steps were also initiated in the Council of Europe Parliamentary Assembly to create an associated status for the Central Asian OSCE countries and the North African Mediterranean countries which are linked to the OSCE as 'Mediterranean partners for cooperation'. The Council's membership was made to match more closely that of the OSCE, thereby answering the criticism that the OSCE is 'better' than the Council of Europe because its membership is more inclusive. In connection with this, the Council of Europe also established a *political process* for monitoring basic commitments certain countries made at the time of admission to membership.[36]

At the same time, the Council of Europe sought to expand its activity respecting minority rights and inter-ethnic issues, issues of ever increasing concern. Just as the CSCE gave increasing attention to these subjects (most notably in the 1990 Copenhagen Document, the 1991 Report of the CSCE Meeting of Experts on National Minorities, Geneva, and the mandate for the High Commissioner on National Minorities, adopted in Helsinki in July 1992), the Council of Europe followed suit. On November 5, 1992, the Council of Europe opened for signature the European Charter for Regional or Minority Languages; on February 1, 1995, the Council of Europe's Framework Convention for the Protection of National Minorities also opened for signature.

The European Charter for Regional or Minority Languages codifies an obligation for member states to guarantee minorities specified rights regarding their mother tongue. The treaty advances somewhat the existing norms on minority language use. Of note, the treaty's commitments are presented as a 'menu' from which states parties must agree to adopt a minimum of thirty-

[36] Currently, Albania, Bulgaria, Croatia, Latvia, Macedonia, Moldova, Russia, Slovakia, Turkey and Ukraine are participants in this special monitoring process.

five; as a result, there is not necessarily a core of commitments equally bind-ing on all states parties. The enforcement mechanisms also are fairly soft: states parties undertake to make regular, public reports on their implementa-tion of the treaty, and these reports are reviewed by a committee of experts nominated by the states parties. No real remedies are specified for violations.

The very title of the Framework Convention suggests the hesitancy with which the Council's member states approach the task of codifying the rights of national minorities. In fact, it is debatable whether this treaty really advances minority rights norms. Many of the treaty's Articles begin with the conditioned formulations (*e.g.*, the Parties 'undertake to adopt, where neces-sary . . .' or 'shall endeavor to ensure') that are pervasive in OSCE texts. There are also relatively soft provisions for implementation: after an initial report by states parties to the Council's Committee of Ministers, the Committee of Ministers reviews compliance on an *ad hoc* basis and with the assistance of an advisory committee it will establish. Unlike the Council's landmark European Convention on Human Rights and Fundamental Freedoms, the more recent agreements do not provide a right to individual petition, do not provide a right for one state to sue another state for an alleged breach, and do not establish any adjudicatory processes with the authority to issue legally binding decisions. In sum, the recent initiatives of the Council of Europe look a lot more like soft law than hard law.

Would the CSCE/OSCE itself have been more successful if it had been grounded in a hard law framework? The answer is clearly no. First, not one but two hard law alternatives existed in parallel to the CSCE/OSCE. The United Nations included virtually all the participating states, but failed to win them as parties to human rights review mechanisms until after the Cold War ended; even now, some OSCE countries do not accept the Optional Protocol to the International Covenant on Civil and Political Rights. It is not at all clear that the kind of human rights machinery created at the United Nations would have ever acted as a catalyst for change the way the Helsinki process ultimately did. A hard law alternative to the CSCE also existed at the Council of Europe, but the Council of Europe's membership was restricted to European parliamentary democracies; by definition then, it excluded half of Europe and the countries which were most in need of human rights reform. Although, the Council of Europe has succeeded in expanding the community of nations that are party to the European Convention on Human Rights—the quintessential example of a hard law human rights treaty—efforts to expand the Council's norms regarding minority rights have produced relatively soft formulations. Finally, although repeated efforts have been made by some countries to place the CSCE/OSCE on a treaty-based footing, these efforts consistently have failed to gain the necessary consensus to be adopted. In short, the participating states did not see themselves faced with a choice between a soft-law system and a hard-law system, but between a soft-law pan-European system or no pan-European system at all. There is no evidence that this perception has changed with time.

International Labor Organization Recommendations and Similar Instruments

FRANCIS MAUPAIN

INTRODUCTION

This project closely relates to a recent reassessment of ILO standard-setting and means of action that has centered on the need to adjust ILO normative development to the realities and requirements of the global economy in the post Cold War period. The rise of the global market following the fall of the Berlin wall and the completion of the Uruguay Round of trade negotiations refocused attention on one purpose of ILO standard-setting action, in response to the risk of social 'free riders'. As the Preamble to the ILO Constitution states, the 'failure of any nation to adopt humane conditions of labour is an obstacle in the way of other nations which desire to improve the conditions in their own countries'. In the post Cold War context the lack of a worldwide, 'social level playing field' became evident. It also became clear that, notwithstanding its unique tripartite structure, ILO standard-setting was mainly, if not exclusively, addressed to states that in the face of globalization appeared to have a diminishing capacity and will to implement ILO standards efficiently. The re-evaluation was launched in 1994 on the occasion of the 75th anniversary of the organization and culminated at the June 1997 session of the International Labour Conference.

The challenge is to make ILO standards more effective and more relevant to the global economy. Achieving these objectives requires an increase in universal compliance with fundamental standards and the exercise of greater selectivity in the production of new standards. Increased selectivity has been advocated in choosing subjects for the International Labour Conference (ILC) agenda, picking only those that represent a real 'added normative value' to the existing corpus of standards. In addition, a pressing plea has been made for greater use of non-binding instruments, in view of the declining rate of ratification of recently adopted conventions.[1]

---

[1] This decline probably has a number of explanations. It appears from a recent questionnaire to member states that they may be increasingly reluctant to assume new long-term commitments

In his 1994 report on the occasion of the 75th anniversary of the ILO, the Director-General suggested that greater use be made of soft law instruments such as codes of conduct.[2] This suggestion was strongly resisted by the workers' representatives in the ILO, who feared that such a shift might weaken ILO action. They referred to the Tripartite Declaration of Principles concerning Multinational Enterprises and Social Policy, which scholars[3] consider a unique soft law instrument whose substance they support, but whose practical impact they found disappointing due to the absence of an effective monitoring system.

The Director-General's 1997 report to the ILC concentrated on recommendations, directly challenging the argument consistently made by workers in favor of conventions. According to this argument, the higher prestige attached to international labor conventions means that they exercise a greater influence even when they are not ratified. Mr Hansenne suggested that the argument was circular since recommendations could, under the ILO Constitution, have exactly the same impact as a non-ratified convention on states not party to the convention.

This position, although correct, is itself a bit circular since unratified conventions, while they have no more influence than recommendations, have at least the potential to create obligations, however few. In fact, the dilemma is between the marginal advantage that may be gained from sparse ratification and the damage caused to the credibility of the corpus of conventions through a poor ratification record. For the purpose of the present study, however, the Director-General's report made an important point in drawing attention to the fact that although ILO recommendations cannot create international legal obligations, they have some significant features in common with International Labor Conventions.

First, recommendations are drawn up through the same lengthy and careful procedure as conventions. Once a subject has been placed on the agenda of the Conference, its preparation follows the same process of consultations with the entire membership of the organization. Both conventions and

in the social field because of the increased competition resulting from globalization. A second reason is what has been called, in particular by Virginia Leary, 'administrative congestion': governments find it increasingly difficult to 'digest' the various international instruments and reporting obligations attached to them. Finally, the impact of emergent federalism should not be underestimated. The European Union now regroups the ILO member states that had the best ratification record. The E.U. claims that whenever it has exclusive or shared competence over the matters covered by an ILO Convention, its member states are no longer free to ratify it at their discretion.

[2] *Defending Values, Promoting Change*, Report of the Director-General, International Labour Conference, 81st Session (1994). Codes of conduct or codes of practice are designed to give guidance on specific follow-up to member states, employers, and workers in a technical field. They are prepared by experts and approved or endorsed by the Governing Body.

[3] Leary, V., 'Non-binding Accords in the Field of Labor', in Brown Weiss, E. (ed.), *International Compliance with Non-binding Accords* (1997) 250–6.

recommendations are discussed in the tripartite (governments, employers, workers) forum of the ILC, normally at two successive sessions. The organ competent to adopt the instruments (the ILC) and the majority required for their adoption (two-thirds) are also the same. It thus may be said that international labor conventions and recommendations enjoy an equivalent status from the point of view of 'legitimacy' or 'representativity' mirroring the will of the international community.

Secondly, and more importantly, international labor recommendations are subject to the same follow-up requirements as conventions, apart from those designed to monitor the application of ratified conventions. The follow-up mechanism is twofold. First, under Article 19.6 (a), (b), and (c) of the ILO Constitution, a recommendation must be submitted to the competent authority in each member state 'for the enactment of legislation or other action'. In principle this should occur within one year after the adoption of the recommendation. ILO members have to report to the Director-General on the measures taken to submit the recommendation and on the action taken by the competent authority. Secondly, the Governing Body of the ILO, at later appropriate intervals, may require reports on the law and practice of the country in regard to the matters dealt with in the recommendation. The Constitution specifies that the reports are to show the extent to which effect has been given or is proposed to be given to the provisions of the recommendation, and any modifications of these provisions as it has been found or may be found necessary to make in adopting or applying them. Similar reporting requirements are laid down in Article 19.5(e) of the Constitution in respect of conventions which have not been ratified.

There is one difference between the two situations: a member state that has not ratified a convention is required to explain the way in which effect may be given to it by 'legislation, administrative action, collective agreement or otherwise, and stating the difficulties which prevent or delay ratification of such Convention'. In contrast, member states need not specify the mechanism by which it is proposed to give effect to the provisions of a recommendation, but must specify 'such modifications of these provisions as it has been found or may be found necessary to make in adopting or applying them'.

These unusual constitutional features were introduced in the 1946 amendments to the ILO Constitution in order to establish international labor recommendations as fully-fledged instruments of ILO action and no longer as conventions' 'country cousins', in the words of C. Wilfred Jenks. As such, international labor recommendations are an atypical variety of soft law, differing radically from other types of decisions by the ILC, such as resolutions which have no specific legal basis in the Constitution and do not constitute 'international labor standards'.[4]

---

[4] Such resolutions also may constitute 'soft law' to the extent that they establish their own follow-up mechanism. The most significant illustration is the ILO resolution on the situation of

To the extent that the follow-up process is also an assessment process, these atypical features at the same time seem to make them an ideal candidate for evaluating compliance with non-binding instruments. In practice, however, and despite repeated appeals from successive Directors-General, the ILO, until 1998,[5] had not adopted any autonomous or self-contained recommendations. Recommendations instead have been limited to supplementing conventions by addressing a number of details thought to be inappropriate in a binding instrument. This practical obstacle can easily be overcome, however, since unratified conventions can be considered 'proxies' for autonomous recommendations. As previously mentioned, the assessment of the 'steps taken' by members to give effect to the provisions of the instrument is exactly the same with respect to recommendations and unratified conventions. Thus, when the Governing Body of the ILO decides to request a report from member states on an unratified convention and its related recommendation, it is possible to measure the impact of the provisions of the instruments as non-binding instruments whether they are conventions or recommendations.

These observations open the way to examining the extent to which this follow-up mechanism provides a real insight into the degree of compliance with non-binding instruments. The assessment will begin with a review of compliance with a few selected instruments. It will then examine the limits on the information about compliance provided through the ILO machinery, review recent proposals for the development of new instruments designed to promote compliance with fundamental workers' rights within the ILO, and, finally, assess the perspectives for promoting compliance with ILO instruments through mechanisms other than those afforded by the ILO Constitution.

A. CONSTITUTIONAL PROCEDURES TO ASSESS COMPLIANCE WITH SELECTED ILO INSTRUMENTS

The present study is based on a selection of recommendations that entail varying degrees of difficulty in implementation. It draws upon general surveys of reports requested from member states under Article 19 of the ILO Constitution. The ILO Governing Body may decide to require reports under Article 19, paragraphs 5(e) and 6(d) on one or more selected conventions and recommendations. A questionnaire is then sent to member states and the

workers in Israeli-occupied territories (ILC, 82nd session, 1995) on the basis of which the Director-General submits a yearly report to the ILC.

[5] At the 1998 ILC session, an autonomous recommendation was adopted concerning general conditions to stimulate job creation in small and medium-sized enterprises. It is the first instrument on this topic and was overwhelmingly adopted by the ILC with 403 votes in favor, 0 against and 4 abstentions.

resulting reports are analyzed by the Committee of Experts on the Application of Conventions and Recommendations, an independent twenty-member expert panel, with the assistance of the ILO secretariat. Each year, the Committee of Experts' general survey is examined by the Committee on the Application of Conventions and Recommendations of the International Labor Conference. The instruments that have been the subject of Article 19 surveys are almost as many and diverse as the number of existing instruments. A few seem to have specific significance, however, or raise special difficulties linked to the present subject and thus deserve particular attention.

The first example raises a fundamental concern of great contemporary significance, child labor. The second, the Termination of Employment Convention, 1982 (No. 158), relates to a topic which in some way is ideologically at cross-currents with recent deregulation in the labor market. The third subject is a fundamental issue of national social policy, protection of women workers' rights during pregnancy and child birth (maternity protection). The fourth considers instruments dealing with one aspect of occupational safety and health, namely the protection of workers' health. Finally, it is also interesting to touch briefly on instruments that attempt to put into normative terms a subject that is fundamentally a matter of economic policy: the Employment Policy Convention (No. 122) and Recommendation (No. 122), 1964 and the Employment Policy (Supplementary Provisions) Recommendation, 1984 (No. 169).

1. Child labor

The 'protection of children' is specifically mentioned in the Preamble to the ILO Constitution as one of the concerns of the Organization, but until 1999, only the minimum working age had been addressed by international labor standards. It was the subject of no fewer than ten instruments before being consolidated into the Minimum Age Convention, 1973 (No. 138), supplemented by Recommendation No. 146. These two instruments were the subject of a general survey in 1981.[6] The number of replies received from member states was 107 out of a total membership that then stood at 144. After the recent decision of the Governing Body to place the subject of child labor on the 1998 and 1999 agendas of the Conference for the adoption of new instruments to address the worst forms of child labor, the Office produced a law-and-practice report providing additional evidence on compliance with the minimum age instruments.[7] These two different types of reports allow comparison, at a fifteen-year interval, of the trend in compliance and the tools for evaluating it.

[6] ILC, 67th Session, General Survey by the Committee of Experts on the Application of Conventions and Recommendations, Minimum Age, Report 67 III (Part 4B).

[7] Child Labor, Targeting the Intolerable, ILC, 86th Session (1998) Report VI (1).

The 1981 survey on minimum age was based on 100 reports that often gave an imperfect view of the situation. The Committee of Experts noted the gap between legal provisions generally forbidding child labor and actual practices, to some extent reflected in official statistics which showed the existence of child labor, especially in agriculture. When child labor was recognized, it was attributed to poverty and lack of educational infrastructure. The survey referred to data showing that almost all children had entered the labor market in certain regions and that children represented a significant proportion of the labor force in some countries. It underlined the contrast between the very broad recognition of the objectives of Convention No. 138, which are often reflected in national legislation, and the lack of effective measures, including labor inspection, to enforce them. The survey did not go into detail regarding the obstacles to ratification of the Convention. This cursory treatment of what should normally be the main issue of the survey is not surprising in light of the general conclusion regarding the discrepancy between law and practice. Nevertheless, the Committee of Experts insisted that the adoption of standards could prove to be a powerful stimulus to better compliance and thus pleaded for ratification without waiting for resolution of the compliance problems.

The 1996 report on child labor supplemented and strengthened these conclusions, in particular the contrast between the formal acceptance of the standards and their practical enforcement. It thus noted that 'most of the countries surveyed conform to the spirit of Convention 138'. Thus, while only forty-nine countries had by then ratified Convention No. 138, at least 122 countries had legislation prohibiting work by children below the age of 14, and in most cases had corresponding legislation concerning compulsory education. The report stated, however, that the weakness of enforcement mechanisms was a major obstacle to making this protection effective, especially in the informal sector, away from major cities, in agriculture, and in small businesses. The situation was made all the more difficult by the chronic inadequacies of labor inspection, which has to perform many other functions, all with very limited, if not declining, resources and insufficient practical and legal means of action, including lack of adequate penalties. Finally the report noted that the laws relevant to child labor are not well known to employers, parents, and even labor inspectors themselves. For this reason the new instruments which were adopted unanimously by the ILC at its 87th session (1999) require members to make the most intolerable forms of child labor subject to penal sanctions.

2. Termination of Employment

This topic was the subject of one of the most recent self-contained ILO Recommendations, the Termination of Employment, Recommendation,

1963 (No. 119) on which a general survey was conducted in 1974[8] and that later led to the adoption of the Termination of Employment Convention, 1982 (No. 158) supplemented by the Termination of Employment Recommendation, 1982 (No. 166). These two more recent instruments were in turn the subject of a general survey in 1995.[9]

The purpose of Recommendation No. 119 is mainly to state the principle that an employer should not terminate workers' employment unless there is a valid reason for such termination connected with the capacity or conduct of the worker or the operational requirements of the undertaking. This objective, which seeks to balance the interest in job security with that of the efficient operation of the undertaking, is to be achieved through the recognition of the right of appeal to a neutral body empowered to examine the reasons for termination and to make a decision on the validity of the dismissal. In the survey of Recommendation No. 119 conducted in 1973, one hundred ILO members replied, out of the then total membership of 123, one of the highest reply rates. According to the survey, 'new or revised legislation' or generally applicable collective agreements[10] in over twenty countries provided improved protection against unjustified termination of employment; some of these countries had taken similar measures in respect of other safeguards provided for in the Recommendation. The survey also noted that in a number of these cases the Recommendation had provided some guidance or support in the formulation of national provisions. A further comment suggests that survey itself 'may in fact have served as an occasion for some countries to review their law and practice in this field with a view to the possible adoption of new legislation'.

Even though a rather low 20 percent of countries reported that the Recommendation had made an impact, the trend was sufficiently encouraging to justify launching the procedure for adoption of a binding instrument. This eventually took the form in 1982 of a Convention (No. 158) supplemented by a new Recommendation (No. 166) which revised and replaced the earlier one. Ten years after the Convention's entry into force in 1985, the new instruments were the subject of the abovementioned general survey in 1995, at which time the Convention had been ratified by twenty-five member states. From a total membership that then stood at 171, two hundred and two reports were received from one hundred and seven member states. It is interesting to note that the Committee of Experts expressed misgivings about the limits of the survey as a vehicle for evaluation, in particular because only a

---

[8] General Survey of the Reports Relating to the Termination of Employment, Recommendation (No. 119), 1963, ILC, 59th session (1974), Report III (Part 4 B).

[9] Protection Against Unjustified Dismissal, ILC, 82nd session (1995), Report III (Part 4 B).

[10] This refers to the practice in a number of countries whereby a negotiated collective agreement may be extended by legislation or administrative action to apply to an entire sector.

limited number of governments had provided full information on difficulties of application and their intention as regards ratification.[11]

It is striking that the number of countries that have ratified this Convention (twenty-five) is scarcely higher than the number of states that responded to the 1973 survey by indicating that they followed the prior Recommendation (twenty). Soon after the Convention was adopted, it encountered a cross current of deregulation or more flexible regulation in a number of countries. The replies received, however, did not shed any light on possible 'ideological' bias towards the instrument. In fact, the replies were not sufficiently explicit to give any indication of the reasons why there might or might not be compliance with its provisions. The Committee of Experts stated that 'in most of the cases examined, the ratification of the Convention would not appear to be a social objective which is impossible to achieve'. In the absence of better explanations, it speculated that the lack of ratification could be more the result of specific circumstances than 'opposition in principle to the minimal protection afforded by the Convention'. In an effort to promote ratification, it praised the great flexibility of the Convention as regards methods of implementation to preclude possible arguments that it would increase rigidities in the labor market.

In this particular case, at least, it seems that a comparison between compliance with the recent binding instrument and the impact of the non-binding recommendation that preceded it is not necessarily to the advantage of the convention. This may be merely due, however, to a change in the general economic and ideological context surrounding the subject of termination of employment.

3. Maternity Protection

From its first session in 1919, the International Labor Conference began adopting standards that subsequently exercised great influence on national constitutions and the legislation of many countries.[12] Maternity protection is one such area.[13] The Maternity Protection Convention, 1919 (No. 3), however, has been ratified by only thirty-three countries in the eighty years since it was adopted. Convention No. 3 was revised fifty-three years later with the adoption of the Maternity Protection Convention (Revised), 1952 (No. 103) which itself has been ratified by only twenty-six countries, an even smaller number than Convention No. 3. Convention No. 103 was supplemented by a

[11] Protection Against Unjustified Dismissal, op. cit., note 9, at 5.
[12] Maternity protection at work, ILC, 87th session (1999), Report V(1). Maternity and Work, (1994) 4 Conditions of Work Digest.
[13] The term 'maternity protection' refers to a set of measures to ensure that a woman worker who becomes pregnant and/or gives birth will be entitled to a period of leave during which she retains her employment and receives some income replacement. Lim, L., *Better Jobs for Women* (1996), 180–1.

Recommendation, the Maternity Protection Recommendation, 1952 (No. 95). That Recommendation encourages members, *inter alia*, to provide maternity leave for a period of fourteen weeks, while both Conventions Nos. 3 and 103 provide for a minimum period of twelve weeks.

The application of the instruments concerning maternity protection was the subject of a general survey in 1965.[14] The Committee of Experts found that the entitlement to maternity leave was recognized by law or by non-statutory practice in almost all the countries examined, and that in eighty-nine of those countries, normal leave equaled or exceeded the standard twelve weeks set by the two conventions. The conclusion of the Committee was that in many cases national legislation contained standards equal to or even higher than the international standards.

While the two instruments in question have not been widely ratified when measured against the total ILO membership of 174 states, the law and practice of member states present a strikingly different picture of the actual impact of the norms. A recent review, prepared for the ILC (87th Session, 1999) discussion on the question of revising Convention No. 103, revealed, for instance, that only thirty-one of the 152 countries whose legislation has been reviewed by the International Labor Office provide for a period of less than twelve weeks of maternity leave.[15] In more than half the countries (119) the entitlement period is greater than this period and in sixty-two countries (41 percent) it is at least fourteen weeks as provided for in the Recommendation.[16]

Many governments that had not ratified the Conventions indicated that their legislation nonetheless was inspired by the international standards or had been amended in several respects to take account at least partly of those standards. This seems to confirm that international standards have a practical impact on maternity protection legislation in individual countries, due to the fundamental human and social importance of the question.

4. Protection of Workers' Health

This subject, like termination of employment, saw earlier recommendations followed some years later by conventions. The Protection of Workers' Health Recommendation, 1953 (No. 97) lays down general principles applicable to the prevention of all risks of diseases recognized as being occupational or which could be recognized as such and in more general terms applies to hygiene and the workplace environment. The principles cover technical mea-

[14] Summary of Reports on Unratified Conventions and on Recommendations, Maternity Protection, ILC, 49th Session (1965), Report III (Part II).

[15] Maternity Protection at Work: Revision of the Maternity Protection Convention (No. 3) (revised), 1952, and Recommendation No. 95, 1952, ILO, Report V (1), (1997) 35.

[16] Maternity Protection at Work, Report V(1) ILC, 87th session (1999) 37.

sures for protection and the medical examination of workers exposed to special risks, the notification of occupational diseases, and first aid. The Occupational Health Services Recommendation, 1959 (No. 112), is the result of studies made in close collaboration with the WHO on the basis of Recommendation No. 97. As a result, it was possible to include in Recommendation No. 112 detailed provisions on the status and functions of occupational health services.

A general survey was made of these instruments in 1970;[17] eighty-five reports were received from a total membership of 121 at the time. The Committee of Experts' survey noted that a real impact of the two instruments can be seen on the basis of the many improvements introduced or under consideration in the law and practice of member states.[18] The survey noted in particular that occupational health services had been set up in a large number of countries by one or another of the means advocated in Recommendation No. 112, expressing the view that it was in this field that the most remarkable progress had been achieved or was anticipated. The survey referred to the obstacles of lack of appropriate resources and the shortage of doctors and nurses which made it difficult to organize occupational health services, but recognized that numerous changes had been made in national laws and regulations concerning protection measures, particularly since the adoption of Recommendation No. 97. It gave several concrete examples, mainly from Europe, including the adoption by the Commission of the European Communities of a recommendation allegedly inspired by Recommendation No. 97 concerning the survey of workers exposed to particular risk.

The subjects dealt with in these instruments returned in the early 1980s, first in the Occupational Safety and Health Convention, 1981 (No. 155) and Recommendation, 1981 (No. 164), and later in the Occupational Health Services Convention, 1985 (No. 161), and Recommendation, 1985 (No. 171). The report initiating the process leading to these instruments referred to Recommendations Nos. 97 and 112, stating that 'the adoption by the Conference of one or more instruments of a global nature covering occupational safety and health would now form the cornerstone on which the ILO and member States could found their efforts in the years to come'.[19]

The 1981 instruments set forth the principles of national policy to be implemented in the field of occupational safety and health and detailed the action to be taken at the national level. They did not revise or replace Recommendation No. 97. The 1985 instruments on occupational health services, in

---

[17] General survey on the reports concerning four recommendations (Nos. 97, 102, 112, 115) dealing with health, welfare, housing of workers; Report of the Committee of Experts, 54th Session (1970) 229.

[18] Report of the Committee of Experts, ILC, 54th Session (1970) 229.

[19] Safety and Health and the Working Environment (1980), ILC, 66th Session (1980), Report VII(a)(1), 43.

contrast, did build on and consequently replace Recommendation No. 112, whose impact is recognized in the first preparatory report for the new instruments in the following terms: '[t]his Recommendation has served as a guide for the legislation on this subject which has since been adopted by a number of countries and has thus contributed to the extension of occupational health services in all branches of economic activity, not only in the industrialized countries, but also in the developing countries'.[20] Up to now, Convention No. 155 has been ratified by twenty-eight member states, and Convention No. 161 by 17.

5. Employment Policy

The Employment Policy Convention (No. 122) and its supplementary Recommendation (No. 122) were adopted in 1964. They call upon member states 'to declare and pursue as a major goal an active policy designed to promote full, productive and freely chosen employment' (Article 1, paragraph 1) but do not provide any indication about the form or content of such a policy. The Convention simply requires that employment policy shall be implemented within the framework of a coordinated economic and social policy and 'take due account of the stage and level of economic development and the mutual relationships between employment objectives and other economic and social objectives' (Article 1, paragraph 3).

A general survey of the instruments was made in 1971.[21] Forty-five states had already ratified the Convention, but a relatively low number of replies were received (eighty-five out of a total membership of 121). Few of the replies referred to problems arising out of the terms of the Convention. The Committee of Experts explained that there was indeed 'wide acceptance of the principle that an active employment policy as stated in the instruments should be a major goal'. Only one state complained that compliance with the Convention was difficult because it did not give any guidance on the contents of the active policy advocated. The Committee of Experts noted that the two instruments were among 'the most comprehensive and ambitious ever framed by the ILO',[22] and that the Recommendation sets out in some detail the fields in which measures may need to be taken and the types of measures which may be taken. The Committee reiterated that the flexibility of the Convention should make ratification possible for a far greater number of countries. It noted in this regard that the ratification process was well advanced or was being examined in some twenty countries and that eight other countries were committed to pursuing an employment policy. The experts thus predicted

---

[20] Occupational Health Services, ILC, 70th Session (1985), Report V (1), 47.

[21] General Survey on the Reports Relating to the Employment Policy Convention and Recommendation, ILC, 57th Session (1972), Report III (Part 4B), 101.

[22] *Ibid.*, at 108.

that 'half the member States of the ILO will have accepted formal obligations under the Constitution within the foreseeable future'.[23]

This forecast proved to be surprisingly accurate, as eighty-seven countries have now ratified the Convention. On the other hand, this result does not seem to have contributed much to the eradication of unemployment, even after the adoption of the Employment Policy (Supplementary Provisions) Recommendation, 1984 (No. 169), which was designed to respond to new problems and challenges resulting from changes in the world order. Comparing the employment records of countries which have ratified to those of countries which have not could be a somewhat discomforting experience. The success of this instrument in terms of 'compliance' indeed may provide an illustration of the distinction between effectiveness and compliance: the very flexibility of the Convention makes ratification and/or compliance fairly easy to achieve, but high compliance does not necessarily help achieve the underlying objective. Hansenne's emphasis on the need to assess the 'added normative value' of any new instrument whose adoption is contemplated must be understood in this light.

B. EVALUATION OF PRESENT ASSESSMENT PRACTICES

The preceding overview of some surveys made under Article 19 of the ILO Constitution appears sufficient to conclude with some degree of certainty that ILO recommendations, like unratified conventions, can exercise a real influence on national law and practice, with the degree of influence varying widely depending upon the subject matter. What is much more difficult to assess, however, is the existence and extent of compliance in the strict sense of the word. Two obvious shortcomings may be identified in this respect: the first relates to methodology and the second to resource constraints.

As regards methodology, the analysis conducted in the framework of Article 19 surveys is very formal, and it mostly reflects the answers provided by governments, even though employers' and workers' organizations are called upon to provide comments. There is no critical assessment of the real influence of the instrument or, in particular, of causality. It is rarely clear from the surveys whether or not national law and practice that substantially conform to the instrument under consideration were changed *as a result* of the existence of the instruments. The surveys are often evasive about whether conformity pre-existed the instrument itself or had any connection with it. In fact, the influence sometimes moves the other way, from the national to international level, with international labor standards greatly influenced by existing national legislation. Countries which have legislation on a subject try to

[23] *Ibid.*, at 107.

project that legislation during the ILO double-discussion process, as this is easier than trying to find universal solutions. This phenomenon is particularly visible with respect to European Union legislation. Whenever European legislation exists on a particular subject in the form of a regulation or directive, the Commission and, in certain cases, the International Labor Office itself has tended to project this regional 'legislation' onto ILO standards.[24] In such cases, the conformity of E.U. members' legislation with ILO standards is hardly causally linked.

Another methodological limitation relates to the lack of specificity about the reasons for compliance. The surveys contain some routine explanations for non-compliance such as economic difficulties, lack of administrative means, the importance of the informal sector, and so on, but do not give any insight as to the motivation for compliance. It is only indirectly that some reasons may be very tentatively deduced from these surveys as discussed hereafter.

Convenience. ILO instruments, whether conventions or recommendations, go through a long process of international and tripartite (governments, employers, and workers) negotiation. The norms thus constitute a fairly reliable model of reference, because they represent the common wisdom of governments, employers, and workers on the subject. When considering the introduction of new legislation, member states can save time and other resources by conveniently referring to ILO conventions and recommendations. This is well illustrated by instruments in the field of safety and health, which provide a convenient framework of reference for countries seeking to improve their occupational safety and health policy. As stated by the Committee of Experts in a formula which somewhat confirms the uncertainties surrounding the issue of causality:

> whatever may be the interaction between national law and practice on the one hand and international standards on the other, it cannot be denied that Recommendation No. 112, which is reflected in the work of several regional organizations, has crystallized an approach which may be said by and large to result in consolidation in countries where occupational health services were already in existence, the extension of services or plans for their introduction in other countries, *even including developing countries*, and the tendency to institute legislation in place of systems based on agreements or voluntary participation, although this trend is still uncertain.[25]

The same 'convenience' element is present in a different form through ILO technical assistance that helps member states draft labor legislation, an exercise that obviously takes into account relevant international labor instruments.

---

[24] For the reasons referred to *supra* in note 1, it is all the more paradoxical that it contributes to non-ratification of ILO Conventions by E.U. members.

[25] Report of the Committee of Experts, 54th Session (1970), 299, emphasis added.

A sense of moral duty. This factor may particularly apply to instruments that embody little more than a rule of due process, such as the termination of employment instruments. The right of a worker to know why his or her contract of employment has been terminated can be seen as a rather basic requirement of natural justice, but compliance may become difficult where the instruments require a valid motivation and call for the establishment of procedures and bodies to review the validity of this motivation. At this point, the requirement of natural justice may be considered by some as conflicting with the need for flexibility.

The same sense of moral duty or comfort certainly applies to instruments relating to child labor. The great majority of ILO members recognize the validity and desirability of the ILO standards and generally reflect them in their legislation. Lack of compliance is attributed mainly to economic and administrative limitations. The moral dimension, strongly promoted by NGO action and pressure, was confirmed by the Governing Body's unanimous decision in 1998 and the ILC's in 1999 to add more standards to the existing panoply in order to eliminate the worst forms of child labor and subject them to penal sanctions.

Internal and external influences or pressures. Employers' and workers' organizations exercise some influence on the compliance process through the functions endowed upon them by the Tripartite Consultation (International Labor Standards) Convention, 1976 (No. 144). The ILO itself may promote greater compliance through its multidisciplinary field teams, which aim to bring technical advice closer to the constituents of the organization.[26] Counterbalance comes from other external influences such as the international financial institutions which, in some cases at least, have pressed for greater legislative flexibility within the framework of structural adjustment policies. The extent of the NGO influence, particularly active in relation to child labor, is largely a matter of speculation at present.

Finally, it must be underlined that the lack of specificity in ILO general surveys regarding causality and the explanations for compliance does not seem to be inevitable or inherent in this procedure. As noted by the Committee of Experts itself in the general survey on the Termination of Employment Convention, 1982 (No. 158),[27] the lacunae may be due to the way in which the questionnaires to member states are drafted. They usually do not evoke replies that would enable the Committee to carry out a real evaluation. The Committee itself has expressed the hope that 'the report form concerning Article 19 of the Constitution will contain questions, the replies to which would enable the Committee to develop general surveys into the "ideal

[26] An upcoming evaluation of this 'active partnership policy' to be undertaken soon may shed some more light on the extent of such influences.
[27] Protection Against Unjustified Dismissal, Report of the Committee of Experts, ILC, 82nd Session (1995), Report II.

vehicle for evaluation" that they should be, as suggested by the ILO Director-General in his [1994] Report to the ILC'.[28] The same plea was repeated in stronger terms in the Director-General's 1997 ILC report when he pointed out that most surveys, by concentrating on a comparative analysis instead of assessing the practical difficulties and the real impact of the instrument, do not conform to the original intent of the Constitution.

In fact, the questionnaires sent to member states follow perhaps too literally the terms used in the Constitution itself. As regards conventions, they ask a formal question about the extent to which effect has been given to the provisions of the convention in question. Member states are not asked specifically whether their legislation or practice was modified pursuant to the provisions of the convention. It would seem simple to seek more detailed and specific information with respect to the above questions. It would also be possible, and potentially very interesting, to ask for information from governments and employers' and workers' organizations about the extent to which the instrument may have played a role in shaping collective agreements at the national, sectoral, or local level. This seems especially relevant to assessing the validity of the persistent workers' claim that conventions, because of their greater prestige, have a greater impact in practice. It would also be useful and fairly simple to obtain information on decisions of labor and other courts that take inspiration from unratified instruments.

Various obstacles stand in the way of such an evolution. In particular, a new questionnaire, even if theoretically easy to establish, would represent a considerable additional burden. This leads to the second limitation of Article 19 surveys: resource constraints . At first sight, the advantage of the Article 19 assessments is that they are systematic and cover the entire ILO membership. Yet, it will be apparent from the above summary that the rate of return is not always very high and does not seem to be increasing. This should not come as a surprise, as these general surveys represent a significant administrative burden and cost for both the ILO and its members. It would be difficult, if useful, to repeat the exercise at regular intervals for the same instrument in order to gain an idea of the dynamics of compliance; assessment of increased or decreased impact of an instrument over time would enable the organization to assess whether or not the instrument needs revision. It would be even more difficult to develop a new and sophisticated questionnaire for all standards which are the subject of surveys. There may be a trade-off between evaluation and the creation of new standards. The workers' side, in particular, may think that if it is as costly to evaluate existing standards as to create new standards, scarce resources should first be put into the production process rather than into evaluation. After all, even if the degree of impact were limited, it would still be a more productive investment.

---

[28] Report of Director-General, ILC, 81st session (1994).

Child labor standards illustrate the importance of resources and means of action in carrying out a compliance survey with the required degree of specificity. In this instance, information provided through the questionnaires has been complemented by information acquired through ILO technical services and various field projects. This wealth of information, however, is the direct result of extra-budgetary resources granted to the ILO's International Programme on the Elimination of Child Labor to enable it to carry out activities in this field of great popularity with donors.

It thus appears that cost precludes conducting a meaningful evaluation on a regular basis, especially in a context of decreasing financial and administrative resources in the organization. In addition, most members have established priorities for observance of the most significant ILO standards, as reflected in the ILC adoption in June 1998 of a Solemn Declaration on Fundamental Workers' Rights. This Declaration is aimed at strengthening compliance with such rights, whether or not countries have ratified the corresponding conventions. Implementation of the Declaration is subject to existing procedures based, in particular, on Article 19.

C. NEW PERSPECTIVES FOR COMPLIANCE WITH FUNDAMENTAL WORKERS' RIGHTS

As mentioned, the decline in the ratification rate of conventions has attracted new attention to non-binding instruments, but it has also convinced many that ILO conventions are insufficiently binding because their ratification is voluntary. The ILO Constitution expresses the fear, made more acute by the rise of the global market and global competition, that 'the failure of any nation to adopt humane conditions of labor is an obstacle in the way of other nations which desire to improve conditions in their own countries'; hence the proposal to introduce a guarantee of 'internationally recognized workers' rights' within the framework of the World Trade Organization (WTO).

The complete lack of consensus in the WTO on this proposal has returned to the ILO the issue of how to ensure global compliance with fundamental workers' rights. A reference point has been the freedom of association procedure, developed since the 1950s on the basis of the freedom of association principle articulated in the Constitution. The Constitutional guarantee provided the legal foundation for the Committee on Freedom of Association, a tripartite committee of the Governing Body, to examine complaints concerning alleged violations of this principle. In 1994, the ILO Director-General queried whether a similar type of procedure should not be developed as regards other fundamental workers' rights, i.e. freedom from forced labor, child labor, and discrimination. The suggestion to duplicate the freedom of association procedure, whose introduction was deeply rooted in Cold War divisions, was strongly resisted by most governments, as well as by the employers to the extent that it was based on a complaints procedure. The Director-General was able to revive the subject in his report to the 1997 ILC, thanks to the impetus provided by the Copenhagen World Summit on Social Development in 1995 and the Ministerial Conference of Trade Ministers in Singapore in 1996. He suggested adoption of a Declaration accompanied by a suitable follow-up mechanism in order to achieve universal recognition and promotion of fundamental workers' rights even in relation to countries that have not ratified the relevant conventions. The Declaration would recognize that all members have a duty to promote these rights, arising from their voluntary adhesion to the Constitution and its values. The follow-up mechanism would not be based on complaints, as is the case for freedom of association, but on regular reporting and technical assistance. The idea initially met with great suspicion and even open hostility from some governments, but after a year of intensive negotiations it became a reality in June 1998, when the ILO adopted by 273 votes in favor, no vote against, and forty-three abstentions, the ILO Declaration on Fundamental Principles and Rights at Work. Two important points seem to have been particularly instrumental in this outcome. First, members were assured that the Declaration is not legally binding as such, because the commitment of member states did not derive from it but from the Constitution itself. Second, the follow-up, which is a vital part of the system and was the object of much debate, could not be legally faulted because the Constitution's Article 19.5(e) enables the Governing Body, even in the absence of a Declaration, to review the situation in non-ratifying countries. Even though the follow-up is not complaint-based, it is clear that a country's refusal to report will not paralyze the mechanism because the comments of workers' and employers' organizations will enable the ILO to deal with the situation. It thus provides a rather remarkable illustration of the unexploited potential of Article 19. The adoption of the Declaration has been hailed as a development not only for the ILO, but for the international system at large.

D. PROMOTING COMPLIANCE WITH ILO STANDARDS THROUGH NON-ILO MECHANISMS

The previous section mentioned the attempt to introduce universal compliance with 'internationally recognized workers rights' through an appropriate 'social clause' in the WTO. While the subject is beyond the scope of the present study, it should be noted that it did not meet with consensus. It was aimed at ensuring compliance by making worker rights not only automatically binding on all WTO members but also subject to the measures available in the case of violations of WTO obligations.

There are other ways in which external pressure could foster compliance with ILO standards. Some are governmental or intergovernmental, such as the measures aimed at withdrawing the benefit of additional trade concessions within the framework of the Generalized System of Preferences (GSP), or conditioning grants and loans. These forms of external pressure with their basis in ILO standards raise problems regarding the integrity of ILO standards and the ILO's monitoring mechanisms. Without going into detail, the problems are illustrated by the two procedures concerning alleged forced labor in Myanmar, one of which was instituted at the E.U. in Brussels and the other through a complaint under Article 26 of the ILO Constitution. The E.U. procedure, which concluded that the GSP should be withdrawn for violations of forced labor conventions, *inter alia*, was completed before the ILO Commission of Inquiry was established. In international law, the Commission of Inquiry is the only body that may authoritatively pronounce on such violations, subject to review by the International Court of Justice.

Similar opportunities and problems may arise as a result of non-state initiatives. In his 1997 report to the ILC, the Director-General referred to the proliferation of private codes of conduct and labeling initiatives which may boost compliance with ILO standards. It seems likely, for example, that the withdrawal of a licence conferring access to a label important to exports may have a greater deterrent effect than many other measures. At the same time, however, these developments also present certain risks as regards the integrity of ILO standards and objectivity and uniformity in their application. The potentialities may be illustrated by the experience of the Rugmark Foundation, which has been analyzed along with similar initiatives or codes of conduct in a recent ILO publication.[29] The contributions and risks inherent in such private action are described in the ILO Director-General's report to the 1997 ILC. They relate to the reliability of supervision, to the value and meaning of the label which may diminish with the proliferation of such initiatives, and to the integrity and uniformity of their application.

Regarding the first point, the question is whether private initiatives are going to refer to ILO standards as they stand or adjust them to the specific purposes of the initiative. As underlined above, ILO standards derive a considerable degree of international legitimacy and recognition from the fact that they are adopted on a universal and tripartite basis, at the end of a careful preparation

---

[29] Hilowitz. J., *Labeling Child Labor Products: A Preliminary Study* (1997). In September 1996, i.e. 10 months after the start of Rugmark's operations in Germany, some 15% of all Indian carpets exported to Germany (India's main market) were labelled by Rugmark. This gives an overall indication of the scale of the scheme. With a total of 13,000 loomsites currently licensed and thus under inspection, each of the current 13 Rugmark inspectors has the responsibility for 1,000 looms. Each rotating team of two inspectors visits 8–12 looms a day, which allows each team approximately one visit per loom a year, which is obviously far superior to what the state labor inspection can achieve in a developing country with their very limited means and their very wide range of responsibilities.

process. The standards are thus sometimes complex in their formulation, as is the case for instance with the Minimum Age Convention, 1973 (No. 138), where the restrictions are accompanied by many qualifications and exceptions. The same could be said of freedom of association, where the standards laid down in the Freedom of Association Convention, 1948 (No. 87) have been supplemented by an abundant and complex case law dealing with such vital aspects as the right to strike and public service employee strikes. There is a real risk that for the sake of simplicity each private initiative will be tempted either to ignore or to tamper with the standard to make it a simple if not simplistic yardstick.

A parallel issue concerns the fact that, by definition, ILO standards aim at covering all the workers concerned in each country. In some cases, they provide for the exclusion of certain categories of workers, but such exclusions are always justified in terms of the specific objectives of the standard concerned. In contrast, private initiative labels, like codes of conduct, tend to limit the guarantee of the fundamental rights concerned through the labeling of their products to workers who are engaged in export industries and who are not necessarily receiving the worst treatment. They may ignore the sometimes vast majorities of workers who are working for the national market or, *a fortiori*, in the informal sector.

Finally an effective boycott of a product by consumers may have undesirable results with respect to the objective pursued, because of its very effectiveness. In Bangladesh, for example, the threat of possible consumer boycotts resulted in the dismissal of children from textile firms, without any provision for an education or other alternative. In light of these considerations, it was difficult for the ILO, as the Director-General pointed out in his 1997 report, to turn a blind eye to the impact of these initiatives on the integrity and implementation of its own standards. The report went a step further and suggested that to reconcile the potentialities of consumer preferences with ILO concerns, the possibility of creating a voluntary ILO social label through a convention could be studied. This idea raised sharp criticism from some developing countries, which considered it to be an avatar of the defunct social clause.[30]

---

[30] The misunderstanding may have been due to the reference to a 'global' social label. This term was meant to convey the idea that the label should cover a 'package' of fundamental workers' rights to avoid the proliferation of separate labels for each of the rights that would appeal to each particular initiative or interest group. But it was understood to mean that the country rather than the products would get the global label. While the intention was indeed that the system be country-based (since the convention would be open to member states for ratification, which would entail a mutual recognition of the label attributed by each of the ratifying states under the conditions established by the convention), it would still be applied to specific products; and it would be for each country to determine whether or not to give the label to all of its exported products or to some of them only, depending on its assessment of the situation in a particular sector of the industry as regards the package of rights. And as in non-governmental initiatives the attribution of the label would be subject to an independent system of supervision and inspection to be determined by the convention.

The idea is unlikely to be pursued as such in the foreseeable future, but it did have a positive result. It led the ILO Governing Body to request the Office to prepare for discussion in November 1998 a general overview of various kinds of private initiatives intended to promote international compliance with workers' rights. The study presented in November 1998[31] was based on an extensive compilation of existing documentation and on a survey of more than 200 operational and model codes as well as a dozen social labeling programs. Some striking conclusions emerged from the survey regarding, in particular, selectivity in the nature of the labor issues addressed, the absence of uniformity in the definitions, as well as the lack of standardization in methods of implementation. The contents of the codes seem to reflect the concerns of the specific brands of product more than the intrinsic importance of a particular right (thus very little attention is given to freedom of association notwithstanding the fact that it is recognized as an 'enabling' right for the exercise or improvement of other rights). Concerning assessment and verification of compliance procedures, third party assessment seems to be the exception and self-verification the rule. One of the important questions that arises out of these findings is what role, if any, the ILO could play. Requests made to it seem to reflect a need for an external source of reference and legitimacy. Yet, there remain significant differences in views and interests within the Governing Body and some of its groups over the role the ILO could play. These range from a 'minimalist' attitude limiting its activities to research and facilitating further discussion, to a 'proactive' position that could, for instance, involve a statement of good practices regarding both the content of codes and their implementation or verification. Thus far, the Governing Body has agreed to leave some margin of discretion to the Director General to develop research and activities, mainly on an experimental basis.

CONCLUSIONS

Two main conclusions seem to emerge from the above review. First, assessing compliance is by no means an easy task even in the case of unratified international labor conventions and recommendations, despite the fact that Article 19 general surveys offer an ideal tool for such assessment. The existence of this tool is not sufficient to eliminate the practical financial and methodological difficulties inherent in this task. While the surveys provide some evidence that there is indeed some compliance, it would be hazardous to draw more general or 'scientific' conclusions from these surveys as regards the extent and reasons for such compliance.

The second conclusion relates to the difficulties inherent in the two fundamental concepts behind this study, the concept of compliance and the concept

[31] See GB 273.WP.SDL/1.

of soft law. As regards the concept of 'compliance', one may wonder if some other terminology may not be more appropriate to describe what the limited evidence suggests, that in many cases there is a selective impact of some of the normative provisions of the instrument, but not necessarily of the instrument as an integrated whole. The new developments relating to the issue of fundamental workers' rights seem to confirm the trend: the purpose of a declaration as now envisaged would be to promote compliance with the *objectives* or principles of the ILO Constitution rather than with the specific provisions of existing instruments and, in particular, the relevant conventions.[32]

The special status of international labor recommendations also appears to offer an interesting angle under which to revisit the concept of soft law. As longstanding realities in international law, international labor recommendations can hardly be dismissed as not pertaining to the realm of 'law', even though they are not binding and the law does not tolerate degrees of bindingness. The question which arises is whether this recognition can be of some assistance in overcoming objections and shedding more light on the concept and criteria of 'soft law'.

While international labor recommendations share with other soft law instruments or soft law provisions appearing in binding instruments the general characteristic that they leave a wide measure of discretion as to the extent or manner to implement them, they seem to derive their special status in international law from two broad features: the legitimacy in the labor field of the organ which adopts them, strengthened by careful adoption procedures and specific means to promote and verify their implementation. These broad features are obviously inter-related as the legitimacy of the source contributes to the impact of the standard. They could thus be combined under a more general characterization: the institutional capacity to exercise some verifiable influence on state behavior. Seen from that perspective international labor recommendations seem to share with hard law conventions the same basic function.

Extrapolated more generally to the distinction between soft and hard international law, this approach may explain why non-binding instruments which would meet the abovementioned tests qualify as law. The theory would posit that bindingness is not the essence of international law but rather one of the possible expressions of its object and purpose which, more generally, is to exercise a verifiable influence on the behavior of states. In the case of hard law

---

[32] The 'deconstruction' process of the concept of instrument would seem to go even a step further with the prospect of compliance through private initiatives. As noted above, the labeling initiatives would, by definition, tend to link the protection of the worker to the marketing of his/her product and would consequently be limited at least directly to those engaged in the production process of export goods. They would thus create a minimum degree of common social protection—not to speak of solidarity—among export workers in various countries whereas international labor standards by definition aim at creating a common protection between workers in a given country, the assumption being that social justice begins at home.

this influence rests on the consequences which attach to its violations, such as international responsibility. In the case of soft law, the ability to exercise an influence would not derive from 'soft' international responsibility or retaliation, but from the legitimacy of its sources and content as well as on means to exercise an influence. While these tests obviously have to be adjusted to the object and circumstances of each type and object of soft law,[33] they seem to be sufficiently specific to lend themselves to a fairly strict application. They may thus help to overcome the legitimate objections derived from the binary nature of law as well as the frustrations inherent in a 'pot-pourri' approach to soft law.

Inter-American Human Rights Law, Soft and Hard

DOUGLASS CASSEL

INTRODUCTION

The human rights system of the Organization of American States (OAS) appears to offer an attractive test case to compare compliance with 'soft' and 'hard' international law, both primary and secondary.[1] The system has had normative human rights instruments since 1948, when the OAS adopted the American Declaration of the Rights and Duties of Man (the Declaration).[2] Indisputably non-binding at the outset, the Declaration probably remained soft law for at least two and possibly four decades thereafter. In 1969, the

---

[33] The concept of legitimacy could be further elaborated to distinguish two elements: the competence of the organ or body to deal authoritatively with the subject matter from a technical, legal, or political point, as the case may be; and its representativity which qualifies the conditions under which the competence is actually exercised and should be such as to ensure a balanced representation of the various interests concerned by the subject matter from a geographical, sectorial, or other relevant point of view. The capacity to influence state behavior by means other than state responsibility can take the form of administrative incentives (such as reporting); economic incentives (use of the code or standards to promote the product or process); legal incentives (use of hard law forms to channel soft or hortatory provisions).

[1] For definitions of 'primary' and 'secondary' soft law, see Shelton, D., 'Compliance with International Human Rights Soft Law', in American Society of International Law (Brown Weiss, E. (ed.)), *International Compliance with Nonbinding Accords* (1997) 119–27.

[2] Res. XXX, Final Act of the Ninth International Conference of American States, Bogotá, Colombia, March 30–May 2, 1948, at 38 (PAU 1948), reprinted in OAS, *Basic Documents Pertaining to Human Rights in the Inter-American System* (1996) 17.

OAS adopted a comparable hard law instrument, the American Convention on Human Rights (the Convention).[3] The Declaration and Convention protect essentially the same civil and political rights, allowing comparison to be made of state compliance with these two primary normative instruments, one soft law and one hard law. The system's secondary law also takes both soft and hard forms that may be compared. The Inter-American Commission on Human Rights (the Commission) concludes cases by making recommendations which generally have been viewed as non-binding, whereas the judgments of the Inter-American Court of Human Rights (the Court) in contentious cases are legally binding.[4]

In practice, however, the comparisons prove to be extremely difficult, for several reasons. First, compliance with human rights commitments in the Americas has been low for much of the period since 1948; one is thus reduced to comparing the marginal effects of mostly ineffectual instruments and case law. Secondly, human rights in the Americas are governed by complex interactions of domestic law (rights guaranteed by the constitution and other legal instruments) and international hard and soft law (OAS texts, United Nations treaties and declarations, the Geneva Conventions and Protocols, and customary international law). The existence of these overlapping laws complicates the analysis considerably. Thirdly, data are lacking on state compliance at the degree of precision desirable for comparative purposes; one must resort to approximations and estimates. Fourthly, variables such as internal wars, the democratic or dictatorial nature of regimes, the Cold War, and the varying policies of the hemispheric superpower, have had more impact on state compliance than the soft or hard character of Inter-American instruments. Credible analysis of the reasons why American states comply or fail to comply with human rights commitments thus demands familiarity with a variety of contextual factors.

Despite these obstacles, it appears that at least three tentative conclusions can be drawn from a review of Inter-American human rights experience. First, the difference between soft or hard primary law, in isolation, probably has little significant short-term effect on state compliance. Authoritarian regimes and those in power during armed conflicts largely do not comply with fundamental human rights norms, while peaceful democracies tend not to commit gross violations. In both cases, compliance depends on factors other than the 'hardness' of international norms.

Secondly, and conversely, the soft or hard character of the norm does appear to matter in individual cases. States have been more apt to comply with Court judgments and orders than with Commission recommendations.

---

[3] OAS, Official Records, OEA/Ser.K/XVI/1.1, doc. 65, Rev. 1, Corr. 2 (1970), opened for signature, November 22, 1969, entered into force, July 18, 1978 (1970) 9 I.L.M.673, and in *Basic Documents*, *supra* note 2 at 25.

[4] Convention Arts. 67, 68(1).

They do so in part because the Court, unlike the Commission, is a judicial body, and is also the second and final instance in the processing of complaints of human rights violations. Greater compliance with Court orders, then, is due not only to the distinction between soft and hard law, but to the differing nature of the promulgating institutions and their decision-making processes.

Thirdly, there seems to have been a non-negligible, long-term impact on state behavior resulting from hard and soft human rights norms. The overall growth and hardening of Inter-American and other international human rights law can probably be viewed as both evidencing and contributing to a climate in which state human rights violations have become less acceptable and less frequent over time, while international responses to them have gained legitimacy and effect.

Several mutually compatible factors explain this long-term effect. One is that the hardening over time of Inter-American human rights law strengthens its perceived legitimacy and, hence, in the words of Professor Thomas Franck, its 'compliance pull'.[5] Second is the increasing interaction of Latin American governing elites in diplomatic, commercial, and financial fora, sharing a common ideology of democracy, open markets, and the rule of law. These overlapping fora may constitute an informal 'regime' whose culture compensates for the continuing weakness of the OAS and its human rights agencies. Participants in these fora are continually pressed by international issue networks to promote human rights.[6] The result is to encourage compliance through an 'iterative process of discourse' among states, international agencies, and the public.[7] While the impact of this process on compliance cannot yet be measured, by 1998 it had fostered universal participation by Latin American states apart from Cuba in the hard law of the Convention and Court. This expanded participation should, in turn, accelerate the iterative process. At the same time, individual Latin American states are now more democratic and demilitarized than ever. This environment fosters the incorporation of international human rights norms, especially hard norms, into national laws or otherwise, leading to what Professor Harold Hongju Koh calls 'obedience', or voluntary compliance, through a 'transnational legal process' of interaction, interpretation, and internalization.[8]

In sum, the hardening of Inter-American human rights law is interwoven in and complementary to complex regional and national dynamics that have

[5] Franck, T.M., 'Legitimacy in the International System' (1988) 82 *Am.J. Int'l Law* 705, 712; see generally Franck, T.M., *Fairness in International Law and Institutions* (1995), and *The Power of Legitimacy Among Nations* (1990).

[6] Sikkink, K., 'Human Rights: Principled Issue-Networks, and Sovereignty in Latin America' (1993) 47 *Int. Org.* 411.

[7] Chayes, A., and Chayes, A.H., *The New Sovereignty: Compliance with International Regulatory Agreements* (1995) 25.

[8] Koh, H.H., 'The 1998 Frankel Lecture: Bringing International Law Home' (1998) 35 *Houston L.Rev.* 623, 625–6 ('transnational legal process'), and 'Review Essay: Why Do Nations Obey International Law?' (1997) 106 *Yale L.J.* 2599, 2600 n.3 ('obedience').

begun to contribute to improved compliance over time, and will likely continue to do so. These dynamics are neither sufficient nor irreversible, however. Extremes of poverty and inequality continue to plague Latin America.[9] Associated violent crime has reached fearsome heights throughout most of the region.[10] This social cauldron has engendered police killings of street children and common criminals in Brazil,[11] torture and physical abuse of detainees in many parts of Mexico,[12] prison riots and deaths in Venezuela,[13] expansion of the death penalty in violation of the Convention in Guatemala,[14] and mob lynchings of suspected criminals in several countries.[15] If democratization and open economies fail to address these underlying crises, cycles of protest and repression could be renewed, overwhelming advances achieved through legalizing, legitimizing, processing, and internalizing regional human rights norms.[16]

A. THE LAW OF THE INTER-AMERICAN HUMAN RIGHTS SYSTEM

1. Primary Law: The Charter, the Declaration and the Convention

The Inter-American human rights system has developed within the framework of the OAS Charter,[17] approved in 1948 by the same Inter-American conference that adopted the Declaration. While Charter references to human rights are modest,[18] the Declaration protects a wide range of civil and political rights.[19] The same rights are protected by the Convention,[20] generally with greater juridical precision and detail, along with some additional guar-

---

[9] 'On average, the countries of the region suffer from the greatest income inequality in the world.' Inter-American Development Bank, *Facing Up to Inequality in Latin America: Report on Economic and Social Progress in Latin America, 1998–1999* (1998), Introduction, at 1.

[10] *e.g.*, Human Rights Watch, *Human Rights Watch World Report 1999* (1998) 91.

[11] *e.g.*, Ignacio Cano, *The Use of Lethal Force by Police in Rio de Janeiro* (1997).

[12] UN Commission on Human Rights, Report of the Special Rapporteur on Torture and Other Cruel, Inhuman or Degrading Punishment, Mr Nigel Rodley, Visit by the Special Rapporteur to Mexico, UN Doc. no. E/CN.4/1998/38/Add.2 (1998), 15, para. 78.

[13] Human Rights Watch, *supra* note 10 at 147.

[14] *Ibid.*, at 92–3, 125–6.

[15] *e.g.*, *ibid.*, at 124 (Guatemala); US Dept. of State, *Country Reports on Human Rights Practices for 1997* (1998), 668 (Venezuela), and Country Report on Human Rights Practices for 1998 (1999) 3 (Mexico) (accessible at <http://www.state.gov/www/global/human_ rights/1998>).

[16] Buergenthal, T., and Cassel, D., 'The Future of the Inter-American Human Rights System', in Méndez, J.E., and Cox, F. (eds.), *El Futuro del Sistema Interamericano de Protección de los Derechos Humanos* (1998), 539, 554–7.

[17] April 30, 1948, 2 U.S.T. 2394, T.I.A.S. No. 2361, 119 U.N.T.S. 3, amended February 27, 1970, 21 U.S.T. 607, T.I.A.S. No. 6847, amended September 25, 1997.

[18] *e.g.*, OAS Charter Arts. 3(1), 17 and 106.

[19] Declaration Arts. I–X, XVII–XXVII. The Declaration also includes economic, social, and cultural rights.

[20] Convention Arts. 3–25.

antees. Hence one can compare state compliance across a broad range of rights protected by both instruments.

The Convention is a treaty binding on its states parties and is not *per se* binding on non-parties, although many rights it protects are made binding by other conventional and customary law, as discussed below. The Declaration, initially soft, has evolved over time toward hard law. In 1960 it was incorporated into the statute of the Commission, at that time an entity of uncertain status, but which was later incorporated in the OAS Charter by an amendment that came into force in 1970.[21] By this process of double incorporation, the Declaration arguably 'hardened', by becoming part of the legally binding Charter.

The argument that the Declaration had been incorporated in the Charter was first published by a scholar in 1975.[22] The Commission adopted the thesis in 1981[23] and the Court agreed in a non-binding advisory opinion in 1989.[24] Despite these pronouncements, United States State Department lawyers continue to maintain that the Declaration 'has not acquired binding legal force'.[25] Other states clearly viewed the Declaration as soft law prior to the Charter amendments of 1970, and probably continued to see it as soft law until the Commission's statement and the Court's more authoritative opinion in 1989.

2. Secondary Law: Rulings of the Commission and Court

The Commission was established by resolution in 1959. Its statute, first adopted in 1960, defined 'human rights' by reference to the Declaration, and continued to do so after the Commission became an OAS organ by Charter amendment effective in 1970. Once the Convention came into force in 1978, the OAS adopted a new statute for the Commission in 1979, which defined human rights by reference to the Convention for states parties, and to the Declaration for other OAS member states.[26] OAS member states thus were divided after 1978 into two groups, one subject to the Declaration via the OAS Charter and Commission statute, and the other subject to the Convention. Among the states parties to the Convention, some filed the separate declaration required to accept the Court's jurisdiction in contentious

---

[21] See generally Buergenthal, T., 'The Revised OAS Charter and the Protection of Human Rights' (1975) 69 *Am.J.Int'l.L.* 828–35.

[22] *Ibid.*, at 828–35.

[23] Commission Case no. 2141 (USA), Res. 23/81 of March 6, 1981, OAS/Ser.L/V/11.52, doc. 48, para. 16 (1981).

[24] Adv.Op. OC–10/89, 'Interpretation of the American Declaration of the Rights and Duties of Man Within the Framework of Article 64 of the American Convention on Human Rights', in *Annual Report of the Inter-American Court of Human Rights* 1989 (1990), 119–22 paras. 37–48.

[25] *Andrews* v. *U.S.*, Comm'n case no. 11.139, Report 57/96 of December 6, 1996, *Annual Report of the Inter-American Court of Human Rights 1997* (1998), 570, 583 para. 59.

[26] Commission Statute Art. 1.2, reprinted in Basic Documents, *supra* note 2 at 121.

cases. Even these states, however, come before the Court only in cases referred by the Commission or state;[27] otherwise they remain subject only to Commission resolutions. Thus, as of the end of 1999, the thirty-five OAS member states were in the following three groups for purposes of Inter-American human rights law:

> *Declaration States*: eleven states, all in North America and the Caribbean region, remained subject to the law of the Declaration and to the resolutions of the Commission under the Declaration.[28]
>
> *Convention States*: four states were parties to and thus bound by the Convention, but had not accepted the Court's contentious jurisdiction, and thus remained subject only to the law of Commission resolutions, considered soft for Convention states at least until 1997.[29]
>
> *Court States*: twenty states were parties to the Convention and bound by its norms and obligations as hard law, and had also accepted the Court's contentious jurisdiction. They were thus subject to the hard law of judgments in cases referred to the Court, and otherwise to the soft law of Commission resolutions.[30]

For all three groups, the Commission processes individual complaints of human rights violations. The Commission may investigate, assist in settlements, request interim protective measures, issue resolutions on violations, and make recommendations to the state on the merits of admissible complaints.[31] For states accepting the Court's jurisdiction, the Commission also may refer and litigate contentious cases before the Court.[32] The Commission has a wide range of other functions as well.[33]

The Court's functions are exclusively judicial. At the request of an OAS member state or an OAS organ, the Court may render advisory opinions interpreting the Convention or other treaties concerning human rights in the

---

[27] Convention Arts. 51.1, 61.1.

[28] They are Antigua and Barbuda, Bahamas, Belize, Canada, Cuba, Guyana, St. Lucia, St. Kitts & Nevis, St. Vincent & the Grenadines, Trinidad & Tobago (see *infra* note 82) and the United States.

[29] Barbados, Dominica, Grenada, and Jamaica.

[30] These states are Argentina, Bolivia, Brazil, Chile, Colombia, Costa Rica, Dominican Republic, Ecuador, El Salvador, Guatemala, Haiti, Honduras, Mexico, Nicaragua, Panama, Paraguay, Peru, Suriname, Uruguay, and Venezuela. See Commission Press Releases 21/98 (listing Brazil, Haiti, and Mexico among states now accepting the Court's binding jurisdiction), and 7/99, dated March 16, 1999, para. 27 (reporting decision of Dominican Republic to accept Court's binding jurisdiction), both accessible at <http://www.cidh.oas.org>. With regard to Peru, see *infra* note 82.

[31] Convention Arts. 44–51; Commission Statute Art. 20.

[32] Convention Arts. 51.1, 61.1.

[33] Principally they include reporting on the human rights situation in a state, often in conjunction with an on-site visit; requesting advisory opinions from the Court; and conducting studies, promotional and advisory activities. See generally Cassel, D., 'The Inter-American Human Rights System: A Functional Analysis', in Inter-American Court of Human Rights, *Liber Amicorum: Héctor Fix-Zamudio* (1998) 521.

Americas; upon request from an OAS member state, it may also advise on the compatibility of the state's laws with the Convention and other such treaties.[34] In contentious cases referred by the Commission or a state party, the Court may order interim protective measures, adjudicate violations of the Convention, and order remedies and compensation.[35]

B. THE COMPLIANCE CONTEXT

The Inter-American Human Rights system began with soft norms and continued for three decades to rely exclusively on soft law. Only in the last two decades has its law hardened. Even now, significant soft patches remain, a situation that is by no means accidental.

At its founding meeting in 1948, the OAS rejected hard law options for human rights. Three years earlier a more ambitious agenda had been set.[36] Meeting in Mexico City in early 1945, the assembled American states had called for drafting a human rights instrument 'to be adopted as a convention by the states' and declared their support for a system of international protection of human rights.[37]

The climate changed once the war ended. A November 1945 Uruguayan proposal to establish a multilateral mechanism to deal with American governments that 'notoriously and repeatedly violated human rights' was overwhelmingly rejected as 'unacceptable collective intervention'.[38] In 1947, even as the preamble of a new Inter-American Treaty of Reciprocal Assistance recognized that peace is founded on human rights, nearly all American states refused to deem threats to human rights sufficient to trigger inter-state consultations.[39]

By the time the twenty-one American states met to found the OAS in 1948, a majority of Latin American states, plus the United States, were unwilling to accept any legally binding Inter-American human rights law. Only six states supported incorporating the Declaration into the OAS Charter.[40] Proposed Charter articles to declare fundamental rights and to obligate states to ensure their protection were defeated.[41] Only eight states supported a separate

---

[34] Convention Art. 64. [35] Convention Art. 63.1.

[36] See Fenwick, C., *The Organization of American States: The Inter-American Regional System* (1963), 147.

[37] Int.-Am.Conf. on Problems of War and Peace, Mexico City, February 21–March 8, 1945, Res. XL, 'International Protection of the Essential Rights of Man', reprinted in Buergenthal, T., and Norris, R. (eds.), *Human Rights: The Inter-American System* (1982), part I, ch. V, booklet 6, 59–60.

[38] Medina, C., *The Battle of Human Rights: Gross, Systematic Violations and the Inter-American System* (1988), 29.

[39] *Ibid.*, at 31. [40] *Ibid.*, at 38.

[41] *Ibid.*, at 45 and notes 112–14. Art. 3 of the Charter did list OAS 'principles', including 'fundamental rights of the individual' (Art. 3(l) as of 1999). However, the rapporteur stated that the

human rights treaty.[42] A proposal to empower the OAS Council to investigate 'serious' human rights violations, and to enter a state's territory for that purpose, was defeated in committee.[43] A proposal to create an Inter-American human rights court was deferred for study and further consideration,[44] where it would stay for the next twenty-one years.

The OAS did not establish the Commission until 1959, when it was prompted in part by an alleged attempt by the Trujillo dictatorship in the Dominican Republic to assassinate Venezuela's new democratic president, and in part by the victory of Fidel Castro in Cuba.[45] Even then, the Commission was denied authority to investigate or act on individual complaints until 1965,[46] after it had proved its usefulness by denouncing Fidel Castro and helping to secure human rights in the aftermath of the U.S. intervention in the Dominican Republic.[47] The same momentum led to the adoption of the Convention in 1969. Another nine years were required before a diplomatic campaign by U.S. President Jimmy Carter produced the eleven ratifications required for the Convention to go into effect. Additional ratifications and acceptances of the Court's binding jurisdiction trickled in throughout the 1980s and 1990s.

Unlike commerce and military security, human rights do not immediately appear to fall within the traditional, narrow conceptions of state interests. Governments may even view human rights as *contrary* to the interests of many states because, by definition, they are rights of human beings, not of governments, and generally are rights *against* governments. While enlightened public officials have come to recognize that securing human rights can serve state interests—*e.g.*, by promoting stable climates for trade and investment—human rights are viewed by realist scholars as, at best, a low priority for states.

---

juridical value of these principles was merely whatever 'international law assigns to the whereas or introductory part of a treaty'. Ninth Int'l. Conf. Amer. States, Rapporteur of the Committee on Organization of the Inter-American System on the Project of the Organic Pact of the Inter-American System, doc. CD-i-6/48, quoted *ibid.*, at 41.

[42] *Ibid.*, at 38 and note 78.

[43] Ninth International Conference, Bogotá, 1948, Actas y Documentos, Vol. V, 510–15, doc. no. CB–445/C.VI-36, Report of the Rapporteur for the Sixth Committee, translated and reprinted in Buergenthal and Norris, *supra* note 37, part I, ch. IV, booklet 5 at 19, 22.

[44] Ninth Int'l. Conf. Amer. States, Bogotá, 1948, Res. XXXI, 'Inter-American Court to Protect the Rights of Man', reprinted in Buergenthal and Norris, *supra* note 37, part I, ch. V, 89–90.

[45] See generally Medina, *supra* note 38 at 54–8, 67–70; Forsythe, D., 'Human Rights, The United States and the Organization of American States' [1991] *Human Rights Quarterly* 66, 81–2; LeBlanc, L.J., *The OAS and the Promotion and Protection of Human Rights* (1977) 46–8; Cabranes, J.A., 'Human Rights and Non-Intervention in the Inter-American System' (1962) 65 *Mich. L. Rev.* 1164–5; Dreier, J.C., *The OAS and the Hemisphere Crisis* (1962) 70.

[46] Second Special Int.-Am.Conf., Rio de Janeiro, November 17–30, 1965, Res. XXII, Expanded Functions of the Inter-American Commission on Human Rights, reprinted in Buergenthal and Norris, *supra* note 37, part I, ch. V, 163–5.

[47] Cabranes, *supra* note 45 at 1169–73; Medina, *supra* note 38 at 71, 74–5; Forsythe, *supra* note 45 at 84–5.

In areas like trade and arms control, states may opt for soft law because it is more flexible and may facilitate compliance with commitments in which states perceive a mutuality of interest. In matters of human rights the choice of soft law more likely reflects unwillingness to be bound by unwanted commitments. On the other hand, human rights norms have a high and obvious moral content and, at least in the dominant cultures of the Americas, perceived legitimacy. They may thus inherently exert a greater 'compliance pull' even among state officials.[48] They may be attractive to elites, even to some who serve as diplomats for repressive regimes.[49] So, too, their pull has proved to be strong for international issue-networks of non-governmental organizations (NGOs) and others,[50] and for epistemic communities of like-minded professionals.[51] All this, plus the compatibility of international human rights norms with guarantees found in national constitutions and laws, may make them amenable, over time, to voluntary compliance through a transnational legal process of interaction, interpretation, and internalization by national laws, culture, and, ultimately, practice.

The long-term question may be not whether human rights hard law is, in fact, more likely than soft law to induce compliance, but whether it is so perceived by NGOs, issue networks, elites, the media, and even governments. It seems that the binding nature of the norm is significant. Human rights hard law tends to be perceived as raising the moral, political, and, of course, legal stakes of non-compliance. It may also signal expectations of improved compliance over time, raising the floor of the 'acceptable level of compliance'.[52] Through multiple interactions, it may thus achieve a certain self-fulfilling tendency. These observations may apply generally to contemporary human rights norms, but their relative strength in a particular regime depends heavily on the particularities of the states and institutions involved. To those we now turn.

Three particular elements have shaped the choices of OAS member states between compliance and non-compliance with soft and hard human rights law. First is the history of relations between the United States and its neighbors to the south. Second is the predominance until recently of undemocratic regimes in Latin America. Third are U.S. attitudes and policies toward both human rights and international law.

[48] Franck, 'Legitimacy in the International System', *supra* note 5 at 712.
[49] See Forsythe, *supra* note 45 at 73 (OAS human rights regime supported by 'moral interdependence among hemispheric elites').
[50] See generally Sikkink, *supra* note 6 at 411; Keck, M.E., and Sikkink, K., *Activists Beyond Borders: Advocacy Networks in International Politics* (1998); see also Forsythe, *supra* note 45 at 73–4 (OAS human rights regime supported by 'moral leadership by OAS agencies and a shifting coalition of hemispheric states'), 90 (several Commission members 'resigned in protest over state indifference' to Pinochet regime's human rights violations).
[51] See, *e.g.*, Haas, P.M. (ed.), 'Knowledge, Power, and International Policy Coordination', special issue, (1992) 46 *Int. Org.* 1–390.
[52] Chayes and Chayes, *supra* note 7 at 20.

From the founding of the OAS, a history of U.S. intervention in Latin America provoked profoundly anti-interventionist demands to protect state sovereignty.[53] The concerns were made explicit in the OAS Charter[54] and were an important reason for Latin American resistance to binding OAS human rights commitments.[55] The intensity of the sentiment may have faded, but it has not disappeared.[56] In addition, the Cold War weighed heavily against binding OAS human rights norms or enforcement machinery. The U.S. wanted flexibility to support anticommunist regimes, repressive or not, while dictators who sided with Washington against Moscow expected a measure of understanding on their human rights performance.[57] To a lesser degree, the Cold War also provoked occasional support for the Inter-American human rights system. Discrediting Castro and marketing the human rights credentials of the 'Free World' played a role, for example, in establishing the Commission in 1959 and in enhancing its powers in 1965.[58] On the whole, however, the Cold War greatly retarded the development of the system.

In the post-Cold War era, expanding trade and open markets dominate the Americas. While this new emphasis again relegates human rights to a subordinate policy position,[59] it has led nonetheless to a generally more favorable U.S. human rights policy in Latin America. Washington and its free market allies, which now dominate Latin American governments and international financial institutions, see the rule of law as important to stable investment climates.[60] The increased participation in Inter-American human rights hard law and improved compliance, described below, in part reflect this new ideological emphasis.

The second contextual factor is the shift from repression to democracy in the region. While academic debate continues on whether democracies are more likely to comply with international treaty commitments generally,[61]

---

[53] See generally Cabranes, *supra* note 45 at 1147–64; Forsythe, *supra* note 45 at 74, 77.

[54] Charter Arts. 19 and 21, originally numbered Arts. 15 and 17.

[55] Cabranes, *supra* note 45 at 1159–60; Forsythe, *supra* note 45 at 77, 88.

[56] See, *e.g.*, Kramer, F.V., 'Los Derechos Humanos y el Principio de No Intervención' (1991) 13 *Revista Instituto Interamericano de Derechos Humanos* 87.

[57] See generally Forsythe, *supra* note 45 at 74, 79–80, 81, 82–3; see also, *e.g.*, Guatemala: Memory of Silence, Report of the Commission on Historical Clarification (1999), Conclusions, paras. 13 and 14.

[58] *e.g.*, Forsythe, *supra* note 45 at 82–3, 84.

[59] Compare, *e.g.*, Neier, A., 'The New Double Standard' (1996) 105 *Foreign Policy* 91, with Garten, J., 'Comment: The Need for Pragmatism', *ibid.*, at 103.

[60] See generally, *e.g.*, Inter-American Development Bank, *Justice Delayed: Judicial Reform in Latin America* (Jarquín, E. and Carrillo, F. (eds.)) (1998), pp. iv–viii; Statement of Secretary of State Madeleine Albright, OAS General Assembly, June 2, 1998, afternoon session (accessible at <http://www.state.gov/www/statements/1998>).

[61] Compare, *e.g.*, Alvarez, J., 'Foreword: Why Nations Behave' (1998) 19 *Mich.J.Int'l L.* 303, 314, and Franck, T., 'Commentary: Dr. Pangloss Meets the Grinch: A Pessimistic Comment on Harold Koh's Optimism' (1998) 35 *Houston L. Rev.* 683, 698, with Slaughter, A.M., 'International Law in a World of Liberal States' (1995) 6 *Eur.J.Int'l L.* 503, 532.

there should be little dispute that repressive regimes are less likely to comply with international human rights commitments, hard or soft. Military and other authoritarian regimes are more likely to commit gross violations of human rights and less likely to tolerate a free press, NGOs, independent judiciaries, and professional groups, and other such pathways for internalization of human rights norms.

Repressive states are also more resistant to entering into human rights commitments in the first place. At the founding of the OAS, enthusiastic democracies like Guatemala and Uruguay put forward proposals for Inter-American human rights treaties,[62] but a critical mass of repressive regimes, along with the U.S. and anti-interventionist sentiment, helped ensure their defeat.[63] In contrast, an increase in OAS members with popularly elected leaders was a factor contributing to the creation of the Commission eleven years later.[64] In most cases, however, authoritarian regimes were important in keeping the Inter-American Human Rights system soft and in delaying effective enforcement and implementation of its hard law, even after the Convention and Court were formally in place.

The third factor of regional importance is the attitude of successive U.S. administrations towards international law and human rights. At least one scholar has suggested that the Inter-American Human Rights system is 'probably best understood' in terms of the dominant, even 'hegemonic', power of the U.S.[65] A more modest and nuanced assessment, made in 1991, argues persuasively that at key decision points the system reflected 'multilateral convergence rather than US dominant power'.[66] Indeed, throughout the Cold War, 'with limited exceptions, the United States [was] less leader than reluctant follower with regard to the OAS human rights regime'.[67] Washington joined with repressive and anti-interventionist Latin American regimes to block a hard law regime in 1948, but had to accept a Commission it did not want in 1959, a Commission whose activism it found inconvenient during the years before and after Jimmy Carter.[68] In the post-Cold War period, the U.S. has tended, albeit unevenly, to support a stronger Commission and Court even while remaining outside the Convention.

U.S. opposition to effective mechanisms throughout most of the system's history reflects a number of factors. These include, principally, traditional

---

[62] *e.g.*, Medina, *supra* note 38 at 35 and note 62, 36–8 and note 78.

[63] Thus, *e.g.*, Uruguay's proposal to create a Special American Chamber to hear human rights cases in the International Court of Justice was successfully opposed by military or authoritarian regimes in Argentina, Bolivia, the Dominican Republic, Ecuador, and Mexico. *Ibid.*, at 37–8 and note 75; see Wiarda, H.J., and Kline, H.F. (eds.), *Latin American Politics and Development* (4th edn. 1996) 79–80 (Argentina), 311–12 (Bolivia), 494 (Dominican Republic), 329 (Ecuador), and 350–2 (Mexico).

[64] Medina, *supra* note 38 at 54 and note 153.

[65] Donnelly, J., 'International Human Rights: A Regime Analysis' (1986) 40 *Int. Org.* 625.

[66] Forsythe, *supra* note 45 at 96.   [67] *Ibid.*

[68] See Medina, *supra* note 38 and Forsythe, *supra* note 45.

isolationist and unilateralist currents,[69] often voiced in terms of domestic sovereignty and state's rights;[70] concerns especially in the early years that international human rights law posed a threat to domestic racial discrimination,[71] Cold War concerns,[72] and, even more in recent years, superpower hubris.[73] U.S. policy toward the OAS human rights system has been further complicated by recurring policy disagreements between the White House and Congress. Congress, on the one hand, was more responsive than the Nixon Administration to the Commission's reporting on human rights violations by the Pinochet regime in Chile while, on the other hand, the Senate was unresponsive to President Carter's appeal for its consent to ratify the Convention.[74]

In sum, the U.S. has played an important role in retarding the development of hard law in the system and in weakening both the Commission and Court. Even today, the Clinton Administration's increased budgetary[75] and diplomatic support for these institutions is greatly undercut by U.S. failure to join the Convention and Court . This posture deprives Commission resolutions of much of the moral force and compliance pull they might otherwise command, while reducing incentives for other states to comply. It has deprived even binding Court judgments of needed diplomatic support, thereby delaying compliance.

It should thus come as no surprise that regional institutions for protection of human rights are weak. The Commission has long been grossly underfunded, and until recently was denied control over selection of its personnel, undermining the competence and independence of its staff. Partly as a result, the Commission's procedures and decisions, until recently, often seemed arbitrary and unfair. During the 1970s and 1980s its case resolutions, and even its proceedings, were commonly ignored by states.

The Court also has been and remains seriously underfunded despite recent increases.[76] Highly politicized election procedures have on occasion selected

---

[69] See generally, *e.g.*, Kaufman, N.H., and Whiteman, D., 'Opposition to Human Rights Treaties in the United States Senate: The Legacy of the Bricker Amendment' (1988) 10 *Human Rights Quarterly* 309.

[70] See, *e.g.*, McDougal, M.S., and Leighton, G.C.K., 'The Rights of Man in World Community: Constitutional Illusions Versus Rational Action' (1950) 59 *Yale L.J.* 60, 72–7.

[71] *e.g.*, Forsythe, *supra* note 45 at 78; McDougal and Leighton, *supra* note 70 at 76.

[72] Forsythe, *supra* note 45 at 79–80.

[73] See, *e.g.*, Huntington, S., 'The Lonely Superpower' (1999) 78 *Foreign Affairs* 35; Franck, 'Dr. Pangloss Meets the Grinch', *supra* note 61 at 691–2.

[74] Forsythe, *supra* note 45 at 85 and notes 47 and 48, 85–6, 87–8, 90–1 and note 65.

[75] The U.S. provided 59% of OAS regular funds of $80 million in 1998, plus $7 million in voluntary funds. U.S. Dept. of State, Background Notes: Organization of American States, March 1998 (1998) 2 (accessible at <http://www.state.gov>). Even as the overall OAS budget had been frozen the last 4 years, *ibid.* at 4, the Court received a 10% increase for 1998. *Annual Report of the Inter-American Court of Human Rights 1997* (1998), 18. In 1998 the U.S. contributed an additional $150,000 to the Commission for a special rapporteur on freedom of expression. U.S. Dept. of State, Press Statement, July 10, 1998 (accessible at http://www.state.gov/www/briefings/statements/1998).

[76] See *Annual Report of the Inter-American Court of Human Rights 1997*, *supra* note 75, 31.

judges whose human rights credentials were questionable.[77] And the OAS 'fails even to monitor, let alone to encourage compliance with Commission recommendations and Court judgments'.[78] Faced with tenuous diplomatic support from the OAS, the Court has managed nonetheless to secure remarkably consistent compliance with its judgments, but only by exercising prudence—some would say timidity—in its jurisprudence.

The institutional shortcomings of the human rights organs might be largely overcome if the OAS itself were either a strong regional regime or seriously committed to human rights. But it is neither. As David Forsythe has noted, '[b]y early 1990 the OAS in general was on the point of collapse. On most issues it was marginalized by most member states'.[79] In such a weak regime the 'fundamental instrument for maintaining compliance with treaties at an acceptable level', namely the 'iterative process of discourse among the parties, the treaty organization, and the wider public',[80] has little chance to work. Nor does the potential threat of exclusion from the club. Until the recent Protocol of Washington amended the OAS Charter to permit suspension of membership rights of states whose democratically elected governments have been overthrown by force,[81] OAS members knew that only communist leanings, not human rights failings, could get them excluded from OAS meetings.

Viewed from a broader perspective, however, the totality of increasing regional diplomatic and commercial interactions—not only the OAS but also Summits of the Americas, Iberoamerican Summits, the Inter-American Development Bank, growing intra-regional trade, and assorted sub-regional free trade agreements—may be in the process of constituting a *de facto*, albeit loosely organized, hemispheric regime. Contemporaneous with and to a degree perhaps causally related to the growth of this regime, there seems to be a common culture developing among Latin American governments, nurtured by ideological trends toward democratization and open markets. This culture, even if not yet truly committed to human rights, at least fosters the making of hard law commitments. By the end of 1998, when Mexico and Brazil, the two most powerful countries in Latin America, accepted the Court's binding jurisdiction, Cuba became the only Latin nation remaining outside the formal Inter-American Convention system. In 1999, however, following the withdrawal of Trinidad and Tobago from the Convention, Peru purported to withdraw from the Court's contentious jurisdiction and did so without any immediate adverse response by OAS political bodies.[82] Even so, interactions

---

[77] For an extreme example, see Cassel, D., 'Somoza's Revenge: A New Judge for the Inter-American Court of Human Rights' (1992) 13 *Human Rights L.J.* 137.

[78] Buergenthal and Cassel, *supra* note 16 at 552 (footnote omitted).

[79] Forsythe, *supra* note 45 at 89.   [80] Chayes and Chayes, *supra* note 7 at 25.

[81] Charter Art. 9 (effective 1997).

[82] In mid-1999, the Convention and Court suffered their first formal defections. On May 26, 1999, following one year's advance notice, Trinidad & Tobago withdrew from the Convention, alleging that Commission review of petitions filed under the Convention unduly delayed the

between states and the treaty regime may continue to increase. If so, compliance is likely to get a boost, while states may increasingly fear exclusion, not from formal OAS membership, but from informal social respectability, or what the Chayes call 'membership in reasonably good standing in the regimes that make up the substance of international life'.[83] If this is an accurate interpretation of recent trends, it is hopeful, but the advances may also be fragile. Rising economies in the region have yet to lift the poorest or to reduce extremes of inequality and there may come renewed cycles of unrest and repression. If so, regional human rights law will not likely carry the day.

C. SCOPE AND METHODOLOGY OF COMPARATIVE ANALYSIS

The remainder of this study undertakes to analyze the performance of OAS member states whose comparative compliance with Inter-American hard and soft human rights can in a limited sense be 'measured'. It focuses on the period 1972–98, for which statistical data are available in the form of annual, numerical 'civil liberties' ratings by Freedom House.[84] The comparative analysis considers the twenty-five OAS member states that by 1998 were parties to the Convention and had previously been subject to the soft law Declaration.[85]

The ten OAS member states subject only to the Declaration throughout this period, and thus excluded from the comparative analysis, are not representative of OAS states with the most serious human rights problems. Seven are relatively small Caribbean states not original members of the OAS. They joined upon gaining independence in the 1960s, 1970s and 1980s.[86] Of the three remaining states, Canada did not join the OAS until 1990. Cuba has formally been a member of the OAS since 1948, but its government has been

---

carrying out of death sentences. Ministry of Foreign Affairs, Republic of Trinidad and Tobago, Notice to Denounce the American Convention on Human Rights, May 26 1998 (on file with author.) On July 7, 1999, Peru purported to withdraw its acceptance of the Court's contentious jurisdiction, effective immediately (Inter-Am.Comm'n H.Rts. Press Release No. 21/99, July 9, 1999), after objecting to recent judgments of the Court concerning Peru. See letter of Ambassador Beatriz Ramacciotti, Permanent Representative of Peru before the OAS, to OAS Secretary General César Gaviria, dated 1 July 1999 (on file with author). In September the Court ruled Peru's purported withdrawal legally ineffective. Case of the Constitutional Court Jurisdiction, Judgment of September 24, 1999; Ivcher Bronstein Case, Jurisdiction, Judgment of September 24, 1999; see generally Cassel, D., 'Peru Withdraws from the Court: Will the Inter-American Human Rights System Meet the Challenge?' (1999) 20 *Human Rights L.J.* 167.

[83] See Chayes and Chayes, *supra* note 7 at 27.

[84] This analysis addresses compliance only with civil and political norms and not with the Declaration's economic, social, and cultural norms because there is little basis for hard law comparison.

[85] See *supra* notes 29 and 30.

[86] Antigua and Barbuda, Bahamas, Belize, Guyana, St. Lucia, St. Kitts & Nevis, and St. Vincent & the Grenadines.

excluded from participation since 1962[87] and since 1964 has taken the position that the OAS 'has no jurisdiction or competence, legally, factually, or morally, over a state that has been illegally deprived of its rights'.[88] The final state excluded is the U.S., whose human rights performance has not been materially affected by the OAS system. The U.S. has to date failed to ratify the Convention despite President Carter's signing the treaty in 1977. As a non-party, it is not subject to judgments of the Court, and has declined to comply with the three resolutions which the Commission through 1998 issued against it under the Declaration.[89]

Comparison of compliance with the Declaration and Convention is complicated by other sources of law that also regulate civil and political rights. None, however, precludes overall analysis of compliance with Inter-American law at the level of generality attempted here. Constitutional bills of rights and domestic legal systems for protection of human rights generally have traditionally been ineffective in most Latin American states. This is clearest in the repressive dictatorships and authoritarian military regimes common in the region until the 1990s (see Tables 7.1 and 7.2 below), but most Latin American democracies have likewise suffered from weak legal institutions.[90] Thus, in most cases until recently, state compliance with a Declaration or Convention norm was probably not because domestic law achieved that result independently.

The principal relevant U.N. treaty, the International Covenant on Civil and Political Rights (U.N. Covenant),[91] had little if any impact on state compliance with the Declaration because the Covenant did not go into force until 1976 and only nine of its eventual twenty-five states parties from the region had ratified it before 1978, when the American Convention came into force.[92] In addition, compared to both the Declaration and the Convention, the U.N.

[87] Res. VI, 8th Meeting of Consultation of Ministers of Foreign Affairs, Punta del Este, January 1962, OEA/Ser.F/II.8 doc.68, O.14, reprinted in Buergenthal, T., Norris, R., and Shelton, D., *Protecting Human Rights in the Americas: Selected Problems* (3rd rev. edn. 1990), 80–1.

[88] *Ibid.*, at 83, quoting letter dated November 4, 1964, from Cuba's Minister of Foreign Affairs, Raúl Roa, to Commission Chairman Manuel Bianchi Gundián.

[89] *Andrews* v. *U.S.*, Comm'n Case no. 11.139, Report 57/96 of December 6, 1996, *Annual Report of the Inter-American Comm'n of Human Rights 1997*, (1998), 570; *Haitian Centre for Human Rights* v. *U.S.*, Case no. 10.675, *Annual Report of the Inter-American Comm'n of Human Rights 1996* (1997), 550; *Roach* v. *U.S.*, *Annual Report of the Inter-American Comm'n of Human Rights 1987–88* (1988), 148.

[90] See generally, *e.g.*, Rosenn, K., 'The Success of Constitutionalism in the United States and its Failure in Latin America: An Explanation' (1990) 22 *U.Miami Inter-Am.L.Rev.* 1; Alvarez, J., 'Promoting the "Rule of Law" in Latin America: Problems and Prospects' (1991) 25 *George Washington J.Int'l.L.& Econ.* 281–331.

[91] December 16, 1966, UNGA Res. 2200 (XXI), 21 U.N. GAOR, Supp. (No. 16) 52, U.N. Doc. A/6316 (1967).

[92] The states and the years of Covenant ratification are as follows: Barbados (1973), Chile (1972), Colombia (1969), Costa Rica (1968), Ecuador (1969), Jamaica (1975), Panama (1977), Suriname (1976), and Uruguay (1970). By 1997 the U.N. Covenant had been ratified by 24 of the 25 states parties to the American Convention. The one exception, Honduras, signed the Covenant in 1966 but had not ratified it by mid-1999.

Table 7.1: Civil liberties country scores as compiled by Freedom House†

	1972–3	1973–4	1974–5	1975–6	1976–7	1977–8	1978–9	1979–80	1980–1	1981–2	1982–3	1983–4	1984–5	1985–6
I. Democratic Transition States														
Argentina (84)*	3	2	4	4	5	6	5	5	5	5	5	3	**2***	2
Brazil (92)*	5	5	4	5	5	5	4	3	3	3	3	3	3	2
Chile (90)*	2	5	5	5	5	5	5	5	5	5	5	5	5	5
Paraguay (89)*	6	5	5	5	6	6	5	5	5	5	5	5	5	6
Suriname (87)*			—	2	2	2	2	2	5	5	6	6	6	6
Uruguay (85)*	4	5	5	5	6	6	6	6	5	5	4	4	4	**2***
II. War States														
Colombia (73)	2	**2***	2	3	3	3	3	3	3	3	3	3	3	3
El Salvador (78)*	3	3	3	3	3	3	**4***	3	4	5	5	5	5	4
Guatemala (78)*	3	2	3	3	3	4	**4***	5	6	6	6	6	6	4
Nicaragua (79)*	3	4	4	4	5	5	5	**5***	5	5	5	5	5	5
Peru (78)*	5	5	6	4	4	4	**4***	4	3	3	3	3	3	3
III. Other Military or De Facto Regimes, or Dictators														
Bolivia (79)*	4	4	5	5	4	4	3	**3***	5	5	3	3	3	3
Dom Rep. (78)*	2	2	2	2	3	2	**2***	3	3	3	2	2	3	3
Ecuador (77)*	3	5	5	5	5	**5***	3	2	2	2	2	2	2	3
Grenada (78)*			4	4	4	3	**3***	5	5	5	5	6	3	3
Haiti (77)*	6	6	6	6	6	**6***	6	5	6	6	6	6	6	6
Honduras (77)*	3	3	3	3	3	**3***	3	3	3	3	3	3	3	3
Mexico (82)*	3	3	3	3	4	4	4	3	4	4	**4***	4	4	4
Panama (78)*	6	6	6	6	6	5	**5***	5	4	4	5	4	3	3
Venezuela (77)*	2	2	2	2	2	**2***	2	2	2	2	2	2	2	2
IV. Other States														
Barbados (82)*	1	1	1	1	1	1	1	1	1	1	**1***	1	2	2
Costa Rica (70)*	1	1	1	1	1	1	1	1	1	1	1	1	1	1
Dominica (93)*			—	—		—	3	2	2	2	2	2	2	2
Jamaica (78)*	2	2	2	2	3	3	**3***	3	3	3	3	3	3	3
Trin. & Tob. (91)*	3	2	2	2	2	2	2	2	2	2	2	2	2	2

† All data were taken from comparative surveys carried out by the Freedom House survey team and contained in *Annual Survey of Freedom Country Scores* 1972–3 to 1998–9, available at http://www.freedomhouse.org/rankings.pdf.

* Years in parentheses after country name indicate year the state ratified the American Convention of Human Rights. Underlined scores printed in bold type indicate the civil liberties score assigned each state for the year it ratified the American Convention.

	1986–7	1987–8	1988–9	1989–90	1990–1	1991–2	1992–3	1993–4	1994–5	1995–6	1996–7	1997–8	1998–9
I. Democratic Transition States													
Argentina (84)*	1	1	2	3	3	3	3	3	3	3	3	3	3
Brazil (92)*	2	2	3	2	3	3	3*	4	4	4	4	4	4
Chile (90)*	5	5	4	3	2*	2	2	2	2	2	2	2	2
Paraguay (89)*	6	6	6	3*	3	3	3	3	3	3	3	3	3
Suriname (87)*	6	4*	2	3	4	4	3	3	3	3	3	3	4
Uruguay (85)*	2	2	2	2	2	2	2	2	2	2	2	2	2
II. War States													
Colombia (73)*	3	3	4	4	4	4	4	4	4	4	4	4	4
El Salvador (78)*	4	4	3	4	4	4	3	3	3	3	3	3	3
Guatemala (78)*	3	3	3	3	4	5	5	5	5	5	4	4	4
Nicaragua (79)*	6	5	4	5	3	3	3	5	5	4	3	3	3
Peru (78)*	3	3	4	4	4	5	5	5	4	4	4	4	4
III. Other Military or De Facto Regimes, or Dictators													
Bolivia (79)*	3	3	3	3	3	3	3	3	3	4	3	3	3
Dom Republic (78)*	3	3	3	3	3	3	3	3	3	3	3	3	2
Ecuador (77)*	3	3	2	2	2	3	2	3	3	3	4	3	3
Grenada (78)*	2	1	1	2	2	2	2	2	2	2	2	2	2
Haiti (77)*	4	5	5	5	4	7	7	7	5	5	5	5	5
Honduras (77)*	3	3	3	3	3	3	3	3	3	3	3	3	3
Mexico (82)*	4	4	4	3	4	4	3	4	4	4	4	4	4
Panama (78)*	3	5	5	6	2	2	3	3	3	3	3	3	3
Venezuela (77)*	2	2	2	3	3	3	3	3	3	3	3	3	3
IV. Other States													
Barbados (82)*	1	1	1	1	1	1	1	1	1	1	1	1	1
Costa Rica (70)*	1	1	1	1	1	1	1	2	2	2	2	2	2
Dominica (93)*	2	2	2	1	1	1	1	1*	1	1	1	1	1
Jamaica (78)*	3	2	2	2	2	2	2	3	3	3	3	3	2
Trin. & Tobago (91)*	2	1	1	1	1*	1*	1	1	2	2	2	2	2

Human Rights

Table 7.2: GJS: Rank among 89 states in 1985 and among 104 in 1991 (1 is most 'free')

	ACHR Ratified	Authoritarian (War years)	1985	1991
I. Democratic Transition States (6)				
Argentina	1984	1976–83	25	23
Brazil	1992	1964–85	38	46
Chile	1990	1973–90	81	36
Paraguay	1989	1954–89, 1989–93	82	32
Suriname	1987	1980–8, 1990–1	—	—
Uruguay	1985	1973–85	21	20
II. War States (5)				
Colombia	1973	1953–8 (war 70–)	41	44
El Salvador	1978	1979–84 (war 80–92)	—	66
Guatemala	1978	1954–85 (war 61–96)	—	45
Nicaragua	1979	1936–79,79–84 (war 78–9, 81–8)	—	49
Peru	1978	1968–80 (war 80–96)	39	62
III. Other Military or De Facto Regimes or Dictators (9)				
Bolivia	1979	1964–79, 1979 1979–80, 80–2	37	33
Dom. Repub.	1978	1963–6	29	38
Ecuador	1977	1970–9	32	16
Grenada	1978	1979–83	—	—
Haiti	1977	1957–90, 91–4	—	—
Honduras	1977	1972–82	—	—
Mexico	1982		45	51
Panama	1978	1968–89	35	37
Venezuela	1977	1948–58	23	31
IV. 'Democratic' States (5)				
Barbados	1982		—	—
C. Rica	1970		16	12
Dominica	1993		—	—
Jamaica	1978		34	35
Trin. & Tob.	1991		28	24

Sources: GJS for 1985 and 1991: Gupta, D.K., Jongman, A.J., and Schmid, A.P., 'Creating a Composite Index for Assessing Country Performance in the Field of Human Rights: Proposal for a New Methodology' (1994) 16 *Human Rights Quarterly* 159–62, Annexes 1 and 2.

Covenant's enforcement machinery, like that of the U.N. human rights system generally, is weak.[93]

In some cases, the U.N. has had more impact on state compliance with human rights norms than the OAS, but these tend to be exceptions.[94] They do not preclude an overall analysis of compliance by twenty-five states over a period of decades. Much the same is true of common Article 3 of the Geneva Conventions, Geneva Protocol II, and other international humanitarian law applicable to internal armed conflicts in Latin America.[95] Their norms have been invoked by international observers in specific armed conflicts,[96] but states did not consider the minimum threshold for applicability of the laws of war to have been reached for most urban insurgencies during the 1970s and 1980s. Indeed, El Salvador and Peru resisted treating guerrillas as belligerents, labeling them instead as terrorists and criminals. While international invocations of the Geneva Conventions may have exerted some moderating pressure, these effects were most likely limited in time and place.

If the combined effect of domestic, U.N., and Geneva law does not amount to a red light, it flashes a yellow light. Perturbations from other sources of law may be non-negligible given the modest direct effect of Inter-American human rights law. What makes the present analysis viable, despite their effects, is its high level of generality.

[93] Unlike the Inter-American system, states are subject to individual complaints for violations of the U.N. Covenant only if they ratify a separate Optional Protocol accepting the competence of the U.N. Human Rights Committee. December 16, 1966, UNGA Res. 2200 (XXI), 21 GAOR, Supp. (No. 16) 59, U.N. Doc. A/63316 (1967). The UN system has no human rights court and the U.N. Human Rights Committee is in most respects weaker than the Inter-American Commission. The U.N. Committee does not make on-site investigations nor, indeed, conduct any investigation at all beyond analysis of the parties' submissions. It is also more distant and less known in most Latin American states than is the Inter-American Commission.

[94] This is not to say that the U.N. human rights system has had no impact in the Americas. While the OAS floundered in Chile, for example, the 1973 coup 'stimulated the first serious rights-protecting initiative' of the U.N. Human Rights Commission in the Americas. Farer, T., and Gaer, F., 'The U.N. and Human Rights: At the End of the Beginning', in United Nations, *Divided World, The UN's Role in International Relations* (Roberts, A., and Kingsbury, B. (eds)) (2nd edn. 1993), 282–3; see also Chayes and Chayes, *supra* note 7, 254–6; Medina, C., *supra* note 38, 262–313. U.N. rapporteurs and experts documented and may have helped stem violence in El Salvador and Guatemala in the 1980s, and U.N. human rights field monitors during the peace processes in those countries held down violations in the 1990s. See, *e.g.*, United Nations, *The United Nations and El Salvador 1990–1995* (1995), 6–10, 13–14, 18–19, and 35–6; United Nations, *The United Nations and Human Rights 1945–1995* (1995), 115 para. 490, 402–3 (El Salvador), 116 para. 494, 487–8 (Guatemala); Human Rights Watch/Americas, *Human Rights in Guatemala During President de León Carpio's First Year* (1994), 117–20.

[95] *e.g.*, Convention Relative to the Protection of Civilian Persons in Time of War, August 12, 1949, 6 U.S.T. 3516, T.I.A.S. No. 3365, 75 U.N.T.S. 287, art. 3; Protocol Additional to the Geneva Conventions of August 12, 1949, and Relating to the Protection of Victims of Non-International Armed Conflicts, June 8, 1977, 1977 U.N.Jurid.Y.B. 135; Case Concerning the Military and Paramilitary Activities in and Against Nicaragua (*Nicaragua* v. *United States of America*), Judgment of 27 June 1986, Int. Ct. Justice, paras. 215–20 (common Art. 3 of Geneva Conventions constitutes customary international law).

[96] *e.g.*, Americas Watch, *Land Mines in El Salvador and Nicaragua: The Civilian Victims* (1986), 76–7; Human Rights Watch, *Human Rights Watch World Report 1990* (1991), 244 (Peru).

D. PRIMARY SOFT AND HARD LAW COMPARED

In general, throughout the Cold War period, state compliance with Inter-American human rights norms, whether Declaration soft law or Convention hard law, was weak, inconsistent, and unreliable, if not openly defiant. The data in Table 7.1 demonstrate this using the seven point scale for civil liberties as estimated by Freedom House during the twenty-seven years from 1972 through 1998.[97] In the Freedom House scale a score of '1' is the most 'free', whereas '7' is the most repressive. Scores of 1 or 2 correspond to democracies with a broad range of freedoms, whereas scores of 3 or higher indicate progressively more repressive regimes. The author of the Freedom House reports explains, '[t]hose rated (3) or below may have political prisoners and generally varying forms of censorship. Too often their security services practice torture. States rated (6) almost always have political prisoners; usually the legitimate media are completely under government supervision; there is no right of assembly; and, often, travel, residence, and occupation are narrowly restricted. However, at (6) there still may be relative freedom in private conversation, especially in the home; illegal demonstrations do take place; and underground literature is published.'[98]

The data are presented by placing the twenty-five American states in four groups. The first group of six states (Argentina, Brazil, Chile, Paraguay, Suriname, and Uruguay) ratified the Convention roughly contemporaneously with their transition from a military or dictatorial regime to a more democratic, elected civilian government. Such states were thus subject to the soft Declaration during their repressive regimes and to the hard Convention only after they began their democratic transitions.

Not surprisingly, the civil liberties scores of the six states before their democratic transitions, while still under the Declaration, are very poor. Of ninety-two such ratings, eighty-one, or 88 percent, are in the range from 3 to 6. None attains a '1'. All the scores of '2' were awarded either for years before military coups in Argentina, Chile, and Suriname, or in the waning years of the mili-

---

[97] Freedom House defines civil liberties as the 'freedoms to develop views, institutions and personal autonomy apart from the state'. Issues relevant to the violent abuses common in recent Latin American history are included, for example equality under the law, with access to an independent, nondiscriminatory judiciary respected by the security forces, protection from political terror and from unjustified imprisonment, exile or torture, whether by groups that support or oppose the system, and freedom from war or insurgency. Also included are free press, debate, and assembly; political, civic, labor, peasant, professional, and private organizing; free businesses or cooperatives, freedom of religion, personal social freedoms, equality of opportunity and freedom from extreme government indifference and corruption. Karatnycky, A., *et al.*, *Freedom in the World: The Annual Survey of Political Rights & Civil Liberties 1994–95* (1995) 672–4.

[98] Gastil, R.D., *Freedom in the World: Political Rights and Civil Liberties 1985–86* (1986) 41.

tary regime in Brazil. After the restoration of democracy, under the Convention, their scores improve dramatically. Only thirty-seven of sixty-seven, or 55 percent, are in the 3–6 range. Of these, twenty-seven are scores of 3, at the 'most free' end of the repressive range. While in theory one might attribute these improvements to the ratifications of the Convention, in reality, as anyone familiar with these countries can attest, they were due to the new democratic governments. This hypothesis is borne out by the absence of any convincing correlation between Convention ratification and civil liberties scores for the remaining categories of states.

The second group consists of five states (Colombia, El Salvador, Guatemala, Nicaragua, and Peru) involved in prolonged guerrilla wars. Each ratified the Convention before entering into the most intense and prolonged periods of conflict. They were thus subject to the hard law of the Convention while at war, whereas they had been subject to the soft law of the Declaration during earlier, more peaceful years. Again, their human rights performance overall is abysmal: of 135 total scores, there is no score of '1' on civil liberties and only four scores of '2'. Whether they were under the Declaration or Convention made no discernible difference: of twenty-six scores under the Declaration, twenty-four were in the range of 3 to 6; of 109 scores under the Convention, 107 were in the range of 3 to 6. What mattered for civil liberties in these states was war or peace, not hard or soft law.

A third group of nine states (Bolivia, Dominican Republic, Ecuador, Grenada, Haiti, Honduras, Mexico, Panama, and Venezuela) all had military, dictatorial, or authoritarian regimes for at least several years since 1948. Two (Dominican Republic and Venezuela) had such regimes while they were subject to the soft law of the Declaration; one (Grenada) had such a regime after accepting the hard law of the Convention; and the rest had such regimes during periods under both soft and hard law. Again, their human rights performance is very poor under both the Declaration and the Convention. Of a total of 241 scores, 191, or 79 percent, are in the range from 3 to 6. For Declaration states, forty-three of fifty-three scores, or 81 percent, were in this repressive range. For Convention states, 148 of 188, or 79 percent, were in the same range.

The final group of five 'democratic' states (Barbados, Costa Rica, Dominica, Jamaica, and Trinidad & Tobago) have not experienced military or dictatorial regimes during the life of the OAS. Their civil liberties scores are notably better than those of the transition states, war states, and authoritarian states. Of a total of 129 scores for the 'democratic' states, only eighteen, or 14 percent, are in the repressive range of 3 to 6. Again, it made little significant difference whether these states were under the Declaration or Convention. Of fifty scores under the Declaration, only four, or 8 percent, were in the 3 to 6 range; whereas of seventy-nine scores under the Convention, only fourteen, or 18 percent, all from one country (Jamaica), were in the 3 to

6 range. Again, what appears to matter most is the nature of the regime, not whether it is under soft or hard Inter-American human rights law.

The same conclusion emerges if one considers only the most repressive rankings of 6 or 7. Of thirty-one such scores among war states and authoritarian regime states, twelve were for Declaration states and nineteen for Convention states. 'Democratic' states had no such scores. 'Transition' states had seventeen such scores, all for periods before restoration of democracy.

Recognizing that the Freedom House scores are methodologically simplistic, judgmental, and subject to accusations of bias,[99] Table 7.2 presents data for 1985 and 1991—the only two years available—from a group of analysts using a more sophisticated methodology.[100] While they provide too little data to draw independent conclusions, their rank orderings of 'free' states roughly correspond to those of Freedom House and are to that extent corroborative.

Overly precise conclusions should not be attempted on the basis of the foregoing analysis, which is not statistically rigorous, of data which are not objective. It may be said, however, that the soft or hard form of Inter-American human rights law seems to have had no direct effect on state compliance in a given year. If there was any direct causal effect, it is difficult to detect. What do appear to matter are factors such as whether the state was under a military or other dictatorial regime, was undergoing a democratic transition, or was involved in a guerrilla war. These, in turn, were conditioned by geopolitical and regional realities. The Cold War fomented wars and repression; its end alleviated both, while making possible new United Nations interventions, which further promoted peace and democratization in El Salvador and Guatemala. After the Cold War, U.S. policy in Latin America again gave greater support to human rights in general and to the Inter-American Human Rights system in particular. The demise of communism and opening of economies also created incentives for Latin American states to move toward democracy and human rights. State incentives have further been altered by the growth of human rights consciousness and non-governmental human rights organizations. Such overarching realities affected human rights performance more than any difference between soft and hard law. Still, the data are consistent with the hypothesis that the hardening as well as the growth of Inter-American human rights law has been both a contributor to and a consequence of the creation of a hemispheric climate less conducive to violations and more hospitable to international human rights protection. This is arguably reflected in the increasing number of states ratifying the Convention and accepting the Court's binding jurisdiction through 1998. It is also likely

---

[99] These scores admittedly reflect 'judgment' by the Freedom House analysts. Karatnycky *et al.*, *supra* note 97 at 674.

[100] Gupta, D.K., *et al.*, 'Creating a Composite Index for Assessing Country Performance in the Field of Human Rights: Proposal for a New Methodology' (1994) 16 *Human Rights Quarterly* 159–62, Annexes 1 and 2.

one factor, among others, in the improved human rights picture in the 1990s as compared to earlier years. For example, the five-year average Freedom House scores for the three most troubled groups of states from the early 1980s to the mid-1990s improved as follows:

Table 7.3. Five-year average Freedom House scores[101]

	1980–4	1985–9	1990–4
Democratic Transition States	4.5	3.6	2.7
War States	4.3	4.0	4.1
Authoritarian Regime States	4.1	3.2	3.2

E. SECONDARY SOFT AND HARD LAW

While the difference between soft and hard *primary* law does not seem to have a direct effect on state compliance, the difference between soft and hard *secondary* law—*i.e.*, between Commission resolutions and Court judgments in individual cases—does seem to matter. States have taken far more seriously their obligations to the Court than to the Commission, although in recent years this gap has narrowed considerably.

Until recently, it was commonplace for states simply to ignore the Commission and its proceedings altogether. During the decade from 1986 through 1995, 'states failed to participate in 122 of 218 cases or more than half of those reported by the Commission'.[102] Fortunately, such extreme non-compliance diminished greatly in the early 1990s and by now has all but ended. From 1991 through 1995, state participation in reported Commission cases rose to over 80 percent. For cases published in the 1996 and 1997 annual reports, state participation at hearings, whether in writing or less frequently in person, reached 100 percent.[103] Merely meeting a state's minimal procedural obligations is clearly far short of compliance with Commission recommendations, and states today are increasingly taking sometimes significant steps towards compliance[104] or reaching Commission-brokered friendly settlements that require meaningful action.[105]

---

[101] Source: Table 7.1. Annual rounded averages were calculated by groups of states. These annual averages were then averaged by five-year periods.

[102] Buergenthal and Cassel, *supra* note 16 at 550.

[103] See cases reported in *Annual Report of the Inter-American Comm'n of Human Rights 1997*, *supra* note 89, 51–880; *Annual Report of the Inter-American Comm'n of Human Rights 1996* (1997), 50–624.

[104] *e.g.*, Bronstein *et al.* (Argentina), *ibid.*, at 241; Moscue and Coicue (Colombia), *ibid.*, at 400; Moreno (Colombia), *ibid.*, at 416; Ribón Avila (Colombia), *ibid.*, at 444; Medina Charry (Colombia), *ibid.*, at 482; García Franco (Ecuador), *ibid.*, at 551; Cruz Gómez (Guatemala), *ibid.*, at 619; Santiz Gómez (Mexico), *ibid.*, at 637; Porfirio Rondín (Mexico), *ibid.*, at 662; Ramón Mavares (Venezuela), *ibid.*, at 844.

[105] *e.g.*, Guardatti (Argentina), *ibid.*, at 232; Colotenango (Guatemala), *Annual Report of the Inter-American Comm'n of Human Rights 1996*, *supra* note 103, 447.

If the Commission fails to secure compliance with its recommendations, it may refer the matter to the Court in the hope that the state will comply with a judicial decision. And states, in fact, regularly comply with Court orders requiring essentially the same actions they eschewed when recommended by the Commission.[106] States have admitted violations and conceded liability before the Court;[107] paid or taken steps toward payment of significant money damages;[108] released at least one victim from prison;[109] and routinely taken or purported to take security measures to comply with provisional orders to protect victims and witnesses.[110] States have not complied as readily with the Court's advisory opinions. Witness that Latin America's most democratic state, Costa Rica, took ten years to comply with the Court's advisory opinion against compulsory licensing of journalists,[111] and the initiative ultimately came not from the government, but from the judiciary.[112] It is probably no accident that state compliance with the Commission resolutions has improved as they have begun to read more like well-reasoned judicial opinions.[113]

The more complete and consistent[114] record of compliance with Court judgments cannot be reduced simply to better compliance with hard than

[106] *e.g.*, Loayza Tamayo (Peru), *Annual Report of the Inter-American Court of Human Rights 1997, supra* note 75, 191, 193–4 para. 4(d)–(f) (Commission recommendations rejected by Peru), 216–17 (Court order), 245 (partial compliance by Peru with court order); Caballero Delgado and Santana (Colombia), *Annual Report of the Inter-American Court of Human Rights 1995* (1996), 135, 136 para. 2 (Commission request), 155 para. 72 (Court order); *Annual Report of the Inter-American Court of Human Rights 1997, supra* note 75, 59, 70–1 para. 66 (court order on reparations), 247 (partial compliance by Colombia with Court order).

[107] Aloeboetoe *et al.* (Suriname), *Annual Report of the Inter-American Court of Human Rights 1991* (1992), 57, 61–2 para. 22; El Amparo (Venezuela), *Annual Report of the Inter-American Court of Human Rights 1995, supra* note 106, 23, 27 para. 19; Garrido and Baigorria (Argentina), *Annual Report of the Inter-American Court of Human Rights 1996* (1997) 75, 80 para. 27.

[108] *e.g.*, Velásquez Rodríguez (Honduras), *Annual Report of the Inter-American Court of Human Rights 1996, supra* note 103, 209, 210 para. 3; Godínez Cruz (Honduras), *ibid.*, at 213, 214 para. 3; Gangaram Panday (Suriname), *Annual Report of the Inter-American Court of Human Rights 1997, supra* note 75, 93 paras. 1–4, 117, 157; Aloeboetoe (Suriname), *ibid.*, at 95, 96 para. 1, 117, 157; El Amparo (Venezuela), *ibid.*, 155, 175; Neira Alegría (Peru), *ibid.*, at 349.

[109] Loayza Tamayo (Peru), *ibid.*, at 245.

[110] *e.g.*, Caballero Delgado and Santana (Colombia), *Annual Report of the Inter-American Court of Human Rights 1997, supra* note 75, 85, 139; Giraldo Cardona (Colombia), *ibid.*, at 145; Blake (Guatemala), *ibid.*, at 151; Colotenango (Guatemala), *ibid.*, at 221; Serech and Saquic (Guatemala), *ibid.*, at 227; Alvarez *et al.* (Colombia), *ibid.*, at 273; Vogt (Guatemala), *ibid.*, at 279.

[111] Advisory Op. OC–5/85, 'Compulsory Membership in an Association Prescribed by Law for the Practice of Journalism', *Annual Report of the Inter-American Court of Human Rights 1985* (1986), 21.

[112] Sentencia No. 2313–95, May 12, 1995, of the Sala Constitucional de la Corte Suprema de Justicia de Costa Rica, in the case of *Róger Ajún Blanco*, Acción de Inconstitucionalidad No. 421-S-90 contra Art. 22 Ley Orgánica Colegio de Periodistas.

[113] See generally Buergenthal and Cassel, *supra* note 16 at 548–9 and n.44, 554.

[114] See, *e.g.*, Honduras' long delay in purported compliance with the Court's damages awards in Velásquez Rodríguez and Godínez Cruz. *Annual Report of the Inter-American Court of Human Rights 1989* (1990), 123, 141; *Annual Report of the Inter-American Court of Human Rights 1990* (1991), 53, 69, 85 and 89; *Annual Report of the Inter-American Court of Human Rights 1991, supra* note 107, 9, 34 and 36; *Annual Report of the Inter-American Court of Human Rights 1996, supra* note 103, 209, 213.

with soft law because at least three complications intervene. First, states initially go before the Commission, and only then before the Court. They may have a natural tendency to wait until their defensive venues are exhausted before complying. This is probably encouraged by the fact that Commission remedies are usually more demanding than those of the Court, giving states added incentive to wait until they come before the Court. Comparative compliance in such a hierarchical context may differ from what might occur if the Court and Commission were parallel or alternative remedies.

Second is the differing nature of the institutions. The Commission is quasi-judicial, while the Court is strictly judicial. States appear to view the Court as inherently possessed of greater prestige because it is a judicial body and thus consider its rulings as entitled to greater respect. Again, comparative compliance before such different institutions likely differs from what might occur if the soft and hard law emanated from the same or equivalent institutions, using equivalent decision-making criteria.

Finally, the better record of compliance with Court judgments may in part reflect timing. Except for its first two judgments in 1988 and 1989 the Court's record of securing compliance in contentious cases has been compiled in the 1990s. By then most states, as noted earlier, were moving toward better human rights performance and greater cooperation even with the Commission. In contrast, much of the inferior record of state compliance before the Commission was compiled during a period when many states took their OAS human rights commitments less seriously.

With such caveats, it is still possible that some degree of compliance with the Court's decisions may be attributed to the difference between soft and hard law, but there are too many variables to allow for reliably and precisely distinguishing the effects of one from the other. Still, the issuance of hard law by a judicial body which is a hierarchically superior 'second instance' to a quasi-judicial body issuing soft law may be present in other international regimes utilizing both soft and hard secondary law. Both factors obtained to some degree in the European regional system created by the European Convention on Human Rights and Fundamental Freedoms until the recent entry into force of Protocol 11; they may also arise in the African human rights system, if recent efforts to establish a human rights court succeed. In such systems, the precise division of credit for compliance may not matter as much as the fact that Court-ordered hard law seems to generate better compliance than Commission-recommended soft law. Such, at least, has been the experience of the Inter-American Human Rights system.

CONCLUSION

The effort to compare compliance with soft and hard law in the Inter-American system demonstrates the inherent methodological complexities of the problem. The closer one looks, the more difficult it becomes to isolate the effect of the nature of the law as formally binding or not from other variables ranging from law-related factors like the nature of the promulgating institution and the lawmaking process, to the state of the world. There is also the chicken-and-egg question of whether Inter-American human rights law contributed to a growing culture of rights in the hemisphere, or resulted from it. The answer, more likely, is that they mutually reinforced each other.

Still, some conclusions seem apparent. First, compared to factors such as war and peace, dictatorial or democratic regimes, and the Cold War, any difference in short-term compliance between soft and hard primary law is slight. Secondly, in contrast, one can plausibly posit at least some difference in short-term compliance between soft and hard secondary law. Finally, in the long run, the hardening of Inter-American human rights law is probably one factor, among others, contributing to an environment in which gross violations of basic norms are less tolerable, more politically costly for governments, and hence less likely. The explanations for this appear to be consistent with scholarly literature on legitimization, iterative processes of discourse within regulatory regimes, roles of international issue networks and epistemic communities, and transnational legal processes of interaction and internalization. However, in the context of human rights, especially in Latin America, those factors need to be viewed in light of economic and social conditions. Severe poverty and inequality, and soaring and uncontrolled crime, risk renewed unrest and repression, potentially dwarfing the comparatively modest gains achieved through hardening of regional human rights law.

Human Rights Codes For Transnational Corporations: The Sullivan and MacBride Principles

CHRISTOPHER McCRUDDEN

INTRODUCTION

Codes of practice for transnational corporations are essentially guidelines conveying, usually in relatively general terms, what a corporation should do in a particular country, or when engaged in a particular type of operation, or where particular types of risk are apparent. The following study concerns codes of practice in the human rights field, in particular the Sullivan Principles regarding corporate activity in apartheid South Africa and the MacBride Principles for business operations in Northern Ireland.[1]

There are five different sources of human rights codes: international organizations, national governments, private initiatives, corporations, and, most recently, coalitions among some or all of these interests.[2] International organizations such as the ILO and the OECD produced codes of practice for multi-national organizations during the 1970s,[3] but they are widely perceived as failures, in part because their requirements are neither legally binding nor effectively enforced.[4] During the 1970s and 1980s several governments developed codes of employment practice for their registered firms with subsidiaries in South Africa: the European Community[5] did so in 1977 followed by Canada[6] in 1985.

Private initiatives came to prominence in the 1980s and continue to be produced. In addition to the Sullivan and MacBride examples, they include the Slepak Principles, the Miller Principles, the Maquiladora Standards of Conduct, the Valdez Principles, the Caux Principles, and the Kyosei Principles.[7] In 1998, the Council on Economic Priorities launched a 'global

---

[1] An expanded version of this contribution was published in (1999) 19 *Oxford Journal of Legal Studies* 167. It should be noted that important codes of conduct also exist in the environmental field and raise many of the same issues. See Zondorak, V.A., 'A New Face in Corporate Environmental Responsibility: The Valdez Principles' (1991) 18 *B. C. Environmental Affairs L. Rev.* 457.

[2] For a more detailed account of the history of codes of practice, see Murray, J., 'Corporate Codes of Conduct and Labor Standards', in Kyloh, R., *Mastering the Challenge of Globalization*, ILO, Bureau for Workers' Activities, Working Paper, Geneva (1998).

[3] ILO Tripartite Declaration of Principles concerning MNEs and Social Policy 1977 (1978) 17 I.L.M. 422; OECD Guidelines for Multinational Enterprises 1976 (1976) 15 I.L.M. 967–79. For earlier considerations of Codes of Conduct see Waldmann, R.J., *Regulating International Business Through Codes of Conduct* (1980), and Horn. N. (ed.), *Legal Problems of Codes of Conduct for Multinational Enterprises* (1980).

[4] For an analysis, see Murray, *supra* note 2. See also, Muchlinski, P., *Multinational Enterprises and the Law* (1996).

[5] Community Code of Conduct for Enterprises Having Affiliates, Subsidiaries or Agencies in South Africa, September 20, 1977, EC Bulletin (1977), no. 9, 51. For a discussion , see Blanpain, R., *Labor Law and Industrial Relations of the European Community* (1991) 207–10. For the effect of the Code in leading to action by the individual member states, see Wellens, K.C., and Borchardt, G.M. 'Soft Law in European Community Law' (1989) 14 *European Law Review* 267.

[6] Statements by the [Canadian] Secretary of State for External Affairs Regarding Sanctions Against South Africa, (1985) 24 I.L.M. 1464.

[7] See Minnesota Center for Corporate Responsibility, *The Minnesota Principles: Toward an Ethical Basis for Global Business* (1992). On the Valdez Principles which relate to the environment, see Pink, D., 'The Valdez Principles: Is What's Good for America Good for General Motors?' (1990) 8 *Yale L. and Policy Rev.* 180. The Slepak Principles related to the former Soviet Union; the Miller Code related to China and Tibet; and the Maquiladora Standards of Conduct code relate to the U.S.–Mexican border operations. On these codes, see Compa, L., and Hinchliffe-Darricarrère, T., 'Enforcing International Labor Rights through Corporate Codes of Conduct' (1995) 33 *Columbia J. Trans. L.* 663 at 672–3, and especially Perez-Lopez, J., 'Promoting International Respect for Worker Rights through Business Codes of Conduct' (1993) 17 *Fordham Int'l L.J.* 1 at 12–23. In addition, the OECD has identified the Caux Principles and

standard' to be awarded to those businesses complying with its ethical stance in the production and sourcing of goods from the developing world.[8] Trade unions also have been active in producing codes, including the 'Basic Code of Conduct covering Labor Practices'[9] adopted in 1997 by the International Confederation of Free Trade Unions and the 1997 Code of Conduct agreed to between the European Trade Union Federation for Textiles, Clothing and Leather, and Euratex.

Corporations produced a flurry of self-regulating codes during the 1990s.[10] Three types of self-regulatory code can be identified. The first group sets minimum standards regarding conditions of work within a company and its associates. Another type supports increased company involvement in human rights in the larger community in which it operates. The third set establishes ethical criteria to guide a company's investments.[11] Some of these codes are criticized as aiming more to protect the company than to further human rights.[12]

Recent codes have been negotiated between corporations and other interests, such as trade unions, NGOs, and governments. A trade union coalition and the international soccer regulatory body, FIFA, negotiated a Code of Practice regarding the production of goods licensed by FIFA.[13] Partly in response to these non-state initiatives, governments have become involved in joint initiatives with companies and NGOs. In 1997, a U.S. presidential task force that included human rights groups, labor unions, and apparel industry representatives agreed to create a code of conduct on wages and working con-

the Kyosei Principles, see OECD, *Trade, Employment and Labor Standards: A Study of Core Workers' Rights and International Trade* (1996), 198.

[8] 'Global Standard for Business Ethics Launched', *Financial Times*, June 11, 1998.

[9] For text, see Gibbons, S., *International Labor Rights—New Methods of Enforcement* (1998), Appendix 3.

[10] See *e.g.* policies of Levi Strauss, Reebok Corp., and Starbucks Coffee Co. On these, see Compa and Hinchliffe-Darricarrère, *supra* note 7 at 674–85, reprinted in a revised form in Compa, L.A., and Diamond, S.F., *Human Rights, Labor Rights, and International Trade* (1996). For a more recent analysis, see Sajhau, J., *Business Ethics in the Textile, Clothing and Footwear (TCF) Industries: Codes of Conduct*, ILO, Industrial Activities Branch, Sectoral Activities Programme, Working Paper (1997).

[11] Frey, B.A., 'The Legal and Ethical Responsibilities of Transnational Corporations in the Protection of International Human Rights' (1997) 6 *Minnesota J. of Global Trade* 153, 177. For an argument in favor of such codes see Baker, M.B., 'Private Codes of Corporate Conduct: Should the Fox Guard the Henhouse?' (1993) 24 *University of Miami Inter-American Law Review* 399. For an up-to-date account, see Varley, P. (ed.), *IRRC, The Sweatshop Quandary: Corporate Responsibility on the Global Frontier* (1998).

[12] Consider the controversy surrounding Nike's and Shell's Codes: see, *e.g.* 'Nike's Asian Factories Pass Young's Muster', *New York Times*, June 25, 1997; S. Glass, 'The Young and the Feckless', *The New Republic*, September 8 and 15, 1997, 20; 'Citizen Shell', *New York Times* (editorial), March 31, 1997, A10 ('About 100 American companies now have such codes. They often go unenforced'). In May 1998, Nike published a new Code of Conduct. For text, see Gibbons, *supra* note 9, Appendix 4.

[13] See text reproduced in (1997) 3 *International Union Rights*.

ditions in factories used by American companies throughout the world.[14] In the United Kingdom, the government's 'Ethical Trading Initiative' is 'supporting collaboration between business and the voluntary sector in promoting ethical businesses, including the development of codes of conduct and ways of monitoring and verifying these codes'.[15] Codes, therefore, in different guises, and with varying degrees of approbation and criticism, have become the subject of increasing worldwide attention.[16] This article focuses on the development and operation of the MacBride and Sullivan Principles, and 'compliance' with them. It argues that the two sets of Principles cast light on some current debates about the appropriateness and potential effectiveness of such codes.

The Sullivan Principles were originally a brief set of principles, drafted in 1977 by the Reverend Leon Sullivan, an African-American Baptist minister, whilst he was a member of the Board of Directors of General Motors Corporation. The Principles were intended to put pressure on American companies with operations in *apartheid*-era South Africa to comply with a set of labor and anti-discrimination standards in their South African operations. The focus of concern in South Africa was the position of the non-white workforce.

In November 1984, a different private group promulgated the MacBride Principles, following the model of the Sullivan Principles. These principles are intended to put pressure on American companies operating in Northern Ireland to adopt a set of anti-discrimination and weak affirmative action goals in their Northern Ireland operations. The focus of concern in Northern Ireland is the need to ensure equality of opportunity in employment between the two main (religious) communities.

The codes are not law. They lack specificity in expression, but law on occasion is similarly indeterminate. The Principles are not law because under any definition of 'law' that requires governmental or inter-governmental approval or involvement in the creation of norms or their acceptance if created by others, the Principles cannot *in themselves* be regarded as law. They were the product of private group activity, and were not subsequently adopted as law by national or international entities capable of doing so. Nor have they been applied by judges in any jurisdiction as a codification of existing law or as having created law by incorporation into individual contracts of employment. No such argument was even made.

---

[14] See Varley, *supra* note 11, 470–5 for text, and 464–7 for commentary. See also 'Apparel Industry Group Moves to End Sweatshops', *New York Times*, April 9, 1997, A11.

[15] White Paper, Eliminating World Poverty: A Challenge for the 21st Century (Cm 3789, November 1997), 64. See further, 'Cook Plans Ethics Guide for Companies', *Financial Times*, January 2/3, 1999.

[16] See *e.g.* OECD, *Trade, Employment and Labor Standards: A Study of Core Workers' Rights and International Trade* (1996) 190–204.

If the Principles had become accepted almost automatically by the companies involved, they might have 'crystallized' into some form of corporate 'common law' of United States firms operating in South Africa or Northern Ireland. However, as will be seen, there has there been considerable resistance to signing them, and a significant number of eligible companies have not done so, despite the activities of investors and others. Controversy surrounding the Principles, particularly the MacBride Principles, has undermined their status, although as indicated below the Principles have become guidelines for United States state and local governments for investment, procurement, or other purposes. In that very limited sense they may be considered to have been incorporated into law in certain jurisdictions through incorporation in governmental decision-making, but they have never been drawn on for these purposes in any non-United States jurisdiction, national or international.

They are essentially *political* principles intended to mobilize, and be an expression of, *political* activity. For them to operate effectively as political tools, the *legal* system needs to tolerate them and give them operating space. The danger lies in the possibility that legal systems may remove the space within which the MacBride and Sullivan Principles operated and thus withdraw the tolerance needed for this type of activity to be effective.

A. THE 'PRINCIPLES' IN CONTEXT

The Sullivan and MacBride Principles focus on labor standards, particularly equality of employment opportunities. They thus attempt transnational regulation of the workplace activities of employers. To that extent they are within a lengthy tradition of international labor regulation, most notably by the International Labor Organization's conventions and recommendations.[17] Although ILO standards are adopted by government, the primary *raison d'être* of such norms is to regulate the activities of private sector employers.

International labor regulations also are part of a more recent, broader movement advocating international human rights. The Sullivan and MacBride Principles were heavily imbued with this perspective, although the content of the Principles seemingly owes more to American than to international norms. To the extent that both texts are perceived to be part of the international human rights system, they fit uneasily into some traditional conceptions of that movement, especially the view that human rights primarily involves the control of states and governments, not private actors. However, the growing concern about economic and social rights brings the role of non-state actors into sharp focus. With deregulation and privatiza-

[17] See ILO, *The ILO, Standard Setting and Globalization: Report of the Director-General*, International Labor Conference, 85th Session, 1997. See the study by Francis Maupain, above, p. 372.

tion, governments shed their responsibilities, exposing the role of the private sector in human rights violations. Conversely, as economic globalization of the world economy gathers pace, and with it the need for countries to encourage inward investment, the power of multi-national corporations to pressure governments becomes even clearer. The role of private actors in human rights compliance thus is increasingly recognized.[18]

Traditionally, consumers, shareholders, trade unions, human rights and environmental pressure groups promoted or enforced labor and human rights standards through governmental or international regulation of private sector actors. Increasingly, however, such groups seek additional means of putting pressure on corporations because of the perceived ineffectiveness of the traditional regulatory approach. Skepticism about governments' ability or willingness to regulate effectively has fueled the development of tactics by citizen groups such as consumer boycotts, socially responsible investing, 'social labeling', and codes of practice.[19] The popularity of ethical business issues among sections of the general public in turn has led companies to perceive that issues of human rights and ethics are also matters of business. To retain the loyalty of consumers, the cooperation of workers, or simply to avoid embarrassment at share-holder meetings, companies need to take such concerns seriously, or at least appear to be doing so.

B. THE SULLIVAN PRINCIPLES

In early 1977, the Rev. Sullivan announced that twelve firms had endorsed a set of six principles to promote racial equality in the workplace for United States firms operating in South Africa.[20] Rev. Sullivan saw the principles as

[18] See, *e.g.*,, Cassel, D., 'Corporate Initiatives: A Second Human Rights Revolution?' (1996) 19 *Fordham International L.J.* 1963 at 1984. Governments may support this movement through inserting 'social clauses' in international trade and investment agreements. See Chin, D., *A Social Clause for Labor's Cause: Global Trade and Labor Standards—A Challenge for the New Millennium* (1998). Social clauses involve the parties promising to comply with particular labor or human rights standards, or risk having trade sanctions imposed. Such social clauses have been considered most recently in connection with the World Trade Organization agreements, the North American Free Trade Agreement, and the moribund OECD Multilateral Agreement on Investment. Additionally, both the United States in the Trade and Tariff Act 1984, s. 502(b), and the European Community, in Council Reg. 3281/94 of December 19, 1994 OJ L348, December 31, 1999, Council Reg. 1256/96 of June 20, 1996 OJ L160, 29 June 1996, and Council Reg. 1154/98 of May 25, 1998, OJ L160, June 4, 1998, unilaterally attach labor and other human rights provisions to their Generalized System of Preferences.

[19] OECD, *supra* note 16, 199–204. On social labeling, see the recent study by Janet Hilowitz, *Labeling Child Labor Products* (1997).

[20] On the operation of the Sullivan Principles, see Hauck, D., Voorhes, M., and Goldberg, G., *Two Decades of Debate: The Controversy Over US Companies in South Africa* (1983); Leape, J., Baskin, B., and Underhill, S. (eds.), *Business in the Shadow of Apartheid: US Firms in South Africa* (1985). For studies which consider the Sullivan Principles in the wider context of sanctions against South Africa, see Price, R.M., *The Apartheid State in Crisis: Political Transformation in*

an alternative to corporate divestment from South Africa, which he had originally proposed to General Motors but had failed to achieve.[21] U.S. corporations with operations in South Africa were invited to sign a declaration indicating their adherence to the Principles. The Statement of Principles was 'amplified' in June 1978 and again in May 1979 to require a more stringent implementation of the Principles and to increase the scope of the Principles. Another amplification issued in November 1984 further extended the requirements, calling for U.S. companies to deal more directly with laws and customs which underpinned apartheid.

1. The Content of the Sullivan Principles

As amplified,[22] the Principles required the 'non-segregation of the races in all eating, comfort and work facilities' (Principle I) and elimination of all vestiges of workplace racial discrimination. Principle II required equal and fair employment practices for all employees. Each signatory undertook immediately to implement equal and fair terms and conditions of employment, provide non-discriminatory eligibility for benefit plans, establish an appropriate and comprehensive procedure for handling and resolving individual employee complaints, support the elimination of all racially discriminatory laws which impeded the implementation of equal and fair terms and conditions of employment, support the elimination of discrimination against the right to form or belong to unions and acknowledge generally the rights of Blacks to form their own unions or be represented by existing trade unions, secure rights of Black workers to freedom of association, assure protection against victimization while pursuing and after attaining these rights, and involve Black workers or their representatives in the development of programs to address their educational and other needs and those of their dependents and the local community.

Principle III required equal pay for all employees doing equal or comparable work for the same period of time. Each signatory undertook immediately to design and implement a wage and salary administration plan applicable to all employees performing equal or comparable work, ensure an equitable system of job classifications, determine the need for and extent of upgrading of personnel and/or jobs in the upper echelons, and implement programs to accomplish this objective in representative numbers at all levels of company

South Africa, 1975–1990 (1991); Hull, R.W., *American Enterprise in South Africa: Historical Dimensions of Engagement and Disengagement* (1990); Orkin, M. (ed.), *Sanctions Against Apartheid* (1990). For a more recent reevaluation, see Rodman, K.A., '"Think Globally, Punish Locally": Nonstate Actors, Multinational Corporations, and Human Rights Sanctions' (1998) 12 *Ethics and International Affairs* 19, 19–41.

[21] OECD, *supra* note 16, 197.

[22] The 1984 text is reproduced in 'United States: Press Briefings and Executive Order' (1985) 24 *I.L.M.* 1485.

operations, assign equitable wage and salary ranges, the minimum of these to be well above the appropriate local minimum economic living level.

Principle IV required the initiation and development of training programs to prepare substantial numbers of Blacks and other non-whites for supervisory, administrative clerical, and technical jobs. Each signatory undertook immediately to determine employee training needs and capabilities and identify employees with potential for further advancement; take advantage of existing and develop new outside training resources and activities, and expand inside training programs and facilities.

Principle V required increasing the number of Blacks and other non-whites in management and supervisory positions. Each signatory undertook immediately to identify, actively recruit, train, and develop a sufficient and significant number of Blacks and other non-whites to assure as quickly as possible their appropriate representation in the management group of each company at all levels of operations; establish management development programs as needed, and improve existing programs and facilities for developing management skills of Blacks and other non-whites; and identify and channel high management potential Blacks and other non-white employees into development programs.

Principle VI required employers to improve the quality of employees' lives outside the work environment in such areas as housing, transportation, schooling, recreation, and health facilities. Each signatory undertook immediately to evaluate existing and/or develop programs, as appropriate, to address the specific needs of non-white employees in the areas of housing, health care, transportation, and recreation; evaluate methods to improve medical care for all non-whites and their dependents; and participate in the development of programs to address the educational needs of employees, their dependents, and the local community. Individual and collective programs had to be considered, in addition to technical education. Employers further undertook to support legal changes to provide for the right of migrant workers to a normal family life, and to help develop non-white owned and operated business enterprises including distributors, suppliers of goods and services, and manufacturers.

The 1984 amplification added an undertaking by employers to use their influence and support the unrestricted rights of Black businesses to locate in urban areas of South Africa; influence other companies in South Africa to follow the principles; support the freedom of mobility of workers to seek employment opportunities wherever they exist; make possible provisions for adequate housing for families of employees within the proximity of workers' employment; and support the ending of all apartheid laws.

Signatory companies undertook to report progress annually to Rev. Sullivan through an independent administrative unit he established. Rev. Sullivan could specify areas to be audited by a certified public accounting firm. All employees had to be informed of the company's annual periodic report rating and be invited to give their input on ways to improve the rating. The utility of the Principles increased in 1978 with the decision to appoint the accounting firm of Arthur D. Little, Inc. to monitor the effects of the Principles. Media reporting and a perceived need to improve corporate image among consumers increased the pressure.

The content of the Principles clearly overlaps with international norms contained in human rights treaties.[23] To that extent the Principles may be seen as a means to secure compliance with these norms, but it is equally clear that the breadth and depth of the obligations in the Principles exceed those in human rights treaties.[24] The Principles in fact owe much of their inspiration and content to the notion held by American civil rights activists of appropriate U.S. corporate social responsibility. The Sullivan Principles thus reflected a sustained attempt to export American civil rights conceptions. It is a relevant difference between this study and most of the other studies in this book.

2. 'Enforcement' of the Principles

The activities of church groups, human rights groups, institutional investors, college and university students, and several state and local governments in the United States gave added weight to the Principles. The Sullivan Principles became benchmarks against which to assess the performance of corporations with which these groups contracted or in which they invested. Despite unanswered questions regarding their legality under United States law,[25] the growth of selective investment and purchasing policies became widespread.

A survey in 1993 found twenty-four states with statutory or policy restrictions on South African investments by their public pension funds.[26] At one extreme, the restrictions absolutely required divestment from any firm doing business in or with South Africa. Another approach limited investment to firms subscribing to the Sullivan Principles. Some laws required an active

---

[23] See: Universal Declaration of Human Rights 1948, Art. 23; International Convention on the Elimination of All Forms of Racial Discrimination 1966; International Covenant on Economic, Social, and Cultural Rights 1966, Arts. 7 and 8; International Covenant on Civil and Political Rights 1966, Art. 26; International Convention on the Suppression and Punishment of the Crime of Apartheid 1973. See also the ILO Equal Remuneration and Discrimination (Employment and Occupation) Conventions of 1951 and 1958.

[24] The requirements of political engagement and funding of social projects clearly exceed international human rights norms.

[25] The literature on this question is considerable. See, *e.g.*, Bilder, R.B., 'The Role of States and Cities in Foreign Relations' (1989) 83 *Am. J. of Int. L.* 821, 822 at note 6 which lists many of the main contributions.

[26] Romano, R., 'Public Pension Fund Activism in Corporate Government Reconsidered' (1993) 93 *Columbia Law Review* 795, 809. For a severe criticism of this development, see Langbein, J.H., and Posner, R.A., 'Social Investing and the Law of Trusts' (1980) 79 *Michigan L. Rev.* 72. For a defense, see O'Brien Hylton, M., '"Socially Responsible" Investing: Doing Good Versus Doing Well in an Inefficient Market' (1992) 42 *American University L. Rev.* 1.

assessment of the degree of compliance, whilst others accepted promised adherence.[27] Where states and localities continued to hold stock in companies with South African connections, shareholder resolutions increased the pressure to make changes, again often by pressing for compliance with the Sullivan Principles.

Other institutional investors took up this approach, particularly religious groups such as the New York-based Interfaith Center on Corporate Responsibility, becoming well-known thorns in the side of several companies. The possibility for the use of this 'enforcement' mechanism arose from the rules of the Securities and Exchange Commission which required public companies to include in the company-funded proxy statement all proper proposals by shareholders. Shareholders had to be given the opportunity to vote on these proposals.[28]

State and local entities also made frequent use of 'selective purchasing' in procurement contracts to bring pressure for change. Indeed the first recorded state or local economic initiative involved the adoption of a binding resolution by the city council of Madison, Wisconsin, to seek purchasing contracts with companies that did not have economic interests in South Africa.[29] Other localities and states followed suit, particularly during the mid-1980s. At the height of such activity, according to research carried out by the Investor Research Responsibility Center, six states had adopted selective purchasing laws or policies as well as fifty-three cities[30] and fourteen other localities. Many decisions simply banned contracting with companies that had business relations with South Africa. In other cases, constructive engagement by companies was deemed permissible and the legislation referred specifically to the Sullivan Principles. The Maryland legislation, for example, used the Principles to provide a set of minimum requirements, compliance with which was a necessary condition for state purchasing from a company. Any bidder for state contracts of more than $100,000 had to certify either that it did no business in South Africa, or that it complied with specified parts of the Sullivan Principles.[31] In most cases, selective purchasing laws were merely one part of a range of economic pressures which the state or locality sought to bring to bear, such as divestment of holdings in South Africa related companies, restriction on which financial institutions a state or locality was able to use, and a ban on the purchase of South African made goods.

[27] See Fenton, H.N., 'The Fallacy of Federalism in Foreign Affairs: State and Local Foreign Policy Restrictions' (1993) 13 *Northwestern J. of Int. Law and Bus.* 563, 569.

[28] As described below, corporate distaste for social policy shareholder resolutions gave rise to efforts to pressure the SEC to change its policy.

[29] Moses, W.F., *IRRC, A Guide to American State and Local Laws on South Africa* (1993) 29.

[30] Maryland, Massachusetts, Michigan, New Jersey, North Carolina, and Rhode Island. De Simone, P., and Moses, W.F., *IRRC, A Guide to American State and Local Laws on South Africa* (1995) 17–22.

[31] Maryland. See Moses, *supra* note 29 at 27. The policies sometimes made exceptions to the ban, such as in the case of the non-availability of other suppliers.

428 Human Rights

3. Impact of the Principles

There is some indication that the Principles had several positive effects: first, that corporations found them useful to give a focus to their social and political activities in South Africa; secondly, that the Principles brought about some changes in conditions for Black workers which may not otherwise have occurred; third, that the Principles led to increased company funding of social causes in the South African community, and fourthly, that they may have increased pressure on the government for the recognition of Black trade unions, an important factor in the development of organized Black politics.[32] It is difficult, however, for the effect of the Principles to be disaggregated from the effect of similar activities undertaken by other countries or from larger political and economic forces operating at that time in South Africa.

Whatever effectiveness may be attributable to the Principles, they could only affect South Africa at the margins. Less than half of the relevant U.S. companies became signatories, and membership declined over time.[33] At the height of their popularity there were 178 signatory firms, but by 1982 the number had declined to 145. Further, in the mid-1980s, the Sullivan Principles came under increasing criticism within the United States, in South Africa,[34] and internationally. In 1985, for example, the U.N. Commission on Transnational Corporations criticized codes such as the Sullivan Principles for not helping the Black majority.[35] Added to this was a sense of rising expectations about the degree of necessary change in South Africa, expectations which the Principles could not hope to meet because of their limited focus.

By the mid 1980s, U.S. companies considered the Principles mostly sidelined, a view that increased with the decision of the United States Congress to impose economic sanctions against South Africa. President Reagan sought to forestall Congressional action by issuing an Executive Order that required larger American firms operating in South Africa to conform to a code of fair employment practices modeled on the Sullivan Principles.[36] Reagan's tactic

[32] For assessments, see Note, 'United States Labor Practices in South Africa: Will a Mandatory Fair Employment Code Succeed Where the Sullivan Principles Have Failed?' (1983–4) 7 *Fordham Int. L.J.* 358, 363–5; Campbell, D.C., 'US Firms and Black Labor in South Africa: Creating a Structure of Change' (1986) VIII *Journal of Labor Research* 1; Kline, J.M., *International Codes and Multinational Business* (1985) 95; de George, R.T., *Competing with Integrity in International Business* (1993) 57.

[33] Note, *supra* note 32, 366–7.

[34] The Code was 'widely derided by South African trade unionists as being completely ineffective against apartheid': *African Business*, January 1986, 16.

[35] Examination of the Activities of Transnational Corporations in South Africa and Namibia, U.N. ESCOR (Agenda Item 3) at 10, 12–14, 20–1, U.N. Doc. E/C.10/AC. 4/1985/5 (1985), cited in Weissbrodt, D., and Mahoney, G., 'International Legal Action Against Apartheid' (1986) IV *Law and Inequality* 485, 501–2.

[36] Executive Order 12532 of September 9, 1985, 50 Fed. Register 36861.

failed, however, and Congress passed the 1986 Comprehensive Anti-Apartheid Act[37] which prevented any new U.S. investment in or loans to South Africa, banned the import of certain South African goods, restricted the landing rights of South African aircraft, and adopted a Code of Practice for those American companies continuing to operate in South Africa. To that extent, the Sullivan Principles were incorporated into legislation, as became particularly clear when the implementing regulations exempted signatories to the Sullivan Principles from some reporting requirements under the Act.[38] The main difference between the Code of Conduct and the Principles lay in the sanctions attaching to the legislation. Failure to comply with its requirements could lead to criminal penalties and administrative sanctions, actions which those administering the Sullivan Principles could not impose.

The focus of the law also was different. In contrast to the Sullivan Principles, which were based on engagement, Congress sought disengagement and viewed the Code of Practice as a less attractive alternative to divestment. The strategy of corporate supporters to stave off pressure for divestment by adopting the Sullivan Principles thus failed. Following Congressional action, many more companies left South Africa and the pressure on others to do so increased. The credibility of the Principles was further undermined by the decision of Rev. Sullivan to disassociate himself from the program in 1987, urging divestment rather than engagement and a total U.S. economic embargo against South Africa. Despite this, the program continued for some years under the administration of an Industry Support Group representing those companies that had signed the Principles.[39] By 1991–2, only fifty signatory firms remained. A year later Nelson Mandela issued the call to lift sanctions and most of them were removed, including those involving selective purchasing.[40]

C. THE MACBRIDE PRINCIPLES

The MacBride Principles are similar to the Sullivan Principles and strongly influenced by their compliance mechanisms, but the two instruments emerged from very different settings. The development of the MacBride Principles must be understood in the context of the Northern Ireland problem as a whole.

Northern Ireland was created in 1920 as a partially self-governing entity in the United Kingdom when Ireland became independent.[41] The largely

[37] Comprehensive Anti-Apartheid Act of 1986 (October 2, 1986), Pub. L. 99–440, 100 Stat. 1086.
[38] United States Department of State Regulations Implementing the Comprehensive Anti-Apartheid Act of 1986 (1987) 26 I.L.M. 111.
[39] Moses, *supra* note 29 at 195.
[40] Maryland, Massachusetts, Michigan, New Jersey, North Carolina, and Rhode Island: see DeSimone and Moses, *supra* note 30 at 17–22.
[41] There is a huge literature, see McCrudden, C., 'Northern Ireland and the British Constitution', in Jowell, J., and Oliver, D. (eds.), *The Changing Constitution* (3rd. edn., 1994).

Protestant majority of the population supported continued membership in the United Kingdom, while the largely Catholic minority sought integration with the south. The experiment of devolved government lasted until the early 1970s, but the experiment was unsuccessful, in part because Protestants regarded Catholics as a threat to the continued existence of Northern Ireland within the United Kingdom, in part because Catholics regarded Protestants as suppressing their national identity and threatening their economic status through systematic discrimination in employment, housing, education, and welfare.

By the early 1960s, a group of largely Catholic activists had created a reform movement that concentrated on eradicating such discrimination, modeled on the United States civil rights movement.[42] This led to some minor reforms, but at the cost of increasing political instability. An influential group within the ruling party viewed the reforms as going too far in the face of unjustified pressure, while a significant number of Catholics saw the measures as too little and too late. Views polarized, leading in quick succession to street demonstrations, civil unrest, the introduction of the British Army in a peace-keeping role, the resurgence of terrorism from Protestant and Catholic para-military groups, the collapse of the Northern Ireland government, the suspension of the experiment in devolution, and the imposition of 'direct rule' by the government of the United Kingdom in 1972. Since then there have been repeated attempts to secure a negotiated settlement.

The Anglo-Irish Agreement in 1985 formalized a largely consultative role for the government of Ireland. Agreement finally was reached to cease para-military activity on both sides, leading to multi-party talks involving all those Northern Ireland political parties which chose to attend and the British and Irish governments. The talks were chaired by former United States Senator George Mitchell, indicating the close interest which the United States has had in attempting to reach a settlement. On April 10, 1998 (Good Friday) the talks reached a successful conclusion. By August 1999, however, the Good Friday Agreement was close to collapse and Senator Mitchell was again prevailed upon to intervene to secure agreement on implementation of the Agreement.

This all too brief account introduces an equally brief description of the principal reforms introduced after the introduction of direct rule in 1972.[43] First, voting rights reform measures removed the gerrymandering of local electoral districts and up-dated voter qualifications to remove property and other requirements that had a discriminatory effect on Catholic voters. Secondly, local authority control for the allocation of public housing was transferred to a central housing authority (the Housing Executive) which

[42] Disturbances in Northern Ireland: Report of the Cameron Commission, Cmd 532 (1969).
[43] On reforms, see McCrudden, *supra* note 41.

largely eliminated the crude religious discrimination of the local authority allocations. Thirdly, the Northern Ireland Constitution Act 1972 introduced new constitutional guarantees against religious discrimination in the operation of government, replacing the previous, largely ineffective provisions in the Government of Ireland Act 1920. Fourthly, reforms in recruitment procedures for the Northern Ireland Civil Service aimed not only to reduce discrimination, but to result in a more representative bureaucracy. The Good Friday Agreement includes a strong element of human rights protection, particularly equality, as a significant part of an agreed peace process. As a result, much has changed in terms of political and economic relationships between Catholics and Protestants.

Economic disparity between Catholics and Protestants remains, however, particularly in the labor market.[44] On almost all socio-economic indicators, Catholics are significantly worse off than Protestants. One of the most dramatic differences that has attracted significant local and international attention is the unemployment differential between Catholics and Protestants. The Catholic unemployment rate has long remained about twice that of Protestants.

Parliament passed legislation in 1976 prohibiting employment discrimination (the Fair Employment (Northern Ireland) Act) in order to address the extensive religious discrimination that existed.[45] The law closely mirrored the United States approach and included the creation of the Fair Employment Agency (FEA) with a mandate to enforce the legislation. The legislative history of the Act indicated that affirmative action was regarded as necessary to tackle the inequality of employment opportunity between Catholic and Protestants, but the legislation itself was ambiguous on the permissibility of affirmative action. By the early 1980s, a significant body of opinion decided there was inadequate enforcement of the legislation[46] and the Fair Employment Agency was increasingly pressured to take a tough enforcement stance. The pressure came primarily from groups somewhat on the political fringe and a few trade unionists within Northern Ireland. Established political parties in Northern Ireland largely avoided the issue, with the exception of the more extreme Unionist parties which strongly opposed both the legislation and its enforcement.

A major problem with the Fair Employment Agency was its isolation, because the mainstream political parties in Northern Ireland were not involved in the issue of fair employment. The main constitutional nationalist

[44] See Standing Advisory Commission on Human Rights, *Employment Equality: Building for the Future*, Cm. 3684 (1997).

[45] On the 1976 Act, see Standing Advisory Commission on Human Rights, *Religious and Political Discrimination and Equality of Opportunity in Northern Ireland: Report on Fair Employment*, Cm. 237 (1987).

[46] See Smith, D., and Chambers, G., *Inequality in Northern Ireland* (1991).

party, the Social Democratic and Labor Party, generally held that the highest priority was access to political power so that those it represented (mostly Catholics) would have access to power. The party leaders expressed scepticism that access to justiciable rights, such as rights against employment discrimination, could be an alternative. In short, they considered that the problems of economic equality could only be managed when the minority participated in Government. Sinn Fein, the political wing of the Irish Republican Army (IRA), took the view at that time that Northern Ireland was inherently unable to reform. Any legislative attempt to bring about reform would be merely cosmetic and was doomed to failure.

1. The Origins of the MacBride Principles

The continuing economic disparities led to several significant developments in the 1980s, including the initiation of a campaign by Irish-American activists and some U.S. human rights groups to put pressure on the British government to act more decisively for equality of employment opportunity. Church-related groups were active and the Irish National Caucus (I.N.C.), 'a lobbying group in Washington, D.C. with a strongly nationalist perspective on the Northern Ireland question',[47] began raising the issue of employment discrimination in 1981. This activism led to an unsuccessful attempt in 1983 to pass federal legislation that would have required American companies with operations in Northern Ireland to comply with a set of fair employment principles modeled after similar pending legislation on South Africa.

The Caucus also was involved in 1983 protests against the award of U.S. government contracts to a Belfast aircraft firm, Short Bros. The campaign did not succeed in stopping the award of the contract, but it had a galvanizing effect on Short itself. Earlier, the Fair Employment Agency had produced a critical report on the company's hiring practices, but was unable to get a response from or even a meeting with an officer of the company. The day the INC issued its first statement about the defence contracts, the company apparently called the FEA's chairman to arrange a meeting that morning with the Managing Director.[48] The lesson that economic pressure worked was not lost on fair employment activists.

The MacBride Principles were launched in 1984. Their immediate genesis may lie in a decision of the New York City Comptroller at that time, Harrison Goldin, to 'generate a Sullivan type proposal'.[49] The New York City

---

[47] Booth, H.E., *IRRC, US Companies and Fair Employment Practices in Northern Ireland* (1988) 39.

[48] Letter from R.G. Cooper, chairman of the Fair Employment Commission, to the author, May 8, 1998.

[49] Booth, *supra* note 47 at 40. The competition between the INC and the Comptroller's Office over responsibility for the genesis of the Principles makes it difficult to reach a conclusion.

Comptroller's Office had a high profile in socially-responsible investment in South Africa, but had not acted on Northern Ireland. The staff member who has worked on the issue since its inception, Patrick Doherty, drafted the final form of the principles and approached the INC for its support. The Principles requested American companies with subsidiaries in Northern Ireland to commit to a series of non-discrimination and relatively weak affirmative action principles. The principles were named after, and sponsored by, Sean MacBride, a controversial Irish statesman.[50] His nationalist and human right credentials gave him unrivaled credibility among the constituency which the leaders of the campaign sought to mobilize—Irish-American groups and United States human rights groups.[51]

2. The Content of the Principles

The clear and obvious model was the Sullivan Principles even though they were beginning to run out of steam and credibility. That was, perhaps, part of their attraction: they were relatively unthreatening, even conservative, but the link forged between South Africa and Northern Ireland was of immense symbolic importance. The content of the principles drew heavily on the American employment discrimination law and avoided the substantial commitments made by signatories to the amended Sullivan Principles to engage politically and to fund social projects.

The Principles aimed in part to ensure that American companies with subsidiaries in Northern Ireland would interpret equality of opportunity to incorporate the idea of affirmative action. The text directly addresses companies operating in Northern Ireland, who are invited to indicate their acceptance by 'signing' them. Employers are to abstain from religious discrimination and to adopt affirmative action. The text is relatively unspecific in articulating expected action generally prescribing goals and ends. Clearly, those drafting the Principles did not want to become embroiled in the raging American controversies surrounding affirmative action and they chose to adopt elements of affirmative action that were relatively uncontroversial. The MacBride Principles, like the Sullivan Principles, were drafted as admonitions rather than as demands. The Principles provided opportunities for corporations to demonstrate their social responsibility. Their promulgation by a private group necessitated the non-binding form and meant that they

---

[50] MacBride was variously a former leader of the IRA during the 1930s, a former Minister of Foreign Affairs in the Irish Republic, founder of Amnesty International, and recipient of the Lenin Peace Prize, the Nobel Peace Prize, and the American Medal of Honor.

[51] Several Northern Ireland co-signatories joined in espousing the Principles: Inez McCormack (a prominent trade unionist continuously involved in employment equality issues, who is from a Protestant background married to a Catholic), Fr. Brian Brady (a Catholic priest who has since died), and John Robb (a respected surgeon from a Protestant background). Sean MacBride died in 1988.

could have no direct legal force, either in Northern Ireland or in the United States.

The targeting of American companies with subsidiaries in Northern Ireland does not mean that the employment practices in American subsidiaries were worse than those of other local companies; indeed, they are likely to have been rather better. American companies were chosen because they were there in substantial numbers[52] and thus offered a useful peg on which to hang a campaign for employment equality. Northern Ireland needed to project a positive image to attract American investors and any threat to continued American investment was deeply troubling to a government struggling with a high unemployment rate and the collapse of core local industries such as textile manufacture and shipbuilding. Secondly, there was a justifiable hope that the adoption of anti-discrimination policies by American companies in Northern Ireland could spread to other firms.

Relatively quickly, however, the Principles became highly controversial for a host of reasons:[53] the explicit linking of South Africa and Northern Ireland, the composition of the group involved in drafting and promulgating the Principles,[54] concern that American pressure might indeed be effective in combating employment discrimination, genuine concern about whether companies operating in Northern Ireland could comply without violating Northern Ireland law due to the affirmative action requirements (weak though they appeared), and concerns that such activity might deter inward investment by new companies, or lead to divestment by companies already operating in Northern Ireland. On the last point, the South African parallels were particularly troubling.

Some suspected the campaign was actually an attempt by Irish Republicans to carry out an 'economic war' against Northern Ireland. Not long before the campaign started, the IRA had begun a violent operation against economic targets in Northern Ireland, appearing specifically to target corporations with outside associations. During the 1970s executives from several corporations were murdered or kidnapped. In these circumstances, major SDLP figures who were campaigning for outside investment joined others in concern that the campaign was supported by those for whom it was another phase of the attacks.

---

[52] Currently, there are 61 publicly traded U.S. companies with subsidiaries operating in Northern Ireland with more than 10 employees, but there are about another 40 firms that are either privately owned or publicly traded but with fewer than 10 employees, about 100 firms in all. These companies account for 6% of the Northern Ireland workforce monitored by the FEC. IRRC, *Fair Employment in Northern Ireland*, Social Issues Service, 1998 Background Report A (1998) 1.

[53] For a representative selection, see Northern Ireland Information Service, *What's Wrong With the MacBride Campaign?* (1990).

[54] Some of those involved were associated with Irish Republicanism. In addition, the use of MacBride's name was deeply troubling to some because of his previous IRA connections and to others because he was perceived as representative of the worst aspects of southern Irish Catholic social conservatism.

Controversy over the legality of the MacBride Principles led to an 'amplification' of them in 1986, again an obvious borrowing from the Sullivan Principles. The MacBride 'amplifications' were intended to address specifically the affirmative action requirements, and to indicate more clearly their relatively weak content, but the controversy refused to go away. The Principles as modified by the amplifications are annexed to the end of this study.

3. Compliance Mechanisms

The main force of the Principles lay not in their content, but in the political weight given to them in the institutional framework that developed in the United States. Nothing equivalent emerged in any other country; it was and is an almost entirely American phenomenon. The strategy initially developed by the New York City Comptroller's Office encouraged shareholder resolutions, together with legislation short of divestment, following the Sullivan approach. The INC preferred a strategy of pressing for federal, state, and local legislation in favor of the Principles, based on their experience. By 1986, a strategy based on both elements was in place. The news media, in particular newspapers and television in Ireland, were actively drawn into the campaign, directing attention to the issues and plotting the growing acceptance of the Principles in the United States during the 1980s. Several elements are worth distinguishing among the activities involved, because they indicate clearly the extent to which the Principles played a mobilizing role. They also suggest the impact of the Principles.

First, several state and local government large pension funds embraced the Principles. In addition, shareholder resolutions, submitted to companies' annual meetings from 1985, grew in numbers each year and put pressure on the parent companies. The New York City Comptroller's Office was at the forefront of this approach. Although none of the MacBride proposals were adopted, they brought a significant amount of publicity to the Principles and some bargaining power for institutional investors to negotiate adherence to the Principles outside the context of the shareholders' meetings. Ford Motor, for example, agreed in 1987 to review and report on its operations in Northern Ireland, leading to the withdrawal of a shareholder resolution.[55] Ford's subsequently published report led to the adoption of several new fair employment policies in its Belfast operation. In 1989, the Comptroller's office persuaded Digital Equipment Corp. 'to become the first company to agree to take 'lawful steps in good faith' to implement the principles, and to allow independent monitoring of its Northern Ireland operations—in exchange for

---

[55] Booth, *supra* note 47 at 48.

the withdrawal of the city's resolution'.[56] Several agreements along similar lines were concluded with other companies having subsidiaries in Northern Ireland.

Shareholder resolutions asking firms to implement the MacBride principles were submitted annually for thirteen years. The New York pension funds alone submitted seven resolutions asking companies to make lawful efforts to implement the Principles, aiming to reach an agreement with the targeted company. As the IRRC has recently observed, however, '[t]he agreements stop short of formal adoption of the principles; generally, companies say they are implementing the principles to the extent they lawfully can do so. Companies with agreements usually have indicated they would cooperate with independent monitoring of their Northern Ireland operations.'[57]

The collection of information about companies in Northern Ireland is an important part of the process. Initially, the information collected was sporadic, and was largely collected and disseminated by the New York City Comptroller's Office or the INC. An attempt was made to involve the Arthur D. Little company, again mirroring the Sullivan Principles, but the company declined. By 1988, the Investor Responsibility Research Center, based in Washington, D.C., was closely monitoring the evolving campaign and producing detailed analyses of the relevant companies. The IRRC had a long-standing relationship with the investor community due to its involvement in South African institutional investment issues. At the beginning of the 1990s, some of the institutional investors involved in the campaign and the IRRC reached an agreement to monitor compliance by employers with the Principles. The effort has involved designating a staff member to conduct periodic inquiries in Northern Ireland and publishing information on the basis of these inquiries for the benefit of the institutional investors and investment managers who handle the institutions' investment portfolios.

Two legal issues of note arose during the 'shareholder resolution' campaign. The first, although of relatively limited general concern, was crucial to the continued vitality of shareholder action at the time. It involved the legality of the Principles' content under the law of Northern Ireland. In a 1986 case in the U.S. federal court, the affirmative action requirements of the Principles were alleged to constitute reverse discrimination against the majority group contrary to the law of Northern Ireland. The case was between the New York City Employees' Retirement System, which had put forward a shareholder resolution on the MacBride Principles, and American Brands, to which the resolution was directed. The company successfully argued before the Securities and Exchange Commission that it could omit the resolution from

[56] Welsh, H., *IRRC, A Guide to U.S. Laws and Legislation in Support of the MacBride Principles 1992* (1992), 51.

[57] IRRC, *Fair Employment in Northern Ireland*, Social Issues Service, 1997 Background Report A (1997) 3.

consideration because of its illegality and the SEC decision was challenged in federal court. The court overturned the SEC decision, held in favor of NYCERS and issued an injunction requiring American Brands to include the resolution in its proxy ballot.[58]

A second legal issue of more general importance involved the scope of the SEC rule that allows companies to refuse to table shareholder resolutions which relate to the company's 'ordinary business operations'. The original standard, articulated in 1976,[59] provided an exception for certain proposals that raised significant social policy issues. In 1992, however, the SEC sent a no-action letter to Cracker Barrel Old Country Store Inc.,[60] that defined 'ordinary business' to include those employment-related shareholder proposals which raised social-policy issues, including matters relating to discrimination and equality of opportunity within a company's workforce. Protracted litigation ended favorably to the SEC, but the appeals court decision left open the possibility of further litigation. In 1996, one of the four SEC commissioners publicly advocated revision of the policy. In practice, companies seldom refused either to include MacBride resolutions in proxy statements or to reach a settlement with the sponsors,[61] but shareholder activists feared that the shareholder resolution approach would be of limited utility in the long term.[62] Finally, after protracted discussion and consultations, the SEC reversed its Cracker Barrel no-action letter position in 1998 meaning that certain employment-related proposals raising significant social policy issues may now have to be included in companies' proxy materials provided they do not seek to micro-manage the company.[63]

The use of hearings at the state legislative level was another means of generating support for the Principles in the U.S. This resulted in part from assiduous lobbying by several organizations, including the Irish National Caucus. In addition, the New York City Comptroller's office, the AFL-CIO, Irish-American trade union groups, and several religious groups have actively promoted the Principles at the state and local levels. State legislatures and localities were persuaded to adopt policies or legislation requiring American companies in which the state invests to insure fair employment practices in their Northern Ireland subsidiaries. New York City pension funds were the first to do so in 1985. Massachusetts took the lead among states in 1985, followed by New York State in 1986, Connecticut, New Jersey, and Rhode

[58] *New York City Employees' Retirement System* v. *American Brands*, 634 F. Supp. 1382 (S.D.N.Y, 1986).

[59] See Exchange Act Release No. 12999 (November 22, 1976), 41 Fed. Register 52994.

[60] SEC, October 13, 1992.

[61] The IRRC has observed that Companies 'have been reluctant to face possible litigation and/or bad publicity on the issue'. IRRC, *supra* note 57 at 3.

[62] See Lazaroff, D.E., 'Promoting Corporate Democracy and Social Responsibility: The Need to Reform the Federal Proxy Rules on Shareholder Proposals' (1997) 50 *Rutgers L. Rev.* 33.

[63] SEC, Amendments to Rules on Shareholder Proposals, May 21, 1998 (Release No. 34–40018), 63 Fed.Register 29106, 17 C.F.R. Part 240.

Island in 1987, Illinois, Michigan, Maine, Minnesota, and Florida in 1988, and New Hampshire and Vermont in 1989.[64] During the 1980s, the campaign appeared to be 'moving faster than did the embracing of the anti-apartheid Sullivan principles in the 1970s'.[65] By 1993 eighteen states, thirty-one cities, and the District of Columbia had adopted legislation of some kind.[66]

State actions diverged. Only one state (Connecticut) required divestment from firms not adopting the MacBride Principles. Massachusetts prohibited investment in firms making weapons for use or deployment in Northern Ireland and required compliance with the MacBride Principles. Most states urged state fund managers to consider the firm's compliance before investing and required compliance studies to be undertaken. The public reporting requirements of some of these laws have been important, giving teeth to the subsequent monitoring effort and, in some measure, helping to keep the issue alive. They have institutionalized the campaign by making annual audits of corporate compliance a bureaucratic responsibility. The general policy of constructive engagement, rather than divestment, reflected closely the view of those in Northern Ireland who advised on strategy. It also reflected the views of the New York City Comptroller who wanted to avoid a repetition of the controversy surrounding divestment from South Africa.

From around 1989, selective purchasing 'emerged as the major new plank of the MacBride campaign'.[67] Cleveland, Chicago, and New York City, followed by New York State, passed legislation linking contract eligibility to companies' actions on the MacBride principles. By 1993, a total of fourteen localities had similar laws or resolutions.[68] The New York City legislation is fairly typical in providing that prospective City contractors with operations in Northern Ireland may lose contract bids if their Northern Ireland subsidiaries are not implementing the MacBride Principles. The approach appears to have concentrated the minds of some company managers previously unwilling to engage with the MacBride advocates.[69] 'Since the law's enactment', reported the New York City Comptroller's Office, 'ten more corporations have reached agreements with New York City to implement MacBride and to co-operate with independent monitoring of their compliance'.[70]

Selective purchasing by state and local governments has given rise to a host of domestic legal issues. Some argue that the U.S. constitution prohibits

---

[64] See Welsh, *supra* note 56; McManus, S.,*The MacBride Principles: Genesis and History and the Story to Date* (n.d.).

[65] 'More Cities Sign on to MacBride Principles' [1989] *Bulletin of Municipal Foreign Policy*, Summer, 33.

[66] Welsh, *supra* note 56.   [67] *Ibid.*, at 1.   [68] *Ibid.*, at 3.

[69] Administrative Code of the City of New York, Section 6–115.

[70] City of New York, Office of the Comptroller, Office of Policy Management, *The MacBride Principles and Fair Employment Practices in Northern Ireland: A Status Report* (June 1993), 2–3. By 1998, this number had risen to 45, according to Patrick Doherty in a telephone interview, June 1998.

imposing such requirements because they involve an impermissible entry by a state into an area of federal responsibility,[71] although similar laws were in operation from the late 1970s and throughout the 1980s to protest apartheid in South Africa. In the end no major constitutional challenges were mounted against linking purchasing with support for the MacBride Principles. Recently, however, the National Foreign Trade Council (NFTC), which represents about 580 U.S. companies, challenged the constitutionality under the U.S. Constitution of Massachusetts' selective purchasing legislation relating to Myanmar (formerly Burma). In November 1998, the United States District Court for the District of Massachusetts held the legislation to be unconstitutional because it impermissibly infringed the federal government's power to regulate foreign affairs.[72] The decision was affirmed on appeal.[73]

Every year since the early 1980s, legislation has been introduced into the federal Congress to give the MacBride Principles some federal authority. One approach would prohibit the importation of an article from Northern Ireland unless documentation was presented at the time of entry indicating that the enterprise which manufactured or assembled such article complied at the time of manufacture with the MacBride Principles. Any United States person with operations in Northern Ireland would be required to ensure the implementation of the Principles. Such Bills were before the House and Senate for action in 1997–8.[74] Another recent approach links adherence to the MacBride Principles or their equivalent to the receipt of federal aid to Northern Ireland, channeled through the International Fund for Ireland, which receives a federal grant each year. A rider to this effect was passed in 1995 by the United States Senate and the House of Representatives, but the Bill was vetoed for unrelated reasons by President Clinton. The principle of adherence to the MacBride Principles was accepted by the Administration, however, and when the United States Congress in 1998 again attached a set of principles, equivalent in most respects to the MacBride Principles, to its funding authorization for the International Fund for Ireland President Clinton signed the bill into law.[75]

---

[71] See Spiro, P.J., 'Note: State and Local Anti-South African Action as an Intrusion Upon the Federal Power in Foreign Affairs' (1986) 72 *Va. L.R.* 813. However, a 1986 opinion from the Office of Legal Counsel of the U.S. Department of Justice concluded that the selective purchasing laws relating to South Africa were probably constitutional. 10 U.S. Op. Office of Legal Counsel 49 (April 9, 1986).

[72] *NFTC* v. *Baker, et al.*, 26 F. Supp.2d 287 (D. Mass., 1998).

[73] 1999 WL 3984 14 (1st Cir. Mass).

[74] Northern Ireland Fair Employment Practices and Principles of Economic Justice Act of 1997, S. 184, HR 178; MacBride Principles of Economic Justice Act of 1997, HR 2833, HR 150.

[75] Omnibus Consolidated and Emergency Supplemental Appropriations for Fiscal Year 1999 Act, 105 P.L. 277, s. 2811, amending the Anglo-Irish Agreement Support Act of 1986.

4. Compliance with the MacBride Principles

The initial purpose of the MacBride campaign was to provide a private method to supervise companies' compliance with fair employment standards, given the extent to which official methods of enforcement in Northern Ireland had proven unsatisfactory. Although the primary group addressed by the Principles was American employers with subsidiaries in Northern Ireland, the more important indirect addressees were the British government and its enforcement institutions. Compliance with the Principles therefore involves considering the actions both of the companies directly addressed and the governmental bodies indirectly addressed. It is also useful to distinguish between the use of the Principles in the United States and the use of the principles in Northern Ireland itself. Finally, we can distinguish the role that the Principles played prior to 1989–90, when the Northern Ireland Fair Employment Act 1976 was substantially strengthened by the Fair Employment Act 1989 from the role that the Principles have played subsequently. They have been influential. It is important, however, not to exaggerate their importance or that of the American political activity surrounding them. The campaign for the eradication of employment inequality in Northern Ireland began in the early 1960s, long before the MacBride principles were drafted. Local political activity on the issue continued unbroken through the 1970s and 1980s. So too, local pressure on the issue is likely to continue irrespective of the continuing success of the MacBride campaign. The MacBride campaign was still important, in United Kingdom terms, because of the extent to which it was taken up by those engaged in local political activity on the issue of employment discrimination.

The synergy between American and Irish political activity was of crucial importance.[76] In the absence of external political support, activists in Northern Ireland were relatively weak, particularly in the context of the campaign for more effective government regulation. Several different organizations in the United Kingdom used the success of the MacBride campaign in the United States to put pressure on the British government to introduce tougher new legislation, particularly in the period between 1984 and 1989. The Principles were used in part as an illustration of what could happen if the British government did not handle the issue effectively. As a former British government minister responsible for fair employment issues has written: '[t]here was no doubt that the British government had to introduce legislation to show the world (or rather Irish-America and Dublin) that employment practices were unbiased'.[77]

---

[76] McCormack, V., and O'Hara, J., *Enduring Inequality: Religious Discrimination in Employment in Northern Ireland* (1990) 35.

[77] Needham, R., *Battling for Peace* (1998), 302.

The MacBride Principles were strongly opposed by the British government. Partly as a result of the MacBride campaign, however, the British government initiated a process to consider the adequacy of government policies dealing with discrimination between the two communities. The United Kingdom was particularly sensitive to bad publicity in the United States about its role in Northern Ireland and this led it to increase funding of the Fair Employment Agency, and to fund the government-appointed Standing Advisory Commission on Human Rights to undertake a substantial investigation of the effectiveness of the Fair Employment Act. The Commission produced an influential report which concluded that substantial reforms were necessary because the 1976 Act was not effective.[78] In 1989, the second Fair Employment Act[79] was adopted, giving the enforcement agency, the newly entitled Fair Employment Commission, broader powers. The law also required limited affirmative action and compulsory monitoring.[80] In effect, the content of the MacBride Principles was incorporated in Northern Irish law, but without any explicit mention of them.[81] Indeed, the Principles have not been mentioned in any legislation or government regulations other than in the United States.

A principal aim of the MacBride campaign was to induce American corporations to accept the Principles and much of the early activity was designed to put pressure on particular companies. By April 1998, the Investor Research Responsibility Center reported that forty-nine companies had reached agreement in some fashion to implement the MacBride Principles; twelve of them ended their ties to Northern Ireland, leaving thirty-seven companies operating in Northern Ireland with agreements, out of the almost 100 eligible companies.[82] Campaigns have been initiated against particular employers such as the Ford Motor Corporation and Gallaher Ltd. (then a subsidiary of American Brands), alleged to be contravening the Principles. The attention given by the MacBride campaign to these companies in turn led to greater attention being given to them by the local official enforcement body, the Fair Employment Agency. The FEA in turn exerted considerable pressure leading to agreements that were designed at least in part to take the pressure off the companies in the United States.

Although the MacBride campaign could have become a turf-battle between the American supporters of MacBride and the FEA/FEC, there developed, instead, a symbiotic relationship between them. On the one hand, the MacBride campaign in part depended on the FEA/FEC for information on

[78] Standing Advisory Commission on Human Rights, *supra* note 44.
[79] On the passage of the legislation, see McCrudden, C., 'The Evolution of the Fair Employment (Northern Ireland) Act 1989 in Parliament', in Cormack, R.J., and Osborne, R.D. (eds.), *Discrimination and Public Policy in Northern Ireland* (1991) 244.
[80] See McCrudden, C., *Fair Employment Handbook* (3rd. edn. 1995).
[81] See Bloomfield, K., *Stormont in Crisis: A Memoir* (1994).
[82] IRRC, *supra* note 57 at 3.

companies, and instances of discrimination, in order to generate publicity in the United States. The IRRC also 'piggy-backed' on the FEC's monitoring process. 'It's less threatening to companies (and less work for them) to say that we just want the same information that they give to the FEC.'[83] The FEA/FEC in turn depended in part on the MacBride campaign to place external pressure on the companies, thus giving it greater importance and weight than its somewhat weak political position in Northern Ireland would alone accord it. Before the MacBride campaign, the FEA was politically isolated. With the development of the campaign it gained a necessary leverage: employers would deal with it or face something worse.

Given its dual role in pressuring the British government and in targeting companies, the campaign adapted relatively easily to its relative success in contributing to the enactment of stronger legislation in Northern Ireland. The campaign demonstrated that it had a continuing role to play by pointing to the expression of strong reservations by the British Labour Party in Parliament about whether the new legislation would be strong enough to accomplish its purposes. It was able to point, as well, to continuing controversies surrounding particular companies after the new legislation was in operation. Finally, it was able to argue that it had a continuing role in putting pressure on the British government to ensure that it did not renege on its legislative commitments.

In the United States, the campaign's utility was undiminished for politicians and pressure groups eager to demonstrate their commitment to a nonviolent role for the United States in Northern Ireland. Although activity continued at the local and state levels[84] and among shareholders, attention shifted to the federal level during the 1990s. Presidential candidates felt the need to endorse the Principles and to avoid falling foul of those advocating them. The change in control of the House of Representatives from Democrat to Republican brought a noted supporter of the Principles to the chairmanship of the House International Relations Committee. He has held hearings on the issue[85] and supported the passage of legislation requiring adherence to the Principles in the allocation of funds from the International Fund for Ireland.[86]

---

[83] Heidi Welsh in a letter to the author, May 21, 1998.

[84] An article in March 1997 mentions that the Principles had been adopted in 16 states and 30 cities. 'Sleepless in Seattle Over Ireland', *The Observer*, March 9, 1997, 26.

[85] Hearings Before the Committee on International Relations, House of Representatives, 104th Congress, March 15, 1995, U.S. Economic Role in the Peace Process in Northern Ireland (1995); Hearings Before the Committee on International Relations, House of Representatives, 106th Congress, March 13, 1997. No similar hearings took place under the Democratic Congressional leadership since key members, including House Speaker Tom Foley and Senator Edward Kennedy were opposed to the MacBride campaign largely due to the influence of John Hume, leader of the Social Democratic and Labour Party in Northern Ireland.

[86] Foreign Relations Authorization Act, Fiscal Years 1998 and 1999, and European Security Act of 1997, HR 1757, s. 1737.

5. Incentives and Disincentives to Compliance

The crucial question for both the companies and the British government is what reactions and beliefs were thought to be important to their self-interest. The incentive structure for individual firms was often somewhat complicated. For American parent companies, the incentives to comply derived from two main considerations: first, the fear of losing state–government contracts or investment and, secondly, in the context of investment, the desire to reduce confrontation with activists, particularly in the United States, where the resulting bad publicity could harm the company's image. There was no major campaign in the United States against compliance, which often initially required only the relatively simple act of 'signing' the Principles. Even when monitoring of the workforce became compulsory under Northern Irish law in the 1989 Act, there was relatively little that a company had to do to comply that it would not have to do to comply with the legislation. Thus, there were few extra costs generated by compliance. There has been a relatively high rate of low-profile co-operation by companies with aspects of the MacBride campaign and a relatively high rate of cooperation with IRRC's independent monitoring. Approximately 75 percent of companies regularly respond at least in some fashion to IRRC's annual surveys. This relationship has evolved in part because there has been relatively little activity against particular companies as a result of disclosing the information, and in part because government authorities in Northern Ireland have not expressed significant opposition to such monitoring activities.[87]

The major disincentives to comply came from the reaction of sections of the local population in Northern Ireland, where the Principles have been seen as highly politicized and controversial. The MacBride campaign was opposed not only by the British government, but also by the Fair Employment Agency,[88] the main Catholic political party (whose leader argued that they created extra barriers to inward investment from the United States), the local business community, sections of the Northern Ireland trade union movement, and initially the Irish government. It is likely, therefore, that local managers would have sought to avoid adverse reaction to the company in Northern Ireland by refusing explicitly to sign up to the Principles.

The incentive structure for the British government was somewhat different. The government relatively early defined the issue as an Irish Republican-based campaign against itself in the United States. It devoted considerable resources to attempting to defeat it, and there was thus a strong incentive to deny that any legislative action was occasioned by the MacBride campaign. Due to the relative success of the campaign in the United States, however, the

[87] Letter from Welsh, *supra* note 83.
[88] The FEA alleged before 1989 that the Principles required unlawful action to be taken.

issue of employment equality in Northern Ireland remained an issue of some importance in both Anglo-Irish and Anglo-American relations throughout the 1980s.[89] The reduction of political pressure in this area and improvement of relations with American public opinion provided the incentive to do something in response to the campaign. Good relations were important if the 'larger prize' of an overall constitutional settlement to the Northern Ireland problem was to be attained with American support. The resulting 1989 legislation denied that it had anything to do with MacBride, but nevertheless implemented its approach.

CONCLUSION

Was the MacBride campaign effective? In part, the answer depends on the basis of comparison. When MacBride was compared to treaties and regional instruments, MacBride was considerably more successful. The European Convention on Human Rights is the only treaty in the area that has been invoked to address employment discrimination in Northern Ireland and it has proven ineffective because the relevant discrimination concerns private sector employment in the main, which is not covered by the Convention. Comparing the MacBride campaign to political activism without the Principles, again political activism with MacBride was the more successful, because the campaign focus was easily identified, clear, and, at least from an American point of view, involved relatively uncontroversial standards. To the extent that the purpose of the MacBride Principles was to put pressure on the British government, it was largely successful in the late 1980s, when new legislation was introduced. And it remains a potentially potent force for change in Northern Ireland should the British government's efforts, or those of its agencies, fail in the future.

Its added value in bringing about change in particular companies is more difficult to estimate, however, given the problem of determining causality, particularly in a context in which the nexus of pressure is mutually reinforcing. Nonetheless, to the extent that it provided a focus for activity which might otherwise have been more diverse and less targeted, it appears that some companies in Northern Ireland were pressed to move further and faster than they would otherwise have done.[90]

In considering the relevance, if any, that this experience has for the proliferation of the codes of practice discussed at the outset, an important point emerges. There is a clear distinction between the use of codes to create political pressure for a change in national laws that in turn modify the conditions on the ground, and the use of codes directly to change conditions in compa-

---

[89] Compare Bloomfield, *supra* note 81.

[90] The clearest evidence is found in policy changes introduced by companies on the display of offensive flags and emblems in the workforce.

nies that are targeted. If the latter is the aim, then such codes need to become institutionalized if they are to be effective. In particular, the institutionalization of effective monitoring is crucial and should be done by an independent body.[91] Funding for such research is required, but not often available for transient issues that attract publicity initially but fade away relatively soon thereafter. MacBride has had a degree of staying power in the United States because of Irish American political power, and because there has been no substantial countervailing force to which United States politicians are beholden. Institutionalization of other codes seems less likely in the absence of these relatively favorable political conditions.

We can note, too, some features of the MacBride and Sullivan Principles, beginning with several areas of similarity. They have both been immensely plastic in their form, diverse in the purposes that they served, and adaptable over time. The form in which they are expressed owes a lot to the traditional form of law, in that they are both rule-based in appearance. So too, the mechanisms for enforcement and pressure have been similar: the importance of shareholder action, public procurement, and legislative backing in making them more effective should not be ignored. These similarities, of course, are no accident: the MacBride Principles were explicitly based on the model of the Sullivan Principles. The similarities go deeper than this, however. In particular, each code's relationship to 'law' is similar. Both codes operated in the twilight zone of legality. They acted as a stimulus to the development of law in their areas of concern, operating like water that seeps into rock and, by continually freezing and unfreezing, creates fissures and cracks that contribute to collapse and its subsequent replacement by something different.

There are also contrasts between the Principles. The Sullivan Principles were explicitly established to encourage corporations to do things questionable under South African law, while the MacBride Principles were ostensibly meant to further existing Northern Ireland law. Paradoxically, however, the South African government tolerated the Sullivan Principles as alternatives to divestment, whilst the British government opposed the MacBride Principles because they considered them likely to lead to divestment.[92]

Of greater impact, however, was the difference in public perception of the two sets of Principles. The Sullivan Principles came to be associated with a somewhat conservative political reaction to South Africa (engagement rather than withdrawal). Ultimately, a significant section of public opinion thought of the Sullivan Principles as creating a defensive wall which protected rather than challenged corporations. In contrast, the MacBride Principles were viewed as a somewhat radical tool for change, partly because the British

---

[91] A point recognized in the recent agreement by Nike to permit independent observers into its plants in Asia, see 'Nike Pledges to End Child Labor and Apply U.S. Rules Abroad', *The New York Times*, May 13, 1998, D1.

[92] McCormack and O'Hara, *supra* note 76 at 37.

government miscalculated in drawing considerable attention to them by its active opposition. This difference in perception has both followed, and contributed to, rather different interests lining up in support of the two sets of Principles. Significant numbers of business leaders in the United States saw the Sullivan Principles as a way of staying in South Africa whilst satisfying external criticism of the role of business in South Africa. Few business leaders have embraced the MacBride Principles due in part to a different perception of the legitimacy of the British government compared to that of South Africa. Many have seen the British government's role in Northern Ireland as attempting in good faith to deal with a difficult problem, whereas the South African government itself was perceived to be the problem.

On the other hand, opposition to the MacBride Principles by the British government and big business has contributed to their continued force among Irish American and other human rights groups, and has given them continuing relevance in Northern Ireland. The challenge role of the MacBride Principles remains even after significant changes. It continues, unlike the Sullivan Principles, to fill in the cracks of existing hard law, in this case the cracks in enforcement, making the hard law more effective and longer lasting. In this sense, the MacBride Principles now operate by shadowing hard law, ready to jump in when (or if) the hard law stumbles or falls.

The final contrast is, perhaps, the most important. The Sullivan Principles became largely irrelevant when they ceased to reflect the aims of the major political forces for change in South Africa. Once constructive engagement by United States corporations had been rejected by those representing the black majority in South Africa, and economic sanctions became their mechanism of choice, the Sullivan Principles were rendered largely irrelevant, though the Principles continued in existence for some time after that. The relative success of the MacBride campaign lies in the extent to which it continues to reflect the preferences of an influential sector of human rights opinion formers in Northern Ireland. Constructive engagement by the United States is still the aim in general, and the MacBride campaign fits into that strategy.

This contrast, however, requires us to focus on a potentially troubling aspect of codes of conduct such as MacBride and Sullivan and, indeed, corporate codes of conduct more generally. Who should make judgements such as these? The two sets of Principles were devised and operated by private interest groups in the United States. On the one hand, this may be a positive development, contributing to the democratization of norm generation and enforcement, replacing ineffective and compromised traditional mechanisms of law creation and enforcement. This development also may be a positive expression of growing grass roots involvement in effective rights enforcement. We may view hostility to such developments cynically, perceiving it to be motivated by the threat which it poses to the monopoly power of national and international legal bodies.

On the other hand, the Principles and their enforcement may rightly be viewed as a controversial development, relying on the aggregation and exercise of power by essentially unaccountable bodies, and permitting the application of national norms originating in one country in situations where the affected interests—particularly the workers affected—are neither consulted beforehand, nor are they subsequently in control of the process of enforcement.[93] The danger of such negative effects may cause some discomfort when the use of similar strategies for ensuring compliance with international norms is contemplated. The political reality is, however, that in the absence of more traditional mechanisms of effective national or international legal action, such developments are, perhaps, inevitable. As Arthurs posits: 'the enfeeblement of the nation state and the failure to produce an effective substitute for the state at the transnational level may refocus attention on local struggles, on indigenous, implicit, and informal lawmaking, on movements which have not become juridified but which actually draw their strength and sustenance from grass-roots involvement.'[94]

ANNEX—THE MACBRIDE PRINCIPLES AND THE 1986 AMPLIFICATIONS (IN ITALICS)

1. Increasing the representation of individuals from under-represented religious groups in the work force, including managerial, supervisory, administrative, clerical and technical jobs.

A work force that is severely unbalanced may indicate prima facie *that full equality of opportunity is not being afforded all segments of the community in Northern Ireland. Each signatory to the MacBride Principles must make every reasonable lawful effort to increase the representation of under-represented religious groups at all levels of its operations in Northern Ireland.*

2. Adequate security for the protection of minority employees both at the work place and while traveling to and from work.

While total security can be guaranteed nowhere today in Northern Ireland, each signatory to the MacBride Principles must make reasonable good faith efforts to protect workers against intimidation and physical abuse at the work place. Signatories must also make reasonable good faith efforts to ensure that applicants are not deterred from seeking employment because of fear for their personal safety at the work place or while traveling to and from work.

---

[93] For a recent discussion of some of these issues, see Report of the Director-General, The ILO, Standard Setting and Globalization, International Labour Conference, 85th Session, 1997, (1997), 29–32.

[94] Arthurs, H.W., 'Labour Law Without the State' (1996) 46 *University of Toronto L. J.* 1, 45, quoted in Hepple, B., 'New Approaches to International Labour Regulation' (1997) 26 *Industrial Law Journal* 353, 358.

3. The banning of provocative religious or political emblems from the work place.
Each signatory to the MacBride Principles must make reasonable good faith efforts to prevent the display of provocative sectarian emblems at their plants in Northern Ireland.

4. All job openings should be publicly advertised and special recruitment efforts should be made to attract applicants from under-represented religious groups.
Signatories to the MacBride Principles must exert special efforts to attract employment applications from the sectarian community that is substantially under-represented in the work force. This should not be construed to imply a diminution of opportunity for other applicants.

5. Layoff, recall and termination procedures should not, in practice, favor particular religious groups. *Each signatory to the MacBride Principles must make reasonable good faith efforts to ensure that layoff, recall and termination procedures do not penalize a particular religious group disproportionately. Layoff and termination practices that involve seniority solely can result in discrimination against a particular religious group if the bulk of employees with greatest seniority are disproportionately from another religious group.*

6. The abolition of job reservations, apprenticeship restrictions and differential employment criteria, which discriminate on the basis of religion or ethnic origin.
Signatories to the MacBride Principles must make reasonable good faith efforts to abolish all differential employment criteria whose effect is discrimination on the basis of religion. For example, job reservations and apprenticeship regulations that favor relatives of current or former employees can, in practice, promote religious discrimination if the company's work force has historically been disproportionately drawn from another religious group.

7. The development of training programs that will prepare substantial numbers of current minority employees for skilled jobs, including the expansion of existing programs and the creation of new programs to train, upgrade and improve the skills of minority employees.
This does not imply that such programs should not be open to all members of the work force equally.

8. The establishment of procedures to assess, identify and actively recruit minority employees with potential for further advancement.
This section does not imply that such procedures should not apply to all employees equally.

9. The appointment of a senior management staff member to oversee the company's affirmative action efforts and the setting up of time tables to carry out affirmative action principles.
In addition to the above, each signatory to the MacBride Principles is required

to report annually to an independent monitoring agency on its progress in the implementation of these Principles.

Commentary and Conclusions

DINAH SHELTON

International human rights law since World War II has utilized a combination of binding and non-binding instruments to set forth human rights guarantees and the obligations of states in regard to them. The United Nations Charter contains references to human rights, including the obligation of member states to take joint and separate action in cooperation with the organization to achieve universal respect for, and observance of, human rights and fundamental freedoms. The first instrument adopted by the member states to define the rights referred to in the Charter was the 1948 Universal Declaration of Human Rights (UDHR), a non-binding resolution of the UN General Assembly. From the beginning, however, the drafters of the UDHR intended that it be the first step, 'a common standard of achievement' that would lead to a binding agreement on the subject. The 1966 Covenants on Civil and Political Rights and on Economic, Social and Cultural Rights fulfilled the drafters' expectations by incorporating the UDHR rights in binding international agreements. The UDHR remains, however, and many assert that its norms have become legally binding on all members of the United Nations as an authoritative interpretation of member states' human rights obligations, or that the UDHR is binding on all states as customary international law through state practice and *opinio juris*.

It is unusual to find human rights norms that exist only in soft law form, given the complex interweaving of treaty and non-binding instruments, global and regional texts. Human rights law also is complicated by the existence of judicial and quasi-judicial bodies that decide cases and build a jurisprudence that itself is a combination of hard and soft law. A decision of the European Court of Human Rights or the Inter-American Court of Human Rights, for example, is legally binding on the state party to the case, but is not binding on other parties to the treaty. In the field of human rights, therefore, it may be useful to attempt to categorize non-binding norms, as follows:

Primary soft law can be considered as those normative texts not adopted in treaty form that are addressed to the international community as a whole or to the entire membership of the adopting institution or organization. Such an instrument may declare new norms, often as an intended precursor to adoption of a later treaty, or it may reaffirm or further elaborate norms previously set forth in binding or non-binding texts. The UN Standard Minimum Rules for the Treatment of Prisoners, adopted by the First United Nations Congress on the Prevention of Crime and Treatment of Offenders, 1955, and approved by the UN Economic and Social Council in 1957 is an example of a primary declarative text, whereas ECOSOC resolution 1984/50 on Safeguards Guaranteeing Protection of the Rights of Those Facing the Death Penalty is a reaffirmation of prior human rights law. The Safeguards text explicitly cites to and calls for application of the fair trial guarantees of Article 14 of the International Covenant on Civil and Political Rights. Sometimes, a non-binding instrument reaffirms a previous non-binding instrument. The United Nations Rules for the Protection of Juveniles Deprived of their Liberty (1990), for example, declare that juveniles should only be deprived of their liberty in accordance with the non-binding UN Standard Minimum Rules for the Administration of Juvenile Justice (Beijing Rules).[1]

In many instances, primary soft law elaborates previously-accepted general or vague norms found in binding agreements or non-binding instruments. The Universal Declaration of Human Rights defines the term human rights as it is used in the United Nations Charter. The U.N. Declaration on the Rights of the Child in turn calls the Universal Declaration of Human Rights the 'basis' for its adoption. The U.N. Declaration on the Rights of Persons Belonging to National or Ethnic, Religious and Linguistic Minorities is comprehensive in its references. According to its preamble, it elaborates standards on the treatment of minorities in a desire to promote the realization of the principles contained in the U.N. Charter, the Universal Declaration of Human Rights, the Genocide Convention, the Convention on the Elimination of All Forms of Racial Discrimination, the International Covenant on Civil and Political Rights, the International Covenant on Economic, Social and Cultural Rights, the Declaration on the Elimination of All Forms of Intolerance and Discrimination Based on Religion or Belief, and the Convention on the Rights of the Child, as well as other relevant international regional and global human rights instruments. As Douglass Cassel shows, the American Declaration of the Rights and Duties of Man has played a role in

---

[1] See also the United Nations Declaration on the Protection of All Persons from Being Subjected to Torture and Other Cruel, Inhuman or Degrading Treatment or Punishment (1975) which excludes 'lawful sanctions to the extent consistent with the Standard Minimum Rules for the Treatment of Prisoners'. More sweepingly, the 1974 Declaration on the Protection of Women and Children in Emergency and Armed Conflict cites to treaty law and non-binding texts without distinction, proclaiming that women and children 'shall not be deprived of shelter, food, medical aid or other inalienable rights, in accordance with the provisions of the Universal Declaration of Human Rights, the International Covenant on Civil and Political Rights, the International Covenant on Economic, Social and Cultural Rights, the Declaration on the Rights of the Child or other instruments of international law'.

the western hemisphere similar to that of the Universal Declaration of Human Rights on the global level: it constitutes an authoritative interpretation of the treaty references to human rights in the Charter of the Organization of American States.[2]

Secondary soft law includes the recommendations and general comments of international human rights supervisory organs, the jurisprudence of courts and commissions, decisions of special rapporteurs and other *ad hoc* bodies, and the resolutions of political organs of international organizations applying primary norms. Most of this secondary soft law is pronounced by institutions whose existence and jurisdiction are derived from a treaty and who apply norms contained in the same treaty. As Douglass Cassel relates, however, even institutions are created by soft law. The Organization of American States established the Inter-American Commission on Human Rights by General Assembly resolution and conferred upon the Commission authority to supervise compliance with the rights and duties contained in the American Declaration of the Rights and Duties of Man, including the power to make recommendations to particular states. Thus, an institution established by soft law received a mandate to apply primary soft law to create secondary soft law.[3] Similarly, the OSCE, studied by Erika Schlager, has no treaty basis and calls on its participating states to adhere to soft law human rights norms. Even less legal authority for creating and applying human rights norms is seen in the case of non-governmental organizations, whose members are self-selecting and whose conduct sometimes lacks the transparency of governmental or inter-governmental entities.

Secondary soft law has expanded in large part due to the proliferation of primary treaty standards and monitoring institutions created to supervise state compliance with the treaty obligations. In some cases, human rights treaty bodies have asserted their implied powers to encourage compliance and have developed a considerable body of secondary soft law. An important source of soft law norms is the set of General Comments issued by many of the U.N. treaty bodies, including the Human Rights Committee and the Committee on Economic, Social and Cultural Rights.[4] General Comments interpret and add detail to the rights and obligations contained in the respective treaties. The complaints procedures of international monitoring bodies such as the Racial Discrimination Committee (CERD), the Human Rights

[2] See *Interpretation of the American Declaration of the Rights and Duties of Man within the Framework of Art. 64 of the American Convention* (1989) 10 Inter-Am.Ct.H.R. (Ser.A).

[3] In the *Loayza Tamayo* case, the Inter-American Court enhanced the juridical value of Commission recommendations, declaring that states parties to the American Convention 'have the obligation to carry out their best efforts to enforce the recommendations' of the Commission as one of the principal organs of the OAS and an organ of protection of the Convention. *Loayza Tamayo* v. *Peru* (1997) 40 Inter-Am.Ct.H.R. (ser.A), para. 80.

[4] See Compilation of General Comments and General Recommendations Adopted by Human Rights Treaty Bodies, U.N. Doc. HRI/GEN/1 (1992).

Committee, the Inter-American Commission on Human Rights, and the African Commission on Human Rights provide another source of soft law, producing recommendations that are technically not binding, although they constitute a determination of whether or not a violation of the human rights treaty has occurred. Similar 'adjudicatory' decisions can be found in resolutions of the U.N. Commission on Human Rights, the U.N. General Assembly, and the OAS General Assembly. Although these decisions apply existing human rights norms generally found in treaties, the interpretations and guidance they give make them an important secondary source of human right standards.

Finally, secondary soft law derives from the increasingly important work of specially appointed individuals or working groups. Both in the United Nations and regional organizations, thematic rapporteurs or *ad hoc* committees have become a common device for monitoring state compliance with particular human rights.[5] Thematic mandates may be based on a particular treaty norm or a primary soft law text. The U.N. Special Rapporteur on Religious Intolerance, for example, has a mandate based on the 1981 General Assembly Declaration on the Elimination of All Forms of Intolerance and of Discrimination Based on Religion or Belief. Rapporteurs create both primary and secondary soft law. The Special Rapporteur on Summary or Arbitrary Executions worked with the U.N. Committee on Crime Prevention and Control in developing a resolution on effective prevention and investigation of extra-legal, arbitrary, and summary executions, adopted by ECOSOC in 1989 and approved by the General Assembly. After the resolution was adopted, the Special Rapporteur announced that he would hold governments responsible for any 'practice that fails to reach the standards set out in the principles'. In his 1993 report, the Special Rapporteur refers to the Declaration on Torture, the Principles on the Use of Force and Firearms by Law Enforcement, and the Standard Minimum rules on the Treatment of Prisoners, and clearly seeks to induce states to comply with all of them.

The U.N. Working Group on Disappearances recommended the adoption of an international instrument on the topic. After the General Assembly complied by adopting the Declaration on Forced Disappearances, the Working Group sent a questionnaire to all states asking what measures had been taken to incorporate in national legislation the principles set out in the Declaration.

---

[5] There are currently special rapporteurs on: extrajudicial, summary, or arbitrary executions; torture; religious intolerance, and discrimination; effects of the illicit movement and dumping of toxic and dangerous products and wastes on the enjoyment of human rights; contemporary forms of racism, racial discrimination, xenophobia, and related intolerance; independence of judges and lawyers; promotion and protection of the right to freedom of opinion and expression; sale of children, child prostitution, and child pornography; use of mercenaries as a means of impeding the exercise of the right of peoples to self-determination; and violence against women, its causes, and consequences. Working groups have been created on the topics of arbitrary detention and enforced or involuntary disappearances.

Not all governments responded with information, but none refused on the basis that the Declaration was not legally binding.

A. THE USE OF NON-BINDING INSTRUMENTS

The United Nations has followed the precedent of the UDHR by adopting numerous non-binding texts as a step towards concluding formal treaties. The practice of a preceding declaration was utilized for the Convention on the Elimination of All Forms of Racial Discrimination, the Convention on the Elimination of All Forms of Discrimination Against Women, the Convention Against Torture and Other Cruel, Inhuman and Degrading Treatment or Punishment, and the Convention on the Rights of the Child. In a few instances, no legally-binding instrument has followed, due to lack of agreement: *e.g.* the 1981 Declaration on the Elimination of All Forms of Intolerance and of Discrimination Based on Religion or Belief and the 1986 Declaration on the Right to Development. In general, however, human rights treaties at the United Nations are preceded by declarations setting forth the normative framework. In some instances, the time lag between adoption of the declaration and the treaty results in strengthening the guarantees, *e.g.* the rights of the child and the elimination of discrimination against women. Where no treaty is concluded, the declaration may become the *de facto* standard invoked to judge the behavior of states.

Non-binding instruments are also used to conclude the increasingly frequent global conferences convened by the United Nations. Declarations resulted from two general human rights conferences, Teheran in 1968 and Vienna in 1993. The Vienna Conference also produced a plan of action. In recent years the U.N. has sponsored specialized conferences on social development, population, children, and women. Most of the conferences adopt platforms or plans of action.

Non-binding norms form the only detailed guidance in many areas of criminal justice. These norms have largely emerged from meetings of the United Nations Congresses on Crime Prevention and Treatment of Offenders, but some have been developed by the U.N. Human Rights Commission. There is some effort underway to translate the Standard Minimum Rules on the Treatment of Prisoners into a binding text, but in general the detail involved in many of these texts may make states unwilling to see them placed in a binding agreement. In addition to the Standard Minimum Rules, the texts include rules on treatment of juveniles, codes of conduct for law enforcement officers, prosecutors, judges, and lawyers. Rules on the administration of justice generally and on the use of firearms further add to the package. The United Nations Economic and Social Council has now compiled the standards into a manual for law enforcement recommended to every state.

United Nations practice distinguishes various kinds of non-binding instruments as well as binding and non-binding texts. In 1962, the Commission on Human Rights reported to ECOSOC on the impact of human rights declarations[6] after debate arose in the Commission over the form of an instrument on freedom of thought, conscience, and religion.[7] The Commission then requested a legal opinion on the difference between a recommendation and a declaration. The Office of Legal Affairs submitted a memorandum in which it said: '[i]n United Nations practice, a "declaration" is a formal and solemn instrument, suitable for rare occasions when principles of great and lasting importance are being enunciated, such as the Declaration of Human Rights. A recommendation is less formal.' The Legal Office added that although a declaration is not binding, 'in view of the greater solemnity and significance of a "declaration" it may be considered to impart, on behalf of the organ adopting it, a strong expectation that Members of the international community will abide by it'.[8] The opinion also recognized that, in so far as the expectation is gradually justified by state practice, a declaration may by custom become recognized as laying down rules binding upon states. In sum, 'in United Nations practice, a "declaration" is a solemn instrument resorted to only in very rare cases relating to matters of major and lasting importance where maximum compliance is expected'.[9] States on the Commission responded to the opinion by deciding to defer a decision on the form of the instrument on freedom of religion until it had determined the normative content. Lack of agreement over substance helped determine the form of the instrument and it took nearly twenty years for agreement to be reached on what became the Declaration on Religious Intolerance.

B. COMPLIANCE ASSESSMENT

Efforts to assess compliance with human rights norms are important to those who seek to know the truth about the quality of government conduct. Compliance assessment can gather evidence that is essential for prosecutions and civil remedies when violations occur. Evidence of non-compliance can lead to pressure on governments for better performance or, in serious cases, to sanctions. Assessment of compliance with human rights norms may also indicate where further standard-setting is necessary.

Human rights is a difficult subject for determining compliance. International human rights instruments do not provide methods or measurements for determining if a state is complying with international norms, nor do they indicate the methodology for comparing different states' human rights prac-

[6] E/3616/Rev.1, E/CN.4/832/Rev.1, Commission on Human Rights, Report of the Eighteenth Session, ECOSOC Supp. No. 8 (1962).
[7] *Ibid.,* at 15, para. 103.   [8] *Ibid.,* at para. 105.   [9] *Ibid.*

tices over time. The very complexity and proliferation of human rights norms could be a disincentive to compliance. On the other hand, many of the norms contained in the different instruments are similar or even identical in language, reducing the number of rights and obligations to a more manageable level.

In the absence of a general statistical protocol, supervisory organs usually try to measure compliance by questioning states about the incorporation of international norms into domestic legal systems. Where there is a procedure of periodic state reports, questions concerning domestic incorporation are routinely asked. Domestic measures, including constitutions, laws, judicial decisions, executive orders and decrees, administrative regulations and other legal norms are reviewed for conformity with the international standard. Such reviews can be important when they inquire into the effective implementation of the laws, including provision of remedies when violations occur.

A comprehensive study assessing the impact of the Universal Declaration of Human Rights since its adoption as a non-binding resolution of the General Assembly on December 10, 1948[10] found that the Declaration had a marked impact on the development of human rights law. Virtually every international human rights instrument, binding and non-binding, contains a reference to the UDHR and it has become the benchmark for subsequent standard-setting. At the 1993 World Conference on Human Rights, more than 100 countries reaffirmed 'their commitment to the purposes and principles contained in the Charter of the United Nations and the Universal Declaration of Human Rights' and emphasized that the UDHR 'is the source of inspiration and has been the basis for the United Nations in making advances in standard setting as contained in the existing international human rights instruments'.[11] The General Assembly emphasized the need to observe the UDHR when it created the post of U.N. High Commissioner for Human Rights, whose mandate is to function within the framework of the Charter and UDHR.[12]

More directly relevant to the issue of compliance by individual states, the study found that more than ninety national constitutions since 1948 contain statements of fundamental rights inspired by the UDHR. More than two dozen constitutions explicitly refer to the UDHR.[13] Annex 2 of the study lists national cases citing the UDHR and includes more than 200 opinions from twenty-seven countries. In sum, the UDHR has served as a model for

---

[10] See Hannum, H., 'The Status of the UDHR in National and International Law' (1995–6) 25 *GA. J. Int'l & Comp.L.* 287.

[11] Vienna Declaration and Program of Action, World Conference on Human Rights, 22d plen. mtg. (June 25, 1993), pmbl, para. 3, 8. U.N. Doc. A/CONF.157/24 (Part 1) at 20–46, (1993) 32 I.L.M. 1661.

[12] G.A. Res. 48/141, U.N. GAOR, 48th Sess., 85th plen. Mtg., pmbl., at 1, U.N. Doc. A/REs/48/141 (1994).

[13] Hannum, *supra* note 10 at 313 and Annex 1.

domestic constitutions, laws, regulations, and policies; has been a source of judicial interpretation, a basis for action by inter-governmental organizations and diplomatic action; and has provided an inspiration to non-governmental organizations and individuals pressing for human rights in domestic law and international forums.

Researching compliance through reference to changes in domestic legal norms has the benefit of ease of application. Counting laws and other domestic legal norms does not, however, reveal whether human rights are in fact respected. Numerous examples can be given of constitutional or legislative guarantees of human rights that have been ignored in practice. Assessment of compliance with international human rights norms requires that a much more difficult analysis be done of the openness of a society and the extent to which a government permits diversity and dissent, refrains from interference with personal liberty, and maintains a socio-economic framework in which basic needs are satisfied. The study by Francis Maupin on ILO standards indicates the gap between law and practice in regard to child labour.

As an alternative to evaluating *de jure* compliance with human rights norms, statistical analysis attempts to assess *de facto* compliance by using indicators deemed significant. Such efforts to measure compliance have led to disagreements over methodology, reliability, and bias. Some monitors count violations of rights where quantification is possible: *e.g.* the number of political prisoners or those summarily executed. The data may differ widely, however, depending on what definition of political prisoner is used.

A second measure of compliance relies on standards that set levels of performance that are deemed to indicate compliance, *e.g.* basing assessments of due process on the number of defence attorneys per population unit. The chosen indicators may vary considerably from one organization to another and are often criticized as arbitrary or subjective. The link between the concept and the indicator is rarely explained, nor is why a particular number is deemed sufficient to indicate compliance.

The growth in use of statistical measures has produced a considerable literature on human rights assessments. One study concluded that 'it is still impossible for diverse scholars and policy makers to agree on the quality of a particular government's human rights performance or to state with any assurance which variables lead to improvements or retrogressions in that government's human rights behaviour, or to predict when such changes will occur'.[14] Amnesty International does not provide a comparative assessment of compliance. It cites government secrecy and intimidation as obstructions to the flow of information that make it impossible to establish a reliable and consis-

---

[14] Lopez, G.A., and Stoel, M., 'Problems of Concept and Measurement in the Study of Human Rights', in Jabine, T.B., and Claude, R.P. (eds.), *Human Rights and Statistics: Getting the Record Straight* (1992) 216, 217.

tent basis for comparison. In addition, the wide variety of mistreatment taking place in different contexts does not allow for ease of comparison.[15]

Disagreement over the content or definition of human rights norms can produce vastly different results in compliance assessment. Agreement is often missing on the definition of each right as well as what constitutes a violation. The definition of discrimination and political prisoner varies from one organization to another and one place to another. One study of indicators found nineteen different ones used to measure discrimination and thirty-nine purporting to measure public participation.

Even if agreement can be reached on the definitions of rights and what constitutes a violation, collecting basic data is difficult. Events-based assessment is biased against states where information is readily available. Repressive regimes may escape condemnation because they are able to prevent evidence from emerging. The countries most in need of study are those least likely to allow information-gathering and thus benefit from the under-reporting of violations.

Compounding the difficulties, many rights depend upon subjective assessments, *e.g.*, the degree to which individuals feel their speech is free, their religious manifestations and electoral processes open. Apart from rights of personal security, violations of human rights cannot easily be counted. Denials of freedom of the press or free choices to marry and found a family can be diffuse and the result of a general 'chilling' effect. A single act of censorship may cause other writers to limit their expression. Quantitative data cannot reveal the reasons for a lack of dissent or diversity.

The methodological problems cited are common to assessing compliance with treaty-based norms and those found in non-binding instruments. The problem of causality, however, seems to be greater in regard to non-binding than binding norms. It is very difficult to know why a state behaves as it does. A downward trend in reported human rights violations could mean an improvement in compliance, success in eliminating opposition, or redirected efforts towards other types of control. The causal link between state behaviour and international human rights norms is difficult to make absent direct acknowledgment by the state of the impact of international norms. In some instances, changes in law and policy can be directly linked to treaty ratification. More often, it is almost impossible to identify the particular instrument containing the norm that led to the change in behaviour.

C. COMPLIANCE WITH NON-BINDING NORMS: THE FOUR STUDIES

The four studies in this section reflect a variety of contexts in which human rights soft law instruments are adopted. The variety exacerbates the difficulties

---

[15] Amnesty International Report (1984) 4.

of assessing compliance. Clearly, much more research is needed; for example, it could be particularly useful to look at compliance with one or more of the relatively free-standing human rights soft law instruments, such as the Standard Minimum Rules on the Treatment of Prisoners or the Declaration on the Rights of Indigenous Peoples, to investigate whether a soft law human rights text not linked to a treaty regime produces substantial state compliance over time. Among the present studies, only the Sullivan and MacBride Principles, adopted by non-state actors to govern non-state conduct, are fully independent of human rights treaty obligations. The CSCE/OSCE, although based on nonbinding instruments, involved states that were all party to one or more human rights instruments containing many of the same guarantees found in CSCE commitments. The American Declaration on the Rights and Duties of Man was adopted pursuant to the human rights provisions of the OAS Charter, while most ILO recommendations are adopted following the conclusion of conventions on the same topics. As Doug Cassel and Francis Maupin indicate, it becomes difficult to separate the impact of the non-binding instruments from the treaty obligations.

The ILO is particularly apt to study since it has been carrying on norm-setting for eighty years. In few other fields has there been as extensive and continuous standard-setting and monitoring of compliance. A unique aspect of this work has been the full participation of non-governmental actors (employers' and workers' organizations) in the creation and enforcement of the accords. The impact of this participation appears significant; indeed all four authors point to the important role of civil society in pressuring states to comply with international human rights commitments. It is notable that here, as in other contexts, non-state actors favor binding instruments, probably due to a mistrust of government intentions and a desire to have norms that can be enforced by injured individuals and groups. In the context of the ILO, trade unions are particularly opposed to any dilution from binding ILO conventions to nonbinding norms, finding that compliance even with conventions is inadequate. It is employer organizations and governments that favor soft law.

The ILO reporting and monitoring system applies to binding and nonbinding agreements, such as unratified conventions and recommendations. In labor, non-binding norms have a variety of purposes and are not always directed to specific conduct that would permit examination of compliance. Many are intended to change public opinion, government policies or influence international society. They frequently contain broad general principles that may be transformed later into specific rules. Compliance assessment is a limited tool for determining the usefulness of such accords in drawing attention to a problem and inducing states to address it, for example, violence against women.

In labor, as in environment, non-binding instruments are used and have the most influence in technical fields where changing scientific data play an important part. The Basic Safety Standards for Protection against Ionizing Radiation, for example, contain provisions similar to those of conventions as regards entry into force, non-compliance, and interpretation. The wide participation of government, the scientific community, and international organizations in the adoption of the standards over a long drafting period led to the adoption of a highly influential, if non-binding, text.

The authors reach very different conclusions on the impact of human rights norms on state behaviour, particularly concerning democratization. Erika Schlager refers to the perceived role of the Helsinki process in ending the Cold War in large part by fostering compliance by Communist countries with international human rights norms. Doug Cassel in contrast views the democratization of Latin America as leading to more than following compliance with human rights norms. Schlager does indicate that the evolution of *détente* made possible the Helsinki meeting, so that the political context also forms a causal first step in the process.

One difference in the two systems is the existence of an express linkage in the Helsinki process between human rights and other state interests, such as security and trade. The cost of non-compliance with human rights commitments became higher in the Helsinki Accords because they were coupled with security and economic concerns. The integration and balance of all the issues in Helsinki was a cornerstone of the process and, as Schlager points out, helped ensure that human rights were not subordinated to other issues. In the Americas, apart from unilateral economic sanctions imposed by the United States government in a few instances, no such link was made and human rights is not always at the forefront of OAS activities. As the linkages in the OSCE have become less important, compliance incentives have similarly decreased.

Compliance within the CSCE context was also fostered by the view of states that the commitments made were binding, albeit politically and not legally binding. The same understanding does not exist with regard to ILO recommendations and has only recently been accepted by most states in regard to the American Declaration. ILO recommendations, however, have an enhanced status under the ILO Constitution, which sets them apart from resolutions of the conference and other decisions. This enhanced status carried with it greater expectation of compliance.

CSCE states apparently preferred non-legally binding texts for different reasons; some sought to avoid domestic political battles over treaty ratification; others viewed some of the obligations as inappropriate for a binding text; and some sought to avoid a hierarchy between the legally binding and politically binding norms. In other words, it was felt that the choice of a treaty or treaties might diminish rather than enhance compliance because some states might fail to ratify the agreement and other states might fail to comply with the norms left out of the treaty.

Potentially, in contexts where human rights norms are not expressly linked with other issues, NGOs may offer incentives to compliance that can be a partial substitute for the linkages created in the Helsinki process. NGO incentives include positive public opinion, legitimacy, and even technical or other assistance to governments. The authors of the studies all recognize and discuss the important role of non-state actors in pressing for compliance and providing evidence of non-compliance.

NGOs and other non-state actors were, of course, at the origin of the Sullivan and MacBride Principles and were instrumental in pressuring companies to sign on and abide by them. Notably, however, many laws supported the Sullivan Principles by allowing investment in South Africa only by firms that accepted the Principles. In some cases compliance assessment was required. Nonetheless, fewer than half the companies doing business in South Africa were signatories to the Principles and remained unregulated until the soft law principles became incorporated, at least in part, in hard law legislation. Failure to adhere to the legislative Code of Practice could result in considerable sanctions. In contrast, the MacBride Principles had an institutional framework for compliance supervision, one that embraced the use of shareholder resolutions. Some successful efforts were made to have independent compliance assessment of companies which accepted the principles, negotiated in agreements with the New York City Controller's Office. Transnational civil rights activities involving United States and Irish groups were significant, because Northern Irish groups on their own 'were relatively weak' according to Chris McCrudden.

Schlager also notes the importance of publication of the human rights norms, which serves to inspire and legitimate the work of human rights NGOs. The publicity given to human rights commitments may even stimulate the creation of such organizations, which in turn can pressure the governments for compliance. Maupain indicates that lack of publicity about child labour laws is an obstacle to compliance with ILO standards on the subject.

The institutional structure and processes supporting the substantive norms are significant factors in compliance. Monitoring is perhaps the crucial element referred to in all the studies. The Helsinki process was effective in promoting compliance because of its follow-up meetings and non-governmental participation; it was strengthened by the linkage of subject matters which encouraged states to raise issues of non-compliance. The ILO has been effective in some of its standard-setting and compliance because of its unique tripartite representation and review process. The ILO survey on Recommendation 119 commented that the process of reporting on implementation itself served to stimulate some countries to review their law and practice for possible changes. ILO surveys also reduce some of the problems of causality, because some governments explicitly state when their legislation has been adopted or amended in response to ILO standards. If they do not volunteer this information, however, the surveys are not designed to elicit causal links, only conformity. Maupain suggests that the causal link may in fact be the reverse of what is expected, that is, in many cases national laws produce the international standards and not the other way around.

The issue of capacity to comply is less an issue in civil and political human rights than in economic, social, and cultural rights or in environmental protection, but is nonetheless a problem in some instances. Many newly independent states in the OSCE lack the institutional and financial ability to comply with norms on the administration of justice and minority rights absent technical and economic assistance. A combination of capacity and willingness appears in the apparent reluctance of ILO members to accept social commitments on workers' rights in the light of globalization. A more direct issue of capacity is seen in the ability of states to enforce their implementing laws on child labour and in the lack of resources to implement the recommendation on workers' health.

It is not clear from any of the studies that the fact of a norm being nonbinding was a significant disincentive to compliance or at least a factor more important than incentives to compliance. One of the most significant incentives to compliance is the moral claim of human rights norms. Governments, corporations, and other entities and individuals are concerned with image. There is no organized campaign against human rights compliance in most countries. For companies signing on to the MacBride Principles, the costs have been low, in spite of opposition from the British government.

CONCLUSION

Soft law is used regularly for international human rights norm-setting, either as an ultimate or an intermediate expression of international consensus. In developing human rights treaties, it is now common to pass through a soft law, declarative stage. Probably even more common is the 'secondary' soft law that is not preliminary or declaratory in nature, but is intended to be the ultimate and authoritative determination of a legal question. In this regard, hard law and soft law interact to shape the content of international obligations. Soft law formulates and reformulates the hard law of human rights treaties in the application of this law to specific states and cases. Paradoxically, this secondary soft law may be harder than the primary soft law declaring new standards.

Soft law is clearly useful in enunciating broad principles in new areas of lawmaking, where details of obligation remain to be elaborated. In addition, soft law can be seen as a necessary mechanism related to the traditional consensual nature of international law formation, which allows hard law to be made and imposed only on those who agree. Even where there is overwhelming consensus on the need for action and on the negative impact that inaction will have on all states, norms cannot be imposed on objectors. Soft law can express standards and broad international consensus when unanimity is lacking in state practice and thus the will to establish hard law is absent. Ultimately, as compliance increases soft law may serve to pressure the few non-consenting states to comply with the majority views.

Perhaps surprisingly, states rarely contest the legitimacy of soft law norms. In 1991, Cuba wrote the Working Group on Arbitrary Detention questioning the legal grounds on which the Group was using the provisions contained 'in documents of a merely declaratory nature' or provisions of judicial instruments to which the state in question was not a party to determine the arbitrary nature of a case of detention or imprisonment. The Working Group's response made several claims concerning the juridical basis for using soft law. First, it stated that its mandate extended to the application of 'instruments', evidencing an intention to go beyond treaty norms. Secondly, the Body of Principles on extrajudicial or arbitrary executions, to which Cuba objected, was deemed to be an 'instrument declaratory of pre-existing rights' because many of its provisions set forth and developed principles recognized under customary international law. Thirdly, the Working Group cited the decision of the International Court of Justice in the case *Nicaragua* v. *United States of America* for the proposition that 'consent' of members of the U.N. to the text of declaratory resolutions setting forth customary international law may be 'understood as an acceptance of the validity of the rule . . . declared by the resolution'. The Working Group decided that the Body of Principles, adopted by consensus in the General Assembly, constituted such a declaration and states had therefore accepted its validity. The Working Group also found that the Covenant on Civil and Political Rights had 'declaratory effect' with regard to non-party states.

Whether the norms are binding or non-binding, compliance seems most directly linked to the existence of effective monitoring and independent supervision. The role of non-governmental organizations has been crucial, but without a forum to which to take the results of their investigations and the evidence they gather, they are limited in their effectiveness. In short, it is the synergy between human rights bodies created by inter-governmental organizations and non-governmental organizations that leads to greater compliance by states. The existence of non-binding norms and the consensus that emerges as states begin to comply with them also appears to stimulate the development of legally-binding norms.

The studies indicate that states do comply with non-binding human rights norms some of the time. They also comply with binding human rights norms some of the time. No state is free of human rights problems and it is utopian to think that either international or national human rights norms, binding or non-binding, will ever be complied with by all states all of the time. The use of non-binding instruments in human rights law as a precursor to binding norms probably limits state compliance, because the use of the non-binding form is often a reflection of disagreement over the content of the norm or norms in question. It at least reflects 'unfinished business' in defining the details of the rights guaranteed within the instrument. Subsequent adoption of a treaty is significant for all states, as the adoption indicates the emergence of a consensus on the right or rights. Thus, the treaty may lead to greater compliance by non-ratifying states which participated in the drafting process, as well as ratifying states, due to the fact of negotiating an agreed legally binding norm. It may appear, however, that the state is complying with the earlier non-binding norm. Clearly, the non-binding text is useful to begin the process of consensus, and in some cases may remain the only available text where no agreement can be reached. In the long run, however, non-binding norms in human rights are generally not as effective as binding commitments and the enforcement possibilities that come with them for victims and their representatives.

Chapter 8
Multilateral Arms Control

DINAH SHELTON

Multilateral arms control involves efforts to place limits on the quality and quantity of weapons of war. In respect to the former, at least since the 1868 Declaration of St Petersburg prohibited the use of certain explosive projectiles in time of war, states have sought to fix 'the technical limits at which the necessities of war ought to yield to the requirements of humanity'[1] in order to avoid unnecessary suffering. Throughout the twentieth century, international law moved to prohibit or restrict specific weapons, including asphyxiating or poisonous gases, expanding bullets, poison or poisoned weapons, chemical weapons, biological weapons, and 'certain conventional weapons which may be deemed to be excessively injurious or to have indiscriminate effects'.[2] On the quantitative side, in addition to regulating or prohibiting the use of specific weapons during a conflict, various agreements and understandings have sought to limit the development, stockpiling, and proliferation of weapons during peacetime.

The International Court of Justice summarized the fundamental principles and balance between military necessity and humanitarian considerations in its Advisory Opinion on the Legality of the Threat or Use of Nuclear Weapons:

The cardinal principles contained in the texts constituting the fabric of humanitarian law are the following. The first is aimed at the protection of the civilian population and civilian objects and establishes the distinction between combatants and non-combatants; states must never make civilians the object of attack and must

---

[1] Declaration of St Petersburg of 1868 to the Effect of Prohibiting the Use of Certain Projectiles in Wartime (St Petersburg, November 29–December 11, 1868), reprinted in *International Red Cross Handbook* (12th edn. 1983) 319. See Blix, H., 'Area Bombardment: Rules and Reasons' (1978) 49 *B.Y.I.L.* 31.

[2] See Declaration concerning the Prohibition of Using Bullets which Expand or Flatten Easily in the Human Body (The Hague 1899); The Hague Convention of October 18, 1907 relative to the laying of automatic submarine contact mines (Convention No. VIII of 1907); Geneva Protocol of June 17, 1925 for the prohibition of the use in war of asphyxiating, poisonous, or other gases and of bacteriological methods of warfare; Convention on the Prohibition of the Development, Production and Stockpiling of Bacteriological and Toxin Weapons and on their Destruction of April 19, 1972; Convention on the Prohibition of Military or any Other Hostile Use of Environmental Modification Techniques, of 10 October 1976; and United Nations Conference on Prohibitions or Restrictions on the Use of Certain Conventional Weapons which May be Deemed to be Excessively Injurious or to Have Indiscriminate Effects: Final Act, Convention, Protocols, Resolution, of October 10, 1980.

consequently never use weapons that are incapable of distinguishing between civilian and military targets. According to the second principle, it is prohibited to cause unnecessary suffering to combatants; it is accordingly prohibited to use weapons causing them such harm or uselessly aggravating their suffering. In application of that second principle, states do not have unlimited freedom of choice of means in the weapons they use.[3]

For each state, the issues at stake are of prime importance, concerning sovereignty and survival. National defense being in question, it may be expected that agreements are most carefully negotiated to be precise and sufficiently detailed to provide as much certainty as possible. In such a system, it might be expected that non-binding norms would have little role to play, but the reality is that they serve both as precursors to binding agreements and as subsequent norms to fill in the technical gaps where complex technical regulation is required. United Nations General Assembly resolutions have frequently been a prelude to conventional norms, preceding the conclusion of the partial test ban treaty, the nuclear non-proliferation agreement, the establishment of nuclear-free zones in Latin America, outer space, and the sea bed, and the convention against biological weapons.[4] Resolutions can express public opinion and help create or reinforce international norms. As Barry Kellman describes below, non-binding norms also supplement binding obligations in the protection of nuclear materials.

The studies in this chapter look at the interplay of hard law and soft law in the area of multilateral arms control, from nuclear weapons to land mines. The first study, by David Gaultieri, looks at the various decisions taken by weapons control supplier groups to restrict transfers of specific technology. Barry Kellman then analyses the complex interweaving of hard and soft law for the protection of nuclear materials in order to ensure responsible control over nuclear materials and to prevent nuclear weapons proliferation. Finally, Richard Williamson traces the development of the norm against anti-personnel land mines from soft law to hard law.

---

[3] 1996 ICJ Reports, para. 78, (1996) 35 I.L.M. 827.

[4] See Cot, J.-P., and Boniface, P., 'Disarmament and Arms Control', in Bedjaoui, M. (ed.), *International Law: Achievements and Prospects* (1991) 811, 814.

The System of Non-proliferation Export Controls

DAVID S. GUALTIERI

INTRODUCTION

The international system of weapons control has slowed proliferation and reduced some forms of threats. This study analyzes one element of that system: non-binding export control guidelines as developed and applied by the various 'supplier groups' to block international trade in weapons-related technologies.

Export controls are an integral part of multilateral weapons control. They have effectively stunted the development of nuclear weapons by several less developed states and arguably they have contributed to limiting the proliferation of chemical weapons. Export controls, including those imposed by the supplier groups, have gained in importance in recent years and a great deal of analysis has been devoted to their improvement, even though the spread of technology and the emergence of potential suppliers of weapons technology appear to make restrictive export policies less meaningful.[1] Developing effective controls appears all the more difficult because weapons control is largely becoming a problem of controlling dual-use technologies (technologies with both weapons and legitimate non-weapons purposes) that are difficult to identify and to verify their use for non-weapons purposes.

Export controls operate on three levels. First, restrictions on transfers are included in the major binding multilateral weapons control agreements: the 1968 Nuclear Non-Proliferation Treaty (NPT),[2] the 1972 Biological Weapons Convention (BWC),[3] and the 1993 Chemical Weapons Convention (CWC).[4] Second, key supplier states have formed supplier groups to coordinate and

---

[1] Fischer, D., *Towards 1995: The Prospects for Ending the Proliferation of Nuclear Weapons* (1993) 97.

[2] Treaty on the Non-Proliferation of Nuclear Weapons, opened for signature July 1, 1968, 21 U.S.T. 483, T.I.A.S. No. 6839, 729 U.N.T.S. 161 (hereinafter NPT).

[3] Convention on the Prohibition of the Development, Production and Stockpiling of Bacteriological (Biological) and Toxin Weapons and on Their Destruction, opened for signature Apr. 10, 1972, 26 U.S.T. 583, T.I.A.S. No. 8062, 1015 U.N.T.S. 163 (hereinafter BWC). The BWC is not discussed in detail in this ch.

[4] The Convention on the Prohibition of the Development, Production, Stockpiling and Use of Chemical Weapons and on their Destruction, opened for signature, Paris, January 13, 1993, entered into force April 29, 1997, 32 I.L.M. 800 (hereinafter CWC).

harmonize national export control strategies. The major supplier groups are the Zangger Committee and the Nuclear Suppliers Group (nuclear weapons), the Australia Group (chemical and, to a lesser extent, biological weapons), and the Missile Technology Control Regime (MTCR; regulation of transfers of ballistic missile technology). Supplier groups are an important, albeit informal and voluntary, part of the international regime to control WMD. The Australia Group, for example, is generally considered part of the regime to control chemical weapons although it is entirely separate from the CWC. Third, supplier states enact domestic legislation restricting exports as required under weapons control treaties to which they are parties and pursuant to the voluntary guidelines propounded by the supplier groups.

The export restrictions in weapons control treaties, such as Article III(2) of the NPT, are classic 'hard law', but the export control guidelines developed by the supplier groups are not. Supplier group arrangements share several features. First, they are neither created by nor the subject of a treaty or other positivist source of international law. With the exception of the Zangger Committee, no supplier group is formally linked to an international treaty that addresses the same subject. Second, the guidelines they develop have not been codified in a treaty, are entirely voluntary, and are implemented domestically subject to the will of the supplier group member. Third, supplier group membership is highly self-selective. Fourth, the norms emanating from supplier groups are not the product of a transparent, deliberative procedure. Fifth, there is no express consequence for non-compliance nor procedure to address compliance concerns. Sixth, none of the supplier groups is administered by an international organization.

There are, of course, many reasons why supplier groups adopted and continue to maintain their informal and non-binding status. Supplier group members have consistently demonstrated a preference for the current structure, perhaps a result of security concerns, and rarely have taken steps to formalize or further institutionalize the various supplier groups. Some of the reasons for the current system are historical and highly contextual. For example, the Australia Group was formed in quick response to the horrors of chemical weapons seen in the Iran–Iraq war and because, in 1984, no treaty as yet explicitly banned the production or use of chemical weapons.

Other reasons for the present system are practical. First, export controls consist mainly in the development of lists of technologies whose transfer should be restricted under domestic law. Conventional wisdom holds that a large, formal institution based on a binding treaty will be less nimble and slower to respond to new situations, such as rapid technological innovation. Second, a formalized regime is likely to lose some stringency as export control lists will be subject to review from more states and fewer items will be subject to controls. Amendments and other changes will also be more difficult to negotiate. Thus, supplier group members view the current, informal structure as possessing a flexibility and responsiveness that would be sacrificed if the obligations were binding. Similar reasons underlie the preference of supplier groups to restrict their membership to the major supplier states.

The adoption of non-legally binding export controls in an informal context is also the result of political concerns, such as the internal security of supplier group members and the need for confidentiality during the development of supplier group guidelines. There also may seem to be little need to make supplier group guidelines binding. Supplier group members are typically so self-selected and share enough objectives that members can have a high degree of confidence that other members will implement the guidelines. Even though the guidelines are non-binding and unenforceable on the international plane, they become binding and enforceable once they are transformed into domestic law. Members thus can easily verify that the voluntary guidelines have been implemented and will be enforced through the domestic law of other members.

Despite its advantages, the structure and membership of the supplier groups has for decades drawn objections from the developing world. Supplier group arrangements often exceed the binding norms of the weapons control treaties, such as the CWC or NPT, and are agreed to by a small minority of powerful industrialized parties to those treaties. The disparity between treaty requirements and more stringent supplier group guidelines creates legal tensions and complicates global weapons control cooperation. The current system, in the developing world's view, erects unnecessary barriers to technology transfer, allowing supplier states to protect their markets in sophisticated technologies.[5] The conflict is sharpest where a developing country is a party to a multilateral treaty but is denied a transfer based on a more stringent supplier group guideline to which that state never acceded.

The issue here goes beyond compliance with the non-binding guidelines of the supplier groups. It is important to ensure that export controls are effectively integrated into the larger regime of international weapons controls. Export controls, by themselves, will not stanch proliferation; rather, they play an important role in slowing the development of weapons programs and buying time for other modalities of the weapons control regime to function.[6]

Whether an export restriction emanates from a treaty or a supplier group guideline, there is a general perception that compliance is high among supplier group members. This is different than saying that export controls have been effective in preventing proliferation; such a statement would be difficult to make. Even assessment of supplier group compliance with the guidelines is qualified by several factors. First, it is exceedingly difficult to measure

[5] See Müller, H., *The Nuclear Trade Regime: A Case for Strengthening the Rules in Nuclear Non-Proliferation and the Non-Proliferation Treaty* (1990) 19–21.

[6] See Dunn, L.A., 'On Proliferation Watch: Some Reflections on the Past Quarter Century' (1998) *The Nonproliferation Review* (Spring-Summer) 66.

compliance, because so many weapons technologies can be used both for legitimate commercial purposes and for weapons development. Second, the absence of a mechanism to monitor technology transfers and verify compliance is an obvious impediment. Yet, because supplier groups are self-selected and consist of industrially advanced states that share similar characteristics and interests, a certain degree of compliance can be assumed. In other words, supplier group members are the types of states that are most likely to comply with their own guidelines.

Finally, the efficacy of supplier group restrictions will inevitably be affected by the extent to which there is a perceived proliferation threat from a particular weapon. In that connection, while it might be said that export controls applied to nuclear technology have been fairly effective as evidenced by the few countries that have successfully developed a nuclear weapon, it should be noted that the technology required to establish a nuclear capability is highly sophisticated and relatively easy to track. To a somewhat lesser extent, the same might be said about restrictions on the export of missile technology under the MTCR. In contrast, the greater accessibility of the required technologies and their dual-use character make it difficult to say whether the Australia Group controls have significantly slowed the proliferation of chemical and biological weapons.

Even if a high degree of compliance could be demonstrated, this study suggests that supplier groups must possess legitimacy and normative validity to continue to be effective in an era when developing world cooperation and participation will be essential to broader non-proliferation objectives. Export controls ultimately may be weakened, not by waning relevance or a lack of efficacy, but by flaws in the elaboration and implementation of the supplier group guidelines. The current system possesses little discernible structure and few procedures. Current and potential supplier group members have difficulty assessing the effects of the group and calculating their interests when making the decision to comply or join. In addition, supplier group decisions adversely affect non-members; those states believe that they are being denied economic opportunity by a secretive regime whose processes and decisions are not subject to scrutiny and they are not likely to respect the controls promulgated by supplier groups.

North–South tensions have supplanted the former East–West balance of terror. Although export control guidelines draw powerful normative support from international agreements, their legitimacy and effectiveness are undercut by their informality, their secrecy, and their discriminatory, cartel-like operation. One possible approach to alleviate North–South tensions, while also maintaining the efficacy of export controls, is to impose trade restrictions pursuant to a non-discriminatory, legitimately established export control regime.

Numerous practical reasons support the coordination of export controls under a more formal regime. Export controls require high levels of cooperation and coordination operating within a complex web of agreements and arrangements touching on international security, disarmament, non-proliferation, and international trade. Global interdependence across agreements and issue areas makes it nearly impossible to achieve export control objectives through informal, *ad hoc* responses. According to Chayes and Chayes, 'these developments . . . engender a demand for regulatory norms. . . . The traditional attributes of effective foreign policy in the security area—flexibility, energy, secrecy, etc.— tend to give way before the growing importance for the new sovereignty of predictability, reliability, and stability of expectations.'[7]

Leaving aside the debate over the necessity of highly technical improvements, such as revising control lists or improving national export control policies, this study concentrates on procedural and institutional responses that may engender greater confidence in a cooperative context and improve the long term prospects of compliance with export controls. The first part of the study describes the various supplier groups and the requirements of any weapons control treaty that they supplement. The subsequent section describes why the lack of procedural and substantive legitimacy weakens the current system. The third part suggests possible regime-oriented responses to close the legitimacy gap of the various supplier groups. The final section presents the conclusions.

A. THE INTERNATIONAL SYSTEM OF EXPORT CONTROLS

1. Nuclear Weapons

The 1968 Nuclear Non-Proliferation Treaty (NPT) is the centerpiece of the international regime to control the proliferation of nuclear weapons. The regime also includes the Statute of the International Atomic Energy Agency,[8] national safeguards agreements that govern verification under the treaty, and the operation of two supplier groups: the Zangger Committee and the Nuclear Supplier Group. Relevant export controls include those contained in the treaty itself and the guidelines developed by the supplier groups.

The objectives of the NPT are to (a) halt the spread of nuclear weapons, (b) promote nuclear disarmament, and (c) promote the peaceful use of nuclear technologies and materials. The NPT is intentionally discriminatory; it distinguishes between states that tested a nuclear device prior to 1967 (nuclear weapons states or NWS)[9] and non-nuclear-weapon states (NNWS). NWS

---

[7] Chayes, A., and Chayes, A.H., *The New Sovereignty: Compliance with International Regulatory Agreements* (1995) 124.

[8] Statute of the International Atomic Energy Agency, opened for signature October 26, 1956, 8 U.S.T. 1095, T.I.A.S. No. 3873, 276 U.N.T.S. 3 (entered into force July 29, 1957).

[9] There are five such states: China, France, the former Soviet Union, the United Kingdom, and the United States. Four former Soviet republics have nuclear weapons within their territory: Russia, Belarus, Kazakhstan, and Ukraine.

agree (a) not to assist or encourage any NNWS in acquiring nuclear weapons, (b) to share the benefits of peaceful application of nuclear power for civilian purposes, and (c) to attempt to curb the nuclear arms race at an early date. The NNWS agree to (a) not receive, manufacture, or otherwise acquire nuclear explosive devices, either directly or indirectly; and (b) accept international safeguards on all their peaceful nuclear activities, under the auspices of the International Atomic Energy Agency (IAEA), including reporting requirements, on-site inspections, and other means to verify that nuclear materials, equipment, facilities, and information are not used to further nuclear explosive purposes.[10]

The NPT restricts the international transfer of nuclear weapons, nuclear material, and equipment. NWS cannot transfer nuclear weapons or nuclear explosive devices 'to any recipient whatsoever'. Nor may a NNWS receive nuclear weapons or nuclear explosive devices, or the control thereof, from 'any transferor whatsoever'.[11] Article III(2) is the first and arguably most significant multinational agreement to control exports of nuclear materials and equipment. Under Article III(2), each State Party:

undertakes not to provide: (a) source or special fissionable material, or (b) equipment or material especially designed or prepared for the processing, use or production of special fissionable material, to any non-nuclear weapon State for peaceful purposes, unless the source or special fissionable material shall be subject to the safeguards required by this article.[12]

Thus, both NWS and NNWS must safeguard the transfer to any NNWS of (a) source or fissionable material, or (b) equipment or material designed or prepared for the processing, use, or production of special fissionable material for peaceful purposes. States Parties are also encouraged voluntarily to report their import and export activities with respect to specified equipment and non-nuclear material used in the nuclear industry.

To interpret and effectively to implement Article III(2),[13] a group of ten supplier states, commonly known as the Zangger Committee, began meeting in 1971 to develop a list of materials that, if transferred to a NNWS, would uniformly 'trigger' IAEA safeguards.[14] This list includes components, equipment, and materials necessary for the nuclear fuel cycle, but does not ban transfers of sensitive technologies such as enrichment and reprocessing equipment. To export nuclear material or equipment to NNWS that are not NPT

---

[10] NPT, *supra* note 2, Arts. I, IV and V, VI, II, III (respectively).

[11] *Ibid.*, Arts. I, II (respectively).   [12] *Ibid.*, Art. III(2).

[13] Most Art. III(2) ambiguities have been adequately resolved over a long period of NPT practice. See generally Müller, H., 'The Future of the NPT: Modifications to the Nuclear Non-Proliferation Treaty Regime' (1992) 14 *Harv. Int'l Rev.* 10–12.

[14] IAEA Doc. INFCIRC/209 (September 1974). See also Berkhout, F., 'The NPT and Nuclear Export Controls', in Howlett, D., and Simpson, J. (eds.), *Nuclear Non-Proliferation: A Reference Handbook* (1992) 45.

parties, supplier states must require that trigger list items will not be diverted to nuclear weapons and that the recipient state has negotiated a safeguards agreement with the IAEA. Furthermore, suppliers must seek assurances from recipient states that any trigger list items will not be re-exported to a third state unless safeguards are effectively applied in that state.

The Zangger Committee is a forum for the exchange of information about exports, or licenses for exports, to any NNWS not party to the NPT. Committee members submit annual reports of such exports which are circulated on a confidential basis among the members. The Group's decisions are taken by consensus, have no formal status under international law, and are not legally binding upon its members. Understandings reached by the Committee are communicated to the IAEA and are implemented through coordinated unilateral decisions of governments in their national export legislation.

The Zangger Committee draws discernible authority from the NPT, meaning its guidelines apply only to NPT-specified items and its restrictions cannot be applied any more strictly to ostensibly compliant NPT adherents, even if their proliferation motives are suspect. In light of the fact that the Nuclear Suppliers Group has adopted all items on the trigger list and agreed to require full-scope safeguards as to those items, the Zangger Committee may become less significant, though it might retain a technical, advisory role in support of the Nuclear Suppliers Group.[15]

To rectify some shortcomings in the Zangger Committee, and in direct response to India's successful nuclear explosion in 1974, the Nuclear Suppliers Group (NSG or 'London Club') was formed in 1975 to draw up a list of materials, equipment, and technology more comprehensive than the Zangger Committee's trigger list. The NSG is not the subject of a single formal agreement; instead the original fifteen members exchanged bilateral notes accepting the guidelines. The NSG encourages all countries to apply the guidelines, but will only accept new members upon the unanimous agreement of all current members. The NSG has no permanent location, although many meetings are held in Vienna.[16] No formal institution or organization monitors or enforces NSG guidelines, but Japan serves as a point of contact and oversees the application of dual-use guidelines.

The NSG's main accomplishments are: (1) to add sensitive nuclear technology related to enrichment or reprocessing, and not just hardware, to the list of regulated items;[17] (2) to bring France, then an NPT holdout and not a

---

[15] Goldblat, J., *Arms Control: A Guide to Negotiations and Agreements* (1994) 88.

[16] Search of the United States Arms Control and Disarmament Homepage on the World Wide Web, http://pa.acda.gov/negotiat.htm (March 24, 1996).

[17] Members were to exercise 'restraint' with respect to such transfers, a policy that basically amounts to a rule of no transfers. Müller, H., 'Export Controls: Review of Article III', in Simpson, J., and Howlett, D. (eds.), *The Future of the Non-Proliferation Treaty* (1995) 133.

member of the Zangger Committee, within the system of export controls; and (3) to regulate nuclear materials beyond those specified by Article III(2) of the NPT.[18] Transfers of items on the NSG list would trigger full scope IAEA safeguards when exported to any NNWS not party to the NPT.[19] The NSG's Guidelines for Nuclear Transfers[20] require the recipients of trigger list items to provide effective physical protection for these items and to pledge not to use them for the manufacture of nuclear explosives.[21] If materials are diverted or if supplier/recipient understandings are violated, NSG members should consult promptly on possible common action.[22]

Drawn up in secret by only seven supplier states, the NSG Guidelines engendered great resistance and distrust among developing countries as a discriminatory regime to deny technology. Developments in the 1980s and early 1990s suggested that the Guidelines needed major revisions and led to greater support for the organization. Proliferants adapted to the new rules, choosing to purchase dual-use equipment rather than listed items that would require safeguards, and utilizing consultants for technology transfer and indigenous capabilities. In addition, the activities of Iraq and, later, North Korea demonstrated that NPT membership and apparent good standing did not necessarily indicate compliance or good faith. These apparent cracks in the foundation led several countries to call for stronger export controls, including full safeguards as a condition of supply.

In 1992, the NSG's twenty-seven members met in Warsaw to review and strengthen supplier arrangements for the transfer of sixty-five categories of dual-use items. The most significant change was the requirement of full-scope safeguards as a condition of supply of nuclear material, equipment, and technology. The 1992 Warsaw Guidelines provide that NSG parties should not transfer equipment, material, or related technology: (1) for use in a nuclear explosive activity; (2) for use in an unsafeguarded nuclear fuel cycle activity; (3) when there is an unacceptable risk of diversion; or (4) when the transfer is contrary to the objective of averting proliferation.[23] The latter two controls go well beyond the requirements of the NPT and give suppliers broad latitude in assessing exports to both NPT and non-NPT non-nuclear weapons states.

---

[18] Müller, H., 'Export Controls: Review of Article III, in Simpson, J., and Howlett, D. (eds.) *The Future of the Non-Proliferation Treaty* (1995) at 132–3.

[19] For a thorough discussion of NSG 'trigger list' items see Pilat, J., 'The Major Suppliers', in Potter, W. (ed.), *International Nuclear Trade and Nonproliferation: The Challenge of Emerging Suppliers* (1990).

[20] IAEA Doc. INFCIRC/254.   [21] See generally Berkhout, *supra* note 14.

[22] See Timerbaev, R., Monterey Institute of International Studies Rep., *Eye on Supply: A Major Milestone in Controlling Nuclear Exports* (Spring 1992).

[23] Guidelines for Transfers of Nuclear-related Dual-use Equipment, Materials and Related Technology, April 3, 1992, 31 I.L.M. 1101. See Domke, W.K., 'Proliferation, Threat, and Learning: The International and Domestic Structures of Export', in Van Leeuwen, M. (ed.), *The Future of the International Nuclear Non-Proliferation Regime* (1995) 215.

2. Chemical Weapons

Export controls are also an important part of the international effort to ban chemical weapons. The CWC has the most comprehensive international regulation of a weapon of mass destruction. While the CWC contains explicit limitations on the export of chemicals, a supplier group that pre-dates the treaty, the Australia Group, applies a separate set of controls that have remained in effect even after the CWC's entry into force.

The CWC explicitly requires disarmament, obligating States Parties to declare and destroy existing chemical weapon stockpiles and production facilities.[24] The CWC has not adopted the NPT distinction between weapons states and non-weapons states. Through a rigorous set of reporting requirements and on-site inspections, including both 'routine' and short notice 'challenge' inspections, the CWC seeks to verify that States Parties do not initiate or resume chemical weapons production and storage.

The CWC restricts transfers of dual-use chemicals (CW); the CWC does not restrict the transfer of CW-related equipment. The chemicals regulated by the CWC are placed on three 'Schedules', with Schedule 1 chemicals posing the highest risk to the treaty's purposes. Any transfer of weapons agents or their precursors among States Parties must be for purposes not prohibited by the CWC. States Parties may not assist, encourage, or induce anyone to engage in any activity prohibited under the treaty.[25] A State Party may transfer Schedule 1 chemicals outside its territory only to another State Party and only for research, medical, pharmaceutical, or protective purposes; re-transfers to a third state are prohibited. The transferring and the receiving States Parties must notify the Technical Secretariat, the CWC's administrative and monitoring organ, of such transfers as well as make annual declarations regarding the previous year's transfers.[26]

Chemicals listed on Schedule 2 can only be transferred to or received from States Parties. This restriction will take effect three years after the CWC enters into force; during the interim, each State Party must require an end-use certificate for transfers of these chemicals to states not party to the CWC. Export restrictions of precursor chemicals listed on Schedule 3 of the Annex on Chemicals apply only to transfers made to States not party to the CWC. For these transfers, each State Party must adopt measures to ensure that the transferred chemicals are used only for purposes not prohibited under the CWC and obtain a certificate to this effect from the receiving state.[27] States Parties must also 'review their existing national regulations in the field of trade in chemicals in order to render them consistent with the object and purpose of the CWC'.[28]

[24] CWC, *supra* note 4, Art. I(2–4); Art. IV(6); Art. V(8). [25] *Ibid.*, Art. I(1)(d).
[26] Verification Annex, part VI(2–6). [27] *Ibid.*, part VII(31–32); part VIII(26).
[28] CWC, *supra* note 4, Art. XI(2)(e).

Inspired by the horrific use of CW in the Iran–Iraq war and under U.S. initiative, the Australia Group was formed in 1984 by fifteen key supplier countries in order to improve the exchange of information, harmonize measures already taken, and consider new, stricter means of controlling the international traffic in CW technology.[29] In the absence of a treaty banning CW, it was thought that export controls would be the best means of increasing the cost and difficulty of developing an offensive CW program.[30]

The Australia Group now includes over thirty nations, and other states have voluntarily agreed to impose similar controls. Originally, Australia Group guidelines exhorted members to require formal licenses to export a core list of nine chemicals, essentially banning the transfer of these key chemicals. The Australia Group now controls more than fifty chemical precursors, many of them dual-use, as well as specified CW-related production equipment.[31] The Group has also issued an informal 'warning list' of dual-use CW precursors, bulk chemicals, and CW-related equipment. Members develop and share the warning list with their chemical industry and ask it to report on any suspicious transactions. This simple plan was modified following the Gulf War to require formal licenses to export items on the 'warning list', except for exports to other Australia Group members. The Group, which meets twice a year in Paris,[32] has added biological weapons to its sphere of concern by establishing export controls on certain microorganisms, toxins, and equipment and by warning industry, the scientific community, and other relevant groups of the risks of inadvertently aiding BW proliferation.[33]

The Group operates informally, and its decisions are not enforced through any outside mechanism. Decisions are based on consensus. Informal agreements within the group facilitate information sharing and uniform notification of export license denials.[34] They are transformed into recommendations to the member states, which have great latitude in implementing the guidelines in their domestic export control legislation. Thus, just like the NSG and the MTCR, Australia Group measures are not embodied in a formal agree-

---

[29] See Van Ham, P., *Managing Non-Proliferation Regimes in the 1990s: Power, Politics, and Policies* (1993) 29. See also Bernauer, T., *The Chemistry of Regime Formation: Explaining International Cooperation for a Comprehensive Ban on Chemical Weapons* (1993) 41.

[30] Burck, G.M., and Floweree, C.C., *International Handbook on Chemical Weapons Proliferation* (1991) 553.

[31] See Yuan, J.D., *Nonproliferation Export Control in the 1990s* (1994) 8–9. The full text of the Australia Group guidelines and lists of regulated items is located at the United States Arms Control and Disarmament Homepage on the World Wide Web, <http://pa.acda.gov/negotiat.htm>.

[32] Floweree, C.C., 'Current Chemical Weapons Proliferation: An Introduction', in Findlay, T, (ed.), *Chemical Weapons and Missile Proliferation: With Implications for the Asia/Pacific Region* (1991) 70.

[33] Robinson, J.P., 'Chemical Weapons Proliferation: The Problem in Perspective', in *ibid.*, at 26, note 34.

[34] U.S. Congress, Office of Technology Assessment, Proliferation of Weapons of Mass Destruction: Assessing the Risks, OTA–ISC–559 (August 1993) 88, Table 3–3.

ment and do not carry the weight of law. The Australia Group has no secretariat or governing body.

3. Ballistic Missiles: The Missile Technology Control Regime

Countries wishing to establish a formidable weapons capability must contend with the difficulty of delivering their weapons at long range. Past experience with proliferation demonstrated that many countries developed intercontinental ballistic missiles by importing missiles, importing key components, or by participating in joint ventures with missile producing countries, particularly during the 1970s and through the mid-1980s.[35] The projected legacy of this missile proliferation and its 'multiplier effect' is that fifteen developing states will soon possess ballistic missiles.[36]

Ballistic missile proliferation is not the subject of any international agreement. Instead, key suppliers formed the Missile Technology Control Regime (MTCR) in 1987 to restrict exports of missile components and technology capable of delivering both conventional and mass destruction weaponry. The core founding states in the MTCR are those of the G-7 (Canada, France, the United Kingdom, Italy, Japan, Germany, and the United States). In all, twenty-nine supplier countries belong to the MTCR or adhere to its export guidelines; this represents nearly every potential missile supplier with the exception of China and North Korea.[37]

The original MTCR guidelines were meant to cover only transfers of equipment and technology that could contribute to a missile system capable of delivering a nuclear weapon.[38] In 1992, the restrictions were extended to missiles capable of delivering chemical and biological agents, regardless of range or payload. The guidelines specify two categories of items that are listed with great detail in the Equipment and Technology Annex. For the highly sensitive items in Category I, which includes complete rocket systems and missiles exceeding the 300 kilometer/500 kilogram threshold, major subsystems, and production facilities, equipment, and technology, 'particular restraint' will be exercised and 'there will be a strong presumption to deny such transfers'. Transfers will only be authorized on rare occasions if: (1) binding government-to-government assurances are made by the recipient state

---

[35] Forsberg, R., *et al.*, *Nonproliferation Primer: Preventing the Spread of Nuclear, Chemical, and Biological Weapons* (1995) 62–3. For a thorough discussion of the MTCR and its subsequent impact on these nascent missile programs see Kellman, B., 'Bridling the International Trade of Catastrophic Weaponry' (1994) 43 *Amer. Univ. L. Rev.* 755, 820–3. See also Spector, L.S., 'Nuclear Delivery Systems in the Threshold States: Assessing the Role of "Second Tier" Suppliers', in Potter, W. (ed.), *International Nuclear Trade and Nonproliferation* (1990) 76–85 (detailed account of missile capabilities of threshold, non-declared nuclear states).
[36] Van Ham, *supra* note 29, 24.   [37] Forsberg *et al.*, *supra* note 35 at 76, fig. 6.
[38] See U.S. Congress, Office of Technology Assessment, Proliferation of Weapons of Mass Destruction: Assessing the Risks, OTA–ISC–559 (August 1993).

addressing the item's future use and stating that the item will not be re-transferred and (2) the transferring government takes full responsibility to ensure that the item is put to its stated end-use. These rules place an unprecedented burden on supplier states, which means that, with respect to these items, the rules almost always mean 'no export'.[39]

Category II addresses eighteen types of items, including, *inter alia*, propulsion components, flight control systems, avionics equipment, etc. Most of these items have multiple legitimate uses and can be transferred, but 'restraint will be exercised' and transfers will be considered on a 'case-by-case basis'. Though greater flexibility is built into the Category II rules, transfers will be denied if there are proliferation concerns. Finally, transfers of design and production technology associated with Category I and II items will be subject to as much scrutiny as national legislation permits.[40]

The MTCR is a non-binding arrangement that propounds voluntary guidelines on the transfer of technology. The guidelines are applied unilaterally by members and 'the decision to transfer remains the sole and sovereign judgment' of the participating state.[41] MTCR members meet as a plenary at least once per year; records of meetings and negotiations are confidential. Significant decisions, including membership applications, require consensus. The recruitment of potential members can result from bilateral consultations and fact-finding missions by MTCR delegations. Non-member participation is accomplished by seeking voluntary adherence to MTCR guidelines and through MTCR seminars and workshops that can be attended by non-members. The MTCR has no formal structure and is not a formal organization.

B. THE SUPPLIER GROUP LEGITIMACY GAP

With the partial exception of the Zangger Committee and its express relation to the NPT, weapons control supplier groups lack most of the characteristics of a formal and binding weapons control agreement open to adherence by all states. To the extent these characteristics are missing, it becomes more difficult for a supplier group to establish its legitimacy. Legitimacy is a jurisprudential construct that helps to explain why, even in the absence of a coercive power or other motivation, most states comply with their international legal obligations most of the time.[42] A legal rule is legitimate, and will be seen as

---

[39] Speier, R., 'The Missile Technology Control Regime' in Findlay, *supra* note 32 at 120.

[40] See MTCR Guidelines, paras. 1, 4.

[41] Agreement on Guidelines for the Transfer of Equipment and Technology Related to Missiles, agreed April 26, 1987, modified at Oslo, July 1992 (1987) 26 I.L.M. 599, 600 (hereinafter MTCR Guidelines), Section 2 reprinted in Findlay, *supra* note 32 at 149–161.

[42] See Henkin, L., *How Nations Behave* (2nd edn. 1979) 47 ('[A]lmost all nations observe almost all principles of international law and almost all of their obligations almost all of the time').

such, when it emanates from a fair and accepted procedure, is applied without discrimination, and comports with minimum standards of fairness and equity.[43] A rules system that is legitimate is most likely to engender habitual, uncoerced compliance among states.[44]

Although a supplier group can be an element of a larger regime that includes a binding agreement, such as the CWC regime or the NPT regime, none of the supplier groups exhibit the characteristics of a more formal arrangement. They lack:

- a treaty or otherwise binding legal accord that prohibits proliferation activity or creates affirmative non-proliferation or disarmament obligations;
- a secretariat or formal organization;
- transparent, democratic processes for the elaboration, amendment, and administration of regime requirements;
- a mechanism for verifying members' compliance;
- a formal mechanism to raise grievances, resolve disputes, or address violation of guidelines by a member;
- a procedure for states to petition to join the group and accede to its norms; and
- a formal link to the United Nations or other international political body as a means to address instances of non-compliance.

Without the foregoing or some combination thereof, the supplier groups lack a rules system likely to engender widespread compliance. They therefore will not be seen as legitimate legal institutions and their efficacy may be compromised.

Supplier groups, including the Australia Group, also lack a nexus between the obligations they impose and clear rules of process about how those obligations are formulated, interpreted, and applied. In other words, the supplier groups do not promulgate their restrictions in the context of a procedural and institutional framework with clearly defined 'rules about rules'; as a result, the rules they impose are less likely to obligate.[45] This suggests that soft law institutions like the Australia Group may be less likely to compel compliance with their norms than hard law agreements like the CWC with its formal system of export restrictions and clearly defined processes.

Moreover, while the informality of these groups gives their members flexibility and allows them to respond to special proliferation issues, their nonbinding character and their lack of a verification and enforcement apparatus

---

[43] Chayes and Chayes, *supra* note 7 at 127.

[44] Franck, T.M., 'Is Justice Relevant to the International Legal System?' (1989) 64 *Notre Dame L. Rev.* 945, 947. See also Franck, T.M., *The Power of Legitimacy Among Nations* (1990).

[45] Franck, T.M., 'Legitimacy in the International System' (1988) 82 *A.J.I.L.* 705, 752 (citing H.L.A. Hart's criticism of the international legal system).

mean that each group is subordinate to the will of any individual member. They can also be undercut by uneven and ineffective national implementation.

The current debate over the Australia Group in the CW context demonstrates several aspects of the North–South tension. The Group has expressed full support for the CWC but, despite the CWC's entry into force, the Australia Group, including the United States, has declared that its members will continue their informal cooperation and the maintenance of Australia Group export controls—even those controls that are potentially incompatible with Article XI of the CWC. The CWC is a universal agreement and maintaining a discriminatory export control scheme is viewed by many as anathema to the treaty's guiding principles.[46]

Developing states view the Australia Group's continuing existence under the current terms as a perpetuation of discrimination: 'More critically, the imposition of export controls, even when they are designed in an even-handed form and applied without insidious discrimination, evokes profound resentment from the developing states, who see the tactic as a lingering tool of hegemony wielded by wealthy economic imperialists.'[47] Continued application of extra-treaty controls even casts a negative light on the controls imposed by the treaty itself and adversely affects the perception of the CWC as a whole.

Many view the Australia Group as representing one of the major problems with the export control system. The Group establishes supplier group guidelines, which result in national controls that are more stringent or expansive than the export restrictions enumerated in multilateral treaties covering the same subject. In other words, supplier group norms may be inconsistent with the norms codified in weapons control treaties addressing the same issues.[48]

Norms tend to be more legitimate when they enjoy widespread consensus; this legitimacy may be further enhanced if the norms are codified in a formal agreement. The international legal system is consent-based, and states are more likely to cooperate and comply if they have had the opportunity to assent at every stage. In this sense, the norms expressed in nearly universal treaties like the NPT or CWC enjoy normative legitimacy.

Neither the NSG's nor the Australia Group's controls have any express relation to a formal agreement, yet their guidelines negatively impact on many states that do not belong to either group. Their guidelines often do not

---

[46] See 'Australia Group Ponders Future of Chemical Controls', *Export Control News*, June 30, 1994; Stern, J., 'Lethal Compounds: The New Chemical Weapons Ban', *Brookings Rev.*, June 22, 1994, at 32; Bertsch, G.K., and Cupitt, R.T., 'Nonproliferation in the 1990s: Enhancing International Cooperation on Export Controls', *Wash Q.*, Autumn 1993, at 53.

[47] Koplow, D.A., and Schrag, P.G., 'Carrying A Big Carrot: Linking Multilateral Disarmament And Development Assistance' (1991) 91 *Colum. L. Rev.* 993, 1056.

[48] Norms are generalized 'prescriptions for action in situations of choice, carrying a sense of obligation, a sense that they *ought* to be followed.' Chayes and Chayes, *supra* note 7 at 113 (emphasis in original).

enjoy the agreement of much of the affected community and, accordingly, enjoy less normative authority. Where the supplier group controls are closely linked to a treaty, such as the Zangger Committee's link to Article III of the NPT, the controls have greater claims to legitimacy. Legitimacy, of course, cannot necessarily be equated with efficacy; the NSG was established to address some perceived shortcomings in the Zangger Committee and is generally perceived as the more effective export control mechanism. Thus, while probably less legitimate, the NSG is more effective. The development of legitimate norms, procedures, and institutions can only promote, but cannot guarantee, conditions that foster compliance and cooperation.

Enhanced legitimacy in the export control system should be pursued. Regime members must have a clear sense of what conduct is prohibited as well as the justifications supporting those restrictions. States exercising export restraints should be able to justify their actions as consistent with the legal rules; conversely, states should have advance knowledge and understanding of the restriction and believe in its validity. Restrictions that cannot be identified with a clearly expressed norm become problematic. If supplier group guidelines more closely tracked treaty requirements, the text of the relevant weapons control agreement would identify the relevant norm and provide an authoritative formulation.

C. REGIME-ORIENTED APPROACHES TO STRENGTHEN NON-PROLIFERATION EXPORT CONTROLS

Regimes supported by binding legal obligations and formal institutions are more likely to affect state behavior and coerce compliance with the norms of weapons control. Regime theorists suggest several reasons why states form regimes to address concerns in a particular issue area, including international security.[49] Principally, regimes result in the formation of legal institutions and cooperative alliances that better facilitate communication and cooperation among states. Therefore, it might be useful to look at the system of export controls through the lens of regime formation to identify elements that might enhance the system.

---

[49] The most oft-cited benefits to forming a regime are: legitimating and delegitimating certain types of state actions; reducing transaction costs; establishing clear standards of behavior for states to follow; creating conditions conducive to orderly multilateral negotiations; facilitating linkages among issues within regimes and between regimes; improving the quality of information that governments receive; reducing incentives to cheat; enhancing the value of reputation; and creating conditions for decentralized enforcement by facilitating monitoring. Keohane, R., *After Hegemony: Cooperation and Discord in the World Political Economy* (1984) 244–5; See also Slaughter Burley, A.M., 'International Law and International Relations Theory: A Dual Agenda' (1993) 87 *A.J.I.L.* 205, 220 (Table 1 and accompanying text); Jervis, R., 'Security Regimes', in Krassner, S. (ed.), *International Regimes* (1983) 173; Smith, E.M., 'Understanding Dynamic Obligations' (1991) 64 *S. Cal. L. Rev.* 1549.

A wide range of options is available to address the previously discussed shortcomings in the current system of export controls. An often discussed option is the creation of a single, comprehensive export control regime that would integrate the various existing export controls into a formal agreement and establish an international organization to administer the treaty and monitor compliance. Another, less comprehensive, option would be to encourage the existing supplier groups to adopt some of the characteristics of more formal regimes. The subsections that follow suggest ways that supplier groups could adopt the elements of a more formal legal regime to enhance their legitimacy and validate the norms they propound.

1. Elaborate an Export Control Treaty and Establish an International Export Control Organization

Treaties like the CWC and NPT, and their attendant institutions and procedures, illustrate the trend in international law toward complex regulatory agreements that involve the establishment of an authoritative organ, separate and distinct from the member states, that is capable of overseeing treaty implementation and ensuring fulfillment of the objectives of the treaty. In the area of export controls, such an organ would presumably derive its authority from a binding, non-discriminatory international agreement that perhaps incorporates (or coordinates) the guidelines of the existing supplier groups and fills any gaps. A formal agreement should definitively enumerate the responsibilities of member states, both supplier and recipient, and rely less on the voluntary adoption of domestic measures by individual member states.

The major supplier groups, despite their complexity, multinationality, and relationship to existing treaties and secretariats, lack a central, administrative authority. Perhaps the most important function of a new export control agreement would be the establishment of an institution with the authority and capability to monitor compliance with all non-proliferation export controls. This organ would be vital to the objective application of standards; to the gathering and centralization of information; and to resolving disputes either between member states or between member states and itself. Establishing a single non-proliferation export control organization would also achieve administrative efficiencies and economies of scale and eliminate redundant functions among the existing supplier groups.

International organizations focus and intensify the importance of legal norms, both procedural and substantive. They are inherently more legal in that they propound rules and procedures for decision-making that often enjoy great validity and legitimacy. They also promote discourse by providing a clear record of decisions; resolutions are passed; and policy debates flesh out, and memorialize, the interpretation and application of regime norms.[50]

---

[50] See Chayes and Chayes, *supra* note 7 at 125–6.

An international organization in the area of export controls would complement the other modalities of weapons control by facilitating conferences and negotiations to discuss emerging issues, providing a platform to link export controls with other non-proliferation initiatives. By all accounts, at least within the past few years, the supplier groups are dedicated to frequent meetings and continuing, critical review of their lists; a formal organization could facilitate this process.[51] If properly constituted, a new organization need not result is a loss of flexibility or capacity to respond to technological changes or emerging threats. A permanent organ with a skilled secretariat can also help to coordinate national implementation of regime norms.

2. Increase Supplier Group Membership and Eliminate Discrimination

Short of creating an elaborate new export control regime, incremental steps could be taken to improve the current system and close the legitimacy gap. The limited membership of supplier groups creates practical and political difficulties and is the foremost challenge to their legitimacy. Practically speaking, the current supplier groups are weakened by not including all major and emerging suppliers. Politically speaking, their discriminatory, cartel-like membership undermines the entire system of export controls and threatens its long term prospects.

As weapons technology spreads, firms and scientists in many more states become capable of assisting other states in developing WMD requiring greater consensus on export controls. All states with the relevant technologies should be consulted and encouraged to apply supplier group guidelines. That is not occurring, as some major and many emerging suppliers are not members of the various supplier groups. The nature of international trade and the inherent destructiveness of weapons of mass destruction mean that even a single major defector or non-participant can undermine the entire system.

With regard to nuclear proliferation, several key states have not accepted NSG guidelines, the most notable being China. Other emerging supplier states of concern are: South Korea, Taiwan, Singapore, Turkey, Brazil, and Mexico, and some former Soviet republics. In the area of chemical weapons, China, India, Mexico, Romania, South Africa, and South Korea do not apply Australia Group guidelines and continue to export CW precursors to potential proliferants. The MTCR also could be strengthened by expanding its membership. Outliers such as North Korea, some former Soviet Republics, and China create a tremendous gap in coverage. However, the MTCR continues to expand rapidly and its stated goal is global adherence.[52]

---

[51] Fischer, D., *Towards 1995: The Prospects for Ending the Proliferation of Nuclear Weapons* (1993) 115.
[52] See MTCR Guidelines, *supra* note 41, section 7.

Increasing the membership of these arrangements will be difficult. The emerging suppliers did not participate in the formulation of these guidelines and, if they were to join now, they would be presented with a *fait accompli* and would have a limited ability to amend the guidelines. This situation would likely engender resentment and reduce the legitimacy of the entire endeavor. Moreover, many of the states whose participation is now sought were once the targets of these export restrictions themselves.[53]

Further measures will be required to eliminate discrimination; merely inviting additional major and emerging suppliers to join the supplier groups is unlikely to be enough. Discriminatory regime structures are now widely challenged, as seen in the abandonment of the have/have not distinction in the CWC, the struggles over this issue at the 1995 NPT Review Conference, and the persistent debate over the structure of the permanent membership of the United Nations Security Council. It is unlikely that the current system of export controls can be maintained over the long term. Although less-industrialized recipient states might not pose a threat as proliferators, the global weapons control effort depends on their support.

If membership is expanded, the U.S. and other major suppliers may be forced to accept adverse decisions in the interests of legitimacy and fairness. This is not to say, however, that major suppliers should not continue to play a vital, although somewhat reduced, role in developing norms, building consensus and working to strengthen the regime. Loss of leadership need not be the cost of consensus and legitimacy. Potential negative effects from increased membership could perhaps be mitigated by voting rules, whereby consensus would not be required for all decisions.

3. Develop Clear Procedures and Improve Transparency

The current system must become more transparent by establishing norms and creating obligations for its members through a more formal, open process. While enshrining supplier group restrictions in a treaty would accomplish this, at the cost of diminished flexibility, more modest techniques to increase transparency are available. The objective should be to de-mystify the process and make supplier groups less of a 'club'.

Supplier group proceedings could be opened to outside parties, such as relevant non-governmental organizations (NGOs), while addressing security concerns related to the dissemination of military and industrial information. This step would minimize secrecy, alert the public and affected nations to controls before the rule is adopted, and permit outside monitoring of supplier group actions.[54] Supplier groups could also develop and publish rules of pro-

---

[53] Williamson, R.L., 'Law and the H-Bomb: Strengthening the Nonproliferation Regime to Impede Advanced Proliferation' (1995) 28 *Cornell Int'l L.J.* 71, 139.

[54] Sands, Ph. (ed.), *Greening International Law* (1994) p. xx.

cedure; publish the minutes or some record of proceedings; or publish decisions and the results of rule making procedures.

4. Enforce Supplier Group Norms

The supplier groups lack dispute resolution procedures and sanctions to deal with violations. The international system of export controls might function better if it had institutions and formal procedures at its disposal to respond to compliance concerns. Unlike loose supplier group arrangements, a binding charter with formal enforcement mechanisms provides powerful incentives to cooperate. The process would be transparent and a matter of record, making it harder for the offending member to disguise its non-compliance and object to the application of the sanction.

States also would risk substantial damage to their reputations for refusing to comply, especially given the high profile of accusations of illicit weapons transfers; this damage to reputation could affect the state in other issue areas. Additionally, a finding of non-compliance and open censure from a permanent organ can have greater effects than similar accusations from even the most powerful states.

The exclusionary structure of the current system may be ill-equipped to serve its purpose. The post-Cold War era is characterized by international cooperation and multi-polarity. Reliance on the United States as a single hegemon for norm enforcement seems inadequate. Moreover, with its web of international entanglements, the United States can ill afford to expend valuable political capital to enforce export controls against every state that acts against U.S. interests, continually hinging its relationship with that state on the single issue of non-proliferation. It is therefore essential that an export control regime possess the necessary institutions and procedures to permit states to share information, cooperatively address compliance concerns, and require regime members to justify their suspect conduct through a series of interactions.

Despite this complex system of fail-safes and compliance inducing mechanisms, there remain situations where states make a calculated decision to violate regime norms. After moving through the various iterations, and after all the proffered justifications have been rejected, egregious and willful violations may necessitate sanctions.[55]

CONCLUSION

The imperatives of the international political system are changing dramatically. The institutions of weapons control must do the same. While there is

[55] Chayes and Chayes, *supra* note 7 at 28.

global support for efforts to rid the planet of mass destruction weaponry, some of the norms of international weapons control are implemented by a discriminatory and exclusionary system of export controls. For weapons control to succeed in the next millennium, policy makers must acknowledge that the Cold War dynamics that once justified the current system no longer exist.

The international export control system must be made legitimate in the eyes of the developing world to prevent widening the North–South cleavage on this issue. Restructuring these groups according to the principles of universality and transparent, democratic process can properly address developing world claims that supplier groups are illegitimate.

Legitimacy should not be sought for its own sake, however. Supplier groups are vital to slowing the spread of instruments of destruction and legitimating reforms must be weighed against losses in regime efficacy and the ability to respond to new proliferation threats. This study merely suggests that, despite the possibility of some short term weakening, the export control system could be improved. Elaborating stronger norms linked closely to weapons control agreements, expanding regime membership on a non-discriminatory basis, establishing an export control organ, and adopting formal, transparent procedures will result in a stronger regime and encourage new levels of cooperation.

Protection of Nuclear Materials

BARRY KELLMAN

INTRODUCTION

The worldwide protection of nuclear materials is an urgent global priority. To oversee that protection the international community has developed a highly nuanced international regulatory system comprised of both treaty law and soft law. The complexity of the system is due to the tension and balance between the need for states to implement near-uniform technically detailed standards to avoid catastrophic risk, on the one hand, and their reluctance to adhere to international standards, stemming from their jealous guarding of their nuclear capabilities, on the other hand. Treaty law forms the overarching structure of the system, expressing the strategic commitments of states parties which cede some measure of sovereignty to achieve international consensus. Recommendations of the International Atomic Energy Agency

(IAEA) balance various competing interests and enable relevant actors to fulfill necessary assignments without materially recasting the philosophical or military foundations of international security.

IAEA recommendations take up where treaties leave off, filling in gaps by furnishing the elaborate detail of protective measures. They are not seen to intrude on sovereignty because they are recommendations. They enable a complex regulatory system to function smoothly without mandatory reliance on a cumbersome treaty-making or amending process while still allowing the option of (re)negotiating a treaty when consensus is available. Recommendations do not stand alone, independently of treaty obligations, and only rarely serve as precursors of binding obligations; instead, they follow treaty agreements generally and, because of this underpinning of 'hard law', they are widely accepted and implemented.

This study explains the roles of treaties and soft law, the limitations and accomplishments of each, and the mesh they form to protect nuclear materials. The first part describes the context of nuclear materials protection and explains why an internationally-propounded regulatory system is crucial. The second part presents the treaties that establish the framework for controlling nuclear materials generally and suggests some limitations on a regulatory system that relies exclusively on treaties. The remainder identifies how soft law binds together the complex regulatory system of nuclear materials protection.

A. THE NEED FOR NUCLEAR MATERIALS REGULATION

Most nations and even some sub-national groups could use known and available techniques to make a nuclear explosive device with nuclear materials of suitable quantity and quality.[1] Most of the materials and equipment needed to make a nuclear bomb are readily available and the rudimentary techniques to make a crude weapon are no longer a mystery. The crucial tasks involve assembling the core of fissile material, either plutonium (Pu) or uranium (U–235 and U–233).[2]

The most serious risk posed by loose nuclear materials is their use in a nuclear bomb, but other possibilities also are extremely threatening. A group with nuclear materials but without the capability to make a nuclear bomb still could easily produce a radiological weapon, *i.e.*, a simple chemical explosion that disperses radioactive dust over a wide area.[3] A small group could cause massive deaths by packing conventional warheads and bomb casings with

---

[1] Roberts, G.B., *Five Minutes Past Midnight: The Clear and Present Danger of Nuclear Weapons Grade Fissile Materials* (1996).

[2] DeVolpi, A., 'Fissile Materials and Nuclear Weapons Proliferation' (1986) 36 *Ann. Rev. Nuclear Particle Sci.* 84.

[3] Perera, J., 'Iraq-Disarmament: A Simple Weapon with Deadly Application' [1995] *Inter-Press Service*, November 9.

radioactive material, without creating an actual nuclear explosion. Iraq tried to develop radiological weapons, and Chechen separatists allegedly tried to disperse radioactive Cesium–137 in a Moscow park.[4] In 1985, the Conference on Disarmament called for a convention to prohibit radiological weapons and reaffirmed the prohibition against new weapons of mass destruction.[5]

About 1,000 metric tons of plutonium exist today; over twenty states possess or control separated plutonium either for military or commercial use. France, China, Russia, the United Kingdom, and the United States have accumulated over 250 tons of weapon-grade plutonium in deployed or surplus weapons, as well as about 1,500 tons of highly-enriched uranium (HEU).[6] The United States and Russia, which together account for almost 90 percent of the nuclear materials used in weapons, each will have about fifty metric tons of surplus plutonium and hundreds of tons of HEU from dismantled nuclear weapons by 2003.[7] On the civilian side, 330 metric tons of reactor-grade plutonium will be separated from spent fuel worldwide and will be available for use by 2003.[8] Of the roughly 650 tons of plutonium that exist in commercial programs, approximately 530 tons are contained in untreated spent reactor fuel, while roughly 120 tons are stored in weapons-usable form or recycled as fuel awaiting potential use.[9]

To put these numbers in perspective, a single nuclear weapon can be made with as little as eight kilograms or about eighteen pounds of weapons-grade plutonium (the lower the grade of plutonium, the more required) and approximately twice as much highly enriched uranium is needed.[10] By any measure, there is enough nuclear material to make tens of thousands of nuclear weapons.

Illicit trafficking in nuclear materials has escalated in recent years; the IAEA identified 213 incidents in the five years preceding March 1998.[11] Most

[4] Rathmell, A., 'Iraq's Two-Faced Policy', *Jane's Intelligence Rev.*, March 1, 1996, at 6; Hibbs, M., 'Chechen Separatists Take Credit for Moscow Cesium-137 Threat', *Nuclear Fuel*, December 4, 1995, at 5.

[5] See United Nations, A/RES/40/90 (December 12, 1985). Despite the General Assembly reaffirming that position in 1997, A/RES/51/37 (January 7, 1997), the Conference has not established an Ad Hoc Committee on this matter. The status of work on radiological weapons is reflected in paras. 79–82 of the 1992 report of the Conference to the General Assembly (CD/1173).

[6] Berkhout, F., *et al.*, 'A Cutoff in the Production of Fissile Material' [1994–5] *Int'l Security* 167, 168.

[7] Committee on Int'l Security & Arms Control (CISAC), National Academy of Sciences, *Management and Disposition of Excess Weapons Plutonium* (1994) 40.

[8] Stemming the Plutonium Tide: Limiting the Accumulation of Excess Weapon-Usable Nuclear Materials: Hearing Before the Subcomm. on International Security, International Organizations and Human Rights of the House Comm. on Foreign Affairs, 103rd Cong., 2d Sess. (1994) 83.

[9] Perkovich, G., 'The Plutonium Genie' [1993] *Foreign Aff.* 153.

[10] See generally Congressional Research Serv., Library of Congress, *Nuclear Proliferation Factbook* 475 (prepared for the Committee on Governmental Affairs of the United States Senate).

[11] IAEA, Incidents in the IAEA Database on Illicit Trafficking Confirmed by States, 1998–03– 02.

incidents point to security breakdowns in former Warsaw Pact states, especially Russia.[12] The ascendancy of Russian criminal organizations has rendered access to nuclear materials easy. Nuclear installations have doors that are unlocked, lack fences, or have fences with holes, and are overseen by guards who are inadequately equipped and have little incentive to resist intruders.[13] The theft and sale of all types of military equipment have reached startlingly high levels, and senior Russian officials have admitted the likelihood of nuclear terrorism, including theft of nuclear materials.[14] The problems are even more severe in other former Soviet Republics where research reactors, uranium fabrication facilities, and nuclear submarine bases are not monitored by a capable regulatory infrastructure.[15] Recommendations for strengthening physical protection systems include making standards mandatory for domestic uses, raising those standards, and requiring international inspections or enforcement mechanisms to provide international assurance that states are in fact applying stronger standards.[16]

Protecting fissile material is vital to prevent proliferation by alleviating concerns over unauthorized access and theft.[17] At least four reasons justify an international agency having some authority over nuclear materials protection. First, there is a compelling need for uniform application of protective standards and methods. The global non-proliferation effort rests on a finely-crafted political commitment to afford access to peaceful nuclear technology while reducing diversion of nuclear materials. The numerous obligations implied by this commitment are more likely to be fulfilled if states believe that those burdens are shared by other states. Moreover, uniform application of standards and methods enables more efficient verification of compliance; if each state had discretion to set its own standards, verification would be virtually impossible.

The second objection to broad state discretion pertains to the divergence of technical capabilities. While some states could undertake sophisticated programs to protect their nuclear materials, other states, if left on their own, would be limited by their lack of financial or technical resources. For this reason, international efforts are needed to assist states to build safe and efficient

---

[12] Bukharin, O., *The Threat of Nuclear Terrorism and the Physical Security of Nuclear Installations and Materials in the Former Soviet Union*, Monterey Inst. of Int'l Studies, Occasional Paper No. 2 (1992).

[13] Lambert, S.P., and Miller, D., *Russia's Crumbling Tactical Nuclear Weapons Complex: An Opportunity for Arms Control* INSS Occasional Paper 12 (1997).

[14] Bluth, C., 'Russia's Nuclear Forces: A Clear and Present Danger?' [1997] *Jane's Intelligence Review*, December 1.

[15] See generally Allison, G.T., *et al.*, *Avoiding Nuclear Anarchy: Containing the Threat of Loose Russian Nuclear Weapons and Fissile Material* (1996).

[16] See Bunn, G., Physical Protection of Nuclear Materials—Strengthening Global Norms, <http://www.iaea.or.at/worldatom/inforesource/bulletin/bull394/bunn.html>.

[17] Kellman, B., and Gualtieri, D., 'Barricading The Nuclear Window— A Legal Regime to Curtail Nuclear Smuggling' [1996] *U. Ill. L.R.* 667.

nuclear energy facilities. Such assistance would be harder to promote and regulate if each state had discretion to determine its own needs without consistent and uniform application of criteria.

The third objection pertains to the enforcement objective of protective measures which is, of course, to prevent diversion of nuclear materials. If states could establish their own standards, then proliferators or criminal organizations would seek out the states having the most lax standards. Diversion potentially threatens every state because diversion of critical nuclear materials from a state having lax standards could threaten any state that the proliferators chose to target. Every state therefore has an interest in maintaining high protective standards in every other state. Only a mechanism of global regulation can maintain consistently high standards. As the IAEA has recently recognized: '[t]he need for international co-operation becomes evident in situations where the effectiveness of physical protection in one State depends on the taking by other States also of adequate measures to deter or defeat hostile actions against nuclear facilities and materials, particularly when such materials are transported across national frontiers'.[18]

The final objection to leaving protective measures to each state pertains to the need for coordinated investigations of wrongful activity. When the security of nuclear material is jeopardized, states must cooperate to track down the wrongdoers with modalities of assistance that range from sharing information to extradition of apprehended suspects. Material may have to be tracked using shared techniques for identifying the source of nuclear material.

B. THE TREATY FRAMEWORK OF NON-PROLIFERATION REGULATION

The essence of nuclear non-proliferation is maintaining secure control of the fissile material necessary to make a nuclear bomb so that states and non-state groups do not gain weapons capability. Denial of such capability to a particular state prevents proliferation and helps assure other states that they need not be overly concerned with that state's nuclear propensities. It is unrealistic, however, to build a policy on the basis of absolute denial of access to fissile materials because the same materials and much of the same equipment and processes are needed to generate nuclear energy for non-weapons purposes.

Non-proliferation policy, therefore, balances the competing interests of providing access to materials and technology for commercial nuclear energy purposes in return for verifiable pledges not to pursue proscribed military ambitions. States without a nuclear weapons capability may receive assis-

---

[18] IAEA, INFCIRC/225/Draft Revision, The Physical Protection of Nuclear Material and Nuclear Facilities, April 24, 1998, 2.

tance in developing nuclear energy only if they eschew military applications of nuclear technology and agree to have their civilian applications closely monitored.

Two formal and intertwined treaties form the basis of non-proliferation. In 1957, the Statute of the International Atomic Energy Agency (IAEA) established the IAEA as an affiliate of the U.N., authorizing it to sponsor atomic energy research and development.[19] The IAEA Statute established the international regulatory authority over nuclear materials and technologies. Later, the Nuclear Non-Proliferation Treaty of 1968[20] expressed the strategic commitment of most states that the number of nuclear weapons states should not increase. The NPT established the policy framework for non-proliferation, requiring that non-nuclear weapons states (NNWS) accept IAEA verification of their nuclear non-proliferation commitments. The obligations that flow from these treaties are binding for states parties, but an examination of these two pillars of the non-proliferation system and other relevant treaties demonstrates that they are not fully capable of addressing the tasks of protecting nuclear materials.

1. Establishment and Operation of the IAEA

The IAEA was the first specialized international organization to be directly involved in verifying multilateral arms control obligations. It comprises three principal organs: the Conference of all IAEA member states; the Board of Governors; and the Secretariat, headed by a Director General who administers the IAEA as well as on-site verification activities. The IAEA provides a framework for interaction on nuclear issues and for elaboration and refinement of the international nuclear regime; it is a forum for discussion, exchange of views, and the formulation of initiatives relevant to peaceful nuclear uses; and it provides services relative to the use and control of peaceful nuclear development. To do so, the IAEA manages technical cooperation, research, and development programs for promoting civilian nuclear applications. In addition, the IAEA works cooperatively with regional bodies, including bodies established by nuclear-free zones and the European Atomic Energy Commission (EURATOM).

---

[19] The Statute of the International Atomic Energy Agency, October 26, 1958, 8 U.S.T. 1093, 276 U.N.T.S.3 (entered into force July 29, 1957). There are 125 member states to the IAEA Statute. The IAEA is not a party to the NPT nor was it created by the NPT. The NPT builds on the system established by the IAEA, notably the power to conduct safeguards.

[20] Treaty on the Non-Proliferation of Nuclear Weapons, July 1, 1968, 7 I.L.M. 809, 21 U.S.T. 483, T.I.A.S. No. 6839, 729 U.N.T.S. 161 (entered into force March 5, 1970). The NPT has over 175 states parties. The NPT regime consists of: national safeguards agreements negotiated on the basis of the NPT model safeguards agreements contained in *The Structure and Content of Agreements Between the Agency and States Required in Connection with the Treaty on The Non-Proliferation of Nuclear Weapons*, IAEA Doc. INFCIRC/153 (May 1971).

2. The Nuclear Non-proliferation Treaty (NPT)

The NPT is the cornerstone of international efforts to ban the transfer or acquisition of nuclear weaponry. The IAEA establishes and administers safeguards to ensure that nuclear materials, equipment, facilities, and information are not used to advance military purposes.

The NPT obligates each NNWS to accept international safeguards under IAEA supervision, including reporting requirements, installation of monitoring equipment, and on-site inspections.[21] Safeguards enable the IAEA to detect diversion (any use of safeguarded items in violation of a condition of a safeguards agreement)[22] of significant quantities of nuclear material from peaceful activities to manufacture nuclear explosive devices. The likelihood of timely detection deters diversion. NPT safeguards engender confidence about the nature of each state's nuclear activity and expedite international cooperation concerning nuclear energy development.

Each state party with nuclear energy capabilities must negotiate comprehensive as well as item-specific bilateral agreements with the IAEA pursuant to the framework of IAEA guidance document INFCIRC/153.[23] As of December 13, 1996, 180 states had entered into safeguards agreements.[24] The IAEA and each state party also negotiate subsidiary agreements with more detailed procedures, such as the control measures to be applied at nuclear facilities.[25] An objective of these agreements is to require the state to enable the IAEA to verify the security of nuclear materials. These agreements are not treaties, but are generally regarded as binding.

Each state party must provide the IAEA with information concerning nuclear material subject to safeguards and the features of facilities relevant to safeguarding such materials. The NPT reporting requirements apply if nuclear material is being produced, processed, or used in any nuclear facility, or is outside a facility, or if the facility is expected to contain safe-

---

[21] NPT, Art. III.

[22] INFCIRC/26.

[23] The Structure and Content of Agreements Between the Agency and States Required in Connection with the Treaty on the Non-Proliferation of Nuclear Weapons, IAEA Doc. INF-CIRC/153 (May 1971). Agreements that apply safeguards to a specific item of nuclear equipment or quantity of nuclear material in a nuclear weapon state are established by INFCIRC/66. See Scheinman, L., 'Nuclear Safeguards and Non-Proliferation in a Changing World Order' (1992) 23 *Security Dialogue* 39. See also Edwards, D.M., 'International Legal Aspects of Safeguards and the Non-Proliferation of Nuclear Weapons' (1984) 33 *Int'l & Comp. L.Q.* 1.

[24] IAEA, 1996 Annual Report, Annex: situation on December 31, 1996 with respect to the conclusion of safeguards agreements between the Agency and non-nuclear-weapon states in connection with the NPT. <http://www.iaea.or.at/worldatom/program/safeguards/96tables/safenpt.html>.

[25] See generally Wilmshurt, M.J., 'The Adequacy of IAEA Safeguards for the 1990s', in Fry *et al.* (eds.), *Nuclear Non-Proliferation and the Non-Proliferation Treaty* (1990).

guarded nuclear material.[26] Fewer than 1,000 facilities worldwide fulfill this definition.

Each state party must permit the IAEA to inspect every facility to which reporting requirements apply. Routine inspections are undertaken to verify: (1) that reports are consistent with records; (2) the location, identity, quantity, and composition of all safeguarded nuclear material; and (3) information on the possible causes of material unaccounted for, shipper/receiver differences, and uncertainties in records.[27] Access for routine inspections is generally limited to strategic points, that is, any location where key measurements related to material balance accountancy are made and where containment and surveillance are executed,[28] as well as to accounting records that must be kept under the national safeguards agreement.[29]

In 1997, the IAEA Board of Governors proposed a new model Additional Protocol (INFCIRC/540) aimed at tightening safeguards agreements, particularly in the area of information disclosure.[30] INFCIRC/540 requires disclosure of information about and access to: (1) aspects of states' nuclear fuel cycles (from mines to waste) where nuclear material is present; (2) all buildings on a nuclear site; (3) fuel cycle-related research and development; and (4) manufacture and export of sensitive nuclear-related technologies.[31] The Additional Protocol also calls for the collection of environmental samples apart from declared locations as the IAEA requests and a more streamlined inspector designation and visa-issuance process.

3. Other Treaties

In addition to the IAEA Statute and the NPT, other treaties pertain to the protection of nuclear materials. The most significant is the Convention on the Physical Protection of Nuclear Material,[32] discussed below (p. 499). Of less direct relevance are the Convention on Early Notification of a Nuclear Accident;[33] the Convention on Assistance in the Case of a Nuclear Accident

[26] INFCIRC/153, *supra* note 23, para. 106. See generally, Gualtieri, D., *et al.*, 'Advancing the Law of Weapons Control—Comparative Approaches to Strengthen Nuclear Non-proliferation' (1995) 16 *Mich. J. Int'l L.* 1029.
[27] INFCIRC/153, *supra* note 23, para. 72.
[28] *Ibid.*, para. 116.
[29] *Ibid.*, para. 74(a). Specifically, IAEA inspectors may examine all records kept pursuant to *ibid.*, paras. 51–58.
[30] See Fischer, D., Safeguards: Past, Present and Future, October 1997, <http://www.iaea.or.at/worldatom/in. . .urce/bulletin/bull394/fischer.html>.
[31] Hooper, R, The Systems of Strengthened Safeguards, <http:www.iaea.or.at/worldatom/inforesource/bulletin/bull394/hooper.html>.
[32] Convention on the Physical Protection of Nuclear Materials, March 3, 1980, 18 I.L.M. 1419, T.I.A.S. 11080 (entered into force February 8, 1987). As of July 31, 1997, there were 57 parties, 56 states, and EURATOM.
[33] Entered into force on October 27, 1986. As of July 31, 1997, there were 77 parties, 74 states, and 3 organizations.

or Radiological Emergency;[34] the Convention on Nuclear Safety;[35] and, recently, the Joint Convention on the Safety of Spent Fuel Management and on the Safety of Radioactive Waste Management.[36] These treaties cover specific issues within the context of non-proliferation policy and they demonstrate that the treaty mechanism has continuing vitality in cases where states believe that it is important to impose binding obligations on themselves and can achieve consensus as to the content of the obligations. Each of the treaties contains obligations that prior to the treaty were soft law, and each of them has led to additional and more detailed IAEA recommendations.

Mention should also be made of the proposed Convention on the Suppression of Acts of Nuclear Terrorism.[37] The draft Convention defines nuclear terrorism and obligates states parties to cooperate in preventing such acts by prohibiting illegal activities, exchanging information, and adopting necessary physical protection measures. Moreover, states parties will be required to establish jurisdiction over defined offenses and to extradite or prosecute alleged offenders. Mutual legal assistance obligations are stipulated in order to prevent, suppress, uncover, and investigate offenses and to institute criminal proceedings.

4. Limitations of Treaties

For at least three reasons, the detailed obligations associated with protecting nuclear materials are not entirely implemented through treaty law. The first reason concerns the sheer volume of these obligations and the difficulty of reaching consensus on them. The international community established a regulatory framework that calls for the negotiation of safeguards to protect nuclear material, but the treaty-making process is ill-suited to promulgate literally thousands of highly technical details that must change with advances in technology. Rendering the vast quantity of requirements obligatory via treaty would be extremely difficult. By authorizing the IAEA to issue recommendations, the international community avoids the potentially intractable problems of negotiation and consensus-building.

[34] Entered into force on February 26, 1987. As of July 31, 1997, there were 73 parties, 70 states, and 3 organizations.

[35] Entered into force on September 20, 1994. As of July 31, 1997, 39 states had deposited an instrument of ratification, acceptance or approval, 25 of which have at least one nuclear installation that has achieved criticality in a reactor core. 27 further states have signed the Convention but are not contracting parties.

[36] See (1997) 36 I.L.M. 1431. 62 countries voted in favor of the Convention and two voted against, with three nations abstaining. Pakistan and New Zealand are the only two countries to vote against the Convention and China, Russia, and India were the abstaining nations. The Convention was opened for signature at the IAEA's 41st General Conference. As of February 9, 1998, 30 states have signed the Convention.

[37] See U.N. Ad Hoc Comm. established by G.A. Res. 51/210 of December 17, 1996, 1st Sess. February 24–March 7, 1997, Convention on the Suppression of Acts of Nuclear Terrorism, Draft submitted by the Russian Federation, A/AC.252/L.3, January 28, 1997.

Secondly, the treaty mechanism is inappropriate because of the high level of sensitivity associated with controlling nuclear materials. Implementing and fulfilling the manifold protective tasks require national authorities to coordinate sensitive policies among domestic military and energy agencies. Because nuclear materials have clear military relevance, are indispensable to domestic energy production, and are scarce and require exceptional technical sophistication to produce and use, most governments regard nuclear materials as ultimate manifestations of national sovereignty. Accordingly, the international regulatory system would be politically unacceptable if premised on mandatory state obedience to IAEA-issued directives. Such mandates would be viewed as intolerable intrusions on sovereignty.

Thirdly, in most states, nuclear energy is produced by non-state commercial entities not directly regulated by international law or organizations. Under well-accepted legal principles, international law applies to states that, in turn, have sole legal power over private commercial entities. Even if states were prepared to accept binding IAEA authority over their nuclear activities, the IAEA could not, itself, require that private enterprises carry out specific tasks regarding nuclear materials. By issuing non-binding 'recommendations' that each state party may adopt as domestic regulations, oversight of private industries can be accomplished without intruding on state sovereignty.

C. IAEA RECOMMENDATIONS TO PROTECT NUCLEAR MATERIALS

The international regulatory system to protect nuclear materials is a complex interweaving of treaty and soft law. Treaties establish the structure of the system and regulate transnational aspects of nuclear materials protection. Soft law, in the form of IAEA-issued specifications concerning the thousands of minute details relevant to nuclear materials, are recommendations that states are not legally bound to adopt,[38] but that are, in fact, widely accepted. Recommendations thus come in where treaties leave off, furnishing the elaborate detail of protective measures without intruding on sovereignty.

Recommendations can call for the establishment of national bureaucratic bodies without prescribing responsible agencies. The IAEA can oversee the behavior of private nuclear enterprises but still leave to each state the implementation of tasks required to make the recommendations legally binding. Specific IAEA recommendations can be incorporated into a binding treaty if there is sufficient political consensus; until such consensus is achieved, the recommendations usually achieve a remarkable level of uniformity.

---

[38] See Phuong, H.V., 'Legal Aspects of the Transport of Radioactive Materials' (1979) 21 *IAEA Bulletin* 13.

The process of promulgating IAEA soft law is the subject of uniform prescription.[39] The IAEA has created five advisory commissions with harmonized terms of reference to prepare and review all recommendatory documents; the Secretariat has assigned to each of these bodies a Scientific Secretary who coordinates the work of the body with the relevant Agency policies and programs, and has appointed a technical officer for the preparation of each document.[40]

The IAEA helps member states to comply with safety standards through technical co-operation (TC) programs in the form of experts' services, equipment, and training. The current safety-related TC program includes more than 100 national, regional, and inter-regional projects devoted to radiation and waste safety. In addition, a large number of workshops and training courses are organized and fellowships granted through TC funding. The IAEA has set up an advisory peer review service to evaluate national physical protection systems at state request. Four missions under the International Physical Protection Advisory Service (IPPAS) were carried out in 1997, and again in 1998. The IAEA also assists states in the development of legislation and establishment of regulatory systems.[41]

The system to protect nuclear material demonstrates various interwoven roles for soft law. First, each state must develop a system of accounting and control of nuclear material and keep records; the content of that system is defined by IAEA soft law recommendations. Secondly, each state must implement physical protection measures against theft or unauthorized diversion of nuclear materials and against the sabotage of nuclear facilities or loss of materials in transit; these measures stem from both treaty obligations and soft law recommendations. Thirdly, soft law recommendations specify how states should transport nuclear materials, both domestically and internationally, in order to avoid hazards. In many instances, the recommendations applicable to international transit have been adopted by other international bodies which have promulgated them as their own soft law. Fourthly, the management of spent nuclear fuel and radioactive wastes is now governed by a new treaty whose promulgation suggests novel aspects of the treaty/soft law relationship.

1. State Systems of Accounting and Control (SSAC)

Each NNWS should establish and maintain a system of accounting for and control of all nuclear material so that the state and the IAEA can maintain a

---

[39] For the most recent detailed and informative overview of this system, see IAEA Measures Against Illicit Trafficking in Nuclear Materials and Other Radioactive Sources, Report by the Director General, GOV/INF/818, September 5, 1997.

[40] IAEA, Preparation and Review Process of Safety Standards Series Documents, August 26, 1997, <http://www.iaea.or.at/ns/rasanet/standards/preprevpro./htm>.

[41] Elbaradei, M., Physical Protection of Nuclear Materials, November 1997, <http://www.iaea.or.at/worldatom/in. . .bulletin/bull394/elbaradeiart.html>.

current picture of the materials' location and movement to verify that such materials are not impermissibly diverted. The objectives of an SSAC system are: (1) to identify and track all nuclear material in order to detect any possible losses or unauthorized use or removal; and (2) to provide a basis to apply IAEA verification techniques as the state and the IAEA have agreed.

Each facility is divided into material balance areas (MBAs). A book inventory of the quantity of material in each MBA is maintained by recording measured flows into and out of the area at key measurement points. The IAEA may verify records during inspections, and the correspondence between the contents of the MBA and these records is the basis for judging whether any material is unaccounted for. Material unaccounted for is then evaluated by statistical methods in order to establish, with a reasonable confidence, if significant losses or diversions have occurred.

The IAEA recommendations pertaining to state systems of accounting and control are 'soft law' contained in IAEA/SG/INF/2.[42] These recommendations urge each state to: (1) establish an administrative authority and assign to it necessary tasks; and (2) impose obligations on private industries that possess, use, or store nuclear materials. Both the establishment of an administrative authority and the imposition of requirements on private industry are the responsibility of the state as sovereign and any prescription on how it should carry out those obligations could be viewed as an unwarranted intrusion on sovereignty. Yet, it is important that all states carry out the specific details of accounting and control in a virtually uniform manner so that the IAEA can verify those efforts and so that each state can rely on the representations of every other state. The strong interest in uniformity coupled with inability of the IAEA to prescribe state systems has led the IAEA to promulgate non-binding recommendations on the subject.

The IAEA recommends that each state establish an administrative authority to undertake and supervise its safeguard responsibilities, including accounting for and control of nuclear material. While the structure of that authority is entirely a matter of state discretion, the authority should be empowered to promulgate provisions governing the possession, transfer, and use of nuclear material, to ensure compliance with the state's safeguard objectives, and to serve as the point of contact with the IAEA.

The state should enact domestic legal obligations to ensure that it meets its nuclear material accounting and control obligations. It is recommended, but not obligatory, that enactment of legal measures addresses: (1) requirements for construction and authorization for operation of all nuclear facilities; (2) conditions for revocation, suspension, or modification of authorization to construct and operate facilities and to process, use, or transfer nuclear material; (3) identification of non-compliance; and (4) enforcement measures.

---

[42] See IAEA Safeguards: Guidelines for States' Systems of Accounting for and Control of Nuclear Materials, IAEA Safeguards Information Series No. 2, IAEA/SG/INF/2 (1980).

The Authority should establish an SSAC information system to collect and process information reported by facility operators to the Authority, and prepare declarations for evaluation internally and for submission to designated bodies as necessary to satisfy international obligations. Accordingly, the SSAC information system should contain a list of current facilities, a record of data on nuclear material inventories possessed at each location, data on transfers including inventory reports of domestic and international shipments, and a record of inspection data required to review any possible losses including discrepancies between shippers and receivers and measurement uncertainties.

The Authority should establish a comprehensive audit and inspection program to assure operator compliance with the requirements of the accounting and control system. The program should ensure that each facility operator has the capability to discharge its responsibility to account for and control nuclear material in satisfaction of appropriate requirements, and enable the state to derive assurance through independent verification at facilities by the Authority, that the accounting and control measures implemented by the facility operator are effective. The Authority also should establish criteria for assessment of the operator's capability and performance and the results of SSAC inspections and evaluations.

The Authority should formulate an inspection scheme to review nuclear license applications to determine the applicants' capability to perform required accounting and control functions, determine if its standards of nuclear materials accounting and control have been satisfactorily implemented and performed, and evaluate reports to identify abnormalities, measurement uncertainties, unaccounted for material, and shipper/receiver (S/R) discrepancies.

Each state should provide adequate technical assistance in the area of material accounting and control to enable operators to fulfil the Authority's requirements. Assistance may aim at establishing adequate measurement systems, incorporating non-destructive assay techniques as well as data processing and analysis procedures, making available international standards, and establishing surveillance measures. A number of states have their own research and development programs to improve accounting for and control of nuclear material and may be asked to cooperate in disseminating the results of such activities.

Every facility should institute a system to meet its SSAC requirements. Initially, facility owners should inform the Authority of their organizational units responsible for developing, approving, and implementing nuclear material accounting and control. Facility operators should provide information on facility design and operations involving nuclear material in sufficient detail to permit evaluation of the adequacy of the facility. These details should include identification of the facility type, its arrangement, nuclear material used, and features relevant to nuclear material accounting and control. The facility accounting and control system should include: assignment of responsibilities, a system to record and report nuclear material inventories and transfers, appropriate procedures to carry out required tasks, and an information processing system to timely evaluate data and identify anomalies.

2. States' Physical Protection Systems

A state system of physical protection is essential to avert the theft of nuclear materials or an act of sabotage. The government of each state is responsible for establishing and operating a comprehensive physical protection system for nuclear materials and facilities. International cooperation remains crucial, however, especially where the effectiveness of physical protection in one state depends on other states taking adequate measures to deter or defeat hostile actions against nuclear facilities or materials.

The role of non-binding norms in this context is especially interesting. In 1972, the IAEA issued 'Recommendations for the Physical Protection of Nuclear Material', subsequently revised. In light of concerns that such soft law was insufficient to protect against diversion or sabotage, states negotiated the Convention on the Physical Protection of Nuclear Material,[43] which came into force in 1987. It established a framework for international cooperation in the physical protection of civilian nuclear material while in storage and international transport.[44] To provide further guidance concerning the physical protection of nuclear materials at facilities, the IAEA revised its earlier recommendations in 1993.[45] Thus, soft law *both* preceded a treaty, establishing the policy and the basic regulatory modalities for the treaty, *and* succeeded the treaty, providing substantial detail on the requirements which should be met by nuclear material physical protection systems.

The purposes of the Convention on the Physical Protection of Nuclear Material are to avert the potential dangers of the unlawful taking and use of nuclear materials; adopt appropriate and effective measures to ensure the prevention, detection, and punishment of such offenses; establish effective measures for the physical protection of nuclear material; and facilitate the safe transfer of nuclear material.

The Convention calls for international cooperation to assure the physical protection of civil nuclear material during international transport. Article 3 requires states parties to take appropriate steps under their national law to

[43] Convention, *supra* note 32.

[44] See generally International Physical Security Standards for Nuclear Materials Outside the United States, Committee on Foreign Affairs, U.S. House of Representatives, Reports to Congress Pursuant to s. 604 of the Omnibus Diplomatic Security and Anti-Terrorism Act of 1986 (P.L. 99–399), 1988.

[45] The revisions are contained in INFCIRC/225/Rev.3.

ensure that international transport of nuclear material is protected at the minimum level of physical protection provided in recommendation INFI-CIRC/225. During international transport of the most sensitive (Category I) material, special precautions are to be taken: the sender, receiver, and carrier must make prior arrangements so that escorts constantly oversee the material under conditions that assure close communication with appropriate response forces.

In Article 4, states parties agree not to engage in or authorize the import or export of nuclear material unless they have received assurances that such material will be protected during the international transport at the agreed levels. They also agree not to allow the transit through their territory of nuclear material between states that are not parties to the Convention unless they have received assurances that this nuclear material will be protected during international transport, and to apply within the framework of their national law the agreed levels of physical protection to nuclear material being transported from one part of the state to another through international waters or airspace.

The Convention also provides for international cooperation in the recovery of lost or stolen nuclear materials. Article 5 provides that in the case of theft, robbery, or any other unlawful taking of nuclear material or credible threat to do so, states parties shall, in accordance with their national law, upon request cooperate with and assist each other, to the maximum extent feasible, in the recovery and protection of such material. States parties should thus co-ordinate their efforts through diplomatic and other agreed channels; render assistance, if requested; and ensure the return of stolen or missing nuclear material.

The IAEA recommends other physical protection measures in INF-CIRC/225/Rev.3 (1993).[46] Under these recommendations, the state and the IAEA should agree on the intensity and form of the IAEA's assistance to a state's physical protection systems based on the state's assessment of the threat of unauthorized removal of nuclear material and of sabotage. The IAEA recommendations classify nuclear materials into three categories in order to determine the appropriate level of physical protection measures. For each category, a state's physical protection system should establish conditions to minimize the risk of unauthorized removal of nuclear material or for sabotage, and should provide information and technical assistance to support the state to locate and recover missing nuclear material and to minimize the effects of sabotage. These objectives apply in the context of protecting facilities and shipments.

Each state should identify physical protection requirements including hardware (security devices), procedures (the organization of guards and the

---

[46] See generally Leigh-Phippard, H., 'The Physical Protection of Nuclear Material', in Howlett, D., and Simpson, J. (eds.), *Nuclear Non-Proliferation: A Reference Handbook* (1992) 57.

performance of their duties), and facility design. Among the recommended measures are provisions to limit access to nuclear material to a minimum number of well-trained individuals carrying indications of appropriate registration. All individuals in a facility should be under surveillance at all times, and records should be kept of how long they spend in sensitive areas. The perimeter of a protected area should consist of a physical barrier with a supplementary surveillance system and exit routes should be fitted with alarms, a twenty-four-hour guarding service, and a patrol with two-voice communication. Finally, emergency plans of action should be prepared to counter threats and to ensure that, during evacuations, nuclear material is not improperly removed.

INFCIRC/225/Rev.3 recommends measures that include storage in a 'strong room' within an inner area of a protected area; cleared areas at the perimeter of the protected area with illumination sufficient for observation; periodic external and internal guard patrols; arrangements for response by an armed external emergency team as needed to counter an armed attack; an independent and duplicated transmission system for two-way voice communication to link guards, their headquarters and reserve forces; access to inner areas limited to persons whose trustworthiness has been determined; protection of inner areas with alarms and locks; persons and packages entering or leaving inner areas subject to search; minimum entry of private vehicles to the protected area; constant surveillance of persons in storage area; and control of keys and locks.

The transport of nuclear material is probably the operation most vulnerable to nuclear material theft or sabotage. INFCIRC/225/Rev.3 provides that physical protection for any transport of nuclear material should minimize the total time the nuclear material is in transit; minimize temporary storage and transfers from one mode of transportation to another; avoid regular shipment schedules, and protect schedule and route information; and require advance determination of the trustworthiness of all individuals involved.

To protect nuclear materials during international transport, INFCIRC/225/Rev.1 recommends prior agreement on international jurisdiction; prior arrangements between shipper, receiver, and carrier; minimum time in transits and transfers *en route*; avoidance of regular patterns and areas of natural disaster or civil disorder; use of individuals whose trustworthiness has been determined; arrangements for emergency response forces, as needed, to prevent successful theft or sabotage; use of escorts or guards; two-way radio or frequent telephone communication to provide periodic communication while in transit; closed and locked vehicles, compartments or freight containers; checking of locks and seals; search of load vehicles, and notice to shipper of the arrival or non-arrival of the shipment.

3. IAEA Safe Transport Regulations to Prevent Transport Hazards

In 1961, the IAEA first promulgated Regulations for the Safe Transport of Radioactive Materials for domestic transit of nuclear materials;[47] a separate set of recommendations applies to the international transit of nuclear materials.[48] The IAEA Recommendations have been adopted by the U.N., by all international organizations concerned with the transport of hazardous goods,[49] and by a great number of states. These recommendations are accompanied by advisory material suggesting how best to carry them out, but they are written as regulations, simplifying their incorporation into national regulatory schemes. Such recommendations thereby help to harmonize national requirements.

Radioactive materials in transport pose four unique hazards: contamination, irradiation, heating, and criticality. Ensuring the safe transport of radioactive materials has both technical and administrative aspects. Technical requirements focus on design features for packages, supplemented by special loading requirements based on the information on the package labels. Further protection against hazards is provided by containment and, in some cases, by limiting the amounts of nuclear material that can be transported in specified types of packages. The regulations specify maximum surface temperatures for packages of radioactive materials. Suitable design features protect against the effects of heat generated within the package.

The regulations, in general, hold the consignor responsible for design safety and for the correct assembly of the package. The consignor is also responsible for complying with the labelling and marking requirements, for issuing a certificate stating that the contents are correctly identified, packed, labeled, and marked, and in proper condition for transport, and for including particulars of the consignment in the transport documents. The carrier should provide necessary controls during transport and storage in transit. Additional operational control measures require transport workers to segregate packages from persons and sensitive materials according to the information carried on the package labels. The number of packages in a single vehicle, vessel, aircraft, or storage area should be kept below allowable limits in order to control the

---

[47] The Transport Regs. underwent comprehensive revision in 1964, 1967, 1973, 1985, and most recently in 1995. See IAEA, Historical Development of Safety Standards, <http://www.iaea.or.at/ns/rasanet/standards/bakgrd.htm>.

[48] IAEA Code of Practice on the International Transboundary Movement of Radioactive Waste (1991) 30 I.L.M. 556.

[49] In 1993, the IAEA's recommendations were adopted and supplemented by the IMO Code for the Safe Carriage of Irradiated Nuclear Fuel, Plutonium, and High-Level Radioactive Waste in Flasks on Board Ships. IMO Assembly Res. A. 748(18) (November 4, 1993). The Code is itself a voluntary Code of Practice. See Kwiatkowska, B., and Soons, A., 'Comment, Plutonium Shipments—A Supplement' (1994) 25 *Ocean Dev. & Int'l L.* 419. See also Pedrozo, R., 'Transport of Nuclear Cargoes by Sea' (1997) 28 *J. Mar. L. & Comm.* 207.

radiation level as well as to prevent criticality. Access to any suspected package is restricted.

If there is a release, an expert should assess the contamination, and necessary additional steps should be taken to minimize the consequences of any release. Many national authorities have established detailed plans for reporting and handling emergency situations during the transport of hazardous materials. Advice on appropriate emergency planning for radioactive materials is provided in an existing IAEA document and in a manual of guidance.[50]

4. Spent Fuel Management

In September 1997, the nations represented within the IAEA adopted the Joint Convention on the Safety of Spent Fuel Management and on the Safety of Radioactive Waste Management to assure protection of radioactive waste and spent fuel resulting from civilian, but not most military activities.[51] This first international instrument on the safe handling and storage of spent fuels and radioactive waste is a hybrid of hard and soft law which emphasizes international cooperation while recognizing that national measures are key to achieving and maintaining safety. When ratified by twenty-five states, including fifteen having an operational nuclear power, it will be binding on those states; in the interim, and as applied to all other states having IAEA safeguards agreements, the Spent Fuel Convention represents a set of recommendations.

Each contracting party must take appropriate steps to ensure adequate protection against radiological hazards to individuals, society, and the environment at all stages of spent fuel management. Overall, a contracting party must consider internationally-endorsed criteria and standards, and must implement quality assurance programs, including national safety requirements; a licensing system for all management activities, prohibitions against unlicensed facility operation; a system of institutional control, documentation, reporting, and regulatory inspections; the effective enforcement of regulations; and a regulatory body with adequate power and resources to fulfill its responsibilities.

For existing facilities, all 'reasonably practicable improvements' must be made to upgrade safety. In determining proper design and construction of new facilities, each party must minimize all possible radiological impacts. A safety and an environmental assessment must be performed prior to facility construction. Facilities may be operated only with a license that is 'conditional on the completion of a commissioning program demonstrating that the facility, as constructed, is consistent with design and safety requirements'.

---

[50] IAEA, Emergency Response Planning for Incidents During the Transport of Radioactive Materials.

[51] See *supra* note 36.

License holders are primarily responsible for the safety of spent fuel and radioactive waste management; each contracting party must supervise each license holder in meeting its responsibility.

Each contracting party must report the measures it adopts to comply with the Convention, addressing spent fuel management policy and management practices; radioactive waste management policy and management practices; and the criteria used to define and categorize radioactive waste. Reports should also include a list of the spent fuel and radioactive waste management facilities subject to the Convention, their essential features, main purpose, and location; an inventory of all spent fuel or radioactive waste subject to the Convention that is stored or has been disposed of; and a list of nuclear facilities being decommissioned and the status of decommissioning activities.

With regard to the risks associated with transboundary movement of dangerous radioactive materials, contracting parties must develop programs to ensure that movement proceeds consistent with the Convention and other relevant binding international instruments. Specifically, any transboundary movement must be properly authorized and transpire with prior notification and consent of the destination state which may consent only if it has the technical and administrative capacity, as well as the regulatory structure, necessary to manage the spent fuel or radioactive waste.

CONCLUSION

'Soft law', at least in the context of nuclear materials protection, has flourished over four decades of Cold War confrontation, addressed concerns about proliferation and nuclear safety, and more recently responded to threats of nuclear terrorism. In this field, where treaty-making would be excessively cumbersome but the exercise of state discretion would lead to inconsistency, where the tasks are countless and technical yet the stakes could literally be planetary survival, 'soft law' has evolved to fill a variety of crucial niches.

Given the highly technical nature of this regulatory field and the secrecy regarding levels of state compliance, the efficacy of IAEA recommendations are not precisely measurable. Certainly, numerous recent smuggling incidents suggest the need for more effective recommendations, but this should not lead to a conclusion that the 'soft law' mechanism is inappropriate. On the contrary, it is difficult to imagine how this system could have been implemented without resort to methods that were implicitly obligatory without rising to the level of a formal treaty.

If adherence by a large number of states, indeed virtually the entire planet, is a measure of success, then IAEA recommendations on nuclear materials protection have been successful. If growth of the regulatory system and maturation of substantive controls is a measure of success, then again these rec-ommendations are successful. And of course, if avoiding nuclear catastrophe is a measure of success, then these recommendations have been successful at least up to the time of this writing.

All evidence suggests that resort to the 'soft law' mechanism to protect nuclear materials was not an explicitly deliberate choice. Yet, in hindsight, it is virtually impossible to imagine how this system could have evolved in any other way. Function has dictated legal form.

International Regulation of Land Mines

RICHARD L. WILLIAMSON, JR.

INTRODUCTION

Anti-personnel land mines cause widespread suffering. The nature of efforts to control their deployment globally and the high degree of success of some of those efforts provide an opportunity to study the development of inter-national norms and compliance with international obligations under unusual circumstances. They also suggest several factors influencing the choice of a binding or a non-binding instrument to embrace new international norms.

Over 100 million land mines remain to be cleared around the globe.[1] The problem is particularly severe in Cambodia, Afghanistan, Angola, and the former Yugoslavia, but adverse effects also are felt in dozens of countries on four continents. A study by the U.S. Department of State estimated that there are 150 casualties a week from anti-personnel land mines, or over 7,000 per year.[2] The victims of land mines are usually civilians, with casualties some-times occurring years or even decades following the military conflict during which the mines were laid. As detailed below, many of the wounded die and survivors often require leg amputation. In addition to the toll in lives and per-manent injuries, land mines disrupt agriculture and commerce in several countries, enough to be a major impediment to reconstruction and economic growth. Globally, mine clearance will take decades and significantly divert international aid resources from other pressing humanitarian and develop-ment purposes.

---

[1] U.S. Department of State, Bureau of Political-Military Affairs, *Hidden Killers: The Global Problem with Uncleared Land Mines* (1993) ii.

[2] *Ibid.*, 2–4.

This study briefly explains land mines and the problems they cause. It reviews the international community's response, with a special emphasis on the role of non-governmental organizations (NGOs) in mobilizing efforts to control land mines. It then investigates the role of compliance with soft law instruments in the anti-personnel land mine context, and speculates on the reasons treaty instruments are strongly preferred.

The development of international norms against land mine use has not followed the usual pattern of embodying ideals in legally non-binding documents followed by treaty obligations. With that pattern, compliance with soft law instruments can be assessed in comparison to compliance with norms articulated in the subsequent hard law instruments. Instead, the relevant communities have sought to place stringent restrictions on land mines in hard law instruments almost from the beginning. That effort has been partially successful, although the matter is not fully resolved. Nevertheless, the developing regulation of land mines contributes to our understanding of the development of soft law norms; the relationship of compliance questions to norm formulation; and the interplay between soft law norms, hard law instruments, and evolving custom. In addition, the land mine story illustrates the interplay between two substantive branches of international law: humanitarian law's 'use' controls on a particular weapon and arms control's restrictions on possession and transfer of that weapon.

A. THE TYPES AND USES OF LAND MINES

Land mines consist of a charge of explosives, a triggering device that is activated when moved or subjected to pressure, a detonator that begins the explosive process by mechanical action or electrical charge, and a plastic case. Simple mines can be very inexpensive, costing well under U.S.$10 when purchased in large quantities.[3] More sophisticated and substantially more expensive mines have better triggering devices, may have larger shaped explosive charges and directed shrapnel, and may self-destruct or self-disarm after a time if the mine has not been previously detonated.

Two types of land mines are commonly manufactured: anti-personnel mines and anti-tank mines. They differ in several ways. Anti-personnel mines have a much smaller explosive charge and are much easier to trigger. They can be used in far greater numbers and over wider areas because they are considerably cheaper than anti-tank mines. The latter tend to be concentrated

---

[3] Some unconfirmed reports put the cost of Russian and Chinese mines at $3.00 each. The Brazilian manufacturer Quima Tupan sold its AP NM AE TI model for $5.80. Human Rights Watch and Physicians for Social Responsibility, *Land Mines: A Deadly Legacy* (1993) 56. This study, while partially out of date, contains the best single collection of information on the land mine problem. Another good early overview is contained in Boutros-Ghali, B., 'The Landmine Crisis; A Humanitarian Disaster', *Foreign Affairs* 8 (Oct./Nov. 1994).

around defensive positions, roads, and bridges where they are sometimes set off by trucks or tractors, but pose far less threat to civilians than anti-personnel mines.

Land mines were used and first named in the American Civil War, when large explosive charges were sometimes set off under enemy lines by tunneling or mining under them. Anti-personnel land mines were first used extensively during World War I to protect anti-tank mines from efforts to disarm them by enemy forces. Their use greatly increased during World War II and has continued in a series of subsequent regional conflicts.

For decades, land mines were used primarily in defensive roles to protect fixed positions. While all weapons utilizing explosive force can injure or kill, land mines were considered relatively benign compared to weapons such as land and ship-borne artillery, tank shells, or air-delivered bombs. These 'offensive' weapons possessed far greater explosive power and allowed the military to project force at great distances. They were seen as a greater military threat and also a greater threat to civilian populations because of what seemed be their inherent inaccuracy.

In the recent campaign, anti-mine advocates decided to exempt anti-tank mines from their efforts to bar the production, sale, and use of anti-personnel mines because anti-tank mines pose much less of a problem and the political obstacles to their control are far greater. Military commanders in many countries continue to perceive a utility in having anti-tank mines, but far less in preserving anti-personnel mines. A similar cost-benefit and political analysis led anti-mine advocates to agree to an exception for 'command-detonated' land mines, *i.e.*, those that are remotely detonated by purposeful contemporaneous human decision, and cannot be triggered merely by stepping on them.

Anti-personnel land mines are extremely cheap compared to the cost of other weapons, making it feasible for established military forces and insurgent groups to acquire them in very large numbers, and to use them in offensive roles, *e.g.*, fully surrounding a village, making it necessary for the villagers to flee, or disrupting agriculture or local commerce by placing them in fields or across trails and roads. Their use is greatly assisted by mechanical devices that strew them at high speed.[4]

From the humanitarian perspective, another adverse feature of anti-personnel land mines is that the explosive charge is intentionally small enough to wound but not kill the enemy soldier. By requiring medical attention and other assistance, the wounded soldier keeps additional military personnel out of the active conflict. Undoubtedly, it is more humane to wound an enemy soldier than to kill him outright, but if a lone civilian triggers the device, the victim may bleed to death, not having comrades and medics to attend to the

[4] An example of a high speed system is Italy's Istrice vehicle-mounted mine-scattering system, which can dispense up to 1,750 mines a minute. Human Rights Watch, *supra* note 3, at 41.

wound. Modern military forces often can provide the soldier victim with rapid transport to field hospitals, whereas the civilian is likely to lack prompt medical attention, leading to infected wounds requiring amputation.

A third adverse feature is that mine casings are now made of plastic instead of metal, and minimal metal parts are used in the triggering and detonating mechanisms. Plastic, unlike metal, gives off no readily detectable magnetic field. Coupled with the small size of anti-personnel land mines, this fact makes even simple contemporary mines extremely difficult to locate, greatly increasing the cost and risk of removal. Moreover, plastic is more difficult than metal to detect with medical x-ray equipment, complicating wound treatment.

Finally, with the arguable exception of certain 'smart' mines, anti-personnel land mines pose long-term risks. Recently, for example, a girl in Egypt reportedly was killed by a land mine planted by Rommel's troops in 1942.[5] The longer strewn land mines remain without being removed, the greater the likelihood that they will be covered with soil or overgrown with vegetation, making them much harder to detect.

The carnage from past land mine use is horrific. The U.N. Secretary General's 1995 report estimated that in 1995, there were 110 million land mines deployed, with two million new ones added annually.[6] While estimates vary considerably, there are, at a minimum, several thousand casualties each year, and the yearly toll could be as high as 26,000, roughly half of which are fatalities. The way land mines are triggered makes severe leg injuries the most common consequence for those who survive, leading almost invariably to amputations. The U.S. Agency for International Development estimates that there are 70,000 civilian and soldier amputees in Angola alone,[7] many of whom are children. Outfitting amputees with efficient crutches and proper prothesetic devices, and providing them with rehabilitation, retraining, and on-going medical attention improves the victims' chances of being productive members of society, but the cost is a severe financial drain on their families or on society. Unfortunately, even these ameliorations are unavailable to most victims in developing countries.

The global cost of mine clearance will be massive. It can cost up to 100 *times* as much to locate and remove a mine as it does to purchase and implant one. The U.N. estimates mine clearance costs between $300 and $1,000 per

[5] Meyers, S.L., 'One Step at a Time: Why Washington Likes Land Mines', *New York Times*, August 24, 1997, at Sect. 4, 5. Another report was less certain about whose mine it was, and only asserted that the girl had been injured. Simmons, A., 'Stop the Haggling Over Land Mines', *Chicago Tribune*, September 18, 1997, 25.

[6] Zehm, G.E., '"Perverse" Weapons: Regulations on Mines Face Review', *Deutsche Press-Agentur*, September 22, 1995.

[7] Office of Foreign Disaster Assistance, USAID, Situation Report No. 3 (July 1, 1996), quoted in Africa News Service (July 3, 1996); Accord, United Nations Department of Humanitarian Affairs, *Land Mines* (1995) 18.

mine,[8] a difficult figure to understand unless one considers the sophisticated equipment, the extensive number of highly-trained personnel, and the high support and logistics costs involved in the clearance efforts. In the absence of massive outside assistance, some countries, particularly Cambodia and Angola, have no prospect of clearing their land in the short term. Indeed, absent technological breakthroughs in mine location and removal that would allow far more efficient clearance than is possible at present, foreign assistance organizations can anticipate spending several hundred million dollars a year in coming decades on mine removal. That is a significant portion of the world's total expenditures for development and humanitarian assistance. Unfortunately, although research is taking place in several countries, no miracle clearance technology seems to be on the horizon.

The economic and social consequences of not clearing mines may be even worse than the heavy cost of removal. In several countries, land mines have rendered much of the best agricultural land unusable. Much of Libya's grazing land cannot be exploited because of mines laid during World War II. Moreover, mines placed along roads and trails have become a significant impediment to rural commerce. Even international peacekeeping has suffered, as mines have prevented international military forces and peacekeeping observers from fulfilling their duties in several countries, especially Angola.[9]

B. SLOW INTERNATIONAL RESPONSE

While the harm from land mines steadily grew after World War II, it took considerable time before land mines became a major humanitarian and international political issue. There were several reasons for this. First, land mines were regarded in Western military circles as defensive weapons, no less humane in their effects on enemy combatants than many other classes of light armament. Placed in marked or mapped zones for later retrieval, land mines could be argued to pose less of a risk to civilians than mortars, artillery, and barrage rockets which are difficult or impossible to use with real precision, thus often causing extensive 'collateral damage'. It took time to recognize a gradual but significant change in the method and extent of landmine deployment, deriving from a change in the nature of international conflict, with a shift away from cross-border engagements between professional military forces toward civil wars and insurrections, albeit often with outside assistance. Civilian harm ceased being merely an unintended consequence of military battle, as techniques such as 'area denial', to which civilians are particularly vulnerable, became prevalent. Indeed, in several civil wars,

[8] Human Rights Watch, *supra* note 3, at 251.
[9] This conclusion is based on interviews with U.S. State Department and international organization personnel.

terrorizing civilians and de-populating areas were the intended purposes of mine usage.

Secondly, the international community had to contend with many other pressing international security matters, including the cold war, several actual wars, horizontal and vertical nuclear proliferation, and the use or threat of chemical and biological weapons. In addition, ever more countries were seeking ballistic missiles and other sophisticated delivery systems. Thirdly, agreement was reached, as discussed below, to place certain restrictions on land mine use in Protocol II to the 1980 Convention on Prohibitions or Restrictions of Use of Certain Conventional Weapons Which May be Deemed to be Excessively Injurious or to Have Indiscriminate Effects (CCW).[10] In the wake of that agreement, the international community may have felt it had taken some useful steps and could turn its attention to other matters. Finally, many of the countries now recognized as having severe land mine problems were closed to Western news media and were the scenes of massive human rights violations or intense fighting. The serious residual problems caused by mines only came to light after the situation had stabilized.

C. POLITICAL HISTORY OF RECENT INTERNATIONAL CONCERN

For a decade following the negotiation of Protocol II to the CCW, there was little further action on anti-personnel land mines. Political interest in land mine control almost simultaneously re-emerged in the 1990s from two different communities. On the one hand, the International Committee of the Red Cross (ICRC), the United Nations, national foreign assistance programs, and private humanitarian assistance organizations became increasingly concerned with caring for wounded civilians and former soldiers. On the other hand, human rights organizations reporting on abuses in particular countries, such as El Salvador, began to observe and include information on the impact of land mine use. In the United States, first the Vietnam Veterans of America Foundation (VVAF) and then Human Rights Watch (HRW) became heavily involved in land mine issues. They remained the leaders of the U.S. campaign, which eventually numbered some 235 non-governmental entities, including veterans, religious, human rights, humanitarian aid, peace, and arms control organizations. They were also key players in the international campaign, which ultimately totaled over 1,000 organizations with affiliates in fifty-five countries. The cam-

---

[10] Protocol on Prohibitions or Restrictions on the Use of Mines, Booby Traps and Other Devices ('Protocol II') to the United Nations Convention on Prohibitions or Restrictions on the Use of Certain Conventional Weapons Which May be Deemed to be Excessively Injurious and to Have Indiscriminate Effects (1980), reproduced (1980) at 19 I.L.M. 1524; U.S. Department of State, *Treaties in Force* (1997).

paign became an increasingly sophisticated effort, with detailed studies, massive database collection, multiple language versions of popular comic books, and extensive and heavily used Internet web pages supplementing the traditional articles, rallies, and letter writing campaigns. The involvement of celebrities and international leaders, especially Nelson Mandela and Princess Diana, resulted in considerable media and press coverage.

Prior to the great explosion of public interest in 1991, governments had made some efforts to assist victims and later to clear mines. This was in part a response to urging by the ICRC and the UNGA, and in part the result of domestic pressure being brought by the fledgling anti-mine campaign.

The first serious attempts at mine control came in 1991. VVAF officials, who had a contract with the U.S. government for victim assistance in Cambodia, raised their concerns with U.S. Senator Thomas Leahy who earlier had sponsored legislation authorizing funding to assist mine victims abroad. VVAF personnel pointed out that mine clearance and victim assistance were being overwhelmed in Cambodia because new mines were being laid more rapidly than existing ones could be cleared. They suggested mounting an effort to de-legitimize mines and ban them. Leahy introduced legislation requiring a one-year suspension on land mine exports.[11] With no serious Administration opposition, the Congress passed the 1992 Leahy–Evans Land Mine Moratorium Act, banning the sale, export, or transfer abroad of land mines.[12] The same year, the European Parliament passed a resolution calling on member states to adopt a five-year export moratorium.[13]

By 1993, the pace of action on land mines greatly accelerated. The U.S. Land Mine Moratorium Extension Act extended the ban for another three years. France announced that it had not shipped land mines since 1985 and would no longer do so. It also called for a world-wide moratorium. By the end of the year, the U.N. General Assembly (UNGA) recommended that all nations adopt a moratorium on land-mine exports.[14] The UNGA also called for a review conference of the CCW. By the following year, the Spanish, Slovak, Swiss, Argentine, Israeli, British, Czech, and Russian governments announced various bans or restrictions on their export of mines.[15]

In March 1995, the U.S. finally ratified the CCW,[16] which it had signed in

---

[11] Information in this para. is based on interviews the author conducted with NGO officials and Congressional staff members.

[12] P.L. 102–484, §§ 1364–65 (1992), 106 Stat.2561–63.

[13] 'Resolution on the injuries and loss of life caused by mines', Res. B3–1744/92 (December 17, 1992) [1992] O.J. C161/62.

[14] UNGA Res. 48/75 K (December 1993).

[15] A full run-down on the steps taken by various governments can be found at present on the web-site of the Vietnam Veterans of American Foundation, one of the two leading U.S. NGOs dealing with land mines matters <http://www.vvaf.org>.

[16] See *supra* note 10. Ratification of the CCW was held up over U.S. opposition to Protocol III on incendiary weapons. In the end, the U.S. ratified the CCW and Protocol II, but not Protocol III.

1982. U.S. ratification made it possible for the U.S. to participate fully in the initial CCW review conference session held in the Fall of 1995 in Vienna. In May 1996, amendments to Protocol II, further restricting the circumstances of land mine use, were adopted by the review conference.

During this period, a shift in emphasis became evident in unilateral national statements on anti-personnel land mines. From a focus on restricting exports, nations increasingly announced restrictions on their own deployment of mines. Some supported a total ban including destruction of existing stocks. The first such statement came in November 1994, when the Dutch government announced that it would destroy nearly half a million stockpiled land mines and would support a total ban as the ultimate goal.[17] In March 1995, the Belgian government passed domestic legislation banning land mine use, production, procurement, sale, and transfer. Later, the Belgian and Dutch governments announced a joint operation to destroy stockpiles.

By 1996, several more states joined the trend toward full or partial moratoria on mine exports, including Russia and South Africa, both previously active exporters.[18] Resolutions calling for the regional or global abolition of land mines were adopted by, *inter alia*, the UNGA, the Organization of African Unity, and the Organization of American States. In May 1996, Human Rights Watch reported that thirty-four nations had expressed support for a total ban on land mines.[19] In September, the six Central American heads of state declared their region a mine-free zone. By October 1996, some form of restriction beyond export limitations had been announced, and in some cases adopted into law, by Canada, Switzerland, Australia, Germany, Luxembourg, Portugal, and South Africa.[20]

By this time, the U.S. government was under intense domestic pressure to do more about land mines, but the Executive Branch had three concerns. The first originated with the military, which did not place great stock in anti-personnel land mines generally, but wanted an exception for the Korean Peninsula, given the size of the North Korean forces and the close proximity of Seoul to the demilitarized zone. Secondly, the Pentagon felt that most of the harmful consequences of land mines—including the considerable casualties among U.S. forces in Vietnam when they retreated across previously-mined areas—were caused by 'dumb' mines, those with simple mechanical triggering devices that remain active for years or decades after being implanted. They reasoned that the problem was susceptible to technological solutions such as mines that exploded automatically after a set number of days, and mines that were triggered electronically by batteries that would gradually run down, thus effectively disabling them. The U.S. military

---

[17] See VVAF chronology, note 14.   [18] *Ibid.*
[19] See Human Rights web site at <http://www.hrw.org>.   [20] *Ibid.*

wanted to retain the right to use such 'smart' mines.[21] Developing countries countered that the practical effect would be to deprive them of inexpensive mines and they would either have to do without or pay industrialized countries a considerable amount to acquire smart mines.

The third major difficulty for the U.S. was the belief, widely held in the State Department and the Arms Control and Disarmament Agency, that the key to the problem was mines sold by a few states, notably Russia and China, but also India and Yugoslavia. In the view of these officials, a treaty that had widespread adherence by states that were not the source of the problem, but without adherence by states causing most of the difficulties, was worth very little. Worse yet, it could take the pressure off the states on which it should fall most heavily.[22] The upshot was the announcement by President Clinton on May 16, 1996 of a revised U.S. policy favoring the total ban on land mines as an ultimate goal, while reserving the right to use them in Korea, and to use smart mines elsewhere.

In October 1996, a strategy session was held in Ottawa among governmental representatives and NGOs. Governmental participation turned out to be far greater than the organizers expected. The meeting called for early negotiation of a global ban, with the goal of a treaty signing ceremony in Ottawa in late 1997. In turn, the U.S. pressed for the issue to be taken up at the Committee on Disarmament (C.D.), rather than at a separate treaty-writing conference. The UNGA approved a U.S.-sponsored resolution calling on all states to complete negotiations on a legally binding instrument banning the production, stockpiling, use, and transfer of anti-personnel land mines;[23] however, U.S. efforts to have that done in the C.D. failed because the Canadian approach had gained too much momentum.

The first preparatory conference for a treaty based on the Canadian approach was held in February 1997 in Vienna. By that date, the ICRC reported that fifty-three states had publicly expressed support for a total ban, twenty-eight of those had already put a halt to use of anti-personnel land mines by their own forces, and fifteen were in the process of destroying existing stocks.[24]

Formal negotiations on a treaty began in September 1997 in Oslo. The U.S. decided to attend at the last moment, but was unable to garner significant support for the limitations and reservations it wanted. The final treaty text was opened for signature in Ottawa in December 1997. In less than a year, on September 16, 1998, Burkino Faso became the fortieth nation to ratify, with the result that the treaty entered into force on March 1, 1999. As of August

---

[21] The information in this para. is largely taken from interviews with personnel in several Executive Branch agencies, though some of it has subsequently appeared in the press.

[22] *Ibid.*

[23] United Nations A/RES/51/45, part S (January 10, 1997).

[24] See the website for the International Committee of the Red Cross <http://www.icrc.org>.

1999, 135 states had signed the treaty, and eighty-four had ratified, including former exporting states such as South Africa and the United Kingdom.[25] However, key producing or using countries, including the U.S., China, Russia, both Koreas, India, Pakistan, Iran, Iraq, and Yugoslavia are neither parties nor signatories. Efforts are currently underway, led by the U.S., to negotiate an export ban at the C.D., which would take the form of a treaty parallel to the Ottawa agreement, but which could garner participation from many of the non-parties to the latter treaty.[26] Prospects for this approach are uncertain.

D. LAND MINES UNDER INTERNATIONAL LAW

Until the 1950s land mines were not an issue in intergovernmental discussions of humanitarian law, and virtually nothing was written on the subject by scholars or other commentators. Land mines were not addressed directly in international conventions. Of course, general principles of customary international law banned the use of inhumane or indiscriminate weapons and those that targeted civilians. Many of these principles were codified in Additional Protocol I to the Geneva Convention. The existence of such principles has not been sufficient, of course, to prevent the indiscriminate use of anti-personnel land mines, or even to prevent the deliberate targeting of civilians.

Morris Greenspan, the British/American law of war expert, is widely credited as the first to argue, in his 1959 work *The Modern Law of Land Warfare*, that offensive use of mines would violate existing humanitarian law principles. At the time, this drew no substantial attention because, as previously noted, mines were regarded as defensive weapons. In retrospect, Greenspan proved to be prophetic.

Land mine use increasingly became a problem for humanitarian law experts, particularly within the International Committee of the Red Cross and certain governments. Support gradually grew for a convention that would forbid or restrict the use of specific weapons, including land mines, providing additional substance to the limits imposed by customary international law and Protocol I. The end result was the 1980 CCW.[27] Protocol II of that treaty forbids the indiscriminate use of land mines, *i.e.*, use 'not on, or directed at, a military objective', or use that would be expected to cause damage to civilians which would be excessive relative to the military objective. The Protocol also banned most uses of mines in populated areas, imposed

---

[25] For a current, though non-official list of signatories and parties, see the ICRC website, <http://www.icrc.org>.

[26] UN Disarmament Conference Ends on Controversial Note, AFP (Sept. 8, 1998).

[27] See *supra* note 10.

some restrictions on the remote delivery of mines, required records be kept of mine fields, and mandated that once the conflict ceased these records be shared with adverse and other affected parties.

If all states and insurgent forces had adhered scrupulously to these provisions, there would not be a widespread land mine problem. But many states are not yet party to the CCW and Protocol II, some states parties have violated the provisions, and contesting sides in civil wars, guerrilla groups, and other insurgents certainly have not complied. Moreover, effective map-making and record-keeping are difficult in times of armed conflict even when a military force genuinely intends to do so. Mines are sometimes lost or placed incorrectly, and soldiers sometimes set them in convenient locations and not in the locations in which they were told to place them.

The 1995 CCW review conference addressed some of these problems. Among other things, the parties agreed to amend Protocol II by (a) requiring that all new mines have at least eight grams of iron to make them more detectable, (b) barring mines that cause superfluous injury, (c) requiring that remotely delivered mines, whose location is far harder to map than implanted devices, self-destruct or disarm with sufficient reliability that, *inter alia*, only one in 1,000 is operational 120 days after implantation, (d) declaring that the requirements applied to 'all parties to a conflict', not just states, and (e) banning the transfer of any mines prohibited by the Protocol.[28]

Such measures would no doubt be very helpful if fully implemented. By 1995, however, virtually all concerned groups in the NGO community and most governments, including the U.S., had changed their approach, recognizing that use restrictions or prohibitions on use—typical humanitarian law approaches—were not sufficient. Rather, they realized, approaches more akin to arms control were necessary, *i.e.*, measures forbidding the manufacture and ownership of weapons systems, and their transfer to others. Humanitarian law approaches, of course, could suffice if there were *never* any violations; *e.g.*, if no one ever used chemical weapons, the threat they pose would be eliminated. But humanitarian law approaches do not have a perfect compliance rate, both because they require restraint at exactly the time when the temptation to use a weapon is the greatest, and because some of the decision-making is necessarily carried out at levels far below the political leadership. In contrast, a nation cannot misuse weapons it does not possess, with the result that there has been growing interest in controlling the acquisition and dissemination of weapons systems. Thus, in the case of chemical weapons, the insufficiency of clear humanitarian law prohibitions on use of

---

[28] Protocol on Prohibitions or Restrictions on the Use of Mines, Booby-Traps and Other Devices as amended on May 3, 1996; text at United Nations CCW/CONF. I/16. These amendments to Protocol II entered into force December 3, 1998. However, many important states have not ratified or otherwise adhered to these amendments, including the U.S., which was one of the most important sponsors.

chemical weapons led to a convention forbidding ownership. In the case of land mines, however, although there was considerable support for the need to conclude arms control-like measures, there was considerable objection to doing so within the CCW and its protocols.[29]

The U.S. and many other states agreed that more needed to be done on land mines, though they differed greatly on the details and the tactics. The U.S. favored taking up the question in the C.D., because an arms control approach was being contemplated, and because the Chinese and Russians are active members of the C.D. Most other nations favored acting outside the C.D. in the belief that progress could be made faster in a forum devoted only to the one issue. Moreover, some nations sympathetic to the U.S. position argued that the C.D. had an already crowded agenda, including the negotia-tion of a new agreement on the cessation of production of nuclear materials for non-peaceful purposes. Others have long resented the significant role of the nuclear nations in the C.D. and the fact that most states are not repre-sented in that body. A few states no doubt also enjoyed participating in a process in which the U.S. could be portrayed as isolated and obstructionist.[30] In the end, the U.S. effort to channel the negotiations through the C.D. and to avoid a separate forum were unsuccessful. With the Canadian/NGO approach rapidly gaining momentum, the U.S. decided at the last minute to participate in the Oslo talks, but was unable to have the text modified in ways that it felt would make adherence possible.

The Ottawa treaty bars the manufacture of land mines, prohibits their export except for the purpose of destruction, forbids the laying of existing mines, requires mines in existing mine fields to be removed, and mandates the destruction of existing stockpiles. It contains requirements for reporting on compliance, and very limited provisions for challenge inspections and dispute resolution. The treaty entered into force on March 1, 1999, with later com-pliance dates for some of its substantive provisions.

While adherence to the agreement is likely to continue to grow rapidly, it will be many years if at all before the Ottawa agreement is adhered to by all the relevant states, *i.e.*, the major manufacturers, exporters, or users of land mines. This will leave a murky legal situation. Many states will be party to the treaty. Many more will have signed but not ratified and will not be bound by its specific provisions, but will be subject to the duty of a signatory not to defeat the object and purpose of the treaty. Yet other states are bound to the CCW and Protocol II, and some of those will also be bound to the 1996 amendments. A few states will remain outside all treaties dealing directly with mines. Finally, there is some possibility that the United States will be suc-cessful in having the C.D. negotiate a treaty ban on exports which would both supplement the export ban in the Ottawa treaty with more detail and better

---

[29] Interviews, see note 11.   [30] *Ibid.*

verification measures, and provide a treaty instrument to replace the various unilateral declarations by non-Ottawa parties. Such states will be barred from exporting mines, but not from their manufacture, possession, or use.

Already, some international law experts are asserting that some or all of the provisions of the Ottawa treaty have become customary international law, or have become so for all but persistent objectors.[31] The utility of such assertions is doubtful in this field, unfortunately, given the poor record of compliance with existing customary law prohibitions on non-indiscriminate use and non-targeting of civilians.

E. SOFT LAW ON LAND MINES

There are no non-binding instruments negotiated by the relevant parties that would constitute a soft law arms control instrument.[32] The UNGA has adopted several resolutions on land mines, but it is not clear that these resolutions meet the definition of soft law. The resolutions clearly are not binding and they have the requisite unanimous or virtually unanimous support to be thought of as soft law, but it must still be asked whether they contain non-binding declarations of norms. Some of the resolutions call on states to complete negotiations on a binding international agreement that would impose a permanent ban on production, stockpiling, use, and transfer of anti-personnel land mines.[33] It seems highly doubtful that the states voting for these resolutions thought they were setting forth normative standards for the conduct of nations. Instead, they probably assumed they were encouraging the negotiation of an agreement which would set forth such norms.

UNGA resolutions also have called on states to adopt moratoria on the export of anti-personnel land mines and request additional states to enact export bans.[34] These seem to constitute norm-creation, as they purport to set standards for nations' primary conduct, whether or not the states become party to a binding treaty, and thus are not entirely hortatory.

Assuming that the UNGA resolutions encouraging a cessation on land-mine exports are considered soft law, they have a mixed but increasingly

[31] For a discussion of the process of treaty law eventually emerging as customary law in the land mine context, see Benesch, S., *et al.*, 'International Customary Law and Antipersonnel Land Mines: Emergence of a New Customary Norm' [1999] *Landmine Monitor Report* 1020–36.

[32] These special non-proliferation-related export control regimes are discussed in greater detail in the study by Gualtieri in this volume.

[33] See, *e.g.*, UNGA Res. 51/45 S (December 1996); UNGA Res. 52/L1 (October 1997).

[34] The first such resolution was UNGA Res. 48/75 K (December 1993), which '[c]alls upon States to agree to a moratorium on the export of anti-personnel landmines'. Subsequent resolutions included 49/75 D (December 1994), 50/70 O (December 1995), and 51/45 S (December 1996). The last of these '[c]alls upon States that have not yet done so to declare and implement such bans, moratoriums or other restrictions—particularly on operational use and transfer—at the earliest possible date'.

effective compliance rate, *i.e.*, exports have either ceased or are a tiny fraction of what they were in the period before the norm was articulated. No one disagrees with that assessment, though experts are in disagreement whether there was some non-compliance in the 1993–6 period by the states that had declared export bans, particularly Russia and China.[35]

Compliance can mean more than avoiding violations of the norm itself. It can include measures taken by states to give full force and effect to the norm. As noted above, many states have adopted unilateral export bans or limitations and implemented them through national legislation. Not all motion has been forward, however. While the U.S. Executive Branch continues its moratorium on exports, the legislatively-imposed moratorium was repealed by the Congress.[36] Thus, some future Executive Branch could legally export mines. Compliance with a soft-law norm also might be measured by demonstrations of increasing support for the norm, which can be seen not only in the development of a hard law instrument embracing the same norms, but also in increasing the number of states which support the soft law norm but remain outside the treaty. On that score there has also been progress, as several states that refused to sign the Ottawa agreement have since declared export bans. For example, Pakistan has done so, and South Korea, which already had an indefinite moratorium, reportedly is actively considering a permanent ban.[37]

The more important norms concerning mines are those contained in international treaties, *i.e.*, the CCW and its Protocol II, and the Ottawa agreement. It is too soon to tell how widespread compliance with those instruments will be and, in particular, whether compliance with the treaty norms will be better than with the soft law norms. The only point of direct comparison will be compliance by Ottawa parties with the non-export provisions of the treaty compared to compliance by the non-parties with the soft-law norm on non-export.

In the past two years, compliance with both the treaty norm and the non-treaty norm against exporting anti-personnel land mines has been quite good. However, there have been allegations of shipments to Sudan and Afghanistan by Iran, a non-signatory that has declared it no longer exports mines. Iraq, another non-signatory, has made no declaration of national policy against exports. There are persistent rumors of small-scale Chinese and Russian exports, although these are almost certainly the result of weak export controls rather than a secret national policy in favor of continuing exports. Thus, the early, highly preliminary results suggest either no significant difference or somewhat better compliance by the treaty parties than by the non-signatories

[35] Author interview with officials.
[36] S. 1236 of 105 P.L. 261 (112 Stat. 1920) repealed s. 580 of the Foreign Operations Act of 1996 (104 P.L. 107, 110 Stat 751).
[37] 'Pakistan not to Export Anti-personnel Landmines', AFP (March 13, 1997); 'South Korea Considers Ban on Landmine Exports', AFP (October 5, 1998).

with the norm against mine exports. To date, however, there has been no serious test of the soft law norm, which will come when a country or insurgent group with funds approaches a former producer and requests a large-scale shipment. Will poor producers like India, Pakistan, or North Korea—to say nothing of newly hard-pressed pariah states like Yugoslavia—be able to resist the temptation when they will break no treaty obligation if they make a lucrative export?

Soft law instruments are commonly regarded as easier to negotiate and conclude than hard law instruments. One might ask, therefore, why no relevant government or NGO was pressing for early adoption of a non-binding agreement as an alternative to the negotiation of a treaty. Conversations with a number of the key leaders of U.S. and foreign NGOs, with working-level personnel in the U.S. Executive and Legislative Branches, and with foreign governmental officials reveal a common belief that a treaty would receive a greater degree of compliance than would a non-binding instrument. No one expected compliance problems to disappear—compliance with existing norms concerning mines is not good, even though some of them are contained in binding humanitarian law instruments—but it was expected that compliance would be comparatively better with a treaty than with a soft-law instrument. Some consideration was given to a soft-law alternative. At one stage, NGO organizations thought they might have to resort to a MTCR-like export regime as a way-station toward a binding instrument to govern exports of mines, with restrictions on ownership and deployment coming later. That possibility was set aside, given the very rapid progress in convincing governments to accept a treaty approach. As one leading NGO official put it, 'why not grab the brass ring when it suddenly appears to be in your grasp?' Similarly, the U.S. and U.K. had floated the possibility of a non-binding export control regime in 1995–6, but that proposal garnered no support. Also, just prior to the Oslo negotiations, the U.S. State Department gave substantial thought to pressing for a non-binding agreement, but decided that it was too late for such an approach to have any prospect of success, given the momentum that had built for a treaty.

While momentum and the belief that a treaty was superior because it would result in better compliance were the most important reasons for the outcome, it may be useful to speculate on possible additional factors. First, the subject of land mines already had a substantial history of being addressed by treaty, including Protocol II and its subsequent amendments. It may have been simply a matter of habit; the relevant governmental officials continued to use the methods of international law creation they were accustomed to using. Several participants in the process suggested this and there is no doubt some truth to it. However, it is not entirely dispositive: much the same might be said concerning nuclear commerce, which had been dealt with in treaty form, *inter alia* by the Nuclear Non-proliferation Treaty (NPT), the Tlatelolco Treaty (establishing a Latin American Nuclear Weapons Free Zone).[38] Yet habit did not prevail when the Nuclear Suppliers Guidelines were negotiated as a non-binding instrument was utilized.

Secondly, it might be said that the preference for a treaty followed from the context: there were existing use restrictions in binding international conventions. Those use restrictions proved inadequate and arms control approaches were needed to strengthen the regime. It might have been difficult to explain to the public why one would attempt to bolster a weak binding regime by adopting a non-binding one. Thirdly, there was no need for secrecy, as there had been with the negotiation of the NSG, Australia Group, and MTCR agreements, nor would there be the need to make frequent amendments, both of which are sometimes considered additional advantages of soft law instruments over binding ones. Finally, and perhaps most significantly, there were no important states declaring that they would cooperate in a non-binding agreement, but not in a binding one. In contrast, during the initial consultations leading to the negotiation of the Nuclear Suppliers Guidelines, France made clear that it would not consider participation in a binding regime, as that would be too similar to the NPT, which at that time it was rejecting.

It is also important to consider what factors were not important in selecting a treaty over a soft law instrument. First, it was not because the treaty needed or included compliance-enhancing provisions, although compliance with the norm was assumed to be better with a treaty. The Ottawa agreement does contain reporting requirements, but a soft-law instrument also might have included them. Secondly, while it would have been difficult to include intrusive verification or dispute-resolution provisions in a soft-law instrument, the Ottawa treaty is rather weak in those areas, with no verification provisions except for a limited possibility of challenge inspections utilizing a clumsy procedure. The German and French governments wanted tougher provisions on verification and dispute resolution, similar to those in the Chemical Weapons Convention, but were unsuccessful because of third world opposition to intrusions on their sovereignty and the concomitant concern that really stringent provisions would reduce the number of states willing to become parties. Instead, in what may be an unprecedented step, a group of NGOs, acting under the umbrella of the International Campaign to Ban Land Mines and headed by Human Rights Watch, have taken on a major role in monitoring compliance with the treaty, carefully culling the public record and field reports from their own resources (selectively aided, one hears, by intelligence information provided by friendly governments).[39]

---

[38] See *supra* note 31.

[39] The Landmine Monitor program has produced its first report. Those interested in the current state of compliance with landmine control efforts will find it contains a wealth of material. See International Campaign to Ban Landmines, *Landmine Monitor Report 1999* (1999).

CONCLUSION

The relationship between compliance and norm-creation is an interesting one in the case of land mines. Specifically, the land mine case shows the importance, sometimes seen in other arms control and humanitarian law contexts, of obtaining voluntary early compliance by some key states with an ideal long before it has become the majority view, let alone become a non-binding or binding norm. As noted above, many relevant states decided not to export mines well before the UNGA urged them to adopt a moratorium. Indeed, as noted above, a number of states had gone considerably further prior to the opening of the Oslo talks and had ceased production, halted deployment to their military forces, and even begun to destroy existing stocks of anti-personnel land mines. It may well be that this 'compliance first, agreement afterward' trend will increase in the future, particularly where, as here, governments are under intense domestic political pressure to do something about a problem publicly perceived to have a significant moral component, and where exercising leadership helps build support for the emerging norm. Alternatively, one might explain this as the arising of a 'soft customary norm'. Just as there is a distinction, useful if not always clear, between soft law and hard law in the realm of negotiated international instruments, an analogous distinction may arise in customary international law. One might postulate that a 'soft' customary norm against mine exports was in the process of forming and began to result in compliance even before there were either soft law or hard law norms embraced in UNGA declarations or treaty instruments.

Commentary

ABRAM CHAYES and DINAH SHELTON

Multilateral arms control is a subject area where reciprocity and conflict of interest predominate. Each nation possesses strong incentives for successful surprise defection from an arms control agreement while at the same time risking damage to fundamental national security interests should defection by another state occur. Each state is therefore likely to seek to maintain its own flexibility while binding others to arms limits. Potential or actual hostility between states make trust hard won, secrecy important, and verification essential.[1] Arms control thus provides a model for understanding cooperative interactions between states over time.[2]

Arms control agreements vary considerably in their approach towards regulating weaponry. Some, such as the 1925 Geneva Protocol on Chemical Weapons (C.W.),[3] create a 'non-use' regime, permitting their parties to retain or increase their C.W. arsenals. Other agreements establish geographic limitations upon the deployment or positioning of weapons, and do not mandate any numerical reductions.[4] Some arms control arrangements constrain the testing or development of new types of weapons, but do not prohibit continued production or deployment of the existing types.[5] Several international agreements, notably the 1968 Nuclear Non-proliferation Treaty (NPT),[6] are designed to restrict the spread of the weapon, without directly limiting the weapons capability of those states that already possess the specified arms. In other instances, an international instrument establishes numerical ceilings upon the parties' permitted weaponry.[7] To date, the international community

[1] As Kenneth Abbott has described, arms control agreements share many characteristics of models drawn from game theory, in particular the Prisoner's Dilemma and the Stag Hunt. Abbott, K. W., 'Trust but Verify: The Production of Information in Arms Control Treaties and Other International Agreements,' (1993) 26 *Cornell Int'l L.J.* 1. Each state in such an interaction has incentives to cooperate with the others, but each may also have incentives to act independently, affecting the others negatively. States may enter into an agreement to manifest and reinforce their cooperation, with the agreement serving to increase certainty, raise the costs of breach or defection. The same conflicting incentives will remain at work, however. Thus, each state has reason to observe the agreement, but each may also have reason to defect from the obligations. In such mixed-motive situations, information regarding the structure of the interaction, the incentives perceived by other states, and the compliance of others with their obligations are crucial to international cooperation. Information on compliance is particularly important. States will be reluctant to enter into agreements without clearly defined mechanisms for the ongoing production of reasonably timely and reliable information on these matters. Such mechanisms may determine the success of an agreement in practice. Verification techniques range from research in publicly available documents through external observation to espionage. See Chayes, A. H., and Chayes, A., 'From Law Enforcement to Dispute Settlement: A New Approach to Arms Control Verification and Compliance' [1990] *Int'l Security* 147, 155.

[2] See Smith, E.M., 'Understanding Dynamic Obligations: Arms Control Agreements' (1991) 64 *S. Cal. L. Rev.* 1549.

[3] Protocol for the Prohibition of the Use in War of Asphyxiating, Poisonous or Other Gases, and of Bacteriological Methods of Warfare, June 17, 1925, 26 U.S.T. 571, 94 L.N.T.S. 65.

[4] These include: Antarctic Treaty, December 1, 1959, 12 U.S.T. 794; Treaty on the Prohibition of the Emplacement of Nuclear Weapons and Other Weapons of Mass Destruction on the Seabed and the Ocean Floor and the Subsoil Thereof, February 11, 1971, 23 U.S.T. 701; and Treaty on the Prohibition of Nuclear Weapons in Latin America, February 14, 1967, 22 U.S.T. 762.

[5] Treaty Banning Nuclear Weapons Tests in the Atmosphere, in Outer Space and Underwater, August 5, 1963, 14 U.S.T. 1313.

[6] Treaty on the Non-proliferation of Nuclear Weapons, July 1, 1968, 21 U.S.T. 483, 729 U.N.T.S. 161. On the general subject of non-proliferation see Dunn, L., *Controlling the Bomb* (1982) and Schiff, B.N., *International Nuclear Technology Transfer* (1983); Spector, L.S., *Nuclear Proliferation Today* (1984); id., *The New Nuclear Nations* (1985); id., *Going Nuclear* (1987); id., *The Undeclared Bomb* (1988); and Spector, L.S., and Smith, J.R., *Nuclear Ambitions* (1990); Cohen, S.P. (ed.), *Nuclear Proliferation in South Asia* (1991).

[7] In some cases the ceilings are so high that little is required in the way of dismantling existing weapons. The two SALT I documents (the 1972 Anti-Ballistic Missile (ABM) Treaty and the

has crafted its nuclear non-proliferation policies almost exclusively in support of the goal of preventing countries from acquiring nuclear explosives.[8] Only a few agreements, such as the 1972 Biological Weapons Convention (BWC) purport to abolish a category of weaponry.[9]

For much of the period since 1945, the major weapons and weapons systems developed and deployed have reflected the strategic considerations of the bipolar Cold War. The domination by the major powers of the structures of international security can be seen even in multilateral agreements like the NPT. As the established post-war structure could be upset by the proliferation of weapons of mass destruction, multilateral arms control in the post-war era came to focus on those weapons. The NPT, the BWC, and the Chemical Weapons Convention all focus on weapons of mass destruction. Other major multilateral arms control issues, such as the strength of conventional forces in Europe, fell outside the realm of fundamental security issues during much of the post-war era. The subject of conventional weapons was not addressed seriously until the Conventional Forces in Europe (CFE) negotiations began in the late 1980s and proceeded to a successful outcome.

It could be expected that in such an area of international concern, formal and detailed binding agreements would be sought, leaving little role for soft law. Contrary to expectations, however, some of the most elaborate 'soft' international law is in this area. On some issues there is an express preference for non-binding arrangements.[10] The United Nations General Assembly has adopted significant resolutions on disarmament, often on referral from the Committee on Disarmament, where a few powerful states play a key role.[11] For some issues, there has been a marked interplay between soft and hard

1972 Interim Agreement on Strategic Offensive Arms and the 1979 SALT II Treaty essentially fit this description.

[8] Williamson, Jr., R.L., 'Law and the H-bomb: Strengthening the Nonproliferation Regime to Impede Advanced Proliferation' (1995) 28 *Cornell Int'l L.J.* 71.

[9] See also Convention on the Prohibition of the Development, Production and Stockpiling of Bacteriological (Biological) and Toxin Weapons and on Their Destruction, 1015 U.N.T.S. 163; see also Convention on the Prohibition of the Development, Production, Stockpiling and Use of Chemical Weapons and on Their Destruction, January 13, 1993 (1993) 32 I.L.M. 800.

[10] The international coalition against land mines, for example, is against the Committee on Disarmament taking up the issue of export controls, because it feels that a binding agreement would be weak in content and would dilute the generally effective suppliers' regime that currently operates.

[11] A resolution declaring, *inter alia*, that '[a]ny state using nuclear and thermo-nuclear weapons is to be considered as violating the Charter of the United Nations, as acting contrary to the laws of humanity and as committing a crime against mankind and civilization'. G.A. Res. 1653, U.N. GAOR, 16th Sess., Supp. No. 17, at 4, U.N. Doc. A/5100 (1961) was adopted by a vote of 55 yes, 20 no, and 26 abstentions. The Soviets voted for it; all the other nuclear powers, joined by most NATO countries, voted against it. A decade later, 72 nations voted in favor of a UNGA resolution that 'solemnly declares . . . the permanent prohibition of the use of nuclear weapons'. G.A. Res. 2936, U.N. GAOR, 27th Sess., Supp. No. 30, at 6, U.N. Doc. A/8730 (1972). The U.S.S.R. voted in favor, China voted no, and the three Western nuclear powers and virtually all other Western nations abstained.

norms. The non-proliferation regime, for example, has a treaty supplemented by a series of subordinate implementing measures that are legally binding in various ways. For example, each non-weapons state party that imports peaceful nuclear materials must execute a bilateral safeguards agreements with the IAEA.[12] These safeguards agreements are themselves supplemented by subsidiary non-binding standards, guidelines, and facility attachments that draw their legal authority from the safeguards agreement itself. Decisions of the IAEA Board of Governors and commonly accepted interpretations of certain treaty provisions also have normative impact.

Following the entry into force of the NPT, an NPT Exporters' Committee (the Zangger Committee) was established under IAEA auspices. The purpose of the committee was to establish a list of materials and equipment which could not be exported by an NPT party without IAEA safeguards, consistent with the terms of Article III(2)(b) of the NPT. The Zangger 'trigger' list was derived in part from a list which had been used by informal agreement among Western nations[13] and in turn served as the nucleus for the Suppliers' Guidelines, discussed in the prior chapters.[14] In contrast, the Missile Technology Control Regime is a non-binding undertaking unrelated to a treaty. It was initially entered into by some Western states to halt the spread of ballistic missiles and technology along with space launch technology, which could be used for ballistic missiles.[15]

The weakness of treaty institutions, or the absence of treaty obligations may explain some of the recourse to soft law. In the case of the Chemical Weapons Convention, the Australia Group[16] has been created by supplier states to serve as a focal point for coordination of export control of dual-purpose items in the chemical and biological fields. Likewise, the Nuclear Supplier Group (NSG)

[12] See The Structure and Content of Agreements Between the Agency and States Required in Connection with the Treaty on the Non-Proliferation of Nuclear Weapons, IAEA Doc. INF-CIRC/153 (May 1971). A party to the NPT with nuclear materials on its territory must place them under the safeguards system according to the terms of INFCIRC/153.

[13] See Bertsch, G.K., *et al.*, 'Multilateral Export Control Organizations', in Bertsch, G.K., *et al.* (eds.), *International Cooperation on Nonproliferation Export Controls* (1994) 41, 41–4.

[14] See Communications Received from Certain Member States Regarding Guidelines for the Export of Nuclear Material, Equipment and Technology, IAEA Doc. INFCIRC/254/Rev. 1/Part I (July 1992) (1992) 31 I.L.M. 1232. These are in the form of a series of identical letters to the Director General of the IAEA and not a legally binding agreement.

[15] See Guidelines for Sensitive Missile—Relevant Transfers (1987) 26 I.L.M. 599, 600; Mahnken, T.G., 'Ballistic Missile Proliferation: Seeking Global Solutions to Regional Problems' (1991) 14 Disarmament 1, 11.

[16] The Australia Group is an informal cartel among the leading chemical exporting countries that has met regularly since 1985, but is not based upon a treaty. Participants undertake to align their individual national export control policies to prohibit the export of suspicious, weapons-related substances and to pool their intelligence-gathering activities in resistance to the threatened proliferation of chemical weapons. U.S. Arms Control and Disarmament Agency, Fact Sheet: Australia Group Export Controls on Materials Used in the Manufacture of Chemical and Biological Weapons (1993); Roberts, B., 'Controlling Chemical Weapons' (1992) 2 *Transnat'l L. & Contemp. Probs.* 435, 444.

issues guidelines for export of nuclear weapons-related items as a necessary complement to the safeguard controls as part of the universal effort to prevent proliferation. The Missile Technology Control Regime serves a similar purpose in an area where no major multilateral arms control instrument exists.

The problem in the suppliers' groups is one of legitimacy. As Gualtieri indicates, the normative and institutional framework is one-sided, being imposed on willing buyers by unwilling sellers. In contrast, the nuclear safeguards involve a reciprocal arrangement where both sides accept constraints emerging from a treaty but detailed in non-binding guidelines. Importers receive material and assistance if they accept safeguards through elaborate institutional arrangements. The shortcoming is that the bargain is not coterminous with the problem of nuclear weapons, being directed at peaceful uses of nuclear materials.

A discriminatory regime, whether it is the nuclear weapons 'club' or the technology suppliers' group, probably lacks long term stability. The supplier controls are somewhat confrontational. This lack of a multilateral or truly international character may prove fatal to their sustainability in the long term. The supplier-only approach and the massive exporting interests involved risk weakening the consistency and steadfastness of the mechanisms, especially when competing national interests are at stake. Long-term stability and efficiency require that arms control regimes be built upon mutual interests and relationships, not confrontation. On the other hand, the small number of countries with advanced technology can make for an efficient regime. The enormous cost of developing, testing, deploying, and maintaining advanced delivery systems is a major constraint on advanced proliferation. Indigenous development and manufacture of a delivery system is nearly always more expensive and takes far longer than purchasing an identical system from a nation which has already developed and deployed it. The delivery system problem is thus far more pressing if the countries already possessing them are prepared to sell whole delivery systems, major components, or relevant technologies to the threshold states. Getting such states not to do so is probably easier than bringing in the buyers as well.

Recourse to non-binding norms may reflect a lack of consensus on the issues that makes it impossible to conclude a binding agreement or, conversely, a degree of consensus among a small number of like-minded states which find a binding agreement unnecessary. The export control regime, for example, began as an informal understanding among certain countries about exports to the Eastern bloc, based on a common understanding of the items that should be controlled, and the countries that should be subject to the controls. To some it appeared that the time required to conclude a treaty was prohibitive, assuming it would ever enter into force,[17] and a multilateral treaty structure was unnecessary.

[17] A treaty on export controls, the Geneva Convention on the International Traffic in Arms, was concluded in 1925 but never entered into force.

Recourse to non-binding agreements may also reflect the degree of uncertainty inherent in the subject. Soft law is particularly important to dynamic or complex agreements that are structured to allow consensual changes in the obligations in order to fulfill the object of the treaty when there are expected but uncertain changing conditions. Uncertainty may arise because changing economic relations or technological capacities creates future risk to anticipated gains from cooperation. Arms control agreements create this sort of risk. States also may be uncertain about important facts that underlie the choices made. Implementation of an international agreement may require continued revision of the terms of its obligations as knowledge is acquired. Similarly, states may recognize a shared risk, but not know the precise level or consequences of the risk, because of the complexity of the issue, and thus they may be uncertain about the proper strategy or response to adopt.

Arms control requires cooperative collective action in the face of changing technologies[18] and evolving security relationships. Such action is often based on cooperative review of performance under the agreement. Static arms control agreements become obsolete because they fail to provide for changing weapons technologies.[19] Soft law can make an important contribution because it can more quickly respond to changing weapons technologies that create uncertainty about the risks of the future strategic situation and the mechanisms to minimize them. It may work well especially in conjunction with formal binding agreements that allow the flexible evolution of obligations and give assurances to the parties of the continued viability of the relationship. Such complex arrangements can assist in the establishment of evolving relationships among states, which can facilitate a variety of mutually beneficial responses to technological, political, and economic changes.

Compliance in the field of multilateral arms control is generally good, whether the norms are in hard or soft form. Legally binding norms create a compliance pull deriving from the legitimacy of their form and the process by which they are created, stimulating a sense of obligation.[20] There is thus a link between the collective conclusion by states that an international norm exists

---

[18] Negotiators of arms control agreements frequently find that the strategic instability they seek to remedy has arisen from 'technological creep'. Newhouse, J., *War and Peace in the Nuclear Age* (1988) 223.

[19] See Duffy, G., *Compliance and the Future of Arms Control* (1988) 9.

[20] Professor Franck notes: '[t]he legitimate rule pulls toward compliance because those addressed perceive themselves as perpetually interacting parties engaged in a secular community with rules and rule-based institutions within which the rule-induced benefits of safety, order and predictability promote the aggregate well-being of the community. The just rule gets its capacity to pull toward compliance from the agreement of the parties of a moral order on principles governing the fair allocation of finite resources among individuals. Obviously, rules of the secular state, or of the secular community of states, exert their most powerful pull toward voluntary compliance when they are generally perceived to be both legitimate and just, and a legitimate rule may pull less powerfully toward compliance when it is seen to be unjust.' Franck, T.M., *The Power of Legitimacy Among Nations* (1990) 242.

and the motivation of an individual state to comply with the norm. That normative pull due to form is lessened with non-binding norms because by definition they are not legally binding.[21] As such, compliance should be better with legally binding norms than with non-legally binding ones, all other things being equal. Some evidence in the arms control cases supports this view, suggesting that a norm in a treaty may induce more conforming state behavior than one that is purely non-binding: thus compliance with the treaty-based ban on supplying nuclear weapons is better than compliance with the missile control technology regime, where there is no related treaty. A treaty concluded subsequent to the non-binding agreement can further exercise a pull towards compliance.

All other things generally are not equal, however, and other elements and interests may provide incentives to compliance that outweigh the loss caused by putting the norm in a non-binding instrument. First, the strength of the norm itself can be sufficient that states feel obliged to comply; *i.e.*, the moral claim attaching to compliance or the stigma attached to violating the norm can outweigh the non-binding form of the instrument in which the norm is contained. The 'weapons taboo' or normative content as an incentive to compliance with a non-binding norm is illustrated by the early phases of the proscription against land mines. Such norms of prohibition may be efficient because there is no need to apply the elastic concept of military necessity that governs most restraints during warfare.

The successful stigmatization of a category of weapons such as land mines may be comparatively rare, but it is important because it denies any legitimate use of a technology against military targets. Even emerging bans can have consequences, causing states to hesitate before developing weapons systems.[22] This is in contrast to restrictions on particular uses of weapons which did not preclude development of the weapon itself because various legitimate uses remained possible. The development of the norm against land mines was based upon this logic. Members of the International Campaign to Ban Landmines called for a total prohibition that would make detection of violations easy rather than a complex set of restrictions on how mines would be used or what types of mines could be deployed.

Institutionalizing the norm in treaty law confers a degree of legitimacy on the claim that the weapon is indiscriminate and cruel and strengthens the norm. Harold Muller has argued that 'the sheer existence of a regime puts an "extra" burden of proof on regime opponents because in discourses about

---

[21] It should be noted that Franck rejects the standard jurisprudential efforts to categorize international norms as 'legal' or 'not legal', finding such efforts only marginally relevant to the evaluation of international norms. *Ibid.*, at 33–4; see also Franck, T., 'Legitimacy in the International System' (1988) 82 *Am.J.Int'l L.* 705 (developing an earlier version of his legitimacy theory).

[22] See Harris, P., 'British Preparations for Offensive Chemical Warfare 1935–1939' (1980) 125 *Journal of the Royal United Services Institute for Defence Studies* 61.

proper behavior of states and other regime actors, the regime structure serves automatically as the frame of reference.'[23] Institutionalization may also create a legal and political constituency committed to the regime, providing an additional source of opposition to employment of a prohibited weapon. In the case of land mines, appeals to the public conscience were made linking land mines to chemical and biological weapons, long stigmatized as 'weapons of mass destruction'.

While some argue that weapons are only banned that have little or no military utility, based on rationalist theories of self-interest, the role of norms is particularly important in changing the calculations of what is useful and sufficient in a weapon.[24] The campaign against land mines sought to counter the view that land mines are useful and shift the burden of proof to proponents to justify using mines, not because they are useful—the test for unregulated weapons—but because they are necessary or decisive. As special justifications become required, the search for less controversial alternatives begins, perhaps resulting in increasingly less reliance on the ostracized weapon. Moreover, the campaign may politicize the weapon to the extent that political decisions sometimes outweigh strictly military calculations.

Similar, but less successful, efforts have been made to delegitimate nuclear weapons, including the World Court Project of various non-governmental organizations which hoped that the International Court of Justice would declare the threat or use of nuclear weapons to be a violation of customary international law.[25] A major disincentive to compliance is the advantage and status offered by possession of nuclear weapons and other systems not held by potentially hostile states. Nuclear weapons in particular have the allure of international power. In addition to prestige and influence, proliferation motives include regional rivalries and other security concerns. The moral claim is unavoidably but seriously flawed by the NPT's inherent discrimination; the same is true of MCTR and other restrictions on technology transfer. They divide the world into two classes of countries, those allowed to have the weapons and technology and those that are not allowed to possess them. At

---

[23] Müller, H., 'The Internalization of Principles, Norms and Rules by Governments: The Case of Security Regimes', in Rittberger, V. (ed.), *Regime Theory in International Relations* (1993) 383.

[24] The calculations of what would be an 'adequate supply' of chemical weapons allowing their use during World War II were highly influenced by the norm against their use. The ban meant that any use had to be decisive and not just useful. See Price, R. and Tannenwald, N., 'Norms and Deterrence: The Nuclear and Chemical Weapons Taboos', in Katzenstein, P. (ed.), *The Culture of National Security: Norms and Identities in World Politics* (1996) 114–52.

[25] Some argue that the mere possession of such weapons violates international law. See Meyrowitz, E.L., 'The Laws of War and Nuclear Weapons' (1983) 9 *Brook. J. Int'l L.* 227; Campbell, A.W., 'The Nuremberg Defense to Charges of Domestic Crimes: A Non-Traditional Approach for Nuclear-Arms Protesters' (1986) 16 *Cal. W. Int'l L.J.* 93; Corwin, D.M., 'The Legality of Nuclear Arms Under International Law' (1987) 5 *Dick. J. Int'l. L.* 271. But see McFadden, E.J.G., 'The Legality of Nuclear Weapons: A Response to Corwin' (1988) 6 *Dick. J. Int'l. L.* 313.

least for some states, it is an unjust rule because it promotes the inequality of states.

A second factor that can overcome the loss of compliance pull with non-binding norms is the institutional arrangement created to support the norm through information-exchange, confidence building, monitoring, and verification of compliance. These can be vitally important to improving compliance. Institutional arrangements can help establish a continuing relationship within which each party becomes progressively more transparent, a crucial factor in securing compliance with non-binding norms. In this regard the land mine case has little to offer, being a prohibitive norm without a compliance structure. The prospects for compliance would be greatly increased with the adoption of verification or compliance mechanisms. States can, of course, utilize verification techniques unilaterally, without any explicit arrangements, as the United States and the Soviet Union did during most of the Cold War. But agreed measures can increase the effectiveness of verification.

Mutual assurance mechanisms are similar, but involve each party gathering and providing information about itself and its activities to others. By doing so, it demonstrates its continued compliance with the terms of an agreement, thus forestalling defensive defection. Assurance techniques can range from simple certifications of relevant facts to the provision of otherwise confidential internal documents and physical evidence. Including specific arrangements in an agreement can often increase the effectiveness of assurance, while supporting continued cooperation in other ways. By agreeing to an explicit assurance procedure, states can manifest a clear desire for cooperation and can commit themselves to give specific assurances in the future. Such an *ex ante* commitment should increase the confidence of other states, making them more willing to enter into an agreement. Negotiation of an explicit assurance provision at the outset also allows the parties to harmonize their needs and capabilities before situations engendering concern have arisen, avoiding disappointment and the escalation of suspicion later on. An explicit assurance procedure can increase the effectiveness of the interactive communications essential to the success of the strategy. Some governments may anticipate internal opposition to the giving of assurances, fearing that the assurance strategy will be characterized as a sign of weakness. In these circumstances, an explicit *ex ante* provision can be extremely useful.

As the verification and assurance examples indicate, institutional arrangements can generate relationships and interactions that reinforce a norm, providing prospects for engagement rather than accusation. A good example is the confidence building measures built into the arrangements pursuant to Basket II of the Helsinki Final Act. The Conference on Security and Cooperation in Europe designed devices to build confidence within the heavily armed European area in the context of conventional as well as nuclear forces.[26] The 1975 Helsinki Final Act contained limited 'confidence and security-building measures' (CSBMs) of this sort, including advance notice of very large military maneuvers. The 1986 Stockholm review conference greatly expanded these measures, including pre-notification of smaller and more varied maneuvers, longer notice periods—up to two years for very large exercises—and mandatory observers. The Stockholm Document also authorized challenge inspections in case of suspected violations.[27] Most recently, in 1990, thirty-four states of the CSCE adopted the Vienna Document, reiterating and expanding upon the Stockholm CSBMs.[28] The Vienna Document calls for expanded information exchanges, including plans for new weapons systems and military budgets; provides for consultation and assurance procedures in cases of unusual military activity and 'hazardous incidents'; expands the right of inspection; establishes a new communications network; and reduces the thresholds for pre-notification.[29] These activities are supported by the Conflict Prevention Centre of the CSCE, established under the Charter of Paris for a New Europe.[30] These arrangements included on-going notifications, inspections, and other systematic exchanges of information. They became independently important and within a decade eliminated the possibility of a surprise conventional attack in Europe. The soft law normative framework was successful because of the institutional arrangement that made it part of the on-going military suppositions. The Suppliers' Groups operate in a similar fashion with non-binding norms. The cooperative process of information sharing among the states in the groups makes the systems effective and helps rationalize internal conflicts of interest over sales of weaponry.[31]

[26] Conference on Security and Cooperation in Europe: Final Act, August 1, 1975, (1975) 14 I.L.M. 1292, 1297 (incorporating document on confidence-building measures and certain aspects of security and disarmament) provided the basis for later developments.

[27] Document of the Stockholm Conference on Confidence- and Security-Building Measures and Disarmament in Europe, September 19, 1986, reprinted in *Sipri Yearbook 1987: World Armaments and Disarmaments* (1987) 355 (entered into force January 1, 1987). See Borawski, J., *et al.*, 'The Stockholm Agreement of September 1986' (1987) 30 *Orbis* 643.

[28] Vienna Document 1990 of the Negotiations on CSBMs Convened in Accordance with the Relevant Provisions of the Concluding Document of the Vienna Meeting of the CSCE, November 17, 1990, reprinted in *Sipri Yearbook 1991: World Armaments and Disarmaments* (1991) 475.

[29] *Ibid.*, at 477.

[30] Charter of Paris for a New Europe, November 21, 1990, (1991) 30 I.L.M. 190, 207; Supplementary Document to Give Effect to Certain Provisions Contained in the Charter of Paris for a New Europe, (1991) 30 I.L.M. at 209, 212.

[31] U.S. export controls reflect tension between those favoring business growth and those favoring national security, reflected in the fact that six different federal agencies—Commerce, Defense, Treasury, Energy, State, and Customs—are involved. The Export Administration Act of 1979 (EAA) requires the Commerce Department to maintain a commodities control list setting forth the licensing restrictions for exporting strategic goods and technology. Export Administration Act of 1979, Pub. L. No. 96–72, 93 Stat. 503, 50 U.S.C. app. §§ 2401–2420 (1994). See Swan, P., 'A Road Map to Understanding Export Controls: National Security in a Changing Global Environment' (1993) 30 *Am. Bus. L.J.* 607, 611–51, and Morehead, J.W., 'Enforcing Export Controls: Improving the Effectiveness of U.S. and Multilateral Export Controls' in Bertsch, G.K., and Elliott-Gower, S. (eds.), *Export Controls in Transition* (1992) 128, 128–30.

Compliance is enhanced when issues and states are interrelated in a complex mutually reinforcing regime where international cooperation can overcome collective action problems involving uncertain or changing risks.[32] International regimes arise when states develop shared expectations of behavior, and those expectations lead to consistent practices converging around specific principles, norms, rules, and decision-making procedures.[33] Robert Keohane posits that states will construct regimes when coordinated action across a range of collective interests will allow otherwise impossible specific agreements on particular important issues.[34] Regimes establish a framework for evaluating compliance with specific agreements, improve sharing of information, and reduce the transaction costs of reaching specific agreements on specific issues.[35] Regime norms specify general 'standards of behavior defined in terms of rights and obligations' for state actors.[36] Regime norms generate common customs, practices, standards, and usages, and more explicit rules that may or may not be formalized in a treaty.

Reciprocity also plays a critical role in motivating states to comply with perceived international obligations. Parties to arms control agreements aim to minimize the threats posed by a potentially changing strategic context. They try to develop relationships designed to minimize risks of defection by the non-complying party by establishing mechanisms to allow resolution of a

---

[32] See Williamson, Jr., R.L., 'Building the International Environmental Regime: A Status Report' (1990) 21 *U. Miami Inter-Am. L. Rev.* 679, 740–3. As Professor Williamson describes them, complex international regimes frequently deal with topics that have far greater potential for conflict, including those which deal with vital international security or core economic interests. They generally cover a number of interrelated problems, unlike simple regimes which usually deal with a single issue area. Complex regimes are often highly controversial. The parties to such a regime may well have a common set of values or interests. Yet unlike simple regimes, where the problems are usually extrinsic to the governments of the various participating states, the problem to be dealt with by complex regimes is often the behavior of the holdouts, the countries which have not joined the regime. Building a consensus which will make the regime more nearly universal and restraining or at least influencing the behavior of the nonparticipants are often self-conscious objectives of the regime participants. In complex regimes, the legal arrangements may be far more detailed than in simple regimes. Complex regimes often involve the use of several treaty instruments and/or established bodies of customary international law. Often, one or more international organizations play an important role. They are sometimes given decision-making powers in areas otherwise thought to be matters of national sovereignty. In furthering the norms of the regime, major actions may sometimes be taken by the participant states which they have no legal duty to perform. These nonlegal mechanisms may include the provision of financial or other practical assistance, diplomatic coordination, intelligence sharing, the imposition of export controls, discretionary sanctions, or even military force.

[33] Krasner, S., 'Structural Causes and Regime Consequences: Regimes as Intervening Variables', in Krasner, S. (ed.), *International Regimes* (1983); Haggard, S., and Simmons, B.A., 'Theories of International Regimes' (1987) 41 *Int. Organization* 491; Dougherty, J., and Pfaltzgraf, R., *Contending Theories of International Relations: A Comprehensive Survey* (3rd edn. 1990) 172–6; Young, O., 'International Regimes: Toward a New Theory of Institutions' (1986) 39 *World Pol.* 104.

[34] Keohane, R., 'The Demand for International Regimes', in R. Keohane (ed.), *International Institutions and State Power: Essays in International Relations Theory* (1989) 101 at 110.

[35] *Ibid.*, at 111.   [36] Axelrod, R., *The Evolution of Cooperation* (1982) 1103–8.

dispute while minimizing the disruption of the ongoing relationship. Special norms arise from agreements, arrangements, and other patterns of interaction between the parties applicable in the relational context.[37] These often induce parties to comply with rules that otherwise would have no binding legal force, in part because of the expectations of other states.[38] States are less likely to behave in a manner radically different from the expectations of other states because the number of states involved in arms control efforts often is relatively small, enhancing the importance of reputation. States that thwart general expectations of compliance with international obligations may rapidly find themselves losing the benefits of international cooperation.

Civil society can play a role to reinforce the norms and induce compliance, although unlike the areas of human rights and environment, and even to some extent the subject of trade and finance, multilateral arms control remains predominately an area dominated by states. In the 1960s, organizations like SANE and Mothers Strike for Peace were influential in campaigning for a test ban treaty. The non-governmental scientific community has always played a major part in the debates over national security policy, But in recent years, the role of NGOs has been less prevalent. In this regard, the campaign to ban land mines may reflect change or it may be idiosyncratic and derived from the successful effort to place land mines on the international agenda as an issue of human rights and humanitarian concerns rather than arms control.[39] Each of these factors is reflected in the cases in the chapter.

The lack of access to the policy process and the lack of information because of government secrecy in matters of national security can be overcome by creating communities of experts outside of government able to monitor states' compliance with or violation of desired or established norms of behavior. Communities of scientific experts have played an important role in delegitimizing weapons and policing violations. These epistemic communities have been prominent in opposition to chemical warfare. Civil society was at the center of the campaign to ban anti-personnel land mines. The generation of concern was accomplished by the production of information about the scope of land mine use and its effects, defining it as a 'global crisis'. The statistics created a new social issue widely disseminated through new information technologies. Networks spawned by the land mine coalition established the issue as one of global concern. Members of the coalition even served as official members of state delegations to international negotiations. This degree of involvement by civil society is unprecedented in the weapons field.

[37] G. Gottlieb, 'Relationism: Legal Theory for a Relational Society' (1983) 50 *U. Chi. L. Rev.* 567 at 568–9.

[38] *Ibid.*, at 581; Bilder, R., *Managing the Risks of International Agreement* (1981) 24–6.

[39] Contrast the high profile given land mines by non-governmental organizations concerned with human rights and humanitarian law, including veterans groups, with the almost complete lack of attention paid the debate over ratification of the Comprehensive Test Ban Treaty by the United States.

The fields of land mines and conventional arms control are two of the most important examples of reliance on soft law in the area of arms control. In each case, however, the soft law norms ultimately evolved in a binding international treaty—the Land Mines Convention and the treaty on Convention Forces in Europe (CFE). They thus illustrate one of the most important functions of soft law arrangements. They can be seen as large-scale confidence building measures. They provide an opportunity where, at little risk, states can demonstrate their reliability and trustworthiness and can work out technical details of substance and procedure in a practical setting. Thus they can generate the political will, originally absent, for entering into legally binding arrangements.

A discriminatory regime, whether it is the nuclear weapons 'club' or the technology suppliers' group, probably lacks long term stability. The supplier controls are somewhat confrontational. This lack of a multilateral or truly international character may prove fatal to their sustainability in the long term. The supplier-only approach and the massive exporting interests involved risk weakening the consistency and steadfastness of the mechanisms, especially when competing national interests are at stake. Long term stability and efficiency require that arms control regimes be built upon mutual interests and relationships, not confrontation. On the other hand, the small number of countries with advanced technology can make for an efficient regime. The enormous cost of developing, testing, deploying, and maintaining advanced delivery systems is a major constraint on advanced proliferation. Indigenous development and manufacture of a delivery system are nearly always more expensive and take far longer than purchasing an identical system from a nation which has already developed and deployed it. The delivery system problem is thus far more pressing if the countries already possessing them are prepared to sell whole delivery systems, major components, or relevant technologies to the threshold states. Getting such states not to do so is probably easier than bringing in the buyers as well.

Chapter 9

Conclusions: Understanding Compliance with Soft Law

EDITH BROWN WEISS

The international community increasingly relies on soft law to address common problems across many different subject areas. Some of the instruments are negotiated by governments; others by the private sector. As Reinicke and Witte noted in Chapter 2, globalization has been driven by the private sector; and it inevitably means increased use of non-binding legal instruments. Given the growing use of soft law, it is important to understand the extent to which states and nonstate actors comply with non-binding legal instruments, the factors that affect compliance, and the strategies available to increase compliance.

In the first chapter, Shelton distinguished between four categories of instruments based on whether the form was binding or non-binding and whether the content was binding or non-binding. This served as a basis for categorizing instruments and for clarifying hypotheses related to compliance. The distinction drawn based on the form of the instrument and the instrument's purpose is an essential parameter in framing our understanding of compliance. Some instruments are intended to be binding, that is to cause states and other targeted actors to modify their behavior. In other cases, formal agreements may be technically binding, but contain only hortatory language, which suggests that the purpose is to encourage but not require modifications in behavior. Some instruments are non-binding but are intended to modify behavior, or at least to lead to changes in behavior. In other cases non-binding instruments may be intended to be just that—nonbinding in their effect. For this last case, they may state desired behavior not to bind the actors but perhaps to build a consensus that could lead to binding obligations. These purposes may be captured in the following diagram, which relates purpose of the instrument to the form of the instrument:

Table 9.1 Relationship Between the Form and Purpose of an Instrument

Form	*Purpose*	
Binding	Modify Behavior	Encourage Specified Behavior
Non-binding	Modify Behavior	State Desired Behavior

The author thanks Dinah Shelton and Daniel Ernst for helpful comments.

The research project has largely focused on non-binding instruments whose purpose is to modify behavior, namely those instruments coming within the bottom left box. Hence the focus on *compliance* with soft law.

Chapter 1 set forth certain hypotheses regarding compliance with soft law. In light of the subsequent chapters, it is now possible to assess the extent to which these hypotheses may be valid. The literature analyzing compliance with informal social norms informs the analysis of soft law. Several of the initial hypotheses in the study of soft law are consistent with the postulates in the informal social norms literature.

The research into and analysis of compliance with binding international legal instruments is also relevant, for it provides a framework for asking the question what difference it makes whether an instrument is binding. The results from the case studies on compliance with soft law indicates that the answer is mixed: in some cases the binding instrument evokes much greater compliance, in others there may be little difference, and in still others a non-binding legal instrument may evoke better compliance than would a binding one. In general the same factors are at play and the pathways through which compliance takes place are the same. But domestic institutions for enforcing law, such as the judiciary, are not available, in the absence of domestic legislation or a customary international law rule, and the various international and national incentives and pressures to comply may often be less. Moreover, it is less likely that the institutions often associated with agreements will be created for soft law instruments.

A. ASSESSMENT OF THE HYPOTHESES

The study began with a hypothesis that the context in which soft law developed would affect compliance with the norm. The case studies support the hypothesis that the circumstances that led to the negotiation of a non-binding obligation affect compliance. For example, in fields populated by international agreements, soft law instruments linked to a binding obligation were more likely to be complied with than were those not so affiliated. The chapter on multilateral arms control agreements notes that the decision of the International Atomic Energy Agency (IAEA) Board of Governors setting forth the required content for agreements negotiated between parties to the Nuclear Non-proliferation Treaty (NPT)[1] and the IAEA was more likely to be complied with because the parties were legally obligated to conclude such an agreement. Similarly the requirement in the U.N. Convention on the Law

[1] Treaty on the Non-proliferation of Nuclear Weapons, opened for signature July 1, 1968, 21 U.S.T. 483, T.I.A.S. No. 6839, 729 U.N.T.S. 191 (entered into force March 5, 1970).

of the Sea (UNCLOS)[2] to give effect to 'generally accepted standards' increases the likelihood of compliance with the non-binding standards set forth for marine pollution by the International Maritime Organization (IMO).

Even where a soft law instrument is not directly linked to a binding instrument, its placement within the context of a complex international regime may enhance compliance. For example, compliance with the Nuclear Suppliers' Guidelines, which is part of the highly complex regime for preventing the proliferation of nuclear weapons, has apparently been better than with the Missile Technology Control Regime (MTCR), which is entirely self-standing. Similarly compliance with the driftnet fishing ban is high, despite the large number of potential fishing vessel violators. This may be at least in part because of existing national coastal legislation, regional declarations, and statements, and the 1989 Wellington Convention on the Prohibition of Driftnet Fishing in the South Pacific.[3] When the subject matter is one in which events happen rapidly and the landscape changes quickly, the chapter on financial instruments indicates that some degree of compliance may occur even in the absence of direct links to international agreements or to a regime involving such agreements.

Part of the context for the negotiation of a soft law instrument is the degree of consensus that exists about the norms. Generally the research confirmed that consensus about the norm positively affected compliance. The United Nations General Assembly (UNGA) Resolution calling for a moratorium on driftnet fishing was effective because the resolution reflected a widespread consensus on the underlying norm. This was reflected in unilateral actions, regional conventions, and several United Nations General Assembly resolutions. The actions helped several states to adopt strong enforcement measures. Several major driftnet fishing states—Italy, Korea, and Japan—took voluntary measures to limit driftnet fishing as a result. The case study on land mines reveals the importance of the emergence of a shared consensus among a significant population even before a non-binding or binding instrument is concluded. Because the MacBride Principles in Northern Ireland reflected a shared consensus about the norm, they influenced the British government (which initially strongly opposed the Principles) to pass legislation and to put pressure on individual American corporations to 'sign up' to the Principles. The sharply differing experiences with compliance in the private sector with the MacBride and the Sullivan Principles may partly reflect a different consensus on the underlying norms. In the Antarctic Treaty regime, the parties

---

[2] United Nations Convention on the Law of the Sea (UNCLOS), December 10, 1982, U.N. Doc. A/CONF.62/121 (1982) 21 I.L.M. 1245.

[3] Wellington Convention on the Prohibition of Driftnet Fishing in the South Pacific, 1989 (1990) 29 I.L.M. 1454.

are assumed to share the common norm of protecting the Antarctic, which provides an underlying consensus for the recommendations and other soft law measures that are adopted. In contrast, APEC's lack of consensus contributes to weak compliance.

Several hypotheses were introduced regarding the effect of the content of the soft law instrument on compliance with it. The case studies confirmed that if it was costly to comply with soft law, either because of economic costs or the lack of technical, administrative, or other capacity, compliance was less likely. This did not mean, however, that bans (which require refraining from certain action) were necessarily complied with better than positive obligations requiring action. Rather, within those obligations requiring positive actions, a country's or actor's capacity to comply with the obligation affected the likelihood of compliance. For example, those states engaged in driftnet fishing needed to have the capacity to fish through other methods. The United States provided assistance to Italy, one of the primary culprit states, to develop the capacity to fish with other methods. Similarly, states needed the capacity to comply with the prior informed consent requirements in the non-binding instruments on pesticides and chemicals. Some countries received technical and financial assistance to help them develop their infrastructure and technical capabilities in the management of pesticides and chemicals and thus to comply with the obligations in the non-binding instrument.

Institutional mechanisms for monitoring and supervising compliance with soft law obligations are crucial. The chapters on nuclear non-proliferation and export controls, protection of nuclear materials, human rights, financial instruments, and World Bank operational standards demonstrate this. For example, the non-binding 1975 Helsinki Final Act of the Conference on Security and Cooperation in Europe[4] was influential in promoting better respect for human rights during the Cold War because of the institutional mechanisms in which leaders were called to account for their progress or lack of progress in implementing the soft norms. In the case of driftnet fishing, the non-binding 1991 UNGA resolution called upon states to implement fully a global moratorium on all large-scale pelagic driftnet fishing by the end of 1992. To ensure that this happened, the United Nations set up a supervisory mechanism in which the United Nations Secretary General reported to the UNGA on the resolution's implementation. The UN Food and Agricultural Organization (FAO) and the United Nations Environment Programme (UNEP) monitored the status of high seas driftnet fishing, while states, non-governmental organizations, international organizations with fishing interests, and the scientific community provided information on such fishing, as Donald Rothwell noted. The World Bank's Inspection Panel described by

---

[4] Conference on Security and Co-operation in Europe, Final Act (Helsinki Accords), August 1975 (1975) 14 I.L.M. 1292 . The Declaration on Principles Guiding Relations Between Participating States, July 1992, strengthened the institution (1992) 31 I.L.M.1385.

Laurence Boisson de Chazournes provides a supervisory mechanism for ensuring that the World Bank adheres to its operational standards (policies and procedures) in developing and implementing projects with eligible countries.

B. EXPLAINING COMPLIANCE BY THEORIES
ABOUT INFORMAL SOCIAL NORMS

There is a considerable legal scholarship that addresses compliance in the context of domestic, not international or transnational, law. Some of this literature addresses compliance with informal social norms, with voluntary arrangements, and with non-contractual relationships. The theoretical postulates in this literature must inform analysis of compliance with soft obligations in international law. In general, the scholarship indicates six important postulates for the present study: (1) if there is a continuing long-term relationship among the participants in which they must interact, they are likely to comply with their commitments; the existence of a binding contractual relationship is unnecessary; (2) the concern about 'reputation', particularly in the market place, may render binding contracts unnecessary; (3) compliance with legally non-contractual relationships is most successful when supported by established social norms; (4) a shared desire to maximize welfare and minimize transaction costs may lead to compliance with informal norms without the need for legal enforcement; (5) the threat of sanctions, such as resort to legal enforcement of binding norms, may increase the likelihood of compliance; (6) institutional structures which encourage transparency and accountability, even if informal, further compliance with informal allocation norms. Each of these postulates has relevance to 'soft' international law.

1. The Force of the Continuing Relationship Among Participants

In contract law, the conventional wisdom has been that commercial relationships must be carefully set forth in light of legal requirements and must consider the possibility of enforcement for non-performance of the obligation. Clear rules as contained in contract law will lead to desirable outcomes, and the threat of litigation will deter breaches of the agreement. Litigation is available to resolve any disputes that may arise. Macaulay and others in the law and society movement have challenged this wisdom.[5] They contend that hard

[5] Macaulay, S., 'An Empirical View of Contract' [1985] *Wisc. L. Rev.* 465; MacNeil, I.R., 'Relational Contract: What We Do and Do Not Know' [1985] *Wisc. L. Rev.* 483;. Weintraub, R.J., 'A Survey of Contract Practice and Policy' [1992] *Wisc. L. Rev.* 1; Esser, J.P., 'Institutionalizing Industry: The Changing Forms of Contract' (1996) 21 *Law and Society Inquiry* 593; McAdams, R., 'Accounting for Norms' [1997] *Wisc. L. Rev.* 625.

contract agreements, which can be enforced, are not essential to successful, continuing business relationships. For them, the important factors are the relationship between the participants and the desire to maintain an ongoing business relationship. Using legal sanctions to settle a dispute about a breach of contract is costly and often ends the business relationship between the parties.

To be successful, non-contractual relationships generally assume that there are permanent dealings between the parties, that these dealings involve long-term mutual dependence, that there is either an ingrained traditional morality that covers their behavior or that they must deal face-to-face in a community with the participants so that group pressure can be put on delinquents. The extra-legal sanctions that can be levied by the community are essential to ensuring compliance with the informal rules by the participants.

Compliance by states and by nonstate actors with soft law instruments may be likened to compliance by commercial actors engaged in a long-term business relationship. The non-binding instruments are generally designed to influence the behavior of states and other actors for numerous years or indefinitely. States must interact with each other constantly in the international system. In this sense they are engaged in an ongoing business relationship. However, the theory suggests that for non-binding instruments the states may need to be engaged in a somewhat tighter relationship, either one focused on the issues that are the subject of the agreement or otherwise linked together closely in their disparate dealings.[6] In the case of binding international agreements, the agreement itself provides the forum for this more focused long-term interaction, through meetings of the parties, committees, secretariats, and other such devices.

The existence of the long-term relationship makes it more likely that group pressures, whether from other states or from civil society, may be brought to bear to elicit compliance with the instruments. Indeed the availability of measures other than legal sanctions to promote respect for the soft law measures is essential.

This analysis finds strong support from those who argue that the most important way to induce compliance with specific obligations in hard or soft law is to link states and other actors together in a process that requires them to interact continuously over time.[7] Thus, the supervisory institutional mechanism for the Helsinki Final Act joined the participants together in a process of review and accountability that ensured the states would be confronting

---

[6] Sometimes it will be necessary to link issues together to create the continuing relationship, as in the Helsinki process. See the discussion of Erika Schlager, this volume, pp. 346-72.

[7] Chayes, A., and Chayes, A.H., *The New Sovereignty: Compliance with International Regulatory Agreements* (1995). Chayes and Chayes argue that a useful approach for getting compliance among vastly diverse states is to 'start with a low obligational ante, and then increase the level of regulation as experience with the regime grows'. *Ibid.*, at 16.

each other over a long period of time. It also provided a long-term focus for the activities of nongovernmental organizations. In the context of International Labor Organization (ILO) recommendations, the ILO participates with employers' and workers' organizations in carrying out the recommendations, as by providing technical assistance. Maupain suggests that various internal and external influences and pressures affect compliance and advocates that non-binding declarations be accompanied with follow-up mechanisms to create a process that would encourage compliance.

2. The Reputation Factor

Several theorists point to the importance of 'reputation' either in inducing acceptance of a norm that has not yet been fully internalized by the community or of complying with an established but uncodified norm.[8] For the reputation factor to be important, there must be a consensus about the worth of engaging in or abstaining from a specific act, a risk that someone will detect engagement in the act, and that this detection will be publicized throughout the relevant community.[9] The underlying assumption is that the individual needs the approbation of the relevant community. Merchants, for example, are concerned about their reputation in the market place.

The strategies of compliance with binding international agreements, which focus on transparency—such as monitoring, national reports, public access to information about the instrument, and nongovernmental participation in the monitoring process—are important to implementing the long-term relational view and to making reputation an important factor in promoting compliance. As the case studies reveal, they are equally applicable to soft law instruments, if states and other actors desire.

Both the case studies on controlling nuclear supplies and on the MacBride Principles reveal the importance of the reputation factor in inducing compliance. In the context of nuclear supplier states, Gualtieri argues that states face a risk of 'substantial damage to their reputations for refusing to comply'. This is especially the case because of the gravity of an illicit weapons transfer accusation. Gualtieri observes that 'this damage to reputation could affect the state in other issue areas'. In the context of the MacBride Principles in Northern Ireland, McCrudden argues that one of the reasons so many United States corporations made agreements in accordance with the Principles was 'the desire to reduce the hassle of dealing with activities, particularly in the United States, when the bad publicity which would result could harm the company's image'. In human rights, the moral factor attached to the norm

---

[8] Macaulay, S., 'The Use and Non-use of Contract in the Manufacturing Industry', in Macaulay, S., *et al.* (eds.), *Contract: Law in Action* (1995); McAdams, R.H., 'The Origin, Development, and Regulation of Norms' (1997) 96 *Mich. L. Rev.* 338.

[9] McAdams, *supra* note 9 at 357.

may enhance the reputation factor in inducing compliance.[10] The reputation factor may also induce countries to conclude non-binding instruments. States may not enter into binding agreements because of the risk of noncompliance, since noncompliance could adversely affect their reputation. Compliance with non-binding instruments would enhance a state's reputation, since a state would be known to comply even if it had not assumed a binding obligation.[11]

3. Consensus on the Underlying Norm

The literature suggests that compliance with non-contractual relationships is most successful if there is consensus among the participants on the underlying social norm(s). These norms are informal standards of behavior which individuals feel obligated to follow, because of 'an internalized sense of duty, a fear of non-legal sanctions, or both'.[12] The norms at issue are more informal than most of those studied in the cases in this book. These include the self-imposed informal rules that govern professional groups like lawyers, doctors, and accountants, the informal norms that arise to coordinate social exchanges among members of a community, or other customs, conventions, and mores that arise. For community members to respect these informal norms, the members need to have a consensus about the norms. This may be more likely to the extent that the community is close-knit and homogenous. It is also helpful if the participants value norms of cooperation and of neighborliness, for they are then more likely to work together independently of a formal legal arrangement.[13]

From the literature, we may hypothesize that consensus about the norms incorporated in an international soft law instrument is essential to inducing compliance.[14] As noted, this was one of the initial hypotheses of the study and it was confirmed by the case studies. The case study on APEC demonstrates that valuing a norm of cooperation and neighborliness is not sufficient; there must be agreement on the underlying norms, such as environmental protection.

Soft law instruments sometimes help to develop the very consensus on norms that is fundamental to compliance and set the stage for a binding agreement. In other cases, such as land mines, it may be important, as Williamson argues, to get early voluntary compliance with the norm, such as a ban on land mines, before either the non-binding or binding instrument is negotiated.

---

[10] See Shelton, D., 'Human Rights Governance', in Simmons, P.J., and Oudraat, C. de J. (eds.), *Managing a Globalizing World: Lessons Learned Across Sectors* (forthcoming).

[11] The author is indebted to Andres Rigo for this observation.

[12] McAdams, *supra* note 9 at 340.

[13] See generally Dwyer, J.P., and Menell, P.S., *Property Law and Policy: A Comparative Institutional Perspective* (1998), 440–74.

[14] As the driftnet case study shows, unanimity is not required.

The case studies on non-binding international instruments suggest that the source for developing the norms must be viewed as legitimate by the international community. International labor recommendations, for example, are complied with in part because the organization that developed the standards is viewed as legitimate. Legitimacy of the source for the norm is similarly important for non-proliferation export controls and, as Gualtieri shows, legitimacy is increasingly questioned. Moreover, a consensus on the norm tends to give legitimacy to the norm. Perceived legitimacy in turn fosters compliance.

4. Maximizing Welfare and Increasing Efficiency

According to scholars in the field of law and economics, private actors comply with non-binding, non-legal social norms because they are engaged in a mutual pursuit to maximize their own welfare. They may choose to structure their relationship in accordance with social norms when they feel that it is necessary to maintain flexibility in their dealings with one another.[15] Rather than rely on 'law and order' to guide behavior, they may find it more efficient to agree upon informal social norms and develop their own cost-effective approach to maintaining compliance with them. The argument that informal social norms are relied upon because it is more efficient than relying on formal legal instruments must implicitly rest upon the assumption that the norms are equitable. Otherwise, participants would not be willing to comply with them, unless coerced.[16] In the classic *Order Without Law* Robert Ellickson studied cattle ranchers and cattle trespass disputes in Shasta County, California, to explain why ranchers have relied on informal social norms rather than legally-defined and binding rules and on their own system of punishing bad behavior and rewarding good behavior rather than on law enforcement.[17] The approach maximized their welfare and with fewer transaction costs than enforcement by the legal system. Ellickson argues that a common approach to ensuring compliance with informal norms is informal coercion through increasingly coercive self-help measures.[18] The system works because it can operate efficiently.

The case study on money laundering illustrates this concern with efficiency. Simmons argues that soft law is unavoidable at this time because states are unwilling to forgo their domestic rules to fight money laundering in a binding international regime. Financial practices and market conditions are rapidly

---

[15] Bernstein, L., 'Symposium: Law, Economics, and Norms: Merchant Law in a Merchant Court: Rethinking the Code's Search for Immanent Business Norms' (1996) 144 *U. Penn. L. Rev.* 1765, at 1770.

[16] For the importance of the equity obligations in international law, see Franck, T.C., *Fairness in International Law and Institutions* (1995).

[17] Ellickson, R.C., *Order without Law: How Neighbors Settle Disputes* (1990).

[18] *Ibid.*, at 55–64.

changing and agreement upon monitoring and surveillance mechanisms in a binding agreement is unlikely. Most importantly, cooperation with the financial sector is key to compliance. The financial operators, much like the ranchers in Ellickson's study, think that they can run their businesses more efficiently and better than under a binding legal regime imposed on them by governments.

5. The Threat of Legal Enforcement

Some of the literature on informal social norms points to the importance of having sanctions available as a credible threat in the background in order to encourage compliance with informal social norms. Both Ellickson and Ostrom, respectively writing about cattle ranchers in Shasty County and common pool resources such as ground water, emphasize the importance of having graduated sanctions available that participants in the informal norms can use collectively to induce compliance by individual members.[19] This analysis is consistent with that concerned with compliance with binding agreements. For certain situations where the intent to comply is lacking, the credible threat of sanctions may induce compliance. In the international setting, there is an issue of whether the threat of sanctions is in fact credible in many situations.

In some instances individuals may have to resort to outside legal enforcement of existing legal rules which would otherwise govern in the absence of informal social norms. In the context of the cattle ranchers, participants could appeal to the outside legislative rule regarding grazing and could threaten to enforce it as a way of bringing pressure to comply with the informal social norms. The option to resort to external law may or may not be open to a disgruntled participant in a regime of informal social norms. Moreover, to the extent that the participants are tightly linked together, it may be difficult to exercise any such right. Retaliation or other negative rewards could follow. Since it is usually a disgruntled or a minority participant who objects to the social norm, the system for ensuring compliance with informal social norms may under certain circumstances have to be very repressive.[20] Partially to counter this, the process by which the norm is developed needs to be regarded as legitimate by participants. In international soft law, the remedy for the participant objecting to the non-binding norm is to bring pressure on the body that developed the non-binding instrument, which may not be possible, or to bring pressures stemming from other relationships in which the participants are joined.

[19] *Ibid.*, and Ostrom, E., *Governing the Commons: The Evolution of Institutions for Collective Action* (1990).
[20] See Tushnet, M., 'Everything Old is New Again: Early Reflections on the "New Chicago School"', [1998] *Wisc. L. Rev.* 579 (providing thoughtful critique).

6. The Institutional Setting

For informal social norms, research indicates that the institutional setting affects compliance. From her research on voluntary common pool allocation systems, such as ground water aquifers, mountain pastures, in-shore fisheries, and surface water irrigation institutions, Elinor Ostrom suggests that certain conditions are necessary for effective systems.[21] These include clearly defined boundaries for the resource at issue, monitoring of behavior and access to information, opportunity for affected individuals to participate in modifying the operations rules, access to low-cost arenas for resolving disputes, and graduated sanctions imposed by fellow participants (as discussed above, p. 544).

The case study by Joyner on Antarctica points to the importance of the institutional setting. All of the soft law, whether adopted as recommendations before 1995, or as one of the several forms of soft law distinguished after 1995, is adopted by the Antarctic Treaty Consultative Parties (ATCP) within the context of the Antarctic Treaty. This institutional setting can be used as desired to hold governments accountable for complying with specific soft law instruments. ATCP governments can provide pressure for compliance by each other with the Antarctic recommendations.[22]

The experience with the Helsinki Accords also points to the importance of the institutional context for monitoring compliance with the norm and holding governments accountable. As Schlager notes in her case study of the Organization for Security and Cooperation in Europe (OSCE), the Helsinki Final Act 'set in motion a process devoted to the review of actual implementation of the Helsinki agreements by the participating States'. The follow-up and intersessional meetings between 1975 and about 1990 evolved 'into a forum where Western governments . . . could raise the cases of beleaguered human rights activities in Communist countries'.[23] In human rights, the strength of the regional institutions contributes to greater compliance, as both Shelton and Cassel note.

The case studies on the World Bank by Boisson de Chazournes and Wirth make similar points about the importance of the institutional setting in securing compliance with soft law developed within the institutions. The IAEA provides the institutional setting for the recommendations that cover the many minute details relevant to protecting nuclear materials. According to Kellman, the recommendations come in where the treaties leave off. There is

[21] Ostrom, *supra* note 19.
[22] However, this does not necessarily enlist compliance by relevant third party countries which may not view the norms as legitimate.
[23] Schlager, E., at p. 355.

substantial compliance with them, because of the institutional setting and the link to the treaties.

One significant distinction between the case studies and the analysis of domestic compliance with informal social norms is that nongovernmental organizations and the global civil society often play important roles in fostering compliance with international soft law. They can provide important input into relevant institutions and put pressure on governments and other actors to comply. They are part of the institutional context. To be sure, not all nongovernmental organizations or other nonstate actors may work toward compliance, but all are part of the institutional context in which compliance or noncompliance with soft law occurs.

C. APPLYING RESEARCH ON COMPLIANCE WITH BINDING AGREEMENTS TO SOFT LAW

Since 1992 a growing body of scholarship has focused on understanding compliance with international agreements, particularly international environmental agreements.[24] In 1999 the United Nations Environment Programme developed a working group concerned with 'enforcement' of international environmental agreements. The literature offers many insights, mostly but not always consistently, into understanding compliance by states with international agreements to which they are a party. The present chapter draws largely on the analysis and empirical research by Brown Weiss and Jacobson and their international authors on national compliance by eight states and the European Union with five international environmental agreements that had been in force for a significant period of time.[25]

1. The Factors Affecting Compliance

The study of national compliance, *Engaging Countries*, identified four broad categories of variables to explain compliance: characteristics of the activity involved; characteristics of the agreements; the international environment; and factors involving the countries. While the factors interacted with each to produce a combined effect on compliance, they could nonetheless be

---

[24] See, *e.g.*, Brown Weiss, E., and Jacobson, H.K. (eds.), *Engaging Countries: Strengthening Compliance with International Environmental Accords* (1998); Chayes and Chayes, *supra* note 7; Victor, D.G., Raustiala, K., and Skolnikoff, E.B., *The Implementation and Effectiveness of International Environmental Commitments: Theory and Practice* (1998); Koh, H.H., 'Why Do Nations Obey International Law?' (1997) 106 *Yale L.J.* 2599; Rüdiger, W. (ed.), *Enforcing Environmental Standards: Economic Mechanisms as Viable Means* (1996).

[25] Weiss and Jacobson, *supra* note 24. The countries were Brazil, China, Cameroon, Hungary, Italy, Japan, Russian Federation, United States, and the member states of the European Union. The agreements covered both pollution control and natural resource conservation.

addressed separately in order to clarify their relative importance. The research in this present book on soft law changed one important variable: the characteristic of the agreement. All instruments studied in the present book are soft law instruments. Most soft law instruments were concluded by national governments or intergovernmental bodies, although several were concluded by private or quasi-governmental bodies. This study asks what difference it makes to change the variable of the binding nature of the agreement.

The first category of variables refers to the characteristics of the activity targeted by the instrument, whether binding or nonbinding. The research on compliance with binding instruments confirmed the conventional wisdom that the fewer the number of actors involved, the easier to regulate, and the more positive the effect on the benefit–cost ratio of complying. There is no evidence in the chapters in this study that suggests the results are different for soft law instruments. To the contrary the material by Gualtieri on the Zanger committee that oversees the exports of nuclear materials and equipment supports this result. The literature on compliance with binding agreements suggests that compliance of major parties is crucial rather than compliance by all parties, unless there is no set of parties that would have major impact on the outcome of the agreement.[26] The study of the Financial Action Task Force (FATF)[27] and its recommendations confirms the special importance of compliance by the most industrialized countries with respect to rules for detecting and discouraging money laundering. This is not to suggest that compliance by other countries is not important, for it is, especially in the long term. Moreover, the actions of all countries contribute to international momentum in both hard and soft law for compliance with the legal instrument.

The characteristics of an international legal instrument, whether hard or soft, matter. For countries to comply with both hard and soft law, they must feel the obligations are equitable.[28] The chapters on soft law support this and offer no evidence to the contrary. It is also frequently argued that the more precise the statement of the obligation, the easier it is to ensure compliance. However, research on compliance with binding agreements suggests the situation is more complicated than this simple formulation. Certainly it is easier to assess compliance if the obligations are precisely stated; the ability to easily assess compliance may promote compliance. For some activities and

---

[26] This is arguably the case for certain international agreements to conserve resources located within states, such as World Heritage Sites or wetlands. Convention for the Protection of the World Cultural and Natural Heritage, November 16, 1972, 27 U.S.T. 37, T.I.A.S. No. 8226. Ramsar Convention on Wetlands of International Importance Especially as Waterfowl Habitat, February 2, 1971, 996 U.N.T.S. 245, U.K.T.S. No. 34.

[27] Financial Action Task Force on Money Laundering, established G–7 Summit, Paris 1989, Organization for Economic Co-operation and Development, <*http://www.oecd.org/fatf*>.

[28] Jacobson, H.K., and Brown Weiss, E., 'Assessing the Record and Designing Strategies to Engage Countries', in Weiss and Jacobson, *supra* note 24. Franck, T., *Fairness in International Law and Institutions* (1995).

certain circumstances, however, compliance may be better with a more generally stated norm than with a very precisely stated and complicated obligation.[29] As Jacobson and Brown Weiss noted, '[t]wo generalizations emerge. One is that precise and relatively simple obligations are easier to comply with than precise and complicated ones. The other is that stating obligations precisely cannot override other factors that work against compliance.'[30] Similarly for soft law, some obligations such as those included in the Sullivan Principles as described by McCrudden are appropriately general in content but this may not adversely affect compliance with them.

One of the important characteristics of many binding agreements is that they require national reports from member states. These serve both to monitor compliance with the agreement and to educate countries about actions needed to comply. Non-binding instruments may be subject to similar reporting procedures. Maupain notes in his analysis of international labor recommendations that member states are required to report on the extent to which they have given effect to the specific convention and its related recommendation, and that 'it is possible to measure the impact of the provisions of the instruments as non-binding instruments irrespective of whether they belong to the Convention or to the Recommendation category'.[31] Simmons notes that the Financial Action Task Force (FATF), which concluded forty recommendations to control money laundering, has adopted a system of mutual review in which each member's laws and efforts are reviewed by a FATF and considered by the full task force membership. Recommendations are monitored through annual self-assessments with members subject to on-site inspection.[32]

While the characteristics of the instrument with regard to monitoring, supervision, and evaluation have important effects on compliance, the variable of whether the instrument is binding or sets forth binding obligations, or whether it represents soft law, does not seem by itself to determine these aspects of the instrument. Indeed the case studies suggest that it is more important to have effective supervisory mechanisms in place for compliance than to have a binding agreement.

Other characteristics of the agreement that are important to compliance relate to the secretariat, inclusion of incentives such as funds, technical assistance and training, and sanctions. As the case studies of the FATF and of the Helsinki Accords indicate, it is possible to include sanctions among the measures available to encourage implementation of non-binding measures.

---

[29] Brown Weiss, E., 'Understanding Compliance with International Environmental Agreements: The Baker's Dozen Myths' (1999) 32 *University of Richmond L. Rev.* 1555–89.

[30] Jacobson and Weiss, *supra* note 24 at 524.

[31] Maupain, F., *supra* p. 375.

[32] Simmons, B.A., *supra* pp. 256–7.

Similarly, an array of incentives can be included. However, it is more likely that both incentives and sanctions will be invoked for binding agreements. The agreement may even provide for incentives and sanctions, such as special funds or denial of treaty membership benefits. In adopting recommendations pursuant to a binding agreement, states may be able to take advantage of the agreement's provisions to encourage compliance with the non-binding instrument as the case studies on Antarctica and labor reveal.

The international environment is important for compliance with both hard and soft law. The international environment includes a suite of factors: international conferences, global media and public opinion, international nongovernmental organizations, international financial institutions, and international organizations. In international environmental law, the international environment 'may well have been the most important factor explaining the acceleration in the secular trend toward improved implementation and compliance . . . in the late 1980s and early 1990s'.[33] The analysis of codes of conduct, particularly the MacBride and the Sullivan Principles, points to the important role that the surrounding environment plays in affecting compliance. To promote compliance with the MacBride Principles, pressures were put on the British government and on American employers with subsidiaries in Northern Ireland. Similarly pressures from the international environment were used to promote compliance by the former Soviet Union and by eastern European countries with the Helsinki Final Act.

The presence of leader countries is important to compliance with both hard and soft law. Research on hard law indicates that leader countries are essential to the negotiation of international agreements and to promoting compliance with them. These countries generally have more resources than other countries and are thus in a position to play a catalytic role.[34] Several of the case studies on soft law point to the importance of 'leader countries' in negotiating the soft law instruments and promoting compliance with them. For example, the United States led the debate in the United Nations General Assembly about the global moratorium on driftnet fishing. Early on it took measures to enforce the ban domestically and on the high seas, which measures were influential in persuading other states such as Japan and Korea to cease driftnet fishing. In the context of money laundering, the United States has pressured the international community to harmonize national money laundering rules. In the Conference on Security and Co-operation in Europe (CSCE) Helsinki process, the United States took the lead in systematically raising cases of political prisoners and divided families to then Soviet and Romanian officials to secure their release or right to leave. In the context of controlling nuclear weapons exports, the supplier states took the lead in negotiating guidelines to regulate themselves and in complying with these guidelines.

[33] Jacobson and Brown Weiss, *supra* note 24 at 528.   [34] *Ibid.*, at 537.

Finally, the factors involving the countries themselves are at the heart of understanding compliance with binding agreements. These factors include such parameters as the country's previous actions concerning the subject of the agreement, history and culture, physical size and variation, and number of neighboring countries; fundamental factors such as the economy, political institutions, and attitudes and values; and proximate factors such as administrative capacity, leadership, nongovernmental organizations, and knowledge and information. These same factors affect implementation and compliance with soft law. The most significant difference is that some of the pathways for enforcing compliance at the national level, namely through courts, may not be available for non-binding legal instruments. Only if the international soft law obligation has been codified as a binding obligation in domestic law will courts be available to enforce violations. Cassel noted that in the Inter-American human rights system, '[c]ourt ordered hard law seems to generate better compliance than Commission-recommended soft law'.[35]

In general the case studies do not provide the material necessary to assess the importance of national factors to compliance with soft law, because they do not address compliance of specific countries with a particular non-binding legal instrument. In some cases the soft law instruments are negotiated by the private sector and enforced by the private sector. Thus, it is difficult to reach definitive conclusions. The research on compliance with international agreements suggests that the country factors are critical, and there is no reason in the case studies to think that the same does not apply to soft law negotiated by governments.

The empirical research on national compliance with international agreements found that compliance by a particular country with a given agreement is not static; rather it changes over time.[36] In general there is a secular trend toward improved compliance, although particular developments such as political instability or dramatic economic changes can alter this for a given country. Again, the logic suggests that the same would apply to compliance with those soft law instruments negotiated by governments or concluded in the context of an international regime. As Schlager and Cassel note, compliance with human rights norms may positively affect political institutions, which in turn facilitate greater compliance.

2. Compliance as a Function of National Intent and Capacity

Compliance with both hard and soft law is affected by two important factors, which are related to the proximate factors in the category of national characteristics just discussed. These are the intent of a state (or nonstate actor) to

---

[35] Cassel, D., *supra* p. 417.
[36] Jacobson and Weiss, *supra* note 24 at 512–15.

comply; and the state's (or nonstate actor's) capacity to comply. Both dimensions may change over time for any given state and any given international agreement; the same applies to soft law instruments.

Countries join international agreements for a variety of reasons. Some clearly intend to comply with the obligations they assume. Others may be unaware of the measures necessary to implement and comply with the agreements. While the Foreign Ministry may have joined the agreement, the relevant ministry for implementing the obligations may be unaware of this. Or one part of the national government may intend to comply, while another does not; or subnational units of government may have no intention of complying even if the national government may intend to comply. A state may even cynically join a binding agreement with no intention to comply. In some cases, intent is a matter of priority; complying with other obligations may take priority over those contained in a particular international agreement.

All of these conditions seem to apply also to states and soft law instruments. The difference is that the variable of the binding character of the instrument or of the obligation may affect a country's intent to comply. Most of the case studies suggest explicitly or implicitly that a binding obligation, or a link to a binding obligation, is viewed by governments as preferable to a separate non-binding instrument for inducing the targeted actors to change their behavior. Even Simmons' analysis of the Financial Action Task Force, which notes that its success stems not from the nature of the instrument setting forth the standards for efforts against money laundering but from the attention to monitoring and assessment, recognizes that the top priority of the FATF is 'to get a legally binding commitment from states on the broadest possible principle—that money laundering . . . should be considered a crime'.[37]

Williamson's analysis of the Land Mines Convention confirms the importance that countries attach to a binding agreement. Countries believe other countries are more committed to fulfilling the obligation not to use land mines if the obligation is binding upon them. The binding or non-binding character of the obligation thus is a variable that is at least perceived to affect intent to comply significantly. Notably, however, fairly widespread compliance with a practice against using land mines preceded the negotiation of a binding convention.

In some situations, however, the intent of countries to comply may actually be stronger for a soft law instrument than for a binding one. Countries could be unwilling to commit to a binding obligation or, if committed, unable to garner the support needed to comply with all of the obligations. This could be due to a recalcitrant Congress unwilling to adopt implementing legislation or to provincial or local governments unwilling to abide by the obligations. To the extent that the soft law instrument provides flexibility in meeting the

---

[37] Simmons, *supra* note 32, at p. 263.

obligations, and provides for supervisory and monitoring mechanisms, it may encourage better compliance with its norms than if it were a binding instrument. The FATF, for example, has been more successful as a soft law instrument than a binding instrument would have been at this time. This is consistent also with the literature on informal social norms, referenced earlier.

Similarly, the ISO 14000 standards for environmentally sound operation of industries and the MacBride and the Sullivan Principles have arguably been more effective as soft law instruments than as principles that companies are legally obliged to follow. Were the requirement to follow ISO 14000 standards to become binding upon companies as a result of national legislation, for example, new business for certifying compliance might emerge to accommodate those companies interested only in 'paper' compliance.[38] Thus, the variable of the 'soft' nature of the obligation or of the instrument does not necessarily dilute a country's intent, or a nonstate actor's intent to comply with the norm.

The research on compliance with binding agreements indicates that a country's capacity to comply with the obligations in the agreement is a critical factor. Many assets are important for effective compliance, including an effective and honest bureaucracy, economic resources, and public support.[39] When countries join international agreements, they have varying degrees of these assets, and the assets change over time, sometimes in response to external events. To the extent that countries lack the capacity to comply with international agreements, it is important to provide the means for doing so. This could include financial assistance, technical assistance, training, and access to markets.

The case studies support the proposition that having the capacity to comply with soft law is a critical factor. The chapters on driftnet fishing, pesticides and chemicals, international labor standards, and IAEA standards to protect nuclear materials demonstrate this. Moreover, as the case studies indicate, technical assistance, capacity building, and financial assistance can be made available by countries to build capacity to comply with soft law, as well as with binding agreements. For example, the IAEA helps member states to comply with safety standards through technical cooperation programs that consist of expert advice, equipment, and training. Technical and financial assistance helps countries develop the expertise and infrastructure to comply with requirements for transboundary trade in pesticides.

Developing the capacity to comply with soft or hard law instruments can also positively affect a country's or a nonstate actor's intent to comply. In

[38] Brown Weiss, E., and Weiss, Jr., C., 'Transnational Norms of Environmental Behavior and the Spread of the Industrial Ecology Ethic', in Brown Weiss, E., McCaffrey, S.C., Magraw, D., Szasz, P.C., and Lutz, R.E. (eds.), *International Environmental Law and Policy* (1998).
[39] Jacobson and Weiss, *supra* note 24 at 538.

part externally provided assistance or other incentives may modify priorities within the government, so that as the country builds the capacity to comply, it also increases its intent to comply. It may empower individuals in the bureaucracy through the process of building their ability to comply with the obligations.

As with hard law, it is essential to view compliance as a process that changes over time. A country's intent and capacity can and do change over time. The intent and capacity of nonstate actors also change over time. This suggests that while general assessments of compliance with a soft law instrument can be made, they will always be characterized by variations over time by individual states and by specific nonstate actors.

D. ENHANCING COMPLIANCE WITH SOFT LAW

What, then, does the scholarship on compliance with hard law and with informal social norms tell us about enhancing compliance with soft law? The research suggests that while it is essential to use compliance strategies that are tailored to the intent and capacity of the individual states and other relevant actors to comply with particular instruments, it is also essential to develop and maintain the processes joining the participants and to elaborate mechanisms of accountability among states and other relevant actors. Developing and maintaining a consensus on the norm is crucial.

If the soft law instrument is intended to be binding in the sense of modifying behavior, all of the strategies identified for both binding agreements and for informal social norms merit review. The precise measures needed to further compliance with soft law will change over time, and, as in the case of international agreements, will need to be tailored to the characteristics of the problem and to the characteristics of those expected to comply with the nonbinding instruments. Civil society has an especially important role in furthering compliance with soft law, or in building the consensus needed for negotiating binding legal instruments.

Editor's Concluding Note: The Role of Non-binding Norms in the International Legal System

DINAH SHELTON

The studies in this book evidence the complexity of the modern international legal system, confirming the presence of a multiplicity of actors in the making of international norms and promoting compliance with them. Commitments are made among states and by states with inter-governmental and non-governmental organizations. Business entities, governmental authorities lacking treaty-making powers, and epistemic communities also contribute to the elaboration of international norms. With new actors and new issues, the developing international order, like the modern regulatory state, is increasingly bureaucratized and utilizes numerous methods to express expectations of behavior.

The expanding variety of actors and instruments does not seem, however, to have fundamentally changed the nature of international law, despite debate and controversy. The studies in this volume indicate that law matters and that states continue to choose carefully those obligations that they wish to make legally binding. In this consent-based system, declarations, resolutions, memoranda of understanding, and other non-binding instruments are not adopted as law, soft or hard, although they frequently are intended to alter the behavior of their targets. While they often encompass strong political commitments or moral obligations, indeed commitments and obligations that are stronger than many legal obligations, they become international law only when they emerge in customary international law or are incorporated into a treaty. On the domestic level, however, non-binding international instruments often become a source of law even before they are obligatory on the international level.

Those who enter into agreements consciously determine the form as well as the content of the agreement, at least when the authors are states that can choose the form and content, in contrast to international organizations and other actors that in most cases can adopt only legally non-binding texts. States employ non-binding instruments for various reasons when legally-binding commitments are unwanted or unavailable. In most cases, non-binding instruments are related to a treaty in some manner, either as a precursor or as a subsequent elaboration of technical terms or expected performance. Where non-binding norms precede a legally-binding agreement, the former helps shape the consensus that leads to a legally binding accord. In contrast, where a prior treaty explicitly refers to subsequent elaborative instruments, the latter may acquire a legal basis.

Subject matter has an impact on the choice of binding or non-binding norms, although less, perhaps, than expected. In the field of human rights, soft law usually preceded hard law in the past, helping to build consensus on the norms. Thus, the Universal Declaration of Human Rights led to the two Covenants on Civil and Political and on Economic, Social, and Cultural Rights. The Conventions on race, women, children, and torture all were preceded by declarations. The situation has changed now that the 'easy' topics on which there was widespread consensus have been completed and there are fewer treaties being concluded on the global level. Instead, the United Nations increasingly adopts declarations without subsequent treaties. At the same time, regional institutions continue to formulate legal obligations, with concomitant efforts to secure compliance, perhaps because it is easier to achieve consensus in the shared culture of regional systems and also to agree upon stronger institutions; human rights courts exist only on the regional level. Regional adoption of soft norms also has an important role.

Arms control shows less shift from global to regional commitments, although there are some such efforts as shown by the regional establishment of nuclear free zones. More than in the human rights field there is an intertwining of hard and soft law, with non-binding commitments foreseen by hard law instruments, thus conferring upon the soft law a stronger legal nature. In some instances, like the missile technology control regime, the soft law instrument is deliberately chosen as a substitute for hard law, rather than as a precursor or subsequent gap-filler. In trade, on the other hand, regional mechanisms generally are instituted to secure compliance rather than to create new norms. Incentives to defect are strong, but the possibility of retaliatory measures acts to dissuade defection. In some instances, soft law acts as a substitute for or pre-emptive of, hard law, as with ISO and the Sullivan/MacBride Principles.

In the environmental field, statements of principles coming from global conferences have stimulated the conclusion of both legally binding and non-binding instruments, with peaks of regulation following the Stockholm and the Rio conferences. An ecosystem approach has stimulated a strong move towards regional efforts, with the conclusion of numerous regional seas agreements, a series of agreements on the Alps, comprehensive regulation by the European Union, and major agreements elaborated within the context of the UNECE, the OAU, ASEAN, and other regional institutions. Soft law often follows these agreements, as with the Convention on Migratory Species, acting to fill in gaps, bring in non-state actors, or allowing provisional solutions where there is scientific uncertainty about the proper course of action.

In some instances, like the prior informed consent procedure, soft law commitments precede the conclusion of a binding treaty, but this seems less a deliberate policy than it does in the field of human rights.

As the conclusions of Professor Brown Weiss indicate, compliance with soft law commitments can be impelled by factors similar to those that affect compliance with treaty or customary obligations. The studies done for this book concentrated only on the international aspects of the problem. Clearly, much research needs to be done on the factors within countries, those impacting on will and capacity, that may be as or more important than the international aspects of the issue. For example, it may be asked whether compliance is better in states where individuals or groups can sue to enforce international commitments. Such issues were not part of the current study.

The compliance levels indicated by the various studies ranged from very high to very low, and sometimes varied within a single instrument. For example, the FAO found very high compliance with the requirement that states designate national authorities for the PIC procedure, but far less compliance with the application of the procedure in practice. The authors of the driftnet fishing and Antarctic studies indicated very high compliance with the normative measures involved. At the opposite extreme, there was very weak compliance with APEC environmental norms and problems with money laundering norms as well. Other studies reported mixed results.

The factors that seem to explain the differences are well described in Professor Brown Weiss's conclusions. In particular, the content of the norm, the legitimacy of the process by which it is adopted, the international context, and especially the institutional follow-up seem to impact on state decisions to comply or not comply with the norms in question. Institutional monitoring, supervisory mechanisms, and follow-up may be even more important in the context of non-binding norms, where the compliance pull attributable to law is missing.

The considerable recourse to and compliance with non-binding norms appears to represent a maturing of the international system. The on-going relationships among states and other actors, deepening and changing with globalization, create a climate that may require that fewer expectations of behavior be set forth in formal legal obligations. Formally non-binding norms or informal social norms can be effective and offer a flexible and efficient way to order responses to common problems. While they are not law, such norms have an indispensable place in the modern legal system.

Index

Agenda 21 11, 161
Allott, P. 106–7, 114
Antarctica 10, 110, 112, 229, 239–40, 537–8
  recommended measures 163–96
arms control, *see* multilateral arms control
Asia-Pacific Economic Cooperation Forum
    303–29, 337, 341
Australia:
  money laundering initiatives 246
  Group 468, 475–7, 479–80

bank secrecy 247
bats 206–7, 210–11, 215
Bilder, R. 65–73
Boisson de Chazournes, L. 281–303, 333

capacity 46–7, 155–6, 241, 461, 550–3
capacity-building 58, 155–6, 241, 496
Cassell, D. 112, 393–418, 450, 458
Charney, J. 23, 115–18
Chayes, A. 471
chemical weapons 475–7, 479–80
chemicals 146–63, 225
child labor 376–7, 456
Chinkin, C. 21–42, 94, 115
civil society 95, 97–8, 153–5, 355, 532
    see also non-governmental organizations,
      non-state actors
codes of conduct 154–5, 176, 389–91, 418–49
Commission on Sustainable Development 11
common but differentiated responsibilities 7,
    89
common concern of humankind 176
compliance
  Agenda 21 234–5
  and the rule of law 8–9
  assessment 454–7, 518–21
  capacity 46–7, 155–6, 241, 461, 496, 550–3
  certification 275–7
  content of obligations 14–15, 400–1, 542–3
  costs 248, 276–7
  defined 5
  domestic 231–5
  factors affecting 13–17, 117–18, 180,
    239–42, 261–2, 279–80, 317–27, 358–60,
    384–7, 394–5, 414, 416–17, 444–7,
    457–61, 526–33, 539–53
  form of instrument and 9–10
  international 228–30
  mechanisms 15–16, 54–6, 131–4, 155–61,
    177, 215–18, 256–9, 291–7, 343, 374–5,
    383–4, 435–9, 529–30, 548

pull 116, 176, 179, 395, 401, 526–33, 540–1
Rio Declaration 231–5
theories 43–64
conflict resolution 362–8
Cooper, R. 77–8
cooperation 65, 84–7, 91, 521–2
Council of Europe 10, 370–1
cranes 110, 199, 201, 207–8, 211–12, 216, 236
crime 7, 103, 104–5
  money laundering as 257, 260–1
curlew 208–9, 212–14, 216–17, 236
customary international law 1, 32–3, 95, 102,
    112, 115, 176, 229, 300, 331, 336–7, 449,
    454, 528

definitions:
  compliance 5
  declaration 454
  driftnets 121
  effectiveness 5
  globalization 102–3
  implementation 5
  international law 5–6
  monitoring 5
  norms 5
  prior informed consent 146–7
  standards 5
  treaty 174
democracy 365–7, 402–3
dispute settlement 243
Downs, G. 44
driftnets 110, 112, 121–46, 224–5
  characteristics 122
  compliance with ban 138–44, 239, 537
  defined 121
  European Union actions 141–2
  General Assembly resolutions 126–31
  moratorium on use 129
  U.S. actions 139–41
  use of 123

election monitoring 365–7
employment policy 382–3
enforcement 130, 131–4, 177, 222, 227, 258,
    355–8, 426–7, 485, 537, 544
environment 104, 306–9
environmental impact assessment 178, 228,
    286–7, 299
environmental law 3, 121–242, 285–7
  regional norms 309–16
environmental management standards
    263–5, 267–70

epistemic communities 62–3, 242, 401, 532
European Union:
   actions on driftnet fishing 141–2
   actions on prior informed consent 157–8
   eco-management and audit scheme 272
   money laundering initiatives 259

financial activity 244–5
financial mechanisms 201, 221
Finnemore, M. 99
fisheries 104, 121–42
Food and Agriculture Organization 110,
   142–63, 226
force, use of 102
foreign direct investment 79, 83–4
forfeitures 246
Forsythe, D. 405
future generations 176

globalization 22, 75–114, 372
   defined 102–3
   link to environment 311
   responses to 82–90, 105–9
   as threat to sovereignty 81–2
global public policy 90–7
Greenpeace International 134–5
Gualtieri, D. 112, 466–86, 525

Haas, Peter 1, 43–64
Helsinki process, *see* Organization for
   Security and Cooperation in Europe
Hoffman, J. 81
human rights 3, 105, 111, 112, 345–463
   complaints procedure 398
   compliance 406–18, 454–61, 457–61
   customary international law 449
   General Comments 33, 451–2
   Inter-American system 393–418
   OSCE 346–72
   rapporteurs 452–3
   right to housing 33
   UN Covenants 33

incentives 58–61, 89, 135–8, 155–6, 220–1,
   240, 247, 272–3, 277, 343, 443–4, 528,
   549
indigenous peoples 287–8
Inter-American Commission on Human
   Rights 394–5, 397–400, 403–5, 415–18,
   451
Inter-American Court of Human Rights
   394–5, 397–9, 403–5, 415–18
interdependence 75–81, 103
International Atomic Energy Agency 225,
   241, 491, 495–504
international conferences 28
international criminal law 111

International Court of Justice 6
International Crane Foundation 207
international institutions 52–4, 152–3, 224–6,
   265–7, 303–29, 460–1, 529, 538, 545–6
International Labor Organization 27, 345,
   372–93, 422, 456, 458–61
international law:
   actors 6, 297–301, 554
   consensual basis 66
   enforcement 7, 130, 131–4
   on landmines 514–17
   remedies for breach 116
   role of 7–8
   sources 6, 21–5, 113–14, 115, 174, 554–6
   states 5–6
   subject matter 6–7
   universal international law 23
   see also soft law
International Law Association 226
international organizations 2, 3–4, 12, 28,
   174
International Organization for
   Standardization 112, 236–7, 263–81,
   337–41

Jacobson, Harold 2
Joyner, C. 110, 112, 163–96, 229
jus cogens 40

Kellman, B. 243, 466, 486–505
Kiss, A. C. 223–42
Klabbers, J. 23–4
Koh, H. H. 76, 96, 395
Koskenniemi, M. 39

landmines 105, 111, 505–21
law:
   compliance and form 9
   preference for 9–10,
   role of 7–8, 12
legitimacy 478–81, 525, 527–9
linkages 56–7, 271–2, 311, 358, 459–60,
   536–7
Lipson, C. 43

McBride Principles 29, 419–49, 458–61
McCrudden, C. 29, 418–49, 460
maternity protection 379–80
Maupin, F. 27, 372–93, 456, 458
Mekouar, A. 110, 112, 146–63, 229
memorandum of understanding 10–11
   legal status 204–6
   on migratory species 207–9, 236–7
   on port state control 226–7, 235–6
migratory species 110, 196–223, 241
Missile Technology Control Regime 468,
   470, 477–8

money laundering 110, 244–63
monitoring 54–6, 131–4, 177, 256–9, 274–9, 405, 462
multilateral arms control 3, 105, 342, 465–533
  export controls 467–86
  landmines 505–51
  protection of nuclear material 486–505

nesting 57
non-governmental organizations 6, 28–9, 35, 109, 207, 267, 287, 289, 316–17, 401
  role in promoting compliance 134–5, 219–20, 240, 355–7, 385, 460
non-state actors 6, 22, 35–6, 96
  monitoring compliance 54–6, 134–5
  norm-creation by 29, 48, 113–14, 226–8, 510–14, 528
  participation in legal process 13, 99, 111, 267, 301–2
  structuring globalization 78–81
  as target of norms 16, 47–9, 460
normative ambiguity 70
nuclear weapons 471–4, 490–1, 492

occupational health and safety 380–2
O'Connell, M. E. 100–14
Organization of Eastern Caribbean States 125
Organization for Security and Cooperation in Europe 3, 15, 40, 64, 112, 332, 346–72, 451, 458–61
  background 347–8, 360–1
  commitments 349–50, 352–4
  confidence building measures 529–30
  implementation review 361–2
  legal status 350–2
  limits 368–70
Organization of American States 393–418
Organization of Economic Cooperation and Development 79, 231
ozone depletion 239–40

pacta sunt servanda 8, 62
peer pressure 245
precaution 112, 176, 182
prior informed consent 146–63, 228–9
  compliance with norms on 156–61, 240
  defined 146–7

Reinicke, W. H. 75–100, 103, 535
recommended measures 163–96, 229
  adoption process 165–9
  approval 166–9
  compliance 175–81, 239
  implementation 169–70
  legal status 164, 170–5

regimes 2, 7, 481–5, 531, 537
reporting 7
resettlement 288–9
Roht-Arriaza, N. 110, 112, 337, 339
Rosenau, J. 106–7
Rothwell, D. 110, 112, 121–42
rule of law 106–7

sanctions 1, 51–2, 135–7, 177, 240, 243, 258, 261, 428–9, 460, 539
scientific uncertainty 13
Schlager, E. 112, 346–72, 451, 459
Shelton, D. 1–18, 95, 111, 449–66, 535, 554–6
Shine, C. 27, 110, 196–223
Siberian cranes, *see* cranes
Simmons, B. 244–63, 330
social constructivism 61–4
soft law:
  characteristics 94–5, 204–6, 373–5, 519
  codes of conduct 154–5, 176, 418–49
  content 14, 39–40, 267–70, 349–50, 396, 433–5, 538
  context 536–9, 539–41
  desirability 23–4, 93–4, 523
  distinguished from hard law 11, 421–2
  flexibility 13, 109–10, 175, 330–1, 400
  forms of 4, 25–31, 37–8
  gap-filling by 10, 111, 270–1, 333–4, 375, 466, 487, 495, 524
  hardening of 31–4, 289–90, 334–5, 339–40, 397, 399
  intention of parties 38–9
  legitimacy 478–81
  precursor to hard law 10, 180, 182–3, 206, 229–30, 453, 466
  primary and secondary 27, 449–53
  proponents of 34–5
  rejection of 23–4, 71–2
  role of non-state actors 28–9, 95, 99, 134–5, 223, 224–8, 340–2
  targets of 35–7, 284–5, 331, 418–21
  use of 3, 41–2, 102, 176, 237–9, 262–3, 280, 344, 401, 461–2, 519–26
sources of international law 6, 21–5, 113–14, 115, 174
South Pacific Forum 123–5
sovereignty 85, 97, 99–100
  globalization as a challenge to 81–2
states:
  creation of non-binding norms 223–4
  dominance of 102
  federal 45
  foreign policy 67–8
  fragmentation 101–2
  interdependence 103
  reporting 7
  role in international system 6

subsidiarity 92–3, 98
Sullivan Principles 29, 418–49, 458–61

technology 7
trade 3, 79, 103–4, 243–344
    liberalization 304, 305
    pesticides and chemicals 110, 146–63, 335
transparency 13, 93, 301–2, 484–5
treaties 88–9
    amendment 331–2
    limitations 494–5, 524–5
    and non-party states 12

United Nations:
    Environment Program 110, 142–63, 225
    General Assembly 110, 122, 126–31, 138,
        224–5, 517
    human rights activities 345
United States:
    action on driftnets 139–41
    Antarctic Treaty depository 167
    approval of Antarctic measures 168
    human rights policies 402, 403–4
    landmine policy 512–13

money laundering initiatives 246, 247–8
    role in APEC 304, 321–2
    sanctions against South Africa 428–9

verification 274–6, 529–30

Weber, M. 81
Weiss, E. B. 2, 535–53
Wendt, A. 96, 97
Williamson, R. 105, 505–21
Wirth, D. 243, 330–44
Witte, J. M. 75–100, 535
women:
    violence against 31–3
    workers' rights 387–91, 418–49
World Bank:
    Inspection Panel 33, 292–7, 336
    Operational Standards 281–303, 333–7
World Health Organization 226
World Meteorological Organization 226
World Trade Organization 387–8

Zangger Committee 467, 471–4, 524
Zarsky, L. 303–29, 337, 342

Ingram Content Group UK Ltd.
Milton Keynes UK
UKHW020247180423
420349UK00004B/303